GW00708696

Special Edition

Using Microsoft® Exchange™ Server

Que®

Special Edition

Using Microsoft® Exchange™ Server

Sal Collora • Kent Joshi • Mark Kapczynski
Ruben Perez • Ed Roberts

QUE®

Special Edition Using Microsoft Exchange Server

Library of Congress Catalog No.: 95-73276

ISBN: 0-7897-0687-3

98 97 4

Interpretation of the printing code: the rightmost double-digit number is the year of the book's printing; the rightmost single-digit number, the number of the book's printing. For example, a printing code of 96-1 shows that the first printing of the book occurred in 1996.

Screen reproductions in this book were created by using Collage Plus from Inner Media, Inc., Hollis, NH.

Credits

PRESIDENT
Roland Elgey

PUBLISHER
Joseph B. Wikert

EDITORIAL SERVICES DIRECTOR
Elizabeth Keaffaber

MANAGING EDITOR
Sandy Doell

PUBLISHING MANAGER
Fred Slone

SR. TITLE MANAGER
Bryan Gambrel

ACQUISITIONS EDITOR
Al Valvano

ACQUISITIONS COORDINATOR
Angela C. Kozlowski

PRODUCT DIRECTOR
Stephen L. Miller

PRODUCTION EDITOR
Mike La Bonne

EDITORS
Charles K. Bowles II
Judy Brunetti
Don Eamon
Phil Kitchel
Mary Anne Sharbaugh
Kathy Simpson
Midge Stocker

DIRECTOR OF MARKETING
Barry Pruett

ASSISTANT MARKETING MANAGER
Kim Margolius

TECHNICAL EDITORS
Mark Streger, Ablaze Business Systems
Robert Green

OPERATIONS COORDINATOR
Patricia J. Brooks

EDITORIAL ASSISTANT
Andrea Duvall

BOOK DESIGNER
Kim Scott

COVER DESIGNER
Dan Armstrong

COPYWRITER
Jennifer Reese

PRODUCTION TEAM
Steve Adams
Chad Dressler
Jennifer Earhart
Jessica Ford
Trey Frank
Amy Gornik
Jason Hand
Sonja Hart
Clint Lahnen
Bob LaRoche
Michelle Lee
Laura Robbins
Bobbi Satterfield
Paul Wilson
Jody York

INDEXERS
Brad Herriman
Craig Small

Composed in *Century Old Style* and *Franklin Gothic* by Que Corporation.

Acknowledgments

It has been a long time in the making, but it is finally here: Microsoft Exchange Server. I can remember my first Exchange beta. It was labeled EMS TR1, which stood for Enterprise Messaging System Test Release 1. I received this beta in December 1993. Two-and-a-half years later, Exchange has finally been released and many companies have been busily attempting to deploy the latest in Microsoft Messaging Technology.

I wrote this book to appeal to several types of end users. Of course, a major focus of the book is toward the Exchange system administrator. However, I have included several chapters and sections of chapters that will guide MIS managers through the overall effect Exchange can have on their environment. Exchange encompasses so many areas of the business. From the Exchange universal inbox, you will have "information at your fingertips," as Bill Gates has said.

I especially want to thank some people, for without the support from these individuals and their companies, I would not have been able to write this book. From Microsoft, I thank **Elaine Sharp**. Elaine is part of the core Exchange product team, responsible for developing and delivering this product. I thank **Mark Spain** and **Fred Rodriquez**, also from Microsoft. Mark and Fred provided me with up-to-the-minute software builds of the Exchange product. In addition, their support in answering my questions and issues with the product has contributed a significant benefit to the content of this book.

One cannot write a book like *Special Edition Using Microsoft Exchange Server* without a development environment. I thank **Ralph Smalldino** from NEC and **Kurt Kyle** from Compaq for providing enough servers to build an effective lab. From this lab, we were able to model the types of environments you will certainly encounter in deploying Exchange. It was interesting to note how easily we were able to integrate and manage all of the NEC MIPS servers with all Compaq Intel servers. We had no problems in software supportability across platforms. One additional point to make: Exchange runs great on a Proliant 4500@133mz with 300M of RAM and 12G of RAID 5 hard drive space. Can I keep this as my desktop, Kurt?

I also thank the wonderful third-party ISVs who supported me with technical information and software code to show how Exchange is more than an e-mail system. There are far too many names to mention, and I surely would forget to include some. So I again thank all of the third-party Exchange ISVs for their support.

I also thank my friends and coauthors, **Ruben**, **Sal**, **Kent**, and **Ed**; I could not have done it alone. Thanks for the hard work and patience in working with me.

I thank Que for the opportunity to write this book. We had a short time-frame to deliver the completed book, but we did it. Thanks **Al** and **Stephen** for your support!

I thank my good friend and manager, **Benjamin Goldfarb**, from Nestle USA MIS. Thanks for letting me come in late after working to meet a deadline. Thanks for having confidence in me.

Without a doubt, my biggest supporter was my wife, **Jenna**. Thanks for your patience and encouragement in helping me finish this book. Thank you for the wonderful late night dinners and hot cups of coffee to help get the author team through the work before the deadline. I love you!

If I have left anyone out, I am very sorry. With so many people having affected my work in writing this book, I am bound to forget someone's name. I will just say thank you for helping and your compensation for your support can be found under the cover of this book. The sheer body of work speaks for itself.

Mark J. Kapczynski
Chairman, Los Angeles Windows NT User Group
mark@lantug.org

About the Authors

Sal Collora is a network specialist. While working at LMU, he developed integration of messaging technologies for the LMU network infrastructure. The WAN consists of over 2,000 nodes with 4,000 users. Each student, faculty, and staff member has his or her own e-mail address. He also maintained a combination of cc:Mail, MS Mail, POP3 Mail, and Sendmail to provide communication between users.

Before leaving LMU, Sal was responsible for the new architecture mandate. This mandate consists of migrating LMU from a Novell Netware-dominated environment, to an NT-dominated environment citing Microsoft's SMS technology and Exchange as the answer to the lack of such robustness under Netware. Exchange was to be the key component of the migration. Sal realized the existing cc:Mail infrastructure could not grow with the campus network.

With over three years of messaging experience at LMU, and the ability to integrate a variety of systems, Sal also provided further insight into the practical deployment of Exchange in the enterprise.

Sal is currently working for Rubin Postaer and Associates, an advertising firm in Santa Monica. He is responsible for all worldwide development and networking infrastructure. His plans are to replace the current Quickmail system and migrate from existing MS Mail post offices with a multi-platform, NT/Exchange-based messaging infrastructure.

Kent Joshi has over 10 years of technical experience, ranging from network design to management to sales.

He earned his network design and tuning experience at The Joshi Group, Inc. (pertinent clients include Nestlé USA). There he built, tuned, and upgraded over 80 Windows NT Servers for corporate and remote offices. He also used Performance Monitor on over 100 systems to identify bottlenecks, provide capacity planning information, tune 32-bit applications, and reduce SQL operation times.

At the Utah Department of Transportation, he optimized DEC network and system workflow for the Contract Procurement Department.

At the Engineering-Science Department, a Subsidiary of Parsons Engineering, he set up, administered, and tuned a nationwide Novell network.

He also worked for Microsoft Corporation, where he provided pre- and post-sales consulting for several Microsoft accounts. He served as the technical advisor for the Western Region Account Execs, where he was recognized as the Outstanding Representative in the Western Region.

At the IBM Corporation, he managed a team of representatives who installed and supported networked IBM systems for local clients.

Mark Kapczynski has seven years of computer experience as the director of information technology for Digital Genesis, a senior network systems architect for Computer Dynamics, Inc., and as both a UCLA student and a manager of information technology for the NeuroPsychiatric Institute. Mark is the founder/chairman of the LA County Windows NT/ Microsoft Networking Users Group where he conducts monthly meetings to discuss current issues and solutions. During his studies at UCLA, he was on staff as a network administrator and computer lab assistant for the UCLA School of Medicine, where he began working in October of 1990. Mark developed databases for Paramount Pictures to track film production information. He implemented a system to maintain computerized records for Global Investments, an investment group. Mark specializes in client/server LAN/WAN networking systems; database design and administration for finance/accounting, inventory control, and data warehouse systems; multimedia application presentations using the Internet, CD-ROM distribution, and on-line services; and Information Technology Consulting

Ruben Perez holds a bachelor of arts degree in Classical Civilizations from UCLA. He comes from a very diverse computer technology background. Early experience working at Pacific Data Images with the digital visual effects artists evolved into a love for digital media production. Ruben directed multimedia CD-ROM projects at a large Los Angeles-based multimedia firm. Along with creative direction, he also architected messaging integration on a multimedia production LAN consisting of Macintosh, Windows, and Silicon Graphics workstations. Ruben is an expert in Internet technology and new media design. Currently, he owns Digital Genesis, an Internet technology and content development firm based in Santa Monica, CA. The firm specializes in creative and technical design for both the public Internet and private Intranets. Though a young company, Digital Genesis is rapidly maturing within the industry, with clients such as Capitol Records, Nestlé USA, Microsoft, Compaq, and many others.

Drop Ruben a line at **ruben@dgenesis.com**. He is always in the mood to talk and welcomes any feedback.

Ed Roberts is a senior systems engineer at Ingram MicroArchitecting, a large-scale rollout for group scheduling and conferencing with Microsoft Schedule+ and Exchange. This rollout involves integration with Microsoft Exchange/Schedule+ to a Mainframe-based mail system and Lotus Notes.

He was a regional systems manager, Intergraph Corporation, where he was responsible for the integration/migration of a Microsoft Mail and UNIX Sendmail/SMTP messaging environment. This environment covered the western United States, Alaska, and Hawaii, with over 300 workstations and 40 mobile users in 10 offices.

Ed is a Microsoft-certified systems engineer specializing in Microsoft Mail and Microsoft TCP/IP. He has more than 10 years of computer experience, ranging from personal computers, medium range UNIX workstations and servers, to VAX and IBM mainframe connectivity.

We'd Like to Hear from You!

As part of our continuing effort to produce books of the highest possible quality, Que would like to hear your comments. To stay competitive, we *really* want you, as a computer book reader and user, to let us know what you like or dislike most about this book or other Que products.

You can mail comments, ideas, or suggestions for improving future editions to the address below, or send us a fax at (317) 581-4663. For the on-line inclined, Macmillan Computer Publishing now has a forum on CompuServe (type **GO QUEBOOKS** at any prompt) through which our staff and authors are available for questions and comments. The address of our Internet site is **http://www.mcp.com** (World Wide Web).

In addition to exploring our forum, please feel free to contact me personally to discuss your opinions of this book. You can reach me on CompuServe at **76103,1334** or on Internet at **slmiller@que.mcp.com**.

Thanks in advance—your comments will help us to continue publishing the best books available on computer topics in today's market.

Stephen L. Miller
Product Development Specialist
Que Corporation
201 W. 103rd Street
Indianapolis, Indiana 46290
USA

Contents at a Glance

Table of Contents

IV Exchange Client Software and Scheduling

Introduction

- The strategic features of Exchange
- How Exchange integrates into the Enterprise
- Where Exchange goes from here

Microsoft Exchange Server is one of the most strategic products from Microsoft. On a small scale, it's a robust intraoffice mail and groupware system, integrating with the other desktop applications. On a larger scale, it's positioned to be the messaging backbone for a large organization. Exchange, in essence, becomes the brain of the mail system. It provides connectivity and management of user accounts for the entire enterprise, as well as for the gateways into legacy mail systems. ■

What Are the Strategic Features of Exchange?

Exchange has been in development for over two years. Finally out on the shelves of computer stores, Exchange is a vision into the future of messaging technology. Exchange provides revolutionary functionality at a low end-user cost. Let's review some of these features.

A Universal Inbox

The universal Inbox is not a revolution, it's a reality. No other product has been able to implement this vision. The Inbox is the gateway to information for Exchange users. The Inbox also allows users to access their electronic mail, personal calendar, electronic data interchange, document management and document imaging systems, electronic workflow, electronic forms, outside information stores, and more.

The Inbox is extensible by using the MAPI v1.0 standard published with Exchange. MAPI provides the programming interface that allows applications to leverage the Inbox or other Exchange components.

Single Network and Mail Logon

Exchange is based on two pieces of software—the Windows NT operating system and a component of BackOffice. NT supports a domain architecture for directory services. When users log into a domain, their user ID and password are maintained through their entire use of the network. Exchange relies upon the same network user ID and password from the NT domain, which provides a one-time logon to the end users and a one-time account creation for the network administers.

Server-Based Message Rules

Exchange provides support for *server-based* rules. Users can configure rules to execute on their Exchange home servers to forward messages to particular individuals, reply with an "out of office" note when appropriate, and message routing to specific folders to ease Inbox organization. The process runs on the Exchange Server and doesn't require a user to be logged in.

The server rules can apply to applications that are leveraging Exchange. Outside information stores, for example, will have a server agent configured from the client. The next time the user logs into the system, the server agent runs to retrieve information for the user.

MS Office Desktop Application Integration

Numerous features show the MS Office desktop application integration. For example, from every office application you can send the document directly from within the application. The document even can be sent into a public folder.

The Exchange client software also provides a Microsoft Fax application to support faxing directly from an office application. Each toolbar in Exchange allows for customization. The essence of integration is that Exchange maintains the office application standard and extends the Windows desktop operating system. It supports MAPI, TAPI, OLE, right-mouse button use, drag-and-drop editing, rich text formatting, paste special, and shortcut menus.

From within the office applications, all document routing is handled by the MAPI exchange transport. Another function is the capability to create an e-mail merge directly from the office applications.

Multiple Mailbox Connections

Mailbox is an advanced feature for LAN-based mail systems. Mailbox allows users to access multiple information stores from a single network logon, which is customizable from the client or server to support multiple users who are accessing multiple stores simultaneously. The feature is beneficial for managers and their assistants. Managers can configure their information store to allow their assistants to simultaneously access their information store. This capability makes it convenient for managers who are out of town, to allow their assistants to access their mail and forward messages, send replies, and so on. The convenience comes for the assistants, because they can access this information from their own Inbox, without logging onto the network as their manager.

Remote Access to Mail Information Store

The exchange client is designed to sense line-connection speed and transfer less data over dial-up connections. The exchange client increases the efficiency of the connection. The client software downloads only mail message headers first on a remote connection. Message bodies are downloaded as needed. Additionally, Exchange provides an estimated time to download your request and the capability to schedule a download of your e-mail messages.

Public Folders and Replication

Public folders are central repositories of common information. This public folder is a component of the groupware functionality of Exchange. Exchange users can post messages, applications, forms, and so on into the public folders, which are replicated throughout the Exchange enterprise. Rather than sending a mail message out to many users, you can use public folders. A user can post to a folder, and then view the legacy of the original posting. It provides active threading of the messages.

Public folders can be replicated down to the client PC to facilitate off-line creation and reading. Permissions also can be set to restrict access to certain folder contents. The public folder replication is architected to minimize the amount of data to be replicated. Indexes exist to the public folder content. The index is available across the enterprise. Information is replicated from one Exchange public folder server to the next. A set of folders is known as a replica. Exchange manages the public folders replication and replicas.

Digital Signature

Exchange is rich with security. The Digital Signature is a means to digitally authenticate the user sending the mail message. The security model allows for any user to sign individual messages, based on public and private key RSA encryption. The keys are managed centrally by an Exchange Key server process. This management allows keys to be distributed to individual users from a common server.

Electronic Forms Designer

An electronic forms designer is included with the Exchange client. From the client, just select the Forms tool and wizard to step you through the creation of a new form. The forms designer is easy enough for end users to create basic forms and powerful enough for developers to create form-based applications. The form can be routed to multiple recipients, used to store data locally, or connected to an external data source.

Roving User Support

The server-based information message store can be accessed from any client at any point of connection within the enterprise. Multiple clients can simultaneously access the same server message stores.

Multiple Language Support

The Exchange client and server was localized for international use. The message will be transmitted in the native format. For example, someone in the U.S. writes in English, and a recipient in Germany also sees the message in English. The application software is in the native language of German. Exchange will be supported in over 20 languages.

Group Scheduling and Time Management

Part of the Exchange client and server is a scheduling and group calendaring system: *Schedule+*. Schedule plus integrates with the Exchange message store on the client and on the server. It combines daily, weekly, and monthly views with a planner and contact manager. The Schedule plus system can be integrated into legacy systems such as Profs Calendar by way of an external Exchange gateway.

Schedule plus allows objects such as audio/video equipment or conference rooms to be scheduled into meetings as resources without creating individual mailboxes for each item.

Schedule plus also includes a reference wizard, named the "Seven Habits Tool." This is a logic tool designed to assist you in time management and task planning with prioritization.

An additional function of Exchange and Schedule plus is the integration with Microsoft Project for time and project management.

Single-Seat View for Administration

This feature allows you to manage the entire Exchange enterprise from one location.

Server Monitors with Automatic Process

These monitors continually poll the server connectors, services, message stores, and more. They can be configured to either alert an administrator or automatically handle the situation.

Integration with NT Performance Monitor

Using native Windows NT performance and tuning tools, you can understand the current state of the Exchange processes.

On-line System Backup

Because Exchange is up and running 24 hours a day and seven days a week, you must be able to back up the system on-line. Exchange allows you to perform on-line backups without being forced to alert users. For the users, it's business as usual.

Support for 1984 and 1988 X.400 Standards

Exchange is the only Message Tranfer Agent to support both 1984 and 1988 X.400 standards simultaneously, offering flexibility in designing the Exchange architecture for the enterprise.

Migration Tools for Profs, All-in-One, CC:Mail, MS Mail, and SMTP Mail Systems

Microsoft realizes that many other systems are in use today. Therefore, Microsoft provides all the tools needed to develop and implement a migration from the various competitive mail systems.

Message Routing

Message routing provides multiple routes to transfer mail between servers and connectors. If one link between WAN sites goes down, Exchange has fault-tolerance that is integrated to automatically reroute mail to a secondary route.

The Role of Exchange in the Enterprise

Exchange promises to be the mail system for the enterprise. Exchange can handle directory synchronization of all the legacy mail systems, including most LAN-based mail systems. Exchange leverages the features listed previously to provide a complete messaging solution for the 21st century. Large corporations can use Exchange as a fault-tolerant mail system and take advantage of the universal Inbox to gateway into existing workflow applications, electronic forms, document management systems, electronic data interchange, and much more.

The Future of Exchange

Exchange has been in development for over two years. Finally out on the shelves of the computer stores, Exchange is a vision into the future of messaging technology. Exchange provides revolutionary functionality at a low end-user cost. The future of Exchange includes: close integration with the Web with a WEB Connector to access mail and public folders from a browser; an NNTP or Internet News Connector to post and read Internet newsgroups from the Exchange client; and POP3 or post-office protocol mail support from a POP3 client, accessing Exchange servers. Exchange initially will affect the MS Mail community as a tremendous upgrade. It has been two years, but it's worth the wait.

Who Should Use This Book

This book is aimed at network/system administrators and messaging specialists who are responsible for installing, configuring, and maintaining an Exchange backbone. MIS managers will be interested in using this book as a source of information to understand how to leverage a decision that their corporation makes in deploying Exchange. Areas of interest are electronic forms, application development, scheduling, third-party add-ons, and electronic document interchange. Additionally, coverage of application development is included for administrators who need to build custom programs by using the Exchange e-mail and groupware messaging APIs.

How to Use This Book

This book is divided into five sections. The first two sections are intended for a general audience, and the last three sections depend on an understanding of the previous sections.

Part I: Introduction to Microsoft Exchange

Part I welcomes you into the world of Microsoft Exchange. As described briefly in the preceding sections, Exchange is a completely revolutionary client/server messaging system. Part I presents a complete overview about how Exchange integrates into and is used in your environment.

Chapter 1, "Overview of Microsoft Exchange," introduces the concepts of working with client/server messaging, groupware, document management, and the universal Inbox. This chapter also highlights many new features available with Microsoft Exchange.

In Chapter 2, "Understanding Exchange's Organization and Sites," you learn about the types of server configurations and Exchange services available in architecting your solution.

Chapter 3, "Exchange's Integrated Server Components," provides a more in-depth look at the wide array of client and server functionality.

Chapter 4, "Integrating with a Windows NT Server," discusses the relationship between Windows NT Server and Exchange. This chapter identifies the integration of Exchange into NT and the dependencies on the NT operating system.

Part II: Migrating and Installing Exchange

Part II is the core of the book. This collection of six chapters streamlines all of the planning essentials for migrating to or deploying a new Exchange architecture.

Chapter 5, "Designing Exchange Topology," introduces you to the methodology and thought process needed to develop the Exchange architecture. This is an overview chapter for planning requirements.

Chapters 6 through 8 step you through a series of examples and planning guides to deploy Exchange by itself, as a migration from MS Mail, integrating with legacy systems, and planning connections to external mail systems.

Chapters 9 and 10 prepare you to actually install the software in a primarily Windows NT network. Additionally, these chapters discuss the requirements for deploying Exchange in a Novell network environment.

Part III: Exchange Administration and Configuration

In Part III, you learn how to configure all of the Exchange services, connectors, message transfer agents, links to external systems, public folders, and address routing. This part also focuses on the administration of Exchange. Key elements are creating mail boxes, performance-tuning Exchange servers, security and fault tolerance, and troubleshooting Exchange problems.

Chapters 11 through 14 discuss the core administration setup, configuration, and use of the main components of the Exchange server.

Chapter 15, "Creating and Configuring Recipients," exemplifies how to create a mailbox and NT domain account for an Exchange user, which also includes distribution lists and foreign-mail system custom recipients.

Chapters 16 and 17 walk you through the configuration and setup of public folders. Public folders are the information stores that contain groupware information. This information is then replicated and synchronized throughout the Enterprise.

Chapters 18 and 19 go over how to migrate and interoperate with MS Mail for PC and Macintosh networks. Exchange includes several custom features to support this integration.

Chapters 20 and 21 similarly discuss configurations of the gateway to external mail systems, including X.400 and SMTP recipients.

Chapters 22 through 26 discuss day-to-day operations with Exchange. Various troubleshooting techniques are exemplified. The performance-tuning chapter details how to use a load simulation tool to predict future messaging loads on the servers. This part has a great deal of information. Many sections are used as reference guides.

Part IV: Exchange Client Software and Scheduling

This part discusses the client components, including client electronic mail, the universal Inbox, and the scheduling or group calendaring application.

Chapters 27 and 28 show the ways to deploy client software components and the various configuration options. Additionally, they discuss many of the rich sets of tools for end-user productivity.

Chapters 29 and 30 discuss the calendaring functions. This again covers software installation and the end-user tools.

Part V: Third-Party Integration and Application Development

Part V presents some other uses for the Exchange architecture.

Chapter 31, "Implementing Third-Party Integration Tools," shows the many independent software vendors who are developing solutions.

Chapter 32, "Using Electronic Data Interchange," discusses how EDI applications can be architected by using the Exchange topology and support for industry standards.

Chapter 33, "Introduction to Exchange Forms Development," begins to exemplify ways to develop custom forms to replace paper in the enterprise. This chapter discusses many of the programming issues associated with developing these custom forms.

Conventions Used in This Book

Que has over a decade of experience writing and developing the most successful computer books available. With this experience, we learned which special features help readers the most. Look for these special features throughout the book to enhance your learning experience.

Several type and font conventions are used in this book to help make your reading easier.

- *Italic type* is used to emphasize the author's points or to introduce new terms.
- Screen messages, code listings, and command samples appear in `monospace typeface`.
- Code and other information that the user is asked to type appears in **`bold monospace type`**.

TIP Tips present short advice on a quick or often-overlooked procedure. These tips include shortcuts that will save you time.

NOTE Notes present interesting or useful information that isn't necessarily essential to the discussion. A note is used to provide additional information that may help you avoid problems, or to offer advice that relates to the related topic.

CAUTION

Cautions look like this and serve to warn about potential problems that a procedure may cause, unexpected results, and mistakes to avoid.

PART I

Introduction to Microsoft Exchange

CHAPTER 1

Overview of Microsoft Exchange

- The history of Microsoft Exchange
- The key components of Microsoft Exchange Server
- The role of Microsoft Exchange in a business Enterprise
- Considerations before rolling out Exchange
- Definitions and terms used in Exchange
- The general features that Microsoft Exchange Server offers to administrators
- The features of Microsoft Exchange Client
- Introduction to MAPI

Microsoft Exchange Server is the next-generation messaging system from Microsoft Corporation. This highly revered, much-awaited server product, which has been in development since 1993, represents the latest trends in electronic mail, workflow, and client/server groupware technology. This integrated client/server messaging system provides e-mail, scheduling, electronic forms, document sharing, and a robust application-development framework.

Microsoft has been beta testing Exchange Server for nearly three years and has maintained a strong level of commitment to the delivery of this product. Despite the many delays, Exchange is here; it will affect the way in which we communicate and share information into the next century.

The main focus for Exchange is to provide interoperability for all key legacy systems. Legacy systems are the large mainframe or host based mail system, including PROFS, All-in-One, and MS Mail. In addition, Exchange provides integrated connectivity for Internet Mail (SMTP), cc:Mail, and X.400 standards.

Microsoft has developed a robust messaging architecture that permits communication among the various e-mail systems that are in the marketplace today.

This chapter introduces the core components of the Microsoft Exchange Server and Client. The chapter presents an overview of the functions that the server and client offer, as well as examples of how the technology can be used in a variety of environments.

In addition, the chapter provides some basic definitions of terms used in Exchange. The key features of Exchange will be introduced to provide a framework for later understanding of how this technology is implemented and used in a production environment.

The Development of Microsoft Exchange

The following sections describe some of the history of the creation of Microsoft Exchange Server for Windows NT.

Change in Vision: Electronic Mail to Information Exchange

Electronic mail has been in existence for many years. The original electronic mail systems—including PROFS, SYSM, and Memo—resided on UNIX-based host computers or IBM mainframes. The single host, whether it was a mainframe or a minicomputer, was an enterprise solution. All users connected to the system to perform all facets of their online work. These systems, which are still running today, are text-based and provide centralized processing.

As local-area networks (LANs) have become more mainstream, workgroup computing has grown. Sales of personal computers have increased dramatically, leading to the widespread use of wide-area networks (WANs) to link workgroups. These systems have been growing for the past five years in conjunction with the push for PC computing. These systems are distributed and offer the end user features of a global e-mail address list and text messages with support for file attachments.

Exchange introduces client/server messaging and information exchange to the computer industry. Heterogeneous information can be distributed and managed globally so that information is at users' fingertips. Messages now incorporate electronic forms, documents in various file formats, and shared repositories of information (see fig. 1.1).

FIG. 1.1
E-mail has come a long way from the host-based systems of the past to the client/server solutions that are available today.

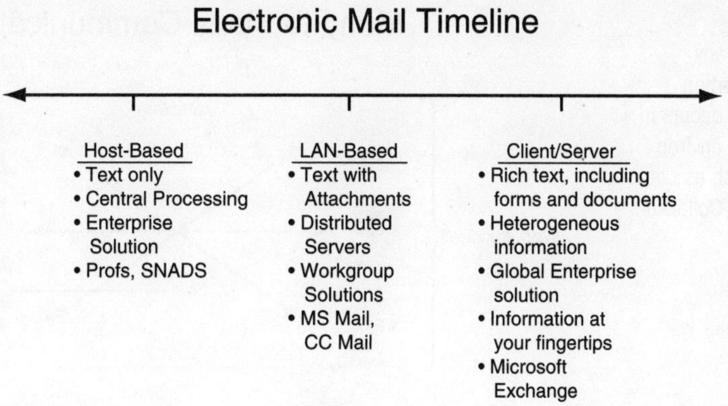

Methods of Electronic Communication

Electronic communication employs several methods of information distribution:

- *One-to-one communication.* One-to-one communication typically occurs in e-mail environments when one user sends a message to another user (see fig. 1.2). The recipient then responds to the message or stores the information for future use.

FIG. 1.2
Typical e-mail transactions embody one-to-one communication.

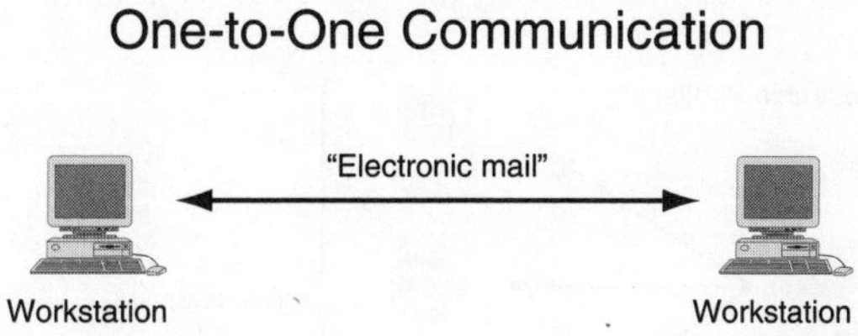

- *Many-to-many communication.* Many-to-many communication (see fig. 1.3) also is commonly known as *groupware*. Products in the genre include Lotus Notes, Collabra Share, and Mesa Conference Plus. The key feature of this form of communication is the fact that threaded conversations are maintained in a group discussion database. All users can simultaneously post to one location that is accessible to the other users.

FIG. 1.3
Many-to-many communication commonly occurs in groupware environments, such as Lotus Notes and Collabra Share.

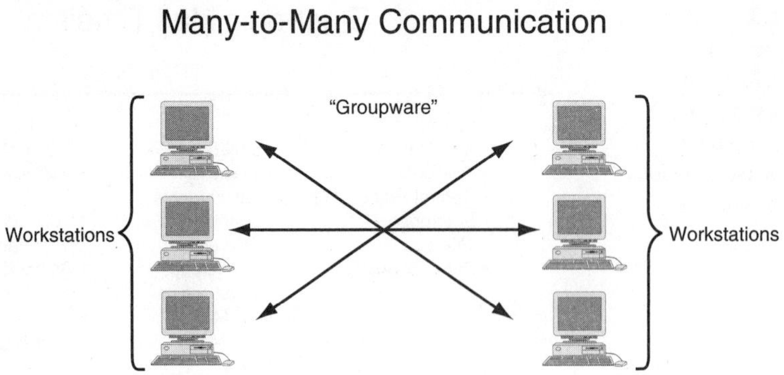

- *One-to-many communication.* One-to-many communication (see fig. 1.4) also is referred to as *electronic publishing*. With the advent of the Internet—in particular, the World Wide Web—a new form of information distribution has surfaced. Many users access information from a single repository that is made available by the central authority. The key is that from one location many people can access the same information.

FIG. 1.4
Internet services such as the World Wide Web have popularized one-to-many communication.

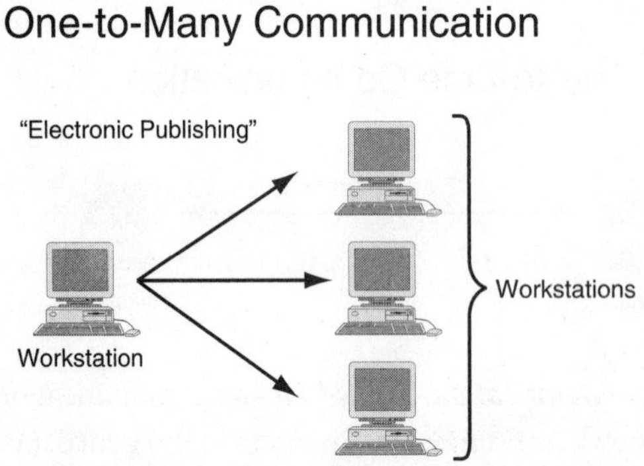

Introduction to Exchange Server's Key Components

The key components of Microsoft Exchange Server include the base message transports, scheduling, group information sharing, and electronic forms design (see fig. 1.5). The following sections explain how these components interoperate or work together with Exchange Server architecture.

FIG. 1.5
Exchange's components provide a robust messaging system that provides ease of use for administrators and end users alike.

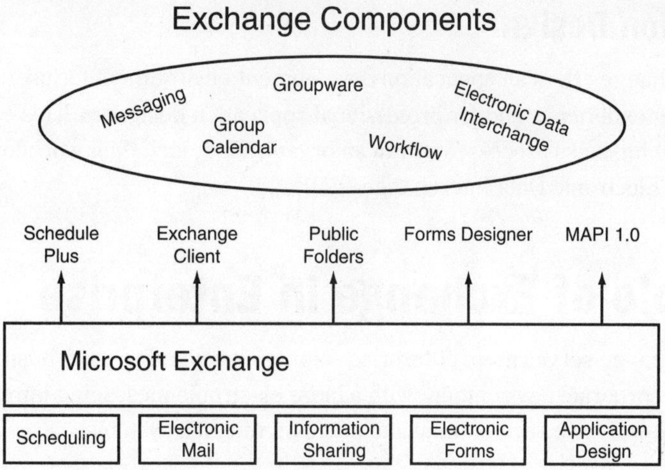

Scheduling

Exchange includes an integrated calendar and scheduler that allows users to manage their personal time, manage their contacts, organize day-to-day tasks, and coordinate group meetings.

Messaging Services

The heart of Exchange is its capability to manage client message creation and routing with Message Transfer Agents (MTAs). An MTA is the tranport system moving messages from one mail server to another. Exchange includes the feature set of the delivery, the routing, and the directory services associated with the messages.

Group Information Sharing

In addition to the one-to-one communication method used in e-mail messages, Exchange allows the user to post information on a bulletin board, track customer accounts from a shared contact-management database, and access product information from a reference library.

Electronic Forms

Exchange provides an Electronic Forms Designer (EFD) that allows users to create simple forms quickly and to generate custom views of the information stored in Exchange Information Stores. In addition, administrators can use the forms capabilities to manage the Information Stores.

Application Design

Exchange offers an application-development environment for users who have no programming experience and for professional application designers. This environment can automate business processes within an organization, including workflow, information routing, and Electronic Data Interchange (EDI).

The Role of Exchange in Enterprise

Exchange serves as an enterprise solution in several ways. A business enterprise consists of a corporate environment with a large electronic messaging infrastructure. An enterprise will have several thousand users on the mail systems.

The Exchange client component on the recipient's PC receives information that is pushed to it from the creator or source. (Microsoft currently provides this level of functionality with versions 3.2 and 3.5 of MS Mail.) Exchange goes beyond the push model by providing a shared repository for storing information that is on call for the user. This repository allows users to pull information down to their workstations when they need that information. By providing both push and pull technology, corporations are not constrained by the distribution mechanism. Exchange provides a complete solution.

Corporations and small businesses that have already adopted the Microsoft standards of back-office products, including Windows NT and SQL Server, are in a great position to integrate Exchange into their environments. Exchange extends the Microsoft vision for a single user ID and network logon. With Exchange, your Windows NT domain logon also is your integrated messaging logon ID and inbox.

Exchange addresses several key business issues: information overload, limited mail systems, and ease of use and integration with existing aplications. More information is available at our fingertips than ever before. The application model that Microsoft Exchange uses provides a client/server application architecture with a universal inbox that centralizes access to information. On the surface, Exchange is the next-generation mail system from Microsoft; however, it goes beyond to provide the framework for information management into the next century. Exchange is a long term messaging solution. It will impact future decisions to implement technology in the enterprise.

Universal Inbox for Information and Applications

The concept of the universal inbox has been around for years, but the capability to deliver such a product is revolutionary. The Exchange inbox is the user's gateway to information. From this inbox, the user can send and receive e-mail messages. The inbox also provides links to existing e-mail systems, fax servers, document imaging and storage applications, in-house applications, and more (see fig 1.6).

Many users have already been exposed to the Exchange interface in Windows 95. This interface provides both the universal inbox and the capability to customize forms and views. Microsoft is banking on users' acceptance of this user interface. Their business strategy is focused on users adopting this application model.

FIG. 1.6
Exchange's universal inbox with application folders enables users to access data from several applications.

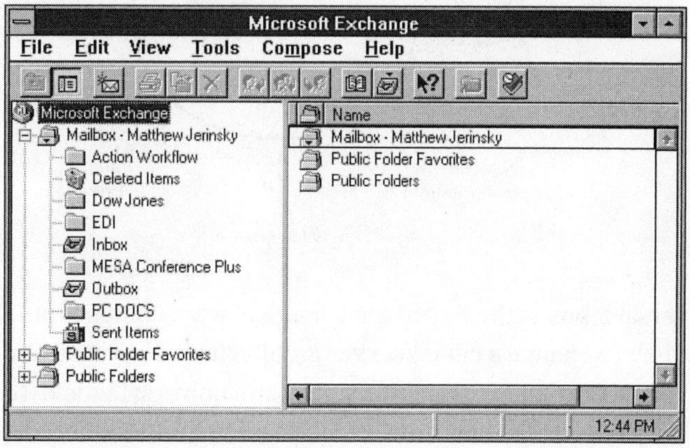

The key to the Exchange inbox is the fact that Microsoft provides the gateway to all your company information. Third-party software developers are leveraging or pursuing business opportunities on this foundation by building their applications on top of this technology; these applications appear as folders. The vision is to provide one standard location and interface for accessing information, regardless of format. Developers are even working on integrating voice-mail systems into Exchange. If you have a multimedia PC with an integrated sound system, you can access your voice mail as e-mail.

The universal inbox is not revolutionary (see fig. 1.7). Apple has had this functionality in its operating system for more than a year. Apple's PowerTalk, however, has not been very successful due to lack of developer support for the interface. Interestingly, Microsoft will provide a Macintosh client for Exchange. In addition, Microsoft will develop the functionality to allow Macintoshes to communicate with Exchange via PowerTalk.

CAUTION

Macintosh Exchange Client does not support the electronic forms of Exchange, due to the fact that the forms are Visual Basic executables. Microsoft does not have any immediate plans to directly support VB on the Macintosh platform.

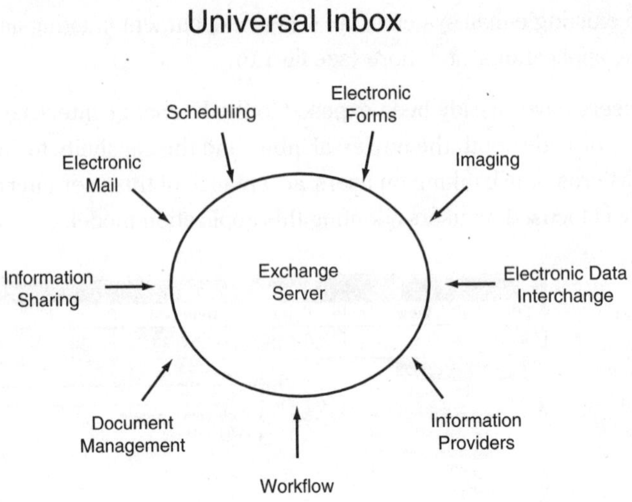

FIG. 1.7
The universal inbox gives you access to all your data in one place.

The universal inbox is the key to the Client software component. This functionality is facilitated by Exchange's client/server architecture. Microsoft and third party developers are writing application to take advantage of the universal inbox. To the end user, they only have to have one application in order to access the information that they need.

NOTE The universal inbox provides the framework for all the application types discussed in the following sections. Microsoft Exchange does not ship with all these third-party applications; you need to purchase them separately. ■

Electronic Mail Electronic mail is the basic foundation for the universal inbox. Users can send and receive e-mail; users can work online and offline, as well as over network connections or dial-up connections. Exchange Server generates a Global Address List to facilitate easy addressing of messages. The Client software provides several other functions that are discussed in the next section in this chapter.

Electronic Forms Many businesses need to reduce the number of paper forms that they use, for many reasons. One reason is that cutting paper consumption helps the environment. In addition, the use of electronic forms cuts data entry in half, reducing the chance for errors, reducing costs, and making people more productive.

Microsoft developed a forms package to be used in conjunction with MS Mail versions 3.2 through 3.5; Exchange expands on that package. Forms now are tightly integrated into the heart of Exchange Client and Server. Forms are routed to a user's inbox as a regular e-mail message. When the user opens the message, the electronic form is executed, displaying the information captured in the package.

Exchange also provides a robust environment for form design, as well as central form-management capability.

Workflow Workflow technology, which is derived mostly from imaging systems, seeks to establish strict steps for a business process, with limited or no choice for individuals to change the business rules. Exchange with workflow goes beyond forms routing to address several workflow-application issues, such as status tracking, work management, deadline management, ad-hoc initiation of workflow processes, negotiation of dates, and autonomous reassignment of work.

Workflow has two parts: routing and true workflow. On the routing side, Exchange offers basic routing functionality via the Messaging Application Programming Interface (MAPI). On the workflow side, Exchange takes a modular approach, providing interfaces that enable workflow developers to design solutions that will run with their database engines. Exchange is an ideal platform for workflow applications because of its MAPI foundation, directory services, and Information Store.

Companies such as Action Technologies are extending the forms capabilities by providing workflow technology for the Exchange inbox. Users will be able to access workflow databases directly from their inboxes. Users must have the Action Technology software installed as part of their Exchange inbox.

Imaging Imaging expands the capability to support multiple file types and provides a strong mechanism for reading, distributing, and annotating information. In the Exchange environment, you can integrate at the information viewer level in order to access public folder data objects from the client. With Object Linking and Embedding (OLE) support, you can drag and drop the actual image into the message. On the server, images are stored as objects in the Information Store.

Companies such as PC DOCS are providing solutions for electronic document distribution. Documents stored in the PC DOCS library will be accessible from the Exchange inbox via PC DOCS interchange. This way, users who do not have the PC DOCS client software can still review and edit the information in the PC DOCS library.

Document Management Document management (which also can be referred to as document imaging) consists of scanning documents into a system, archiving the images, and creating full-text indexes of the content. Document management now extends into the realm of multimedia and OLE objects.

Information Sharing Group discussion databases and threaded conversations are some of the growing technologies that are collectively known as groupware. Threaded discussions show the hierarchical history of the original message combining all of the subsequent replies to the original message. Exchange facilitates this "pull" technology in its public folders, which are accessible from the inbox.

Scheduling Exchange leverages the universal inbox to manage appointments, tasks, events, and contacts. A user can arrange a team meeting by creating a message about the meeting in Schedule+ and then sending the message to the recipients via Exchange. Schedule+ is the Microsoft group calendering software application that ships with Exchange and MS Office. When a recipient opens the message, he or she can accept the meeting based on their availability. In this case, Exchange handles the integration into the recipient's online schedule and books the meeting. In addition, a note is sent back to the person who requested the meeting, confirming the addressee's attendance.

See Chapters 29 and 30 for more detailed discussion about Schedule+.

▶ **See** "Integrating Schedule+ with Exchange Server," **p. 705**

▶ **See** "Using Advanced Schedule+ Components," **p. 717**

The advantage is that from one location, you can plan your meetings and maintain contacts. The contact lists are directly tied to the Exchange Personal Address Books and the corporate Global Address List.

Electronic Data Interchange One the hottest and most-talked-about uses of messaging is Electronic Data Interchange (EDI). Most corporations use EDI applications to exchange messages that contain information about orders, sales, and inventory.

Third parties are providing support for financial transactions via Exchange. Microsoft's intent is to provide support for EDI domestically (with X.12) and internationally (with EDIfac). Exchange does not provide native X.435 support, but support in MAPI will provide X.435 functionality in the client.

Exchange provides a rich architecture for use in EDI transactions. Together with the integration with Microsoft SQL Server and other Microsoft application environments, Exchange will prove to be a very solid, useful, and cost-effective EDI solution.

Information Providers Using the universal inbox metaphor, information providers such as Dow Jones, Reuters, News Wire, and Lexis-Nexis can deliver up-to-the-minute information feeds to a user's desktop. Then the user can use this information in other inbox applications, including forms, workflow, and imaging.

You can use Fulcrum's Find for MS Exchange as a search engine. This product supports advanced full-text indexing and retrieval capabilities for folders, attachments, and data in forms. By contrast, Verity provides Topic Agents, which runs on the Exchange server to continually poll and search data within public folders, as well as external information providers. The results of these searches show up in the user's inbox as a new e-mail message.

Exchange is a great platform for information providers for a several reasons:

- Exchange has built-in replication capabilities, which can make your information available to your enterprise.
- Because it is built on the client/server model, Exchange allows support for slow links, WANs, and remote connections.
- Exchange has the server-based rules to poll for information. These are processing running on the Exchange server to search for information defined by the user. The user does not have to be connected to the server in order to activate the rules.

Fax Routing Third-party products from Right Fax and Octel provide a gateway for DID-supported fax boards, such as Troutdale Boards. Faxes can be sent and received from a central location and routed to and from the Exchange client. This process eliminates the need to provide individual modems and phone lines at users' desktops.

Microsoft also supports its own fax gateway product for MS Mail. Moreover, the Exchange client for Windows 95 can leverage the Windows 95 Microsoft Fax software, which is bundled with the operating system. This way, a user can leverage existing aliases and contact lists in the local directory to send e-mail and faxes from one location. Microsoft Fax also supports binary attachments.

Understanding Client/Server Architecture

In a shared-file mail system, the post office on the server is passive. The messaging activities are performed by a client acting on the passive file server. This type of mail system has been the extent of LAN-based e-mail systems today.

Shared-file mail systems have three inherent problems:

- Limited extensibility
- Limited security
- Excessive network traffic

Every change that is made to the passive server's file structure must be followed by changes in the client component. This requirement makes it very difficult to administer and to configure additional applications to leverage the infrastructure.

The security model is a major breaking point for shared-file mail systems. Clients must have full read and write privileges on the entire file structure. All users must be able to read and write to another user's post-office box and mail files.

In a shared-file system, each client must poll the server continually to check for new messages. This application process adds a constant flow of traffic that will slow the system.

Shared-file, LAN-based e-mail equates to most v1.0 products (see fig. 1.8). Typically, the first release of a product is not the version that you really want to use; you need to let the product mature. Exchange is the incarnation of these original mail systems. Exchange addresses the issues left behind by your existing message tools. Exchange is a v1.0 product, in other words, brand new product, but it offers a legacy of five years of shared-file system e-mail.

FIG. 1.8
Historically, shared-file, LAN-based mail systems have been the standard for many organizations.

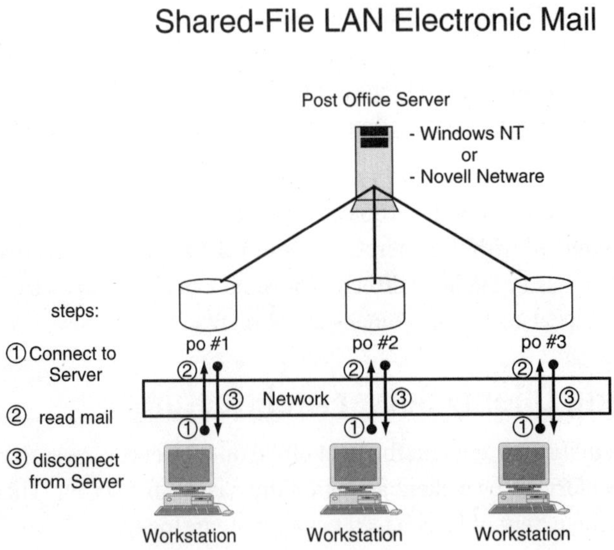

N O T E Interestingly, Microsoft did not use its own shared-file e-mail system; Microsoft used its client interface on top of a proprietary system called Xenix mail. To prove its commitment to the Exchange product, Microsoft has since moved all its internal mail systems to Exchange.

Client/Server Mail Advantages In contrast to shared-file systems, Exchange is a true client/server mail system. Exchange supports client/server standards, including Remote Procedure Calls (RPC), Distributed Computing Environment (DCE), and Open Software Foundation (OSF).

Unlike the clients in a shared-file system, the clients in client/server applications share responsibilities and tasks with the server component. This arrangement allows the application to exploit the total computing power of both client and server by splitting processing of an application between the front-end client and the back-end server. These components work together to accomplish the processing requirements of the application.

This distribution of processing allows the application to be more extensible and more secure, and also decreases network traffic. Client/server mail systems effectively address the limitations of shared-file systems' mail servers.

Exchange's architecture allows for dynamic changes to the server component. The communication between client and server is not affected. In MS Mail versions 3.2 through 3.5, for example, you cannot update the Global Address List (GAL) while users are still connected to the post office and accessing the GAL. Exchange manages all the connections as it simultaneously manages the GAL. Exchange can update the GAL without any negative impact on the client.

Because Exchange runs on top of Windows NT, it maintains the C2-level security of NT. C2 is a government approved security standard for the NT operating system. The United States Department of Defense issues this certification based on criteria meet in the development of the product. With Exchange, each client no longer needs to have full read and write privileges on the file structure. When the client connects, the user is authenticated to access only those files for which he or she has rights.

Because Exchange is a process on the server, the client does not always need to be connected; Exchange can still perform scheduled tasks on the Information Store. Exchange uses Remote Procedure Calls (RPCs) to reduce the network traffic. A client makes an RPC request to execute a command on the server; the server then processes the command and returns a response. A client can continually poll the server for new messages, but it is not required for the functionality of Exchange to deliver or process mail (see fig. 1.9). Each process is independent of each other.

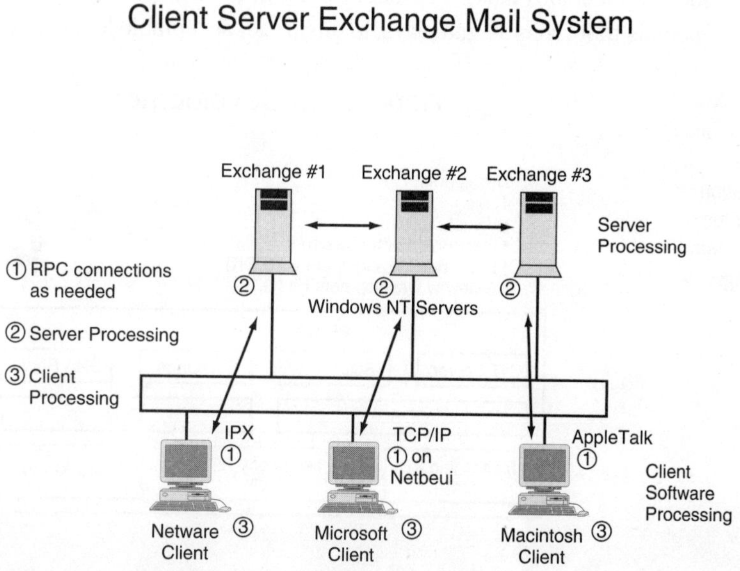

FIG. 1.9
The client/server mail system architecture reduces network traffic by using RPCs.

Exchange's client/server architecture is very extensible with custom applications using Windows Open Systems Architecture (WOSA) development standards. Whether you are using products from third parties or developing your own applications, you can facilitate integration with Exchange by using Open Database Connectivity (ODBC), Object linking and embedding (OLE), Windows NT operating system, SQL server, and MAPI development standards.

Application-Development Platform

Microsoft provides several ways to develop applications for Exchange. Through its use of standard APIs or interfaces to core Exchange processes, Microsoft has positioned Exchange as a flexible application-development platform. You can leverage Exchange for developing applications on top of its messaging infrastructure.

Messaging Application Programming Interface (MAPI) and Telephony Application Programming Interface (TAPI) are two of the programming interfaces exposed or made available for developers. Exchange offers a wonderful framework for application development, because it has a tight integration with the Windows NT operating system. In addition, if you adhere SQL, ODBC, and OLE development, you will have Microsoft standards for development. Using all of the Microsoft standards, provides for seemless integration between applications.

Microsoft ships two developer kits for the Exchange product (see fig. 1.10): the Gateway Development Kit (GDK) and the Exchange Development Kit (EDK). The Gateway kit allows connectivity vendors to develop solutions that provide administrators a consistent look and feel for management of new integration. The Exchange kit addresses the fundamentals that cross all gateways, to ensure an acceptable level of performance.

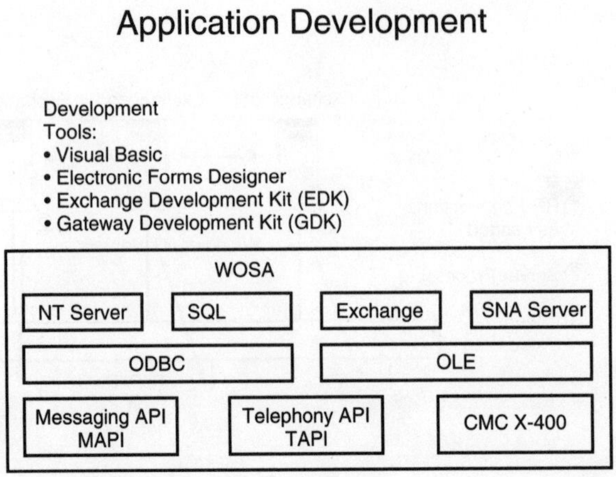

FIG. 1.10 The GDK and EDK provide a robust application-development environment for Exchange.

Data Security

As more people depend on e-mail for communication, the need to authenticate mail increases. Exchange offers three levels of security. Exchange manages the user accounts and the Information Store activity. Exchange also builds off the NT C2 security and incorporates several additional security mechanisms to protect the data stored on the server, the data on the client PC, and data in transit.

Exchange provides for RSA digital key encryption (see fig. 1.11), which is used to authenticate the user who is sending the message. When a user "signs" a message, the signature guarantees that the name associated with the message is the actual name of the author.

FIG. 1.11
Digital signatures provide enhanced security by authenticating the identity of the author of a message.

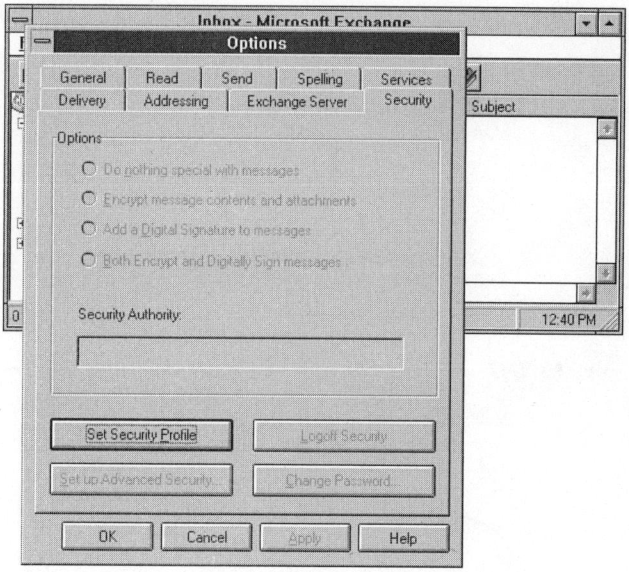

In addition to the digital signature, you can enable digital encryption of messages. Exchange uses an algorithm called CAST, developed by Northern Telecom. Security is discussed further in Chapter 21.

Support for Remote Users

Exchange enables users to work offline. Users can use Exchange Client from their PCs via remote network access (dial-up connections) or while they are disconnected from the network. Exchange was designed to use RPC calls, which are designed to sense the line speed and optimize performance.

Exchange can be used over asynchronous connections, including ISDN, PPP, SLIP, X.25, and regular modem connections (see fig. 1.12). This form of Exchange connectivity holds true for client-to-server connections as well as server-to-server connections. Additionally, security can be implemented when using NT's Remote Access Services for dial back and challenged dial-in via the NT C2 security. This figure shows a matrix for time and speed options for connections. Ultimately, increasing time or speed, increases costs.

FIG. 1.12
Remote-access solutions enable users to work offline and enable servers to talk to each other over ISDN and related technologies.

Remote Access Solutions

Network link	Bandwidth	Approx. Cost
PPP dial-up line	modem speed	$20-30/month
SLIP dial-up line	modem speed	$20-30/month
Dedicated SLIP or PPD	modem speed	$200-300/month
56k Line	56 kb/s	$150-300/month
PPP ISDN	128 kb/s	$100/month
T1	1.544 Mb/s	$2,000/month
T3	44.184 Mb/s	$70,000/month

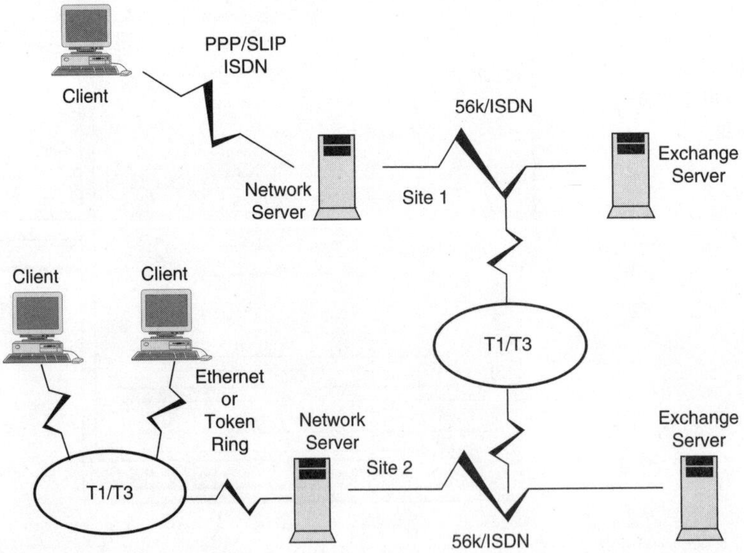

Support for Industry Standards

Exchange supports X.400 standards via an integrated X.400 connector. In addition, Exchange supports existing MS Mail X.400 gateways. Exchange does have its own version of the X.435 standard for EDI functionality. As mentioned earlier, X.435 is supported via third-party developers. No special requirement is necessary in deploying Exchange in an X.400 environment.

▶ **See** Chapter 20, "Configuring X.400 Connections," for a detailed explanation of the Internet Connector, **p. 499**

Exchange ships with the Internet Mail Connector, which allows you to send and receive messages over the Internet. You also can use the connector for internal communication between Exchange sites or between Exchange and MS Mail post offices. This function alone is worth buying Exchange for; it is a huge improvement over the original MS Mail SMTP gateway.

The SMTP support in Exchange now includes full Multipurpose Internet Mail Extensions (MIME). The preceding version was a DOS-based system; now it is a 32-bit service running under NT.

Gateway Support

NOTE An in depth discussion of gateways and connectors can be found in Chapter 24, while an overview can be found in Chapter 3. ■

Microsoft guarantees that all your existing MS Mail gateways will interoperate with Exchange. Your investments in those gateways will be preserved if you want to continue using them. As more Exchange connectors are released, however, you may consider deploying them as upgrades. The existing gateways will communicate with Exchange via the Exchange to MS Mail Connector.

Exchange delivers on Microsoft's commitment to interoperate with legacy systems. Microsoft sees Exchange as an effort to migrate the 4 million users of PROFS and DEC All-in-One to its client/server mail system. Microsoft will settle for providing backbone connectivity among all these systems.

There is tremendous support from the third parties to develop gateways for Exchange. The integrated monitoring and centralized administration of Exchange offers it as a robust solution for the enterprise.

Administration of the Exchange Environment

The administrative model for Exchange centers on the standard of high availability. Exchange must be available 24 hours a day, 7 days a week. The support model is such that local site administrators can manage and control local functionality, while enterprise administration can be performed from any node.

Centralized Administration Console Exchange provides a Microsoft Backoffice Standard Administrative interface. This includes tools to stop and start the Exchange application running on a given server. This interface enables you to manage the Exchange server from any location on site or off site. With Windows NT Remote Access Service, you can dial in remotely to monitor or configure Exchange.

Monitoring More Than Messages Exchange provides tools that help you administer servers and all the gateways and connectors. Exchange enables you to track a message throughout the enterprise through the Link Monitor and the Server Monitor. The Link Monitor allows you, from anywhere on the network, to monitor the status of any of the links or connectors along any message route. The Server Monitor allows you to check the status of any of the multiple Exchange services that are running on one or more servers.

Automatic Routing and Directory Synchronization Exchange is designed to provide automatic message routing. The logic for choosing the best route is built into the server components. The Exchange server looks at the destination address, compares the address with its knowledge of the site connectors, and forwards the message to the next site or connector. You can customize part of this intelligence for your environment, including route costs, bandwidth use, and overall performance. Exchange allows you to determine the route of any given message. You can configure Exchange to know the costs associated with various routes; Exchange then chooses the most cost-effective way to transfer a mail message. This feature is especially useful for budgeting and planning WAN connections.

▶ **See** Chapter 17, "Using Directory Replication and Synchronization," for more information on these topics, **p. 405**

In addition to routing messages, Exchange creates and updates the Global Address List. Formerly a nightmare of any MS Mail administrator, directory synchronization is completely managed by Exchange. You no longer have the problem of trying to update a global address list when someone is simultaneously accessing the file—another outstanding benefit of the client/server messaging architecture. Migrating from MS Mail is discussed in Chapter 7.

Exchange offers some great new updates for current MS Mail administrators. In addition to providing more features, Exchange helps administrators reduce costs and plan for future architecture enhancements.

Considerations Before Installing Exchange

Exchange offers several exciting features for enterprise messaging. You need to consider several issues, however, before you actually purchase the software, hire the consultants, and order the hardware. The following sections discuss those issues.

Connectivity Issues

NOTE Chapter 5, "Designing Exchange Topology," will go into detail on planning resources. ■

Exchange supports a variety of wide-area networking connectivity options. Exchange does not care which protocol you use, because it runs on top of Windows NT, which supports TCP/IP (the Internet's native protocol), IPX (the Novell protocol), and NetBEUI (the default Microsoft protocol). For special gateway connectivity to the Internet, you need TCP/IP; for connectivity to PROFS, you may need SNA or DLC protocols.

You can achieve connectivity between sites over asynchronous connections, including Windows NT Remote Access (RAS), 28.8-Kbps modems, ISDN connections to the Message Transfer Agents, and X.25 TP/x connections that use Exchange site connectors. These connections are available primarily because of the tight integration of Exchange with the Windows NT operating system. You also can use Exchange's X.400 support over an X.25 connection into most Value Added Networking (VAN) providers for international connections. Your choice depends on price, existing infrastructure, and corporate direction. Figure 1.12, which appears earlier in this chapter, shows the speeds and costs of various access options.

Costs and Roll-Out Issues

NOTE Chapters 4-10 will give you a better idea of exactly what to consider when rolling out various pieces of Exchange functionality. ■

The following sections discuss some of the most important issues that you need to review before you install Exchange.

Hardware and Software Costs You must consider several expenses. In addition to the actual servers, you may need to purchase routers, hubs, and several other WAN-related hardware components. If you want to use Exchange to communicate with the Internet, you need a router and a dedicated high-speed line to an Internet access provider. These costs can grow quickly and may limit the effectiveness of Exchange if you don't plan ahead.

Software probably will be the cheapest part. Microsoft offers several attractive packages that enable you to acquire licenses for a minimal cost. The Microsoft Open Licensing Program (MOLP) and Select Program for volume license purchasing give you lowest cost options. In addition, Microsoft bundles Exchange Client with every copy of Windows 95.

Security Models A key element of administration is the security model. Who will be responsible for creating user IDs? Who will moderate public folders? Who will define the configuration for replication of information? You need to address these questions.

Naming Conventions One interesting issue is how to name things. What do you call the servers, domains, and sites? You will fight the battle to choose names that indicate the country, state, and city; the NT domain; the job function; and the like. All these names must follow a logical thought process. Be sure to get agreement and support for naming conventions, because changing them is not easy; you really get only one shot.

Consulting Services You should seriously consider hiring a consulting firm to assist you. Many firms are part of the Microsoft Exchange Beta (Early Adopters) program and, therefore, have experience with the product. The logic is to spend the money up front to over-engineer the roll out. You do not cut costs early on. This is a significant undertaking and things will not work the way you think.

The planning sections of this book will provide insight based on experience gained through working with Microsoft and the Early Adopters Program. This information will help you effectively plan your roll out. Topics ranging from the financial perspective to the architecture across the corporate WAN will be addressed.

Comparison with Lotus Notes

Many critics attempt to compare Lotus Notes and Exchange directly, but no comparison can be made; Exchange far exceeds the functionality of Notes. The two products can compete as groupware solutions, but Exchange provides an entire messaging infrastructure to connect with legacy systems and heterogeneous environments.

NOTE Exchange provides tight connectivity with Notes, so Exchange and Notes can coexist effectively in your environment.

Notes Advantages Lotus Notes has a few advantages over Exchange when it is used as groupware. The product is mature, and Lotus has made several enhancements in it over the years. One exciting new feature is the World Wide Web gateway. From a Web browser, you can access Notes databases.

In addition to Notes' base functionality of providing groupware solutions inside any enterprise, many organizations have adopted an information distribution channel by providing Notes databases of information or direct feeds from their product support. Companies such as SAP, currently use Notes as a means to support their product.

Integration with Notes The preceding section briefly discusses some of the advantages of Notes over Exchange as a groupware solution; no doubt, the same functions will be available in Exchange over time. Microsoft sees PROFS and All-in-One as being fiercer competitors than Notes. Exchange actually interoperates quite easily with Notes.

As we have introduced the notion of the universal inbox and gateways, so too will there be a Notes gateway. Notes, as a product, has adopted MAPI as a development platform. Notes has been gradually moving away from its previous standard of Vendor Independent Messaging (VIM). Notes forms using WOSA API's will cross communicate with MAPI ODBC forms from Exchange. Both applications will share a common data source, despite different user interfaces.

Notes and Exchange can provide a complete solution today for a corporate messaging and groupware. Don't think that by migrating to Exchange, you will lose your Notes investment. The Notes gateway provides information crossover. Notes also supports MAPI, so you will gain a common development platform. These two products will be tightly integrated, thereby improving the market for groupware.

Explaining Important Exchange Concepts and Definitions

Before you use Exchange, you should understand some key concepts and definitions. Following are several terms with which you should become familiar:

- *Microsoft Exchange Client/Viewer:* The program that you use to read, write, and manipulate the mailbox and folders.
- *Directory:* A hierarchical structure of objects that represent each component of the organization, such as the organization itself, recipients, and more.
- *Address Book:* A list of names, addresses, or other information. Names can include users, distribution lists, and public folders. You have access to at least two address lists, one global list, and one Personal Address Book.
- *Recipient:* The receiver of a message or form. A recipient can be a user, distribution list, or public folder.
- *Custom Recipient:* A recipient outside your enterprise. To send Internet mail through the Internet connector to `joe@foo.com`, for example, use `[smtp:joe@foo.com]` as the custom recipient.
- *Information Store:* The back-end database that contains all messages and data located on the Microsoft Windows NT server that houses the Exchange server.
- *Security Descriptor:* Permissions information attached to every object under the Windows NT server. Security descriptors tell the operating system who has access to a certain resource, whether that resource is a file, a service, or an application.

Explaining Exchange Server Administrative Features

Microsoft Exchange Server offers the following key features to the administrator:

- Centralized administration
- Connectivity
- Adaptability and flexibility
- Security
- Monitoring

The following sections describe these features in detail and provide practical examples of each feature to help you learn how Exchange provides a robust messaging architecture.

Exchange takes advantage of all Windows NT Server 3.51 features. Tools such as Event Viewer, Server Manager, RPC Ping, and Dr. Watson can prove very useful to the administrator for troubleshooting Exchange. In addition, Exchange takes full advantage of NT Server 3.51 C2 security. Exchange also inherits NT Server's scalability and protocol robustness. Exchange successfully leverages all the reasons you installed NT Server in the first place.

Centralized Administration

Microsoft Exchange Server administration is performed from a single location with a program called Administrator. This program gives the server administrator a graphical representation of all directory objects on any site for which he or she has permission.

This utility is used to define the hierarchical structure of organization's messaging infrastructure. You can define and set properties for elements such as connections to other mail systems, recipients, servers, and addressing templates.

The advantage of centralized administration is that it enables you to see the entire object tree or hierarchy of information and make any addition, move, or change in an easy, straightforward manner, regardless of the location of the server. If your company merges with another company that has a Microsoft Mail messaging infrastructure in place, for example, the Exchange administrator can add the Microsoft Mail connector, and connectivity would be available to all specified users on all specified servers. The convenience of adding functionality from a central console is apparent in this case.

Connectivity

NOTE For more information about connectors, see Chapter 3 and Chapters 20-22. ■

Exchange offers a wide variety of connectivity features. Through its connectors and gateways, Exchange allows users to exchange mail between different e-mail topologies and different messaging protocols. This includes the host's mail systems using SNA, internet mail systems using SMTP, foreign host systms using X.400, and between Exchange sites using TCPIP, IPX or NetBEUI. The following connectors are included with Exchange:

- Microsoft Mail for PC Networks
- Microsoft Mail for AppleTalk Networks
- X.400
- SMTP

In addition to the aforementioned connectors, gateways for Exchange extend your reach. Exchange supports its own gateways and Microsoft Mail (PC) gateways as well. Following are just a few of the gateways that are available for Exchange from third parties:

- cc:Mail
- DEC All-in-One
- FAX
- PROFS/OfficeVision
- CompuServe
- MHS
- SNADS

Regardless of the origin of messages, all messages in a user's mailbox look exactly the same. The addition of connectors and gateways is transparent to the user. That fact is a key advantage of Exchange. A user's data is collected and consistently formatted in a universal inbox.

Like incoming mail, outgoing mail routed through connectors and gateways is transparent to the user. The administrator creates custom recipients that reside in address books alongside regular Exchange recipients.

When a connector is installed to allow communication to the Microsoft Mail post office, for example, Exchange clients can immediately send and receive mail by addressing the message to the MS Mail user the same way that they do when they send a message to another Exchange user. When Lisa's boss says, "Please send a memo to George Roberts at the new office," Lisa can fire up her Exchange Client and send the memo directly to

George Roberts, because his name is in the address book. Likewise, Lisa shows up in the MS Mail post office, and George can easily send her a message.

Environment Adaptability and Flexibility

Exchange can be used in many environments: Small LANs, large WANs, and everything in between. Because Exchange integrates tightly with Windows NT Server, it has the same scalability. Exchange is a great starting point for organizations that are just establishing a messaging infrastructure, as well as for institutions that are looking for increased functionality and robustness by switching to a new product or adding a new product to the mix.

Exchange provides the functionality not only to connect to other messaging systems and protocols, but also to allow the administrator to migrate mail and user account information from other mail systems.

Exchange supports the following mail systems:

- DEC All-in-One
- IBM PROFS/OfficeVision
- Microsoft Mail for PC Networks
- Microsoft Mail for AppleTalk Networks
- Lotus cc:Mail

Various tools are used to move data from one system to another. These tools show Exchange's flexibility; they allow the administrator to use the tool with which he or she is most comfortable to achieve the specified task. These tools are:

- *Extraction tools.* These tools copy directory, message, and scheduling information from an existing system. Your cc:Mail post office MLANDATA, CLANDATA, and USR files would be run through the tool, dumping all the data into a file and keeping all pointers intact.
- *Migration tool.* This tool imports the data created with the extraction tools in Exchange. You would run the migration tool on the file output by the extraction tools. The user information would go into the address books, and the data would be moved to the Information Store.
- *Administrator program.* You can use the import and export options in the main Administrator program in place of the preceding tools. These options allow you to use the tools with which you are most comfortable.
- *Custom tools.* Exchange allows you to write custom command files that perform

certain functions. These files can be tied in with the NT Server scheduling system to perform certain duties at certain times. If you have limited hardware capacity and want to import cc:Mail entries from different post offices over a certain number of days, you could write custom scripts that perform those tasks without overburdening your network or server. You also could write scripts that manipulate the extraction tools to feed only certain parts of the data to the migration tool.

As you can see, Exchange provides the flexibility to be suitable for large and small environments, and the adaptability to import data from other messaging programs to provide integration with heterogeneous environments. Exchange is capable of providing messaging solutions for any size organization with any combination of exisiting mail systems.

Security

Exchange not only leverages all the security features of Windows NT Server, but also includes added security mechanisms that provide even more protection against unauthorized use of the system and that encrypt the data that is being transmitted. Exchange Server has the following additional security functions:

- *Authentication.* When users access the Exchange server, they can be prompted for their domain password before they are allowed access to the system. This arrangement prevents anyone from going to a user's desk while he is away and accessing that user's files. Secondly, the logon process ties into the use of a single logon and password to all files and servers in a domain which is standard under Windows NT Server.
- *Access control.* Windows NT Server security descriptors are attached to every object in a domain. These security descriptors include files, services, applications, and any other object in the system. This concept extends directly into Exchange. A good example of access control is the ability of users to allow other users to access pieces of their mailboxes. If Jane wants her assistant to be able to access the Meeting Notes folder in her mailbox, she can simply set the properties of that folder to allow access. Any Windows NT Server or Exchange object that Jane owns is under her control; she can grant access to any user.

  ▶ **See** Chapters 27 and 28 for more information on Exchange Client features, **pp. 657** and **685**

- *Encryption and digital signature.* Data that resides on disks, as well as data in transmission over the network, is protected by an encryption algorithm. The benefit of encryption is that it keeps prying eyes from seeing your data and reading your mail as it is being passed over the network.

  The encrypted data also carries a digital signature, ensuring that the person whose name appears in the From field is the actual originator of the communication, whether it be a form, an e-mail message, or a scheduling request. Remember that Exchange is not just an e-mail package. If someone posts an offensive message in a public folder, you can track that person down, because his or her digital signature is attached to that object.

- *Auditing.* Any change to system resources is logged and can be viewed with the NT Server Event Log. This system can log how many new mailboxes are created and who created them; it also can keep track of how many messages are posted so that administrators can perform capacity planning. In some cases, especially when new services are being offered, statistical analysis must be performed so that management can be sure that it has allocated enough resources to the system.

Monitoring

Further building on a solid NT Server foundation, you can monitor Exchange processes in several ways, using such standard NT Server tools as Dr. Watson, Pview, RPC Ping, and Windows NT Server Manager. Three tools that are specific to Exchange are used to monitor a variety of Exchange information:

- *Link Monitor.* In a multiserver network, communication links must be constantly verified to ensure the integrity of the system. Link Monitor ensures the functioning of these links by sending e-mail messages and confirming the delivery of those messages. This tool is very useful in systems that have gateways or connectors, as well as in multiple-site configurations.

  In addition to ensuring link integrity, Link Monitor measures the round-trip time of the message, thereby helping administrators keep the lines of communication clear and to spot potentially overloaded segments of the network. This tool could be very useful when several Exchange servers are in operation. By looking at the logs, the administrator may notice that one server has a higher degree of latency than the others. He or she then can look for ways to alleviate the traffic and move it to another server. Link Monitor also can find overloaded network hardware by means of the same round-trip-time trials.

- *Server Manager.* This tool can be used to monitor the Exchange processes running on a server. If a process should hang, become corrupted, or otherwise become inoperable, the administrator can set an action to be taken. The process can be restarted or shut down, or no action can be taken at all.

- *Performance Monitor.* When Exchange is installed, additional counters are added to the Performance Monitor that allow the administrator to monitor various statistics, such as queue size, threads in use, and server throughput.

Performance Monitor is essential to running a good messaging framework. If, for example, the Message Transfer Agent process dies and messages are queuing up rapidly, you can set a threshold in Performance Monitor that tells the system to page you in the event that the queue grows to more than 100 messages. Then you could use Server Manager, Event Viewer, or Dr. Watson to find out what exactly went wrong and restart the process. As you can see, a combination of these tools can help you out of a tight spot.

This section concludes the overview of the server features. This information should make the examples used later in this book much clearer to you. Things like centralized administration, tight security, and robust monitoring tools that all take advantage of your Windows NT Server training and experience will be discussed in more detail.

Introduction to Exchange Client Components

The Microsoft Exchange Client components consist of Microsoft Exchange Viewer, Microsoft Forms Designer, and Microsoft Schedule+. From the client software, you can create custom applications using MAPI, giving you an unlimited client. Several sample applications are included on the Microsoft Exchange CD-ROM.

The Exchange Viewer provides a consistent look and feel across all the supported platforms; it has the capability to arrange disparate sources of information and data types in a coherent GUI design. You can have spreadsheets, voice-mail messages, word processing documents, and expense reports all organized on one screen.

The client also allows you to place filing, printing, viewing, deleting, and other functions on convenient button bars. These button bars keep the desktop uncluttered and yet allow the desktop to contain many pieces of information.

Folder Types

When you use the Exchange Viewer, you have control of several folders that are displayed off of the Microsoft Exchange root folder tree. These folders are very similar in layout to Windows Explorer, which ships with Windows 95, and to the File Manager in Windows 3.1 and Windows NT.

The three main folder types are:

- *Mailbox.* The Mailbox folder, listed first under the root, serves as the traditional inbox that most e-mail packages have. The main difference in Exchange, however, is that this folder holds much more than e-mail; it also can contain all the data types previously mentioned in the beginning of this chapter. After reading the data, the user can move the data into several other folders or have it automatically moved to other folders based on certain rules, which are discussed later in Chapter 27, "Installing and Configuring the Exchange Client."

- *Personal folders.* These folders allow the user great flexibility in organization. Some people like to organize documents by author, for example; others like to organize by subject. Personal folders also allow users to store the information on their hard disks for use offline. All mail in the mailbox is kept on the server until it is saved on the user's hard disk. Suppose that you're going on a trip. Before you leave, you log on to the Exchange server and get all your documents from the server. You then save the documents to a private folder for review offline. You can compose your replies, and when you connect to the Exchange server the next time, those outgoing messages are sent on their way. In addition, the folder views are synchronized next time you logon on to your Exchange server.
- *Public folders.* Public folders facilitate the sharing of information. Each client who has access rights can read information stored in public folders. The administrator can assign read, write, and delete access to information contained in a public folder.

In addition, the creator of the information creates a view to standardize the look and feel of the information. For example, in many firms there exists a document on all the bulletin boards containing what job openings exist at the company. With Exchange, you could create an Access database that would hold standard information and simply create a form that resided in a public folder. People could then browse the information in a standard way and all data would be updated whenever the database is updated.

Organizing Information

As mentioned earlier in this chapter, Exchange enables users to organize information according to their taste. Exchange provides some features to make this process much easier. Those features are described in the following sections.

Views A *view* is simply a way to order information. Information can be sorted by author, keyword, date, or subject.

Two kinds of views are available: folder views and common views. *Folder views* order information in individual folders. If you have a private folder called Peter which contains all mail from Peter, you can define a view that sorts all the objects in the folder by date. Then you could change the view for the folder to include a secondary sort criterion, such as subject. The data then would conform to the view only in that folder. *Common views* are views that can be applied to any folder. You can define a view called Date and apply it to many folders at the same time.

In addition, Exchange provides many predefined views, and Exchange is also flexible enough to allow you to create views on custom fields. If a public folder has a database element that contains a logical (Y or N) field, you can create a view that sorts all the Yes records before all the No records.

Rules and Auto-Assistants *Rules*, which exist in many of today's popular mail packages, specify that certain actions be performed on certain objects if they meet certain criteria. In regard to a folder called Peter, you can establish a rule that says, "If author = Peter', put element in folder Peter'."

Auto-Assistants allow you to have rules in effect even when you aren't logged on. If you go away on vacation, you can have a message that gets sent back to the person telling him or her that you are away, or if the message contains a certain keyword in the subject you could have your mail forwarded to someone else to take care of it. These are only a couple of examples of how to use rules to make things run more smoothly.

The Finder The Finder is a powerful search engine that allows you to specify criteria for finding items in any or all of your folders. This feature is extremely useful when you remember either the subject or a keyword but can't remember who sent the message or what the actual content was. You can have the Finder look for the message in all your folders.

The Finder runs in the background and is treated like any other running program, allowing you to continue working while the search is under way.

Once you are presented with the objects that meet the specified criteria, any action you take on those objects takes effect in the actual folders the objects reside in. For example, you can use the Finder to retrieve all messages 30 or more days old. Once they are brought up in the Finder window, you can select all of them, and click the delete button. They will all be removed from their respective folders.

Other Exchange Client Components

Three more components of the Microsoft Exchange Client environment are the Exchange Forms Designer, the Custom Application Environment, and Schedule+. These tools, combined with the Exchange Viewer, provide a solid client framework for networked messaging applications.

The Microsoft Exchange Forms Designer The Forms Designer allows the administrator (and any other user when granted permission) to create custom forms that can replace paper forms. Most companies have standard forms for requesting vacation time, for example. Why not create this form online, store it in a public folder, and allow the user to fill out and send it to you for processing? In addition, you can create a Visual Basic program to take the data off the form and store it in an Access, FoxPro, or SQL Server database for later retrieval and manipulation.

Imagine putting office-supplies requisitions in an electronic form. You could tally the total cost of office supplies for a month quickly by using OLE to create an Excel table from the Exchange data.

You do not have to be a Visual Basic guru to use forms, but having (or acquiring) the necessary knowledge allows you to extend the functionality of Exchange beyond the transfer of information.

The Application Design Environment (ADE) The ADE is a very flexible, non-code-based system that generates applications by using a combination of forms and custom folders. ADE is the extension to the Forms Designer, which is described in the preceding section.

Several examples of custom applications appear on the Exchange CD-ROM in the EXCHANGE\FORMS directory. You can build applications from these templates.

Schedule+ Microsoft Schedule+ provides a group calendar and group scheduling and contact-management tools that take the personal information manager to the new level. The tight integration with Microsoft Exchange Server allows the user to communicate and schedule with anyone in the organization. This tight integration has not been seen before between a set of diverse applications.

▶ **See** Chapters 29 and 30 for more information regarding Schedule+, **pp. 705** and **717**

Schedule+ functions not only as a group scheduler, but also as a personal scheduler and a contact-management system. You can group and sort information based on any criteria. You also can allow other people to view your schedule, so as to cut down on repetitive e-mail messages requesting meetings. How many times have you had to cancel a meeting just because one person couldn't make it? With Exchange, you'll know beforehand that that person can't attend, because you can see his or her schedule.

Another good application for this technology is to set up schedules for meeting rooms. Users can see whether a certain room is free at a certain time and, if so, make a reservation.

Understanding Exchange Client Components

The client side of Microsoft Exchange has three core components: Exchange Client or Viewer, Schedule+, and the Forms Designer. You can design custom applications by using the Messaging Application Programming Interface (MAPI).

You will understand how these components fit into the Exchange architecture and what the interrelationships of the components mean to you. The Exchange Client structure will help you understand how to more effectively use all the features of Exchange to improve productivity.

The following sections discuss the following topics:

- MAPI
- The Exchange Client
- Schedule+
- The Forms Designer

Figure 1.13 shows the various Client components and how they communicate with Exchange Server.

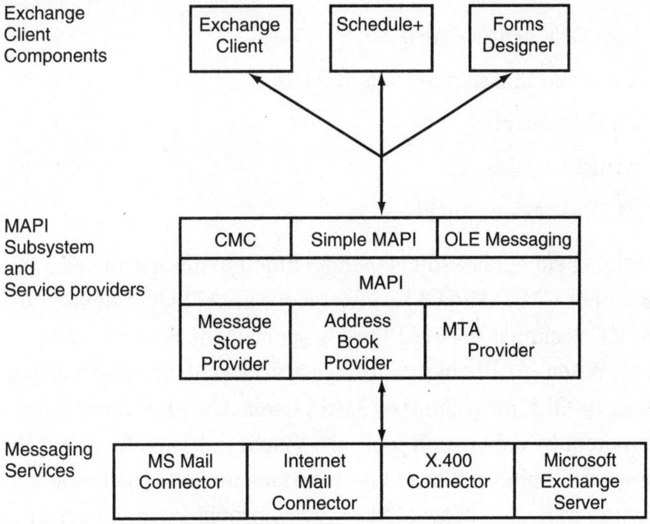

FIG. 1.13
The Exchange client/server architecture has MAPI acting as the glue for the integration of the client with the server.

MAPI

MAPI (Messaging Application Programming Interface) is a set of functions that can be called by C, C++, and Visual Basic programs through Windows Dynamic Link Libraries (DLLs). MAPI allows custom programs that can control and manipulate Exchange objects (see fig. 1.14). MAPI is a powerful extension to Exchange providing support for developers to enhance the core functionality built into Exchange.

FIG. 1.14
The MAPI framework provides the map for designing Exchange applications.

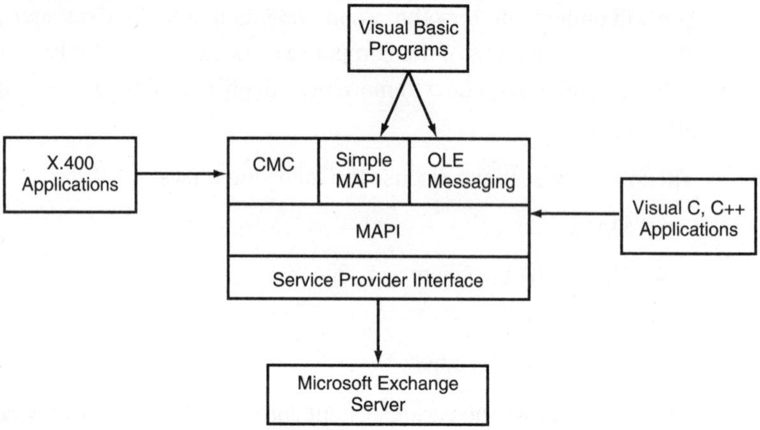

MAPI has five components:

- Simple MAPI (sMAPI)
- Common Messaging Calls (CMC)
- OLE Messaging
- MAPI
- MAPI Service Providers

When the client application is using a function library, messaging services are processed by sMAPI or CMC. The CMC interface is an API layer defined by the X.400 API Association. CMC is similar to sMAPI but is specially designed to support cross-platform development. When MAPI objects are being accessed and manipulated, client requests are serviced by OLE messaging or MAPI itself. The OLE messaging component allows development by using such tools are Visual C, Visual C++, and Visual Basic; MAPI itself is a powerful, object-oriented C++ interface that allows complex manipulation of folders, forms, and messages. The MAPI service providers then perform the requested actions for the client and pass back action through the MAPI subsystem to the MAPI client.

TIP In addition to the tools and sample applications provided by Microsoft, many utilities for Exchange are available from third-party companies. These utilities, which are discussed in Chapter 31, consist of gateways, connectors, Visual Basic custom controls, and administrative utilities.

Third-party developers, such as Lotus Development Corporation, have switched from proprietary messaging standards, such as Vendor Independent Messaging (VIM), to MAPI for designing messaging applications. This fact shows the strength of the MAPI standard and is a harbinger of the plethora of development tools that will emerge for designing MAPI applications.

MAPI is the glue that allows client applications to converse with the server to build a robust communications architecture.

Understanding How the Exchange Client Talks to the Server

The Exchange Client—the user interface to the Exchange Server—is where the user interacts with the server and performs all messaging functions.

Using standard MAPI calls, the Client communicates via RPCs to the public Information Store of the Exchange server to retrieve shared messages and forms; communicates via RPC to the private Information Store of the Exchange server to retrieve private folder information; and presents the information in a consistent, organized fashion.

The method of communication between the Viewer and the Exchange server is Remote Procedure Call (RPC). An RPC is a routine that transfers functions and data between client and server computers. RPCs allow users to access data on other server computers transparently, as though the data were local to a user's computer (see fig. 1.15). To a user, all data access through the user's computer looks just like local data.

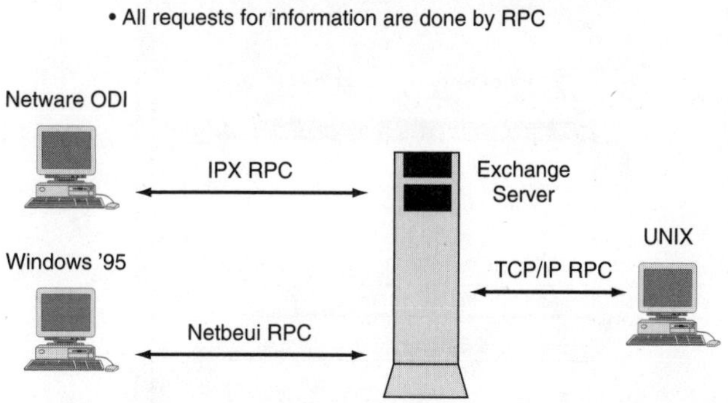

FIG. 1.15 RPC transactions can operate over any protocol and allow for the "push" and "pull" features of Exchange.

RPC gives transparency to the user and provides flexibility for the administrator by supporting many network protocols and methods of communication. The supported network protocols are:

- IPX
- NetBEUI
- TCP/IP

The supported methods of communication are:

- Named pipes
- NetBIOS
- Windows Sockets

When the user loads Exchange Client, it uses RPC to ask the server for all the objects to which the Client has permission. The Client knows which services to connect to by using a profile. A *profile* contains the configuration information about the MAPI service providers (address book, transport, and store providers) that a user wants to use when starting an application, which in this case is the Microsoft Exchange Client. The same situation holds true for Schedule+ information.

Figure 1.16 shows the profile screen where users can add services to a profile to extend functionality to an existing configuration. Multiple profiles can be used for the same Exchange client. If a user wants to keep all faxes separate, for some reason, he or she can configure a profile that connects only to his or her faxes. A user also might want more than one profile if he or she has two mailboxes: one for personal use and one for administrative use.

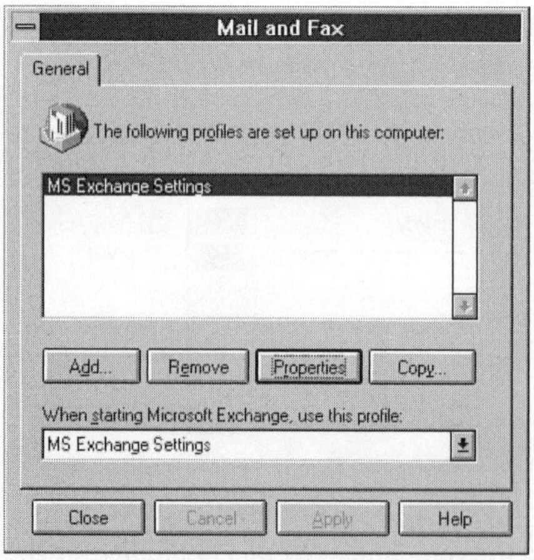

FIG. 1.16
Exchange allows for several profiles per user.

Clicking the Properties button brings up the dialog box shown in figure 1.17, where the user can select the information service to modify.

Clicking the Properties button in this dialog box displays the dialog box shown in figure 1.18. This dialog box has a series of tabs that enable the user to define properties that pertain to the selected information service.

FIG. 1.17
The Exchange Client can have many information sources, such as a Microsoft Exchange Server, an MS Mail post office, or Microsoft Fax.

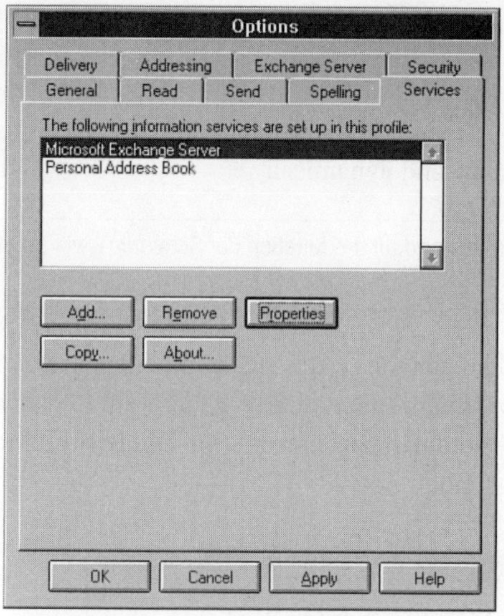

FIG. 1.18
The Service properties dialog box is where all the recipient options are configured.

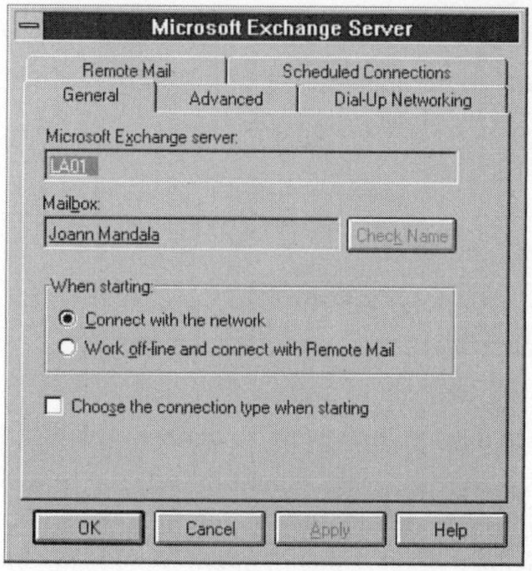

As you can see in figure 1.18, the General tab contains such information as which Exchange server to connect to, which mailbox to connect to, and whether to use local or remote mode.

The client/server nature of Exchange allows remote connections to be transparent to the user. Exchange leverages Windows NT and Windows 95 features of dial-up networking by providing the Dial-Up Networking tab. In many e-mail systems, you must use a separate client for remote access and reconcile your mailboxes. This situation is not the case with Exchange. The architecture of the client components of Exchange allow for a single client, dial-in or networked, through the use of RPC and MAPI.

Snapping Schedule+ into Exchange Server

Schedule+ is the component of the Exchange Client that allows users to plan meetings, track contacts, create to-do lists, and make appointments. Exchange enables users to share this information easily and dynamically.

TIP A step-by-step guide to using this and all the functions of Schedule+ will be discussed in Chapter 30.

In addition, Schedule+ (like all other Exchange components) is tightly integrated to the server so that you can do things automatically. If you want to plan a meeting by sending an e-mail message to all the potential participants, you can use the Meeting Wizard, included with Schedule+ (see fig. 1.19).

FIG. 1.19
You can use the Microsoft Schedule+ Meeting Wizard to schedule group meetings.

All this integration comes at a price, however. To achieve this tight integration, Microsoft had to make the Windows 3.1 version incompatible with the new NT and Windows 95 versions, due to the addition of hooks needed to tie the Schedule+ software to Exchange. You must make some sacrifices to take advantage of the advanced client—server architecture of Exchange; this is one of them.

If you used a plain e-mail system, you would then have to gather all the responses and find out which people can attend and which people can't. Schedule+ automatically checks to see whether the meeting time conflicts with someone's schedule.

A hidden public folder under the Recipients container or directory service for the Exchange site, called Free/Busy Information, contains the Schedule+ information for every user who has used Schedule+. You can view this folder in the Administrator program by pulling down the View menu and choosing Hidden Recipients (see fig. 1.20).

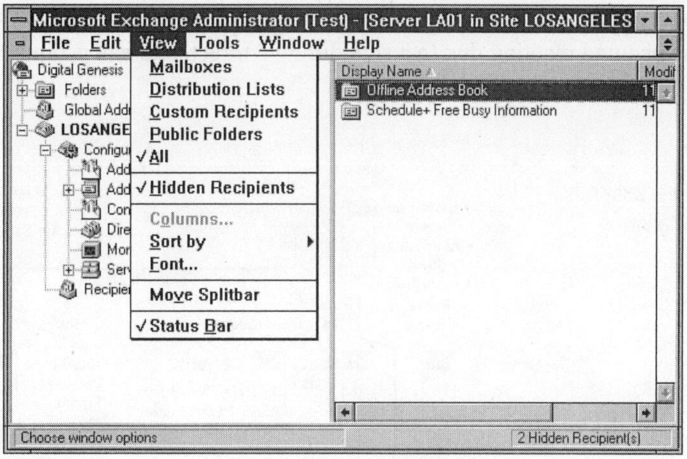

FIG. 1.20
You can configure the Administrator program to allow the viewing of hidden folders.

When the Schedule+ Free/Busy Information folder is in the current window, you can set its related properties. Figure 1.21 shows a sample of these properties.

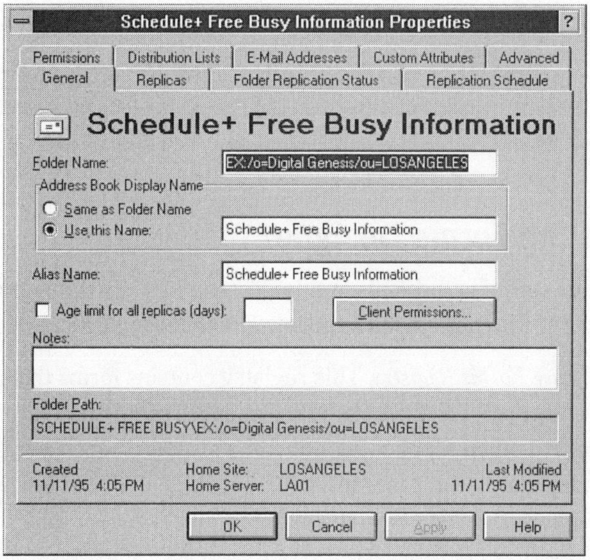

FIG. 1.21
You configure the Schedule+ Free/Busy information in the properties window.

In multiple-server environments, Schedule+ Free/Busy Information is propagated through the Schedule+ Free/Busy Connector. This NT service allows users from one site to schedule meetings with users at other sites transparently. When a user is inviting potential participants to a meeting, the Global Address Book provides the off-site names, while Free/Busy Connector gathers the remote site scheduling information. Figure 1.22 shows this layout. Schedule+ alerts the user even if a remote site participant is unable to attend the planned meeting due to a scheduling conflict, and will prompt the user to enter another suggested time.

FIG. 1.22
Schedule+ Free/Busy Connector Dataflow.

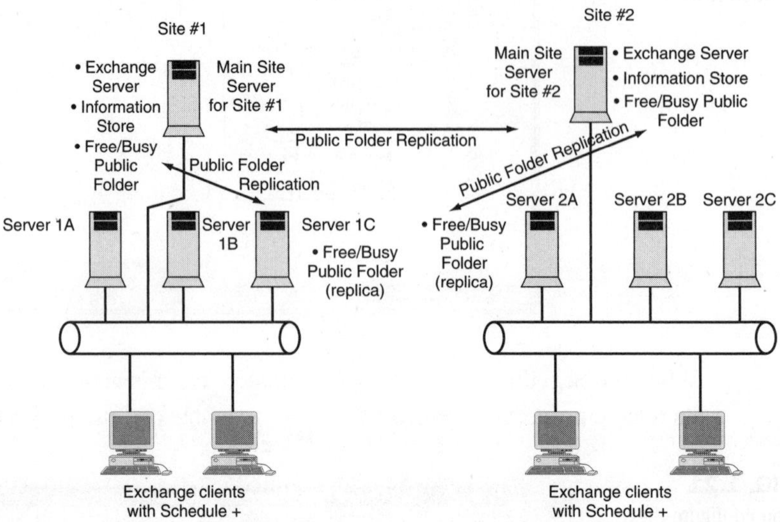

NOTE All replication information is controlled through the Properties windows of all relevant components. Configuring replication is described in detail in Chapter 17.

Integration of the Forms Designer

Forms can be stored in three places: the Enterprise Forms Registry, the Personal Forms Registry, and the Folder Forms Registry. The following list describes these elements:

- *Enterprise Forms Registry.* This registry contains forms that are distributed across the enterprise—for example, office-supplies requisition forms. Most companies use a standard office-supplies vendor and a standard paper form. When you use an Exchange form, the paper form can be eliminated, and forms can be sent directly to the authorizing party or to the office-products vendor itself.
- *Personal Forms Registry.* This registry houses all the forms that the user uses to accomplish personalized tasks. If an Exchange user needs to send out meeting summaries that follow the same format and go to the same people, he or she can use a custom form that contains all the addressees and all the appropriate fields.
- *Folder Forms Registry.* This registry contains forms that post data in pubic folders. This feature can be used between divisions and departments. In many organizations, a lack of communication exists between divisions. For example, Production

may not be ready for some of the demands of Engineering, due to lack of communication. By using custom forms, Engineering can keep Production informed by using a status form or action form to keep the entire company aware of what that division is working on. The form makes entering the data easy. The form can be customized to the user's liking.

By providing a simple graphical user interface, the Forms Designer allows users to create forms without the need for complex programming.

It may be difficult to believe, but the Forms Designer is a front end to Visual Basic. Simply drawing the fields in the form sends the proper commands to Visual Basic to create the executable form.

Like all other Exchange objects, custom forms have properties. Through these properties, the Viewer integrates with the Forms Designer. By setting event properties, the user controls which actions trigger certain events.

Custom Application Programming with MAPI

Exchange Client applications aren't limited to those that ship with Exchange. Because Exchange uses MAPI, you can design applications that take advantage of Exchange's underlying folder architecture.

Custom applications can use MAPI to perform such tasks as open a public folder and drop in data, search data, delete items, and examine the contents of folders. All actions are subject to the permission that the application has for any given object. If the program is running with a certain user's permissions, but that user doesn't have the ability to delete data, the application cannot delete any data.

MAPI also can be used to add functionality to a form created with the Forms Designer. You can write a program that takes data from a custom form, imports that data into Excel, performs some calculations, sends the user the compiled results in an e-mail message, and then faxes a copy to another recipient.

From Here...

This chapter welcomed you to the world of Microsoft Exchange, introducing the key features of Exchange and providing an overview of the concepts of Exchange. For further information, read the following chapters:

- Chapter 3, "Exchange's Integrated Server Components," explains what makes up the Server and provides a basis for further understanding the administration of Exchange.

- Chapter 5, "Designing Exchange Topology," covers the planning of back-end systems that make up Exchange and the layout of sites.
- Chapter 9, "Installing Exchange Server," describes some concerns that you need to address before installing the software.
- Chapters 27 through 30 describe, in detail, how to use the Client and Schedule+.

CHAPTER 2

Understanding Exchange's Organization and Sites

- The three tiers of the Microsoft Exchange Server hierarchy
- General considerations in linking sites to build an organization
- General naming strategies to consider when building your own Exchange enterprise

Microsoft Exchange Server is designed on a three-tiered model. The entire collection of Microsoft Exchange servers within a company is called the *organization*. To facilitate administration and maximize performance, the organization is separated in distinct groups of servers called *sites*. Each site consists of what are called *site resources,* which are the individual Exchange servers themselves and the recipients who reside on those servers. Understanding this hierarchy and the underlying network architecture that supports it is crucial to the implementation of Exchange in any company. This chapter is designed to provide an overview of these concepts in order for you to start thinking about how each element will apply in your specific situation.

Exchange and a Company's Organization

The largest administrative unit in Microsoft Exchange is the organization. All Exchange servers in an association or company are included under the heading of organization. An Exchange organization can be a single-room office with a couple of servers or a huge, multinational facility with dozens of servers at great geographical distances (see fig. 2.1). Regardless of the situation, often there will be other types of messaging systems to which Exchange must communicate. These systems are not considered part of the Exchange organization, though they may play an integral part in your company's overall messaging scheme.

FIG. 2.1
A Sample Microsoft Exchange Organization.

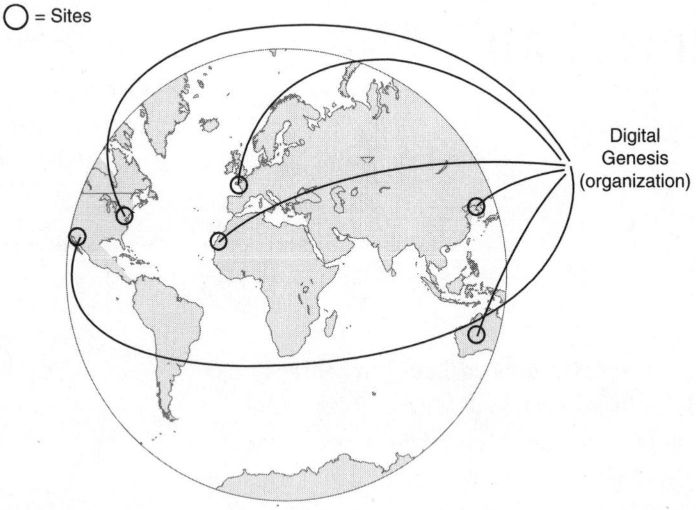

Exchange Server Sites

Sites are Exchange's second tier. They represent a logical grouping of several Microsoft Exchange Server computers. Servers in a site work together to provide messaging services to a set of users. Within a site, all servers can easily share information and can also be managed as a collection.

There are several other advantages to having multiple servers grouped into one site:

- Centralized administration. You do not need to log on to each server in order to perform administrative functions on any of the servers in a site.
- Directory information is automatically replicated between servers in a site. No additional connectors are required for this functionality.
- A user needs only to be added once to gain user access to resources on all servers within a site.
- Easier access to information resources. A user can access a relevant bulletin board without having to know its specific server location within a site.

Defining Site Boundaries

With all of these benefits, you might be inclined to put every Exchange server in one site. For several reasons this is not always the best solution. Therefore, defining where one site ends and one site begins is worthy of some serious consideration (see fig. 2.2). Variables such as network bandwidth, physical links, protocols, network traffic, operating systems, and, of course, cost will affect where site lines are defined in your enterprise. Also, it is important to plan your site boundaries well because it is difficult to reassign them once they are created.

FIG. 2.2
Sample site boundaries.

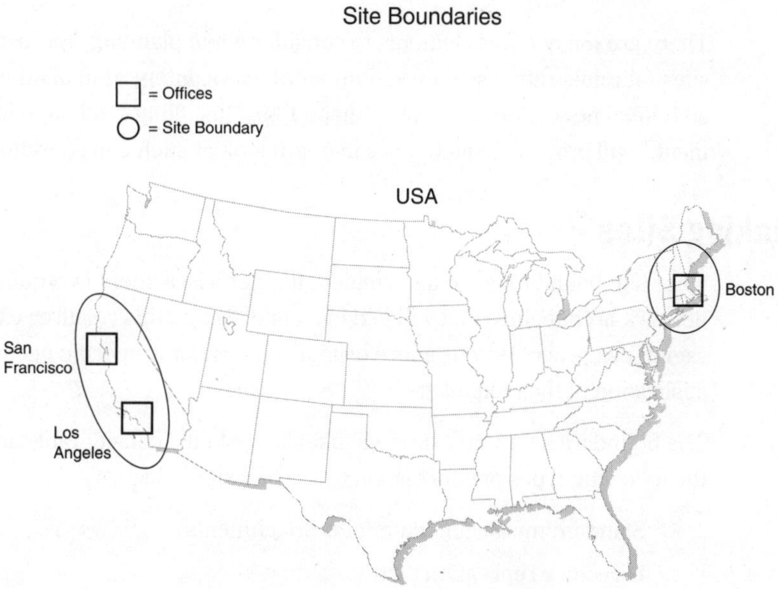

There are some general requirements that must be met by all servers within a site:

- All servers in a site must be able to communicate via Remote Procedure Calls (RPCs). RPCs can communicate over the network by using the various Microsoft Windows NT—supported protocols, inlcuding TCP/IP, IPX, NetBEUI, and DLC. Generally, this means that all the servers must be on the same LAN or WAN. But if you do have a large network spanning geographical boundaries and that network connection supports communication via RPCs, then you could define those servers to all be within the same site (provided the other following requirements are met).
- High bandwidth connections are required for server communication within a site. The definition of high bandwidth is somewhat arbitrary, but for our purposes we consider 128 Kb/s to be the absolute minimum bandwidth for reasonable intrasite communication. Basically, the connection must be fast enough to allow efficient RPC connections between servers. Of course, the bigger the pipe, the better the performance.
- The network connection must be permanent. The links between all servers in a site must be up at all times.
- All servers must exist in the same Windows NT security context. This means all servers must be in the same Windows NT domain or within a trusted domain. Exchange servers in a site must be able to authenticate each other in order to share information.

There are many other elements to consider when planning Microsoft Exchange Server sites (administration schemes, number of users, integration of other messaging protocols, additional network traffic, etc.). Chapter 10, "Installing Exchange in a Netware Environment," will provide a much more in-depth look at such considerations.

Linking Sites

Once site boundaries are determined, further assessment is required to establish the network architecture that will join each one. Again, this requires extensive study of messaging usage across your entire organization and any specific needs determined by your application of the technology.

The boundaries between sites will usually sustain a considerable amount of traffic due to the following types of information traversing site links:

- Standard messaging data (plus attachments)
- Directory replication data
- Public folder replication (or connections to public folders replication if not configured)

There are two primary Exchange components used to connect sites:

- Site connector
- X.400 connector

Site Connector This connector is designed for sites located on the same LAN. A site connector is a Microsoft Exchange built-in connector to facilitate the transfer of messages between two Exchange servers. This connector is an integrated software component to the server. The site connectors use RPC calls to communicate with the other Exchange servers. Site connectors are unlike the Internet or X.400 connectors, in that they will support any Microsoft networking protocol or any Exchange messaging address space or directory services. The key is that the Exchange servers have connectivity between the sites.

The site connector is the most efficient method of site interconnection, but the sites must be able to communicate at high bandwidth using remote procedure calls. Also, because the sites must authenticate each other during communication, they must belong to the same Windows NT domain (or be part of a trusted domain).

There are two major advantages to using a site connector instead of an X.400 connector:

- Efficient communication between sites because messages do not need to be converted from the Exchange internal format.
- Easy configuration since one does not need to define a network transport (RPC communications are transport independent).

X.400 Connector Conditions often mandate the use of the X.400 connector for site links. X.400 connections are used for several reasons. One reason is that your enterprise has a connection to a Value Added network provider in order to send secure messages to a business partner. X.400 is the standard protocol for the VAN connections. The other reason is if your enterprise is quite large, you may configure Exchange to use the X.400 address space as the directory service for the messaging backbone. X.400 provides a standards-based address space, ensuring the longevity of the messaging system in the large enterprises. Microsoft itself uses Exchange with an X.400 backbone to support all 20,000 of its users.

Generally, if any of the following conditions apply, you will need to opt for the X.400 connector:

- Your remote site is not on the same logical LAN. This could mean you are using an asynchronous connection, X.25, or are connecting to a site at a different enterprise.

- You want to use a public or private X.400 system as your messaging backbone.
- You want all Exchange communications to fully comply with the 1984 or 1988 X.400 standards.

Messages routed through an X.400 connector must be converted to X.400 standard for messaging interchange. However, the wide range of connectivity options provided more than makes up for the slight loss in network efficiency.

Site Resources

Site resources are the third tier in the Microsoft Exchange hierarchy. This tier consists of two main elements:

- Servers. The physical hardware and software package that operates Exchange.
- Recipients. The elements toward which all messaging data is directed.

Servers

Server machines may wear many hats in an Exchange environment. An Exchange server can at the same time perform any number of the following tasks:

- Hold local users' mailboxes
- Hold public folders in a local information store
- Be a connection or gateway to other Exchange sites, MS Mail post offices or foreign systems.
- Be a "bridgehead" server for directory replication between sites

Also, the server might hold the following additional Windows NT supporting tasks:

- Support dial-up users via remote access lines
- Be a Windows NT domain controller

To avoid overloading any one server, an optimal situation would be to have a dedicated server for each of the preceding tasks. However, in real-world situations this is often neither practical, nor cost effective. A major goal in planning an Exchange hierarchy is to master the art of load balancing across several machines. Subsequent chapters will discuss these techniques more closely.

Recipients

It is important in a discussion of Exchange hierarchy to consider the very entities of which directories are created. Recipients are the foundation of an Exchange messaging system. We are the reason that messaging technology exists in the first place. Microsoft Exchange server defines the following four types of recipients:

- Mailbox

  Called the "inbox." It is the most common type of recipient. One is usually assigned to each user. Mailboxes are recipients within the messaging site or local post office.
- Custom recipient

  These are recipients outside the messaging site. One common custom recipient would be an Internet user with an SMTP e-mail address, i.e., user@domain.
- Distribution list

  This type of recipient is actually a group of other recipients (either mail boxes or custom recipients). Messages sent to a distribution list are delivered to each recipient on the list.
- Public folder

  A public folder is a recipient with the added functionality of allowing the received messages to be shared among many users in an enterprise.
- Hidden recipients

  Hidden recipients can send and receive mail but they do not show up in the address book. Naturally, hidden recipients are not propagated in directory replication.

Each recipient is handled as an individual object by Microsoft Exchange Server during directory replication/synchronization. Each can be assigned individual trust levels (see discussion in Chapter 6, "Planning Connections to Microsoft Mail Systems") to determine whether its directory entry will be replicated to other sites in an organization.

Each recipient has many different properties and details which can be set by the administrator, but such discussion will occur somewhat later in this book (see Chapter 15, "Creating and Configuring Recipients").

Exchange System Naming Conventions

A good naming strategy is crucial to the efficient operation of a Microsoft Exchange system. Each object in a Microsoft Exchange directory is identified by a unique name. This is called the Distinguished Name and it is set when the object is first built, i.e., when you create a new mail box, install a new server, add a new connector, etc. With a good naming strategy you will be able to quickly pinpoint the object anywhere in your organization.

Good references on which to build names are traditionally as follows:

- Geographical locations (New York, Melbourne)
- Company structure (manufacturing, distribution)

Cute or comical names get old quickly and generally do not provide sufficient information for the widest possible range of personnel to understand your structure.

Microsoft Exchange Message Route

A well-designed Microsoft Exchange system within a reasonably large organization will reflect skillful interweaving of various messaging technologies. Message routing is the process through which a message eventually reaches its intended recipient. Because of Exchange's connector and gateway options, efficient message routing can and will be an intricate process throughout your enterprise. This section will cover basic routing concepts in order to start giving you a feel for how Exchange handles messages.

Fortunately for the end-user, the complex message routes are abstracted into the single inbox metaphor. As a system administrator, however, it is essential for you to understand all the possible instances of message routing in order to be able to create the most efficient routes in your Microsoft Exchange Organization.

The key elements involved in a routing process are as follows:

- Message Transfer Agent
- Directory Service
- Connectors and Gateways

How Routing Works

To route a message correctly to an intended recipient, Exchange needs to know not only the address of the intended recipient, but also information that describes the path to that destination. This is accomplished by two crucial pieces of addressing data:

1. Recipient Address

   The name of the specific mailbox toward which a message is intended. It must be in the standard of the recipient system, e.g., an Internet SMTP address would be **'user@domain'**.

2. Address Space

   Address space entries identify a certain type of message that a connector is responsible for routing. Typically, these entries are a subset of a complete address, identifying the route a certain message will take. Exchange takes each address space entry as a filter to determine whether a message should be sent through a connector or gateway.

Directory Names and X.400 Originator/ Recipient Addresses

Microsoft Exchange uses a subset of the X.400 Originator/Recipient (O/R) to identify individual recipients. The X.400 O/R address is comprised of attributes that define a specific recipient by country, organization, common name, and a variety of other information.

A Routing Overview

Here is the step-by-step logic taken during routing of a message within an Exchange site:

1. The routing process commences when an Exchange Server's MTA receives a message. The message can be derived from a user's mail box, a connector, or another MTA.
2. If the message's destination is specified by a Directory Name, then the MTA compares the site information of the message (part of the directory name) to the local site. If they do not match, then the recipient is on a different site and the message is routed by the process described in the following section.

   If the message's destination is specified by an O/R address, then the MTA compares the site information of the message (part of the O/R address) to the local site. If they are not the same, then routing proceeds to another site (next section).

NOTE If the recipient is a distribution list, the list is separated into its component recipients. Each recipient then enters this routing process independently.

3. If the DN or the O/R address matches the local site, then delivery commences. For recipients on the local server, the MTA ensures delivery directly to the information store.

   For recipients on a different server in the site, the local MTA transfers the message to that server's MTA, which then ensures delivery to the information store.

If at any time an MTA encounters a connection problem with a connector, it will retry the transmission periodically until delivery is successful or until the time-out limit is exceeded. If the time-out limit is exceeded, then the message is returned as non-deliverable (NDR).

Routing Between Microsoft Exchange Site and Foreign Systems

Here is the step-by-step logic taken during routing of a message within an Exchange site:

1. The routing process commences when an Exchange Server's MTA receives a message. The message can be derived from a user's mail box, a connector, or another MTA.
2. The recipient's address is compared to the local site. If they match, the message is delivered as in the previous list.
3. If the sites do not match, MTA will match the recipient's address space to an available connector or gateway.

   For example, if the recipient has an SMTP address, the MTA knows how to route it through an Internet Mail connector.

   If more than one such connection is available, then one is selected based on routing costs.
4. The MTA sends the message through the selected gateway.
5. The message is delivered according to the process of the receiving system. If the receiving system is an Exchange site, the message will be routed as noted in the previous list. Every other messaging system will have its own delivery methods.

NOTE Often there may be multiple message routes to a particular destination. In this case, the appropriate route is chosen by the *routing cost* of that destination (see following section).

Understanding Routing Tables

Routing tables contain all the information a message transfer agent needs to determine where to send messages. Every time you make a change that affects message routing, you will be prompted to rebuild the routing table in order for the change to be saved. Routing tables can be rebuilt manually though a button on the MTA property sheet.

Routing Attachments with Messages

Attachments are routed simultaneously with a message. All necessary file format conversions are handled by the appropriate MTAs through which the message passes. Exchange does have intelligent attachment handling when dealing with distribution lists. Only one instance of an attachment is sent to each mailbox. This eliminates wasted disk space to maintain exact duplicates of an attachment for several users in a same site.

Using Distribution Lists

Distribution lists allow a group of recipients to be addressed by sending one message. For instance, sending a message addressed to a distribution list named "accounting" would be received by all members of that list. Lists are established and modified by the administrators.

▶ **See** Chapter 15, "Creating and Configuring Recipients," for more information on creating distribution lists, **p. 345**

An individual user can also join appropriate lists from within his or her Exchange Client.

From the Exchange server standpoint, lists themselves are individual directory objects. This means they can each have specific properties attached to them and are replicated by directory replication and synchronization.

A message sent to a distribution list is treated as a single entity until it is split into its component recipients. When configuring a distribution list's properties, you define an expansion server where the list splits into its components.

Here is the process:

1. A user addresses and sends a message to a distribution list.
2. The message is routed as normal to its intended recipient (in this case, the distribution list).
3. The list object is routed to an Exchange server set as this list's Expansion server. At this point, the list is broken down into its component recipients.
4. Each message to the component recipients is routed individually.

Redundant Site Links, Routing Cost, and Load Balancing

For large organizations it is often efficient and safe to establish multiple links between certain sites. This not only increases the system's fault tolerance, but also can be used to balance messaging traffic between sites. Often there will be specific links which receive an extraordinary amount of large traffic. Message routing in this situation demands establishing a priority for whatever connections will receive the traffic. This will be discussed more in-depth in the site planning section of this book. There are some general considerations for situations where alternative routes should be established.

- Available Network Bandwidth. Links with more robust bandwidth will generally receive the bulk of messaging data between sites. An asynchronous modem link would usually be used as a backup, for example.
- Cost of Connections. Certain types of connections (such as the use of private X.400 connections) are less cost efficient and should be used only when other connections are overloaded or unavailable.

A variable called Routing Cost is assigned to each connection (in its property sheet) and used by Exchange message transfer agents to determine the path of a message. The cost of each route can be any number between 0 and 100. A route that costs 0 will always be used first if it is available, and a route that costs 100 will only be used if no other routes are available. Default value for all connectors is one. If two or more connections have the same routing cost, then messaging load will be roughly split equally among them.

In the DGENESIS organization, for example, a number of connectors are set up to connect servers in site LOS ANGELES to site BOSTON. In the connectors' property sheets we establish links between the following Microsoft Exchange servers:

1. A site connector over a T-1 line between servers BOSTON01 and LA01. We assign this link a routing cost of 1.
2. A site connector over the same T-1 line between servers BOSTON04 and LA07. We also assign this link a routing cost of 1.
3. An X.400 connector over a private network between server BOSTON02 and LA02. We assign this link a routing cost of 2.
4. Finally, we have one last resort Dynamic RAS X.25 connection between BOSTON01 and LA07. We assign this link a routing cost of 100 due to its inherent monetary cost of message transfer and limited bandwidth.

Messages will normally traverse the first and second site connections. Their routing cost is equal, so Exchange will attempt to distribute message load across both connectors evenly. Under heavy message loads where message cues on both site connectors 1 and 2 are long, Exchange will commence to utilize connector number 3 (X.400). In the rare situation where all three above connectors are disabled (e.g., the T-1 link is down and the BOSTON02 is off-line for repair), Exchange will engage connection number 4 as a last resort.

Load Balancing is the fine art of crafting your system's connections to best handle your diverse system traffic. By considering the above and many other variables, you will able to design an efficient and fault-tolerant system for your enterprise.

Address List and Directory Management

A listing of all available recipients, i.e., a global address list, is of great value to a user. From the standpoint of a network administrator, however, maintaining an accurate and timely address list can be one of the greatest challenges. Traditionally, Microsoft Mail has had a history of difficulties in implementing such functionality, and not since the arrival of Exchange has there been a bigger push for excellence in this area.

This section will overview the essential components of Exchange's directory architecture. Additionally, you will learn important concepts about directory synchronization that will aid in planning and implementing Exchange in your enterprise.

The Directory Service is the primary component responsible for directory manipulation in Microsoft Exchange. The Directory Service uses Directory System Agents (DSAs) that are the subprograms responsible for executing specific changes to a directory structure.

Maintaining a useful, up-to-date directory involves managing user addresses within an Exchange site, between sites, and between your enterprise and the other systems with which you pass information. If, for example, a user is added on one server, you as the administrator need to decide which other site directories should reflect that change and configure appropriate connectors to facilitate the process. By administrating a combination of system processes you will be able to detail how directory information propagates through your system.

There are two principal Exchange operations that carry out directory management tasks:

- Directory Replication
- Directory Synchronization

Directory Replication

Directory replication is the process by which all the Microsoft Exchange servers in an enterprise will share directory information. To maintain a useful user directory, updates must be accurate, timely, and available to all appropriate users.

Directory Replication Within a Site

Directory replication between servers in the same site is automatic (see fig. 2.3). Each server holds a local copy of the directory for that site. When you as the administrator modify a mailbox at one server, that change is automatically distributed to all servers in that site. Usually it takes about five minutes for new information to propagate across a site.

FIG. 2.3
Directory replication within a site.

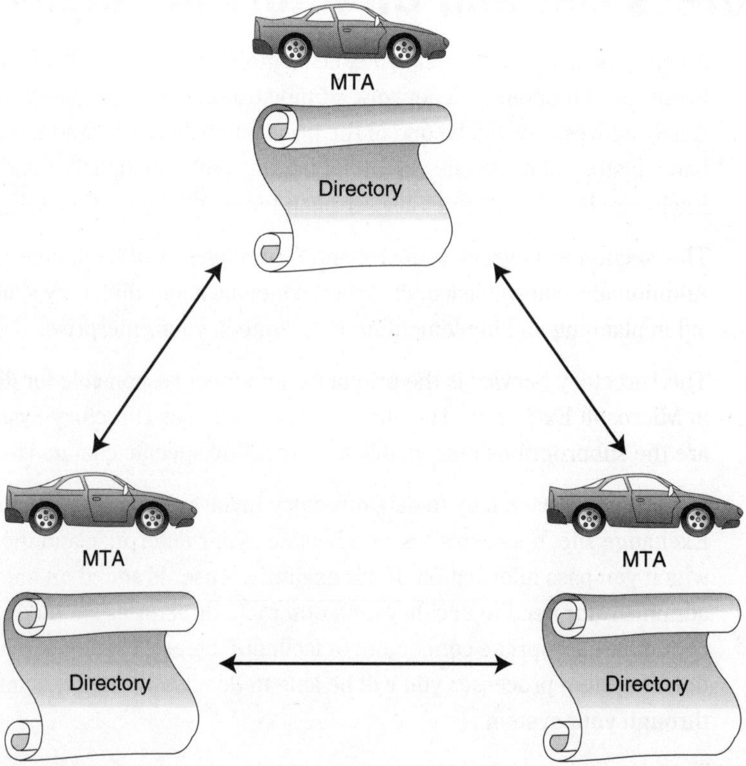

By default, all directory information is included in replication. This means an exact duplicate of each server's entire directory structure is exchanged during replication. This is efficient within a site due to the high bandwidth network connections typically found between servers. By the same token, network connections between sites are typically much lower bandwidth, so passing entire directory lists is not the most efficient method of maintaining timely address lists.

Directory Replication Between Sites

Directory replication between sites is not an automatic process. For two distinct sites to share directory information, there needs to be a specific connector established. This gives you the option to filter what data is actually replicated and what remains unique to that site.

Directory replication between sites can occur if the sites are on the same logical LAN, WAN links, or public and private messaging links (see fig. 2.4). Therefore, public X.400 systems, or even the Internet, can be the transport for your directory replication information between sites.

Directory replication across sites occurs asynchronously and is scheduled in the administrator program. Only one server in each site can be configured to either send or receive replication information. However, one server can be set up to both send and receive the data. Servers that act as the connection boundaries for directory replication are known as the "bridgehead servers."

There are two steps to resolve before directory replication occurs across site boundaries.

1. Decide what specific directory information you wish to exchange with other sites.
2. Act upon that decision and configure each site so only the desired information is replicated.

Replication Trust or Sensitivity Levels Each directory object (such as mailboxes, public folders, or distribution lists) can be individually assigned a parameter called replication trust level or sensitivity level. These trust levels determine whether or not a certain object will be replicated to a certain site.

Example: The trust level for replication from the Boston site to the Melbourne site is set to 50. You can create a user mailbox in Boston and set its trust level to 51 and information about that recipient will not be propagated to the Melbourne site in the directory replication process.

FIG. 2.4
Directory replication between sites.

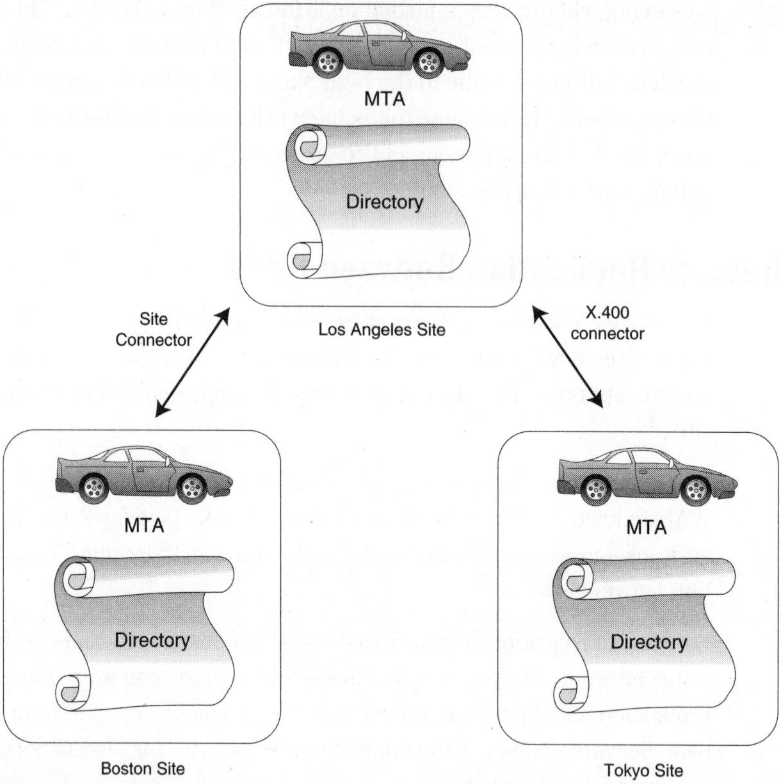

Directory Replication Tables

Directory replication tables are maps that describe the replication links between servers in a site. This is useful mainly when adding new servers. For instance, you bring up Server XYZ in a site, and then the directory replication tables are updated to include this server. The next time replication occurs, server XYZ can send and receive updates to all other servers in the site.

Directory replication tables also map links between servers in a site and the bridgehead server. This server is the one machine responsible for receiving directory updates from remote sites.

Directory Synchronization

Perhaps a greater challenge than replicating directory data between Exchange servers is synchronizing directory data with other messaging systems. Typically, this situation arises when linking Exchange to an existing Microsoft Mail network or to a foreign system through an external gateway. Exchange Server supports synchronization with any mail system that uses the Microsoft Mail for PC Networks version 3.x directory synchronization protocol.

Directory synchronization (dir-sync) is optional and it ensures that each directory (or post office for MS Mail) has an up-to-date address list. The dir-sync process is streamlined by propagating only the changes between systems and not the complete address lists.

Because Exchange's directory synchronization is based on the MS Mail dir-sync protocol, let us first examine the architecture of that system before proceeding (see fig. 2.5). MS Mail directory synchronization involves the following core components:

- Directory synchronization server—A single MS Mail post office assigned to the task of synchronizing directories.
- Directory synchronization requestor—Every other post office on the network that shares addresses with the dir-sync server.
- Server address list—The master list of all users that is maintained on the dir-sync server.
- Dir-Sync Server—The directory synchronization server (there can be only one dir-sync server in a site) collects address list updates from requestors, updates the master directory list, and then sends out the resulting updates to each requestor.
- Dir-Sync Requestor—These systems send local directory updates to the designated dir-sync server (note: when the requestor is also a server it sends messages to itself). Requestors also obtain address updates from other requestors through the dir-sync server.

NOTE On a dir-sync server, the master address list is stored separately from local address information. Therefore, when a local address is changed on the machine operating as the dir-sync server, it will communicate that change to itself as would any other requestor.

FIG. 2.5
Directory synchronization within a Microsoft Mail system.

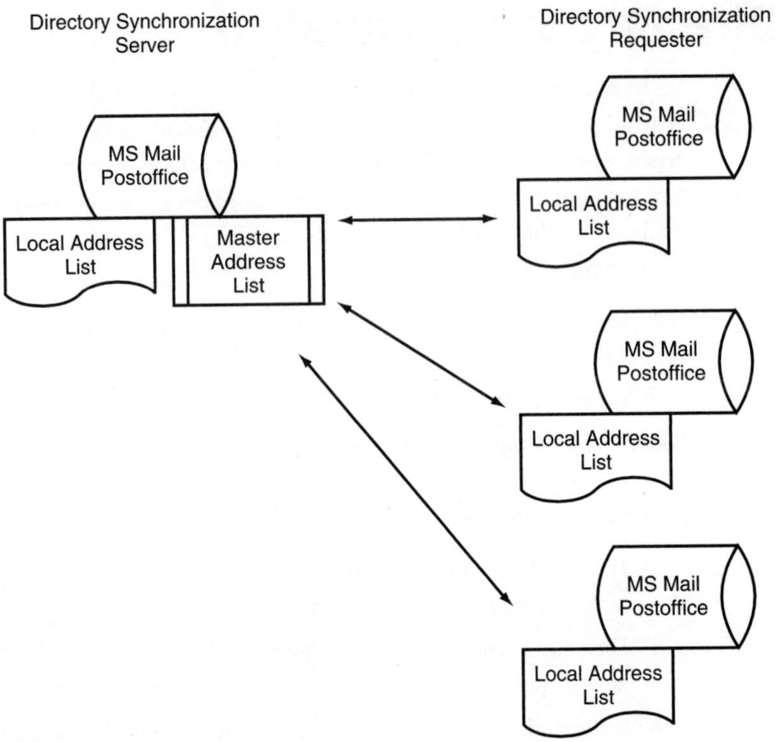

Microsoft Exchange server contains a component, the Microsoft directory synchronization agent (DXA), that can function in either the server or the requester role (see fig. 2.6). As with MS-Mail networks, you can set up only one directory synchronization server in each Exchange site. Instead of having a server address list, Exchange uses its standard server directory.

NOTE Microsoft Mail for AppleTalk networks can participate in directory synchronization with the Microsoft Exchange Connection Gateway installed on the appropriate MS Mail (AppleTalk) server. This connection includes a requester program that will function exactly as any other MS Mail requester.

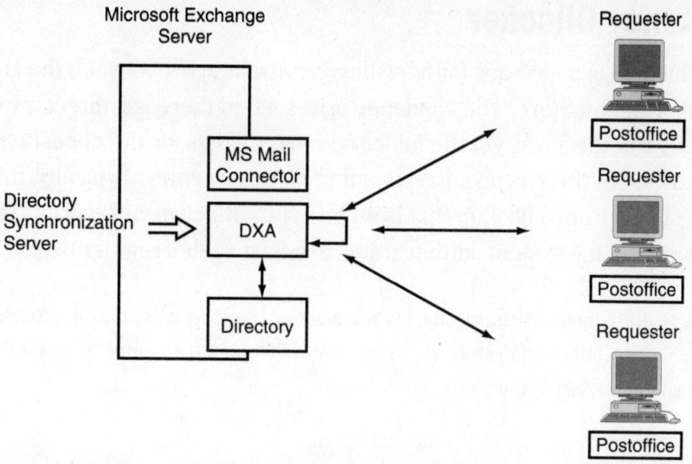

FIG. 2.6
Microsoft Exchange directory synchronization agent.

Part I Ch 2

Directory Synchronization with Foreign Systems

Foreign mail systems can also participate in directory synchronization provided they can import and export addressing information using the Microsoft Mail 3.x directory synchronization protocol.

In essence, the foreign system then becomes another requester and is seen as such by the directory synchronization server.

The following is a description of how a foreign requester participates in directory synchronization:

1. The foreign requester creates its own list of address updates and puts them into system messages.
2. The address updates are submitted to the dir-sync server via the appropriate gateway or transport.
3. The dir-sync server receives and incorporates the updates into its master directory list. A new message reflecting address changes is generated.
4. The message containing the updates is transmitted once again via the appropriate gateway to the foreign requester.
5. The foreign requester processes the changes into its local address list.

Consistency Checker

This tool is necessary for adjusting inconsistencies between the Directory and the Public Information Store. The challenge arises when there is a directory entry for a particular folder in the store, yet the folder no longer exists, or the opposite situation where a folder exists, but there is no corresponding directory entry. Typically, this is due to information restored from a backup that is out of sync with current records. The consistency checker is run by the system administrator to adjust such irregularities.

NOTE The consistency checker will create a directory entry only if a folder exists in the public information store. However, never will it create an entry in the public information store if an entry exists in the directory.

Understanding the X.500 Directory Service

Microsoft Exchange server directory architecture is based on the 1988 X.500 directory service recommendations. The X.500 directory structure outlines a logical directory object organization scheme, each object's attributes, and how they relate to one another. X.500 is a widely accepted standard, and with its application Exchange can participate in directory data sharing with many different systems.

Exchange defines additional object classes and attributes beyond X.500 standards in order to provide users more descriptive directory entries. For example, Exchange directories can support the following attributes which X.500 does not:

- Individual titles, e.g., president, MIS director
- Additional phone numbers
- Custom attributes defined by the administrator
- Organization charting information
- Alternate recipients

From Here...

This chapter has introduced you to some concepts surrounding the use of organizations and sites in Microsoft Exchange. These concepts included:

- Organizations, sites, and linking sites to one another
- Site resources such as servers and recipients

- Naming conventions
- Message Routing
- Redundancy
- Directory management functions such as synchronization, replication, and trusts

Grasping conceptual aspects of Exchange discussed in this chapter will help you understand the installation and configuration examples discussed in later chapters. The following chapters contain related information to some of the items talked about in this chapter:

- Chapter 5, "Designing Exchange Topology," gives detailed information pertinent to the topics discussed in this chapter.
- Chapter 17, "Using Directory Replication and Synchronization," goes in-depth on those topics. Having read this chapter, you are better prepared to understand the configuration of these components.
- Chapter 25, "Monitoring Exchange Sites," takes the enterprise-wide view of keeping an eye on entire sites in an organization.

CHAPTER 3

Exchange's Integrated Server Components

- The components of Exchange Server
- How components communicate with each other
- What connectors are and how they work
- How connectors can be used in various Exchange environments

Exchange server comprises four fundamental system services that run under Windows NT server. Together, these services handle all basic client/server interaction, user lookups, message transmission, and storage of information in public and private folders. With these four core components, an Exchange server can function as a stand-alone unit. All other components are optional and are designed specifically to facilitate information transfer to other Exchange servers and other external information systems. ■

Exchange's Four Central Components

This chapter is designed to provide an overview of the Exchange server's four central components and describe how they communicate with each other and with other optional components. The following are the integrated server components (see fig. 3.1):

- System Attendant
- Message Transfer Agent
- Information Store (public and private)
- Directory

FIG. 3.1
The Integrated Exchange Server performs all the functions needed in the Exchange environment.

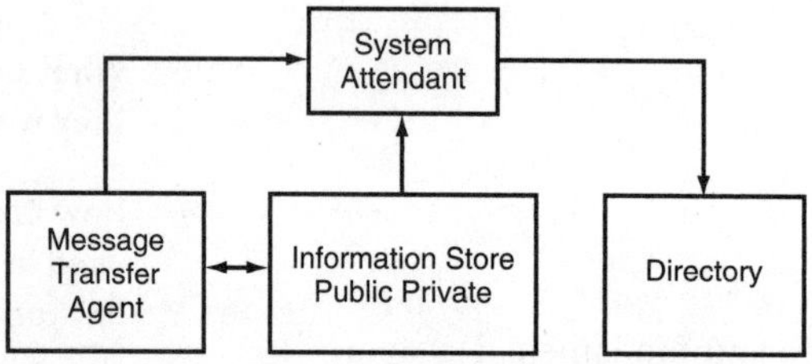

Introduction to System Attendant

▶ **See** Chapter 12, "Directory and System Attendant Configuration," for more detailed instructions on System Attendant implementation, **p. 269**

This service performs general maintenance tasks. It functions much like the central nervous system for an Exchange server. Its operation is required in order for Microsoft Exchange processes to run. The System Attendant tasks are as follows:

- Monitor status of messaging connection between servers. This includes assisting in monitoring the state of links between servers in one site, two different sites, and between different systems.
- Gather information on each server in a site (such as what services are running) to assist in running messaging monitoring tools.
- Build routing tables in a site.
- Verify directory replication information and correct inconsistencies.
- Maintain information logs about sent messages for tracking purposes.
- Generate e-mail addresses for new message recipients you create. Default addresses created by the System Attendant are MS-Mail, X.400, and SMTP. Additionally, if you have any third-party gateways installed, the System Attendant will create appropriate addresses for those systems.

The principal reason for communication between the System Attendant and other Exchange components involves logging messaging activity. Message logs are kept for all messages arriving and departing from the Exchange server. The following are the components that make up the communication between Exchange services:

Agent	Function
Message Transfer Agent	The Message Transfer Agent notifies the System Attendant that it received or sent a message for delivery to other systems or sites.
Information Store	The Information Store communicates its messaging activity for logging by the System Attendant. This includes notice that it has received or sent a message for local delivery, i.e., on the same server.

Introduction to Message Transfer Agent

▶ **See** Chapter 13, "Message Transfer Configuration," for an in-depth discussion of MTA topics and issues, **p. 299**

The Message Transfer Agent (MTA) comprises the foundation of Exchange server's communication infrastructure. The MTA handles message transport to other servers, other sites, or foreign systems. In addition to being the transport vehicle for messaging information, it also maps addresses, routes them, and performs message format conversion to other system's standards.

Being the principal message transport mechanism, the MTA communicates with all other Exchange components, as shown in the following minitable:

Component	Communication
Directory	The MTA uses the directory to look up a user address. The directory instructs the MTA to submit mail from other sites' directories (to perform directory synchronization).
System attendant	The MTA tells the SA to log each instance of a message transfer.
Administrator Program	From the Administrator Program, the MTA receives requests to manipulate messages in the queue.
Information Store	The information store submits messages for delivery to other systems and is notified to receive new mail by the MTA.

continues

continued

Component	**Communication**
Microsoft Mail connector	The MTA is notified of new mail to handle.
Directory synchronization	The MTA is directed to send directory-related component messages from foreign systems.

Introduction to the Information Store

See Chapter 14, "Information Store Configuration," which provides a complete description of all facets of configuring the IS, **p. 311**

The Information Store (IS) is the end of the line for all messaging data transmitted successfully to an Exchange server. This includes both private messages sent to individual users and public information folders intended for viewing by many users. The IS maintains data in two distinct databases—the Private Information Store and the Public Information Store.

In addition to message storage, the IS handles local delivery of messages (when both sender and recipient are on the same server), replicates public folders, and enforces storage limits. The following is a list of the principal functions of the MTA. The MTAs communicate with the following Exchange components.

Component	**Communication**
Message Transfer Agent	The IS contacts the MTA to accept new incoming mail, to deliver new outgoing mail, and to resolve addresses intended for gateways.
Exchange Clients	To the client the IS announces the arrival of new mail. Also the IS accepts new mail submitted for delivery from the client.
Directory	The IS uses the directory to look up addresses, get user mailbox information, and create directory entries for public folders.
System Attendant	When the IS either receives or sends a message, it notifies the System Attendant so that a log entry is generated.
Administrator Program	The Administrator Program sends instructions to the IS to show statistics about connected users and other storage usage information, e.g., folder sizes. The Administrator Program connects to the IS to view information, logons, and resources.

Component	Communication
Gateways	IS communication to gateways involves the retrieval and delivery of messages to outside systems.

Introduction to Directory Service

▶ **See** Chapter 12, "Directory and System Attendant Configuration," which covers the issues dealing with the directory in detail, **p. 269**

The directory service keeps all the information about users and resources in an organization. This includes a structured view of all server names, mailboxes, and distribution lists in a site. Also, the directory keeps configuration information that other Exchange server components use when mapping addresses and routing messages.

In order to maintain consistency of addressing information across several Microsoft Exchange servers, directory data is automatically replicated among all servers in a site. This replication is carried out through the MTA and administered by the directory service. The directory service also manages directory replication between sites on a scheduled basis (see Chapter 6, "Planning Connections to Microsoft Mail Systems," on directory synchronization/replication).

The directory classifies organization information (servers, mailboxes, etc.) as objects. Being objects, through the administrator program one can specify their characteristics, as well as determine who can use or change them (see Chapter 20, "Configuring X.400 Connections," on Exchange component administration). The following is a list of components of the Directory service and how they commnicate with these Exchange services.

Component	Communication
Other Directories	Directories communicate with other directories within the same site to replicate directory information.
Message Transfer Agent	The directory notifies the MTA in order to send mail to and receive mail from other directories (during directory replication). The MTA looks up addresses and configuration information from the Directory.

continues

Component	Communication
Administrator Program	The administrator program commands the directory to display and modify the address book, list of recipients, user properties, and directory objects (servers, monitors, connectors, etc.). Also, the administrator program can create objects in the directory.
Exchange Clients	Client programs call upon the directory to find a specific user's address and to display the address book, resolve an e-mail name to a full alias, and modify distribution list memberships.
Information Store	The IS uses the directory to look up address and configuration information, get information about mailboxes, and create directory entries for public folders.
System Attendant	The SA uses the directory to look up address and configuration information, build routing tables, generate e-mail addresses for new recipients, and verify consistency of directory information.
Directory synchronization	The directory synchronization component generates component requests to create, modify, and delete custom recipients. Also, it asks to look up recipients and configuration information.
Microsoft Mail connector	The MS-mail connector looks up addresses from Microsoft Mail for PC networks and configuration information in the directory.
Gateways	A gateway uses the directory to replicate directory information and to look up address and configuration information.

The Administrator Program

The Administrator Program is the primary tool for administering Exchange. Though it is not an integrated server component, it does comprise an essential part of the Microsoft Exchange architecture. Further chapters will describe the multitude of functions provided by the administrator program, but this will present you with the basic description of its communication with a few integrated server components. The following is a list of programs controlled by the Exchange Administration program with their associated functions.

Program	Function
Directory	Through the administrator program one can display the address book, the main viewer, lists of recipients, properties of a user, and directory objects. Also, the administrator program allows you to create objects in the directory.
Message Transfer Agent	The administrator program allows you to manipulate messages in the queue.
Information Store	The administrator program allows you to delete mailboxes and show statistics about information storage usage such as number of users logged on. It also provides information on the private and public information stores (connections, logos, resources) and determines schedules for public folder replication.

Integrating Connectors in the Exchange Server

One of the big improvements Microsoft has made with Exchange is the integration of connectors into the server. This feature eliminates the need for external boxes to establish connections to other mail systems.

Connectors allow Microsoft Exchange to exchange information with various messaging systems. They provide tight integration with all the tools and utilities Exchange administrators will be using in the running of the server, such as the Performance Monitor, Link Monitor, and the Administrator Program.

This section will cover the following:

- What connectors and gateways are
- How connectors and gateways fit into the Exchange framework
- How gateways and connectors can be used to link sites
- What connectors and gateways are available

Using Exchange connectors will be an easy transition for anyone who has configured mail gateways for other mail systems. For example, the Simple Mail Transfer Protocol (SMTP) gateway for cc:Mail has many of the same configuration parameters as the Internet Connector. These include whether to act as inbound and outbound gateways, who acts as the administrator, where bounced messages are delivered, and whether attachments are handled via Multimedia Internet Mail Extensions (MIME) compliance or UUENCODE. Being familiar with these terms as well as with Windows NT and 95 properties boxes facilitates configuration. By filling out properties sheets in the Administrator Program, as shown in figure 3.2, you can be up and running without a lot of hassle.

FIG. 3.2
The properties sheet for the Internet Connector gives the administrator many configuration options.

In addition, connectors can be used to link multiple Exchange sites. For example, the Internet Connector can be used effectively in organizations where some departments choose to use Exchange, while others choose other platforms. Many of these organizations standardize on SMTP to transfer messages between departments because most LAN-based e-mail packages have some form of SMTP gateway since SMTP is a non-proprietary Internet standard. These kinds of uses will be explained in a little more detail later in this chapter.

The following connectors will be explained in this chapter:

- Microsoft Mail
- X.400

- Internet
- cc:Mail (available after initial product release)

The Microsoft Mail Connector

Connecting to existing Microsoft Mail systems will be a very common use of Exchange in a large enterprise. With an installed user base of at least four million users, it makes sense that Exchange server would strongly support compatibility with MS-Mail.

▶ **See** Chapters 18–19 for more information on configuring the MS-Mail Connector, **pp. 447** and **481**

Primarily this compatibility comes in the form of the Microsoft Mail connector. This component bridges the gap between standard MS-Mail post offices and Exchange server. Essentially, Exchange emulates the functionality of an MS-Mail post office so other MS-Mail computers see it as just another member of the chain.

MS-Mail is a shared-file, LAN-based messaging system. Messages are sent to servers called post offices to which a user connects to retrieve messages. In order to integrate with this system, Exchange's MS-Mail connector becomes a post office of its own to which any other post office can connect. This allows other Microsoft Mail post offices to continue normal operation (that is, of course, until they are migrated to Exchange as well).

The MS-Mail connector (PC) consists of the following components:

- MS-Mail connector interchange. A system service that handles routing and message transfer between Exchange and the MS-Mail connector post office.
- MS-Mail connector post office (also called a shadow post office). A temporary information store for messages in transit to and from an MS-Mail system. It is often called a shadow post office because it contains no local mailboxes.
- MS-Mail connector (PC) Message Transfer Agent. A system service that handles message transport between the connector post office and the MS-Mail post offices.

  Similarly, the MS-Mail connector can also establish communication with MS-Mail for AppleTalk systems (see fig. 3.3). For connection to MS-Mail for AppleTalk Networks, the Exchange Microsoft Mail connector also includes two additional components:

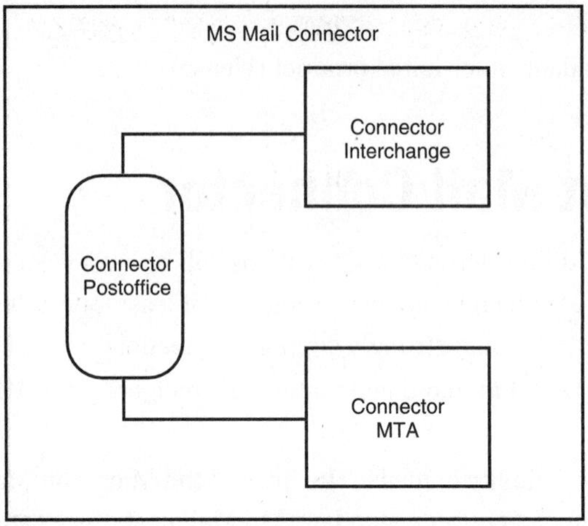

FIG. 3.3
The MS-Mail Connector Architecture.

- MS-Mail connector (AppleTalk) message transfer agent. A system service that operates with the Microsoft Exchange Connection gateway to handle message transfer and translation between MS-Mail connector post office and MS-Mail (AppleTalk) systems (see fig. 3.4).

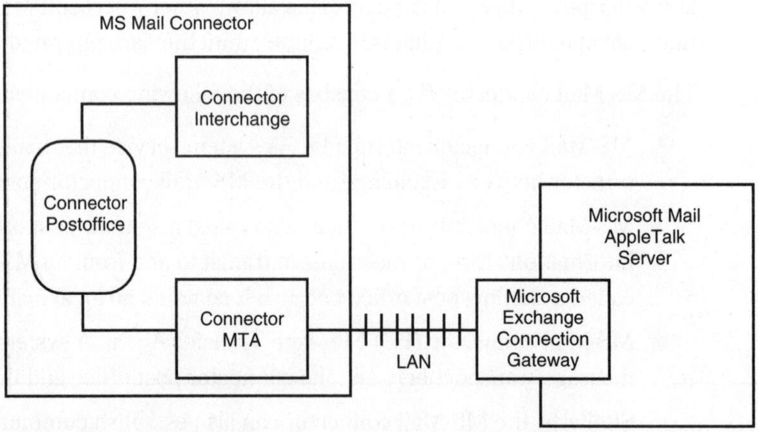

FIG. 3.4
The MS-Mail Connector (AppleTalk) Architecture.

- Microsoft Exchange connection. A gateway installed separately on a Macintosh MS-Mail server. It allows that server to communicate with the Microsoft Mail connector in Exchange.

LAN Connection to Post Offices

In this scenario a Microsoft Exchange server with the Microsoft Mail connector installed is hooked to a LAN running several MS-Mail 3.x post offices (see fig. 3.5).

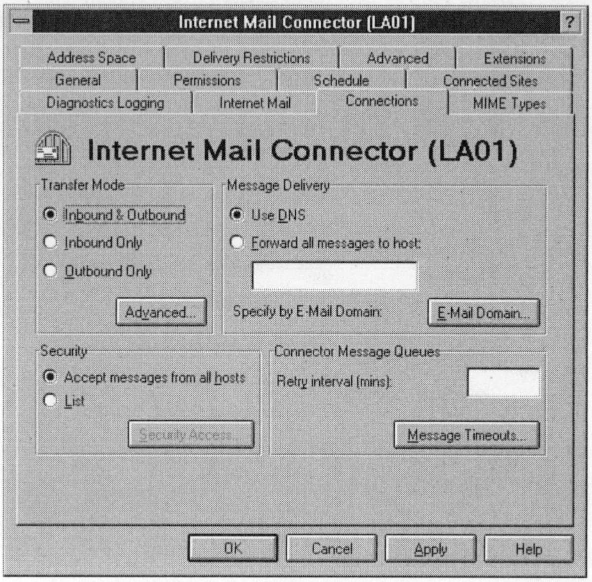

FIG. 3.5
MS-Mail LAN connection.

The following is a typical example of message transfer between both systems:

1. Messages intended for MS-Mail recipients are picked up by the Microsoft Mail connector interchange.
2. There they are translated into MS-Mail format; any OLE or other attachments are converted as required and the message is placed into the connector post office.
3. The MS-Mail connector (PC) MTA pulls the message from the connector post office and delivers it to the appropriate MS-Mail post office.

In the opposite situation, when a message originates from an MS-Mail user, the previous sequence is exactly reversed.

Asynchronous Connection to Post Offices

Microsoft Mail networks not on the same logical LAN can also be bridged with the Microsoft Mail connector. Such connections are commonly established by modem or wide area X.25 links. Exchange's Microsoft Mail connector (PC) MTA can be configured to support asynchronous or X.25 connections (see fig. 3.6). However, a normal Microsoft Mail post office cannot alone handle this connection. There must be an MS-Mail External or Multitasking MTA program set up to provide the modem management and message transfer functions over a remote link.

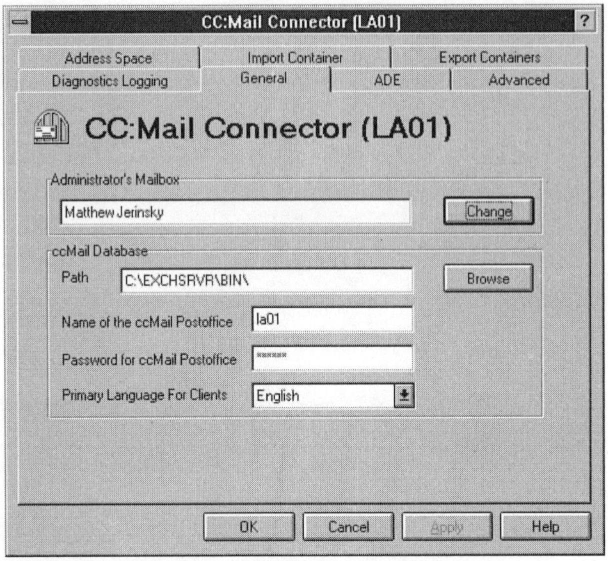

FIG. 3.6
Asynchronous connection to post offices.

Multiple MS-Mail Connector MTAs

A single Exchange server can run multiple instances of the MS-Mail connector MTAs (see fig. 3.7). Each MTA runs as a Windows NT system service that can be stopped and started independently of any other service. The best way to architect such connections is to create one instance of the MTA for each type of network connection. Therefore, one MTA is dedicated to an X.25 link, while another can service a modem link, and still another can connect to a local LAN.

If your organization uses a large number of Microsoft Mail 3.x post offices or they are spread over a wide area, then you would want to set up multiple MS-Mail connectors within your organization.

NOTE It is important to realize that all MS-Mail connectors in a site will use the same e-mail address. From the MS-Mail perspective, each site will be seen as one large post office.

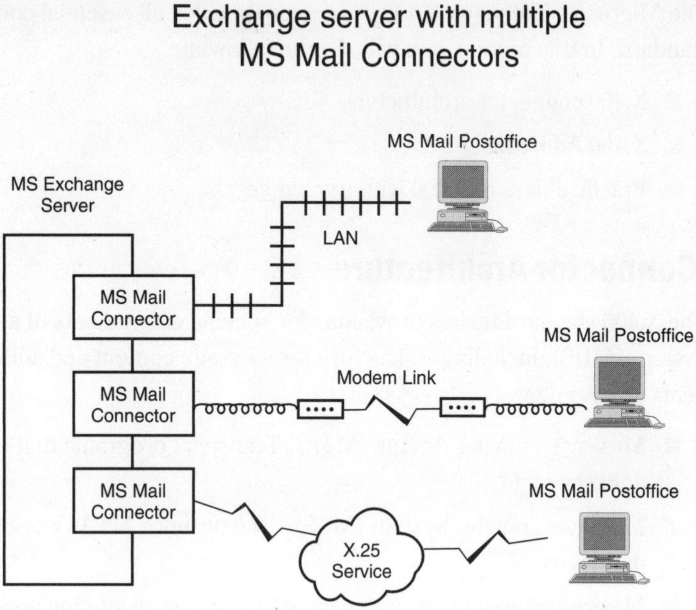

FIG. 3.7
Exchange server with multiple MS-Mail connectors.

Understanding the X.400 Standard

Microsoft Exchange's use of the X.400 standard allows a broad interoperability with a wide range of messaging systems. X.400 is a standard set by the International Telegraph and Telephone Consultative Committee (CCITT). To date there have been three iterations of the X.400 standard (1984, 1988, 1992). The initial release version of Microsoft Exchange supports the 1984 and 1988 standards, with the 1992 version to be supported in later versions.

▶ **See** Chapter 20, "Configuring X.400 Connections," **p. 499**

The X.400 standard defines the basic framework of a message handling system, the structure of the message and its components, and how messages are transferred. It is widely supported and used by most public e-mail carriers and telecommunication providers. Because of its widespread acceptance, many companies have already developed gateways to bridge their messaging systems with X.400. In real-world situations, where network, hardware, and communication standards are not strictly enforced, X.400 provides a common ground for interoperability between messaging systems. Microsoft has assured Exchange's strict conformance to government X.400 standards, which means that Exchange will be a reliable solution for the widest possible number of X.400 connections.

The Microsoft Exchange X.400 connector provides all essential connectivity with this standard. In this section, you will see the following:

- X.400 connector architecture
- X.400 Addressing
- Practical uses of X.400 with Exchange

X.400 Connector Architecture

The X.400 standard makes provisions for specific components of a Message Handling System (MHS), including a structure for message content and addressing. These components are as follows:

- Message Transfer Agents (MTA). Transport programs that execute message delivery
- Message Transfer System (MTS). Two or more MTAs working to transfer messages
- Message Stores (MS). An intermediate message storage area between an MTA and a user agent
- User Agents (UA). A client program designed to send and retrieve messages from an MTA and an MS
- Access Units. Gateways to other messaging systems

Microsoft fulfills each element specified by the X.400 standard. In fact, the whole Message Transfer System design is the basis for Exchange's Server site and organization structure.

When referring to a Microsoft Exchange X.400 connector, one is really describing the use of a Microsoft Exchange MTA configured to connect to an X.400-based system. MS Exchange MTAs are compliant with other MTAs (in another Exchange server or an external system) that comply with the 1984 or 1988 X.400 standards. The Exchange MTA can be extensively configured to negotiate such connection over a wide variety of network transports.

▶ **See** Chapter 13, "Message Transfer Configuration," for more information on MTA configuration, **p. 299**

The Message Store requirement is met by Exchange's public and private information stores.

▶ **See** Chapter 14, "Information Store Configuration," **p. 311**

The User Agents are realized as Microsoft Exchange Client programs currently available on several common platforms.

The Access Units are the many gateways currently available for use with Exchange (PROFS, SNADS, Fax, pager, etc.). Each provides a route into its particular system.

X.400 Addressing in Exchange

Much like an Exchange address is identified by the user at site structure, X.400 addresses are distinguished by unique personal information and information about the system on which they receive messages. A typical X.400 address contains the following information:

> c=US; admd=MCI; prmd=Digital Genesis; o=Los Angeles; ou1=Sales; dn=Davey Kim;

Each element is described in Table 5.1.

Table 5.1 X.400 Addressing Elements

Element	Description
c=US	country
admd=MCI	Administrative Management Domain. Usually the name of your X.400 service carrier.
prmd=	The name of your enterprise.
o=	Organization. Name of the Exchange site.
ou1=	Organizational Unit. The X.400 attribute which helps further identify the remote site.
dn=	Directory Name.

NOTE To appropriately route messages in a site or between sites, Microsoft Exchange uses what is called the X.400 global domain identifier (GDI) of the local site. In order for messages to be routed correctly, the GDI used for a Microsoft Exchange Server cannot be identical to the GDI of a connected foreign system. This will become an issue only when using Exchange to connect to foreign X.400 systems.

Adding Foreign X.400 Addresses into Exchange

As a system administrator, you can use Exchange's bulk import utility to merge a series of foreign addresses into Exchange's global address list. Additionally, the Exchange client allows individual users to enter their own X.400 addresses via an X.400 template.

X.400 addresses for recipients on an Exchange server are automatically created when a new mailbox is created.

Application and Examples of the X.400 Connector

Connecting an Exchange Server site to a foreign X.400 system will be a primary use of the X.400 connector. However, there are a number of connection possibilities afforded by the implementation of this versatile tool. Connections over X.400 can be established to share directory information, replicate public folders, transmit standard messages, or all of the above. The following figure 3.8 gives three examples of such usage.

FIG. 3.8
You can connect an existing MS-Mail server to a foreign X.400 system (through an Exchange server).

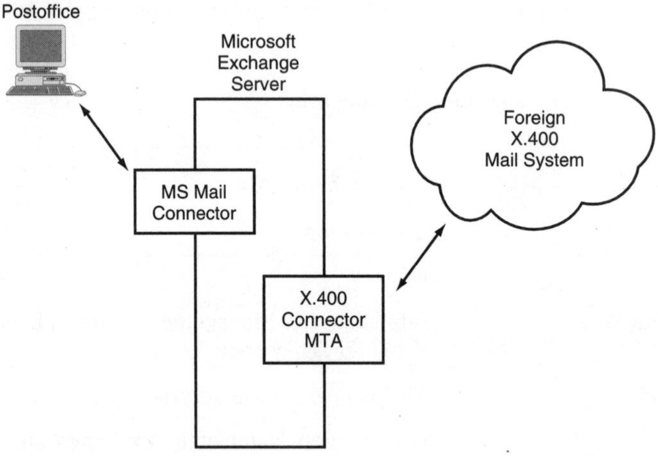

The Microsoft Exchange X.400 connector, in conjunction with the Microsoft Mail connector, can allow users on MS-Mail to access X.400 systems (see fig. 3.9).

FIG. 3.9
You can connect an Exchange Server site to an MS-Mail post office.

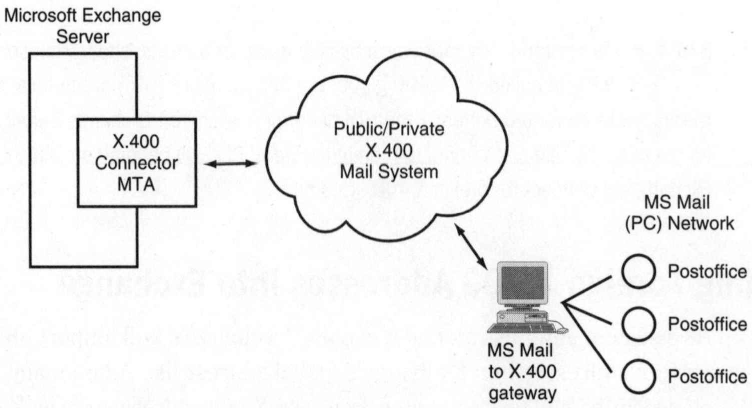

A common use of the X.400 connector in Exchange will be bridging messaging systems that are geographically dispersed. In this example, a Microsoft Exchange server is set up to transfer messaging data with an MS-Mail system using an X.400 connector on one end and a currently available MS-Mail X.400 gateway on the other (see fig. 3.10).

FIG. 3.10
You can connect two Exchange Server sites.

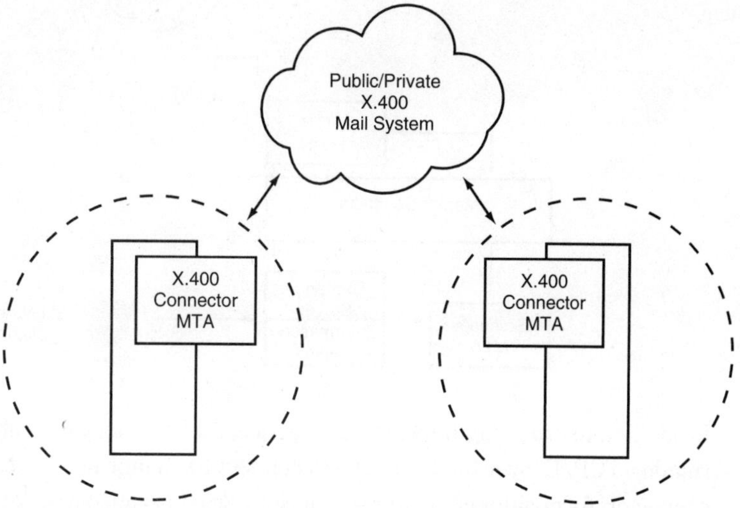

Two Microsoft Exchange Server sites can be linked via a public (or private) X.400 mail system. All that is required is one properly configured message transfer agent at either end. The same technique is applicable over a TCP/IP network with the Internet Connector and is covered in the next section.

The Internet Connector

As its name implies, the Internet Connector provides integrated, native SMTP connectivity to the Microsoft Exchange server. In doing this, Microsoft has eliminated the need for the DOS-based SMTP gateway for Microsoft Mail that lacked robustness, had memory allocation problems, possessed little or no security, and needed external hosts to send out SMTP mail. The gateway was usually run on a 386 and had a hard time communicating with various Internet mailers.

The Internet Connector solves those problems by providing a stable, proven, and secure platform with Windows NT Server. In addition, the Internet Connector can send and receive SMTP mail without the need for external hosts, is MIME-compliant, and provides robust performance.

See Chapter 21, "Setting Up SMTP Connections," **p. 523**

Part I Ch 3

The following diagram (see fig. 3.11) shows how the Internet Connector fits into the Microsoft Exchange architecture.

FIG. 3.11
Internet Connector Architecture.

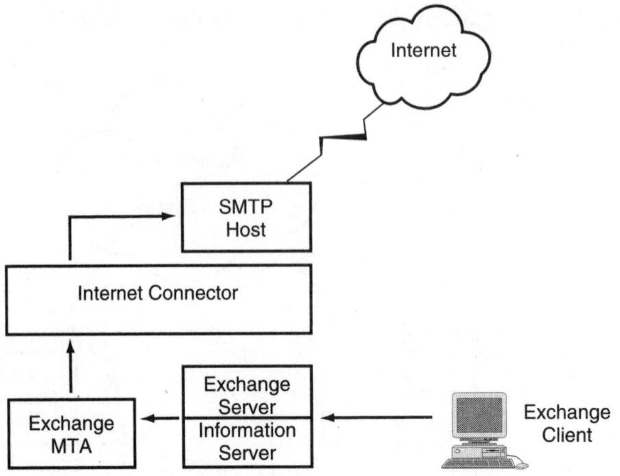

In addition to providing Internet mail service, the Internet Connector allows those users running TCP/IP over the backbone to connect Exchange sites to each other using the connector. As mentioned previously, decentralized organizations often give control of the mail system to the respective department. Many large universities operate this way. These organizations often choose SMTP as the way for disparate mail systems to communicate because it is an Internet standard. Microsoft has recognized that many companies route only TCP/IP over their WANs to maximize router throughput. More information on planning and designing Exchange networks can be found in Chapters 12–16. A diagram showing how to link disparate Exchange sites by using the Internet Connector is shown in figure 3.12.

FIG. 3.12
Connecting Multiple Exchange Sites Over TCP/IP.

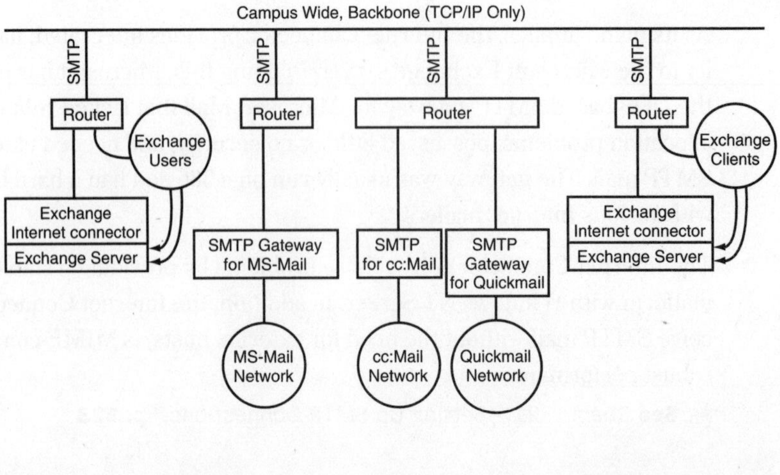

The Internet Connector provides for full integration into environments where security is a big concern. Many companies configure firewalls to protect internal data from hackers on the Internet. In addition to all the security components inherent to Exchange and Windows NT Server, the Internet Connector provides the ability to refuse messages from any specified hosts. This provides protection from many forms of hacking because many hackers use the e-mail system to carry out their work. For example, you might configure the connector to refuse mail from all hosts other than a certain mail relay. That means that a hacker could not send a message directly to your Exchange server and send commands directly to it. By refusing mail from certain hosts, Exchange is flexible enough to fit into existing company security policies. Any hacker would have to compromise the firewall in order to send a message directly to the Internet Connector.

Exchange can also be configured to allow only incoming or outgoing traffic through the connector. This is an important feature because one Windows NT server can only do so many things and complete so many tasks without taking a performance hit. Configuring the connector to only send out mail might be a good idea for a machine that is already overloaded. However, this is not a cause for concern. As long as there is incoming Internet mail added to the Information Store, all Exchange users, including users at other Exchange sites, will receive Internet mail. For example, if you have the Internet connector configured on two servers and configure one to receive-only and the other to send-only, the Exchange users' e-mail addresses will still be the same. Users will not know where the mail came in and don't really care. The connections are completely transparent. Figure 3.13 shows the properties screen where the administrator can configure security and transfer options.

Delving Deeper into the Internet Connector

In addition to fitting into the overall Microsoft Exchange picture, the Internet Connector has an architecture of its own that needs to be explained. When installed and configured properly, the Internet Connector functions as two NT services. One is the "Connector Service" and the other is the "SMTP Service." These two services combine to perform all the tasks of obtaining, transporting, and receiving SMTP messages and all their MIME attachments. The following describes these two services and their functions:

- The Connector Service. This service takes messages addressed to foreign sites from the Information Store and translates them into the standard RFC-822 format. An important thing to note is that this service looks at the property sheets defined in the administrator program to see how things like the message body and any attachments are handled. For example, there are many sites on the Internet that are not fully MIME-compliant, but allow attachments using the UUENCODE format.

This is not the standard Base-64 encoding defined by the MIME standard; nevertheless, it is used in many sites. The Exchange administrator can set up the Internet Connector's properties to use the UUENCODE style of attachments, causing the Connector Service to UUENCODE outgoing messages and UUDECODE incoming messages.

FIG. 3.13
Internet Connector Connections Properties.

For incoming messages, the Connector Service automatically detects the body of the message as being in the RFC-822 format and places it in the Information Store just like any other Exchange message, allowing transparency to the user.

- The SMTP Service. Put very simply, the SMTP Service is like "sendmail" on UNIX. It establishes connections to the remote mail systems, and when authentication is enabled, does all the verification. The one limitation is that Exchange will not act as a relay host, so don't point other hosts at the Exchange server to deliver mail.

  The service can be configured to disallow connections from remote systems, as well as make connections at specified times and intervals. If, for example, your WAN links were being overloaded you could configure the Internet Connector to transfer mail in the late evening only, or at one-hour intervals to provide some breathing room for other data.

Connecting to Lotus cc:Mail

The cc:Mail Connector provides seamless communication between Microsoft Exchange Server and Lotus' cc:Mail product. In recent months, Lotus has embraced the MAPI standard for messaging-enabled applications, switching from their previous Vendor Independent Messaging (VIM) standard. Despite this change in Lotus' strategy, its Post Office Version 8, which supports MAPI, has yet to ship, leaving existing users with VIM-based post offices. The cc:Mail Connector enables connectivity between these post offices and Exchange.

The cc:Mail Connector has many configuration variables enabling the use of the existing cc:Mail tools such as Import, Export, and ADE to enable robust, hassle-free connections to cc:Mail VIM post offices.

cc:Mail users are to be directly imported into the Microsoft Exchange Global Address Book and will appear just like any other Exchange user.

Just as with the Microsoft Mail Connector, a cc:Mail post office is created on the Exchange server, resulting in Exchange server users appearing in the cc:Mail directory like all other cc:Mail users. This gives transparency to the cc:Mail user. As far as he or she is concerned, all users in the Global Address Book are local.

Exchange allows the administrator to set the paths to the standard Import and Export utilities that come with cc:Mail. These utilities are used to import and export directory and message data from the Exchange server to all other cc:Mail post offices in the cc:Mail network. Examples of the uses of this connector are shown in figure 3.14.

FIG. 3.14
Architecture of the cc:Mail Connector.

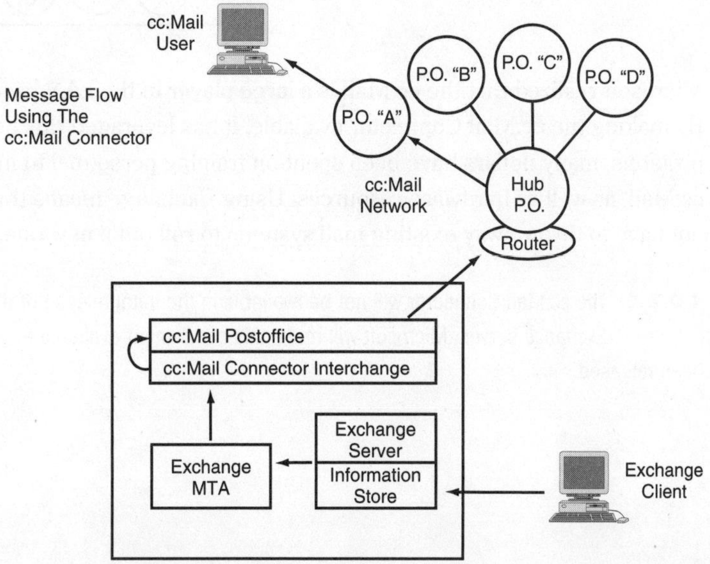

Part I Ch 3

On the cc:Mail side, Exchange looks just like any other post office; by using Automatic Directory Exchange (ADE), all cc:Mail post offices, including the Exchange cc:Mail post office, can be kept up to date as users are added on both sides. For example, if a user is added to the Exchange Global Address book, an ADE message is generated and sent to the master cc:Mail post office. From there, the master cc:Mail post office generates ADE updates through the cc:Mail router to the rest of the cc:Mail post offices. All the cc:Mail administrator needs to do is follow the same directory synchronization procedures used when a new cc:Mail post office is created. The following figure 3.15 explains this concept.

FIG. 3.15
ADE Synchronization between the cc:Mail and Exchange.

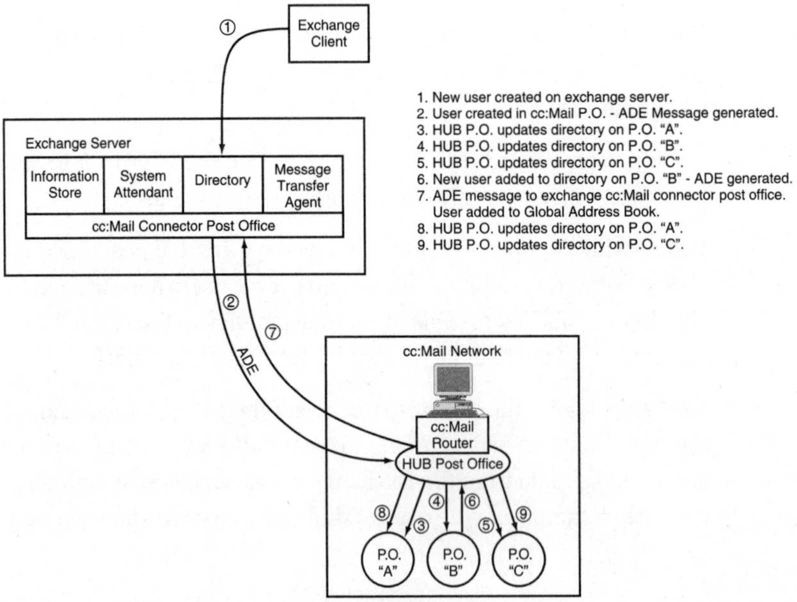

Microsoft realized that the cc:Mail is a large player in the LAN-based messaging market. By making the cc:Mail Connector available, it has leveraged this popularity. In some organizations, many dollars have been spent on training personnel to install and maintain cc:Mail, as well as hardware resources. Using Exchange means that your organization will not have to throw away existing mail systems to roll out a new one.

NOTE The cc:Mail Connector will not be available in the inital release of the Microsoft Exchange server. Microsoft will make this component available after the product has been released.

Understanding Gateways

Gateways provide a way for Exchange to integrate disparate information services into Microsoft's Universal Inbox, using the single Microsoft Exchange Viewer to organize all types of information. These include things such as voicemail, fax, paging, as well as e-mail from other vendors' systems.

Despite the variety of information services that snap into Exchange, the end user sees no difference. To him or her, the addressee is the addressee. A user can address a message and send it, and the addressee might get a page, fax, voicemail, or Internet message. The addressee may be using cc:Mail, PROFS, SNADS, or Microsoft Mail, and the user sending the message would never know because all he or she needs to know is the addressee's name in the Global Address Book.

Using Microsoft Mail Gateways

In addition to native Exchange gateways, Exchange can use standard Microsoft Mail gateways by using the Microsoft Mail Connector described earlier in this chapter. Each gateway uses the Microsoft Mail Connector to exchange data with foreign mail systems. This may be useful for sites with large Microsoft Mail installations that are migrating to Exchange slowly, but want to provide the core messaging functions first and add connectors and gateways later. In addition, some organizations are hesitant to sway from things that work. For example, if the Microsoft Mail gateway to PROFS has been working fine, some may be hesitant to roll out the Exchange PROFS gateway because they haven't had the opportunity to test it and get their staff familiar with it. Figure 3.16 shows how Microsoft Mail gateways fit into the Exchange topology.

In the preceding case, the PROFS gateway for MS-Mail simply talks to the MS-Mail Connector post office. When configuring the PROFS gateway for MS-Mail, you simply point it at the MS-Mail Connector post office and the exchange of information becomes transparent.

With Exchange, Microsoft took those concerns into consideration and provided the flexibility to use legacy systems in the migration to a robust Exchange environment. For the purposes of this book, only the native Exchange gateways will be discussed in detail.

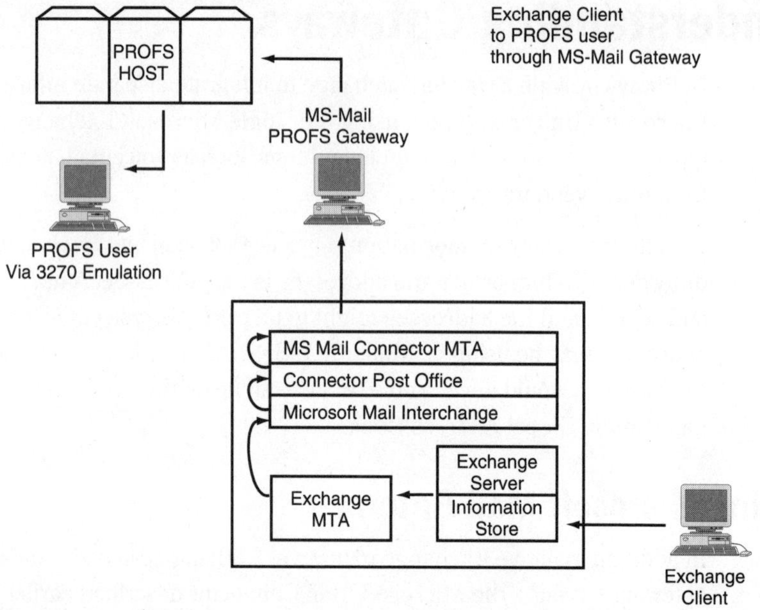

FIG. 3.16
Message flow of Exchange to PROFS using PROFS Gateway for MS-Mail.

Exploring Native Exchange Gateways

The following Exchange gateways will be discussed in the following sections: Voicemail, Fax, Pager, PROFS, and SNADS.

Voicemail

Microsoft's Universal Inbox metaphor is being further developed by the integration of voicemail into Exchange. In some cases, voicemail is quicker and carries less overhead than e-mail. In addition, many organizations have an existing voicemail infrastructure. Many vendors are working to integrate these existing technologies into Microsoft Exchange Server, bringing the concept of the universal inbox into reality.

Octel, a leading provider of Enterprise voice and fax messaging, is bridging the gap between voice and e-mail communications through new technology developed for Microsoft Exchange. Octel Unified Messaging simplifies communications by combining voice and fax messages with e-mail into a single Exchange Server mailbox and providing access to all messages from a telephone or PC (see fig. 3.17). System managers also benefit as the Octel Unified Messaging architecture shares a common database, directory, and administration. Octel Unified Messaging operates on standard PC hardware and is fully compliant with Microsoft NT Server.

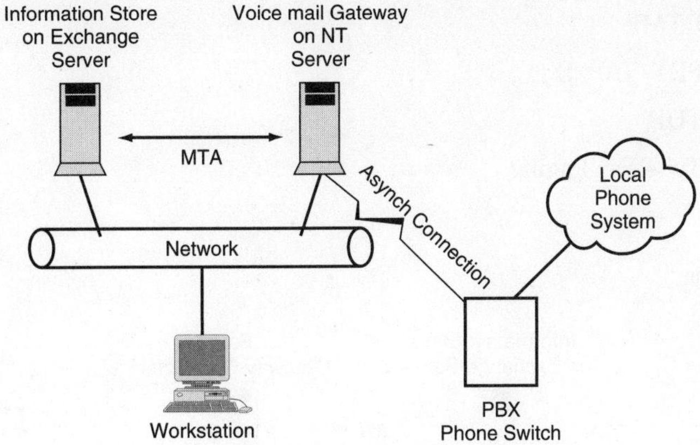

FIG. 3.17 Voicemail Integration with Exchange.

Fax

The Microsoft Exchange Client provides for outbound faxes through Exchange Server or a local modem, but there are fax gateways being developed that tie into the Exchange Server Address Book. This means that users without a local modem can send and receive faxes that come into their inboxes. By interfacing with the PBX at the site, transparent fax capability can be achieved.

Figure 3.18 shows the architecture of the fax gateways. The NT server housing the Exchange server has PBX interface hardware that connects several Direct Inward Dial (DID) lines to the server. The gateway software then links mailboxes with specific fax numbers using the * key on the telephone keypad. For example, if the DID line phone number was 555-3456, each user's individual fax number would take the form of 555-3456*1.

Using this system, the fax gateway can route the message to the proper inbox. This paperless fax system, along with the concept of binary faxes, makes fax integration very robust. Binary faxing allows the user to receive a fully editable document. Rather than faxing a plain image, you can load Word and start editing a fax.

Pager

One of the many add-on products for Exchange is the Integra Wireless Server for Microsoft Exchange. This product allows all Exchange clients to send pages through the Exchange server by adding a custom recipient to their personal address books.

The software works by using modems in the Exchange server to dial access numbers which are set up in the "Gateway Wireless Communications Connector" properties. The gateway supports the following communications protocols:

- DTMF
- PET/TAP/IXO
- TDP
- Two-Way Paging

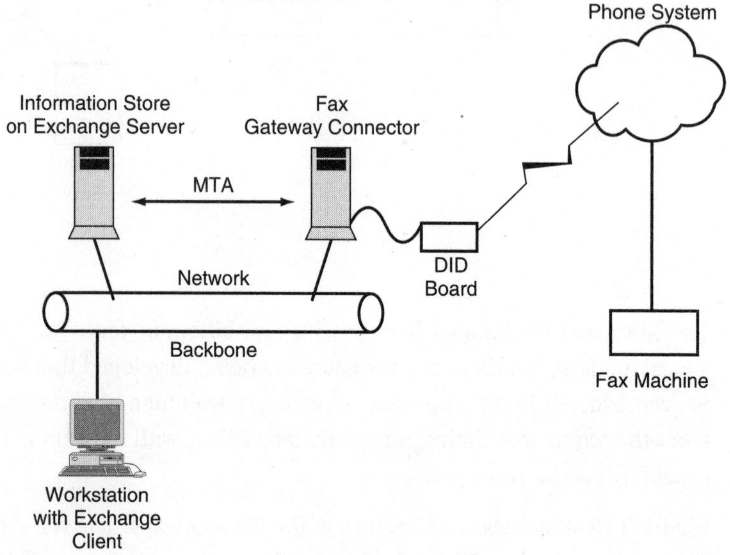

FIG. 3.18
Fax Gateway Connectivity.

Integra Wireless Server is fully MAPI-compliant, and custom applications can be created to take advantage of paging technology. For example, you could write a program that will page you when there are more than five messages in your inbox while you're away from the office. The product fully supports 32-bit OLE automation and includes a 32-bit OCX custom control.

If you have an alphanumeric pager, the Wireless Server can also be configured to send your e-mail directly to your pager. You can also have it send your Schedule+ information to inform you of appointments while on the road.

Integra is the maker of WinBeep for Networks, and has migrated this technology to Microsoft Exchange Server (see fig. 3.19). Like all other native Exchange software, it is configured through the Exchange Administrator Program and integrates with all the standard Exchange administration tools.

PROFS

Attachmate's Zip! Gateway for Microsoft Exchange Server allows seamless integration with PROFS systems. It will allow for the transfer of e-mail, address books, and Free/Busy

Schedule information. The advantage this product has over the standard MS-Mail Gateway for PROFS is that it is tightly integrated with Exchange Server's Administrator Program. You will be able to configure and monitor this gateway in the same way as all the connectors.

FIG. 3.19
Integra Paging Gateway Connectivity.

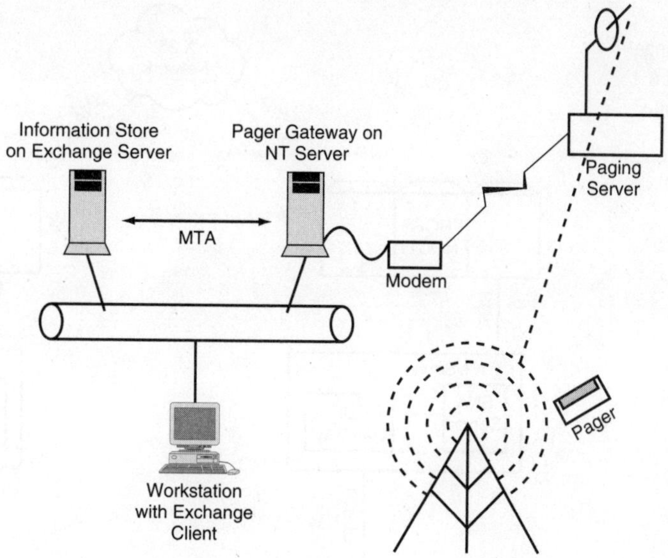

The Zip! Gateway also improves on the standard Microsoft Mail gateway for PROFS by adding real time calendar detail access and directory integration. All of the standard directory synchronization is taken care of by the standard Exchange directory synchronization service.

In addition, just as with the Internet Connector, the Zip! Gateway can be used to leverage PROFS host-based infrastructure. If two sites have SNA APPC connectivity between them, any Exchange messages can be sent over the PROFS backbone as shown in figure 3.20.

The Zip! Gateway uses standard SNA APPC, CSV, CPIC, and LUA APIs and works with the following host platforms:

- PROFS version 2.2.2 or later
- OfficeVision/FM 1.0 or later
- VM/HPO, VM/SP release 5 or later, or any release of VM/XA or VM/ESA
- Microsoft SNA Server

Attachmate's Zip! Gateway is a marked improvement to the Microsoft Mail PROFS gateway, and Microsoft has committed to working very closely with Attachmate due to its knowledge and history of working with IBM mainframe connectivity products. Rather than reinvent the wheel, Microsoft is teaming with other companies, leveraging its distinctive competency in a given area. Microsoft's alliances with third parties is discussed in detail in Chapter 29.

FIG. 3.20
Sending Exchange Messages over a PROFS backbone.

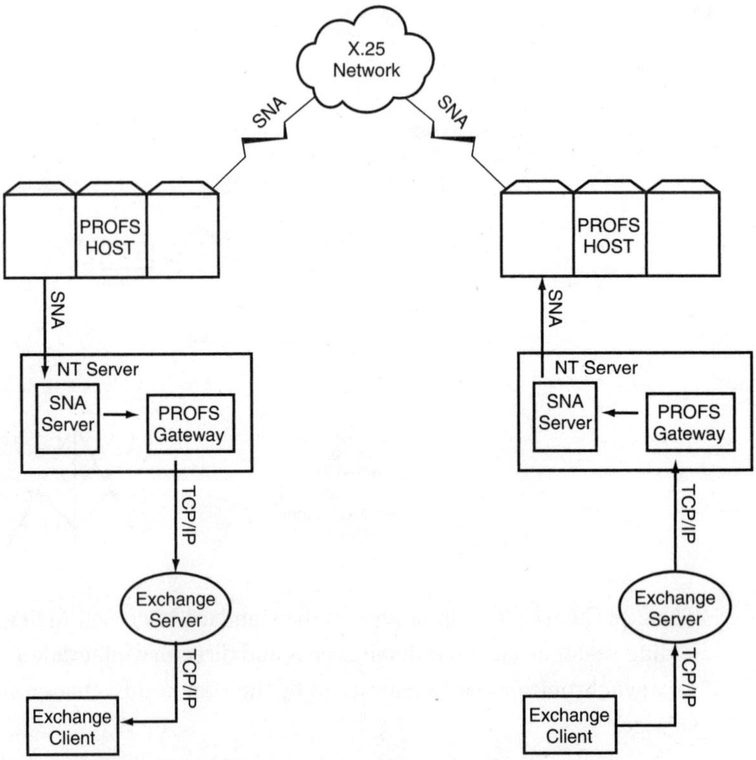

Microsoft sees the PROFS gateway as being very important for organizations looking to migrate existing PROFS users to Exchange, given the recent surge of companies migrating from mainframe-based applications to client/server based systems.

SNADS

Attachmate's Zip! Office Gateway to SNADS allows Microsoft Exchange users to seamlessly communicate with users on existing SNADS platforms. SNADS is the IBM mainframe connectivity protocol over serial connections, instead of using LAN connections.

It is tightly integrated with Exchange Administrator Program, Microsoft SNA Server, and other Microsoft Exchange gateways. Its 32-bit object architecture gives it the ability to scale in large environments as well as perform reliably and quickly.

Similar to the PROFS gateway mentioned earlier, the Zip! Gateway to SNADS allows current SNADS infrastructures to be used to send native Exchange data without the loss of data integrity.

The gateway is compatible with the following platforms:

- IBM Officevision/MVS via DISOSS or OfficePath
- OfficeVision/400
- IBM Mail Exchange
- Verimation Memo

This gateway can be used to both leverage current hardware and software investments in SNADS, or as a migration tool to Exchange depending on your organization's plans and goals.

From Here...

Exchange has a powerful back-end architecture consisting of four components: the System Attendant, the Message Transfer Agent, Information Stores both public and private, and the Directory. In addition, connectors and gateways are integrated into the server to provide seamless connections to external systems.

Both connectors and gateways serve the following needs:

- Integration of Exchange with existing messaging systems
- Integration of Exchange with other information services like voicemail, fax, and paging
- A slow migration path from other mail systems to a pure Exchange environment
- An effective use of existing voice or messaging infrastructure
- Universal Inbox providing transparency for the client

The following chapters contain related information to some of the items talked about in this chapter:

- Chapters 11–14 cover the detailed configuration of the four core components of the server.
- Chapters 18–19 will provide more information on how to plan the migration of your existing Microsoft Mail system to Exchange.
- Chapter 20, "Configuring X.400 Connections," provides detailed information on the implementation of the X.400 Connector.

- Chapter 21, "Setting Up SMTP Connections," will delve into how to connect SMTP systems to Exchange.
- Chapter 22, "Exchange Performance Tuning and Capacity Planning," will explain the steps required to determine capacity requirements of your Exchange servers.

CHAPTER 4

Integrating with a Windows NT Server

- **The core functionality of the Windows NT Operating System**
- **Explanation of the Domain Architecture**
- **How Exchange integrates with the server**
- **How Exchange depends on the server**

Microsoft Exchange Server is part of the BackOffice suite of server products that runs on top of the Windows NT operating system. Windows NT is a 32-bit multithreaded, multitasking operating system. The Exchange Server can leverage this functionality by utilizing as many threads or application processes as needed to provide a robust messaging infrastructure.

You should now have an understanding of the core components and framework for the Microsoft Exchange server and client. This chapter helps you to understand the way Exchange integrates with the operating system. We will also discuss how Exchange can leverage the NT platform to provide a robust and fault-tolerant messaging solution. ■

The Core Functionality of Windows NT

Windows NT is a 32-bit operating system. It provides multitasking and multithreading capabilities. This means that the operating system can simultaneously process multiple requests or instances of an application.

NT is more that just an operating system. It is a framework to develop fault-tolerant client server applications. To enhance the operating system, NT provides a full set of Application Programming Interfaces (APIs) and Software Development Kits (SDKs). The operating system is more than a file and print server; it is an application server. Through the use of the APIs and SDKs, many applications can harness the power of the operating system.

The operating system runs on a variety of platforms including Intel, MIPS, Alpha, and the Power PC. This portable operating system has several key benefits. The following sections cover the benefits in detail.

Multiple Protocol Support

NT provides native support for the following protocols: TCP/IP, IPX, Netbeui, AppleTalk, DLC, SNA, X.25, and X.400(TP/x). This enables the operating system to support a wide array of clients. NT can communicate with Unix, Banyan Vines, DEC Pathworks, Netware, Apple Macintosh, and of course all of the Microsoft networking clients, including MS-DOS, Windows For Workgroups, Windows 95, and Windows NT Workstation.

This feature enables NT to interoperate in a heterogeneous environment. You will not be "trapped" by implementing the NT operating system into one of these environments. NT can offer additional functionality in these situations. The alternative means providing native support which would be very costly or impossible.

For example, NT can be easily added to a Novell Netware environment to provide Remote Networking or Dial-in access. The NT operating system ships with a complete remote access server component integrated with the OS. With Netware you would have to purchase an additional product known as "Netware Connect" to obtain this capability.

In the situation with Exchange, Netware clients can easily access an Exchange server running on NT with native IPX client software installed. Clients communicate with industry standards known as Remote Procedure Calls (RPC) using the Exchange server. NT supports every major communication protocol. Therefore, a client can connect to Exchange using RPCs over TCP/IP or IPX in a Netware environment.

▶ **See** "Installing Exchange in a Netware Environment," **p. 231**

In addition, Microsoft will release a standard for Remote Procedure Calls (RPCs) over AppleTalk, the Macintosh's native communications protocol. In order for a Macintosh workstation to connect to an NT Exchange server, it will make RPCs over TCP/IP or AppleTalk. This functionality shows Microsoft's firm commitment to a Macintosh operating system and recognizes that the Macintosh operating system has an important share in the marketplace (see fig. 4.1).

FIG. 4.1
NT supports most industry standard network protocols.

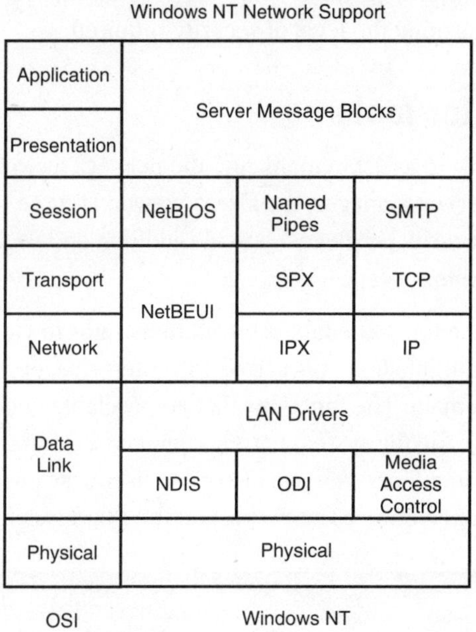

C2 Level Security

Security is a key element of any messaging system. Users want to know that their message will get to its destination without someone intercepting it. Exchange expands upon the Class C2 Level of Security which is at the heart of the NT operating system. The Department of Defense defines this level of security.

Class C2 requires a secure logon, discretionary access control, and full auditing capabilities. The secure logon requires that users identify themselves with a unique logon identifier (user ID) and password. This logon must be validated prior to accessing any system resources.

The discretionary access control enables the owner of a resource, whether it is a file, subdirectory, or printer, to determine who can access the resource. This also defines the level of control the user has over the resource. The owner grants rights to a user or group of users.

Auditing is the capability to log the security information of each operating system transaction to a file based on user ID. This feature provides the capability to detect and record important security-related events or instances in which security was challenged.

C2 security has several other components to its matrix of functionality. However, the Exchange server leverages its core features. Not all aspects of C2 security are required for use with Exchange. You also do not have to use every feature of C2 security when working on or creating a network application operating system. The company using the C2 security system can determine the level of security required.

Integrated Administrator Tools

NT provides several tools to assist in managing the network as well as the operating system. NT includes the Server Manager, the Event Viewer, and the User Manager to manage processes, define security privileges, provide auditing and security logging, and to create new users and groups, respectively.

The Server Manager (see fig. 4.2) enables the administrator to view all of the servers from a single domain, multiple domains across the enterprise, or individual servers and workstations inside a domain. The functions that are available enable you to control the share or access points to the file systems of a server, and to stop and start application processes. Using these functions, you can also close user sessions and manage specialized access via AppleTalk, Netware Gateways, and the File Transfer Protocol (FTP).

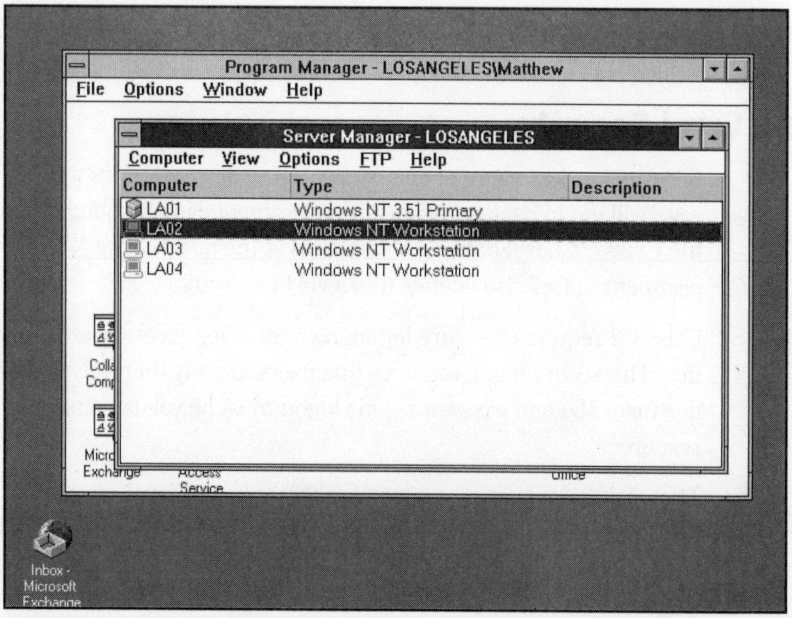

FIG. 4.2
Windows NT Server Manager enables remote management of the network servers.

The event viewer, also known as the event log, is the centralized repository for system, application, and security information for a server or workstation. From a remote console an administrator can pull up the event viewer to see the entries of a network server. All Backoffice certified application must write the events to the event viewer. Events can be informational (blue), cautionary (yellow), and serious (red) in nature. You will be able to tell whether your tape backup has finished properly and at what time of day it completed. From the system, you will see whether there have been any problems related to the operating system and the hardware. From the security log, you can view all of the information predetermined for auditing.

The event will store information related to the Exchange server and all of its gateways, connectors, and external processes. It will also store security information (see fig. 4.3). Exchange itself has a security log which extends the basic functionality provided by the event log.

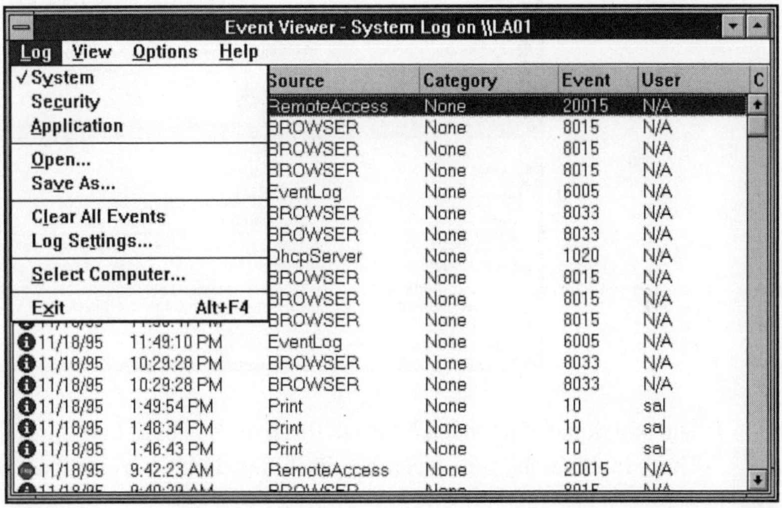

FIG. 4.3
Windows NT Event Viewer records systems, security, and application events from the operating system.

The User Manager is a tool used by the security administrators or domain administrators to create the single domain logon user ID. This ID includes all of the user's application profiles, group memberships profile, and time and workstation restrictions. The User Manager helps you to define trust relationships among domains, define auditing functionality, and general domain user account functions.

From the User Menu, you can select to create a new user, a local group, or a global group. The user ID is the individual ID used in conjunction with the password to be authenticated by the domain to access network resources. Local groups are those residing within the single domain in which they were created. If the domain is referred to as "Boston," all local groups created in this domain will only be able to access resources within the domain. Global groups, however, can be used to provide access to trusted domains. A local group can contain local user IDs, as well as global groups from both the local and trusted domains.

Exchange adds the functionality of creating a mailbox for users at the same time as assigning their domain logon ID (see fig. 4.4). This gives the mail, security, and domain administrators control over the same set of user accounts. In large organizations, this is the responsibility of a Network Security Group. This one group would be responsible for creating the user IDs as well as the appropriate mailboxes.

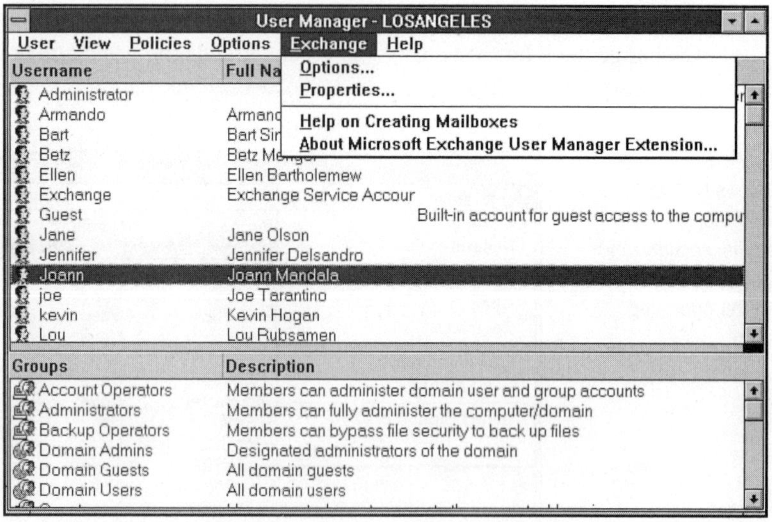

FIG. 4.4
Windows NT User Manager enables you to create domain user IDs, including the Exchange mailbox.

The functionality provided by these three tools is built into the NT operating system. These tools can be run on remote machines, 16-bit workstations, and from the Internet.

Introduction to the Windows NT Domain Architecture

At the heart of the Windows NT network operating system is the fundamental architecture of the Domain Model. A domain is a logical grouping of servers and workstations. One server must be the "Primary Domain Controller" (PDC) and subsequently have "Backup Domain Controllers" (BDCs). NT provides the capability to build servers as "name servers" which belong to the domain. These servers, however, are not responsible for replicating user account and security information throughout the domain. The PDC and BDCs remain synchronized by updating each other's user and security databases at regular intervals 24 hours a day, seven days a week.

The domain architecture consists initially of a single PDC of a single domain. From there, NT architecture can grow in any number of combinations that can include multiple BDCs in a single domain or a number of trusted domains with BDCs and member servers.

Trust Relationships Among Multiple Domains

Trust relationships can be created between multiple domains. Trusts enable users from one domain to be granted secure access to resources in a second domain. This maintains the concept of the single network logon. Users will see no change from a single domain to multiple domains.

Two types of trusts exist: one-way and two-way. One-way trusts are set up to enable users from the second, or "trusted" domain to access resources of the first domain. The second domain, however, has the freedom to create its user accounts and manage its own domain independently of the first domain. This can be illustrated using a distributed administration model in which certain divisions have their own network administration; however, there is a central domain providing corporate-wide resources. The divisional domains can completely administer their own domains without affecting the central domain. The central domain has the capability to enable the divisional domain to access the central resources. This is useful because full administrator privileges can be given out at the divisional level without administrative rights over the entire WAN.

Two-way trusts grant access and administrative functionality among all domains that are in them. This is also known as the Complete Trust Domain Model (see fig. 4.5).

FIG. 4.5
Establishing trust relationships between domains enables one domain to access the resources of another.

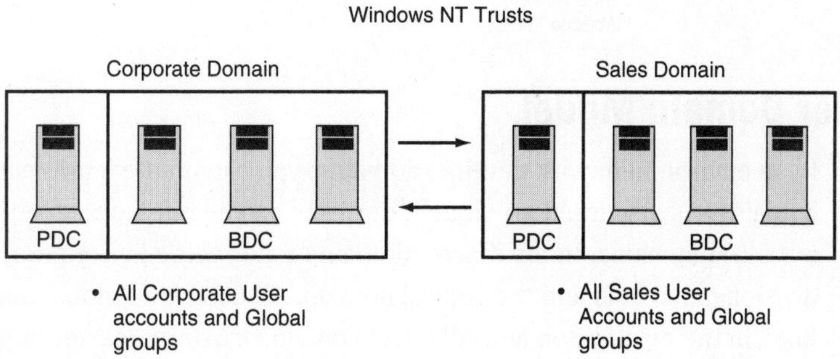

Single Domain Model

A domain is a logical grouping of servers that shares the same user accounts database and provides a single logon for all users to all the servers in the domain. As a comparison, on Novell Version 3.x networks, each server maintains its own user account database or "bindery." In this way, user accounts must be individually created on each server.

The concept of a domain is primarily used for centralized administration. All the servers in a domain are updated with a single action. Regardless of when the user ID is created or modified, all the servers maintain the single logon for the group of servers in the domain.

A single domain only consists of a PDC. For small organizations, additional BDCs can be added to validate user access rights. In the single domain, there are no trust relationships. Small organizations primarily use the single domain. These organizations do not have to be interconnected with other domains. Sometimes corporations use a single domain as a development domain. In this way, they do not affect the production domain. The server in the single domain can communicate with the other domains; however, additional user IDs will be necessary (see fig. 4.6).

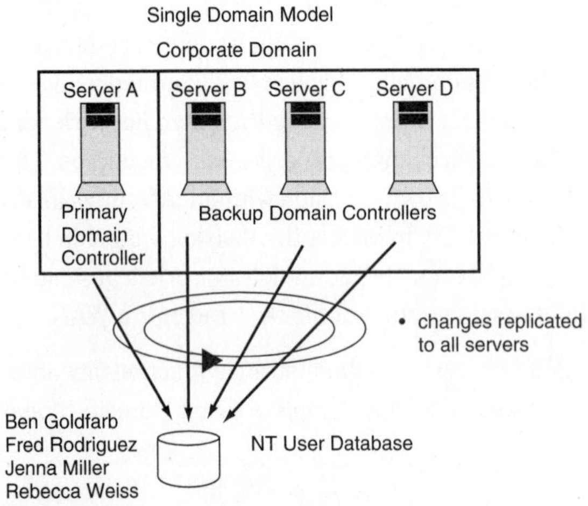

FIG. 4.6
Single Domain Model represents the simplest form of a Microsoft Windows NT network.

Master Domain Model

In an environment with multiple domains, you can create trust relationships between domains. As discussed previously, domains can be interconnected via one-way or two-way trust relationships. In the master domain model, there is a one-way trust between the divisional domains and the central domain. All users and global domain groups are defined in the master domain. All other domains trust the master domain. This model ensures centralized administration for all domains. Again, this model maintains the single network logon by establishing one user account for the enterprise.

For example, in a large organization, the MIS Division manages from a central point. Therefore, the same should hold with the domain architecture. From one location, all users and security are maintained. The master domain referred to as "Corporate" houses all users and global groups. The resource domains, "Sales," "Marketing," and "Legal," only maintain local groups. When a resource is needed from the Sales domain, a local group is created in Sales, and its members include a global domain group from Corporate.

One disadvantage to this model is that performance might decrease as the number of users and groups grows. For this reason, larger domains need to consider the next model (see fig. 4.7).

FIG. 4.7
The Master Domain Model puts global groups and users in the master domain. This Model also places resources in separate domains.

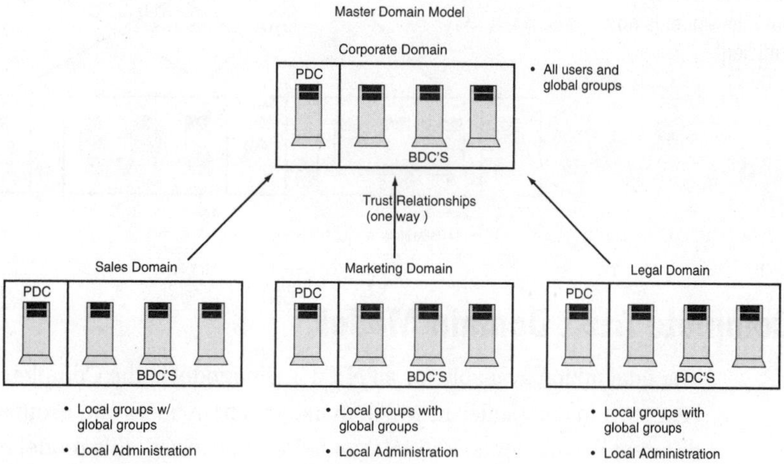

Multiple Master Domain Model

The multiple master domain extends the single master domain into a broader scope. This domain model is typically seen in very large organizations. If your organization has two major corporate headquarters, and many divisions, you might choose to implement the multiple master domain model.

Building on the previous example, the multiple master domain model has two tiers of domains (see fig. 4.8). The first tier interconnects the master domains. "Corporate" and "International" are the two domains. These two domains each house their respective users and global groups. These domains are then configured with a two-way trust. These domains trust each other. Therefore, only one copy of each user ID is needed.

The second tier of domains includes all of the resource domains. These domains each maintain a one-way trust to the two master domains. This model can be scaled to networks with any number of users. You can easily have upwards of 10,000 users supported with this model. The resource domains can then be grouped logically based on function and geographic location. The resource domains also provide for local administration at the divisional level. The disadvantage to this model is that there are more trust relationships to manage. Also, not all user accounts are located in one domain.

FIG. 4.8
Multiple Master Domain Model provides the scalability needed in a large organization when the Master Domain Model is not sufficient.

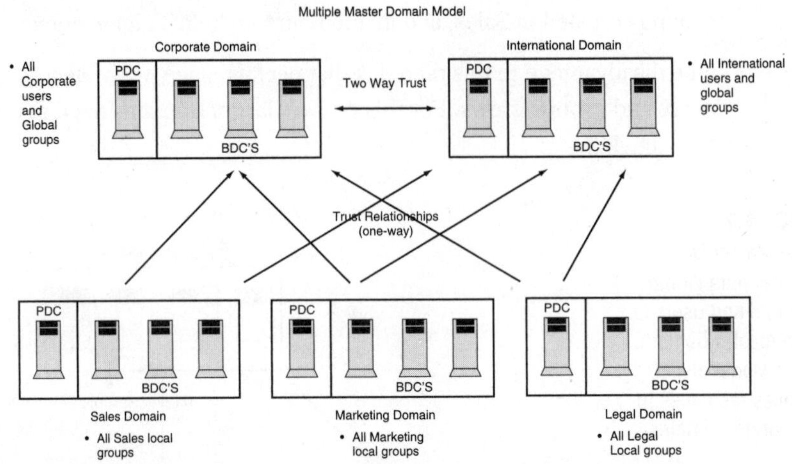

Complete Trust Domain Model

The final option available for an NT domain model is the Complete Trust. This model is best used in companies in which management of users and groups is distributed among different departments. Rather than being centralized, this model extends the administration down to the divisional level. Every domain trusts every other domain on the network. One immediate disadvantage to this model is that an administrator of one domain now has full rights over every other domain in the model. This can lead to security problems. If you are going to use this model, an auditing process could help manage who has made administrative changes on the various domains.

In this model (see fig. 4.9), the resources and the user accounts are grouped into divisions. Again, the only situation in which a Complete Trust is appropriate is when there is a lack of centralized management. This model is not practical for corporations with a large central department. The reason is that the model lacks the security needed for a large enterprise network.

Several options exist for an NT domain model. In Chapter 5, you are given the criteria for selecting which domain architecture to use when planning to deploy Exchange in your environment.

Microsoft also provides a tool through its BBS and Internet site to assist with planning a domain architecture. This tool is referred to as the "Domain Planner." It is a Visual Basic application that steps you through the options when choosing your domain and trust relationships.

FIG. 4.9
The Complete Trust Domain Model is intended for decentralized management and carries many security risks for an enterprise network.

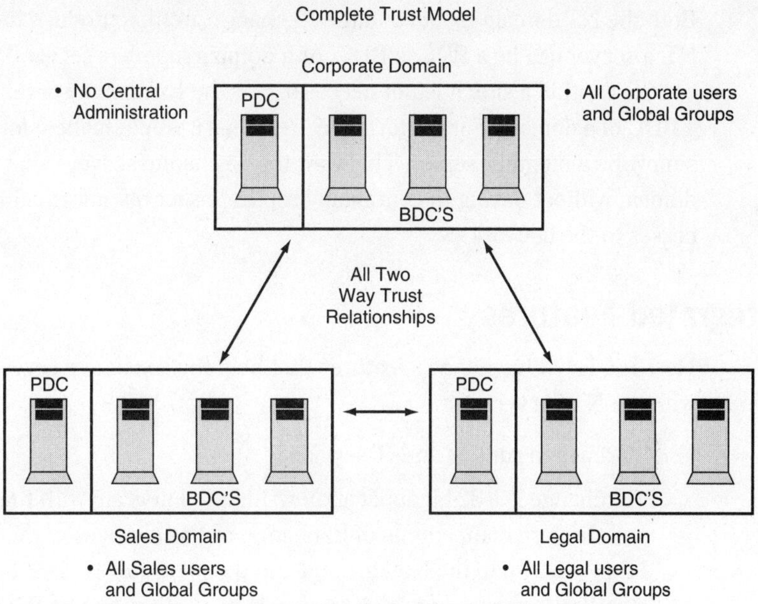

Understanding Exchange and NT Operating System Integration

This section explains how Exchange leverages the NT operating system. Exchange has been created to exploit all the features of Windows NT Server, including all the tools. These tools include the single logon, permissions that can be user defined, the User Manager for Domains, the Event Logger, and the Performance Monitor.

Comparison of NT and Exchange Terminology

Exchange sits on top of the NT OS. However, it has hooks into the OS to provide a robust, high performance messaging system. Not all of the NT terminology applies or directly converts to Exchange terminology. The reason is that the messaging platform has its own architecture.

Exchange uses the concepts of Organizations and Sites, whereas NT uses domains. Organizations are at the top of the Exchange hierarchy. Typically, you find only one Organization name in the entire enterprise. Sites, on the other hand, can be geographic locations, divisions, or functional areas. Sites can also map one to one with domains.

Sites can span across multiple domains, provided that the domains are trusted. This is necessary because a server within a site must authenticate each user.

Both the NT domain model and the Exchange architecture use the term "server." Within NT, a server can be a PDC, a BDC, or a domain member server. Within Exchange, servers exist within a site. It is not necessary for the Exchange server to be either the PDC or a BDC of a domain. For performance reasons, it would be best for the Exchange server to simply be a member server. This way, the Exchange servers share the resources of a domain without having to continually replicate security information or validate user accesses to the network.

Integrated Features

Here is a list of Exchange's features that help the Exchange server to closely integrate with the NT Server.

- Exchange runs as an NT service

  Exchange is a 32-bit application written to integrate with the NT Server. Therefore, all the core components of Exchange run as services of the NT OS. This means that they will run in the background and do not require a user to manually execute their application components. A service is an application that the operating system is aware of and manages its execution. In addition the service will log the activity of the process to the Event Viewer. From the performance monitor you can verify the impact the process has on the operating system. From the Server Manager, you can stop and start the processes.

  The 32-bit architecture of the executable enables Exchange to utilize the multithreaded, multitasking capabilities of the OS. Exchange runs in the background on the server. If a sudden burst of messages is passed to the Exchange server that needs to be forwarded, the executable can spawn more threads to effectively deal with the increased load.

  This integration is only one way in which Exchange leverages the NT operating system (see fig. 4.10).

- Additions to the User Manager for Domains

  Exchange adds functionality to the User Manager for Domains already discussed in this chapter. Exchange places an additional menu item with which you can administer user mailboxes from within the same consistent interface. Additionally, while you are creating users and assigning them group membership for NT file access, a dialog box pops up to add the users' mailbox to Exchange. The user can be added to any Exchange server across the enterprise as long as the administrator has permission to do so.

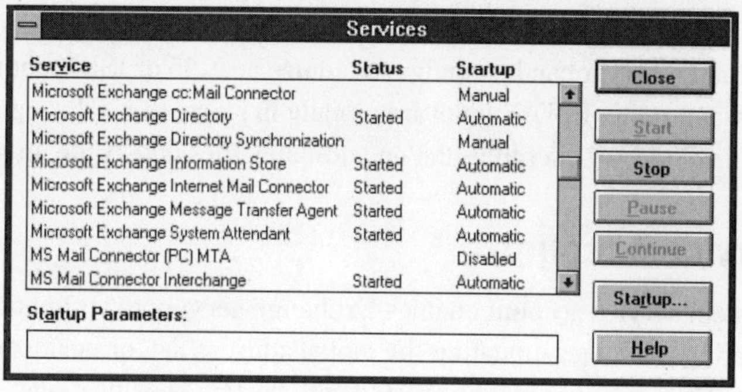

FIG. 4.10
The NT Service Manager enables you to start, stop, and pause services, as well as control their start-up properties.

- Additions to the Performance Monitor

Exchange extends the functionality of the Performance Monitor bundled within NT. This extensive monitoring tool enables you to observe both processor and disk space utilization, memory allocation, page faults, and over a thousand more counters.

Exchange adds some specific counters to the performance monitor which enable the administrator to view statistics of critical elements of the Exchange processes. These include the number of open tables on the message store, cache hits, I/O performance on reads and writes, RPC packets per second, number of bytes sent and received, and more.

Exchange NT Dependencies

Exchange relies on the NT operating system for certain functionality. The major function is that you must create a user account in the operating system for Exchange to run its services. Exchange also can import and export names from the NT domain user database. This facilitates a quick migration to Exchange from your existing NT Network architecture.

Exchange relies on the connectivity that NT provides. Exchange enables all types of clients to connect to its servers. Novell Netware clients, Macintosh, Unix, and all the Windows clients can connect to Exchange using their native protocols. This is made possible through NT's use of RPCs and multiple protocol support.

For remote access solutions, Exchange again relies on the NT OS. NT has an integrated remote access server as part of the operating system. The NT server running Exchange can be configured for a user to dial directly into the server and access Exchange, as well as any other network resources. For performance reasons, it might be more appropriate to set up the remote access server on a dedicated server.

For WAN connections, NT supports X.25 and ISDN without any additional software. An Exchange server can be configured to use an X.25 or ISDN connection to bridge the message route. If WAN links are already in place, these dial-up solutions provide a second level of fault-tolerance and an additional message route, in an emergency.

System Service Account

The system service account enables Exchange servers to authenticate each other when transferring messages, updating the global address list, or performing directory synchronization. This account must be created with certain specifications.

It is important to carefully plan the implementation of this account. You must have a domain model that supports these user accounts. Whether you have trusted or untrusted domain, you must ensure that the Exchange services can be authenticated between servers. If this does not occur, mail will not be forwarded from one system to another.

Security Models

Exchange relies on the C2 level security of the operating system. Any user who attempts to access the system must first be authenticated by the domain. Exchange extends the single logon ID. Therefore, the domain logon also validates users for accessing their Exchange mailbox. As mentioned previously, in the file-sharing mail systems, users had full access to the file system that comprised the post office. Exchange now manages the access to the post office based on the central domain user database.

Exchange itself provides three levels of security. The user accounts are leveraged from the NT user database. From within the Exchange Administrator Program, a user account can be specified as a complete administrator, a local administrator, or as a read-only administrator.

▶ **See** Chapter 23, "Exchange Maintenance," for a detailed discussion on Exchange security, **p. 571**

There are many issues related to using Exchange on the NT operating system. NT provides connectivity to almost any other operating system used in the enterprise. NT should not be a point of concern when deploying Exchange. The NT OS interoperates more easily with your existing network operating systems and mail environments than some proprietary systems that communicate with themselves. This is the case with PROFS or OfficeVision. Exchange leverages the NT OS to provide a strong messaging backbone.

From Here...

In this chapter, you learned how Exchange integrates with the NT operating system. For more information, see the following chapter:

- Chapter 10, "Installing Exchange in a Netware Environment," helps you begin to plan your Exchange system.

PART II

Migrating and Installing Exchange

CHAPTER 5

Designing Exchange Topology

- Your topology will have three layers. In this chapter, explanations of those layers and how they interconnect will be discussed.
- Understanding your Users' and Organization's needs
- Understanding your network type and operating structure
- Understanding Exchange sites and e-mail addresses
- Combining all the layers into an Exchange Topology

A successful Exchange implementation requires the proper fit into your organization. This chapter outlines an iterative, eight-step process that is applicable for all company sizes. Of course, smaller companies can choose a smaller, more appropriate set of steps, while larger, international companies will probably benefit from the entire process. However, many of the steps will provide value for all types of businesses. In addition, you may use this plan or create your own.

NOTE The examples presented may not completely match your environment. It's extremely important you recognize your environment's unique elements, especially when installing and naming the organization, site, primary domain, and server. These names cannot be changed without reinstallation.

Step 1: Understanding Your Users

The first step in designing your enterprise is effectively soliciting your organization's information requirements from users and management. Once identified, you can then connect those needs to services offered by Exchange. This step illustrates types of services users require and allows you to match those needs to features within Exchange (see Table 5.1).

Table 5.1 User Needs

Company Role	Needs	Exchange Feature
All functions	Share and organize information (e-mail, documents, schedules, images, reports, forms). Guarantee message confidentiality. E-mail response when out of the office.	Connectivity to other platforms; standard interface across heterogeneous platforms. Encryption. Out of Office Assistant.
Management	Allow secretary to respond to e-mail schedule for others.	Send on behalf; delegate access.
	Distribute company report.	Public folder (BBS).
MIS Support	Solution database.	Custom electronic forms, public folders.
	E-mail connectivity to Unix systems.	Internet Mail Connector.
Field Sales	Remote E-mail access.	Remote connectivity.
Manufacturing	Connectivity to legacy mail system.	MS Mail connector.

Step 2: Knowing Your Network

Your network topology has the greatest influence on Exchange's topology and boundaries. This step identfies the major characteristics of networks and maps some of Exchange's needs to your network's strengths. Contact your network administrator or architect and gather the following bulleted information regarding your network.

Each bulleted section will be described in detail and summarized on a table. If you are already familiar with networking concepts, you can reference the section entitled "Selecting Sites Based on Network Type" and summary table before moving to the next step.

- Types and links
- Size
- Bandwidth
- Protocols

Network Types & Links

There are several types of networks and network links today. When you understand the specific characteristics of your network and its associated links, you'll be able to accurately determine if a particular link is adequate for Exchange's needs.

- Dial-up phone line

  Phone lines are comprised of copper wire mainly used for single users to remotely connect to existing LANs and WANs. They provide an inexpensive, but periodic connection.
- X.25

  X.25 lines are permanent, leased lines proving a connection between LAN segments, i.e., WANs. X.25 is an international standard for packet communication over public data networks.
- Frame Relay

  Frame relay is similar to X.25, but provides better performance than X.25 due to decreased overhead. Frame relay is a method to send packets over private and public data networks to connect LAN segments, i.e., WANs.

- Fractional T-1

  Since T-1 lines can be divided into 24 separate lines or channels, fractional T-1 lines make connecting LAN segments, i.e., WANs, more affordable than using a full T-1. Bandwidth can be expanded all the way to a full T-1 by adding additional channels.

- Integrated Services Digital Network (ISDN)

  ISDN is digital communication over dial-up lines using the ISDN standard. ISDN eliminates the need for a voice digitizer (analog to digital conversion unit) in the telephone company's central office, thus allowing faster throughput than a modem over dial-up phone lines. Typically, ISDN is used by personal computer users at home and some LAN segment connections.

- T-1

  T-1 is a digital link carrying voice or data transmissions and is usually used to connect LAN segments. It also can be used to create private data and voice networks within a company.

- Satellite Communication

  Satellite communication is a wireless communication scheme that provides global data access. Typically used to interconnect LAN spread over a wide, geographic area and/or used to provide a redundant link when land-based lines are unavailable.

- Microwave Communication

  Microwave communication is a wireless link that uses microwaves to connect LANs that are typically on a business, campus, or industrial park.

- ArcNet

  ArcNet networks utilize a star or bus topology with a token-passing access scheme over coaxial cable (RG-62 or RG-59).

- T-3

  T-3 is similar to T-1, but has a higher bandwidth equal to 28 T-1 lines. Each of these channels can be divided and grouped into smaller portions. Typically, T-3s are used as high-speed WAN links.

- Thin Ethernet

  Thin Ethernet uses a linear bus topology with Carrier Sense Multiple Access with Collision Detection (CSMA/CD) over thin coaxial (10Base2) or twisted-pair (10BaseT) cable.

- Thick Ethernet

  Same topology and access method as thin Ethernet, but over thick coaxial cable (10Base5).

- Token Ring

  On a Token Ring network, all the computers are connected physically as a star and electrically as a ring. It uses a token-passing access scheme over shielded or unshielded twisted pair (UTP) wire.

- 100BaseT Ethernet (Fast Ethernet)

  Fast Ethernet uses the CSMA-CD communication scheme and comes in two flavors (100BaseT4 and 100BaseTX) depending on the type of UTP cable in place. Stations connect to 100BaseT hubs in the same way they connect to 10BaseT hubs. Typically, Fast Ethernet is used in LANs and WANs.

- 100VG-AnyLAN

  Proposed by IBM and Hewlett-Packard, 100VG-AnyLAN uses the same Ethernet frame format but replaces CSMA-CD with a deterministic protocol called the Demand Priority Access Method (DPAM). DPAM is conceptually similar to the token-passing method in Token Ring networks. 100VG-AnyLAN is used in the same types of networks and linking as Fast Ethernet.

- Fiber Distributed Data Interface (FDDI)

  Communication over a fiber-optic cable usually uses the FDDI standard. This standard is similar to the token-passing technique of Token Ring but operates at a much higher speed. Typically, FDDI is used as a backbone interconnecting lower speed LAN, e.g., Ethernet or Token Ring; connections to WANs; or to provide direct, high-speed attachments for routers and hosts.

- Synchronous Optical Network (SONET)

  SONET is a standard for high-speed communications over fiber-optic cable. It is a network transport (like Ethernet) and has a bandwidth equivalent to 48 T-3 lines. Like T-3, SONETis used to connect WANs together.

- Asynchronous Transfer Mode (ATM)

  From the standardization process of International Telecommunication Union (ITU) comes ATM, which was designed to handle voice, video, and data transmission over high-speed fiber-optic links. ATM's strength is that it can transport multiple data streams on virtual circuits operating at different data rates. Initially used as a LAN backbone (like FDDI), ATM is also being used to connect WANs over fiber-optic cable. ATM can use fractional T-1, T-1, T-3, and SONET as its physical medium.

Selecting Sites Based on Network Type

The following tables list all of the network types and links and group them according to bandwidth. As a rule of thumb for the average organization, you'll want to design sites so Exchange servers can communicate over a Type B (Table 5.3) or Type C (Table 5.4) link.

Generally, links having 64 Kbps or less of bandwidth have been classified by this guide as Type A (see Table 5.2). Type B links range up to 1.544 Mbps. All links with bandwidth over the 1.544 Mbps mark are considered Type C.

In certain cases, you may want to examine a smaller bandwidth link over a larger one if reliability is a factor. For example, some high (Type C) bandwidth links may not be as reliable as the low (Type A) links. Because Exchange servers in the same site need a permanent link to communicate, it may be wiser to choose the more reliable Type A link if messaging volume is light.

Keep in mind this is only one piece of information in selecting a site. You will need to analyze other factors such as the number of users per server, message traffic, the volume of public folder replication, and so on. Review the appropriate sections of this guide to gather all necessary information before making your final site selection.

Table 5.2 Type A Network Links

Type	Bandwidth
Dial-up phone lines	2.4 to 57.6 Kilobits per second (Kbps).
X.25	19.2, 56, and 64 Kbps.
Frame Relay	64 to 512 Kbps; newer implementations go to 1.544 Megabits per second (Mbps).
Fractional T-1	Each channel is 64 Kbps. Additional channels can be added up to 24, which equals a full T-1 line.

Table 5.3 Type B Network Links

Type	Bandwidth
Integrated Services Digital Network (ISDN)	64 to 150 Kbps
T-1	1.544 Mbps
Satellite Communication	128 Kbps to 1.544 Mbps
Microwave Communication	1.544 Mbps

Table 5.4 Type C Network Links

Type	Bandwidth
ArcNet	2.5 Mbps
T-3	44.148 Mbps
Thin Ethernet	10 Mbps
Thick Ethernet	10 Mbps
Token Ring	4 or 16 Mbps
100BaseT Ethernet (Fast Ethernet)	100 Mbps
100VG-AnyLAN	100 Mbps
Fiber Distributed Data Interface (FDDI)	10 to 100 Mbps
Synchronous Optical Network (SONET)	51.8 Mbps to 2.5 Gigabits per second (Gbps)
Asynchronous Transfer Mode (ATM)	100, 200, 400 Mbps up to 9.6 Gbps

Network Size

Although this may seem obvious, it's important to determine if you have a small or large network. In basic terms, a small network consists of one or two servers, a few clients, and a single domain or site. A large network contains multiple servers, clients, domains, and sites.

Second, it's important to know how quickly your network is growing and to what extent Exchange is being adopted. In many organizations, e-mail is the universal application that everyone seems to want. The need to exchange information, schedule meetings, and "be in the loop" will overcome even the most technically stubborn user. Along the same lines, the quick adoption of e-mail will sometimes force a reluctant organization to grow its network to reach the needs of its users.

Given this information, it's helpful to draw up a low, medium, and high Exchange adoption or migration plan and include its impact on your network's current size. Manage to the medium, but prepare for the high.

Network Bandwidth

Through careful examination of the underlying physical network, you may determine that existing network connections and bandwidths appear adequate to meet your organization's needs. For the purposes of this design guide, network bandwidth is defined as the amount of data per second that can be transmitted over a communication link. However, it is crucial not only to take into account the size of your links, but also to carefully look at the link's utilization. You may find your network has very large and fast connections; however, they may already be inundated with other network traffic which impedes overall performance of the network link. This is called Net Available Bandwidth (NAB). If your NAB falls to the same capacity as a Type A network link, it may be necessary to increase bandwidth in areas of heavy network traffic.

Another area to monitor is traffic bursts. Traffic bursts are short bursts of data transmission that utilize a majority of the bandwidth for short periods of time. You may find that some network links appear to have low overall utilization; however, during peak periods of the day these connections experience traffic bursts that impede performance.

Knowing or predicting network traffic patterns through a network link allows you to determine whether your link has enough NAB to support additional Exchange traffic.

To predict traffic patterns and prevent them from affecting your network, measure the network bandwidth utilization (how close a network link is to full capacity) and total packets per second (how close bridges and routers are to reaching full capacity).

Monitoring network traffic requires specialized tools such as dedicated network monitoring software like Microsoft System Management Server, packet sniffer, or NT's Performance Monitor. For more information on the specific Performance Monitor counters, please refer to Chapter 22, "Exchange Performance Tuning and Capacity Planning."

Network Protocols

For an effective Exchange topology, you should know which network protocols are used on your network. Exchange offers several types of connectors, but each of them has unique requirements.

For example, configuring a site connector in the Administrator program does not require knowledge or configuration of network transports because all communications happen over Remote Procedure Calls (RPCs). The X.400 connector, on the other hand, requires the existence of TP0/X.25, TP4/CLNP, or TCP/IP.

Another consideration is support for remote clients, e.g., field sales needing remote e-mail access, for which Remote Access Server (RAS) can be used. RAS supports the point-to-point (PPP) protocol that enables any client to use the TCP/IP, IPX, or NetBEUI protocol.

Step 3: Determining a Windows NT Domain Model

This step describes local and global groups, trust relationships, server roles, and domain models. A domain is a grouping of computers and users that eases administration of the computers and user accounts. Windows NT Advanced Servers all share a common user account and security database, thus enabling each user to have a single account that is recognized on all servers in the domain. The domain can also contain other Network Operating Systems (NOSs) such as LAN Manager 2.x and a variety of clients like DOS, Windows, Windows for Workgroups, Windows 95, and NT Workstation.

You can examine the following domain models to create your own domain or examine your existing one. Or you may use Microsoft's Domain Planner Wizard, which is available in the Resource Kit, or call Microsoft.

NOTE Once a domain has been created, you will typically need to reinstall NT to make any changes.

Local and Global Groups

Similar in structure to user accounts, groups allow efficient assignment of access privileges to multiple users within the domain. The two classes of group accounts are:

- Local groups, which are not accessible outside the home domain, but may have global groups from the home as well as other domains as members.
- Global groups, which contain users from the home domain and can be assigned access to resources within the home domain as well as away domains.

Trust Relationships

Windows NT Server supports the ability for one domain to "trust" another domain, thus giving users of the trusted (or account) domain the ability to act as authorized users on the trusting (or resource) domain. It also allows users in the trusted domain to access resources in the trusting domain without re-creating their user ID and other security information a second time. Keep in mind that no matter where network resources are located, users will always log into their home (trusted) domain.

For example, let's say that you own a VCR and your neighbor would like to borrow it and watch a video of Bill Gates speaking about Exchange and the future of messaging technologies. You "trust" your neighbor (a user from a trusted domain) enough to allow him or her entry into your house (resource domain) to use your VCR (a network resource) without making a second key (re-creating security information).

In addition, trust is one-way and not transitive. If domain A trusts domain B, it does not imply domain B trusts domain A. This two-way trust must be explicitly established by a domain administrator. Also, if domain A trusts domain B and domain B trusts domain C, it does not imply that domain A trusts domain C.

While trust relationships are very useful capabilities, they also involve setup and maintenance. It is best to limit trust relationships to a number that satisfies the organization's requirements without creating unnecessary complexity.

NOTE If an Exchange site spans multiple domains, there must be a trust relationship in place so that the servers can establish synchronous Remote Procedure Call (RPC) connections.

Server Roles

A Windows NT Server computer can have one of three roles in the domain:

- Primary domain controller (PDC)

  The PDC maintains the original user accounts database. This database contains all the security information for the domain. The PDC should be physically attached to the most central and high-speed network segment possible. Since the PDC authenticates users and receives updates to the user accounts database, it should never be on an unreliable or periodic network link, such as a wireless network or dial-up line.

- Backup domain controller (BDC)

  The BDCs receive a copy of the user accounts database from the PDC via replication. BDCs also authenticate users and can change their role to a PDC in case of PDC failure.

  If a BDC is replicating over a slow WAN link (less than 128 Kbps) and the PDC and BDC are at least NT Server version 3.5, you may want to examine the BDCs Replication Governor registry setting. This parameter tunes the load placed onto a WAN from replicating the user accounts database.

- Member server

Member servers are not tasked with authenticating users and thus servers are deployed as dedicated file, print, application (e.g., SQL Server), communication (e.g., RAS server) or messaging (e.g., Exchange) machines. Depending on their function, member servers can be connected over all (Type A to Type C) links.

Exchange should be installed on a machine serving either a BDC or member server role. You will not want to place Exchange on your PDC except in special circumstances, e.g., extremely small networks with very light mail volume.

Domain Models

Since Exchange needs a trust relationship to communicate between sites, you'll want to evaluate each domain model based on its implementation of trusts. If a domain model is already in place, evaluate its current trust capacity for an Exchange rollout. To monitor the status of your domain trusts, use the Domain Monitor for Windows NT.

- Single domain model

  This model doesn't use trust relationships. It contains a single PDC and can contain multiple BDCs and member servers. It's the easiest model to manage since user accounts and all groups (global & local) are centralized. Unfortunately, performance may suffer as the size grows toward the domain's capacity (around 22,000 users) (see fig. 5.1).

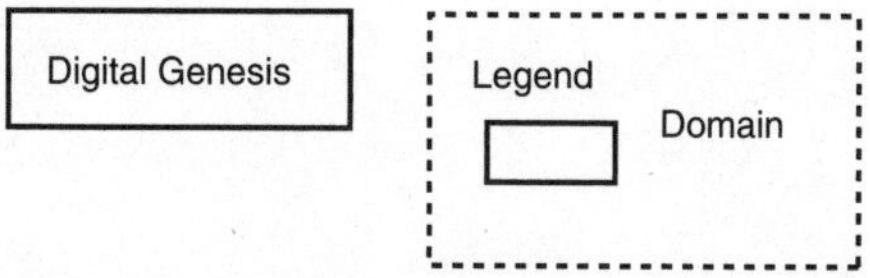

FIG. 5.1
Single domain model.

- Single domain with complete trust model

  Here, each domain has a two-way trust relationship with every other domain in the enterprise. The total number of trust relationships that must be set up is equal to N*(N-1), where N is the number of domains. Each domain has its own user accounts and global groups.

  For organizations that use distributed management or function without a central MIS, this model provides the best fit. Each department within a domain can effectively manage its home domain as well as other domains. However, as the network grows so does the administrative burden of adding additional domains and managing multiple trusts.

  In figure 5.2, Digital Genesis has no central MIS and thus allows each functional department to manage its respective users and groups.

FIG. 5.2
Single domain with complete trust model.

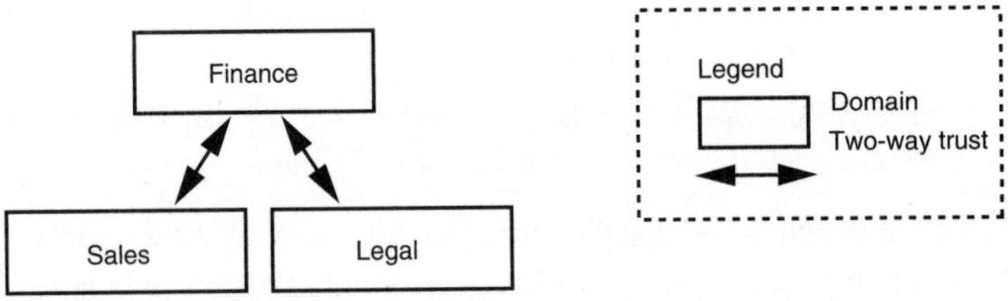

- Single master domain model

  In this model, there are several domains but one serves as the central or master domain. All the other domains are resource domains that trust the master domain via a one-way trust. The resource domains do not trust each other. All user accounts and global groups are contained in the master domain, while the resource domains contain file, print, communication, and SQL servers as well as local groups.

  Due to its centralized nature, this model allows a network administrator to manage all the organization's user ids from one domain, while the local administrators of each resource domain can manage their home domains. One disadvantage is that the single master domain can support networks of only up to 22,000 users and thus may not support explosive growth within an organization.

  In figure 5.3, IBT/Digital Genesis Inc. has centralized its user accounts and global groups within one master domain while organizing its resource domain along geographical locations.

FIG. 5.3
Single master domain model.

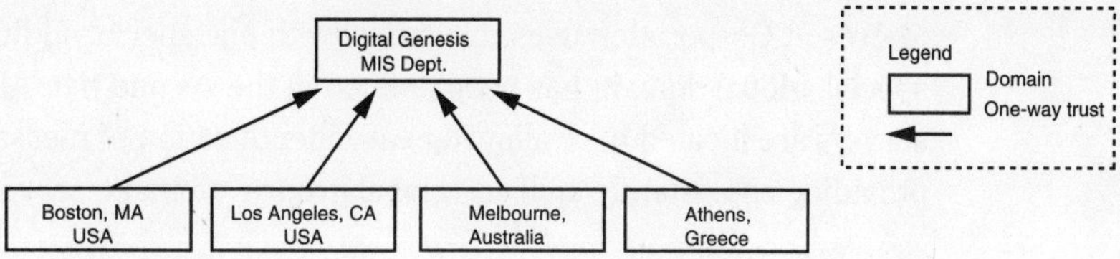

- Multiple master domain model

  This model is organized into two tiers and combines the features from the second and third domain models already mentioned. There are two or more master domains on tier one. Each master domain has a two-way trust to all other master domains. Thus, a user need be defined only once. Each resource domain on the second tier trusts all master domains with a one-way trust. The second tier domains do not trust each other.

  The multiple master domain model scales easily to an organization's growth and works well when a company has a centralized MIS department. In addition, each master domain can support up to 22,000 users each. However, the administrative burden is heavier than the other models due to multiple trust relationships and user accounts dispersed through several master domains.

  In figure 5.4, Digital Genesis has organized its first tier domain structure along geographically independent lines of business. It has offices in Boston, Los Angeles, Melbourne, and Athens. This strategy allows each office to administer its own security database while controlling access to the resource domains. Each of the resource domains is organized along functional departments allowing access to specific departmental resources.

FIG. 5.4
Multiple master domain model.

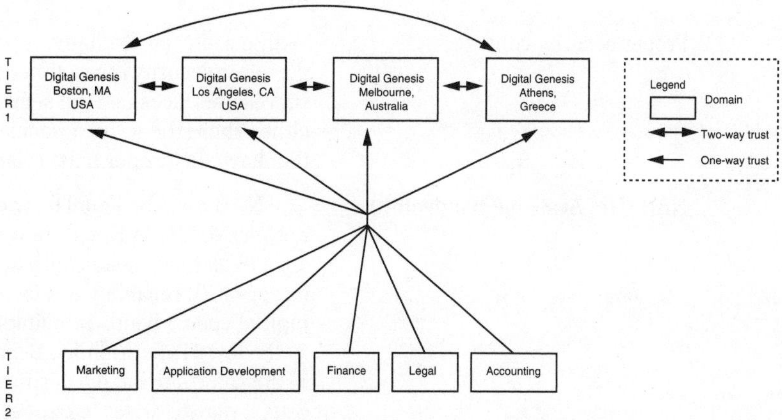

Microsoft Corporation uses this model with one special addition for Exchange. A special, global domain has been defined in the second tier. All Microsoft Exchange servers are located here allowing easy identification of messaging servers and providing consistently applied "global groups" to make server management easier.

Step 4: Selecting Your Sites

This step explains the difference between the critical and discretionary factors for a good Exchange site.

When determining which servers belong to which sites, you must consider two sets of qualifying factors. The first set includes permanent, RPC-compliant connections, plenty of NAB (Net Available Bandwidth), and proper security context. All of these factors must be present to group servers together in one site. The second set of factors are discretionary. They include the fifty server rule, connection cost, connection performance, replication, and company organization. Please refer to the next table for details.

NOTE These examples may not completely apply to your environment. Please carefully consider all pertinent factors before selecting a site and choosing site boundaries. Any changes will require a reinstallation.

Table 5.5 Necessary Site Factors

Factor	Requirements
Permanent, RPC-compliant connection	Servers within a site must communicate over a permanent network link that supports synchronous RPC.
Proper security context	Within a site, all Exchange servers must run under the same security environment. Since all Exchange servers' services use the service account, they must either share the same domain or belong to domains that have the proper trust relationships setup.
NAB (Net Available Bandwidth)	The NAB must be equal to or exceed a Type A network link (>64 Kbps). In certain cases, you may want to examine a smaller bandwidth link over a larger one if reliability is a factor. For example, some high (Type C) bandwidth links may not be as reliable as the low (Type A) links. Because Exchange servers in the same site need a permanent link to communicate, it may be wiser to choose the more reliable Type A link if messaging volume is light.

Table 5.6 Discretionary Site Factors

Factor	Requirements
Fifty server rule	As a rule of thumb, limit your site to contain no more than fifty servers apiece.
Consider large sites	Since Exchange will automatically replicate all changes within a site, consider making your site as large as possible to ease the administrative burden. Remember: It is easier to split than to merge.
Directory Replication	Since network bandwidth is higher within a site than between separate sites, replication will automatically occur more often inside sites. If you wish to manually control replication, place the servers in separate sites.
Bandwidth	If you have a group of servers connected at the same bandwidth, you should consider grouping those servers together in a common site. Place servers connected at a slower bandwidth in separate sites.
Company organization	Naturally, you'll want to group users in the same department or functional unit together. This provides a more effective use of network and Exchange resources.

Step 5: Selecting a Mapping Strategy

Now that network structure has been outlined and you've identified your critical site factors, it's time to choose a mapping strategy. This step describes the major site strategies, basing them on several domain and network examples.

During Exchange's setup, the install program creates several services that start and run based on the context of a user account called the service account. This account is created on the first computer within a site. Other computers within the site are validated by the service account and thus are given access to Exchange's services. All Exchanges computers within the same site must use the same service account.

If you have one domain and one site, you'll want service accounts created in the only domain. For multiple domains within a single site, create the service account in the account domain or whichever domain is handling your administrative domain functions. In a master or multiple-master domain model, the master domain would contain the service account (see fig. 5.5). In a single domain with complete trust model, any domain could contain the service account because it's accessible to all the other domains (see fig. 5.6).

If two sites are in separate domains, one service account can be used for both domains if they trust each other. If they do not, you can use a site connector to serve as a link. In this case you must set up the site connector to connect to the untrusted domain's service account. For example, let's say Exchange Site 1 uses a service account called Service1 and Exchange Site 2 uses Service2. Site 2 must connect to Site 1 with Service1's account name and password. Likewise, Site 1 connects to Site 2 with Service2 (see fig. 5.7).

When laying a site framework over your existing network foundation, consider the following strategies:

- One-to-One Strategy

  For a small organization, consider a one site to one domain approach. This means there is one site within every untrusted domain. A one-to-one strategy is similar to the single domain model. One advantage with the one-to-one approach is that it's one of the easiest to configure and manage. In addition, everything is centralized in one site and one domain. However, it is difficult to scale as you approach 50 servers per site unless you create additional domains/sites and use site connectors. Usually, as an organization grows or plans to rapidly grow, its mapping strategy moves toward a one-to-many technique.

- Many-to-One Strategy

  Another strategy you may consider is mapping many sites into one domain. This is useful when you want to segment a large network due to the fifty server rule or to group servers with similar bandwidths together. Although easy to configure, this strategy may have more management overhead if you choose to connect the sites via one of Exchange's site connectors.

- One-to-Many Strategy

  Larger organizations should consider moving to a one-site-for-many-domains strategy. This is equivalent to moving from a single domain to a single master or from a single master to a multiple master domain model. Since Exchange will replicate all changes to properly trusted domains, a one-to-many strategy is fairly easy to administer and removes the overhead of managing site connectors between untrusted domains. Still, you're limited to around fifty servers per site to maintain an effective Exchange system.

Overall:

- It is not necessary to map all sites to all domains.
- It is best to consider a large site over a small one when mapping sites to domains.
- Only domains containing the Exchange service account need to be mapped.

Review the following two tables to determine the best strategy for your organization.

Table 5.7 Effective Site Mapping

Domain Model	Mapping Strategy	Description
Single	One-to-One	All servers within the site have access to the service account (see fig. 5.5).
Single with	One-to-One	All domains and servers complete trust can access the service account (see fig. 5.6).
Two Single	One-to-One	A server in untrusted Domain Models domain A can access with no trusts the service account in domain B via a properly configured site connector (see fig. 5.7).
Single	Many-to-One	Each site can use its own service account or the service accounts in the other site via a properly configured site connector (see fig. 5.8).
Single Master	One-to-Many	With the proper trusts in place, servers in domain B and C can use the service account because it's located in master domain A (see fig. 5.9).
Multiple Master	One-to-Many	As with the previous mapping, the trust relationships allow all first and second tier servers to access the service account in master domain B (see fig. 5.10).
Two Single	One-to-Many	The trust relationships Master models allow the servers in each with no trusts second tier domain (B, C, E, & F) to access the service account defined in their local master domains (A and D). With a site connector, both untrusted domains' service accounts are linked together (see fig. 5.11).

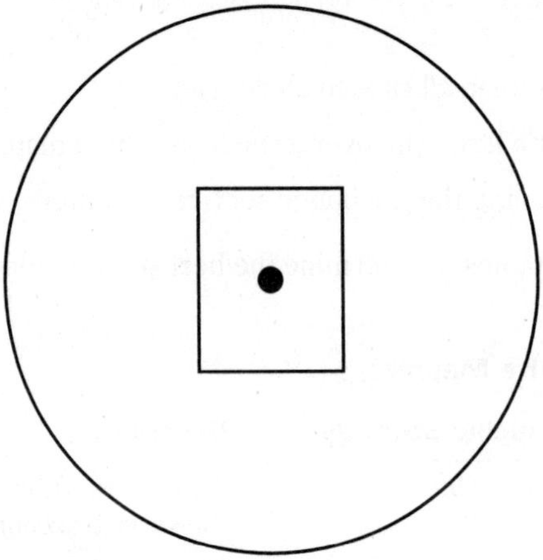

FIG. 5.5
Single domain using a one-to-one strategy.

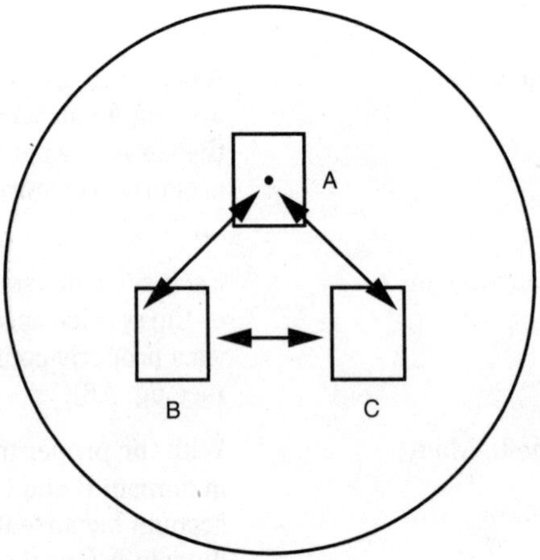

FIG. 5.6
Single domain with complete trust using a one-to-one strategy.

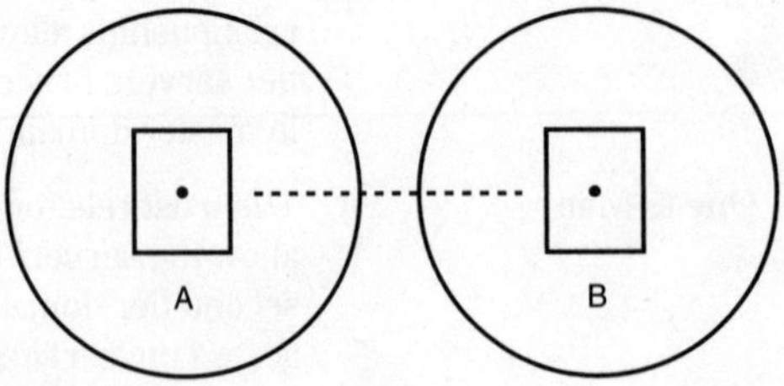

FIG. 5.7
Two single domain models with no trusts using a one-to-one strategy.

FIG. 5.8
Single domain using a many-to-one strategy.

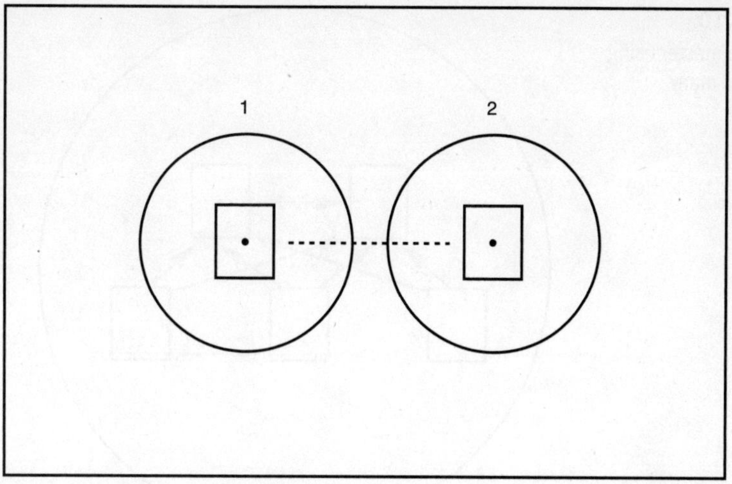

FIG. 5.9
Single master using a one-to-many strategy.

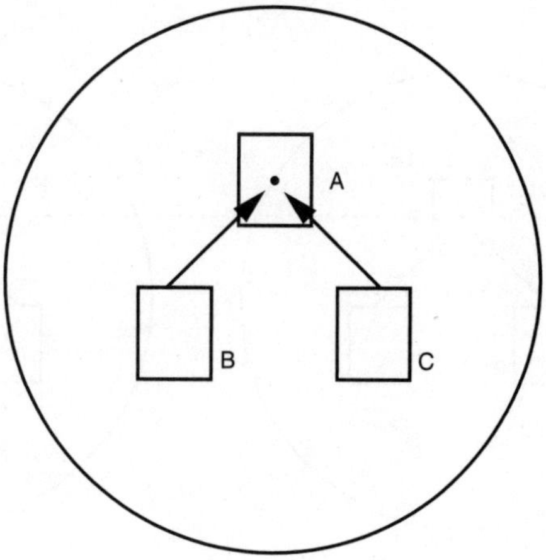

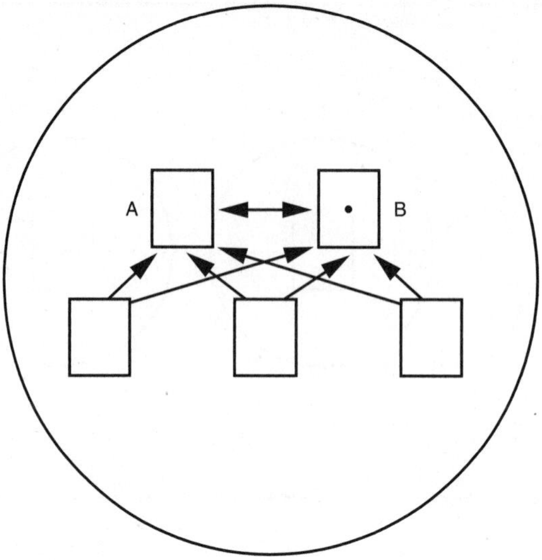

FIG. 5.10
Multiple master using a one-to-many strategy.

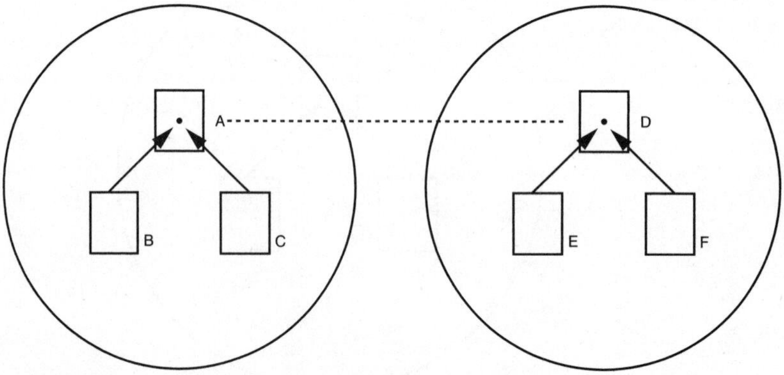

FIG. 5.11
Two single master models with no trusts using a one-to-many strategy.

Step 6: Selecting a Naming Strategy

This step will describe the format, use, and restrictions of e-mail addresses within Exchange.

Just as external messaging standards are necessary for different mail systems to communicate and share information, internal naming standards are just as vital to building a well-run, easily administered mail system. As with many items in this chapter, you must thoroughly plan before implementing a naming strategy because some changes will require reinstallation.

There are three elements of a sound naming strategy:

- It is not affected by a company's natural growth and reorganization. For example, base your naming conventions on geographic location, building numbers, and permanent floor locations. Avoid choosing company attributes that may change over time.
- It is easy to add additional items like sites, servers, users, and other directory objects.
- It is easy to use and administer the system.

Keep these elements in mind as you progress through the different mail systems and standards below.

Organization Name

An organization name should comprise your entire company. When choosing an organization name, be aware that it can be used to generate e-mail addresses for non-Exchange systems. Some system standards restrict the number of characters in an address. In fact, Setup will remove unrecognized characters for the Internet and MS Mail (PC) addresses. The organization name will also be part of the directory names of all directory objects such as mailboxes, public folders, and distribution lists. Organization names can contain up to 64 characters, must be unique, and cannot be changed.

Site Names

A site name can be based on function (sales, distribution), geography (countries, regions, cities), or physical location (building). Site names can contain up to 64 characters, must be unique, and cannot be changed. In addition, they are used by Exchange when generating non-Exchange e-mail addresses.

Server Names

A network uses the server name to identify a particular NT machine. Server names must be unique, can contain up to 15 characters, and cannot include any of the following characters: bullet (•), currency sign (\$), broken vertical bar or pipe (|), section sign (§), or end of paragraph sign (¶). In addition, do not put spaces in the server names if logon scripts are part of your environment.

Mailbox Names

A mailbox name should be easy to identify and similar in form to your organization's internal phone lists. Since mailbox names are listed in Exchange's address book, you may want to create mailbox names that sort properly when displayed. Review the following table for a breakdown of mailbox names.

Table 5.8 Guidelines and Restrictions for Mailbox Names

Field	Guideline	Restrictions
First Name	User's first name	Up to 16 characters, can be changed.
Last Name	User's last name	Up to 40 characters, can be changed.
Alias Name	To route messages to non-Exchange systems, an alias name is used. Identify the external mailsystems within your organization, e.g., PROFS, MHS, MCI Mail, AT&T Mail, and determine their unique requirements, e.g., PROFS can accept up to eight characters for an e-mail address. For best results, the alias name should bear a recognizable resemblance to the original name, e.g., Kent Smith becomes KentSm.	Up to 64 characters can be changed
Display Name	Base this name on how you want it displayed in the Address book and Administrator window. Be sure to consistently use the same format for all names, e.g., Last Name, First Name.	Up to 256 characters, can be changed.
Directory Name	Exchange uses this name to route mail messages. This is an internal name and is not displayed to users or administrators. Exchange will set this to the first alias name specified, but you can use another.	Up to 64 characters, must be unique, can't be changed.

E-Mail Addresses

When Exchange communicates with other (or foreign) mail systems, like the Internet, it must have a valid address format the other mail system understands. A foreign user whose address exists both on a foreign network as well as in the Exchange directory is referred to as a custom recipient. Exchange recipients (including mailboxes, custom recipients, distribution lists, and public folders) that have addresses on foreign mail systems are known as foreign e-mail addresses.

Exchange automatically generates an e-mail address for the following mail systems: X.500, X.400, MS Mail (PC), and the Internet (SMTP). Exchange does this to provide the widest possible compatibility with other messaging systems. Keep in mind that other addresses may be generated if there is a PROFS or another third-party gateway installed.

X.500 Addresses X.500 was designed to provide an international standard for enterprise-wide directory service access. The 1988 X.500 directory service guidelines form the basis of Exchange's directory service. It is in the directory that Exchange stores all X.500 object classes in an X.500 schema.

The directory objects are organized in a hierarchical structure known as the Directory Information Tree (DIT) and they are identified by a unique item called a distinguished name (see example).

The following table shows how the X.500 object name maps to an Exchange object.

Table 5.9 Mapping X.500 Names to Exchange Objects

X.500 Name	Attribute	Exchange Server Object
Country	c=	Country
Organization	o=	Organization
Organizational Unit	ou=	Site Name
Common Name	cn=	Exchange Server Recipient Container
Common Name	cn=	Exchange Server Recipient or directory name

For example, the distinguished name for Kent Smith who has a mailbox in Los Angeles within the Digital Genesis organization would be o=DG/ou=LosAngeles/cn=recipients/cn=KentSm. When you remove the naming labels, you receive the form that Exchange uses: DG/LosAngeles/recipients/KentSm.

Since X.500 doesn't support all object classes and attributes, Exchange also includes support for titles, organization charting information (who reports to whom in an organization), additional phone numbers, arbitrary attributes created by the administrator, and alternate recipients.

X.400 Addresses X.400 is a widely recognized and accepted international standard by the messaging industry. Exchange's compliance with the X.400 standard is important for organizations that want to use e-mail with heterogeneous mail systems as well as those who want to communicate with external companies via public carriers.

X.400 addresses can contain all of the upper- and lowercase letters, all numbers (0–9), a space, left and right parentheses, the plus and equal signs, the comma and the period, the hyphen and the forward slash or solidus (/), and the colon and question mark. In addition, X.400 addresses can contain the following attributes which are listed in hierarchical order:

Table 5.10 X.400 Attributes

Description	Attribute
Country	c=
Administrative Management Domain (ADMD)	a=
Private Management Domain (PRMD) (Exchange organization)	p=
Organization (Exchange server site)	o=
Organizational units	ou1=;ou2=; ou3=; and ou4=;
Common name	cn=
Generation qualifier	q=
Initials	i=
Surname (last name)	s=
Given name (first name)	g=

For example, a valid X.400 address for Kent Smith who has a mailbox in Los Angeles within the Digital Genesis organization would be:

```
g=Kent;s=Smith;o=Los-Angeles;p=dg;a=mci;c=us;
```

This address also represents the minimum information you need to receive e-mail from someone else.

Microsoft Mail Addresses If you will connect to Microsoft Mail for PC Networks or Microsoft Mail for AppleTalk Networks systems, character restrictions are:

Microsoft Mail network name	10
Post office name	8
Mailbox name	8

A valid MS Mail address for Kent Smith who has a mailbox in Los Angeles within the Digital Genesis organization would be DG/LSANGLES/KENTSM. For more information on connecting to MS Mail, please see the "Planning Connection to MS Mail" section within this book. For information on migration from MS Mail to Exchange, please see "Migration from MS Mail."

SMTP Addresses Exchange's SMTP connector is a dependable way to exchange mail transparently with SMTP users as well as with Mail users on other LANs over an SMTP backbone. It also enables Mail users to easily access mail networks such as UUCP, BITNET, and Internet.

When communicating with the Internet or other SMTP systems, look at their particular character or addressing limitations. In general, SMTP addresses can include all upper- and lowercase letters (A–Z), all numbers (0–9), and the hyphen (-). However, spaces are not permitted.

A valid SMTP address for Kent Smith who has a mailbox in Los Angeles within the Digital Genesis organization would be KENTSM@LOS-ANGELES.DG.COM.

External System Addresses If your organization has other mail systems (PROFS, SNADS, and so on), you will want to examine any conditions they place on usable characters and addressing. This way you can properly configure the Alias Name field (see the Mailbox name section) for your particular mail system.

Step 7: Linking Your Sites

Now that you have your sites laid out and the proper e-mail address to share information, the next question is: How do I link my sites? This step explains the methods you can use to link your sites, and discusses the pros and cons of different connectors and how this affects the Microsoft Exchange Server.

Site Connector

The site connector is the most efficient way to connect two sites if they are on the same logical LAN. It also offers the greatest performance because it uses RPC for communication.

Listed on the following table are the pros and cons when using the site connector.

Table 5.11 Pros and Cons of Using the Site Connector

Pros	Cons
Provides automatic load balancing and fault tolerance.	Requires a permanent, high bandwidth connection of at least 56 Kbps or higher (Type B or C link).
Easiest site connection option to configure and manage since a network transport is not involved.	Transmits more frequently than other site connection options. If you are charged for traffic, e.g., frame relay or packet network, you may want to examine another site connection option.
Messages don't need to be translated between sites.	Cannot control message size.
Configures both sides of the connection at the same time.	Cannot schedule connections.
Messages take fewer hops to reach their destination.	Can overwhelm network link when multiple Exchange servers use the same link.

RAS Connector

The RAS connector is useful where there is no permanent LAN or WAN connection, but you can link up to another site remotely. This is usually the case with small branch offices where permanent links are expensive or not available.

You can also use the RAS Connector to provide a redundant connection for sites using one of the other site connection options. For example, you can configure the RAS connector to handle message routing in cases where the primary connector link becomes unavailable.

Table 5.12 reveals the pros and cons when using the RAS connector.

Table 5.12 Pros and Cons of Using the RAS Connector

Pros	Cons
Connections can be scheduled.	Transfer is limited by speed of modem.
Can link sites over an asynchronous, periodic connection.	Link saturation is more likely since all site message traffic is flowing through one dial-up link.

X.400 Connector

The X.400 connector is useful where you are connecting to other sites via slow network links or on private or public packet networks. In addition, the X.400 connector provides compatibility with 1984, 1988, and future MTAs. This means you can communicate via X.400 with companies that are at different stages of implementing X.400 technology.

Microsoft Exchange Server supports X.400 over these OSI transports: TP0/X.25, TP4/(CLNP), and TP0/RFC 1006 to TCP/IP. After configuring to a transport, Exchange routes the message with standard X.400 messaging protocols.

Table 5.13 reveals the pros and cons when using the X.400 connector.

Table 5.13 Pros and Cons of Using the X.400 Connector

Pros	Cons
Connects to foreign, non-Exchange systems that support X.400 standard.	Must configure network transports.
Can schedule connections.	Bottlenecks may appear since all mail traffic is flowing through one central server.
Can determine messaging	Must verify that the existing routing through Exchange's network infrastructure topology (bridges, routers) can support the required protocols.
Message size can be controlled.	

Internet Mail Connector

Although the Internet mail connector can link two sites, its main purpose is to connect to the Internet using the SMTP (Simple Mail Transfer Protocol). Most UNIX systems and any mail systems supporting plain text-RFC 822, MIME (Multipurpose Internet Mail Extensions)-RFC 1521, MS Mail server format, or Uuencode/Uudecode standards can be linked, too.

Listed on the table below are the benefits and drawbacks when using the Internet mail connector.

Table 5.14 Pros and Cons of Using the Internet Mail Connector

Pros	Cons
Can forward all mail to a single host.	Must configure a network transport (TCP/IP).
Can be configured to accept or reject host connections.	Connections cannot be scheduled.
Can be configured to receive inbound or outbound messages or both.	

Microsoft Mail Connector

The Microsoft Mail connector provides seamless connectivity to Microsoft Mail for PC Networks, Microsoft Mail for AppleTalk® Networks, and Microsoft Mail for PC Networks gateways (PROFS, SNADS, Netware, MHS, and FAX). It uses a "shadow" post office that is structured like a Microsoft Mail 3.*x* post office.

The Microsoft Mail connector runs over the following transports: TCP/IP, IPX/SPX, NetBEUI, X.25, Asynchronous, and Remote Access Service (RAS).

Listed on the following table are the benefits and drawbacks when using the Microsoft Mail connector.

Table 5.15 Pros and Cons of Using the Microsoft Mail Connector

Pros	Cons
Can connect directly to another Microsoft Mail post office, allowing you to replace it without additional software.	In most cases, a network transport must be configured.
Allows you to migrate your MS Mail network in phases instead of all at once.	Must verify that the existing network infrastructure (bridges, routers) can support the required protocols.

Step 8: Reviewing Your Plan

Congratulations! You have all the necessary pieces to build a successful Exchange Topology plan that meets your and your organization's needs.

Keep in mind that every time you expand your network or Exchange site, you will need to enter a design phase again to create and implement a plan. Prepare for it by recording any important changes that may occur in the areas described.

From Here...

This chapter has provided a model for designing an Exchange Topology. Depending on your current phase of implementation, you may want to proceed to the following chapters:

- Chapter 7, "Migrating to Microsoft Mail Systems," addresses the challenges and provides solutions for moving your MS Mail network to Exchange.
- Chapter 9, "Installing Exchange Server," will provide step-by-step instructions on installing Exchange in your environment.
- Chapter 27, "Installing and Configuring Exchange Clients," will lead you through the installation steps to set up Exchange clients.

CHAPTER 6

Planning Connections to Microsoft Mail Systems

- **Description of the major components that make up the Microsoft Exchange Server Microsoft Mail Connector**
- **Description of the major components that make up MS Mail 3.x**
- **How to integrate Microsoft Exchange Server into an existing MS Mail 3.x mail environment**
- **Overview of Directory Replication between Microsoft Exchange Server sites**
- **Directory Synchronization between Microsoft Exchange Server sites and MS Mail 3.x mail systems**

By coupling the functions of a Gateway Post Office and the External program, the Microsoft Mail Connector bundled within Microsoft Exchange Server becomes the primary link between Microsoft Exchange Server and Microsoft Mail 3.x (PC and Appletalk). It also provides the connectivity link that ties Microsoft Exchange Gateways and MS Mail 3.x Gateways. This Connector allows Microsoft Exchange Server to route and transfer messages to one or more MS Mail 3.x(PC) systems over LAN, Asynchronous, or X.25 connections.

You can configure Microsoft Mail Connector for message transfer and routing by using components provided with Microsoft Exchange Server. The components built into the Microsoft Mail Connector are comparable to the components in the MS Mail 3.x Post Office and External message transfer programs. The Microsoft Mail Connector components run as services on a Windows NT operating system, which allows for better error logging, memory management, and performance monitoring of the entire messaging system. Integration of an existing MS Mail 3.x system, using the External or the Multitasking MTA programs with Microsoft Exchange Server, can be easily configured to allow a common coexistence of both messaging systems on the same LAN. ■

Microsoft Mail Connector Components

The following three components are located within Microsoft Mail Connector and work in conjunction with each other transparently to transfer and route messages to and from MS Mail Post Offices (see fig. 6.1):

- Microsoft Mail Connector Interchange
- Microsoft Mail Connector Post Office
- Microsoft Mail Connector (PC) Message Transfer Agent (MTA)

Microsoft Mail Connector Interchange

The Microsoft Mail Connector Interchange is a Windows NT service that converts the message from or to MS Mail 3.x format, then routes and transfers messages between Microsoft Exchange Server and the Microsoft Mail Connector Post Office. This process is completely transparent to the users and completed in the background. Configuring the Microsoft Mail Connector Interchange must be done for LAN, asynchronous, and X.25 transport connections. Configuration requires using the Administrator program, in the Interchange tab, to create and set up an Administrator Mailbox to receive delivery status messages, the establishment of a primary language used by the majority of the Post Offices using the Connector, and if MS Mail 3.x clients wish to view or save OLE documents received from Microsoft Exchange Clients, the Maximize MS Mail 3.x Compatibility item must be selected.

Microsoft Mail Connector Post Office

The Microsoft Mail Connector Post Office is a temporary information store for messages in transit. The Connector Post Office is sometimes referred to as a *gateway Post Office* because it is dedicated to message transfer and has no local mailboxes. The Microsoft Mail Connector Post Office sits between the Microsoft Mail Connector Interchange and the Microsoft Mail Connector MTA. Since this Post Office works with messages being transferred both ways through its information store, it temporarily holds messages that have been converted and are waiting to be routed to MS Mail 3.x clients or messages sent from MS Mail 3.x clients, waiting to be converted.

Microsoft Mail Connector (PC) Message Transfer Agent (MTA)

The Microsoft Mail Connector Message Transfer Agent is a Windows NT service that connects to and transfers mail between the Microsoft Mail Connector Post Office and one or more MS Mail (PC) Post Offices. It can execute most of the same operations of the MS Mail 3.x External and Multitasking MTA programs, including message distribution and delivery to users on MS Mail Post Offices. The MTA contains the information for which the direct and indirect connection routing of mail messages occurs between MS Mail 3.x Post Offices. The information is read from a list that is configured through the Microsoft Mail Connector section of the Administrator program.

Once again, all of the preceding components can be configured in the Administrator program, under the Microsoft Mail Connector, within the individual component tab.

FIG. 6.1
Microsoft Mail Connector components.

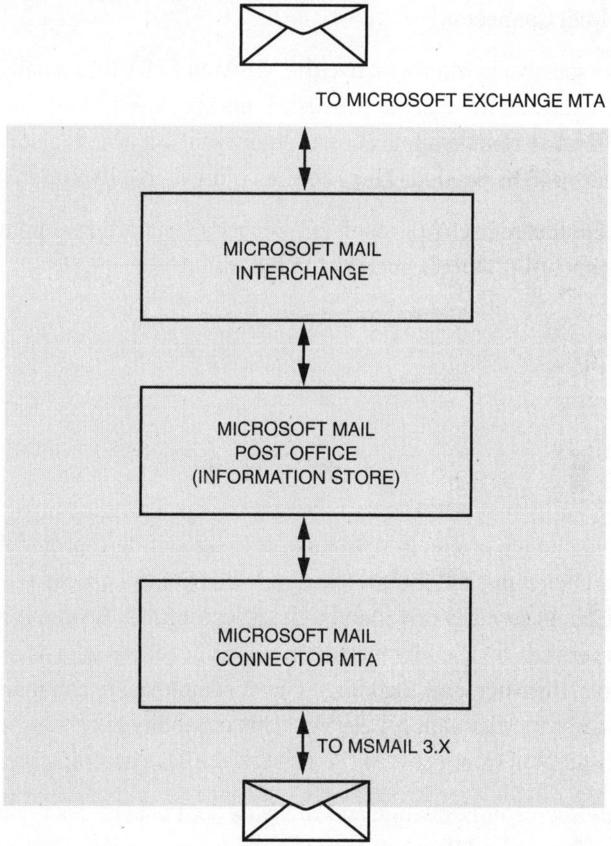

In an MS Mail 3.x environment, the External (Mail Transfer Agent—MTA) and the Multitasking MTA (MMTA) programs transfer and route messages between MS Mail

Post Offices. The programs do not have all of the same advanced features as the Microsoft Mail Connector. However, any existing MS Mail 3.x system using External and the Multitasking MTA programs to transfer and route messages, can easily be integrated with a Microsoft Exchange Server directly, with the help of the Microsoft Mail Connector.

The Microsoft Mail Connector MTA does not completely handle all of the functions of the MS Mail 3.x External or Multitasking MTA. In some cases, the messaging system may still require some of the functions found in the External program.

For example, when MS Mail 3.x Remote users dial in for their messages, they dial into the MS Mail MTA (External), which handles message transfer between Remote users and the MS Mail 3.x Post Offices. With users still using the MS Mail Remote client program, the MS Mail MTA (External) cannot be replaced by the Microsoft Mail Connector. The continued use of the External program will need to be maintained, as well as the Microsoft Mail Connector.

Another perspective is when you use the MS Mail MTA (External); the MTA administers to modem setup and the dial-out process. It also requires its own separate dial-in infrastructure. If other remote applications require dial-out access also, another separate dial-in infrastructure will be needed. This requires quite a bit of communications equipment.

Microsoft Exchange uses Microsoft NT Server's standard remote network hardware that supports standard protocols such as the following:

- PPP
- TCP/IP
- IPX/SPX
- NetBIOS
- AppleTalk

Microsoft Exchange profits from the use of these standard protocols by making it possible to implement and integrate a single dial-in infrastructure to handle all remote communications services provided by the Microsoft NT Server. A multitude of remote access servers can be used by your Remote mail users to gain access to the mail system. For example, the Microsoft Exchange Client remote users can make use of the built-in Remote Access in Microsoft NT Server. This capability allows remote users to dial directly into Microsoft Mail Connector MTA through the Microsoft Exchange Server.

When both Microsoft Exchange and MS Mail 3.x Post Offices reside on the same LAN, you can configure the Microsoft Mail Connector to transfer route messages from the Microsoft Exchange Server MTA, convert the message, and deliver the message to the correct recipient on the MS Mail 3.x Post Office.

When you send a message to a Microsoft Exchange Server destined for an MS Mail 3.x recipient located on the same LAN, the message is received by the Microsoft Exchange MTA. Then, the message is routed by the Microsoft Exchange MTA to the Microsoft Mail Connector Interchange. Here, the message and any OLE attachments are converted to MS Mail 3.x format. The converted message is then sent to the Microsoft Mail Connector Post Office (Information Store) where it is held until the Microsoft Mail Connector MTA picks it up and delivers it to the appropriate MS Mail 3.x Post Office (see fig. 6.2).

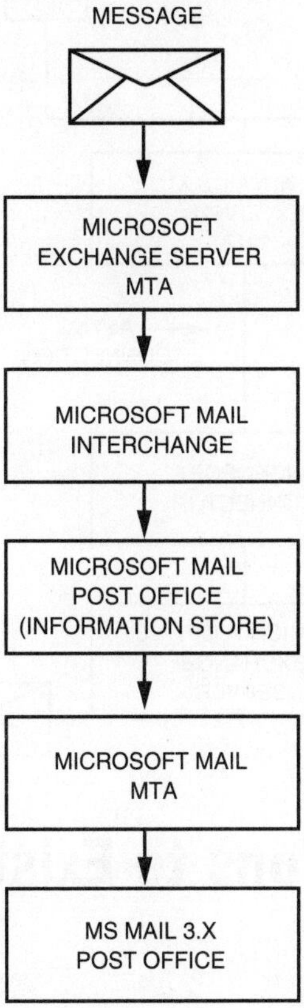

FIG. 6.2
The message transfer process from Exchange Server MTA to MS Mail 3.x.

MS Mail 3.x message delivery can be performed only over a Direct LAN connection. The Microsoft Mail Connector, External MTA, and Multitasking MTA determine their routing information between Microsoft Exchange Server and MS Mail 3.x by the information that is entered into the Address Space. The *address space* is defined as a set of MS Mail 3.x Post Office names, to which mail messages will be routed by the Microsoft Mail Connector. This entry in the address space is also known as an *Instance*.

When connecting MS Mail 3.x over X.25 or Asynchronous services, the External MTA or Multitasking MTA program at the Remote Post Office location will also have to be configured with an instance in the address space of the MTA to connect with the Microsoft Mail Connector (see fig. 6.3).

FIG. 6.3
Basic MS Mail 3.x External (or Multitasking MTA) layout.

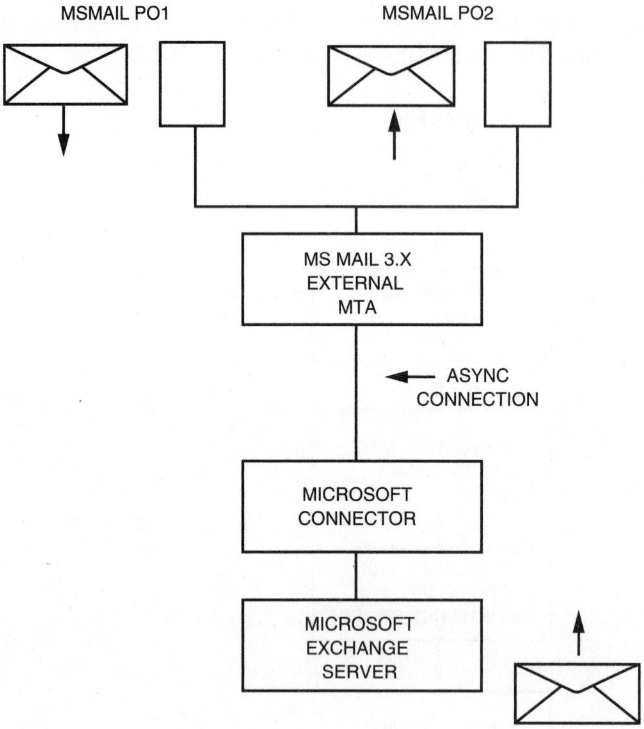

Configuring LAN Connections to Existing Post Offices

The LAN connection happens to be the easiest and one of the simplest types of connections in terms of setup and administration. In this particular case, you don't have to use the External or Multitasking MTA programs at all. Instead, you can use the Administrator program in Microsoft Exchange Server to configure the majority of the message routing and transfer between the Microsoft Mail Connector and the MS Mail 3.x Post Offices.

MS Mail 3.x Post Office

If you have multiple MS Mail 3.x Post Offices on the same LAN, a way to increase the performance of the Microsoft Exchange Server is to configure one of the MS Mail 3.x Post Offices as the direct connection Post Office. This MS Mail 3.x Post Office will be the recipient and sender of messages transferred to and from the Microsoft Exchange Server Microsoft Mail Connector. The Microsoft Mail Connector contains an instance in its address space to route messages to the MS Mail 3.x direct connection Post Office. Additionally, the address space of the Microsoft Mail Connector also specifies instances for all of the other MS Mail 3.x Post Offices located on the LAN as indirect connections. The MS Mail 3.x Post Offices configured as indirect connections transfer messages to and from the MS Mail 3.x direct connection Post Office.

Similarly, the address space of the MS Mail 3.x Post Office that is configured as the direct connection Post Office will also contain entries of indirect connection instances that describe the remaining MS Mail 3.x Post Offices located on the LAN (see fig. 6.4).

FIG. 6.4
Basic LAN connection with direct and indirect route configuration.

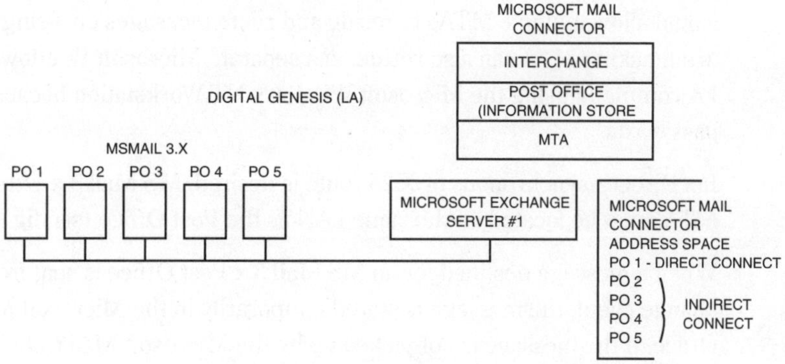

To transfer and route messages correctly, the Microsoft Mail Connector must know about each of the remote Post Offices. Microsoft Mail Connector has an integrated feature that automatically extracts Indirect Routing information from an MS Mail 3.x Post Office. This feature means there is no need to manually configure the routing information for each of the MS Mail 3.x Post Offices connected indirectly to the Microsoft Mail Connector. The only requirement for the automatic upload of routing information is a LAN Connection. Unfortunately, if the MS Mail 3.x Post Office you are trying to connect to is over an Asynchronous or X.25 service, the indirect routing information will have to be input manually through the Microsoft Mail Connector property pages.

Asynchronous and X.25 Connections for Remote Post Offices

You need two components to connect Microsoft Exchange Server and an MS Mail 3.x Post Office over an X.25 or Asynchronous service. The first is the Microsoft Mail Connector MTA, the main routing component of the Microsoft Mail Connector included within the Microsoft Exchange Server. It runs as a service on the Microsoft NT Server. When configured, it contains the routing information in the address space that will be used to route messages to and from the MS Mail 3.x Mail systems.

The second is the MS Mail 3.x External or Multitasking MTA program provided with MS Mail 3.x Server. This program provides the message transfer and modem management functions necessary to communicate over a remote connection within an MS Mail 3.x system. If the MS Mail 3.x External MTA will reside on a DOS computer, this will need to be a dedicated computer. DOS will not allow multiple sessions, or executables, to occur at the same time. Setting up the Multitasking MTA on a Microsoft Windows NT Workstation would allow multiple MTAs to reside and route messages on a single computer. The Multitasking MTA can also reside on a separate Microsoft Windows NT Server if desired. I recommend using the Microsoft Windows NT Workstation because it doesn't require passwords.

If a Direct Asynchronous or X.25 route is desired, MS Mail 3.x External or Multitasking MTA must be located on the same LAN as the Post Office (see fig. 6.3).

When a message destined for an MS Mail 3.x Post Office is sent from a Microsoft Exchange client, the message is stored temporarily in the Microsoft Mail Connector Post Office. If the message is not picked up by the Microsoft Mail Connector MTA and routed to its destination, the message will remain in the Connector Post Office until it times out and is returned to the sender, or it gets picked up and delivered by a LAN connected instance of the MS Mail 3.x External or Multitasking MTA or Gateway (see fig. 6.3)

Using Multiple Microsoft Mail Connectors (PC) MTAs

Each Microsoft Mail MTA instance will react differently depending on the type of connection it uses.

NOTE Each instance is named and registered as a Windows NT service on the Microsoft Exchange Server computer on which it was created and can be started or stopped independently of any other service. ■

Each instance has a primary connection type, although all instances can service LAN-Connected Post Offices. Depending on the number of Post Offices and what their connection types are, it might be more efficient to group the same connection types in the same instance. If the connection types are diverse, multiple instances should be created.

For example, if your network contains 10 LAN-connected MS Mail 3.x Post Offices and five Asynchronous-connected MS Mail 3.x Post Offices, it would be more efficient to create an instance on the Microsoft Mail Connector MTA for servicing only the LAN-connected Post Offices and another instance for connecting to and servicing the Asynchronous Post Offices.

If there are only two Asynchronous-connected MS Mail 3.x Post Offices and 10 LAN-connected MS Mail 3.x Post Offices, only one instance needs to be created on the Microsoft Mail Connector MTA for the Asynchronous connected Post Offices. Since all instances can service LAN connected Post Offices, the LAN connected Post Offices can then be added to the same instance.

Using Multiple Microsoft Mail Connectors

If your organization contains a large number of MS Mail 3.x Post Offices, you might need multiple Microsoft Mail Connector MTAs for message connectivity between MS Mail 3.x and Microsoft Exchange recipients. Since the same MS Mail E-Mail address is used by every Microsoft Exchange Server in the site, MS Mail essentially views each of the Microsoft Exchange sites as one large MS Mail Post Office. Therefore, it is recommended for routing purposes, that one Microsoft Mail Connector MTA should be used for every Microsoft Exchange Server Site, which subsequently means multiple instances.

Additional Routing Considerations

If you are going to use Multiple Microsoft Mail Connector MTAs, make sure each Microsoft Exchange Server has its own Microsoft Mail Connector MTA. Also, use duplicate address entries in two or more Microsoft Mail Connectors to route messages based on cost. This is useful for redundancy and load balancing traffic across connections and between servers.

Using Exchange Server as a Backbone to MS Mail (PC)

Multiple MS Mail 3.x Sites and individual MS Mail 3.x Post Offices can be coupled into a single messaging system using Microsoft Exchange Server as a Backbone to the existing MS Mail 3.x messaging system. To make this connection, message transfer should first be set up between each of the Microsoft Exchange Server sites and a MS Mail 3.x Post Office. Make sure that each of the MS Mail 3.x Post Offices correctly routes the messages to its destination through the Microsoft Mail Connector. When connected through a Microsoft Exchange Server, this will allow each of the MS Mail 3.x Post Offices to see the other MS Mail 3.x Post Offices as connected indirectly through one or more other Post Offices. If Directory Synchronization has been set up between any of the sites and the MS Mail 3.x Post Offices, all of the new information added to the Microsoft Exchange Server while setting up the message transfer between the sites and the MS Mail 3.x Post Offices will be replicated to each of the connected Post Offices and the information shared by all (see fig. 6.5).

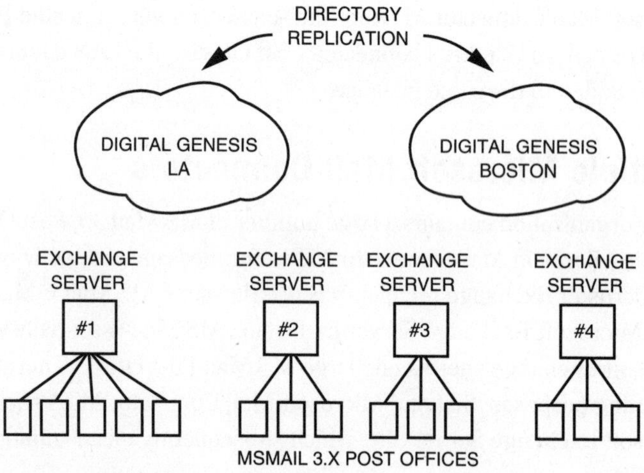

FIG. 6.5
Basic site-to-site backbone configuration.

Using Existing MS Mail (PC) Gateways

Microsoft Exchange Server supports a wide variety of MS Mail (PC) Gateways, which grant messaging services to other messaging systems. Supported MS Mail (PC) Gateways include the following:

- AT&T Easylink
- Fax

- IBM PROFS and OfficeVision
- MHS
- SNADS
- MCI Mail Gateway (M-Bridge for Microsoft Mail for PC (Networks)

All of these Gateway programs come enclosed with Microsoft Mail Server 3.x on an options diskette included with the software. Each of the Gateway programs will require a short installation and configuration process. They are menu driven and easy to follow.

There are two ways Microsoft Exchange Clients can pass information through an existing MS Mail 3.x mail system gateway. First, a typical gateway scenario in an existing MS Mail 3.x environment would find the MS Mail 3.x Gateway software running on a dedicated computer. A MS Mail 3.x Post Office will need to be selected as the Gateway Post Office. All messages destined for the foreign mail system will pass through this gateway Post Office, and vice versa. In order for Microsoft Exchange clients to access the actual Gateway and pass messages to the foreign mail system, the Microsoft Exchange Connector Post Office needs to have the MS Mail 3.x Gateway Access Component installed on it (see fig. 6.6). Secondly, if a Microsoft Exchange Server is selected as the Gateway Post Office, the MS Mail 3.x Post Offices will then be required to hold a Gateway Access component. Either way will integrate a Microsoft Exchange Server into an existing MS Mail 3.x Gateway scenario (see fig. 6.7).

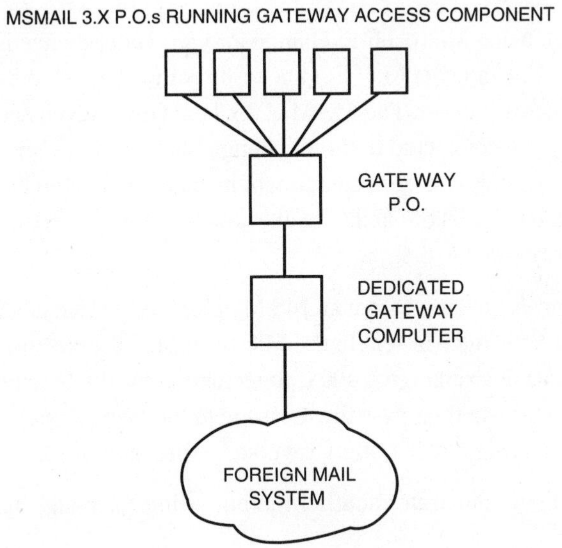

FIG. 6.6
Basic MS Mail 3.x Gateway Layout.

FIG. 6.7
A typical gateway scenario.

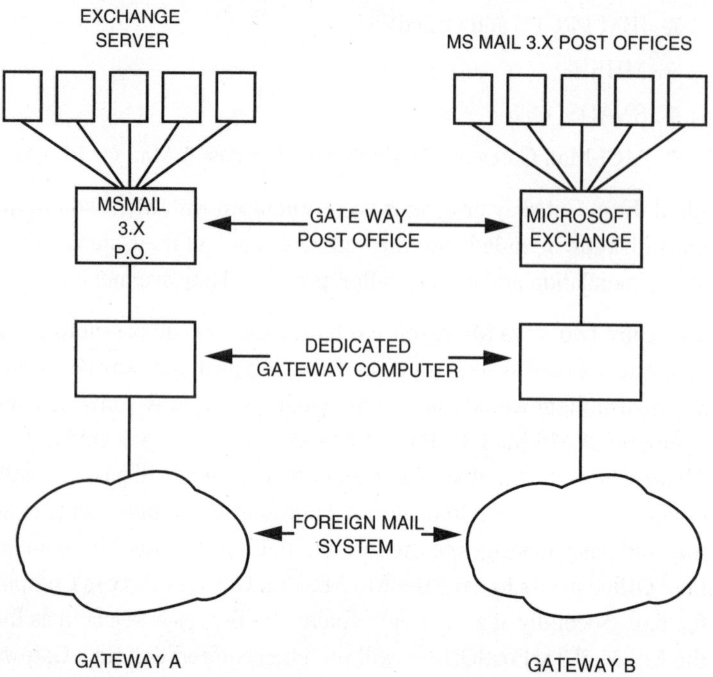

Using Exchange Connectors as Gateways

If you decide on using Microsoft Exchange for your Gateway needs, Microsoft Exchange X.400 Connector or Internet Mail Connector or both will need to be installed on the Microsoft Exchange Server. The MS Mail 3.x Post Office given access to the foreign mail service needs to be connected to the Exchange Server via the Microsoft Mail Connector and must have a gateway access component installed on it. One benefit to using Microsoft Exchange as a gateway is the ability to alleviate the need for a dedicated computer running the gateway (see fig. 6.8).

When a mail message is sent from an MS Mail 3.x Post Office destined for the foreign mail service, the message is sent to the Microsoft Mail Connector, which passes it to either the Microsoft Exchange X.400 Connector and/or the Internet Mail Connector. The selected connector will then pass the message to the foreign mail service. For a message traveling from a foreign mail system, reverse the procedure.

The following figure illustrates another method using Exchange as a gateway.

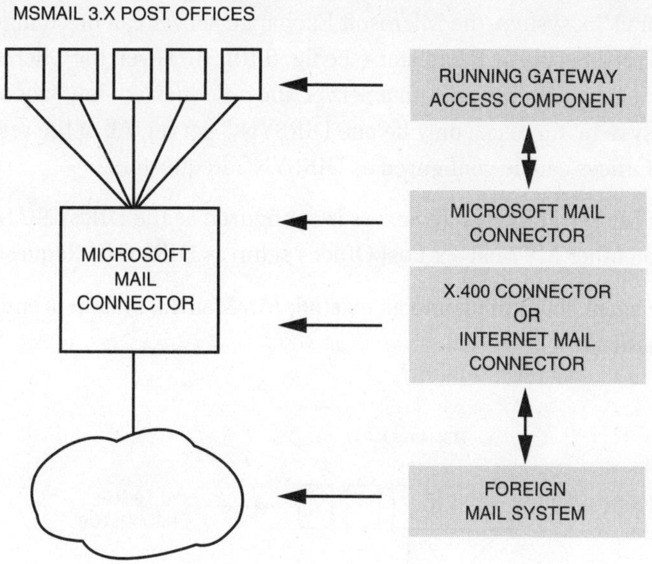

FIG. 6.8
Using Microsoft Exchange as a gateway.

Directory Replication and Synchronization

Directory Replication is the automatic process of replicating the Directory information between Microsoft Exchange Servers within a site. The information that is replicated includes all the information available about an organization's resources and users including mailboxes, public folders, distribution lists, servers, and more. Other components use the directory to map addresses and route messages. Replication can also be configured to automatically replicate all or only the desired amount of the directory information between multiple Microsoft Exchange sites.

Directory Synchronization is the process of keeping a Microsoft Exchange Server directory synchronized with directories from MS Mail (PC) and MS Mail (AppleTalk) systems. This is accomplished by the MS Mail 3.x DISPATCH program included with the MS Mail 3.x Server. Like Directory Replication between Microsoft Exchange Server sites, only the desired information will be transferred.

In order for a Microsoft Exchange Server to accomplish Directory Synchronization with a MS Mail 3.x mail system, the Microsoft Exchange Server must be running the MS Mail 3.x Directory Synchronization Agent. The Directory Synchronization Agent on a Microsoft Exchange Server plays one of two roles depending on the mail system environment, DIRSYNC Server or DIRSYNC Requester (see fig. 6.9). On an existing

MS Mail 3.x system, the Microsoft Exchange server can be configured as either a DIRSYNC Server or Requestor (see fig. 6.10). However, the Microsoft Exchange Server cannot be configured as both a Server and a Requestor simultaneously. On a MS Mail 3.x mail system, there can only be one DIRSYNC Server. All of the rest of the MS Mail 3.x Post Offices can be configured as DIRSYNC Requestors.

If the Microsoft Exchange Server is configured as the DIRSYNC Server, it can synchronize all other MS Mail 3.x Post Offices setup as DIRSYNC Requestors.

Once again, integration into an existing MS Mail 3.x system is entirely conceivable and not difficult.

FIG. 6.9
Using Microsoft Exchange as a DIRSYNCH server on an existing MS Mail system.

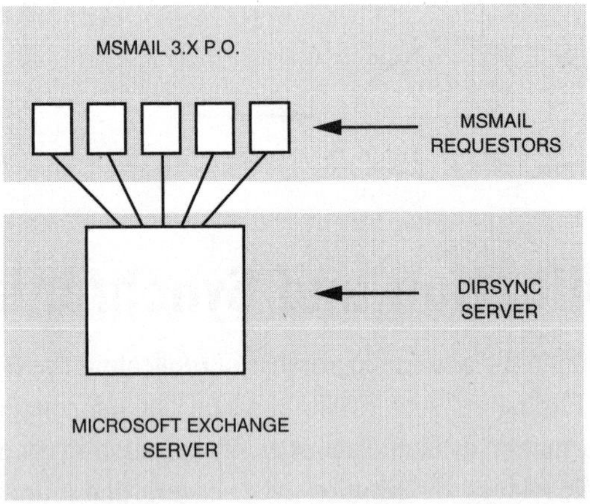

FIG. 6.10
Using Microsoft Exchange as a DIRSYNCH Requestor on an existing MS Mail system.

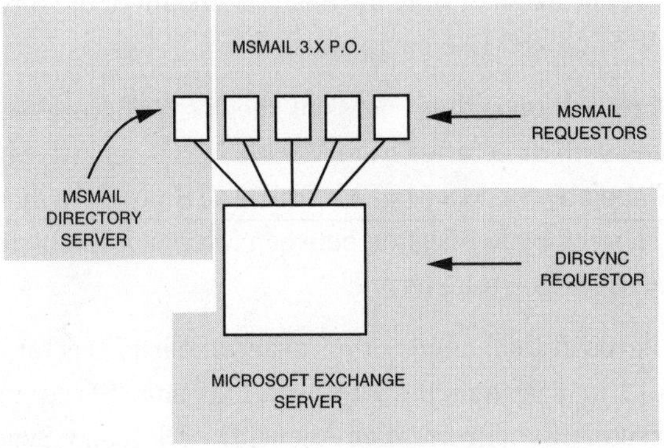

From Here...

This chapter has addressed the topic planning your Microsoft Mail Connector. For more information, refer to the following:

- Chapter 7, "Migrating to Microsoft Mail Systems," which details the migration process, including the use of the Migration Wizard.
- Chapter 8, "Planning and Migrating to External Systems," which describes other mail systems that can communicate with Exchange.
- Chapter 19, "Setting Up Microsoft Mail for AppleTalk Networks," which explains how to connect Exchange to an existing AppleTalk network.

CHAPTER 7

Migrating to Microsoft Mail Systems

- Before you start: Migration Strategy and Planning
- The Migration Elements: Migration Assistant and Source Extractor, Connectors, MTA, DXA
- A Sample Migration—a Three-Phase Model
- Connecting Exchange clients to MS Mail Post Office
- Connecting Exchange clients to Exchange Server
- Using Exchange Server with Mail clients
- Using Exchange Server with Mail and Exchange clients
- Using Exchange Server with Exchange clients
- Using the Migration Wizard

Migration is the act of moving users from one messaging system to another. This can include mailboxes, mail, addresses, and schedule information from your existing system.

In the past, mail migration was not considered something for the "faint-footed." However, Microsoft Exchange is packed with migration features that support multiple scenarios for interconnecting to other Mail systems. Tools like Migration Wizard simplify the migration process and ensure a smooth transition to Microsoft Exchange. ■

Migration Strategy and Planning

Microsoft Exchange Server has many migration tools to be used with Microsoft Mail (PC). As you plan your migration you will need to consider the following:

- What level of migration—coexistence, mailbox migration, mailbox creation, or a combination of these will be best for your organization?
- Should all users be migrated, or only a subset of users?
- Do users have all the hardware necessary or will migration occur in phases?
- What connectivity issues need to be addressed?
- Which users should migrate first?

Migration Levels: from Full Migration to Coexistence

There are three levels of migration: coexistence, mailbox creation, and mailbox migration. The type you choose depends on how much data you want to move from your existing system to Microsoft Exchange:

- Establish coexistence with an existing system.

  This level enables users on both MS Mail and Exchange to exchange mail. You have a chance to test connections between the two systems; addresses are extracted from the existing system and added as custom recipients in Microsoft Exchange. This provides a foundation for migrating users to Microsoft Exchange, usually before actual migration.
- Create new Microsoft Exchange Server mailboxes without data.

  At this level, only user account information is copied from the existing system. This will create empty mailboxes and, as an option, Windows NT accounts. This approach is used to migrate users without migrating their data, either with a plan to migrate their data later, or to skip migrating the data altogether.
- Migrate mailbox contents.

  At this level, mailbox contents are copied (not moved) from the MS Mail to Microsoft Exchange Server mailboxes. The contents include messages, attachments, and calendars. This enables the user to use Microsoft Exchange without any data loss. This can follow coexistence and mailbox creation, or it can be combined with those steps for a quick migration.

You can use one of these three migration levels exclusively, or you can use all three as part of your migration plan. For example, after you install your first new Exchange server, you can migrate addresses from MS Mail. For a test run, you can create new mailboxes without data. Once your testing is complete, you can migrate the mailbox contents to the new mailboxes and have the users upgrade their clients to Microsoft Exchange-based clients.

The following list describes issues associated with a migration from MS Mail to Exchange:

- Migration testing shows that high volumes of data can take weeks or even months to migrate.
- Hardware used for the existing system needs to be freed up in early phases for redeployment during later phases.
- Existing messaging applications are needed in some departments until they can be replaced with Microsoft Exchange public folders and custom form functionality.
- Not all departments have the budget to upgrade at the same time.
- The group in charge of Microsoft Exchange implementation is small and can't afford to bring in extra resources for a quick migration.
- The help desk group is small and can't handle the short spike of requests a quick migration is likely to create.
- Some departments don't have the hardware or system software to upgrade now.
- Microsoft Exchange is being tested in a pilot stage first.
- Microsoft Exchange clients are not available for all platforms or networks.

The following is a list of the types or levels of migration from MS Mail to Exchange. You should choose the proper phase for your organization:

Single-phase migration

Gives users some of the enhanced features before migration, while you are planning and testing the enterprise design.

Multi-phase migration

Gives all users a common user interface as you migrate mailboxes in stages.

Multi-phase migration with dual access

Enables users to retrieve mail from their old mailboxes after their mailboxes have been migrated to Microsoft Exchange Server.

Taking into consideration the previous two lists, you should be developing an idea of the migration strategy for your organization. As you plan your organization's new messaging infrastructure, you'll probably want to break down the project into steps. The major steps of the migration process can be divided as follows:

- Connect Microsoft Exchange Client to existing systems
- Create directory and mailbox entries
- Extract and load accounts
- Set up directory synchronization
- Set up connectivity with gateway
- Migrate server contents
- Move user's data
- Update the directory

Now that you are aware of the issues, phases, and steps to migrating MS mail to Exchange, keep in mind the effect of these items on your organization. The next section will take the previous lists and apply them to an actual organization.

Introduction to the Three-Phase Method

Large organizations might consider phased migrations, concentrating on more challenging sites prior to the major Exchange roll-out. There may also be longer periods of coexistence with legacy mail. Smaller organizations by contrast would most likely be able to do a very quick migration—almost instantaneous.

If you belong to a large organization, your migration plan will probably take place in three basic phases:

- Installing Exchange Server centrally
- Migrating users and/or branch offices and coexisting with legacy systems, like MS Mail.
- Completing migration in remote locations

Sample Migration with a Three-Phase Method

A three-phased approach is used to simplify the task of migration. Inside each phase may be numerous individual tasks. On a high level, these three phases will apply to any organization. The following sample will be used to walk you through the migration process for an actual organization.

Digital Genesis has its headquarters in Los Angeles, and offices in Boston, MA and another in Melbourne, Australia (see fig. 7.1). The two American offices are connected over a T1 line. The headquarters and Australian office are connected over a wide area X.25 network that uses X.400 services.

FIG. 7.1
A sample migration—using the three-phase method.

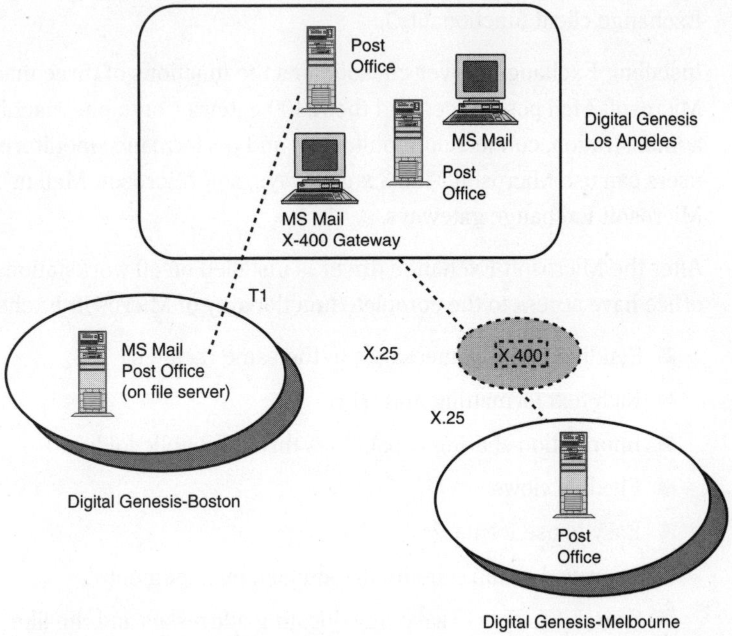

Its e-mail system consists of four Microsoft Mail post offices: two in Los Angeles, one in Boston, and one in Melbourne. In this example, all the PCs are using the Microsoft Mail driver and the Microsoft Windows 95 operating system. This enables its to use the Microsoft Exchange client with its existing Microsoft Mail post offices.

Phase One: Migrating Headquarters to Microsoft Exchange

Headquarters installs a Windows NT-based server with Microsoft Exchange Server on an existing Novell network. Then, using the built-in Migration tool, the company migrates its Microsoft Mail post offices at headquarters to Microsoft Exchange.

The Migration tool converts Microsoft Mail messages, Personal Address Book data, attachments, private folders, and meeting requests to the Microsoft Exchange format and creates new accounts on the Microsoft Exchange system. Microsoft Schedule+ 1.0 calendar files are automatically updated by the Microsoft Exchange group scheduling function. Because the X.400 gateway is integrated into Microsoft Exchange, this capacity is automatically installed with the initial setup.

At headquarters, they simultaneously start installing the Microsoft Exchange Server driver on each of the Windows 95-based workstations to access the Microsoft Exchange Server. Those still using the Mail 3.x driver can continue to communicate with other users of Microsoft Mail and Microsoft Exchange, but without the enhanced functionality provided by Microsoft Exchange. (See Table 7.1 for a comparison of Mail client versus Exchange client functionality.)

Installing Exchange Server consolidates the functions of three machines, the two Microsoft Mail post offices and the X.400 gateway, onto one machine. It also adds one stop administration, connection monitoring, and performance monitoring. Microsoft Exchange users can use Microsoft Mail 3.x gateways, and Microsoft Mail users can use the Microsoft Exchange gateways.

After the Microsoft Exchange driver is installed on all workstations, users in the L.A. office have access to the complete functionality of Microsoft Exchange, including:

- Sending multiple messages to the same recipient
- Rich text formatting and OLE
- Information-sharing capabilities through public folders
- Flexible views
- Easy-to-use forms
- Improved group scheduling and task management
- Searching tools to save time locating addresses and the like

Microsoft Exchange users in L.A. can continue to communicate with their counterparts in Boston and Melbourne. This enables the company to migrate in stages while still enabling all users to:

- Exchange mail messages with attached files and embedded objects
- Exchange meeting requests and free/busy information
- Take advantage of improved group scheduling and task management capabilities.

Table 7.1 Client Feature Comparison After Phases of Migration

Feature	A	B	C
Rich text support	x	x	x
Auto reply	x	x	
Access to public folders		x	
Flexible views		x	x

Feature	A	B	C
Delegate access		x	
Remote functionality	x	x	x
Rich searches	x	x	
Group Scheduling	x	x	x
Easy-to-use forms	x	x	x
Central forms registry	x		
OLE 2.0	x	x	

A—Microsoft Mail 3.x client/Microsoft Mail post office
B—Microsoft Exchange client/Microsoft Mail 3.x post office
C—Microsoft Exchange client/Microsoft Exchange Server

Phase Two: Coexistence

Next, the company installs Microsoft Exchange Server in the Los Angeles office, and combines existing users of the two Microsoft Mail post offices on that server.

The organization still uses MS Mail post offices at the remote locations. Using the Microsoft Exchange Server as an MTA between the Microsoft Exchange Servers and the MS Mail post offices offers different advantages:

- *Auto routing*. The server automatically configures itself for efficient routing.
- *Load Balancing*. If one communication link fails, the MTA will automatically reconfigure itself to balance the load over the remaining communication links.
- *Least-cost routing*. Enables administrators to assign costs to communications lines so the MTAs can intelligently route information over the line with the lowest cost. Combined with load-balancing, this provides the highest availability of lines at the lowest cost.

Digital Genesis also installs Microsoft Exchange drivers on all PCs at headquarters to access the Microsoft Exchange Server. At the end of phase two, all users in L.A. and Boston have access to the complete functionality of the Microsoft Exchange system. They can also continue to exchange messages with users in Melbourne via the X.400 connector through a "pass-through gateway." Mail Connector manages the directory exchange between Microsoft Exchange and Microsoft Mail during this coexistence phase.

Phase Three: Completing the Migration

In the final migration phase, the Melbourne office installs NT Server and Microsoft Exchange on both the server and the workstations. This consolidates the Microsoft Mail 3.x post office and Mail gateway onto one server. Now, users across the enterprise have full use of Microsoft Exchange's rich functionality and are able to share information with everyone else in their organization, anytime.

The company has realized the cost savings of consolidating the functions of nine machines into three and have condensed the administration for all three offices onto one Windows NT-based workstation. They have a consistent enterprise-wide messaging and information exchange system with the features catalogued in the following list and can install additional Microsoft Exchange gateways to extend these capabilities beyond the enterprise:

- AutoSignature
- Blind carbon copy (BCC)
- Universal inbox in Windows 95
- Rich text
- Views
- Schedule+ 7.0
- Built-in remote client

Implementing Client Migration

The Microsoft Exchange Windows clients can be used as clients for Microsoft Mail (PC) post offices. This is done by adding the Microsoft Mail service provider to the profile. This can be done before migration or before and during phased migration to move users to the new client while retaining the post office infrastructure.

Even if only the clients are migrated to Exchange, they will enjoy all the benefits listed at the end of the previous section. With this strategy, all users will also have a consistent user interface.

To install Microsoft Exchange client, users need the Profile Wizard, included with the client setup software. The Profile Wizard pulls default information for connecting to the post office from the MSMAIL.INI file.

NOTE To use the MS Mail Post office, also called the MS Mail provider, you will need to make the Microsoft Mail (PC) provider the default for the client profile; for this you use the Setup Editor. The Setup Editor allows complete configuration of the Exchange client prior to installation on the user's PC. This is also true for installing the Microsoft Exchange provider.

After the client software is installed on the user's PC, the user then imports the contents of the Microsoft Mail Message File (MMF) file into the Exchange inbox format. If the MMF file is in the post office the user should first move the MMF file to the local disk or a viewable network share before importing the contents. If the MMF file is left on the post office, the contents will be migrated to Microsoft Exchange when the mailbox is migrated.

Once a user begins using Microsoft Exchange client, there is no easy way to migrate the messages they receive to an MMF or mailbag file. He or she can copy the messages to a shared folder and then retrieve them with the old client, but this does not guarantee privacy of the messages.

When you migrate the user's mailbox to Microsoft Exchange Server, you have two options:

- Switch the profile over to connect only to Microsoft Exchange (single provider).
- Switch the profile to connect to Microsoft Exchange and the old post office (dual provider).

Implementing Server Migration

The Mail Server or Exchange Server is the "provider." A single provider option is full migration from one messaging server to another. A dual provider strategy is one in which both messaging systems coexist and two servers or providers are used.

One-Step Migration

Depending on the size of your organization and your human resources, you may be able to do a one-step migration. This can happen overnight, on a weekend, or on company shutdown time. If your organization can't tolerate the down time or doesn't have the resources to migrate everyone in a weekend, phased migration is the best choice.

Instant migration may be better for your organization if

- There is little or no existing data to move from the old system.
- You have enough human resources to migrate everyone in a night, weekend, or during a traditional down time.
- All hardware and system software are in place.

One-step migration takes extra planning in the areas of

- Replacing existing workflow applications
- User and help desk training
- Preparing for roll out and resource needs
- Preparing for contingencies

Should you choose to go with a single mail provider, like Exchange Server, the single provider option provides for these scenarios:

- Every mailbox on the post office is migrated
- Only some mailboxes on a post office migrate, and their addresses change

Update the global address list and the directory. Mail sent to the old addresses from the personal address books and personal address lists will be returned as non-deliverable (if you delete the old mailbox) or pile up in the old mailbox.

With a multi-phase migration, you have two "providers," MS Mail Post office and Exchange server, for instance. A Dual Provider provides for these scenarios:

- All mailboxes are migrated and addresses are changed.

  The users can still connect to the old post office and get mail that is sent to their old address, but as the global address list gets updated, new messages sent to them are routed to their Microsoft Exchange Server mailbox.

- Some mailboxes are migrated and addresses are not changed.

  Routing on the Microsoft Mail connector is not updated so that mail sent to these users from Microsoft Mail users still arrives at their old mailbox, but messages sent from Microsoft Exchange Server users are delivered to the new mailbox. The users can now send mail from their Microsoft Exchange Server mailboxes and use Microsoft Exchange Server public folders.

The drawback of these options is that the profile must be edited three times: first when the client is installed, again when the Microsoft Exchange Server provider is added, and again when the Microsoft Mail (PC) provider is removed.

When configured for dual providers, the use of the MS Mail provider should be limited to retrieving mail for the old mailbox. Mail addressed with the MS Mail address book will be delivered and can be replied to. Choose the Reply to All option on mail messages addressed to both Microsoft Mail mailboxes (not as Microsoft Exchange custom recipients) and Microsoft Exchange mailboxes will fail to reach the Microsoft Exchange mailboxes.

If the message is sent to Microsoft Mail mailboxes as custom recipients, the client transfers the message to the Microsoft Exchange server. The Microsoft Exchange server updates the Microsoft Exchange mailbox addresses when it transfers the message to the MS Mail Connector so they can be replied to by Microsoft Mail recipients.

Upgrading to Microsoft Exchange and the MS Mail Provider

Now that we have discussed the one method for migration to Exchange, we will now discuss migrating the MMF files from MS Mail into the Exchange format. In addition, we will discuss issues associated with upgrading from Schedule+ v1.0 clients to Exchange Schedule+ v7.0 clients.

Migrating MMF Files from Microsoft Mail for PC Networks 3.5 Microsoft Exchange client users must migrate their mail message files to a personal folder file. When MMFs are stored on a post office, you can use the MMFClean utility to manage their size and the age of messages (how long a message will be kept on file before it is automatically deleted). Personal folder files should not be stored on the post office.

The MMF Migration tool does not delete the MMF when it creates the personal folder file, move MMF files locally, or delete them after their contents are migrated to personal folder files.

Schedule+ Coexistence with the MS Mail Provider Users who switch to the Microsoft Exchange client must also switch from Schedule+ 1.0 to Schedule+ 7.0. When they run Schedule+ 7.0 for the first time, it will migrate their CAL (Schedule+ 1.0 calendar format) file to SCD (Schedule+ 7.0 calendar format) file.

Schedule+ 7.0 can read CAL, POF (Schedule+ 1.0 post office free/busy times), and SCD files, but Schedule+ 1.0 can only read CAL and POF files. If your users make heavy use of Schedule+, switch everyone over to the new client at the same time. If some people switch to Schedule+ 7.0, the rest will not be able to view their calendars or act as their coworkers' delegate.

Migrating Partial Post Offices Migrating everyone off of a post office at the same time is not always possible. Some users are waiting for hardware upgrades. The migration might be a pilot test or a limited rollout. When migrating partial post offices, the following considerations are necessary:

- Routing to old post offices must be maintained so that the remaining users continue to receive mail.
- Mail sent to migrated mailboxes that passes through Microsoft Mail (PC) gateways will be delivered to the Microsoft Mail (PC) mailbox, or returned as undeliverable.
- Directories in Microsoft Mail (PC) and with Microsoft Mail (PC) gateways that have the old mailbox address have to be updated immediately—the old address is invalid.

- For users who are still on Microsoft Mail (PC), any mail they received in the past from a migrated user can be replied to, but the reply will be delivered to the Microsoft Mail (PC) mailbox or returned as undeliverable.
- For users who are still on Microsoft Mail (PC), any Personal Address Book or Personal address list entries they have for migrated mailboxes are invalid.

NOTE No routing changes are required or allowed when doing a partial post office migration. The mailboxes remaining on the post office need mail addressed to them to continue to be delivered.

Part of your migration plan needs to include how many mailboxes at a time will migrate to Microsoft Exchange servers. As a general rule, migrating the whole post office (every mailbox) will be easier to plan for, implement, and maintain than migrating a partial post office. Migrating a partial post office is more likely to occur during a pilot or limited roll out, when the number of users is small and the issues are easier to solve or work around. The following section explains why this is so, and gives examples of each of these scenarios.

Migrating Whole Post Offices If you migrate every mailbox on a post office, you can maintain original Network/Post office/Mailbox Microsoft Mail address for each old mailbox as one of the proxy or e-mail addresses of the new mailbox. This has many advantages:

- With limited routing changes, mail continues to be delivered without interruption.
- Mail sent to migration mailboxes that passes through Microsoft Mail (PC) gateways will be delivered.
- Directories in Microsoft Mail (PC) post offices and foreign systems connected to them with Microsoft Mail (PC) gateways that have the old mailbox address do not have to be updated immediately—the old address is still valid.
- For users who are still on Microsoft Mail (PC), any mail they received in the past from a migrated user can be replied to.
- For users who are still on Microsoft Mail (PC), any Personal Address Book or Personal Address List entries they have for migrated mailboxes is still valid.

PC Mail Pass-Through Retaining the original e-mail address provides for pass-through from Microsoft Mail (PC) gateways. The Microsoft Mail connector post office must have an access component for the gateway installed. Because the Microsoft Mail type addresses for migrated mailboxes have not changed, the mail will be routed from the gateway to the Microsoft Mail connector, and from there to the Microsoft Exchange mailbox.

Personal Address Books for Users Who Haven't Migrated Personal address book entries function similarly to replies. For Microsoft Mail (PC) users, their personal address book addresses continue to work for migrated mailboxes because the addresses are the same.

Migrated personal address book entries will work for Microsoft Mail (PC) mailboxes that have not migrated. This means that if you do not update your personal address book with the new Exchange e-mail addresses, some e-mail will still be directed to MS Mail mailboxes that no longer exist. Mail addressed to mailboxes that have since migrated will get routed to the Microsoft Mail connector. The Microsoft Mail connector does not have a post office configured with that address and will return the mail as undeliverable. This undeliverable mail can be re-addressed from the Microsoft Exchange server global address list and be delivered normally.

There is no tool that updates the user's personal address book entries as changes are made in the Microsoft Exchange server global address list. To prevent undeliverable mail, users can remove all personal entries of the type, MS, from their personal address book after the entries are migrated to Microsoft Exchange mailboxes.

The Migration Package Elements

The following sections cover the main elements of Microsoft Exchange's Migration package. This package allows you to implement Exchange into environments with legacy mail systems. These tools assist with the extraction of e-mail addresses from the legacy systems and import them into Exchange.

The Migration Tools

There are several tools that assist with the migration from MS Mail to Exchange. These tools include the functionality to extract mailbox information from the legacy system. In addition, there is a server component called an MS Mail "server" post office. This post office resides on the Exchange server and can only be accessed by the Exchange and MS Mail MTAs.

The Source Extractor There is a Source Extractor for every system such as MS Mail, PROFS, and the like. The Source Extractor extracts users, inboxes, folders, and address books from the source mail systems.

The following list is the components of the source extraction tool used to convert extracted addresses into the Exchange format and provide support information for the migration process. Other components include the directory agent to facilitate the dirsync process via the Exchange MS Mail server post office. Several other components include the free/busy connector to allow for group scheduling information and the passthrough connectivity to interconnect with Exchange.

- The Migration Assistant

  The Migration Assistant converts all extracted data from the source system to Microsoft Exchange.
- The Migration Wizard

  Microsoft Exchange includes a Migration Wizard to guide administrators through migration. There is an option included for one-step migration.

The Microsoft Mail Connector The term *Connector* has taken the place of the Microsoft Mail Transfer Agent (MMTA) in MS Mail. The Connector is the main link between users of Exchange and Microsoft Mail (PC), as well as MS Mail gateways and Exchange gateways. There are three components to the Microsoft Mail Connector:

- *Connector MTA.* Connector MTA is a message transfer agent, similar to the MTA. It routes mail between a Microsoft Mail post office and the Connector post office, a Microsoft Mail gateway and the Microsoft Exchange server.
- *Connector Post Office.* Connector post office is the data file structure used to store messages in transit between users of Microsoft Exchange, Microsoft Mail, and gateways.
- *Microsoft Mail (PC) Interchange.* MS Mail (PC) Interchange manages the transfer and translation of messages stored in the Connector post office to the Microsoft Exchange MTA and vice versa.

Together, these components make up the Mail Connector, allowing Microsoft Exchange users to transparently send and receive messages and files, meeting requests, and free/busy information with users on MS Mail.

Directory Exchange Agent The Directory Exchange Agent (DXA) in Microsoft Exchange enhances directory synchronization with flexible scheduling, better time zone management and update scheduling. Its multithreaded design improves throughput. Because the DXA includes multiple server support, the directory synchronization load is distributed across multiple "dirsync" servers for increased reliability and faster response. This reduces address list maintenance, increases security, and assures that updates occur more promptly.

Microsoft Schedule+ Free and Busy Gateway The Microsoft Schedule+ Free and Busy Gateway enables users who remain on Schedule+ version 1.0 using MS Mail 3.x servers to see free/busy information in the planner view of users who are on the new release of Schedule+ on the Microsoft Exchange Server computer, and vice-versa. The data from each server platform is replicated across the connector to appear to users on the other platform.

Passthrough Connectivity Microsoft Exchange Server offers hardy group distribution list support and enables MS Mail users to send messages to X.400 and SMTP environments through the Microsoft Mail Connector. Messages sent from the MS Mail 3.x users through the Microsoft Exchange Server computer can use the Microsoft Exchange X.400 Connector and the Internet Mail Connector to interchange messages with these environments. Alternatively, Microsoft Exchange users can send messages through any of the Microsoft Mail gateways, through the Microsoft Mail Connector.

Using the Migration Wizard

You can use the Migration Wizard to migrate one or more mailboxes on a Microsoft Mail for PC Networks post office. When each mailbox on the post office is migrated, you have a choice of what information to migrate.

The following is a list of available components to migrate into the Exchange environment. The list covers the components from the actual mailbox containing data to the schedule+ file and then the group or shared folders and the personal address book entries on a user's local PC.

- Messages, attachments, private folders, and contents of mail message files (MMF)
- Schedule+ data
- Shared and group folders
- Personal address book entries

NOTE Make sure there is no mail activity during migration.

The following preparations are recommended before migrating in order to ensure safe migration of data:

- The Migration Wizard and necessary files are installed with the Administrator program.
- Install the Microsoft Exchange Administrator program on a Windows NT computer with the Setup program.
- Compare free hard drive space on the server to the post office volume.

  The server should have plenty of available space, at least twice as much as the post office volume. If free hard disk space is less than twice the post office volume, you should watch available space with the Performance Monitor during migration. Stop migration if free space reaches less than 5MB.

- Shut down the Microsoft Exchange server MTA, connector, and gateway services.

  Modify or shut down any server monitors that would restart these services. If these services are running while using the Migration Wizard, and you need to restore your Microsoft Exchange server from backup, any mail they delivered during the failed migration attempt is lost.

- Shut down any MTA, external, or gateway programs that connect to this post office.

  MTA and external programs can be restarted after modifying their .INI file or command line options so they do not connect to this post office. The Migration Wizard requires that no mail be delivered to mailboxes during migration.

- Disconnect the clients.

  All users on both the post office and the Microsoft Exchange server must exit and log off of their client programs. Use your network software with Microsoft Mail (PC) to check for connections to the post office share. Use the Administrator program on the Microsoft Exchange server to check Mailbox Logons and Public Folder Logons property sheets in the server's private and public information store properties respectively.

- If you are copying the post office to the Microsoft Exchange server for migration, copy it now. Once the copying is finished, you can restore MTA, external, gateway, and client connections.

- Back up the Exchange server information store and directory.

  Back up the post office. However, this is not a requirement because data on the post office is read, not deleted. You need read and write access to the post office because a datestamp is modified in each MMF as it is migrated.

To create the user list from a Microsoft Mail (PC) post office:

1. (Optional) Map a drive letter or connect to a file server where the post office resides. You will need read and write access to the share or volume and have the name and password of the administrator.
2. In Program Manager, choose Microsoft Exchange.
3. In the Microsoft Exchange group, choose Microsoft Exchange Migration Wizard.
4. Select Migrate from Microsoft Mail for PC Networks, and choose the Next button.
5. Read the informational screen and choose the Next button.

6. In the Path to MS Mail Post office box, type the path to the post office.

   or

   Choose the Browse button to specify the path to the post office.
7. In the Account Name box, type the mailbox name of an administrator on the post office.
8. In the Password box, type the password for this mailbox and choose the Next button.
9. Select Two Step Migration and choose the Next button.
10. Select Extract a User List File and in the User List to Be Created box, type the path and file name of the new user list

    or

    Choose the Browse button to specify the path and file name.
11. Choose the Next button.
12. In the Select Which Accounts You Would Like to Migrate box, choose the mailboxes you want to migrate.

    or

    Choose the Select All button to select all mailboxes.
13. Choose the Next button to create the user list file.

You can make changes as needed in the user list file. If you need to change the directory name of a mailbox, do it before the mailbox is created. Other fields can be changed now in this text file, or later. To change them now, follow the process as outlined in the following paragraphs. To change them later, use the Administrator program to change them one at a time, or use the Directory Import command to change them in a batch mode.

To modify the user list file:

1. Make a backup copy of the user list file. You will need it later.
2. Open the user list file with a text editor.
3. Delete the first two lines that have post office information and save the file as text.
4. Open the modified user list file with a database program. The file is text, comma delimited, and the first row contains field names.

   The fields in Table 7.2 are in the user list. (The first two fields can't be changed, and the first six need to be kept in the same order.)

Table 7.2 User List Fields

Field	Contents
SFS_UserName	The mailbox name or alias of this mailbox in the post office. Do not change this.
SFS_FullName	The full or display name of this mailbox in the post office. Do not change this.
MigrateUser	Should be "Y" if mailbox is to be migrated and "N" if the mailbox should not be migrated.
Obj-Class	This field should be "mailbox." Other valid values are "remote" for custom recipients and "dl" for distribution list.
Mode	Describes what should be done with this object—"create," "modify," and "delete" are valid options. The default is "create."
Common-Name	The directory name of the mailbox. This can't be changed later without deleting the mailbox and re-creating it, so change it now to match your naming convention.
Display-Name	The display or friendly name as seen in the address book.
Given-Name	The first or given name of the mailbox's user.
Surname	The surname or last name of the mailbox's user.
Home-Server	The home server of the mailbox. You can move a mailbox within the site later without difficulty, but you should decide where each group of mailboxes is to be created.
Comment	This is the address book comment. It can be used to distinguish between two people with the same or similar names, or for notes about contacts for Schedule+ resources.
Assoc Windows-NT Account	Each mailbox needs an associated Windows NT account that has user access. On a Schedule+ resource account this can be a Windows NT group or account that is responsible for managing the resource, or the administrator who is going to sign into the account once to set up forwarding rules and Schedule+ access permissions.

** You can add additional directory import fields after Assoc-NT-Account.*

5. After it is modified, export the file in CSV format.
6. Open the modified file and the backup file with a text editor. Copy the two lines from the backup file to the top of the modified file. Save the file as text.

After creating the user list and modifying it, you can migrate mailboxes from the post office to your site. This does not delete the mailboxes or remove mail, it only copies the information to the Microsoft Exchange servers where the new mailboxes are created.

To migrate mailboxes from a post office to a Microsoft Exchange server with a user list, follow these steps:

1. (Optional) Map a drive letter or connect to a file server where the post office resides. You will need read and write access to the share or volume and have the name and password of the administrator.
2. In Program Manager, choose Microsoft Exchange.
3. In the Microsoft Exchange group, choose Microsoft Exchange Migration Wizard.
4. Select Migrate from Microsoft Mail for PC Networks, and choose the Next button.
5. Read the informational screen and choose the Next button.
6. In the Path to MS Mail Post office box, type the path to the post office.

   or

   Choose the Browse button to specify the path to the post office.
7. In the Account Name box, type the mailbox name of an administrator on the post office.
8. In the Password box, type the password for this mailbox and choose the Next button.
9. Select Two Step Migration and choose the Next button.
10. Select Use a User List File to Do a Migration and in the Existing User List File box, type the path and file name of the modified user list.

    or

    Choose the Browse button to select the file.
11. Choose the Next button.
12. Select the import options based on your needs (see Table 7.3).

Table 7.3 Import Options

Option	Description
Information to Create Mailboxes	Create mailboxes for the selected users in the user list file.
Personal E-Mail Messages	Copy messages and folders from the selected users mailbox and server-based MMF. You can select all messages or set a date range.

continues

Table 7.3 Continued

Option	Description
Shared Folders	Copy all shared folders to the public folder server.
Personal Address Books	Copy PAB entries in the MMFs and put into the selected user's inbox in a special message.
Schedule Information	Copy calendar files from the CAL directory on the post office to a special message in the selected user's inbox.

13. Choose the Next button.
14. In the Enter a Server Name box, type the name of the destination Microsoft Exchange Server computer. Choose the Next button.
15. Select the directory container for the new mailboxes.

NOTE You cannot move a mailbox from one directory container to another after the mailbox has been created. ■

16. If you are using a mailbox template to reduce the work of setting up new mailboxes, choose the Browse button and select the template mailbox from the address list.
17. Choose the Next button.
18. In For Users That Don't Have Windows NT Accounts, choose one of the options (see Table 7.4).

Table 7.4 Options for Users Without NT Accounts

Option	Description
Create Accounts and Generate Random Passwords	Accounts are created with names that match the alias and random passwords. The passwords are written to the file BIMPORT.PSW in the working directory of the Migration Wizard. For users to log on to Windows NT, distribute these passwords to them.
Create Accounts and Use Alias as Password	Accounts are created with names and passwords that match the alias.
Don't Create Windows NT Accounts	No accounts are created and the mailboxes can't be used by anyone until an account is assigned later.

19. In the Choose a Windows NT Domain for New Accounts box, select the domain where the user's Windows NT accounts are located or to be created.
20. Choose the Next button to begin the migration process.

To migrate in one step from a Microsoft Mail (PC) post office, follow these steps:

1. (Optional) Map a drive letter or connect to a file server where the post office resides. You will need read and write access to the share or volume and have the name and password of the administrator.
2. In Program Manager, choose Microsoft Exchange.
3. In the Microsoft Exchange group, choose Microsoft Exchange Migration Wizard.
4. Select Migrate from MS Mail for PC Networks, and choose the Next button.
5. Read the informational screen and choose the Next button.
6. In the Path to MS Mail Post office box, type the path to the post office.

   or

   Choose the Browse button to specify the path to the post office.
7. In the Account Name box, type the mailbox name of an administrator on the post office.
8. In the Password box, type the password for this mailbox and choose the Next button.
9. Select the One Step Migration option, and choose the Next button.
10. Select the options based on your needs (see Table 7.5).

Table 7.5 One-Step Migration Options

Option	Description
Information to Create Mailboxes	Creates mailboxes for the selected users in the user list file.
Personal E-Mail Messages	Copies all messages and folders from the selected user's mailbox and server-based MMF. You can select all or set a date range.
Shared Folders	Select this check box to copy all shared folders to the public folder server of this server.
Personal Address Books	When selected, PAB entries in MMFs are copied and put into the selected user's inbox in a special message.
Schedule Information	Calendar files are copied from the CAL directory on the post office to a special message in the selected user's inbox.

11. Choose the Next button.
12. In the Select Which Accounts You Would Like to Migrate box, choose the mailboxes you want to migrate.

    or

    Choose the Select All button to select all mailboxes.
13. Choose the Next button.
14. In the Enter a Server Name box, type the name of the destination Microsoft Exchange Server computer. Choose the Next button.
15. Select the directory container for the new mailboxes.

NOTE You cannot move a mailbox from one directory container to another after the mailbox has been created.

16. Choose the Next button.
17. Choose one of the options in For Users That Don't Have Windows NT Accounts (see Table 7.6).

Table 7.6 One-Step Migration, Options for Users with No NT Accounts

Option	Description
Create Accounts and Generate Random passwords	Accounts are created with names that match the alias and random pass words. The passwords are written to the file BIMPORT.PSW in the working directory of the Migration Wizard. For users to log on to Windows NT, you need to distribute these passwords to them.
Create Accounts and Use Alias 95 Password	Accounts are created with names and as passwords that match the alias.
Don't Create Windows NT Accounts can't be used by anyone	No accounts are created and the mailboxes until an account is assigned later.

18. In the Choose a Windows NT Domain for New Accounts box, select the domain where the user's Windows NT accounts are located or to be created.
19. Choose the Next button to begin the migration process.

Migrating MMFs

As explained earlier in the migration tools section of this chapter, MMFs can be migrated by the user to personal folder files, or by the Administrator to the private information store, depending on the location of the MMFs. There are a few things to note about MMF migration:

Network Errors

If there is a network failure during MMF migration, the client or Migration Wizard retries the network connection every ten minutes to reestablish a connection. An error message is displayed during this retry time.

Error Log

Any errors during client MMF migration are logged to a file in the client directory with a file name the same as the MMF name and an extension of .LOG. You can view them in notepad or any other text editor.

To import an MMF file with the Windows NT or Windows 16 client, follow these steps:

1. From the File menu, choose Import.
2. In the Specify File to Import window, select the MMF file.
3. In the Import Mail Data window, type the password for this MMF file.

   Select the Import Messages check box to import all messages and folders.

   Select the Import Personal Address Book Entries check box to create a Microsoft Exchange PAB file.
4. Choose OK.

After Using the Migration Tool

Depending on your migration strategy, you will need to delete the Microsoft Mail (PC) mailboxes or hide the post office. It is possible to make a full backup of the updated information store.

From Here...

Exchange's Migration tools, will give you powerful interoperability with existing MS-Mail systems. After planning the steps and phases to migration, administrators, with the help of tools like Migration Wizard, can create a smooth transition to Exchange, so they and their users can sooner get down to the business of information exchange.

- Chapter 6, "Planning Connections to Microsoft Mail Systems," gives you the information you need to have an MS-Mail and Exchange system coexist.
- Chapter 8, "Planning and Migrating to External Systems," rounds out the discussion of how to move data from other kinds of mail systems.

CHAPTER 8

Planning and Migrating to External Systems

- Migrating from a host-based system
- Migrating from SMTP (Internet) Mail Systems
- Migrating from foreign X.400 messaging systems

This chapter's primary focus is on migration to Microsoft Exchange from host-based systems, but also includes a brief overview of Migration strategies from SMTP mail and foreign X.400 messaging systems. This chapter covers both the use of Exchange as gateway to these other systems and the process of transferring users to Exchange as the primary messaging system.

Migrating from a Host-Based System to Microsoft Exchange Server

The first messaging systems were proprietary. For example, PROFS was the most popular proprietary messaging system established. There are about 6 million PROFS users today. Proprietary messaging systems like PROFS were designed to provide messaging within organizations rather than between organizations. Also, with the advent of GUI interfaces, client/server architecture, open systems architecture, and the need for inter-LAN messaging, it is likely that first-generation tools like PROFS will be eclipsed by technologies such as Microsoft Exchange.

Quickly review the benefits of Exchange over a legacy host system like PROFS:

- APIs—Developed to establish interoperability, allowing one client interface and transparency toward different message store, message transports, and directory implementations. Important architecturally for open architecture between disparate LAN systems. Exchange offers the recognized MAPI and CPC interface.
- X.500—Recognized standard for distributed directory system.
- Client/Server Architecture—Client/Server partitions responsibility between client and server, using a standard of remote access calls, allowing the technology to become more efficient, and taking advantage of the price/performance benefit of using distributed PCs, e.g., multi-processor RISC machines, rather than an expensive central host.
- GUI Interface—Now the preference of PC users, the popularity of the Windows interface has set the standard for user expectations, with character-based interfaces à la PROFS increasingly likely to disappear.

In addition to the peceding advantages, new Exchange clients also get to enjoy the advantages of group scheduling, powerful enterprise-wide workgroup applications, and one-stop enterprise-wide administration. In summary, migrating from a host-based system such as IBM PROFS™ to Microsoft Exchange offers several significant advantages, including the potential for enormous cost savings, communication between organizations, and freed host resources.

Review the following for migration from host-based systems:

- Migration Planning considerations
- Migration steps

- Migration elements
- Sample migration
- Client migration
- Host to server migration
- Single versus dual provider strategy
- Migrating partial versus whole post offices

NOTE Information that applies to IBM PROFS also applies to IBM OfficeVision/VM.

Migration Planning Considerations

The following list shows data that you can migrate from IBM PROFS by using Exchange's broad migration features:

- Calendars and reminders
- Nickname files
- Distribution lists
- Mailed documents

Introducing Migration Steps

When a large organization moves to a new messaging infrastructure, it's a good idea to break down the project into a series of steps. The major steps of migration can be divided as follows:

1. Use the MAPI driver (optional).
2. Create directory and mailbox entries.
3. Extract accounts, load accounts.
4. Set up connectivity (gateway).
5. Migrate the server contents.
6. Move the user data.
7. Set up directory synchronization.
8. Update the directory.

The Migration Elements

The following sections cover the main elements of Microsoft Exchange's Migration package. These tools and components of the Exchange system provide an easy and effective way to implement Exchange in your environment. Additionally, the migration tools are used in a similar manner for each e-mail system migrated to Exchange.

The Migration Tool

The following three tools are included with Exchange to provide an easy way for you to migrate from an existing e-mail system to Exchange. These tools extract the e-mail address information from the legacy system and guide you through the conversion and migration into Exchange.

- **The Source Extractor**—There is a Source Extractor for every system, such as MS Mail, PROFS, and so on. The Source Extractor extracts users, inboxes, folders, and address books from the source mail systems.
- **The Migration Assistant**—The Migration Assistant converts all extracted data from the source system to Microsoft Exchange.
- **The Migration Wizard**—Microsoft Exchange includes a Migration Wizard to guide administrators through the migration process. An option is included for one-step migration.

Connectors

The Connector is the main link between users of Exchange and external systems, such as SMTP/MIME/Internet connector for UNIX, X.400 connector, and of course, Microsoft Mail (PC) post offices.

Gateways

The Microsoft Exchange gateway for PROFS/OfficeVision provides seamless message transfer with Microsoft Exchange server. The gateway supports all the features of the existing Microsoft gateway for IBM PROFS version 3.4, but with tighter calendar and directory integration. The PROFS/OfficeVision gateway encapsulates Microsoft Exchange messages sent to other Microsoft Exchange users of a PROFS backbone to maintain data integrity.

Directory Exchange Agent The Directory Exchange Agent (DXA) in Microsoft Exchange enhances directory synchronization with flexible scheduling, better time zone management, and update scheduling. Its multithreaded design improves throughput. Because the DXA includes multiple server support, the directory synchronization load is distributed across multiple "dirsync" servers for increased reliability and faster response. This setup reduces address list maintenance, increases security, and assures that updates occur more promptly. The DXA agent can only function if the proper connectivity exists between the e-mail systems. The DXA operates through the gateway to the legacy e-mail system.

Microsoft Schedule+ Free and Busy Gateway The Microsoft Schedule+ Free and Busy Gateway allows users who remain on Schedule+ version 1.0 and use MS Mail 3.x servers to see free/busy information in the planner view of users who are on the new release of Schedule+ on the Microsoft Exchange Server computer, and vice-versa. The data from each server platform is replicated across the connector to appear to users on the other platform.

Passthrough Connectivity

Microsoft Exchange Server offers hardy group distribution list support and enables MS Mail users to send messages to X.400 and SMTP environments through the Microsoft Mail Connector. Messages sent from the MS Mail 3.x users through the Microsoft Exchange Server computer can use the Microsoft Exchange X.400 Connector and the Internet Mail Connector to interchange messages with these environments. Alternatively, Microsoft Exchange users can send messages through any Microsoft Mail gateway by using the Microsoft Mail Connector.

Using the Migration Wizard

You can use the Migration Wizard to migrate one or more mailboxes on a Microsoft Mail for PC Networks post office. When each mailbox on the post office is migrated, you have a choice of the information to migrate.

A Sample Migration

In this sample, a shipping company headquartered in Los Angeles has branch offices in Dallas and Boston. The headquarters has a mix of IBM PROFS and MS Mail users. Both customer service and accounting departments need constant access to information on the host, communicating by way of the IBM PROFS system. Users in sales, marketing, and both branch offices are all on MS Mail post offices. Both branch offices are connected to the headquarters by T1 lines. PROFS users are linked to Microsoft Mail users through the Microsoft Mail gateway to PROFS (see fig. 8.1).

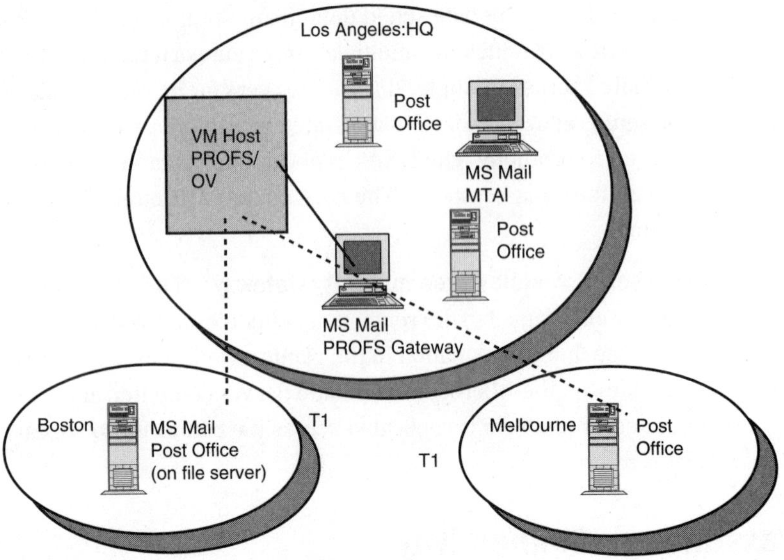

FIG. 8.1
Exchange has connector support for Profs via the Attachmate Zip office gateways for Exchange.

Phase One—Migrating to Microsoft Exchange Clients

First, the Microsoft Exchange client is installed on all workstations over time, both at headquarters and in the branches. Microsoft Exchange clients that work with the Microsoft Mail post offices have the rich e-mail functionality in Microsoft Exchange and are still fully compatible with existing Mail clients.

Exchange client talks to the PROFS host via the MS Mail Connector to PROFS.

Microsoft Exchange is then installed on the Windows NT–based server at the headquarters, and both PROFS users and MS Mail post offices are migrated to the Microsoft Exchange Server. This action consolidates the PROFS gateway and two MS Mail post offices on one Microsoft Exchange Server, combining the functions of three machines on one (see fig. 8.2). (The customer also can continue to use the Microsoft Mail-based PROFS gateway.)

The automated Migration Tool in Microsoft Exchange works with most common host-based systems as easily as it works with LAN-based systems to automatically extract data and convert it to the Microsoft Exchange system.

The following data is migrated from a host-based system to Microsoft Exchange: notes, notelogs, calendars, reminders, and address books (nicknames).

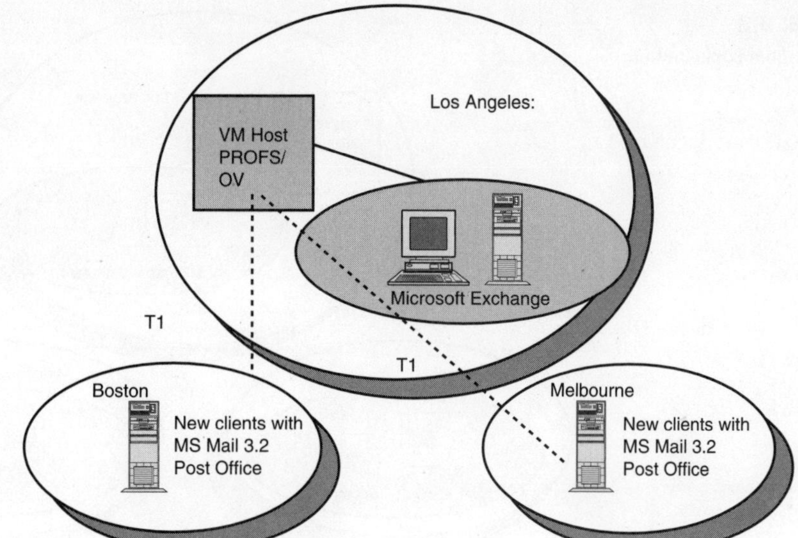

FIG. 8.2
Both PROFS users and MS Mail post offices are migrated to the Microsoft Exchange Server.

The following data is not migrated: personal address information, preferences and settings, and binary file attachments. After all headquarters users are migrated, they have access to the complete functionality of Microsoft Exchange. They also can exchange messages, attachments, OLE objects, and scheduling information with Microsoft Exchange clients who are working against the Microsoft Mail 3.x post offices in the branch offices.

Sending Microsoft Exchange Messages via a Microsoft Mail-Based Gateway

At the headquarters, before the Microsoft Exchange gateway to PROFS was installed, messages were routed to PROFS users from Microsoft Exchange users working against MS Mail post offices through the Microsoft Mail gateway to PROFS. PROFS users also routed their messages back through the Microsoft Mail gateway.

Phase Three—Migrating the Branches to Microsoft Exchange Servers

Windows NT-based servers are added to the networks in both branches and Microsoft Exchange is installed on each server (see fig. 8.3).

FIG. 8.3
The final configuration.

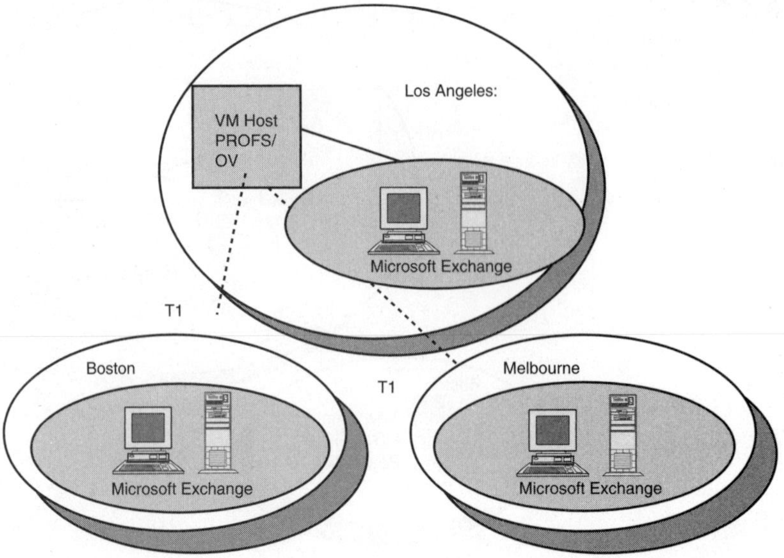

Now the power of Microsoft Exchange is unleashed across the enterprise. All users have access to rich text formatting of messages and exchanged documents, rules, public folders, forms, group scheduling, remote functionality, and more. Relevant customer service and accounting data from the host can be extracted and put in public folders that are available to all or specified users both at headquarters and at the branches. With immediate access to the same information, users across the enterprise can respond faster to market demands and make better-informed decisions.

In figure 8.4, the message originates from PROFS and is routed by the PROFS gateway directly to the Connector post office in-queue, and routed as are all other messages bound for Microsoft Exchange users.

FIG. 8.4
The message flow from IBM PROFS users to Exchange users.

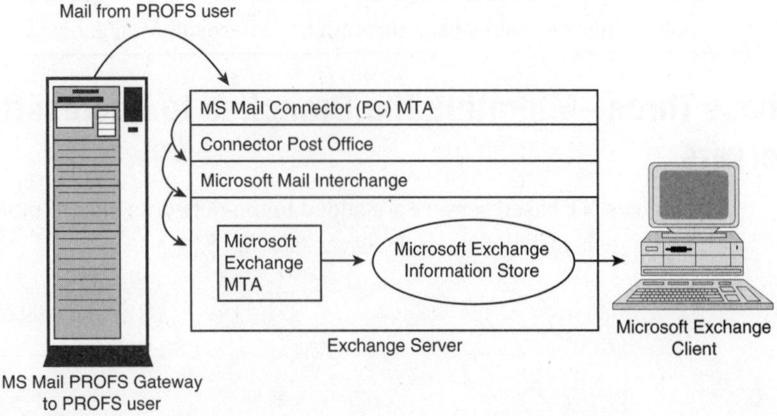

The Role of the Microsoft Mail Connector in Coexistence with PROFS

It's helpful to illustrate the message flow process. When using Microsoft Mail gateways with PROFS, it's a natural development to have Microsoft Mail gateways in coexistence with Exchange Server.

The preceding diagram outlines the flow of a message that originates from PROFS and is routed to the MS Mail user through the Microsoft Exchange gateway to PROFS.

The message is passed through the PROFS gateway to the Microsoft Exchange Information Store. The gateway converts the PROFS message into a standard MAPI message.

When the message arrives in the Information Store, it follows the same message flow as if it originated as a Microsoft Exchange message. Going the other direction, a message from a MS Mail user destined for a PROFS user takes the following route through the Microsoft Mail Connector.

Message Flow from Microsoft Exchange Users to IBM PROFS Users via Microsoft Mail-Based Gateway

In the reverse situation, a message originates from Microsoft Exchange and is routed through the Microsoft Mail Connector to the MS Mail post office with a PROFS gateway installed.

In this case, the message from the Microsoft Exchange user is stored in the Microsoft Exchange Information Store, and is then sent by the Information Store to the Microsoft Exchange MTA. From there, it's routed by the MS Mail Interchange to the Connector post office. The message then is routed from the Connector post office to its final PROFS destination directly by the Microsoft Mail PROFS gateway.

Going in the other direction, PROFS users who send messages to Microsoft Exchange users use the PROFS gateway in MS Mail.

The message from Microsoft Mail is picked up by the MS Mail Connector (PC) MTA and placed in the Connector post office in-queue. Once there, the message is handled exactly the same as all other messages.

Using Client Providers for IBM PROFS

Using a PROFS MAPI client provider for the Microsoft Exchange Client is an alternative to or a variant of multiphased migration. Using Attachmate's ZIP! Office Client Connection product, the Microsoft Exchange Client can be used to connect to the IBM PROFS system, Microsoft Exchange Server, or both systems.

Having Users Drive Migration

With some programming, you can make a multiphased migration user-managed and user-driven. For example, the mailboxes for all users can be created in Microsoft Exchange server computer, but made hidden. When a user accesses his or her new mailbox and no longer needs the IBM PROFS system, he or she can send a special custom form. This form is already addressed to a mailbox. When the message is received, a program creates an account file with the sender's host account information, and then runs the source extractor. After the source extractor is finished, the files are copied to a network share and the Migration Wizard is started in batch mode. It imports the data into the empty mailbox, and logs that this user has been migrated.

How the Source Extractor Works

The IBM PROFS source extractor is a multithreaded application when migrating messages. It runs in a specially defined MIGRATOR VM ID. Each thread takes the next VM ID from the list of VM IDs to be migrated and attempts to autolog on this VM ID. If successful, it invokes the MIGVIZ EXEC from a common mini-disk. This EXEC links to the MIGRATOR's 191 mini-disk, from which it can access the migration parameters and other migration programs. These programs extract the relevant data from notelogs, files, calendars, nickname files, and distribution lists and send the data to a file transfer VM ID. When it completes extracting all the data or when the maximum-wait time limit is reached, the thread goes on to the next unmigrated VM ID in the list.

Preparing to Migrate Data

Before installing the software, you need to create two VM IDs, MIGRATOR and MIGXFER, as described in the following sections. Create either a class B VM ID that can perform the autolog function or a class G VM ID that can perform this function. This ID must have the following:

- A 191 mini-disk to store programs, accounts files, other required data tables, LOG, and STATUS files.
- A LINK to a mini-disk that contains the OFSUAD FILE or a LINK to xxxDBM 191 mini-disk.
- A LINK to a mini-disk that contains the PROFS NICKNAME file and ADDRLIST files.

- (Optional) Pre-ESA systems may need to provide a link to the VM DIRECTORY file, unless some other means exists to perform the AUTO LOGON of VM IDs from the MIGRATOR VM ID.

The following code shows a sample directory entry for the MIGRATOR VM ID:

```
USER MIGRATOR password 4M 8M B
 ACCOUNT
 IPL CMS
 CONSOLE 009 3215
 SPOOL   00C 2540 READER *
 SPOOL   00D 2540 PUNCH O
 SPOOL   00E 1403 A
 MDISK   191 3380 ccc 016 vvvvvv MR readpw writepw
 LINK    xxxDBM   191 395 RR
MIGXFER
```

This class G VM ID may be used to receive the files generated during migration process from the reader to a mini-disk. This VM ID requires a mini-disk large enough to store all notelogs, calendar, mailed documents, and nickname information from the group of users participating in the migration run. Optionally, the Administrator may choose to designate the MIGRATOR VM ID to receive these files, rather than creating a second VM ID. The documentation assumes that there are two VM IDs.

The following code shows a sample directory entry for the MIGXFER VM ID:

```
USER MIGXFER password 4M 8M B
 ACCOUNT
 IPL CMS
 CONSOLE 009 3215
 SPOOL   00C 2540 READER *
 SPOOL   00D 2540 PUNCH O
 SPOOL   00E 1403 A
 MDISK   191 3380 ccc 100 vvvvvv MR readpw writepw
```

Installing the IBM PROFS Source Extractor

To install the Microsoft Exchange Server IBM PROFS source extractor with an MS-DOS 3270 Emulator, use the following procedures:

1. Log on as the MIGRATOR VM ID.
2. Insert the floppy disk with the PROFS Source extractor code into the A drive of the computer.
3. From the a:\ prompt, type **UPLOAD** ***<path to terminal emulation software>*** and press ENTER. Do not include a trailing backslash on the path.
4. Move the file MIGVIZ EXEC to a common mini-disk.
5. Repeat this process for the file transfer VM ID.

Installing the Microsoft Exchange Server IBM PROFS Source Extractor with a Windows 3270 Emulator

If you don't use terminal-emulation software, the files can be transferred to the MIGRATOR's 191 mini-disk with the sample RUNBATCH.EBM macro.

Customizing EXECs After Installation You may need to customize the files MIGLOGON EXEC and MIGLINKP EXEC to work with your system. Before using MIGLOGON EXEC, you must change the variables, rdpass and vmdir. Before using MIGLINKP, you may need to change the text for sysadmin.

Maintaining Directories During a Multiphase Migration During migration, you need to keep directories in both systems current. You can use the migration tools to export and import directory information, as described in the following sections.

Creating Addresses in Your Host System

If you don't have a directory synchronization requestor for your host system, then you need to handle the following:

- Export the mailbox and foreign system addresses from Microsoft Exchange Server with directory export.
- Change the format of the file.
- Import the addresses into your host system.
- Extract Custom Recipients from PROFS.

Mail sent in Microsoft Exchange server computers and incoming mail from Microsoft Exchange Server gateways can be routed to the PROFS addresses. You can use this rather than using directory synchronization but you have to repeat the process on a regular basis to update the Microsoft Exchange Server directory with changes in the existing system directory.

Extract a file of IBM PROFS addresses. Move the file to the Microsoft Exchange Server computer. Import the IBM PROFS address file into Microsoft Exchange server with the Migration Wizard to create custom recipients.

NOTE The custom recipient information is created with PROFS target addresses. If mail sent from Microsoft Exchange Server mailboxes is routed through X.400 or SMTP to reach the PROFS host, you must modify the custom recipient data before importing it to have the proper address type and address.

1. On the computer where you installed the source extractor, log on as the MIGRATOR VM ID.
2. Type **MIGWIZRD** and press ENTER to start the source extractor. The screen displays the following code:

```
Source Extractor for IBM (R) PROFS (R) and OfficeVision (TM)
Microsoft Exchange Server Migration Wizard

The following parameters are specified in MIGPARMS DATA file.

You can change these parameters using this menu, or by using XEDIT.

OV/VM (PROFS) Nickname File: File name:          File type:
Accounts File:               File name:          File type:
PROFS Calendar MIGRATOR vmid (PROFS system only)
Notify VM id                                        : HOWARDS
File Transfer VM id                                 : MIGXFER
Thread timeout (min)                                : 30
Spool Console required                 (TRUE/FALSE) : FALSE
Number of migration threads                         : 05
Replace previously migrated accounts (TRUE/FALSE)   : TRUE
------------------------------------------------------------------

<< BACK     NEXT >>         FINISH          CANCEL      HELP
 F10/F22    F11/F23         F12/F24         F3/F15      F1/F13
```

3. (Optional) In the OV/VM (PROFS) Nickname File field, type the name and file type of the nickname file. If this field is not filled in, the source extractor uses OFSUAD FILE, if access to this file is available.
4. (Optional) In the Accounts File field, type the name and file type of the accounts file with a list of VM IDs for which you want to create custom recipients. If you plan to create custom recipients for all VM IDs, skip this step.

   Anywhere from one to all VM IDs can be specified in an account file. The account file has one VM ID on each line.
5. In the Notify VM ID field, type the VM ID to which alert messages are sent. This VM ID doesn't need to have administrator privileges.
6. In the File Transfer VM ID field, type the VM ID to which all the extractor data should be written.
7. Press the F11 key to continue. The screen displays the following:

```
    Source Extractor for IBM (R) PROFS (R) and OfficeVision (TM)
Microsoft Exchange Server Migration Wizard

What information would you like to migrate?

Type Y to select option, or N to reject it.
```

```
Y Remote addresses creation information (REMADDR FILE)
N Mailbox creation information (MAILBOX FILE)
N Email messages (Notelogs and In-basket)
          From: 1994/10/28 to 1995/10/28
N Schedule information (Calendars and Reminders)
          From: 1995/10/28 to 1996/10/28
N Documents from OFSINDEX FILE
          From: 1994/10/28 to 1995/10/28
N Personal Address Book (Nicknames and Distribution lists)

----------------------------------------------------------------

<< BACK    NEXT >>       FINISH          CANCEL    HELP
 F10/F22   F11/F23       F12/F24         F3/F15    F1/F13
```

8. Set the Remote Addresses Creation Information to Y. Set all other options to N.
9. To continue, press the F11 key. The screen displays the remote address file.
10. Edit the remote address file as needed to remove VM IDs for which you don't want Microsoft Exchange Server custom recipients, or to change the display names. The source extractor uses XEDIT as the editor, and all XEDIT commands and subcommands are available.
11. Press F12 to complete the process.

    This procedure creates REMADDR FILE on the MIGRATOR 191 mini-disk and sends REMADDR PRI and REMADDR PKL to the reader of the file transfer VM ID. The REMADDR PRI and REMADDR PKL files are in ASCII format.

Moving the REMADDR Address to the Microsoft Exchange Server To move the REMADDR address to the Microsoft Exchange Server, take these steps:

1. Log on as the MIGXFER VM ID.
2. Type **MIGXFER** and press ENTER to start the transfer tool.
3. The transfer tool modifies the file named REMADDR FILE to the migration file format and transfers it from the reader to the minidisk. The MIGXFER EXEC also creates MIGXFER BAT, MIGRATOR PKL, and MIGPURGE EXEC on the mini-disk.
4. Download the MIGXFER BAT file to the personal computer.
5. From the personal computer type the following:

    MIGXFER ***<path to your terminal emulation software>***

    to transfer the REMADDR FILE and packing list file to the personal computer as REMADDR.PRI and MIGRATOR.PKL.
6. On the host, type **MIGPURGE** to remove the files from the reader.

7. (Optional) Edit the REMADDR PRI file to remove addresses, modify display names, change the target address type, or add additional directory import fields and data. For example, if you want all the custom recipients to have telephone number data, you can add the field, Telephone-Office1, to the end of the first line in the directory section, and then add telephone numbers to the end of each line of data.

The migration files now can be imported into Microsoft Exchange Server with the Migration Wizard. See the following section, "Importing Migration Files," for the next step.

Creating Mailboxes

The procedure for creating mailboxes is exactly the same as for creating custom recipients except that, in step 8 of the extracting process, set Mailbox Creation Information to Y. A MAILBOX file is created in place of the REMADDR file.

Migrating Data The process of migrating data creates secondary files, and autologs onto the VM IDs that are being migrated. The VM IDs to migrate cannot be in use during the extracting process.

Extracting E-Mail Data To extract e-mail data, take the following steps:

1. Log on as the MIGRATOR VM ID.
2. Type **MIGWIZRD** and press ENTER to start the source extractor. The screen displays the following information:

```
Source Extractor for IBM (R) PROFS (R) and OfficeVision (TM)
Microsoft Exchange Server Migration Wizard

The following parameters are specified in MIGPARMS DATA file.

You can change these parameters using this menu, or by using XEDIT.

OV/VM (PROFS) Nickname File: File name:          File type:
Accounts File:               File name:          File type:
PROFS Calendar MIGRATOR vmid (PROFS system only)  :
Notify VM id                                      : HOWARDS
File Transfer VM id                               : MIGXFER
Thread timeout (min)                              : 30
Spool Console required                (TRUE/FALSE) : FALSE
Number of migration threads                       : 05
Replace previously migrated accounts  (TRUE/FALSE) : TRUE

-----------------------------------------------------------------

<< BACK     NEXT >>       FINISH           CANCEL      HELP
 F10/F22    F11/F23       F12/F24          F3/F15      F1/F13
```

3. (Optional) In the OV/VM (PROFS) Nickname File field, type the name and file type of the nickname file. If this field is not filled in, the extractor uses OFSUAD FILE.

TIP If you are migrating only a few accounts, create an accounts or nickname file with these accounts in it and set the appropriate field to point at the file.

4. (Optional) In the Accounts File field, type the name and file type of the accounts file with a list of VM IDs for which you want to create custom recipients.
5. (Optional) If you are migrating calendars from a PROFS system, enter the corresponding VM ID in the PROFS Calendar MIGRATOR VM ID field. Ignore this step if you are migrating calendars from OfficeVision.
6. In the Notify VM ID field, type the VM ID to which error messages are sent. This VM ID doesn't need to have administrator privileges.
7. In the File Transfer VM ID field, type the VM ID to which all the extractor data should be written.
8. In the Thread Timeout field, type the maximum number of minutes it should take to migrate each VM ID. When this time runs out, the MIGWIZRD EXEC reuses the thread.
9. In the Spool Console Required field, set the value to TRUE to send console updates to the MIGRATOR VM ID to monitor progress.

   Alternatively, set the value to FALSE so that the console updates are not sent.
10. In the Number of Migration Threads, set the number of VM IDs that will be migrated simultaneously. If you set this number too high, it can affect performance and resources on the host computer.
11. In the Replace Previously Migrated Accounts field, set the value to TRUE if you want to migrate data for VM IDs that previously were migrated.

    Alternatively, set the value to FALSE if you do not want to migrate previously migrated VM IDs.
12. Press the F11 key to continue. The screen displays the following information:

```
     Source Extractor for IBM (R) PROFS (R) and OfficeVision (TM)
Microsoft Exchange Server Migration Wizard

What information would you like to migrate?

Type Y to select option, or N to reject it.

 N Remote addresses creation information (REMADDR FILE)
 N Mailbox creation information (MAILBOX FILE)
 Y Email messages (Notelogs and In-basket)
          From: 1994/10/28 to 1995/10/28
```

```
Y Schedule information (Calendars and Reminders)
           From: 1995/10/28 to 1996/10/28
Y Documents from OFSINDEX FILE
           From: 1994/10/28 to 1995/10/28
Y Personal Address Book (Nicknames and Distribution lists)

------------------------------------------------------------------

<< BACK    NEXT >>      FINISH            CANCEL     HELP
F10/F22    F11/F23      F12/F24           F3/F15     F1/F13
```

13. Set the options to Y or N, based on the information you need to migrate. Also, update the date range for each type of information that is being migrated.

CAUTION

The date range doesn't dynamically update. To avoid not migrating recent items, set the To dates to a future date, in case you forget to update them.

14. Press F11 to continue. The screen displays the accounts file.
15. Edit the accounts file as needed to remove VM IDs that you do not want to migrate.

    The status field can have the following three possible values:

    Init—Not migrated yet but will be migrated.

    Timeout—Attempted to migrate VM ID, but reached the timeout limit before migration was finished. Will be migrated.

    Done—Exported data from this VM ID in the past. Will be migrated only if Replace Previous Migrated Accounts field is set to TRUE.
16. (Optional) If you didn't create a small nickname file or accounts file with your list of VM IDs to be migrated, pare down the full list of users to only the ones you want to migrate.
17. Press F12 to start extracting data. The screen displays the following information:

```
Source Extractor for IBM (R) PROFS (R) and OfficeVision (TM)
Migrating mailbox information...
Migrating users...
Max_threads=05. Replace=1
N_input=63
  AUTO SUFINE EXEC MIGRATE MIGRATOR READ
  AUTO STGRAY EXEC MIGRATE MIGRATOR READ



                                                  RUNNING   MSVM7
```

18. When the MIGWIZRD EXEC is finished, type **SHUT** to end the program.

This process creates several items in the reader of the file transfer VM ID, depending on the options selected in the second screen, which are described in the following table:

Item Name	Description
MAILBOX FILE	Information to create mailboxes
<VM ID> PKL	Packing list for the migration files of the VM ID
<VM ID> PRI	Primary intermediate file for the migration files of the VM ID
<VM ID> SEC	Secondary intermediate file for the migration files of the VM ID

These files are stored in ASCII format and should not be edited. For each VM ID there can be multiple primary intermediate files.

Migrating Files to Microsoft Exchange Server To move the migration files to Microsoft Exchange Server, follow these steps:

1. Log on as the MIGXFER VM ID.
2. Type **MIGXFER** and press ENTER to start the transfer tool. The screen displays the following information:

```
    Source Extractor for IBM (R) PROFS (R) and OfficeVision (TM)

    There are 180 K bytes available on A disk.
    Total size of selected files is 1892 K.
    Select a subset of files that can be transferred by editing this file.

          User ID              File Size
 00000 * * * Top of File * * *
 00001 REMADDR                      6080
 00002 MAILBOX                      4960
 00003 EAST03                       1328
 00004 EAST02                      36628
 00005 EAST01                      10064
 00006 CENT01                      98776
 00007 CENT02                     309728
 00008 CENT03                     282512
 00009 CENT05                       4344
 00010 WEST01                      16416
 00011 WEST02                      22004
 00012 CENT04                    1044180
 ------------------------------------------------------------------------
  FINISH                 RECALCULATE                CANCEL
  F12/F24                F10/F22                    F3/F15
 ====>
```

3. (Optional) Select a subset of files to transfer by editing this list. If limited by space on the mini-disk, press F10 to recalculate the total size of selected files.

4. The transfer tool modifies the files to the migration file format and transfers them from the reader to the mini-disk. The MIGXFER EXEC also creates MIGXFER BAT, <VM ID> PKL, and MIGPURGE EXEC on the mini-disk.
5. Download the MIGXFER BAT file to the personal computer.
6. From the personal computer, type **MIGXFER** ***<path to your terminal emulation software>*** to transfer the migration files to the personal computer as *.PRI, *.SEC, and <VMID>.PKL. This step also consolidates all packing list files (PKLs) into one file.
7. On the host, type **MIGPURGE** to remove the files from the reader.
8. If you want, edit the MAILBOX.PRI file to modify information such as directory names or to add additional directory import fields and data. For example, if you want to migrate department information with each mailbox, you can add the field Department to the end of the first line of the directory header, and then add department names to the end of each line of data.

NOTE **Important:** If you need to change directory (common-name) names, do it before importing the migration files. After creating mailboxes, the directory name can be changed only by deleting the mailbox and creating a new one.

Importing Migration Files

The Migration Wizard reads files created by the extractor and automates simple administrative tasks, such as creating mailboxes and custom recipients.

Import the migration files with the Migration Wizard. See Chapter 7, "Migrating to Microsoft Mail Systems," for steps on how to use Migration Wizard.

Migrating from SMTP (Internet) Mail Systems

This section is relevant if your organization currently has a mail system with a proprietary gateway into the Internet or if you use an SMTP POP mail server connected directly to the Internet.

NOTE Any reference in this section about connecting to the Internet also applies to connections with other SMTP-based systems.

The Microsoft Exchange Internet Mail Connector provides connectivity with any SMTP-based mail system. In the past, with a PC-based messaging system, it was necessary to connect a separate SMTP gateway PC to access the Internet or other SMTP system. Exchange is designed to talk to the Internet directly and, because of its other connectors and gateways, is well-suited for use as a gateway for other systems.

You will Encounter two types of migration when implementing Exchange in an SMTP (POP mail) environment, which are described in the following list:

- **System Migration**—Replacing existing SMTP gateways with Exchange servers
- **User Migration**—Transferring POP mail users to Exchange mailboxes

System Migration

You can use Exchange to replace the current SMTP Gateways in your organization. If you currently use the MS-DOS-based SMTP gateway for Microsoft Mail, you want to do this as soon as possible. Exchange provides a far more reliable and efficient method for bridging your organization into SMTP-based systems such as the Internet.

Migrating Users from POP Mail to Exchange

If your organization uses SMTP Mail (POP) mail servers for user accounts, consider the following points about migration to Exchange.

First, POP mail provides the flexibility to check messages from any point on the Internet with several commonly available mail clients (such as Qualcomm's Eudora, or even with an advanced World Wide Web browser, such as Netscape's Navigator). Although Exchange has excellent remote uses support (for all its functionality, such as public folders and so on), it does currently require that you use the Microsoft Exchange client only to retrieve messages. This section provides some suggestions for migrating users to Exchange and beyond.

Building a Parallel SMTP System

Unlike the X.400 connector option of sharing address spaces with a foreign system, this isn't an option in the SMTP world. Therefore, it's not a practical method for gradual migration from a POP mail to Exchange. If you do happen to have a large number of POP Mail users that you want to migrate to Exchange, the best way probably will be to build all your accounts on parallel systems. Then, you have to "throw the switch" and redirect mail to your Exchange server when it's all set up.

For example, for "YOURCORP" organization, the Internet domain is YourCorp.com. We can temporarily set up an offline Exchange server to receive mail at popmail. YourCorp.com for testing. We create all the necessary user accounts on this parallel system, and test for proper routing to this address. Then at a specified time, we modify the entry in the DNS (Domain Name Server) to route all YourCorp.com mail to the machine previously designated as popmail.YourCorp.com.

If you have users that must retain a POP Mail account for some reason (for example, to check mail remotely without an Exchange client), then you can implement the following tricks.

After switching your main organization to Exchange from POP mail, you can concurrently maintain a true POP Mail server to use (popmail.YourCorp.com) for certain user accounts. Then, configure a specific user's mailbox to forward mail to the POP account.

You can accomplish this in the following ways:

A user would configure an Out of Office Assistant from his or her Exchange client to automatically forward mail to his or her POP Mail account when he or she is out of the office.

An administrator can configure an alternate recipient in the user's mailbox's property page to forward mail to a standard POP Mail account. This account can then be accessed from anywhere on the Internet with any standard POP Mail client (Eudora, Netscape Navigator, and so on).

Exchange offers excellent support for remote users, so use these methods only when a remote user does not have access to an Exchange client while on the road.

Migrating from Foreign X.400 Messaging Systems

The X.400 Connector for Microsoft Exchange provides all the connectivity needed for replacing a foreign X.400 system in your organization. This connectivity includes gateways for connecting to any system that uses X.400 standards.

As in connecting and migrating from SMTP mail, there are two kinds of migration, which are described in the following list:

- **User Migration**—Transferring foreign X.400 system users to Exchange mailboxes
- **System Migration**—Replacing existing X.400 gateways with Exchange servers

User Migration from Foreign X.400 Systems

When switching to Exchange from a foreign X.400 system, user migration will probably be a gradual process. During migration there obviously will be some users on Exchange and others still using the foreign X.400 system simultaneously. Microsoft Exchange allows you to share the X.400 address space with a foreign system to provide coexistence during the migration process.

For example, the Melbourne site is connected to the Los Angeles site through a public X.400 network. Originally, the messaging system in Melbourne was a foreign X.400-based system, but now is being migrated to Exchange. Suppose that 65 percent of the Melbourne users were migrated (using the included migration tools) to Exchange. To maintain coexistence, you set up Exchange to share an address space with the foreign X.400 system (in the Site Addressing property page), which means that messages can arrive for users on both Exchange and the foreign X.400 at the same address.

The following list shows the message route in the preceding example:

1. A message from the public X.400 network enters through the Microsoft Exchange X.400 connector.
2. If the user is an Exchange user (or a user on another system connected to Exchange through another connector), the message is delivered normally.
3. If the user isn't on the Exchange system, it will be routed to your foreign X.400 system and delivered to the user in that mailbox.

With this system, users can be migrated to Exchange at your pace, knowing that both systems will run side-by-side provided that you need them to do so. This approach also reduces the amount of non-deliverable messages often encountered when switching over to a new system.

System Migration

Another common system migration scenario is to replace your current MS Mail X.400 gateways with a more robust Exchange server with both the X.400 and MS Mail connectors.

In this scenario, Exchange receives incoming X.400 messages through the X.400 connector, and routes them through, using the MS Mail connector. Because there will not necessarily be any mail user on the Exchange servers, no user migration is needed.

However, the next step is to migrate the users from MS Mail to Microsoft Exchange, but this topic is covered in its entirety in Chapter 6, "Planning Connections to Microsoft Mail Systems."

From Here...

This chapter has covered migrating from the PROFS, X.400, and Internet-based (SMTP) messaging systems. As shown, Exchange can serve as a gateway between itself and your current messaging systems as well as provide a rich set of tools to smoothly migrate your users into Exchange.

- Chapter 6, "Planning Connections to Microsoft Mail Systems," gives you the information you need to have an MS-Mail and Exchange system coexist and eventually migrate fully to Exchange.
- Chapter 15, "Creating and Configuring Recipients," gives you methods of creating new recipients for migration to Exchange.
- Chapter 20, "Configuring X.400 Connections," teaches how to configure a connection to an X.400-based system.
- Chapter 21, "Setting Up SMTP Connections," shows how to configure the Internet Mail Connector.

CHAPTER 9

Installing Exchange Server

- System requirements for Exchange server
- How to prepare to install Exchange sites
- Installation procedures for Exchange
- Installation of additional Exchange servers in an organization

Before proceeding with the Microsoft Exchange Server installation, you should make sure the machine(s) that will be used have the basic resources available to accomplish the task.

The following lists show the minimum hardware and software requirements necessary for installing the Exchange Server:

Hardware:

- a 486–66MHz processor
- 32M of RAM
- 250–500M of free hard disk space

Software:

- Windows NT 3.51 Server
- Windows NT Services for Macintosh
- Windows NT NW-Link protocol
- Windows NT TCP/IP

Microsoft Windows NT Server v3.51 is the base network operating system. The Microsoft NT Server

Service Pack 3 should be installed on the NT Server that will be used, before the beginning of the Microsoft Exchange Server install.

Macintosh Services will be necessary for MS Mail AppleTalk clients to access the Microsoft Mail Connector, which is the liaison between the AppleTalk clients and the Microsoft Exchange Server.

If you want access from a Novell Netware 3.XX or 4.XX File Server, the Windows NT NW-LINK and the NW-LINK NetBios protocol services need to be loaded on the Windows NT Server.

When a new or existing Mail system will be using the Microsoft Exchange Server to transfer messages over the Internet, the Internet Mail Connector will be used. A necessity for the use of Internet Mail Connector is the Windows NT TCP/IP protocol. It must be installed and configured.

The preceding are the minimum requirements. To enhance the performance of the system running the Microsoft NT Server and the Microsoft Exchange Server, at least a 90MHz processor with 64M of RAM should be used. For busy sites, you should use 1G of hard disk space. This disk space requirement does not allow for user mail message stores on the server. Depending on the number of users, you may need to add additional server hard drive storage. ■

Preparing for Server and Site Setups

Before installing the Microsoft Exchange Server, you should gather some relevant information relating to the business or organization. This will include number of users, patterns of e-mail use in the business, geographic locations of the business, managerial style of the IS departments (central or distributed management), and more. You want to discern how the Microsoft Exchange Servers fit into the overall company plan.

The following shows the areas of reference that you should review to help with the design and installation of the Microsoft Exchange Server message system.

- "Before You Begin" in the "Getting Started" chapter of the Microsoft Exchange Server Installation guide.
- Chapter 2, "Understanding Exchange's Organization and Sites," helps you to comprehend what is required for designing single and multiple site Microsoft Exchange Servers.
- Chapters 5–7 help you to understand the issues pertaining to the setup, connection, and migration techniques involved in planning the Connector component installations.

Gathering Information Used during the Installation

During the setup process you are asked to answer questions regarding your organization and the Microsoft Exchange Server. The site-specific information needs to be confirmed. Because some of the information can only be changed by reinstalling the Exchange Server, review the naming schemes that will be used for the message system.

You should know the following information before you begin the installation process:

- An organization name
- The Microsoft Exchange Server Site name
- What role the Microsoft Exchange Server you are installing will play in the organization: making a new site or joining an existing one
- The Microsoft Windows NT Server Administrator account name and password
- The name of the Microsoft Exchange Server Administrators Group

When designing the naming scheme for the Microsoft Exchange Server Message system, use logical names that depict relative information to the end users and IS administrators. Because of the nature of Mail system standards, these names are also case sensitive. To avoid confusion, check each name entered before continuing, these names are used throughout the entire message system.

Setting Up a Single Server

The first Microsoft Exchange Server to be installed in a new site is the most important. All other Microsoft Exchange Server installations within the same site refer to this Exchange Server for configuration information.

The following list refers to the steps to complete the first or only Microsoft Exchange Server in a site or organization:

1. Create the Service Account.
2. Configure the Exchange Server Administrators Group.
3. Install the Exchange Server software.
4. Grant the Exchange Server administrators permissions for the site.

Creating the Service Account

The Microsoft Exchange Server uses the Service Account to run its services on the given Microsoft NT Server. The account is granted the "Log on as a service" right. When creating and joining a new Microsoft Exchange Server within the same site, the Service Account name and password are required to continue with the installation. Microsoft Exchange Server Setup uses this account to transfer the configuration files to the new Microsoft Exchange Server. Furthermore, this account is also used by all Microsoft Exchange Servers in the same site to communicate with one another.

The following steps help you to create the Service Account:

1. Log on the Windows NT Server as the Domain Administrator or equivalent.

NOTE You must log in to the same Domain that holds the system for which you plan to create the account.

2. While in the Program Manager, open Administrative Tools. Then, open User Manager for Domains.
3. From the User menu, choose New User.
4. Enter the information you have listed for the Service Account.
5. Check the box titled User Cannot Change Password.
6. Check the box for Password Never Expires.
7. Clear the box that says User Must Change Password at Next Logon.
8. Clear box that says Account Disabled.
9. Choose Add (see fig. 9.1).
10. Choose Close.

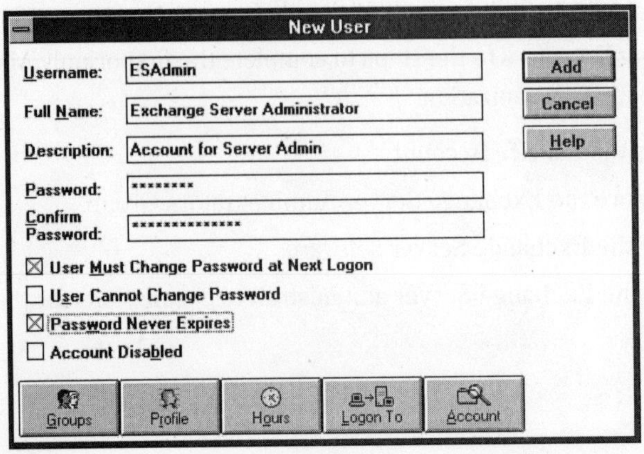

FIG. 9.1
You can add the Service Account.

Creating the Exchange Administrators Group

The Administrators Group should consist of all the Microsoft Windows NT users account information selected as Microsoft Exchange Server Administrators. Members of this group possess the privilege to gain access to the Microsoft Exchange Server Public Folders and Utilities for administrative purposes. This account is a Global Group. You should verify that all users who become a member of this group will receive this privilege.

The following steps help you create the Exchange Administrators group:

1. Log on as a Domain Administrator to the Microsoft NT Server that is in the same domain as the Microsoft Exchange Server. This Microsoft NT Server will be the central location for the administration functions of Microsoft Exchange.
2. In Program Manager, choose Administrative Tools; then, select User Manager for Domains.
3. From the User menu, choose New Global Group. The New Global Group dialog box appears (see fig. 9.2)
4. Type the name and a brief description of the newly created group.

NOTE You will be required to know this group account name later in the installation and setup of the Microsoft Exchange Server. ■

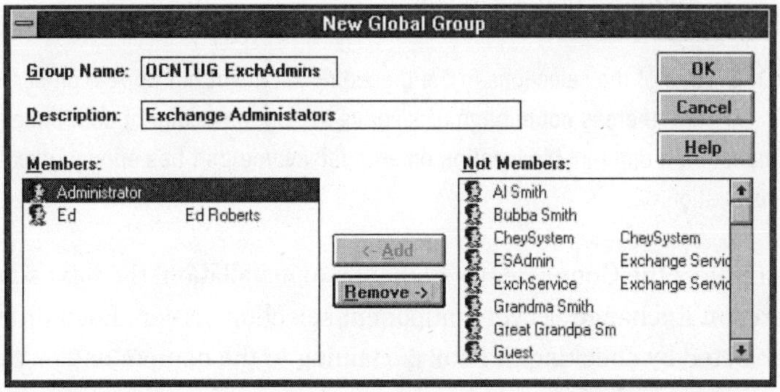

FIG. 9.2
Creating the Exchange Administrators group.

Installing the Exchange Server Software

Before beginning the actual installation, you should verify the following:

- Be sure that the PDC (Primary Domain Controller) is connected and operating.
- Review the proposed Microsoft Exchange Server naming scheme and design layout.
- Check that there is a working CD-ROM drive available as a resource on the Windows NT Server. You will use this drive during the installation process.

The following steps help you to install the Microsoft Exchange Server:

1. Log on to the Microsoft NT Server as the Local Administrator.
2. Load the Microsoft Exchange Server CD-ROM into the CD-ROM drive.
3. Choose the program group Main; then, start Windows File Manager.
4. Scan through and become familiar with the directory structure on the Microsoft Exchange CD-ROM.
5. Locate and change directories to the Setup directory.
6. Locate and change directories to one of the computer types (Alpha, i386, PPC, or MIPS). For example: d:\SETUP\i386.
7. Choose SETUP.EXE; then, press OK to continue past the Welcome dialog box.
8. An Installation Options box appears (see fig. 9.3). Select the desired type of installation and the location to which the files should be copied. The following are the installation options from which you can select:

   - *Typical.* Microsoft Exchange Server will be installed with the most common options.
   - *Custom/Complete.* Microsoft Exchange Server will be installed with only the options you select.
   - *Minimum.* Microsoft Exchange Server will be installed with the minimum required options to run.

NOTE One of the selections in the preceding list might not appear on-screen. The reason is that there is not enough disk space for that particular option. Choose another type of installation or a different file location on another volume that has enough disk space to handle the installation.

If you select the Complete/Custom type of installation, the next screen to appear is the Microsoft Exchange Server component selection screen. Each different component can be selected by checking the box pertaining to the component, or clearing the box if that selection is not desired—depending on the given installation. The following lists the different components and their sub-components available for selection during installation:

- Microsoft Exchange Server—The default location for installation of component files is C:\EXCHSRVR. This can be modified by choosing `Change Location of Files`. If all Server components are to be installed, 67,072K of disk space is required.
- Microsoft Mail Connector—Connects a Microsoft Exchange Server to MS Mail 3.x PC and AppleTalk Networks. This component requires 5,578K of disk space.

- SMTP Internet Mail Connector—Connects a Microsoft Exchange Server to the Internet or some other SMTP compatible service. This component requires 708K of disk space.
- X.400 Connector—Connects a Microsoft Exchange Server to X.400 compatible systems. This component requires no disk space.
- Microsoft Exchange Server Administrator application— The default directory path for installation of the Administrator components is C:\EXCHSRVR\BIN. You can change the directory path if you want a different location. The Administrator software component has no sub-components that are selectable. This component requires 35,124K of disk space.

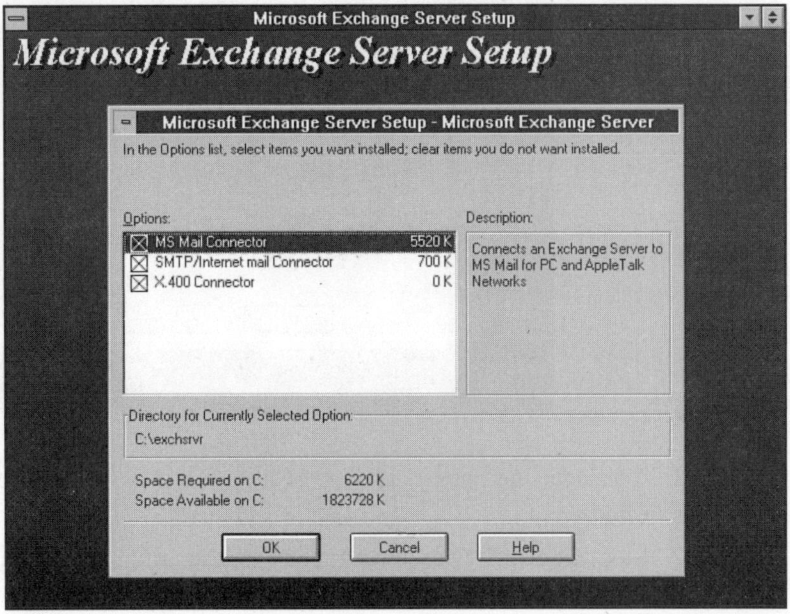

FIG. 9.3
You can select from the Installation Options Box when setting up the Microsoft Exchange Server.

NOTE If a Complete Install is executed, it will require 102,196K of disk space. This does not include disk space for user mailboxes, just the Exchange system files.

9. The Choose Licensing Mode dialog box appears. Select the type of licensing desired. Select I Agree; then, choose OK. The following shows the types of licensing modes from which you can select:
   - *Per Server Licensing*—Enter the number of Client Access Licenses that have been purchased. For concurrent connections, the number entered must be a value greater than zero. Otherwise, Microsoft Exchange Clients will not be able to connect to the Microsoft Exchange Server system.

- *Per Client Licensing*—This type of access is based on the valid ownership of MS Mail 3.x client software and Microsoft Exchange Client.

10. Choose Create a New Site when the Organization and Site dialog box appears (see fig. 9.4). Enter the Organization Name and Site Name. Entering these names is mandatory. Choose continue.

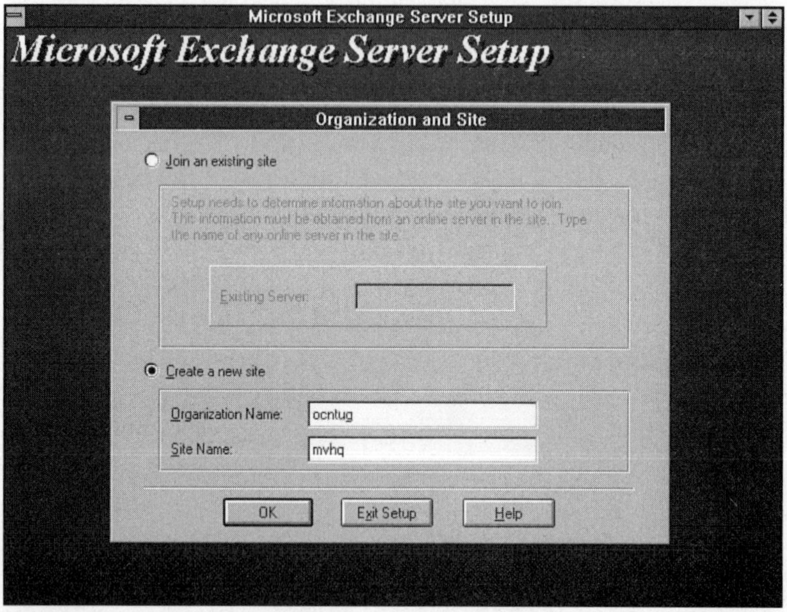

FIG. 9.4
Creating a new Exchange site.

11. A dialogue box appears asking, `Are you sure you want to create a new site?` Choose `Yes`.
12. Next, the Site Services Account box appears asking you to choose the Service account (see fig. 9.5). Enter the Service account name and password created at the beginning of this chapter. Alternatively, you can choose Browse. Then, you can choose the account from the list provided. Choose add; then, click OK.
13. The dialogue box appears confirming that the rights have been granted (see fig. 9.6). Choose OK.
14. To complete the installation, choose OK from the next dialog box. Microsoft Exchange Server Setup then copies the Microsoft Exchange Server files and installs the Services to the selected Microsoft Windows NT Server.
15. The next screen that appears is asking to which Windows NT Program Group the Microsoft Exchange Servers application icons should be installed. The default is Microsoft Exchange Server. Accept the default Program Group; then, enter a new

Program Group name. Alternatively, you can select an existing Program. Then, choose continue.

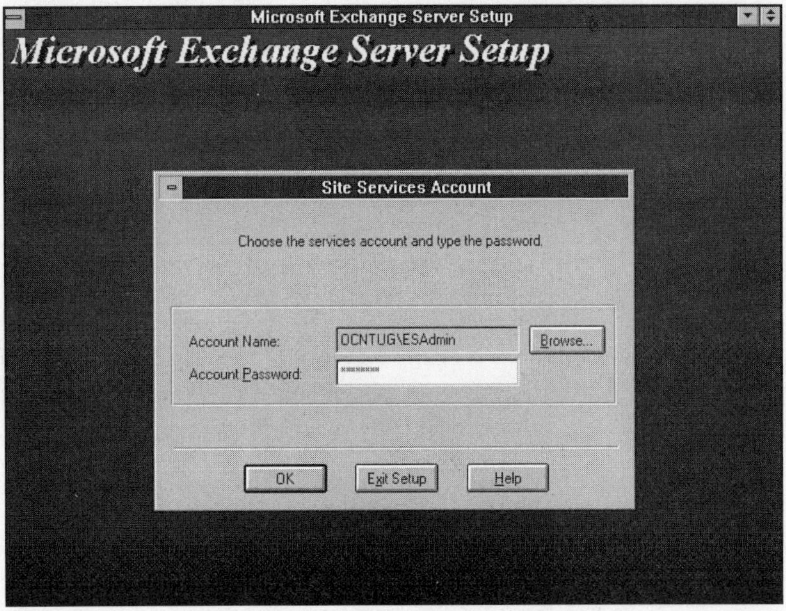

FIG. 9.5
You can enter the Services account name and the appropriate password.

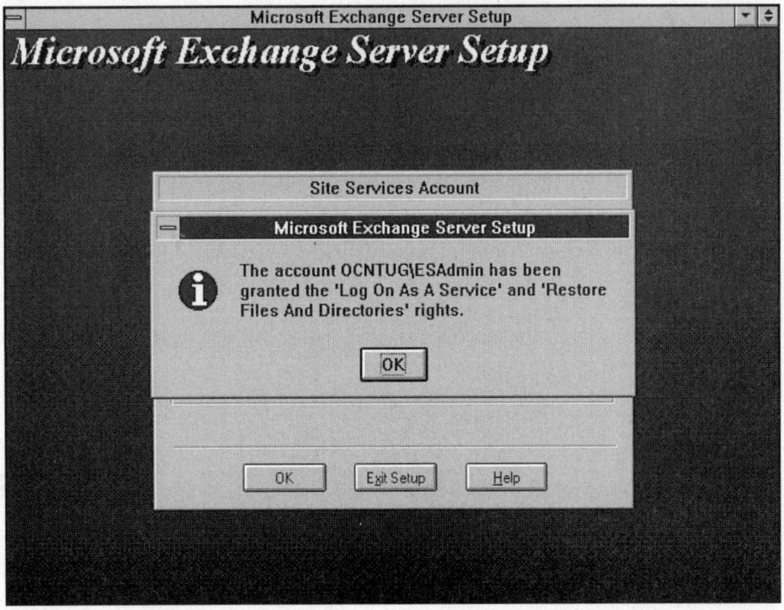

FIG. 9.6
You should verify that the proper rights have been granted.

16. Finally, once the installation is completed, a dialog box appears asking whether the Performance Optimizer Wizard should be run (see fig. 9.7). Select Run Optimizer to have the Performance Optimizer Wizard analyze your hardware configuration. Run Optimizer also arranges files on the Microsoft Windows NT Server for optimum performance.

NOTE Running the Optimizer is critical to the efficient operation of the Microsoft Exchange Server. The Performance Optimizer Wizard does not have to run at this time. However, it should be run before the Microsoft Exchange Server goes into production.

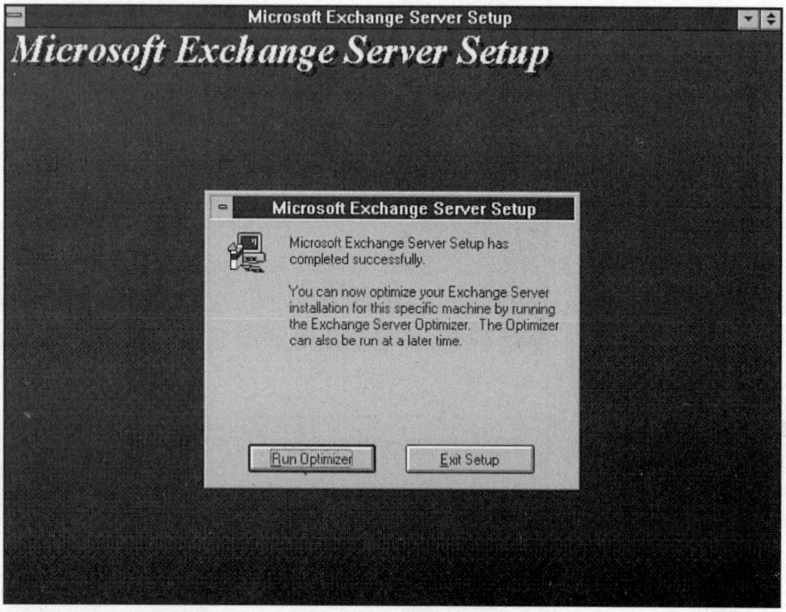

FIG. 9.7
Completing the Setup and Performance Optimizer option will get the Exchange Server up and running.

17. The Microsoft Windows NT Server needs to be rebooted to verify that the Microsoft Exchange Server services that were just installed have taken effect.

This completes the procedures for installing the first or only Microsoft Exchange Server in a single site.

Granting the Administrators Group Permissions for the Site

In order for the Microsoft Exchange Server to be administered, permissions have to be granted to the Administrators Group. The following steps provide a description of procedures for completing this task:

1. Choose the Microsoft Exchange Server Administrations program for the Microsoft Exchange Server Program Group.
2. Connect to the new Microsoft Exchange Server.
3. Select the File menu and choose Properties. Then, choose the Permissions tab. You will see the Permissions Property page (see fig. 9.8). A list of Microsoft Windows NT user accounts for this site appears.

FIG. 9.8
The Permissions page shows Microsoft Windows NT user accounts for this site.

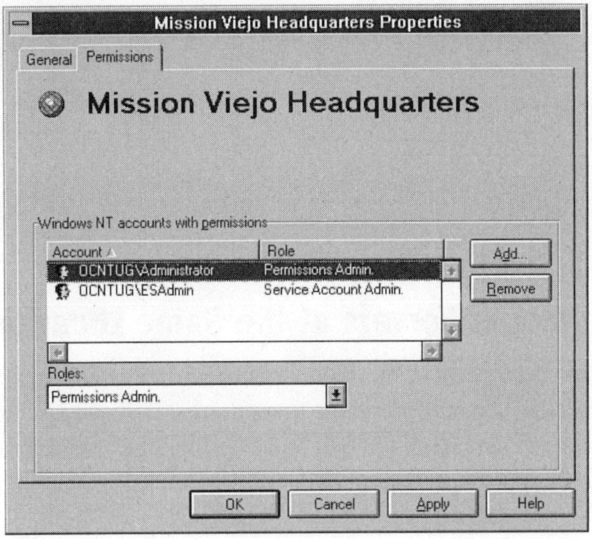

4. Select the Microsoft Windows NT Domain that you want.
5. Select the User(s) or group(s) that are to be added to the Administrators Group from the given list (see fig. 9.9). Alternatively, you can enter manually the User and Group names by typing the Domain Name followed by a backslash. Then, you can type the User account and Group names into the Add Name box, for example, **Domain1\User1**.
6. To continue to designate additional properties, choose Apply to activate the entered properties. Alternatively, you can return to the Administrators window by choosing OK to close the Permissions property sheet. Choosing OK applies the changes as well.

The Administrators Group has now been granted the correct permissions for accomplishing administrative needs.

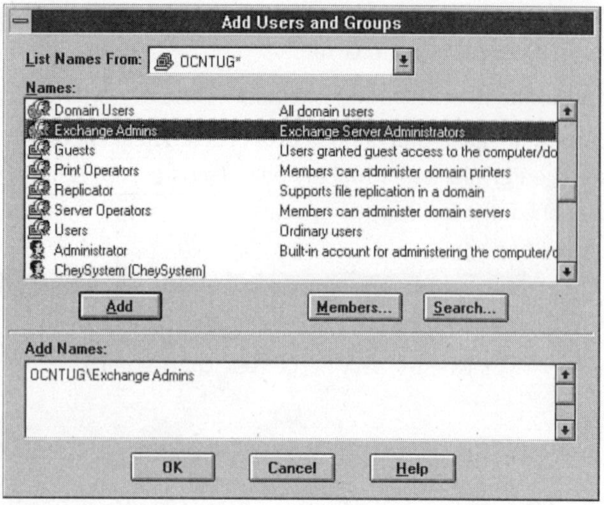

FIG. 9.9
You can choose users and groups that are to be added to the Administrators Group.

Setting Up Additional Servers at the Same Location

The procedures for setting up additional Microsoft Exchange Servers at the same site are similar to the steps taken to create the first or only Microsoft Exchange Server. The major difference between setting up the first and a second Microsoft Exchange Server occurs at step 10 of the directions pertaining to the creation of a new Microsoft Exchange Server site.

When step 10 is reached, and the Exchange Site dialog box appears, choose the Join An Existing Site selection (see fig. 9.10). Then, enter the name of an available Microsoft Exchange Server system. Choose OK. This new server will be added to the existing site. It will receive its configuration file from the existing Microsoft Exchange Server. You should continue through step 12 of the process to create a new Microsoft Exchange Server.

Adding Additional Microsoft Exchange Server Sites within an Organization

If the Organization that you are designing and creating has multiple Microsoft Exchange Server sites, you need to remember the following:

- You need one Microsoft Windows NT Server to have an initial Microsoft Exchange Server created and set up at the site. You must use the steps described earlier in this chapter.
- The existing site must have a Site Connector installed.
- Installation of a Site Connector at the new site is required.

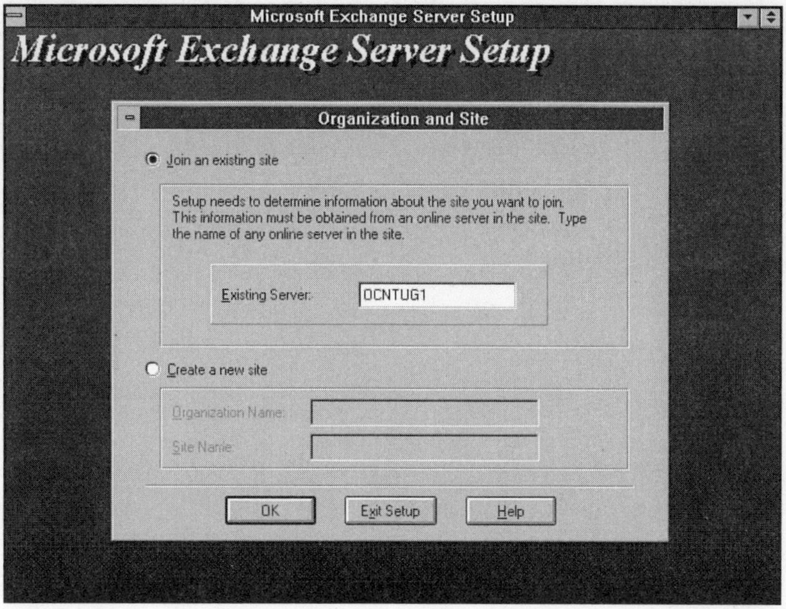

FIG. 9.10
Creating a new Exchange server to join an existing site.

From Here...

The initial installation of the Microsoft Exchange Server has now been completed. The following lists the different chapter references to help you further configure and enhance the performance of the Microsoft Exchange Server.

- Chapter 12, "Directory and System Attendant Configuration"
- Chapter 14, "Information Store Configuration"
- Chapter 16, "Site Connector and Dynamic RAS Connector"
- Chapter 17, "Using Directory Replication and Synchronization"

CHAPTER 10

Installing Exchange in a Netware Environment

- The History of Microsoft and Novell Product Integration
- Server Considerations
- Client Considerations
- Migration Considerations
- Organizational Concerns

There are many issues you must confront when installing Exchange in a Netware environment. They range in nature from technical considerations to organizational concerns.

The History of Microsoft and Novell

Many years before Microsoft created Windows NT, their network operating system platform was a product called Microsoft LAN Manager. Without getting into the details, it didn't sell very well, and Novell captured the networking market with its Netware product line.

As Novell set up shop on corporate Local Area Network (LAN) servers, Microsoft chose to go after the desktop operating system market. Microsoft introduced its Windows 3.0 product. It ran on top of DOS, but was a revolutionary advance in design and function from Microsoft's Windows 286 and Windows 386 environments. Its application software for Windows consisted of Word, Excel, PowerPoint, Mail, Schedule+, and Project. Microsoft also developed Dynamic Data Exchange (DDE) and Object Linking and Embedding (OLE) technology that tied its applications to one another and provided a robust desktop platform.

The two worlds remained separate. Developers of networking technologies continued to leverage Netware's popularity by designing Netware Loadable Modules (NLMs) to run on top of the Netware servers. Many corporations continued to make heavy investments in Netware because it provided the best, most extensible, cost effective networking solution on the market.

As a result of these two companies' abilities in different market segments, there were many Netware networks running with Windows Operating System and Windows applications on the desktop. In fact, several organizations even executed Windows from the Netware server. This enabled administrators to manage users' Windows profiles and Windows application software configurations from any workstation because all initialization files were kept on the server. Since Windows ran on top of DOS, all of the workstation network card and protocol drivers could be loaded in DOS, and a drive letter could be assigned to the Netware volume. Once the connectivity to the server was established, Windows and applications were loaded from the server.

In the past year or two, however, things have changed a bit. Microsoft introduced Windows NT as a network server solution, and Novell acquired WordPerfect and Borland's Quattro Pro spreadsheet. Novell then bundled these applications with its Groupwise e-mail and scheduling package to market a suite called PerfectOffice to compete with Microsoft Office. This was a 180 degree turn from the previous situation. Novell and Microsoft were trying to capture the piece of the business they did not have previously. However, the Novell applications were not accepted by a large number of companies, with the exception of WordPerfect. Novell took a lot a criticism for losing focus on Netware and for not providing adequate support for its core product. This encouraged people to start testing new networking platforms like Windows NT Server.

After those very turbulent years, however, Novell is out of the applications business; and Microsoft is moving further ahead with NT and the applications software that made it such a dominant player in the market.

The dominance of Microsoft Office applications and technologies like OLE are the reasons why Exchange will be successful in any environment, including those with Novell servers. The Exchange client components tie very closely with all the Microsoft products. Third-party companies write applications to the standard Application Programming Interfaces (APIs) that Microsoft incorporates into its products. The underlying networking technology and protocols should not sway you from implementing Exchange. Exchange's client-server model, integration with other Microsoft applications already use, and its open programming architecture will provide a solid foundation for your organization to build a global messaging architecture.

Exchange Installation Server Considerations

There are several things to consider on the server side when implementing Exchange. These consist of:

- Choosing a Network Protocol
- Migrating Users to the NT Servers
- Moving Existing Mail Data
- NT Server Expertise

Choosing a Network Protocol

The NT server that Exchange runs on can communicate over several protocols. The two real choices in the Netware environment are IPX and TCP/IP. NT supports both protocols out of the box, enabling your Netware clients to communicate seamlessly over the already existing network without modifying the client workstation protocols or adding new protocols to your routers.

This leads to an important point. You must have NetBIOS support enabled on all the NT Servers that will be acting as Exchange servers. The reason for this is that the clients will be looking for Exchange servers across the network based on their NetBIOS names. NetBIOS is not required on the workstations, but can be used if desired.

Migrating Users to NT Servers

Since most packages require that you create a separate account for mail, you already have systems in place for generating new accounts. In addition, users are already familiar with the interface; and you, the administrator, are already familiar with all the back-end utilities that go along with running the mail system. You already have backup procedures in place as well. All of this will have to change when you install Exchange. Although your clients will need minimal or no special configuration, the server side of things will be a bit different.

There are a few things you will have to keep in mind. One is that Exchange security is tied to NT domain security. This means that an NT domain login must be created for every account. This will provide the user with powerful permissions features that allow users to delegate certain responsibilities to other users. For example, if you wanted your secretary to be able to access your appointment book, you could do it. You are able to get very granular as to what permissions are assigned to certain users.

Given the above, the biggest job you will have is importing all the current users and data from your current e-mail system.

Although Microsoft provides a bindery migration utility, it will import only the Netware user names and group memberships. The problem with that is in most Netware environments, user names are based on a first initial, last name or first name, underscore, last name standard because spaces are not allowed in Netware user names.

However, in most e-mail environments, the user's full name is listed in the e-mail directory. If you import a bindery from a Netware server, then run the NT User List to Exchange migration utility you will wind up with a list of first initial, last name entries, rather than full names. This is unsatisfactory because you will have to go back and re-key all the user names.

You can overcome this shortcoming, however, by using one of the mail migration utilities that ship with Exchange or a third-party tool. For example, if you have Microsoft Mail post offices spread throughout your Netware network, you can run the Migration Utility and select MS-Mail, and that will create the Exchange users with full names while migrating data. As the Exchange users are created, you can have the utility create the NT user accounts for you, thus making the transition seamless.

Moving Existing Data

When changing from a Netware-based e-mail system to Exchange, moving data is made easier by the Microsoft and third-party data migration utilities. These utilities are:

Using Gateway Services for Netware This standard NT feature allows NT servers to mount Netware volumes. The purpose of this feature is to allow users on Microsoft NT networks to access volumes on a Novell server. The administrator of the NT server logs into the Novell server and mounts the disk as a logical drive. The NT server can then share this device with any NT server user. The same thing applies to printers on the network. You can associate a Netware print queue with an NT print queue and provide seamless access to authorized users on the NT server. While this may seem unconventional in a predominantly Netware environment, it does provide some very interesting functionality. This tool can prove very useful when using the Migration Wizard to move users from a Novell server-based e-mail package like MS-Mail.

If the post office exists on Novell file server NOVELL001, on volume SYS1:, you can mount it on the NT server as drive D:, and just perform your import seamlessly. This functionality is provided by NT Server out of the box. Think of the alternative; you would have to copy all the associated post office files to a workstation and then copy them to an NT server.

Exchange Installation Client Considerations

There are many different ways a client workstation can be configured in a Netware network. For workstations using DOS/Windows 3.1 or DOS/Windows for Workgroups, 16-bit real mode drivers are used to access the Exchange server over IPX or TCP/IP.

In an IPX configuration, the IPXODI driver provides all the needed connectivity to the Exchange server. Through the use of the NWLink protocol on the Exchange server, the IPX client can seek out the Exchange server on the network. Once a connection to the server is established by the Exchange client software, all communication is handled through RPC.

When installing the Exchange client software on a DOS, Windows 3.1, or Windows for Workgroups 3.11 machine, the installation program looks for a file called NETAPI.DLL. It then copies the appropriate RPC communication DLL based on the version of that file.

If you have TCP/IP running across your network already, and all the software is already installed on the workstation, you can have clients use TCP/IP to connect to the server. As long as the stack you use is Winsock compliant, the connection should be seamless.

For Windows 95 clients, using Microsoft's 32-bit IPX and TCP/IP drivers for your network card will provide robust connectivity. If you have these drivers already in place to access the Netware servers on your network, this same set of drivers will be used by the client to access the Exchange servers. One note is to make sure that if you are using the IPX protocol to communicate with Exchange, the Windows NT server will need to have the IPX protocol installed.

The client-server architecture of Exchange eliminates the need to actually mount any volumes of the server. The client communicates with the server via Remote Procedure Calls (RPCs) to provide seamless communication. For example, in the current cc:Mail and Microsoft Mail implementations, the user must provide a drive letter and path to the post office. That means they must be logged into the server and have the proper search paths and drive mappings established to communicate with the post office. With Exchange, all you have to do is configure the client to look for a certain server on the network. RPCs take care of the rest of the communications once the Exchange server is found on the network.

Exchange Migration Considerations

There are many sites that use Netware servers to house their shared file e-mail system. Users have different passwords for login and e-mail. The two systems are completely separate, with the exception of MHS-based systems like Novell's Groupwise, which ties into the bindery or NDS. For these organizations, there are real benefits to installing Exchange.

The movement away from the shared file system to client-server is a real boon to the administrators of those e-mail systems. Keeping database pointers in line, getting clean backups, and shutting down the system to make changes are all things these administrators have come to know all too well.

There are several tools at your disposal to bring Netware users into the Exchange environment. You can use the Migration Tool that ships with Exchange or you can use the Bindery Import Tool that comes with Windows NT Server. The two solutions yield different results that will be explained in the sections that follow. In addition, Gateway Services for Netware allows the NT server housing Exchange to access Netware volumes.

Using the Exchange Migration Tool

When you use this tool to give Netware users access to Exchange resources, that is all the Netware users will have. They are not given logons to the NT domain.

Think of your current LAN-based e-mail system, be it cc:Mail, MS-Mail, or POP. When you launch the client application on your PC or Macintosh, you are prompted for a login name and password, and the back end mail engine authenticates you. This same thing happens when you use the Migration Tool for Exchange.

Exchange can be thought of as an upgrade to your current mail system that will provide so much extra functionality. Microsoft has provided many tools that make Exchange an easy platform to implement regardless of your current server environment.

Although this system lacks the single logon benefit that comes along with running NT Server, it is still very manageable and very robust.

Coexistence of Netware and Windows NT Server

Rather than migrating your existing Netware server-based e-mail system to Exchange, you might consider coexistence. Through Exchange's wide variety of bundled connectors, you can make the most of new technology while keeping your current system up and running. Consider the following real-world example.

ABC's Information Services Department uses Netware servers on the backbone of the campus-wide network. The system has grown to over 5,000 users, all with Netware 3.12 accounts. They use MS-Mail as the messaging platform.

Recently, the MS-Mail infrastructure has been showing signs of weakness because of the load being put on all the servers. The message databases have grown to over 500 megabytes, with thousands of Internet e-mail messages going through two gateways, one for students, one for everyone else.

At the same time, the need to perform database maintenance was becoming prohibitive. If the utilities weren't run every night, the database would get corrupted, causing the entire system to be shut down during peak hours. In addition, data was being lost in the process. Also, the amount of storage needed to run the utilities was getting excessive, causing the need for the entire database to be moved to a separate server for the utilities to be effective. Needless to say, the system was breaking down.

This scenario lead ABC to explore the possibility of migrating the students over to Exchange because of its client-server platform. Rather than 3,000 students sharing one post office file on one Novell server, the company could move to the client-server model. However, they wanted to preserve their investment in Netware, but at the same time wanted to move to Exchange for messaging.

They set up an Exchange server for students to access mail, while still using the Netware server to load Windows 3.1 and house the Exchange client software. They used the Exchange Migration Tool to import the user data and accounts from the existing MS-Mail system so no data loss occurred.

They then called a Microsoft Solution Provider who installed the MS-Mail connector and set up the proper Directory Synchronization in the connector properties so that any new accounts created on the MS-Mail side would be reflected in the Exchange Global Address Book for the students. The Solution Provider gave ABC information on how to get hands-on Exchange training along with some basic Windows NT fundamentals.

Since IPX was the standard protocol loaded on the workstations, there were no workstation issues that needed to be addressed. The Exchange client software was loaded onto the Novell server, and a central program group was created and added to each user's PROGMAN.INI file using a batch file that ran upon login to the Novell server.

The users were then provided with an on-line tutorial using the company's internal World Wide Web pages. These pages helped ease the transition from MS-Mail to Exchange for the users.

By implementing this solution, the company minimized the expertise needed on the Windows NT side of the house by using the migration tools that came with Exchange. In addition, they continued to use their Novell server as a distribution medium as well as a file repository. The login script capabilities of Netware were utilized in rolling out the client software to the workstations.

The one issue ABC must deal with is creating new users on the Novell server. They used to have the MS-Mail user accounts automatically generated through the same script they used to create Netware accounts. They edited this script to create the proper Exchange account information.

Can this be done, and how so? This implementation of co-existing systems can work in many environments. In addition, once the word spreads among the user community about how good the e-mail system can be, you can leverage this demand when proposing a full migration as well as when deliberating the use of Exchange's more advanced groupware features.

Migrating from Netware to Windows NT Server

The introduction of Exchange by Microsoft may prompt the discussion of a complete migration from Netware to Windows NT Server. The reason for this is that for so many organizations, e-mail and group collaboration are the main reasons for having a network in the first place.

Combined with the introduction of Exchange are Windows 95 desktops and the forthcoming release of Windows NT Workstation 4.0. As these 32-bit platforms roll out onto the desktop, migrating file and print services to Windows NT Server may be a more strategic decision. You may already have Microsoft application software. When you combine that with Exchange, and then Windows NT Server and BackOffice, you have a completely integrated Microsoft networking solution.

You should consult a Microsoft Solution Provider for more information about moving your organization off Netware and onto Windows NT Server.

See the upcoming section on Microsoft Solution Providers.

The Role of Systems Integrators and Consultants

Many environments consist of nothing but Netware for file and print services. The organizations that operate in that environment choose Netware because it is very popular and there is a lot of third-party support for the platform. In addition, choosing one platform leverages all the staff training across the organization.

Trying to roll out Windows NT servers to implement Exchange might seem like an impossibility in these environments; however, there are several benefits to using Exchange that have been described throughout this book, and not putting this technology into place due to the lack of expertise in the organization may be shortsighted.

You can turn to the following channels to get Exchange rolled out in your environment:

- Intrapreneurs
- Newsgroups and Web Pages
- Microsoft Solution Providers
- Microsoft Consulting Services

Intrapreneurs

These are the people in the organization who experiment with different technologies on their own time. You know who they are. These people are the ones who can train the other system administrators on NT concepts and work with the management to support an Exchange roll out.

Newsgroups and Web Pages

There are several newsgroups on the Internet that are related to Windows NT and groupware. These are under the hierarchy of comp.os.ms-windows.nt.*. They include such topics as administration, networking, hardware, services, compatibility, and advocacy. These groups are a great resource for getting in touch with people who run NT-based networks.

In addition, there are Web pages solely dedicated to NT technologies that will definitely include Exchange. These sites include:

- **http://www.microsoft.com/**
- **http://www.lantug.org/**
- **http://www.bhs.com/**

Microsoft Solution Providers

There are many consultant agencies and systems integrators that are certified by Microsoft as Solution Providers. Just as the Novell environment has the Certified Netware Engineer (CNE) program, Solution Providers must pass tests and spend a certain number of hours using the platform to be certified by Microsoft.

You can count on these professionals to assist you in planning and implementing Exchange. Most are very familiar with Netware servers and clients because many Windows NT shops migrated from Netware with the help of Microsoft Solution Providers. Contact Microsoft to get a list of Solution Providers in your area.

Microsoft Consulting Services

For those organizations that will settle for nothing but the real article, Microsoft has a division to help you implement Microsoft technology solutions. These professionals provide the soup-to-nuts support with all the backing of Microsoft.

This group is a step up from the Solution Providers because they have access to all the resources of Microsoft including all the constant, up to date training, and experience with the product. This is especially important in the case of Exchange. Many companies have been eagerly awaiting the delivery of Exchange, and Microsoft Consulting Services has the benefit of having gone through the beta testing of the product and all the knowledge gained from that testing.

Organizational Considerations

In addition to the networking and technical considerations involved when installing Exchange in a Netware environment, some organizations will have to undergo serious change in their IS departments, especially in those shops running Netware servers and MS-Mail and Microsoft applications like Excel, Word, and PowerPoint.

These organizations have made such a large investment in Microsoft technologies, but the network server platform has always been Netware. There may be great opposition in the organization to move to Exchange because it means that Windows NT server must be rolled out into the entire enterprise just to upgrade MS-Mail. Some managers will be harboring resentment toward Microsoft for painting them into a corner.

Breaking the Netware Culture

Novell, now rededicated and refocused on expanding its core technology competencies in networking, is strongly marketing and supporting its Netware 4.1 platform with Netware Directory Services (NDS), a global directory service. This rededication has reassured many companies that their Netware investments are indeed safe.

Many Netware shops are starting to outgrow their LAN-based e-mail packages and are looking for more robust client-server solutions for e-mail and groupware. Exchange will function very well in Windows NT and Netware shops alike. Yes, the Exchange server must be an NT server; but as long as the connectivity is provided from the client to the server, there is no problem.

However, connectivity isn't the only problem. In many Netware-dominated shops, Windows NT is not a welcome solution. Since it isn't a Netware server, it takes no advantage of NDS trees already in place, although Microsoft is developing utilities that will allow Windows NT server to be managed as NDS objects.

In addition, users must be migrated to the Exchange server; and more important, staff has to be trained on NT Server because Exchange is so closely tied to the Microsoft operating system. This may be the biggest barrier to entry into Netware environments for Exchange. Many administrators might ask, "Why not use Groupwise for e-mail and groupware?"

Also, since the IBM acquisition of Lotus, Notes is being pushed very aggressively. Notes server can be run on a Novell server, thereby strengthening the resolve of some administrators to keep Windows NT out of their shops.

It is advisable to keep in mind that Exchange will be heavily tied into the operating systems you will run on the desktop, along with the applications being run on the desktop. In the future, the server platform used to file and print services will become less important. What will become increasingly important is the applications that can be run on top of the server operating system.

Exchange ties in very closely with the Windows 95 operating system, as well as the upcoming Windows NT Workstation 4.0 that is currently in beta as this book is being written. As your workstations change from DOS/Windows 3.1 to these newer 32-bit operating systems, Netware's dominance as the back end server will decline because these new Microsoft desktop operating systems make it very easy to participate in NT domains and use the resources within them.

Committing to an All-Microsoft Strategy

Many managers might be wary of committing to an all-Microsoft strategy. Not wanting to put all your eggs in one basket is a legitimate concern; however, you may want to consider the following points:

- Microsoft's Products are tightly integrated vie OLE and MAPI.
- There is tremendous third-party support for NT and Exchange.
- Microsoft's Solution Provider program does not lock you into Microsoft for support.
- Microsoft solutions are competitively priced.

These points address many of the concerns of information technology managers. These concerns stem from the experience of IBM dominance of the mainframe market in the early days of mainframe computing. The solutions were very proprietary, very expensive, and hard to learn. The one thing to remember was that they worked. As long as you stuck with an all-IBM solution, you felt comfortable because everything worked together, and IBM engineers were familiar with the equipment.

Microsoft's product line of today has some of the same characteristics. It is well integrated, and there are many well-trained engineers who know the software.

However, unlike the old IBM, Microsoft has built an open architecture using the MAPI and OLE standards combined with the Win32 SDK to enable third-party vendors to extend the capabilities of the core products.

In addition, there are several channels of support which were outlined above that should allay the concerns of managers. You can feel secure that although you're committing to Microsoft products, you are not dependent on Microsoft for support and extensibility.

From Here...

As you can see, there are many issues you'll have to consider when installing Exchange in a Netware environment. Some obstacles you'll face are technical, some are organizational; but you'll find the robustness of Exchange will be a vast improvement over your existing file-sharing e-mail system.

The areas of concern are as follows:

- Networking Protocol
- User accounts and data migration
- Coexistence or Migration of Netware
- Back end administrator training

With the help of trained professionals, you will be able to work out all these issues and come up with an installation that makes the most sense for your organization. This chapter was intended to provide a starting point for any organization using Netware, to point out the relevant questions.

The following chapters contain more information on topics talked about in this chapter:

- See Chapter 4, "Integrating with a Windows NT Server," to get a more in-depth picture of what goes into creating Windows NT networks.
- Chapter 6, "Planning Connections to Microsoft Mail Systems," will give you the information you need to have an MS-Mail and Exchange system co-exist.
- Chapter 7, "Migrating to Microsoft Mail Systems," will provide the necessary steps to move users and data from an MS-Mail system to an Exchange server.
- Chapter 8, "Planning and Migrating to External Systems," will round out the discussion of how to move data from other kinds of mail systems.

PART III

Exchange Administration and Configuration

CHAPTER 11

Using the Administrator Program

- How to use the main program windows efficiently
- How to use the object types displayed by the Administrator program
- How to use the Administrator program's menus

The Administrator program will become your familiar friend as you work with Exchange. From this program, you can manage an entire Exchange organization. Because Administrator is so versatile, it is also rather ominous-looking at first sight. The dozens of functions that are provided in menus and check boxes tend to be somewhat confusing initially. The primary goal of this chapter is to familiarize you with this application and assist you in navigating it comfortably. Administrator is the most useful tool for Exchange administrators, so learning its tricks now will alleviate many headaches for you in the future. ■

Starting the Administrator Program and Connecting to an Exchange Server

The first step is launching the Microsoft Exchange Administrator application from within Program Manager in Windows NT; simply double-click the application icon. If you have not yet configured a default server, the Connect to Server dialog box appears (see fig. 11.1).

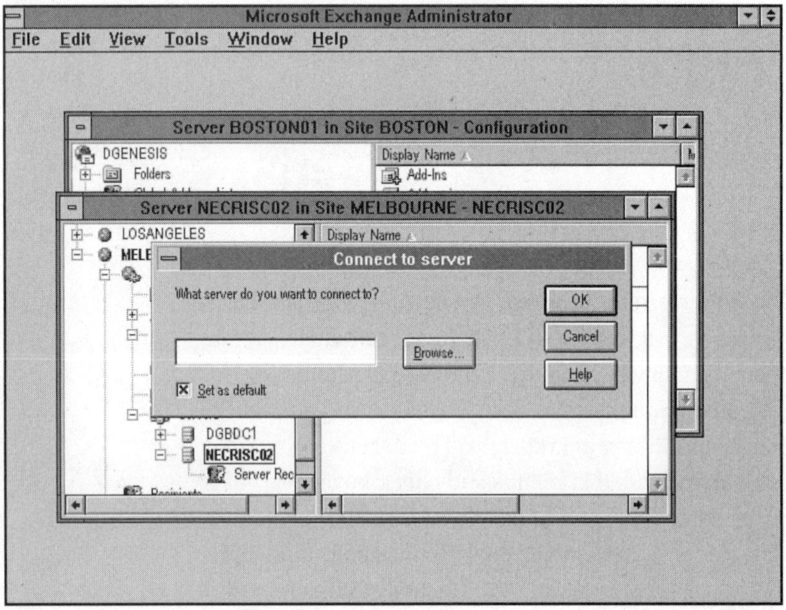

FIG. 11.1
Select your target Exchange server; then click OK.

This dialog box appears repeatedly when you work with Exchange, so you should be familiar with it. The dialog box asks you what server you want to connect to. In the text box, type the name of the server to which you want the administrator program. You must type the server name accurately.

NOTE You must have administrator privileges on the server to which you are trying to connect; otherwise, you will be denied access.

If you click the Browse button, you can view a graphical representation of the Exchange servers within your organization. From this window, you can choose the Exchange server you would like to administer.

The Set As Default check box allows you to designate the selected server as the default connection. The next time you launch the administrator program, you will not be prompted to choose a server; the default Exchange server's window appears. This check box is unavailable until you make an entry in the text box.

Click OK when you finish making your selections. The administrator program attempts to connect to the server. If you typed the name of an Exchange server that does not exist, or if the selected server or its connection is down for any reason, you get an error message and the option to attempt a different connection.

If you have already configured a default server, the connection is made, and you see the Administrator interface, which is covered in the following section.

The Administrator Interface

You can use the Exchange Administrator to view your entire Exchange organization (see fig. 11.2). Like a satellite view of the earth from space, this window presents the big picture of your Exchange hierarchy. You have the option to zoom as close as you want to view any object.

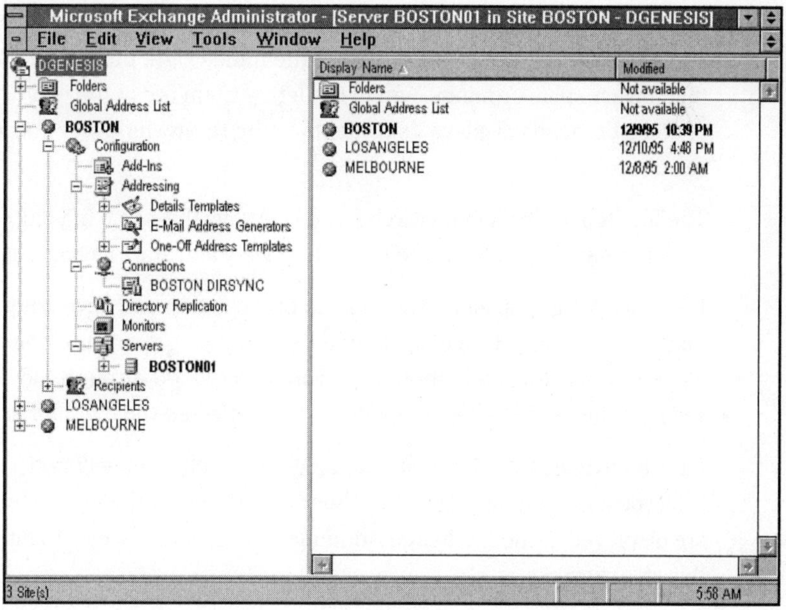

FIG. 11.2 The main Administrator window.

The left side of the window shows your Exchange hierarchy, displaying all the objects in your Exchange organization. The right side of the window displays the contents of the container object that is selected on the left side of the window.

The title bar of the window displays the server name, the site name, and name of the object that is currently selected, in the following format:

Server *name* in Site *name*—Object *name*

Take some time to explore the Exchange hierarchy on the left side of the window, to get a feel for how the elements are organized.

Navigating the Hierarchy Tree

The Exchange site hierarchy window displays all of the components that make up your Exchange site in a treelike fashion. This includes recipients, servers, connectors, and any other Exchange component that you have installed. Navigating this window is much like navigating the directory hierarchy in File Manager or the Windows 95 explorer. Many of the elements or objects in Exchange's hierarchy have multiple levels below them.

A plus sign (+) to the left of an object indicates that the object has branches below it. Click the plus sign to display these branches. After you display the branches, the plus sign turns into a minus sign (–). When you click the minus sign, the branches disappear. Branches that have no plus or minus sign to the left of them are at the end of the tree. Clicking one of these branches displays its contents in the right window of the administrator program, see figure 11.3.

The top item of the site hierarchy tree is always the name of your organization. Double-click the name to collapse the entire tree view and start navigating from the top.

If you are setting up an new Exchange organization and have not yet established connections, you see only a small portion of local Exchange server elements in this default view. As new connectors and other objects are created, go through the administrator window to see how these additional components have affected the overall Exchange hierarchy.

As you navigate the Microsoft Exchange hierarchy, you will notice that every object has an associated graphic icon. The following text shows the hierarchy tree and objects that are displayed in the Exchange Administrator program (refer to fig. 11.3 for an example of this structure):

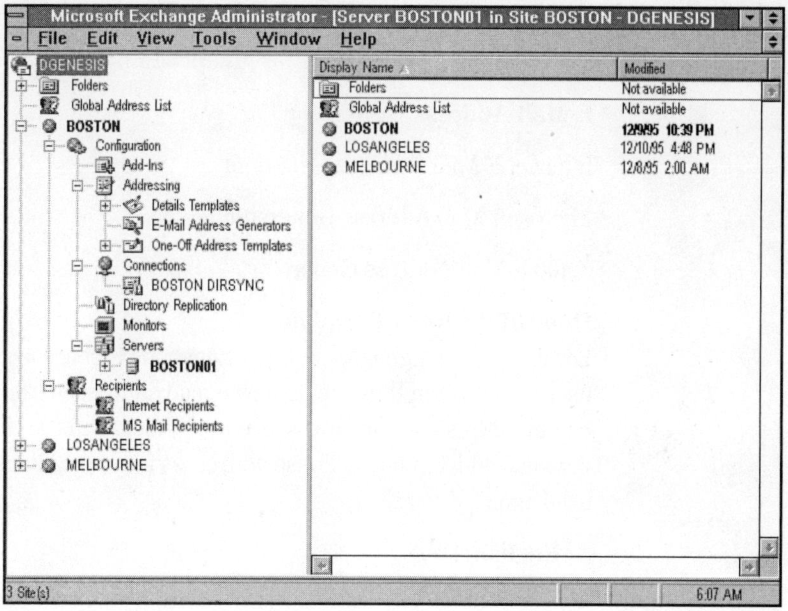

FIG. 11.3
Object hierarchy tree.

Organization
The top of the Exchange server hierarchy

Folders

Global Address List
Lists the all recipients that are contained within your Exchange organization

Site
The name of a Microsoft Exchange Server computer's messaging site

Configuration
Contains optional configuration

Add-Ins

Extension for Internet Mail Connector

Extension for MS Mail Connector

Extension for Schedule+ Free/Busy Gateway

Addressing

Details Templates
Localized (by language/country) templates that define the details that are displayed on recipient objects

English/USA
The default details template for American English

E-Mail Address Generator

Internet E-Mail Address Generator

Microsoft Mail Address Generator

X.400 E-Mail Address Generator

One-Off Address Templates
Localized (by language/country) templates that are used to determine what users input when they create new e-mail addresses from their Exchange Client for addressing mail messages to mailboxes not in the GAL or in the users' personal address book. These addresses are typically used once and then not used again.

English/USA
The default one-off address templates for American English

Connections
Contains all connectors that are used to link Exchange sites with other Exchange sites, with other MS Mail environments, or with other foreign e-mail systems.

Internet Mail Connector
Permits message exchange with Simple Mail Transport Protocol (SMTP) based e-mail systems

MS Mail Connector
Permits message exchange with Microsoft Mail for PC and AppleTalk networks

Site Connector
Creates a messaging bridge between two Microsoft Exchange sites on the same logical LAN

X.400 Connector
Creates a messaging bridge between two Microsoft Exchange sites over an X.400 network or to a foreign X.400 system

Dynamic RAS Connector
Creates a messaging bridge between two Microsoft Exchange sites over a Windows NT Remote Access link

Directory Exchange Requestor
Sets up a Microsoft Exchange server to request directory information from MS Mail or other systems

Directory Exchange Server
Sets up a Microsoft Exchange server to perform as a directory-synchronization server for external mail systems

Remote Dirsync Requestor
A representation of an external mail system's directory-synchronization requestor that connects to the Directory Exchange Server

Directory Replication
Contains all directory replication connectors for this site

Directory Replication Connector
An object that establishes recipient information sharing between sites

Monitors
Contains monitoring tools created to watch over an Exchange organization's servers and the links among them

Server Monitor
Watches the status of a Microsoft Exchange Server's services and provides warnings or alerts if errors occur

Link Monitor
Watches the status of messaging connections between Exchange servers

Servers
Contain a list of the Exchange servers in this site and each of their core components

Server Recipients
Contains all the recipients that call this server home

Directory Service
Controls directory handling within a site

Directory Synchronization
Also called Exchange DXA, this object controls general properties for Microsoft Exchange directory synchronization

Message Transfer Agent (MTA)
Transports messages from one server to another or to external connectors

MTA Transport Stack (RAS, TCP, and so on)
An underlying transport mechanism for use by other Microsoft Exchange connectors

Private Information Store
Stores all messaging data sent to individual mailboxes

Public Information Store
Stores all messaging data posted to public folders

System Attendant
A core Microsoft Exchange service that manages log files and that is required to start other Exchange services

DS Site Configuration
Holds general properties for directory services in an Exchange site.

Information Store Site Configuration
Holds general properties for all the Information Stores in a site

MTA Site Configuration
Holds general properties for all the MTAs in a site

Site Addressing
Holds general site-addressing data used in message routing

Recipients
Contains a list of recipients for this Exchange site

Mailbox
A private receptacle for messaging data

Distribution Lists
A group of individual recipients that can be addressed as a single recipient or e-mail address. This is similar in function to a listserver.

Custom Recipients
Foreign recipients whose mailboxes do not reside on a Microsoft Exchange server

Public Folder
A receptacle where information that is stored can be shared among many users

Microsoft Schedule + Free/Busy Connector
A connector that receives Free/Busy scheduling information from Schedule+ for MS Mail

Menu Overview

The Exchange Administrator program menus are:

- *File.* Enables you to connect to other servers, create new connections and objects, and modify and view object properties.
- *Edit.* Enables you to execute standard Windows functions: cut, copy, paste, delete, and so on.
- *View.* Enables you to choose the type of information displayed in the administrator window and how it is sorted; also allows you to set the aesthetic properties of the display (font, sizes, and columns).
- *Tools.* Enables you to perform various administrative tasks, such as tracking messages and importing Windows NT user lists.
- *Window.* Enables you to perform standard Windows appearance and arrangement functions, such as tiling, cascading, and switching between open windows.
- *Help.* Opens the Exchange online help system and provides Exchange version information.

Exchange Administrator Menus

The following sections describe the Exchange Administrator menus in detail.

File Menu

You will use the Administrator program's File menu (see fig. 11.4) to create the components that comprise an Exchange organization or site.

NOTE If you have two or more Exchange Server connections open at the same time, make sure that the correct window is in the foreground when you create components.

Connect to Server This menu item allows you to administrate a Microsoft Exchange server remotely, as though you were logged into it directly. Although the Administrator program allows you to view all the objects in your organization hierarchy, you cannot alter site connections, mailboxes, connectors, or site servers unless you are directly connected to a server in that remote site with the administrator program.

NOTE You must have administrative access on the remote site to perform remote administrator functions.

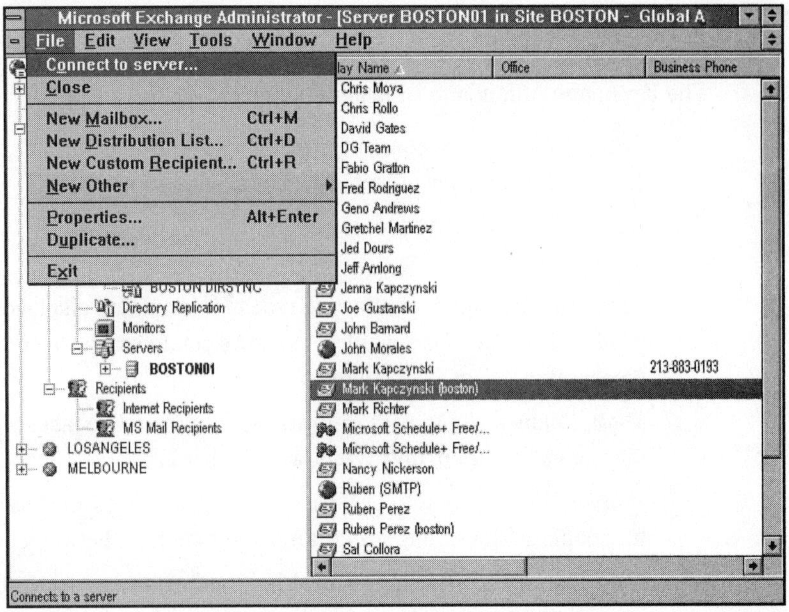

FIG. 11.4
The Administrator program's File menu.

Close This menu item closes the active server connection window that you are using.

New Mailbox This menu item creates a new user mailbox. You must select a recipient container; otherwise, you are prompted to use the standard Exchange recipient container for that site.

New Distribution List This menu item creates a new distribution-list recipient. (You must select a recipient container first.) You must then configure the properties for the distribution list.

New Custom Recipient This menu item creates a recipient in a foreign mail system (MS Mail, SMTP, X.400, or the connected gateway).

New Other This menu item displays the submenu shown in figure 11.5, which allows you to create other types of Microsoft Exchange objects.

The items in this submenu are:

- *Server Monitor.* Creates a process that watches the operational condition of one or more servers in a site; can be configured to generate alerts when certain conditions (such as a stopped system service) occur.
- *Link Monitor.* Creates a process that monitors the state of messaging connections between Exchange sites and servers; the link monitors are configured to create alerts when errors occur.

- *Recipients Container.* Creates custom containers for certain object types. A good example is creating a specific Internet recipient's container that holds all custom recipients that have SMTP addresses.
- *MTA Transport Stack.* Defines underlying transport protocol for each X.400 or Dynamic RAS connector you create. Make sure that you have all necessary transport software set up properly in Windows NT (e.g., X.25 protocol); otherwise, you cannot proceed beyond this configuration point.
- *X.400 Connector.* Defines an X.400 connection to another Exchange site or foreign system. Before you select this item, you must define an MTA transport stack over which this connector is to communicate.
- *Dynamic RAS Connector.* Set up a part-time remote access link between servers. You can set up an RAS connection over modem, ISDN, or X.25 systems if you have the appropriate MTA transport stack installed.
- *Site Connector.* Sets up a connection between two Microsoft Exchange Server sites—typically, on the same logical LAN.
- *Directory Replication Connector.* Creates a directory-sharing relationship between two Microsoft Exchange sites.
- *Dirsync Requestor.* Configures a directory-synchronization requestor that is compatible with any messaging system that supports the Microsoft Mail 3.X directory-synchronization protocol. The Dirsync Requestor is most commonly used to request directory updates from a Microsoft Mail post office that is set up as a directory-synchronization server.
- *Dirsync Server.* Configures a directory-synchronization server that is compatible with any messaging system that supports the Microsoft Mail 3.X directory-synchronization protocol.
- *Remote Dirsync Requestor.* The remote Dirsync Requestor allows a foreign system's dirsync requestor to connect to a Microsoft Exchange dirsync server.
- *Information Store.* Creates a public or private information store for an Exchange server. You can use this option only if a certain server does not currently have an information store of its own or if it has been deleted.

Properties This menu item enables you to view and edit settings for particular Exchange objects or containers. Double-clicking on the individual objects brings up the properties as well.

Duplicate This menu item creates a new recipient object with properties exactly like an existing one. Selecting a distribution list and clicking Duplicate, for example, brings up a new distribution list with a blank name but with all the members of the original list. This option is the same as using copy and paste functionality in other windows-based applications. This option is not available if you have not highlighted or selected a recipient.

Exit This menu item closes all connections to Microsoft Exchange Servers and exits the Administrator program.

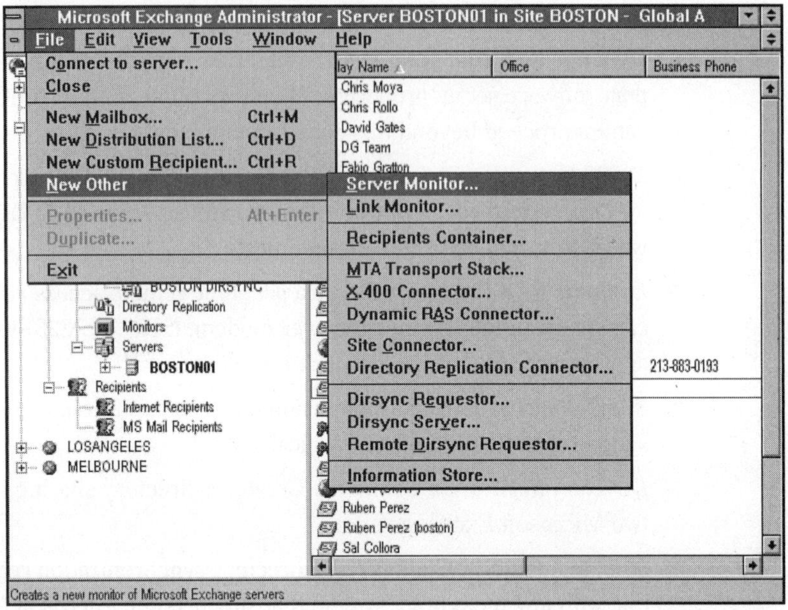

FIG. 11.5
The File–New Other submenu allows you to create many Exchange objects.

Edit Menu

The Exchange Administrator's Edit menu allows you to perform all the standard Windows Edit-menu functions.

Undo This command works only with property text operations (cut, paste, and delete). Because you cannot access the Edit menu while a property page is open, this menu item is just about useless. Press Ctrl+Z instead to undo text commands.

Cut, Copy, and Paste These menu items function as normal windows-based commands for use with text entries. They perform the same functions as in Microsoft Word.

Delete This menu item removes unwanted text entries or directory objects.

CAUTION

Delete operations on directory objects cannot be undone. The only way to recover a deleted object is to restore from some sort of backup.

Select All This command allows you to select an entire group of Microsoft Exchange objects in the Administrator program.

View Menu

The View menu (see fig. 11.6) is designed to filter or sort what information the Exchange Administrator program displays. Mainly, you can choose how to view recipients, thereby making a large Global Address List a more manageable beast.

FIG. 11.6
The View menu filters and sorts objects displayed in the Administrator window.

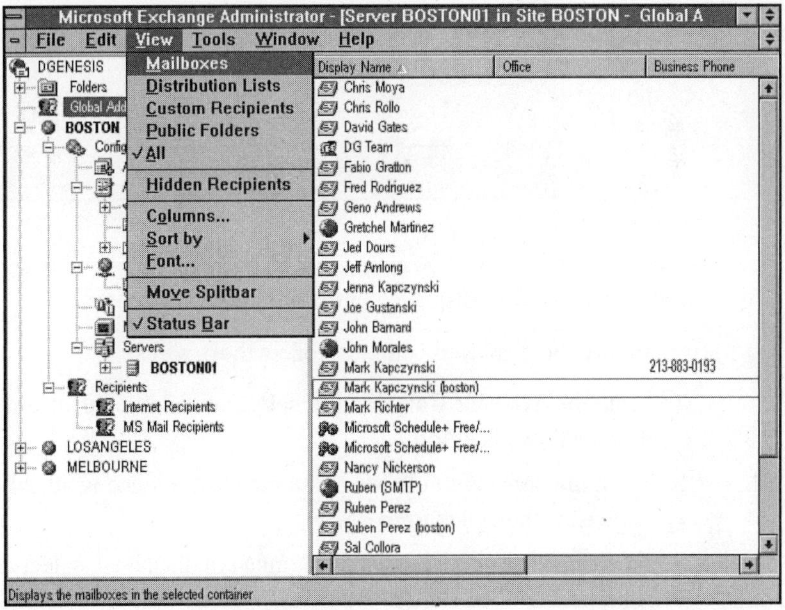

Mailboxes, Distribution Lists, Custom Recipients, Public Folders, and All These menu items all filter the view for the list of Exchange recipients. A check mark appears next to the menu item that you are currently viewing. To view only a particular subset of the recipients, select an option other than the "all" option.

Hidden Recipients This menu item is a filter that adds hidden recipients to any of the preceding viewing filters. Hidden recipients are recipients not seen in the GAL.

Columns This menu item changes the columns of information that appear in the Administrator program's user interface. This item is available only while you are viewing a recipient container. After you click on the Columns button, the dialog box shown in figure 11.7 will appear.

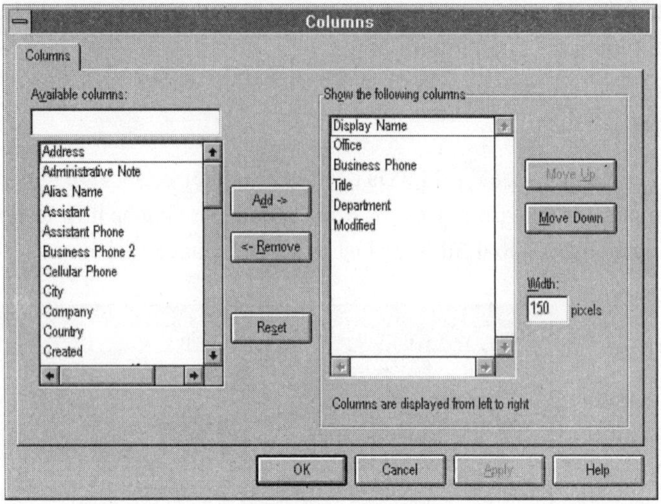

FIG. 11.7
The Columns dialog box allows you to specify what object attributes are displayed.

The left side of the dialog box shows all Exchange recipient attributes. The right column shows which ones are displayed in the administrator program.

To configure the displayed columns, follow these steps:

1. From the Available Columns list, select any additional attributes that you want to display; then click Add.
2. From the Show the Following Columns list, select any attribute that you do not want to display; then click Remove.
3. To change the order in which columns are displayed, select an attribute from the right list and then click Move Up or Move Down.

NOTE Columns are displayed from left to right, even though you set their order from top to bottom.

TIP A better way to set column widths is to use your mouse. In the Administrator program's user interface, drag the mouse pointer over the dividing lines between each attribute column. When the pointer changes to a double-headed arrow, click and drag that column to the desired width.

4. To change the width of a particular column, select its attribute and edit the number of pixels it takes up on the Administrator program user interface window.
5. Click Apply to view your changes immediately on the background window.
6. Click OK to finalize your changes.

Sort By This menu item enables you to organize what you see in the Administrator program user interface. You can sort any Microsoft Exchange object, including recipients.

When you choose this menu item, a sub-menu appears, with two options:

- Sort by Display Name places the objects in alphabetical order by display name.
- Sort by Last Modified Date places the objects in order of the dates (and times) when they were last modified.

Microsoft Exchange remembers every view setting for each object list in the Administrator program user interface. At the same time, you can choose to view your global address list sorted by display name and your connection sorted by date last modified, and you can have your local address list filtered to show only public folders.

Font This menu item will open a Font dialog box that displays your currently installed system fonts. Select a font and then click OK to return to the Administrator program.

Move Splitbar This menu item selects the dividing line between the Exchange site hierarchy and the objects corresponding to the hierarchy in the Administrator program. You can now adjust the window's partition. Use the mouse to drag the line to the desired position; then click to set the line.

TIP Another way to redivide the administrator program user interface is to drag your mouse over the line, then click and drag it to the desired position.

Status Bar This menu item turns the status bar on and off. The status bar displays useful help messages and shows the number of objects in the selected container.

Tools Menu

The Tools menu provides access to various administrative utilities.

Directory Import The Directory Import option allows you to read comma-delimited files and use them to create or modify recipients. These files may contain MS Mail recipients, Exchange recipients, or some other foreign e-mail system recipients. The files will need to be created either by using the Exchange migration tools or by using Directory export tools in the respective e-mail systems. The files contain recipient name and e-mail address information to be used in Microsoft Exchange.

Directory Import Features:

The following is a list of the features you can perform using the Exchange directory import function.

- Import Directory information from another e-mail system or import.
- Add or change personal information for existing mailboxes and other recipients.
- Add members (in bulk) to distribution lists.

Microsoft Exchange includes some useful migration tools that provide similar functionality and are simpler to use. See Chapters 7 and 8 for more information on migrating from other mail systems and use of the migration tools.

Directory Export This menu option creates text files of Microsoft Exchange directory information that can be imported into other messaging systems.

Extract Windows NT Account List This menu item selectively copies data from the Windows NT account list of a trusted domain. Files are stored in the CSV file format, which you can use with the Directory Import command to add and create Exchange recipients.

Extract NetWare Account List This menu item selectively copies user data from a Novell Netware account list. Files are stored in the CSV file format, which you can then use to import into Exchange to create Exchange recipients and Windows NT user accounts.

Find Recipients This menu item allows you to search for recipients anywhere in your organization, based on a variety of criteria. When you choose Find Recipients, the dialog box shown in figure 11.8 appears.

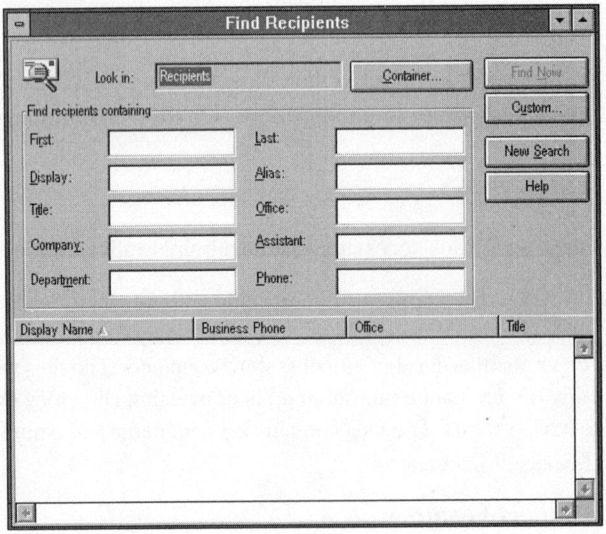

FIG. 11.8
The Find Recipients dialog box allows you to search for a recipient by any attribute.

The top half of this dialog box allows you to specify search criteria; the bottom half displays the result of your searches.

To search for recipients, follow these steps:

1. The Look In box displays the recipient container in which a search will be executed. Click the Container button to display a global list of Exchange recipient containers in your organization; select one and then click OK.

   By default, the Look In box shows the primary recipients container of the server you are connected to.
2. In the Find Recipients Containing section, enter any distinguishing search criteria for the recipient.
3. To search by custom attributes, click Custom, a dialog box opens up, and you can enter your search parameters; then click OK to return to the Find Recipients dialog box.
4. Click Find Now when you finish entering search parameters. All matches of your search criteria are displayed at the bottom of the Find Recipients dialog box.
5. Double-click any listed recipient to view its Exchange properties.
6. Click New Search to clear all search parameters.
7. Click Cancel to close the dialog box to return to the Administrator program.

Move Mailbox This menu item transfers a selected recipient to a different server within the same Microsoft Exchange site. When you choose Move Mailbox, the dialog box shown in figure 11.9 appears.

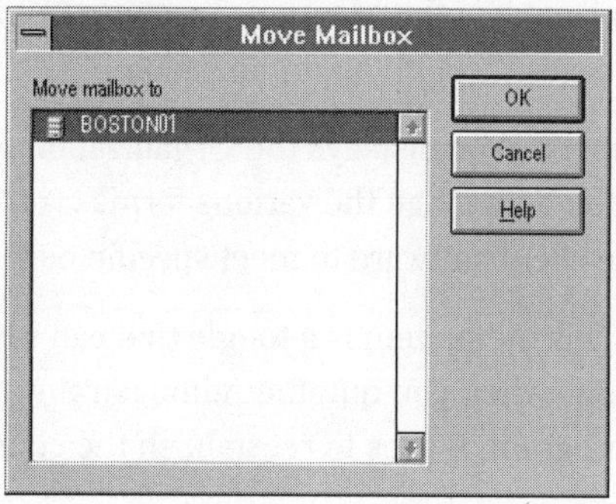

FIG. 11.9
Transfer a mailbox to another server in the site.

Select the Exchange server to which you want to move this recipient, and click OK. The mailbox is transferred to the new server's private information store.

NOTE This menu is unavailable unless you select a recipient from the recipient's container in the Exchange site hierarchy.

Clean Mailbox This menu item deletes messages in a particular user's mailbox, based on several criteria. This command can be useful when an unreasonable number of messages have piled up in a specific mailbox.

Select the criteria that you want to use to delete messages in this mailbox. A message must meet all the selected criteria to be deleted. The criteria are:

- *Age.* All mail older (in days) than the number in the All Messages Older Than (Days) will be deleted. All mail greater in size (in kilobytes) than the number in the All Messages Greater Than (K) box will be deleted.
- *Sensitivity.* All messages have a sensitivity attribute. You can select up to four sensitivity levels. All messages that have the selected sensitivity levels will be deleted.
- *Read Items.* This option is the read or unread status of the messages. You must select the status of messages to be deleted: read, unread, or both.
- *Delete Items Immediately.* This item permanently removes messages from the mailbox.
- *Move Items to the Deleted Items Folder.* This item places the selected messages in that user's Deleted Items folder in the Exchange Client.

Start Monitor This menu item starts the selected server monitor or link monitor. This option is unavailable if a monitor is not selected.

Track Message This option launches the Message Tracking Center, which is a tool for following the delivery of messages through an organization.

Forms Administrator This menu item displays the Organization Forms Library Administrator, which allows you to manage the various forms created using the forms designer tool in the Exchange client software to meet specific messaging needs.

Save Connections on Exit This menu item is a toggle that can save information about your current server connections when you quit the Administrator program. The next time you open the Administrator program, it tries to reestablish the connections to those servers.

Save Connections Now The moment that you select this option, Exchange saves current Exchange Server connections. The next time you open the Administrator program, it tries to reestablish the connections to those servers.

Options This menu item displays two property pages that allow you to set options for Exchange mailboxes and other recipients. The property pages are:

- *Auto Naming.* Allows you to define a method for Display Name Generation and Alias Name Generation.
- *Permissions.* Allows you to set a default Windows NT domain where new mailbox accounts are to be created in addition to other object related permissions.

To set Auto Naming options, follow these steps:

1. Click the Auto Naming tab in the Options dialog box (see fig. 11.10).

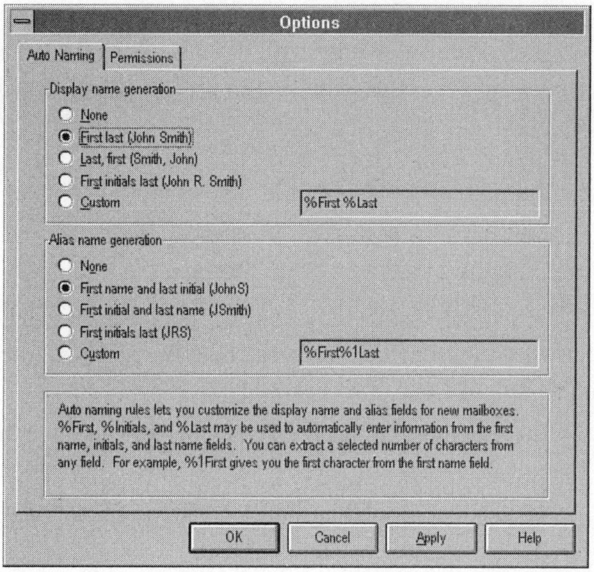

FIG. 11.10
The Auto Naming tab helps you generate mailbox display names.

2. The Display Name Generation section allows you to define how the Administrator program generates display names when the e-mail system administrator is typing or importing new Exchange mailboxes. Choose None to always enter display names manually. Choose Custom to create a specialized entry type or template.
3. The Alias Name Generation section allows you to define how the Administrator program generates alias names when the e-mail system administrator is typing or importing new Exchange mailboxes. Choose None to always enter alias names manually. Choose Custom to create a specialized entry type.
4. Click Apply to set these properties and continue with the other properties.
5. When you finish making settings, click OK to return to the Administrator program.

To set Permissions options, follow these steps:

1. Click the Permissions tab in the Options dialog box.
2. Select the default Windows NT domain for all new mailboxes from the pull-down menu.
3. Choose Show Permissions Page for All Objects if you want the permissions to be displayed in all the property pages of the objects that have them. By default, this box is not checked, and the permissions pages are hidden.
4. Choose Display Rights for Roles on Permissions Page to display the list of rights on the permissions page. *Roles* are sets of rights that define what type of access, and how much, a user or group has.
5. Choose Delete Primary Windows NT Account When Deleting Mailbox to delete the associated Windows NT account along with a mailbox. This box is not checked by default.

CAUTION

Proceed with caution; a deleted Windows NT user can no longer log into the domain for any reason.

6. Choose Try to Find Matching Windows NT Account When Creating Mailbox to have the Administrator program search the Windows NT user list to find the matching account name. This box is checked by default.
7. Click Apply to set these properties and continue with the other properties on the permissions tab.
8. When you finish making settings, click OK to return to the Administrator program.

Window Menu

This menu a standard Windows menu. You can create a new display window for a particular server. Cascade, Tile Horizontally or Vertically, and Arrange Icons function as normal. Refresh requests and update to all window information from the server.

Help Menu

This menu is a standard Windows help menu. The menu contains three standard options:

- *Microsoft Exchange Server Help Topics.* This option allows you to view standard help information on all Exchange interface settings.
- *Books Online.* This option allows you to read the official Microsoft Exchange Server documentation, with searchable indexes and tables of contents, online.

- *About Microsoft Exchange Server.* This option displays version and copyright information.

From Here...

See the following chapters for more information on topics related to the Exchange Administrator program.

- Chapter 12, "Directory and System Attendant Configuration," for managing core Exchange server components.
- Chapter 13, "Message Transfer Configuration," for managing the flow of messages between sites.
- Chapter 15, "Creating and Configuring Recipients," to build the global address list with all types of recipients.
- Chapter 17, "Using Directory Replication and Synchronization," to manage the directory synchronization process.

CHAPTER 12

Directory and System Attendant Configuration

With this section, we begin covering the details for configuring your Exchange server components. First, we will cover the step to set up each Exchange site down to the server level. This will teach you to set site configuration properties as well as general settings for the core components of each Microsoft Exchange server. Subsequent chapters cover configuring additional components and using elements together to develop a complete Exchange organization.

In this chapter, you will learn the step-by-step process of configuring the core component properties.

- **Directory Service Site Configuration**

  Lets you set preferences on Exchange site directions functions

- **Site Addressing**

  Lets you configure site properties that deal with reentry messages to their intended destination

- **Server Configuration**

  Lets you configure general functions

- **Directory Service**

  Lets you configure diagnostics information

- **Directory Synchronization**

  Allows service between exchange and MS Mail and other compatible foreign systems

- **System Attendant**

  Allows other Exchange system servers to run

Configuring Directory Services

Directory Site site configuration allows you to set preferences on Exchange site directory functions. Settings made to this object's properties affect an entire Microsoft Exchange site.

In this section you learn about the following:

- Set tombstone lifetimes
- Set garbage collection intervals
- Generate and schedule the creation of offline address books
- Define the custom attribute for all recipients within an Exchange site

First, let us define some concepts essential to proper configuration of the Directory Service agent.

Tombstone Lifetime

A "tombstone" in Exchange directory terms is a marker representing a deleted directory object. At the moment when you delete a directory object, it is removed instantly from the local server only. All the other Exchange servers that participate in directory replication with this server do not become immediately aware of that object's deletion. Therefore, a "tombstone" marker is created that when replicated to other servers informs them of the original object's deletion. The tombstone lifetime dictates the number of days a tombstone marker exists before it expires and can be deleted from the system.

Here are some considerations for setting tombstone lifetimes:

Situation 1—Frequency of directory object deletion. If you set the tombstone lifetime for an excessively long period of time and you frequently delete objects, there will be a large number of tombstone markers clogging your entire directory replication system.

Situation 2—Length of time a server could be down. For example, you set the tombstone lifetime for a site at seven days. Let's say one server in your site is down for over a week. That server that was down will not be notified of an object's deletion before the tombstone of some directory object is deleted. There will be some directory inconsistencies to correct.

NOTE Tombstones cannot be used to un-delete a previously deleted directory object.

Garbage Collection Interval

The garbage collection interval determines the number of hours between deletion of expired tombstone markers (referred to as garbage). Much like a traditional garbage collection service, this operation is a scheduled removal of expired directory "garbage." Once directory object tombstone markers have expired they are ready ("placed on the curb") for deletion at the garbage collection interval.

Offline Address Book

Remote users can take advantage of Exchange address lists by downloading a current version of the offline address book. This address list is generated from the main address list and the process is managed through these property pages. A remote user uses the offline address book like a standard recipient directory when disconnected from the network. The offline address book contains only the recipients or recipient groups specified by the Exchange administrator. The offline address book object itself is a hidden public folder held in the public information store of a designated Exchange server. There can be only one offline address book per site.

Custom Attributes

Custom attributes pertain specifically to recipients. They are added to represent any extra information you want to have entered when creating recipients. Where standard attributes are *city, state, zip, phone number* a custom attribute can be anything from birthday, age, or hair color, to favorite music or bowling average.

Configuring DS Site Property Pages

In this section, you begin to configure the DS Site property pages. You will find that a wide variety of settings affect how directory functions are carried out it you Exchange site.

The General Page

Figure 12.1 shows the General property page and the various directory settings associated with it.

1. Select the General tab of the DS Site configuration property pages. The General property page appears.

FIG. 12.1
General directory settings for a site.

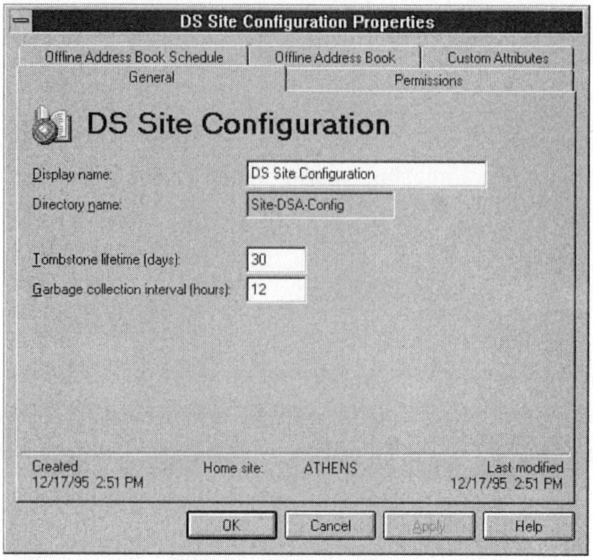

2. Enter a Display name for this object as you want it to be displayed in the Exchange administrator program. By default, this name is DS Site Configuration. The Alias name is set to Site-DSA-Config and cannot be modified.
3. Next to Tombstone lifetime (days), enter the length of time (in days) until a directory object's tombstone marker (see above) expires. By default, this value is set to **30** days.
4. Next to Garbage collection interval (hours), enter the interval (in hours) between deletion of expired tombstone markers. See the preceding page for a more detailed description of the garbage collection interval. By default, this value is set to 12 hours.
5. Click Apply to set these properties and continue with other properties. If you are done with all settings, click OK to return to the administrator program.

The Permissions Page

This property page allows you to define certain Windows NT user accounts that have rights to modify this directory object.

The Offline Address Book Schedule Page

This property page allows you to determine at what intervals a new offline address book will be generated.

1. Select the Offline Address Book Schedule tab of the DS Site Configuration Properties pages. The property page in figure 12.2 appears.

FIG. 12.2
Set the schedule for creating an offline address book.

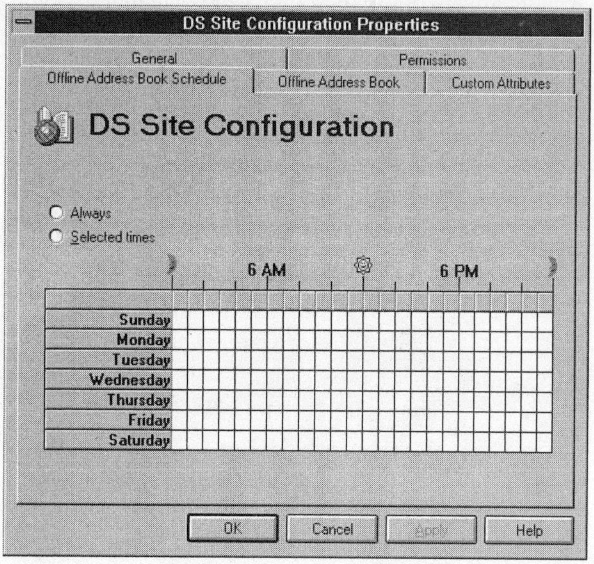

2. Click Always to continually re-generate updated versions of an offline address book. Once a cycle completes, a new one begins immediately.
3. Click Selected times and use the time grid to set specific times when offline address book generation will begin.

   For example: If you know that your remote users connect first thing in the morning to update their offline address books, then set the schedule to begin several hours before you expect most of them to connect. That way the whole generation cycle will be complete, and the address book they download will be as complete as possible.
4. Click Apply to set these properties and continue with other properties. If you are done with all settings, click OK to return to the administrator program.

NOTE Generating an offline address book can often take several hours. If one cycle of offline address book generation carries into the next scheduled generation time, the generation will finish normally, then begin again at the next scheduled time after its completion.

The Offline Address Book Page

This property page defines parameters on how the offline address book will be created. You choose what elements of the directory will be included. If you desire a highly customized list of recipients to be included in the offline address book, then consider creating a recipient container dedicated to offline address book generation.

1. Select the Offline Address Book tab of the DS Site Configuration Properties pages. The property page in figure 12.3 appears.

FIG. 12.3
Set offline address book creation and location options.

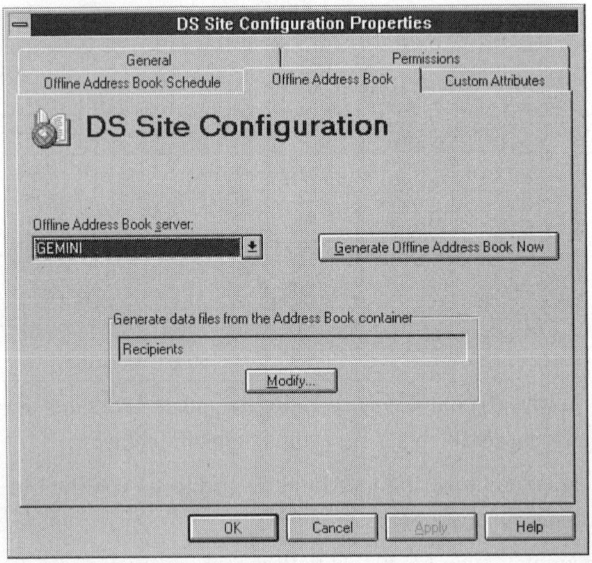

2. Select the Offline Address Book server by using the pull-down menu. This is the server that will actually generate the offline address book and from which a remote user will download the information. By default, this is the Microsoft Exchange server to which you are currently connected.

> **TIP** Since generation of a large offline address book can be a lengthy process, select a lower traffic server (if available) to perform this task.

3. Click Generate Offline Address Book Now to immediately begin the generation of a new offline address book.

NOTE Before an offline address book is available to remote users, it must first be generated. Note your generation schedule to see if the next scheduled cycle falls within an acceptable time frame. If necessary, click the Generate Offline Address Book Now to create it immediately.

4. The Generate data files from the Address Book container box displays which recipient container is used to create the offline address book. Typically, you will use the global address list container in the offline address book for this site. Note that by default the selected container is the recipients from the local Exchange site, not the global address list. Click Modify to select a new recipient container.

   Choose the recipient container you want to use for the offline address book. Click OK to accept your choice.
5. Click Apply to set these properties and continue with other properties. If you are done with all settings, click OK to return to the administrator program.

CAUTION

There must be only one offline address book per Microsoft Exchange site. Replicating the offline address book hidden public folder will create directory errors.

The Custom Attributes Page

This property page allows you to define characteristics that will appear on the Custom Attributes property page of each recipient in the local site. The field can be defined to display any additional information for which you want to create a space.

Creating Custom Attribute fields:

1. Select the Custom Attributes tab of the DS Site Configuration Properties page. The property page in figure 12.4 appears.
2. Type in the names of Custom Attributes 1-10 in the spaces provided. By default these entries are literally named "Custom Attribute 1" through "Custom Attribute 10."
3. Click Apply to set these properties and continue with other properties. If you are done with all settings, click OK to return to the administrator program.

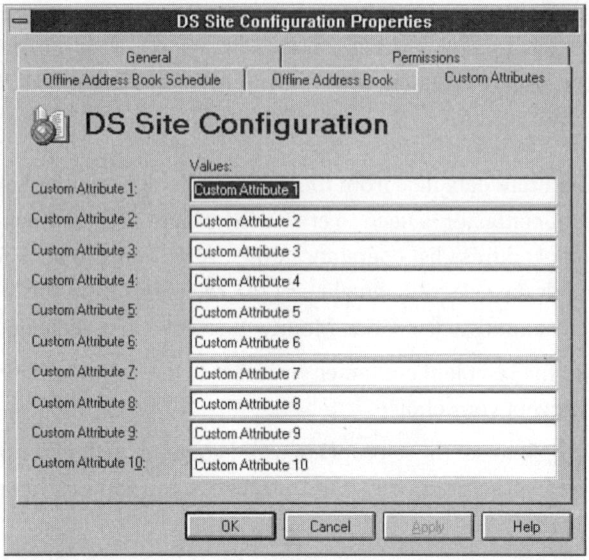

FIG. 12.4
Set the custom attribute whose values you will set in the recipient's properties pages.

Configuring Site Addressing

These sets of property pages allow you to configure site properties that have to do with routing messages to their intended destination within an Exchange system. These options determine which servers will be used to calculate routing tables, and when to calculate those tables. Also, you can use these pages to get an overview of how messaging links are established in you organization.

Configuring the Site Addressing Properties page:

The General Page

In this property page, you can edit this object's Display name and also:

Choose Routing Calculation server. This server will be responsible for processing routing data for this server. The updated routing table will then be replicated to this server.

Choose Share address space with other X.400 systems l (see fig. 12.5). With this option selected, if an incoming X.400 message cannot find its intended Exchange recipient, it will be routed to the system sharing this address space. This option is helpful when running Exchange side by side a foreign X.400 system (for example, during a migration to Exchange). By default, X.400 address space is not shared.

FIG. 12.5
Set general site routing parameters.

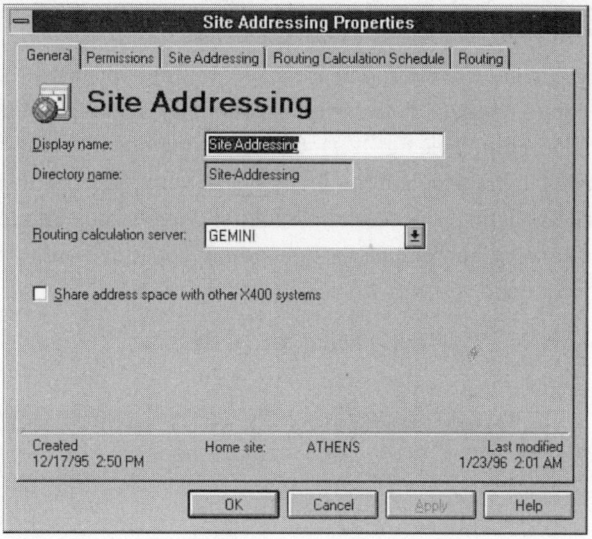

The Site Addressing Page

E-mail addresses are used by the various Exchange gateways and connectors to identify specific directory objects to other messaging systems (see fig. 12.6). In this case, these addresses affect all messages routed to this site. There are three default addresses created each for MS Mail, SMTP, and X.400. If other connectors or gateways are installed, those addresses can be created by default as well.

FIG. 12.6
Set e-mail address entries for the entire site.

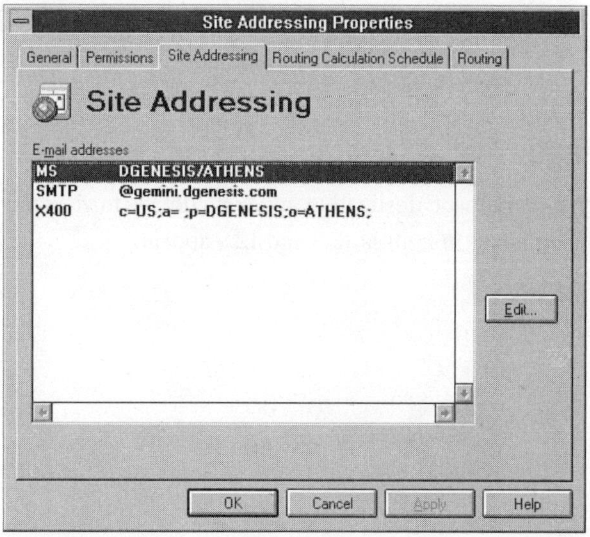

The Routing Calculation Schedule Page

When changes in site configuration are made, routing tables need to be rebuilt in order to maintain accurate message delivery information. By default, routing is calculated once per day at 4 a.m. local time (see fig. 12.7). Generally, the default settings will be more than adequate to maintain up-to-date routing tables in your site; use the manual override when immediate recalculation is necessary. If your site undergoes frequent changes in components (more servers, new connector types, etc.), you may want to increase the routing calculation frequency.

Set the schedule in a standard schedule property page:

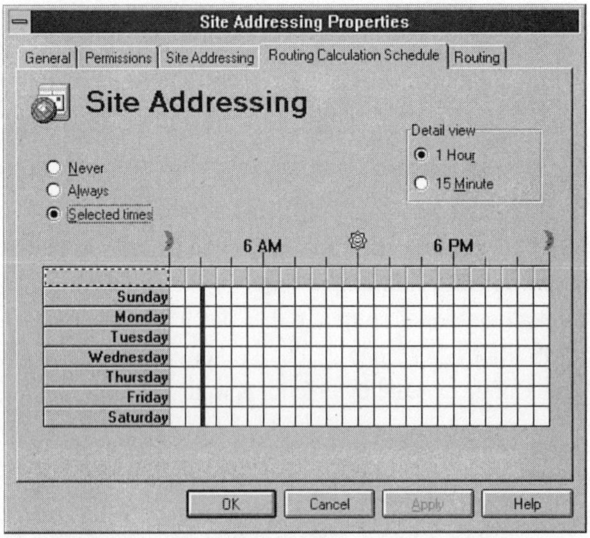

FIG. 12.7
Define a schedule when routing table calculations occur.

The Routing Page

Click on a type of message destination and click details to view the route of such a message. The dialog boxes in figures 12.8 and 12.9 appear.

FIG. 12.8
View the message routes available from this Exchange site.

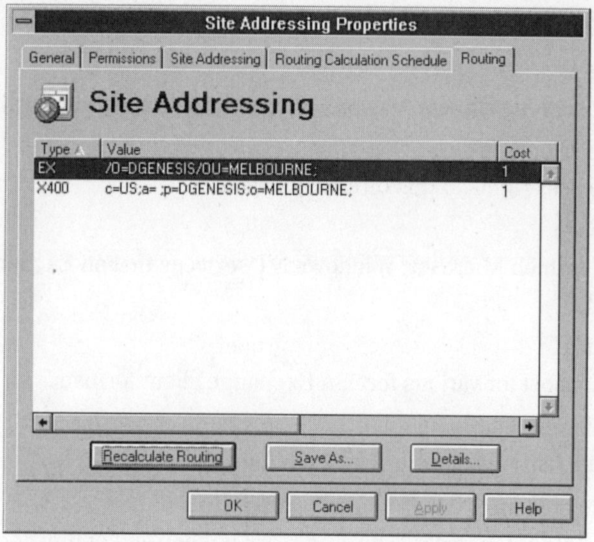

FIG. 12.9
View Routing Details for connector available from this site. *Note the file extensions for this file type.*

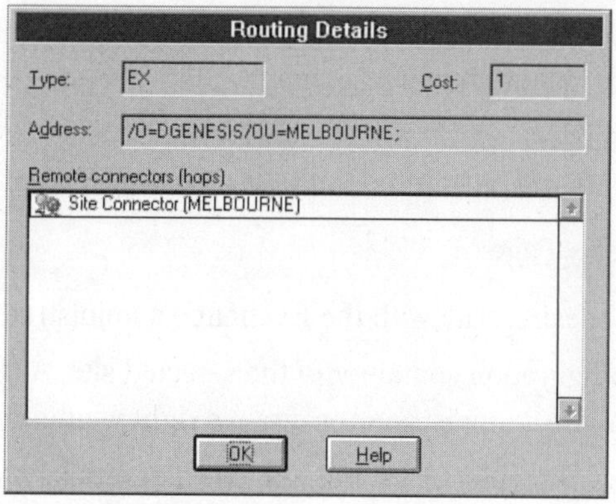

Server Property Pages

Each Microsoft Exchange server has its own set of property pages. Here, you can configure general functions that apply specifically to a single Exchange server.

The following are the property pages for server configuration:

- General
  View server's Directory name. No configuration options available.
- Permissions
  Set access rights to this directory object.
- Services
  Select which Microsoft Windows NT services that an Exchange server monitor will check.
- Locales
  Set support for various foreign Exchange client formats.
- Database Paths
  Set the hard disk location for each information store.
- IS Maintenance
  Schedule automatic information store upkeep and optimizing.
- Advanced
  Toggle circular logging for the directory and information store and configure information store inconsistency adjustment.
- Diagnostics Logging
  Define what events will be entered in the Windows NT event log.

Opening Server Property Page:

1. Navigate to your desired site with the Exchange administrator program.
2. Click on the Configuration container of the selected site. All the site configuration objects appear in the administrator program's right window.
3. Open the Servers container. A list of Exchange servers in your site will be listed.
4. Click the server name on which is the Private Information Store you want to configure (see fig. 12.10). The following list of server objects is visible on the right display window of the Microsoft Exchange Administrator Program.
5. Open its property pages by selecting Properties from the administrator program file menu or by pressing Alt+Enter.

Configuring Exchange Server Properties:

FIG. 12.10
Select the Exchange server to edit, then open its properties.

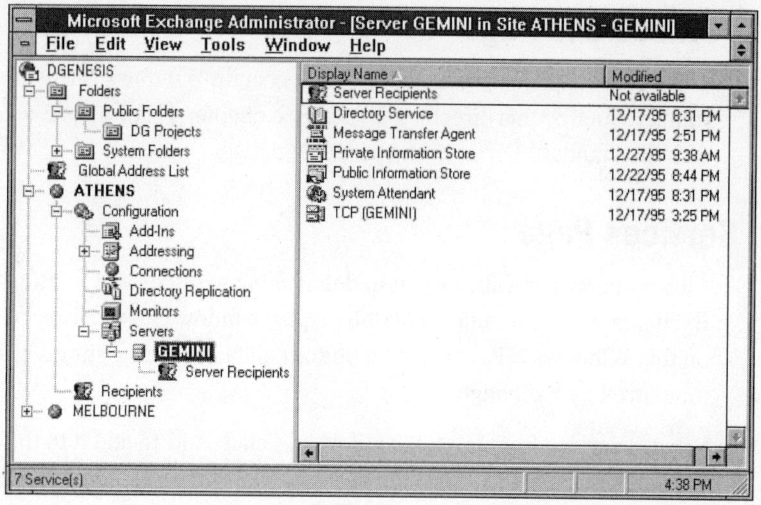

The General Page

This property page displays the server's Directory name and has a space for an additional Administrative note (see fig. 12.11).

The server's directory name cannot be changed without reinstalling Microsoft Exchange.

FIG. 12.11
The server name cannot be changed after Exchange has been installed.

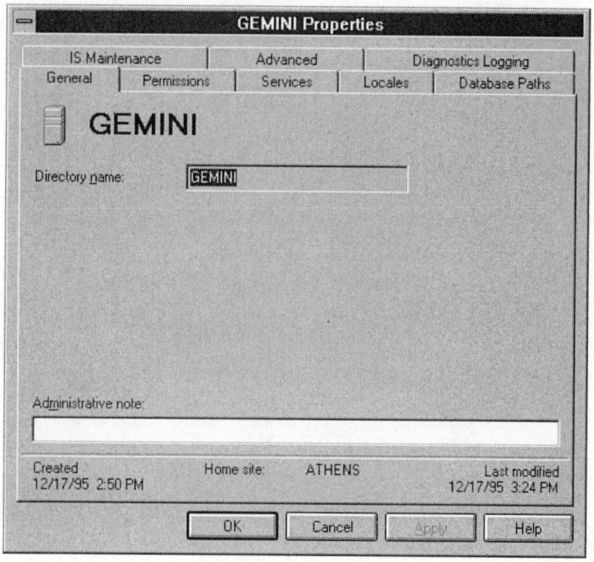

The Permissions Page

This property page allows you to define certain Windows NT user accounts that have rights to modify this directory object. See chapter 11 for a detailed description on working with the standard Permissions property page.

The Services Page

This property page allows you to define what services will be checked by a Microsoft Exchange server monitor. The top display window shows all services currently installed on this Windows NT server. The bottom display window shows all the services currently monitored by Exchange.

Select a service from the top window and click Add to add it to the list of Monitored Services (see fig. 12.12).

Select a service from the bottom window and click Remove to take it off the list of Monitored Services.

Click Default to return to the basic services selected by Exchange Server.

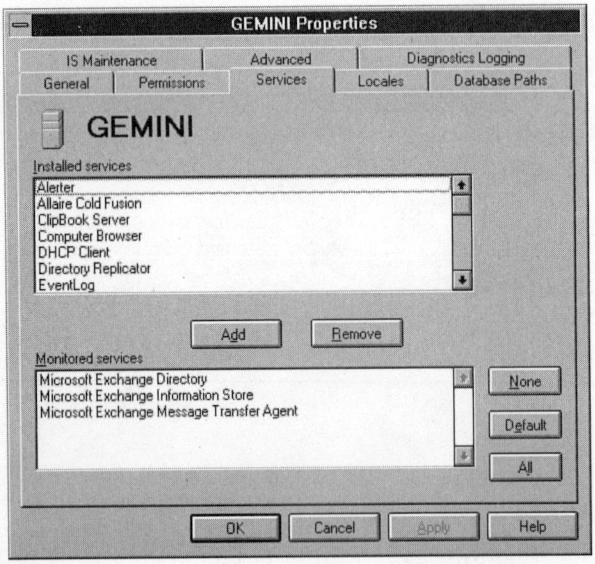

FIG. 12.12
Select the services to be monitored by an Exchange server monitor.

The Locales Page

Locales determine how values (such as date or currency) are displayed in the Exchange client. International settings are determined by the Exchange client settings (see chapter

28, "Understanding User Interface Features") and also affect default sorting order for lists. This property page allows you to activate certain locales from the list of installed locales.

The Installed Locales window displays all the formats currently installed on this Exchange server.

Click Add or Remove to edit the list of Selected Locales.

The Selected Locales window displays what formats are in use (see fig. 12.13).

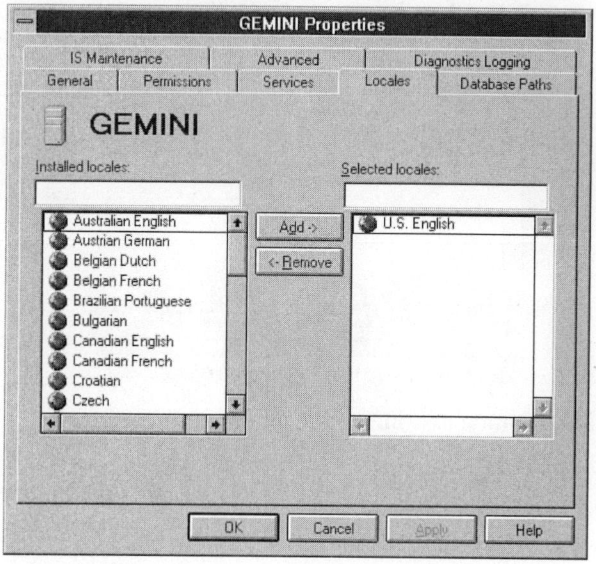

FIG. 12.13
Use this dialog box to add or remove support for various foreign language Exchange clients.

The Database Paths Page

The Database Paths are pointers to the hard disk files where Exchange actually stores information. This property page allows you to set the paths to the directory and the public and private information store files on this server. The paths are set up when you initially install Exchange Server.

The three main Exchange server databases are:

1. Directory
2. Private
3. Public Information Store

Additional information files (see fig. 12.14) store additional Exchange data such as transaction logs.

TIP One basic way to improve Exchange performance is to spread the database files across several hard drives. The Microsoft Exchange Optimizer can assist with this process.

FIG. 12.14
Use this dialog box to view the physical location, i.e., hard disk, for the various types of Exchange.

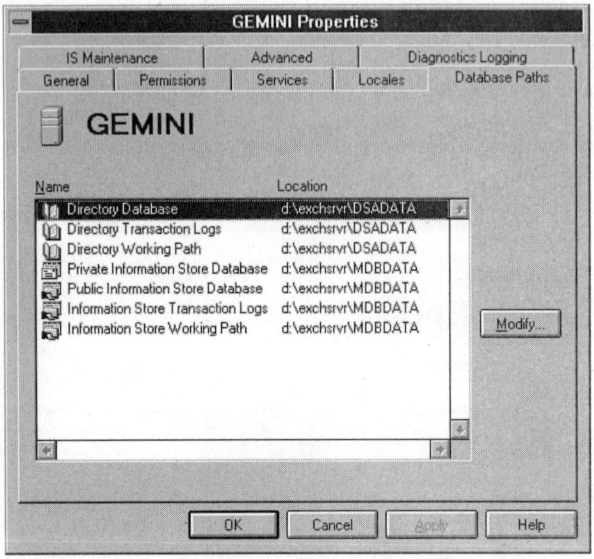

Click the Modify button to bring up the following dialog box.

Browse through your system's file structure and select a location for the database information.

The IS Maintenance Page

Information Store Maintenance optimizes an Exchange server's operating speed. Basic maintenance includes disk defragmentation for improved hard disk performance (see fig. 12.15). Use this page to schedule maintenance for each Exchange server.

TIP Maintenance tasks are taxing on hard drive and overall server performance. Always schedule them at the server's least busy period of the day.

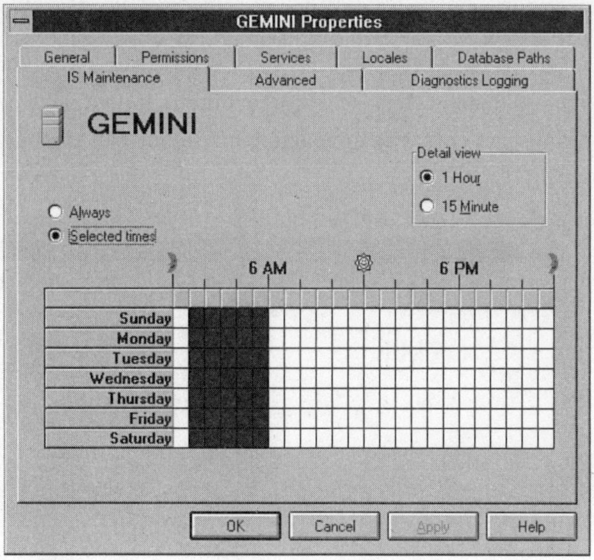

FIG. 12.15
Select the least busy time of the day for information store data upkeep.

The Advanced Page

This property page allows you to configure two advanced options:

- **Database Circular Logging**. Enabling these two checkboxes allows Exchange to write over transaction log files after their data is saved to the database. Use this option to save drive space only if storage space availability is a serious consideration.

CAUTION

If the circular logging options are enabled, you will no longer be able to perform differential and incremental backups (see Chapter 23, Exchange Maintenance").

- **DS/IS Consistency Adjustment**. There are two components to each directory object saved in a server's information store: The object itself and a corresponding entry in the directory. Consistency adjustment corrects errors arising by mismatched information. This feature will either add or delete a directory entry to match the existence or absence of information store information.

This property page allows you to control at what point these inconsistencies are to be corrected.

Select either the All inconsistencies to correct them immediately or select Inconsistencies more than __ days and enter the time an inconsistency can exist before it is automatically corrected (see fig. 12.16).

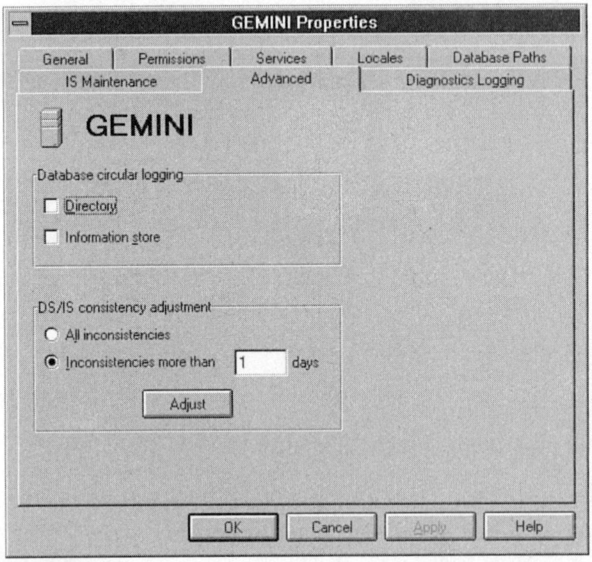

FIG. 12.16
Set general logging and inconsistency adjustment preferences.

Diagnostics Logging

This property page works in conjunction with the Windows NT Event Log to record various "events" that occur within various Exchange services. Various levels of logging determine what constitutes an event and, therefore, what types of information are actually recorded. For troubleshooting purposes, you would want a very detailed record of occurrences and, hence, set a high logging level. However, normally you would want to log only events that are critical, so set a lower logging level for everyday operation (see fig. 12.17). Individual components (for example, Directory, MTA, and Information Store) also have diagnostic logging pages for their individual service, but all services are available through this server property page.

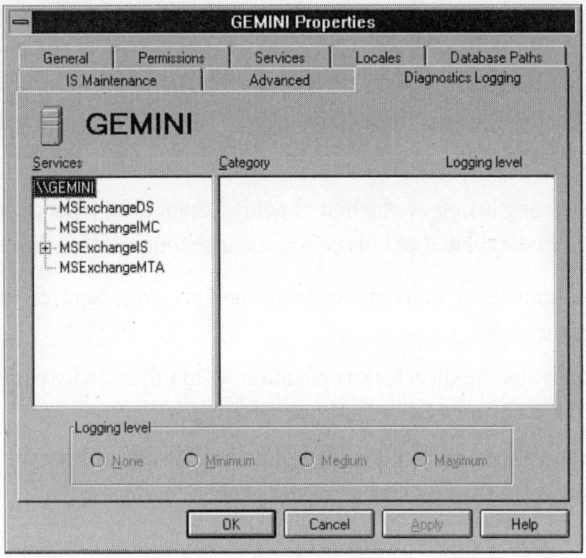

FIG. 12.17 Control log settings for all Exchange services running on this server.

Configuring Directory Service

The Directory Service Properties pages are mainly used for configuring diagnostics information. However, there are two additional functions provided by this object that will be used more frequently during normal operation. These functions are:

- **Manually synchronize directory information within a site**. This operation normally occurs every five minutes; but if changes have been made and you do not want to wait for automatic synchronization, then use this property page.
- **Manually check knowledge consistency**. Knowledge consistency for this local server is its awareness of other Exchange servers within a site and other sites within your organization. This operation is run automatically once daily; but if Exchange servers or sites were added and the local was not aware of those changes, (e.g., the local server was down during that time), then you may not want to wait for the automatic checking and do it manually.

Example

Exchange Server BOSTON01 is brought down for two hours for a memory upgrade. During the time of the upgrade, a new server, BOSTON08, is added to the site. When

BOSTON01 is restored to proper functioning, it will not be aware of the existence of the new server until the Knowledge Consistency cycle is run at the end of the day. Knowing this, the administrator for BOSTON01 runs the Knowledge Consistency cycle manually from the Directory Service Properties pages. BOSTON01 is now aware of the new server's existence.

If an inconsistency is detected when checking manually, it is a good idea to manually execute all processes related to correcting inconsistencies. Use this sequence:

1. Check knowledge consistency from the Directory Service Properties pages and detect the error.
2. Manually update directory replication within the site by running Update Now also from the Directory Service Properties pages.
3. Open the Message Transfer Agent properties for this server and click Recalculate Routing from the General property page.

Although the preceding sequence is optional and will be automatically executed with a 24-hour period, performing the tasks immediately will reduce the possibility of other conflicts or errors.

Opening the Directory Service Properties Pages:

1. Use the Microsoft Exchange administrator program to navigate to the list of servers within the site to which you are connected.
2. Click on an Exchange server within the site, and a list of configuration objects appear in the administrator program's right display window.
3. Select the Directory Service object and open its property pages.

Configuring the Microsoft Exchange Directory Service

The General Page

1. Select the General tab of the Directory Service Properties page (see fig. 12.18). The following property page appears.
2. Click Update Now to request directory updates from all servers in the site. This process automatically runs every five minutes within an Exchange site.
3. Click Check Now to run a knowledge consistency check and detect any changes in servers in a site or sites in your organization. This process automatically runs once a day.

FIG. 12.18
Use these two controls to manually update the local site directory and check knowledge consistency.

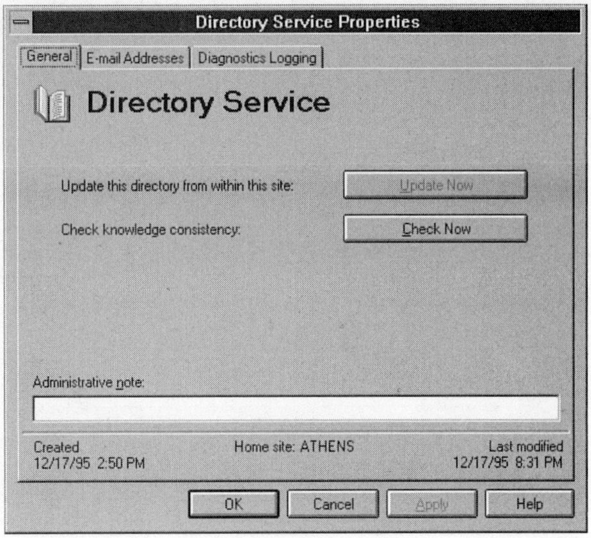

4. Enter any additional Administrative note.
5. Click Apply to set these properties and continue with other properties. If you are done with all settings, click OK to return to the administrator program.

The E-Mail Addresses Page

E-mail addresses are used by the various Exchange gateways and connectors to identify specific directory objects to other messaging systems. There are three default addresses created each for MS Mail, SMTP, and X.400.

Setting public directory service e-mail addresses:

1. Click the E-mail Addresses of the Directory Service Properties pages (see fig. 12.19). The following dialog box appears.

   The three default addresses (MS Mail, SMTP, and X.400) are displayed.
2. Click New to add a specific e-mail address for this directory service. Select an existing address and click Edit to modify it, or click Remove to delete it.
3. Click Apply to set these properties and continue with other properties. If you are done with all settings, click OK to return to the administrator program.

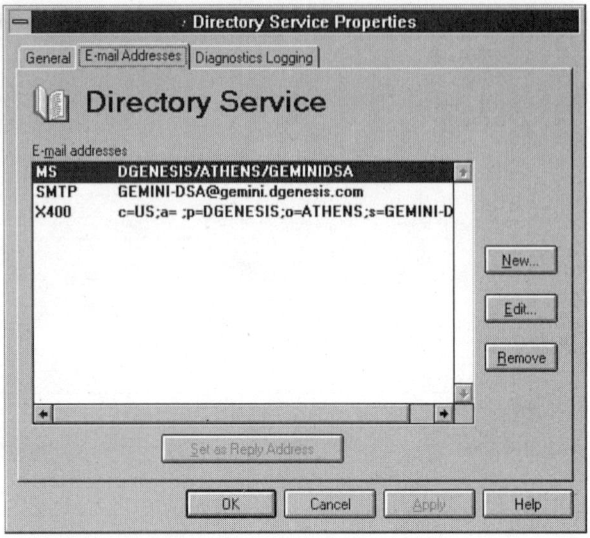

FIG. 12.19
Define any additional e-mail address for this directory object.

The Diagnostics Logging Page

This property page works in conjunction with the Windows NT Event Log to record various "events" that occur within the Directory Service (MSExchangeDS). Various levels of logging determine what constitutes an event and, therefore, what types of information are actually recorded. For troubleshooting purposes, you would want a very detailed record of occurrences within the Directory Service, and hence set a high logging level. However, normally you would want to log only events that are critical, so set a lower logging level for everyday operation (see fig. 12.20).

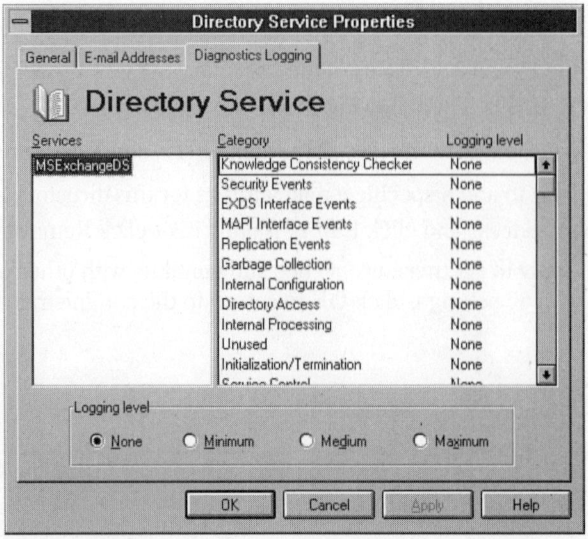

FIG. 12.20
This page controls logging for the directory synchronization service only.

Configuring Directory Synchronization Service

These property pages allow for directory synchronization between Exchange and MS Mail and other compatible foreign systems. For further directory synchronization information see Chapter 17, "Using Directory Replication and Synchronization."

The following are the property pages available for configuration on the directory synchronization service:

- General
- E-mail Addresses
- Delivery Restrictions
- Incoming Templates
- Outgoing Templates
- Diagnostics Logging

Opening the Directory Synchronization Service Properties Pages:

1. Navigate to your desired site with the Exchange administrator program.
2. Click the Configuration container of the selected site. All the site configuration objects appear in the administrator program's right window.
3. Open the Servers container. A list of Exchange servers in your site will be listed.
4. Click the server name on which is the directory synchronization service you want to configure.
5. Click the Directory Synchronization object. Open its property pages.

Configuring Directory Synchronization Service Properties Pages:

The General Page

This property page allows you to view only the current server's name and enter an Administrative note (see fig. 12.21). An Exchange server's name is set when the software is installed and cannot be changed after the fact.

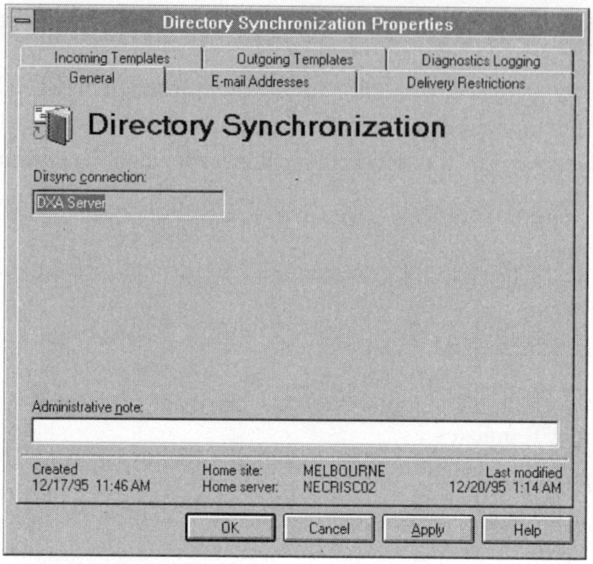

FIG. 12.21 The name of this server cannot be altered.

The E-Mail Addresses Page

E-mail addresses are used by the various Exchange gateways and connectors to identify specific directory objects to other messaging systems. The directory synchronization service receives regular update messages sent to these addresses. There are three default addresses created each for MS Mail, SMTP, and X.400.

The Delivery Restrictions Page

The directory synchronization service executes its functions by the transfer of messages between itself and other systems. This property page assures that only specific users can send messages to the directory synchronization service.

Configuring delivery restrictions:

1. Select the Delivery Restrictions tab from the Directory Synchronization Properties pages (see fig. 12.22). The following property page appears.
2. Use the dialog box to either restrict certain senders or to permit only certain senders.
3. Click Apply to set these properties and continue with other properties. If you are done with all settings, click OK to return to the administrator program.

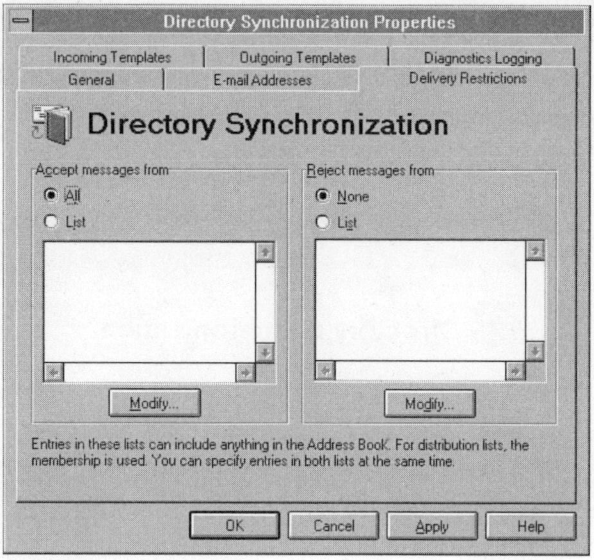

FIG. 12.22
Use this page to prevent unnecessary messages from being sent to this service.

The Incoming Templates Page

In this property page you can define a template that will apply to all incoming directory synchronization messages (see fig. 12.23). See Chapter 17, "Using Directory Replication and Synchronization," for more details on this template and its use in directory synchronization.

FIG. 12.23
Map standard MS Mail attributes to Exchange server recipients.

The Outgoing Templates Page

In this property page you can define a template that will apply to all outgoing directory synchronization messages (see fig. 12.24). See Chapter 17 for more details on this template and its use in directory synchronization.

FIG. 12.24
Map Exchange server recipient attributes to the standard MS Mail attributes.

The Diagnostics Logging Page

This property page works in conjunction with the Windows NT Event Log to record various "events" that occur within the Directory Synchronization Service. Various levels of logging determine what constitutes an event and, therefore, what types of information are actually recorded. For troubleshooting purposes, you would want a very detailed record of occurrences within the Directory Synchronization Service, and hence set a high logging level. However, normally you would want to log only events that are critical, so set a lower logging level for everyday operation.

Configuring System Attendant

The system attendant service must be running in order for most other Exchange system services to run. Stopping the system attendant service, for example, will prompt the halting of several other Exchange services, simultaneously.

Each Microsoft Exchange server within your organization can be configured with different properties.

Configuring the System Attendant Properties pages:

1. Use the Microsoft Exchange administrator program to navigate to the list of servers within the site to which you are connected.
2. Click the server name whose System Attendant object you want to configure.
3. In the right display window, you will see a list of objects pertaining to that Exchange server (see fig. 12.25).

FIG. 12.25
The System attendant is found in the individual Exchange server container.

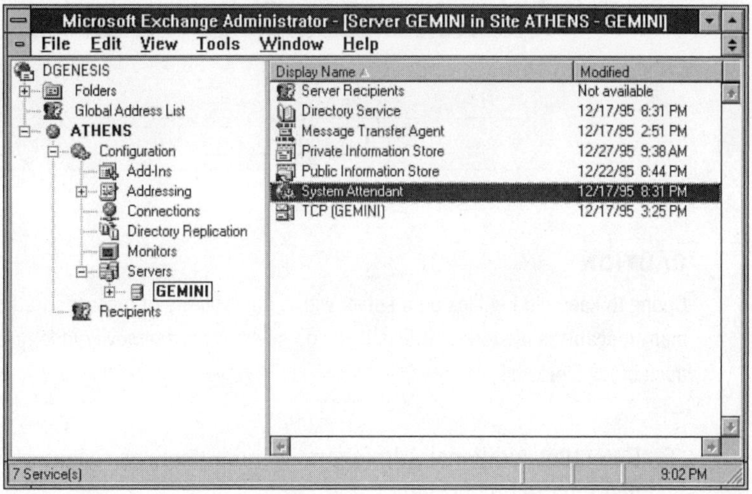

Click the System Attendant object and open its property pages. The property page in figure 12.26 appears.

4. The General page is the first visible property page. The Display name is set as "System Attendant" by default and cannot be changed. Likewise, the Alias name for this object is set to "MicrosoftSA" and also cannot be changed.
5. Under the Message tracking log files maintenance window:
   Click Do not remove old log files if you want the system attendant to keep such log files for an indefinite time. Click Remove log files older than—days to have this system attendant delete message tracking files after a specified number of days has elapsed. Enter the number of days in the box provided. By default, this option is selected, and the log files are deleted every seven days.

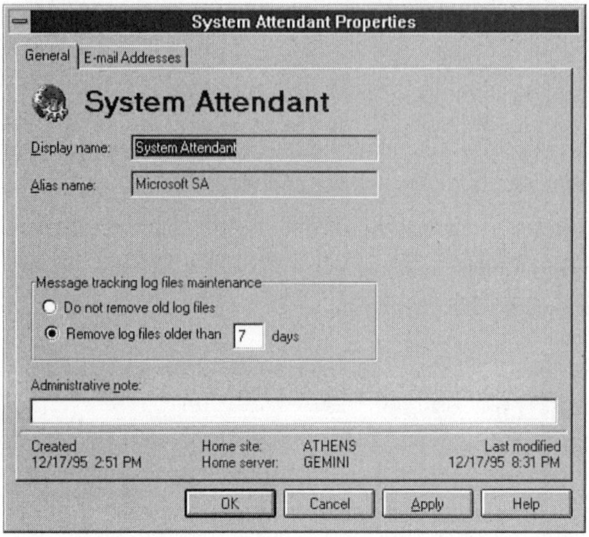

FIG. 12.26
The System Attendant General property page

CAUTION

Opting to keep old log files on a server with a high volume of message traffic could easily take up many megabytes of storage space. If you do select Do not remove old log files, make sure to keep track of log file sizes!

6. Enter any additional Administrative note (such as reasons for keeping all old log files) in the box provided.
7. Click Apply to set these properties and continue with other properties. If you are done with all settings, click OK to return to the administrator program.

Setting E-Mail Addresses for the System Attendant

E-mail addresses are used by the various Exchange gateways and connectors to identify specific directory objects to other messaging systems. The System Attendant, though not capable of receiving messages, is a directory object just the same and has a set of e-mail addresses associated with it. There are three default addresses created each for MS Mail, SMTP, and X.400.

1. Click the E-mail Addresses of the System Attendant Properties page (see fig. 12.27).

   The three default addresses (MS Mail, SMTP, and X.400) are displayed.

FIG. 12.27
The E-mail addresses page displays the three default address for this System Attendant.

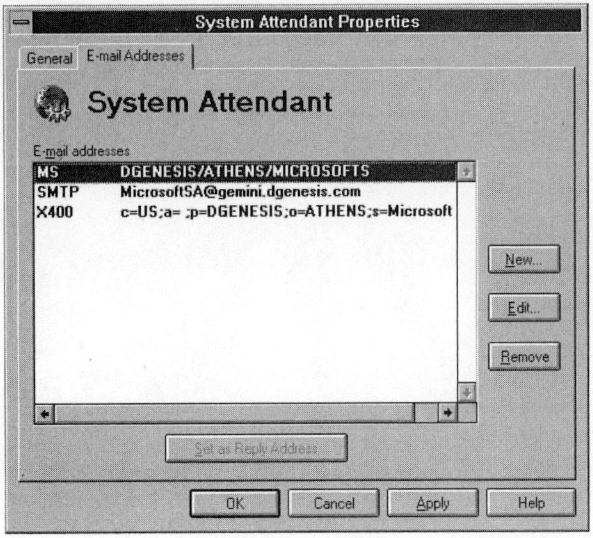

2. Click New to add a specific e-mail address for this system attendant. Select an existing address and click Edit to modify it, or click Remove to delete it.
3. Click Apply to set these properties and continue with other properties. If you are done with all settings, click OK to return to the administrator program.

All other functions of the System Attendant (such as checking directory replication inconsistencies and gathering information about other running Exchange services) are carried out without additional configuration by the administrator.

From Here...

For more information on related items, see the following chapters:

- Chapter 2, "Understanding Exchange's Organization and Sites"
- Chapter 3, "Exchange's Integrated Server Components"
- Chapter 17, "Using Directory Replication and Synchronization"
- Chapter 26, "Diagnostic and Troubleshooting Tools"

CHAPTER 13

Message Transfer Configuration

- Various components of the Message Transfer Agent
- How to perform the MTA Site Configuration tasks
- How to configure the Local MTA Properties

The Microsoft Exchange Message Transfer Agent (MTA) is the key component that provides addressing and routing information and that delivers messages. Proper configuration of MTA settings is important to an efficient Exchange organization. As described in Chapter 3, "Exchange's Integrated Server Components," a message that originates in an Exchange mailbox reaches its destination in only two ways:

- A message is addressed to a user on the same Exchange server and is delivered by the Information Store.
- A message is addressed to a user on a different server or foreign system, and the MTA handles the message transmission.

Unless your organization consists primarily of one or two Exchange servers, the MTAs on various levels are the entities that are responsible for message routing and transmission.

Understanding the Transfer Agent Components

The Microsoft Exchange Message Transfer Agent is primarily a Windows NT service running on each Exchange server in your organization. For connection to Microsoft Mail systems, an additional service called the MS Mail Connector (PC) MTA negotiates message transmission with MS Mail for PC networks.

Configuration of the primary Exchange MTA is handled though two sets of property pages:

- *MTA Site Configuration.* Defines overall settings for message transmission within the entire Exchange site.
- *Message Transfer Agent* (for a specific Exchange server). Defines server-specific MTA settings, such as message size limits and logging levels.

Let's discuss some of the essential parameters involved in performing MTA Site Configuration.

Dead Letter

Any message that is defined as undeliverable by the Message Transfer Agent is classified as a *dead letter*. You can specify a dead-letter recipient (usually, an administrator) from within the MTA site configuration property pages.

Message Tracking

To keep records of Message Transfer Agent activity within a Microsoft Exchange site, enable message tracking. A daily log file is generated and stored in the EXCHSRVR\TRACKING.LOG directory. Message tracking log files are in a text format. The full file name, to use the example, would be : EXCHSRVR\TRACKING\960529.LOG. The individual log files are:

YYMMDD.log

Example

960529.log for MTA activity on May 29, 1996.

Message Queues

Each server has a list of messages that are waiting to be delivered by its MTA. The queues are distinguished as being either private or public Information Store messages. Messages are held in the queue until the MTA can successfully establish a connection with a remote MTA and transfer the messages or until the messages exceed their lifetimes (set in the messaging defaults).

Messaging Defaults

Settings for how (and how long) to transfer a message before certain time-outs occurs are called *messaging defaults*. These values are set in the MTA Site Configuration properties and are used by all MTAs in the site unless a specific connection uses MTA override parameters.

MTA Overrides

Certain connectors—namely, the Dynamic RAS Connector and the X.400 connector—provide for object-specific MTA settings. Use the Override property page to change the default Microsoft Exchange Server MTA attributes when using a specific X.400 or dynamic RAS connector. Keep in mind their existence when you define messaging defaults in the MTA Site Configuration property page. Override property pages are there for developing flexibility in MTA configuration.

Performing MTA Site Configuration

To open the MTA Site Configuration property pages, follow these steps:

1. Navigate to your desired site with the Exchange Administrator program.
2. Click the Configuration container of the selected site (see fig. 13.1). All the site-configuration objects appear in the Administrator program's right window.

FIG. 13.1
The MTA Site Configuration is located in the Configuration container.

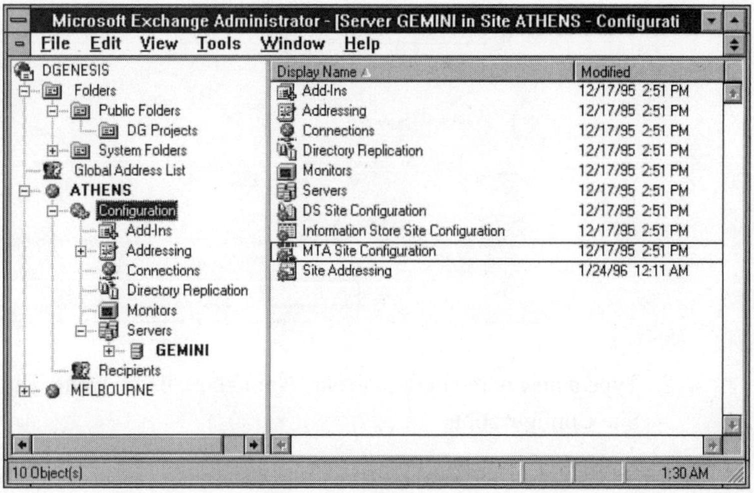

3. Select the MTA Site Configuration object from the list.
4. Open the MTA Site Configuration Object property pages by double-clicking on the object.

At this point, you have three property pages to configure:

- *General.* Sets the MTA site configuration display name and the dead-letter recipient, and enables message tracking.
- *Permissions.* Sets security rights to the MTA Site Configuration object.
- *Messaging Defaults.* Defines connection and transmission parameters for the MTAs in your site.

The General Tab

To configure the General features, such as display name of the MTA Site Configuration Object, follow these steps:

1. Click the General tab of the MTA Site Configuration Properties page (see fig. 13.2).

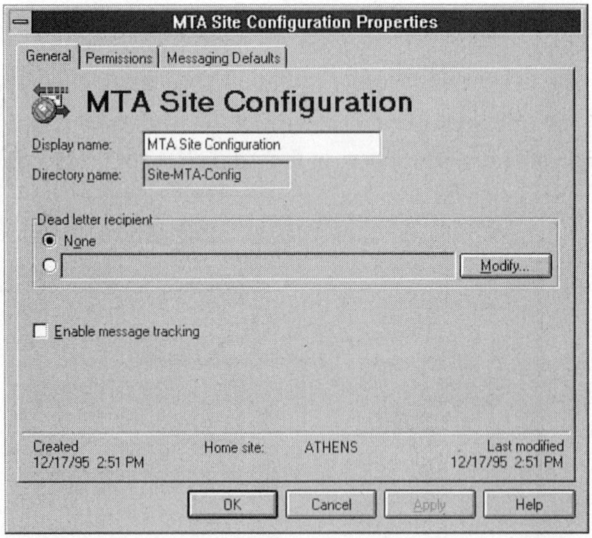

FIG. 13.2
The General MTA site configuration property page.

2. Type a new name in the Display Name box, if you want. The default name is MTA Site Configuration.

NOTE By default, the Directory Name, Site-MTA-Config, cannot be changed.

3. In the Dead Letter Recipient section, click the None radio button if you want all nondeliverable messages to be deleted. By default, this option is selected.
4. Click the Modify button if you want to enter or change a name in the Dead Letter Recipient text box. The Exchange address list appears. Click the radio button next to the name in the box to designate that recipient as the dead-letter recipient.
5. Click the Enable Message Tracking check box to instruct the System Attendant to keep a daily log of all messages processed by the MTA. This check box corresponds to the "Enable Message Tracking" check box in the Information Store Site Configuration property page.
6. Click Apply to set these properties and continue with viewing/changing of other properties.
7. When you finish making settings, click OK to return to the Administrator program.

The Permissions Tab

This property page allows you to define certain Windows NT user accounts that have rights to modify this directory object. See Chapter 11, "Using the Administrator Program," for a detailed description on working with the standard Permissions property page.

The Messaging Defaults Tab

To set the messaging default values for the MTA Site Configuration object, follow these steps:

1. Click the Messaging Defaults tab of the MTA Site Configuration Properties page (see fig. 13.3).

TIP To return to the default Message Transfer Agent settings, click the Reset Default Values button.

2. Enter specific MTA configuration variables, as described in Table 13.1, which follows these steps.

   To the right of each item listed in the table is a box that contains a default numeric value. Replace any value with a number that will be used in establishing a connection through any MTA in the current site.
3. Click Apply to set these properties and continue with other properties.
4. When you finish making settings, click OK to return to the Administrator program.

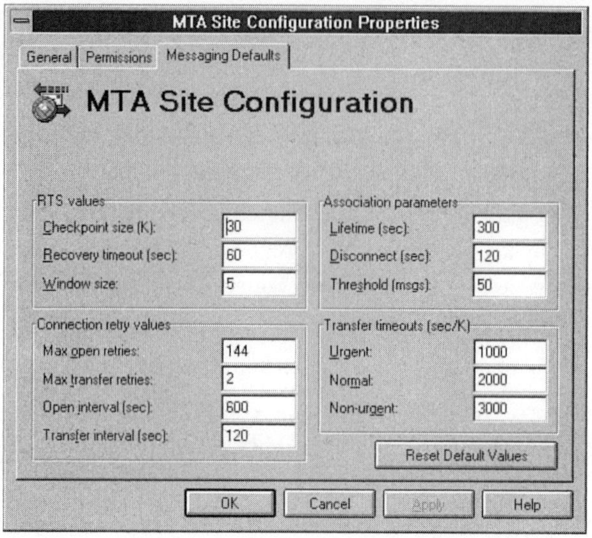

FIG. 13.3 Messaging defaults govern each connection made by the MTA.

Table 13.1 MTA Site Configuration Parameter Values

Variable	Description
RTS Values	
Checkpoint Size (K)	The value (in kilobytes) used to verify packet transmission with returned checkpoints. By default, this value is 30.
Recovery Timeout (Sec)	The time delay (in seconds) before a broken transmission is retried. By default, the delay is 60 seconds.
Window Size	The number of checkpoints (in kilobytes) that can be transmitted without acknowledgment. By default, this value is 5.
Connection Retry Values	
Max Open Retries	The maximum number of consecutive failed attempts before the MTA ceases trying to open a communication channel with a remote MTA. By default, an MTA makes 144 attempts.
Max Transfer Retries	The maximum number of consecutive failed attempts before the MTA ceases trying to transfer a message packet. By default, the MTA makes 2 attempts.
Open Interval (Sec)	The delay (in seconds) between attempts to open a communication channel. By default, the delay is 600 seconds.

Variable	Description
Connection Retry Values	

NOTE If you combine the default 144 Max Open Retries with the default 600-second Open Interval, Exchange waits 24 hours before returning a message as undeliverable.

Variable	Description
Transfer Interval (Sec)	The delay (in seconds) between attempts to retransmit a failed message packet. By default, this delay is 120 seconds.
Association Parameters	
Lifetime (Sec)	The maximum time that an idle connection between MTAs remains open. By default, an idle link is held open for 300 seconds after the last communication.
Disconnect (Sec)	The maximum time allowed for establishing or terminating a connection before the session is ended independently. By default, this time is 120 seconds.
Threshold (Msgs)	The number of messages that must be queued at this MTA before the MTA initiates a link to a remote MTA. By default, 50 messages must be awaiting transmission.
Transfer Timeouts (Sec/K)	
Urgent	The delay (in seconds per kilobyte of total message size) between retries of urgent messages. By default, this delay is 1,000 seconds.
Normal	The delay (in seconds per kilobyte of total message size) between retries of normal messages. By default, this delay is 2,000 seconds
Non-Urgent	The delay (in seconds per kilobyte of total message size) between retries of nonurgent messages. By default, this delay is 3,000 seconds.

The following section discusses configuring Message Transfer Agent properties for each Microsoft Exchange Server.

Configuring Local MTA Properties

Each Microsoft Exchange Server has a Message Transfer Agent. The MTA property pages are designed to configure and manage this service.

First, you must select the MTA from the server within your site. Follow these steps:

1. Navigate to your desired site with the Exchange Administrator program.
2. Click the Configuration container of the selected site. All the site-configuration objects appear in the Administrator program's right window.
3. Open the Servers container by double-clicking on it. A list of Exchange servers in your site appears.
4. Click the name of the server that houses the MTA that you want to configure (see fig. 13.4). The following list of server objects is visible on the right display window of the Microsoft Exchange Administrator program.

FIG. 13.4
The Message Transfer Agent directory object is located inside the server container.

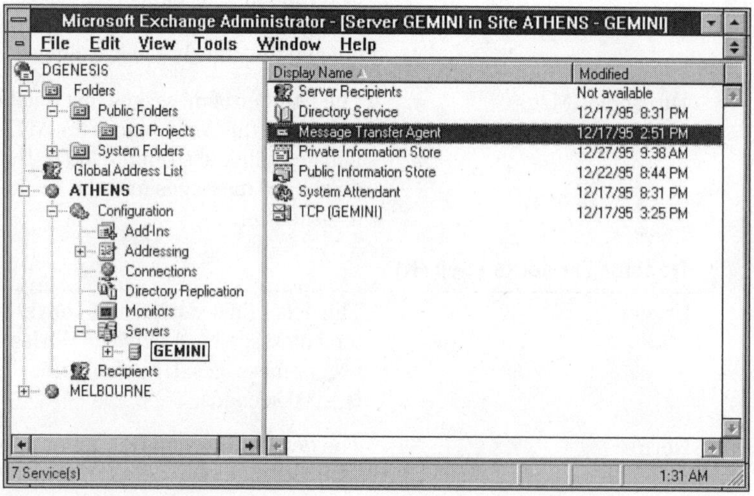

5. Click the Message Transfer Agent object, and open its property pages.

The following three property pages become available for you to configure:

- *General.* Sets local MTA name, password, and general message transmission preferences for this server.
- *Queues.* Lists messages awaiting transmission by the local MTA.
- *Diagnostics Logging.* Sets the level of events that are entered in the Windows NT event log.

The General Tab

To set values for the local MTA name, password, and other general message transfer preferences for this server, follow these steps:

1. Click the General tab of the Message Transfer Agent Properties page (see fig. 13.5).

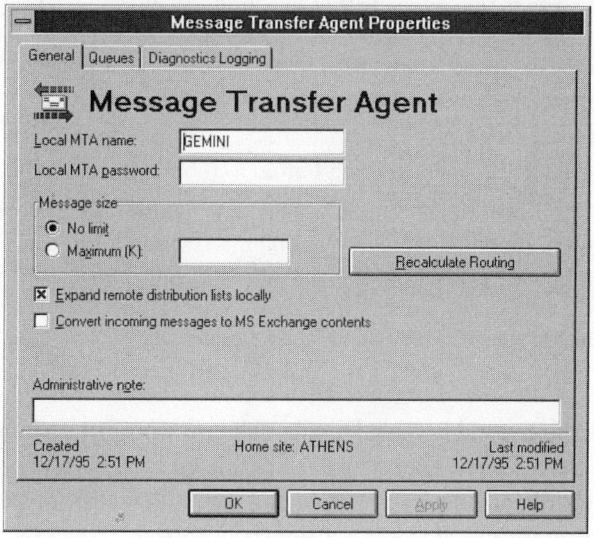

FIG. 13.5 The General Message Transfer Agent property page.

2. Type a name in the Local MTA Name box. This name will be used by remote MTAs (either on remote Exchange servers or foreign messaging systems) to identify this MTA. By default, this name is the name of the Exchange server on which the MTA is installed.
3. Type a password in the Local MTA Password box, if necessary. If you enter a password in this box, any remote MTA (either on remote Exchange servers or foreign messaging systems) must be configured to provide this password for authentication. By default, this box is blank, and no authentication is required of the remote MTA.

Part III Ch 13

NOTE If you decide to change the Local MTA Name or to add or change the Local MTA Password, be sure to take into consideration any previously established MTA connections. All remote sites (and foreign systems, such as X.400) must be adjusted to reflect the new information. Authentication is never required between two MTAs in the same site.

TIP Use these settings as a filter to manage the messaging load for all traffic to and from this server. The upper-limit settings have precedence over message-size settings in individual connectors and recipient objects.

4. In the Message Size section, click the radio button that indicates how you want to restrict the passage of messages through this message transfer agent.

   Click the No Limit radio button to allow this MTA to deliver messages of any size.

   If you want to set a size limit, click the Maximum (K) radio button; then, in the text box, type an upper limit (in kilobytes) for messages that travel through this MTA. Any message that exceeds this size limit will be returned as undeliverable.

TIP Rebuilding routing tables sometimes takes several minutes, so it is a good idea to go through each MTA property sheet, make all changes, and then recalculate routing.

5. Click the Recalculate Routing button to rebuild the routing tables for this MTA. (See Chapter 2, "Understanding Exchange's Organization and Sites," for more information on routing tables.) New routing information for this MTA will propagate to all Exchange servers within the site automatically.

NOTE Routing tables are rebuilt once a day automatically.

6. Click the Expand Remote Distribution Lists Locally check box to force distribution lists created on remote sites to be expanded on this server. When a message is sent to a distribution list by a user on this server, the message is split into its component recipients locally. If this box is not checked, the distribution list is expanded in the remote site, following the configuration in the distribution list's own property pages. By default, this box is checked, and distribution lists are expanded locally.

NOTE Consider both the physical locations of the majority of the distribution list's recipients and the messaging load on the local server. If you choose the default settings, make certain that the local server can handle the extra messaging traffic; expanding large distribution lists can be a considerable load on an already overburdened Exchange server. Also, if you know that the majority of the distribution list's recipients reside on Exchange servers on the remote site, consider allowing the list to be expanded there.

7. Click the Convert Incoming Messages to MS Exchange Contents check box to convert all messages to Exchange's MAPI-compliant format automatically. By default, this option is not selected, and messages are kept in the format in which they arrive at the MTA (such as standard X.400 format).
8. If you want, make an entry in the Administrative Note text box.
9. Click Apply to set these properties and continue with other properties.
10. When you finish making settings, click OK to return to the Administrator program.

The Queues Tab

The Queues tab of the message transfer agent property pages lists messages that are awaiting delivery by the MTA. The two primary windows are Queue Name, which shows the queue that you are currently viewing, and Message List, which displays the messages in that queue. From the Message List window, you can view details about a specific message in the queue, change its priority for delivery, or delete it.

The Message List window has three columns that contain information about a particular message:

- *Originator:* the original sender of the message
- *Submit Time:* the time of the next transfer attempt for this message
- *Size:* the size of the message, in kilobytes

To configure the Queues property page, follow these steps:

1. Click the Queues tab from the Message Transfer Agent Properties page (see fig. 13.6).

FIG. 13.6
Messages waiting to be delivered are held in the queue.

2. From the Queue Name drop-down list, select the message queue to display. The list shows queues for the private and public information stores, as well as for any installed gateways.

NOTE The Internet Mail connector and Microsoft Mail connector have separate queues that you can access through their property pages. ■

3. Select a message, and click Details to view additional information about it.

   The additional message information includes the message originator, submit time, message size, and priority. This button is dimmed if no messages are in the queue.

4. Click the Refresh button to update the Message List window with the latest list of messages in the MTA queue.

5. Click Priority to display the message's priority, and change the priority of the message, if you want. Priority can be low, medium, or high. Messages are sent in order of priority. A message's priority is set when a message is created.

6. To remove a message from the MTA queue, select a message and then click Delete.

7. Click Apply to set these properties and continue with other properties.

8. When you finish making settings, click OK to return to the Administrator program.

The Diagnostic Logging Tab

This property page works in conjunction with the Windows NT Event Log to record various "events" that occur within the message transfer agent. Various levels of logging determine what constitutes an event and, therefore, what types of information are actually recorded. For troubleshooting purposes, you would want a very detailed record of occurrences within the MTA; hence, you would set a high logging level. Normally, however, you want to log only critical events, so set a lower logging level for everyday operation.

From Here...

The Message transfer agent is the key component for routing and delivering messages to their destination. You administrate MTA functions through two main sets of property pages:

1. MTA Site Configuration Settings for an entire Exchange site
2. Message Transfer Agent Settings for an individual Exchange server's MTA service.

See the following chapters for more information on topics related to the MTA.

- Chapter 3, "Exchange's Integrated Server Components," provides an overview of how the message transfer agent integrates with other Exchange components.
- Chapters 15, "Creating and Configuring Recipients," 18, "Setting Up Microsoft Mail for PC Networks," and 20, "Configuring X.400 Connections," cover Exchange connections to other systems and explain how the MTA communicates with gateways and connectors.
- Chapter 26, "Diagnostic and Troubleshooting Tools," discusses troubleshooting the MTAs operation by using Diagnostic Logging.

CHAPTER 14

Information Store Configuration

- **Information Store site configuration—Overall settings for an entire Microsoft Exchange site**
- **Private Information Store server configuration**
- **Public Information Store server configuration and Public Folder Replication**

The Microsoft Exchange Information Stores (public and private) are the databases that hold all Microsoft Exchange messaging information. In addition, the Information Store is the primary storage system for information relevant to users, including Messages, Server-based mailboxes and their contents, Public folders and their contents, Private folders that are stored on a server instead of on a user's computer, documents, forms, and user-defined items.

Important Information Store Concepts

The following concepts will be helpful to understand when proceeding through this chapter:

Top-Level Folder

A public folder created at the highest point in the public folder directory tree. Usually only certain individuals in an Exchange organization are granted the right to create folders at the top of the hierarchy.

Public Folder Instance

A replica of a public folder on a different site than it was created. Users can then connect to the instance of the folder instead of crossing site boundaries (and adding to network traffic) and connecting to a remote site.

Public Folder Affinity

When a user in a local site needs to connect to a public folder only available in a remote site, the choice of connection will be based on the costs assigned to that site containing replicas of that folder.

Information Store Message Tracking

The Information Store is responsible for message transfer between two users on the same Exchange server. To keep a record of Information Store message transfer activity within a Microsoft Exchange server, enable message tracking. A daily log file is generated and stored in the EXCHSRVR\TRACKING.LOG directory. The individual log files are named as follows:

YYMMDD.log

Example

960529.log for Information Store activity on May 29, 1996.

Information Store Site Configuration

Settings made on the Information Store Site Configuration property pages affect all servers within an Exchange site. When first setting up an Exchange site, you should use these property pages.

Opening the MTA Site Configuration Properties pages:

1. Navigate to your desired site with the Exchange administrator program.
2. Click the **Configuration** container (see fig. 14.1) of the selected site. All the site configuration objects appear in the administrator program's right window.

FIG. 14.1
The Configuration container holds all site configuration objects.

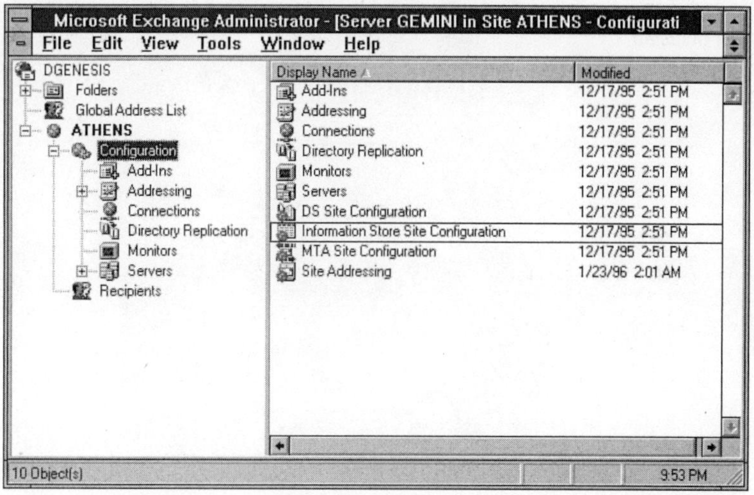

3. Select the **Information Store Site Configuration** object from the list.
4. Open its property pages.

At this point there will be five property pages to configure:

- General

  Set display name, public folder container, and toggle message tracking.
- Permissions

  Set access right to the Information Store Site Configuration directory object.
- Top-Level Folder Creation

  Define which users are allowed to create public folders at the highest level of the public folder directory tree.
- Storage Warnings

  Schedule when notification messages about exceeded storage space are sent to those users in violation of set restraints.
- Public Folder Affinity

  Configure connections to public folders in remote sites.

The General Page

1. Select the General tab of the Information Store Site Configuration Properties page. The property page in figure 14.2 appears.

FIG. 14.2
The Configuration container holds all site configuration objects.

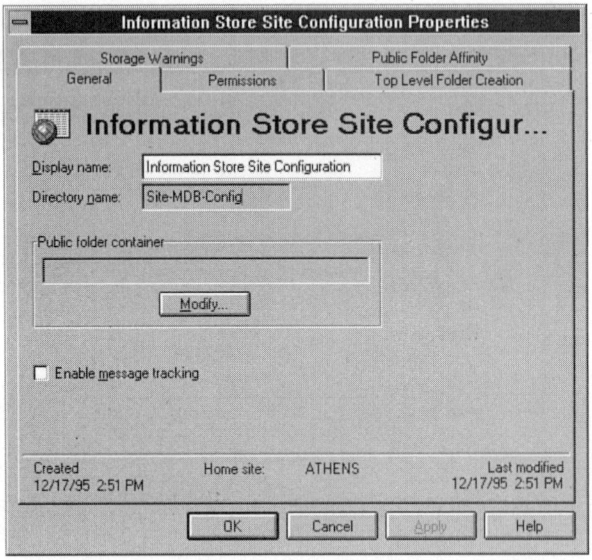

2. If desired, type a new Display Name as you want it to appear in the Microsoft Exchange Administrator program. By default this name is Information Store Site Configuration. The Directory name for this object is Site-MDB-Config by default, and it cannot be changed.
3. The Public Folder container box displays the recipient container in which the Public Folders for this site are stored. By default, this box is blank, and Public Folders are stored in the standard recipients container. Click Modify to bring up a dialog box with a listing of all available recipient containers within this site. Select a container, then click OK.
4. Click the Enable message tracking checkbox to instruct the Information Store to keep a daily log file about all messages processed by the MTA. This button corresponds with the Enable Message Tracking checkbox on the MTA Site Configuration.
5. Click Apply to set these properties and continue with other properties. If you are done with all settings, click OK to return to the administrator program.

The Permissions Page

This property page allows you to define certain Windows NT user accounts that have rights to modify this directory object. See Chapter 11, "Using the Administrator Program," for a detailed description on working with the standard Permissions property page.

The Top-Level Folder Creation Page

This property page can either deny or allow certain users the capability to create public folders on the highest level of the hierarchy.

NOTE Distribution lists can also be specified, and Exchange will use the members of that list to determine top-level folder creation permission.

Configuring Top-Level Folder Creation Properties:

1. Select the Top Level Folder Creation tab from the Information Store Site Configuration Properties page. The property page in figure 14.3 appears.

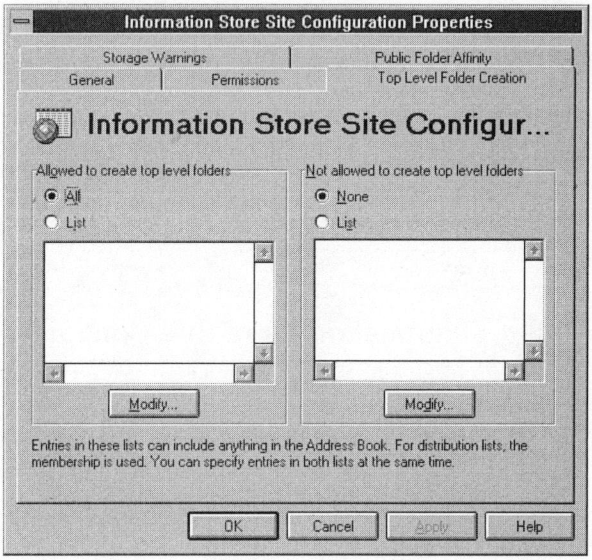

FIG. 14.3 Selectively assign Top Level Folder creation rights from this property page.

The `Allowed to create top level folders` box lists the recipients who are specifically given permission to create these folders. The `Not allowed to create top level folders` box lists the recipients specifically denied permission to create these folders.

2. Click the Modify button under either window if you wish to add or delete recipients from the lists. A standard address list dialog box appears. By default, All can create top-level folders and None are denied permission.
3. Click Apply to set these properties and continue with other properties. If you are done with all settings, click OK to return to the administrator program.

The Storage Warnings Page

The actual storage limits are set in the following property pages for each corresponding recipient type:

- Mailboxes

  Mailbox Advanced property page for each individual user, or a more global storage limit for all mailboxes on a particular server, in the private information store property page.

- Public Folders

  Public Folder Advanced property page for each individual folder, or a more global storage limit for all public folders on a particular server, in the public information store property page.

Set the Storage Warning notification schedule by taking these steps:

1. Select the Storage Warnings tab of the Information Store Site Configuration Properties page. The properties page in figure 14.4 appears.

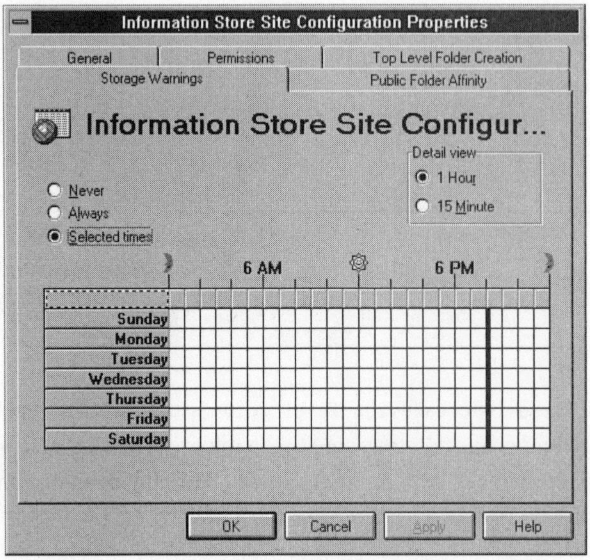

FIG. 14.4 Set the Storage Warnings notification schedule.

2. Select one of the three radio buttons that determine when recipients are notified.

    Never—This effectively disables storage warning notification.

    Always—A storage warning notification is executed immediately when a storage limit is exceeded.

    Selected times—Storage warning notifications are executed based upon the time slots selected on this property page.

> **TIP** If you are using storage limits in a large organization, it is generally not a good idea to select Always and potentially overtax your servers during high-traffic times with a large number of scattered warning messages. Better to schedule a time when messaging load is lower and have them all sent at once.

3. If you choose Selected Times, the Detail view radio buttons become available. Select either the 1 Hour or 15 Minute detail view, and the time grid will change its scale accordingly.
4. If you choose Selected Times, pick the time blocks for connection. By default, storage warning notifications are scheduled once per day beginning at 8 p.m.
5. Click Apply to set these properties and continue with other properties. If you are done with all settings, click OK to return to the administrator program.

The Public Folder Affinity Page

This property page allows you to set up connection to public folders located in remote Exchange sites.

Configuring public folder affinity:

1. Select the Public Folder Affinity tab of the Information Store Site Configuration Properties pages. The property page in figure 14.5 appears.

    The Sites window lists all the sites in your organization. The Public folder affinity window lists all the sites to where a connection may be established in order for a user to connect to a remote public folder. The Cost column displays the relative numeric value assigned to this site. Similar to message routing, the site with the lower cost will be used first.
2. To add a site, select it from the Sites window and click Add. To remove a site, select it from the Public Folder Affinity window and click Remove.

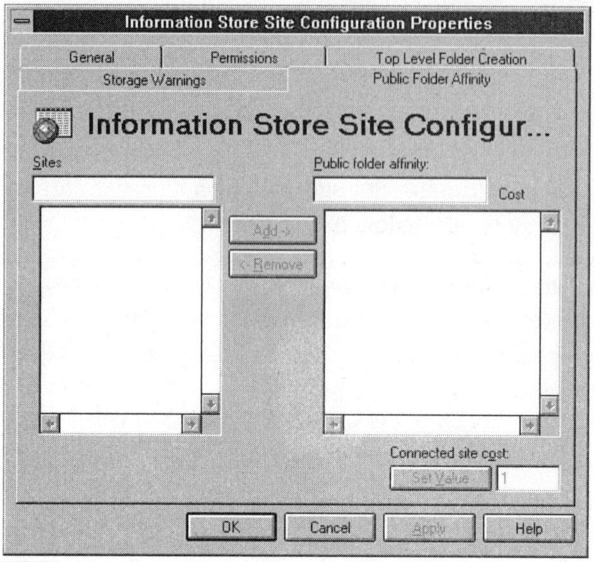

FIG. 14.5
Define how a user connects to remote public folders.

3. Enter the Connected site cost in the box at the lower right if the property page is 0. This site will always be used first if it is available. 1–99: Sites used in numerical sequence, with load on equally numbered sites being distributed evenly. 100: This site will be used only if no other site is available.
4. Click Set Value to save the cost associated with the selected site.
5. Click Apply to set these properties and continue with other properties. If you are done with all settings, click OK to return to the administrator program.

Configuring Private Information Store

Now we will move on to configuring Private Information Store properties on an individual Microsoft Exchange server. The Private Information Store primarily holds data posted to public folders.

- General

  Set global mailbox storage limits; designate a public folder server
- Logons

  View a list of users' connections to the Private Information Store
- Mailbox Resources

  View general settings and amount of storage space used by each mailbox

- Diagnostic Logging

  Set logging levels for tracking down errors and debugging your organization

First you must select the Private Information Store from a server within your site:

1. Navigate to your desired site with the Exchange administrator program.
2. Click the Configuration container of the selected site. All the site configuration objects appear in the administrator program's right window.
3. Open the Servers container. A list of Exchange servers in your site will be listed.
4. Click the server name on which the Private Information Store your want to configure is (see fig. 14.6). The following list of server objects is visible on the right display window of the Microsoft Exchange Administrator Program.

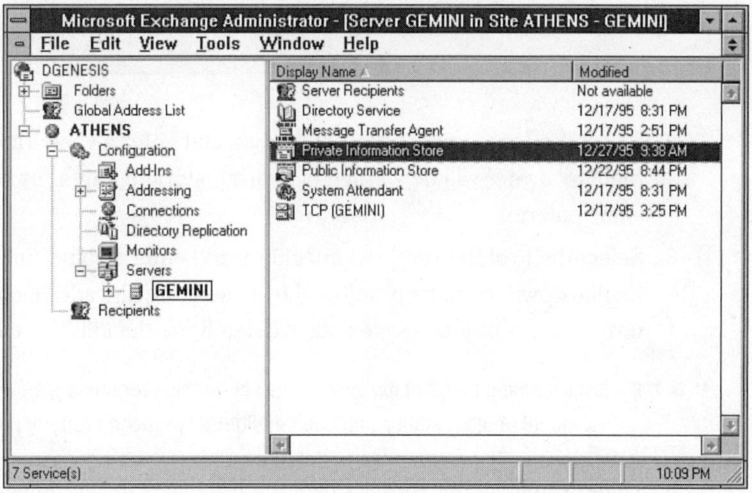

FIG. 14.6
The Private Information Store holds all mailbox data of users on the local server.

5. Click the Private Information Store object. Open its property pages.

The General Page

This property page allows you to set global storage size limits for mailboxes on this server. Also, you can specify a different Exchange server to be responsible for the public folders created by users on this server.

Configuring Private Information Store General properties:

1. Select the General tab of the Private Information Store Properties page. The property page in figure 14.7 appears.

FIG. 14.7
The settings on this page apply to all mailboxes on this server.

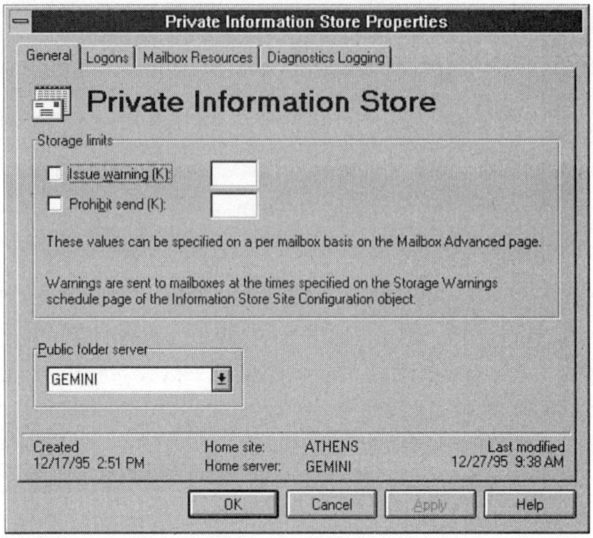

2. Select the Issue warning (K) checkbox and enter a value (in kilobytes) at which a mailbox owner will be warned of nearing storage limits. By default, there is no set value entered.
3. Select the Prohibit send (K) checkbox and enter a value (in kilobytes) at which a mailbox owner will be prohibited from sending any additional outgoing messages until some stored message data is deleted. By default, there is no set value entered.

NOTE Issue warning and Prohibit send limits set on this property page are overridden by individual mailbox settings on each mailbox's Advanced property page.

4. Under Public folder server select the Exchange server in your site on which will be stored public folders created by users on the local server. By default, the public folder server used is the same one on which the folder was created, the current server.

NOTE If you select a server other than the local Exchange server, then you are effectively separating that server's public information and private information stores. Only select a different server if this complies with your overall load balancing plan for this Exchange site.

5. Click Apply to set these properties and continue with other properties. If you are done with all settings, click OK to return to the administrator program.

The message shown in figure 14.8 is an example storage size warning message.

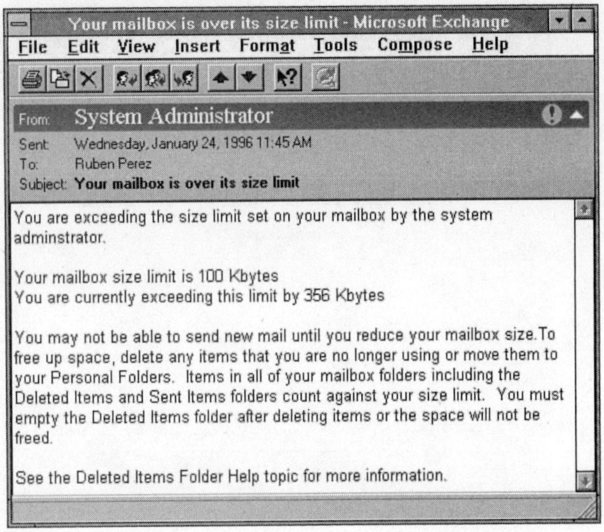

FIG. 14.8
This message is sent when users exceed set storage limits for their mailboxes.

The Logons Page

This property page allows you to monitor the Microsoft Exchange users currently logged into a server. It consists of one main display window that shows all currently connected users. The window is broken down into various columns of information. The specific columns displayed are customizable both by information shown and width on the screen.

Viewing Logon information:

1. Select the Logons tab of the Private Information Store Properties page. The property page in figure 14.9 appears.

   The display window shows all users currently logged on to this Exchange server.

NOTE The Microsoft Exchange System Attendant is always listed in this window as well.

2. Click the Refresh button to update the display window with the latest information.
3. Click the Columns button to edit which columns are displayed and their width in pixels (see fig. 14.10). See the following for a description of each column heading and what type of information it can display.
4. Click Apply to set these properties and continue with other properties. If you are done with all settings, click OK to return to the administrator program.

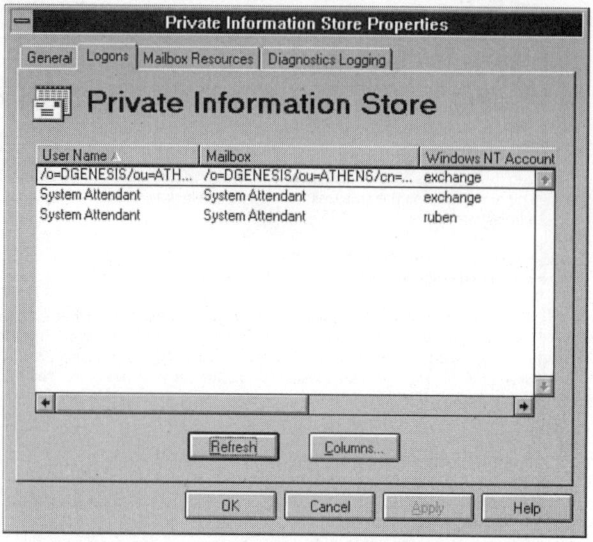

FIG. 14.9
View currently logged on users.

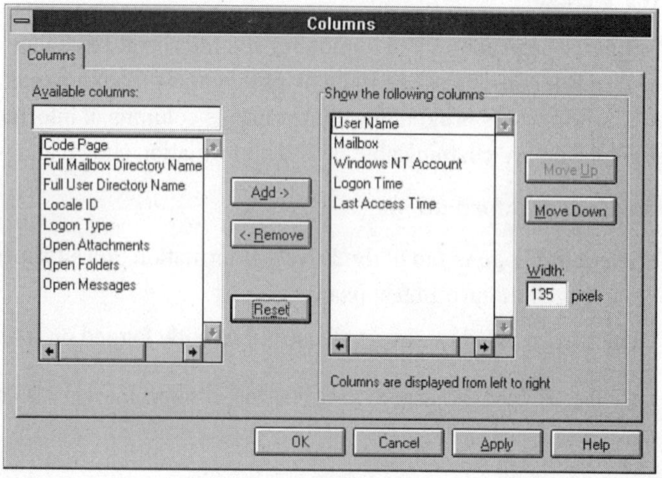

FIG. 14.10
Display Columns available for the Logons property page.

Default Columns

- User Name

  The name (display name) for the user logged on to this mailbox
- Mailbox

  The Exchange administrator program object display name for this mailbox
- Windows NT Account

  The Windows NT account of the user currently logged on to this mailbox

- Logon Time

  The date and time the user logged on to Microsoft Exchange
- Last Access Time

  [to be determined]

Optional Columns

- Code Page
- Full Mailbox Directory Name
- Locale ID
- Logon Type
- Open Attachments

  The total number of attachments a particular user currently has open
- Open Folders

  The total number of folders open within the user's Exchange client for this user
- Open Messages

  The total number of messages a particular user currently has open

The Mailbox Resources Page

This property page allows you to view the physical resources, e.g., hard disk storage space, used by the Exchange mailboxes on the server. It consists of one main display window that shows the mailboxes on the current server. The windows are broken down into various columns of information. The specific columns displayed are customizable both by information presented and width on the screen.

NOTE A mailbox will be displayed in this window only after the first time a user logs on to it. If the mailbox has never been used, it will not appear on Mailbox Resources property page.

Viewing Mailbox Resources information:

1. Select the Mailbox Resources tab of the Private Information Store Properties page. The properties page in figure 14.11 appears.

   The display window shows all the mailboxes on this server that have been used at least once.

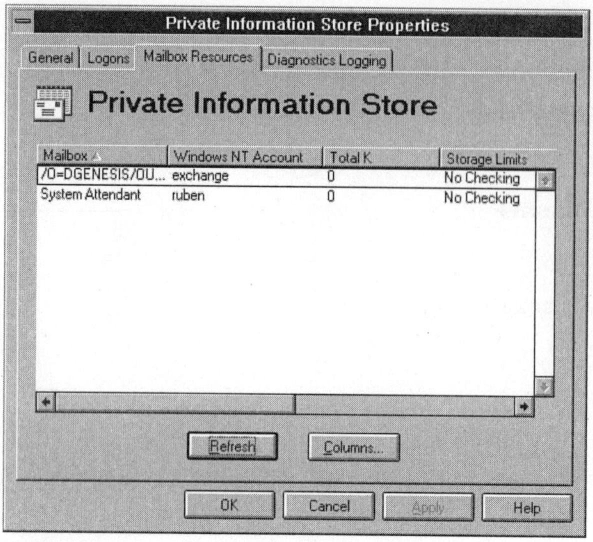

FIG. 14.11 View server resource use on a per-mailbox basis.

NOTE The Microsoft Exchange System Attendant and the Exchange account itself are always listed in this window as well.

2. Click the Refresh button to update the display window with the latest information.
3. Click the Columns button to edit which columns are displayed and their width in pixels (see fig. 14.12). See the following for a description of each column heading and what type of information it can display.
4. Click Apply to set these properties and continue with other properties. If you are done with all settings, click OK to return to the administrator program.

The Default Columns

- Mailbox

  The Exchange administrator program object display name for this mailbox

- Windows NT Account

  The Windows NT account of the user currently logged on to this mailbox.

- Total K

  The total amount of disk storage space (in kilobytes) taken up by the contents of this user's mailbox. This value includes any message attachments.

- Storage Limits

  Any storage limits imposed on mailbox; e.g., Prohibit Send

- Total no. Items

  The sum of all messages and attachments stored in a mailbox

- Last Logon Time

  The last time a user logged on to this mailbox

- Last Logoff Time

  The last time a user logged off from this mailbox

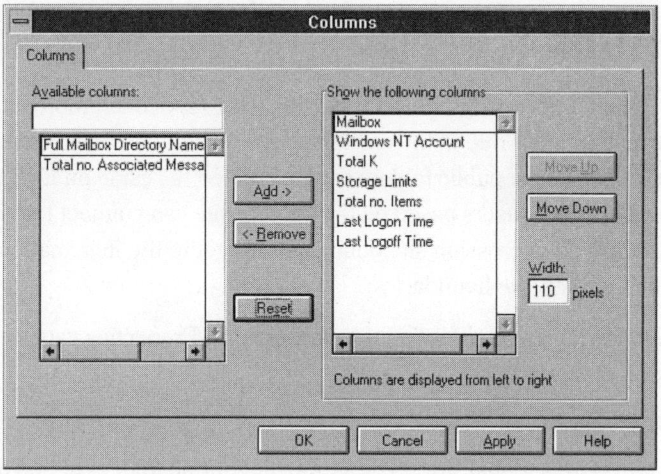

FIG. 14.12 Display columns available for the Mailbox Resources property page.

Optional Columns This property page allows you to view the full e-mail address for the mailbox and the total number of associated messages in this mailbox.

- Full Mailbox Directory Name

  The entire X.400 e-mail address for this mailbox

- Total no. Associated Messages

  The sum of stored views and deferred action messages (messages scheduled to be sent/processed at a later time) in this mailbox

The Diagnostic Logging Tab This property page works in conjunction with the Windows NT Event Log to record various "events" that occur within the Information Store. This property page is identical to that one found on the Public Information Store Properties pages. Various levels of logging determine what constitutes an event, and therefore, what types of information are actually recorded. For troubleshooting purposes, you would want a very detailed record of occurrences within the Information Store, and hence set a high logging level. However, normally you would want to log only events that are critical, so set a lower logging level for everyday operation.

Public Information Store/Public Folder Replication

The Public Information Store Properties pages are much more extensive than the Private Information Store due to the existence of public folder replication. To reiterate this concept, duplicates of public folders can be created to reside on Exchange server on remote sites. Therefore, users based on the remote site can connect to the local copy of the public folder instead of crossing site boundaries to get to the information. This reduces network traffic between site boundaries.

The following are the Public Information Store Properties pages available on each Microsoft Exchange server:

- General

  Impose a global storage limit warning for all folders in this public information store.

- Instances

  Select which public folders to replicate to the local server from remote sites.

- Replication Schedule

  Set the times when public folders on the local server are replicated to the established remote instances.

- Age Limits

  Set the lifetime of public folders or their contents.

- E-mail Addresses

  Define and modify various e-mail addresses for the public information store directory object.

- Logons

  View data about users currently connected to a public folder.

- Public Folder Resources

  View data about quantity of server resources consumed by a particular public folder.

- Server Replication Status

  Monitor each server's participation in public folder replication.
- Folder Replication Status

  Monitor the replication of individual public folders.
- Advanced

  Define the delay between replication cycles when Always is selected for the schedule. Also, define the maximum size of each individual replication message.
- Diagnostics Logging

  Activate various levels of logging for troubleshooting purposes.

The General Page

This property page has only the one option to set a global Issue Warning for all public folders on the local Exchange server (see fig. 14.13).

Setting the General properties:

1. Select the General tab of the Public Information Store Properties page. The following property page appears.

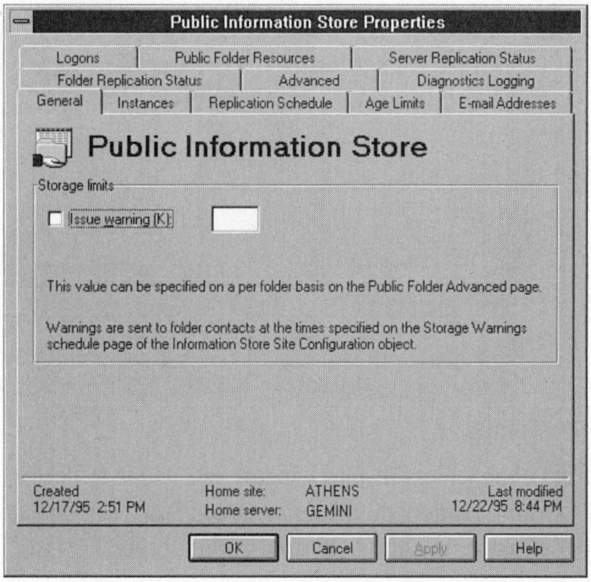

FIG. 14.13
Set a global (for all public folders on this server) public folder size warning.

2. Click the Issue warning (K) checkbox and enter a folder data size (in kilobytes) at which a folder contact will be notified. By default, this option is unchecked. Warnings can also be set at the individual folder level on the public folder's Advanced property page.
3. Click Apply to set these properties and continue with other properties. If you are done with all settings, click OK to return to the administrator program.

The Instances Page

Use this property page to mark public folders for duplication to the local server. Such *instances* of public folders in the local site are actually created through the process of public folder replication (see fig. 14.14).

1. Select the Instances tab of the Public Information Store Properties pages. The following property page appears.

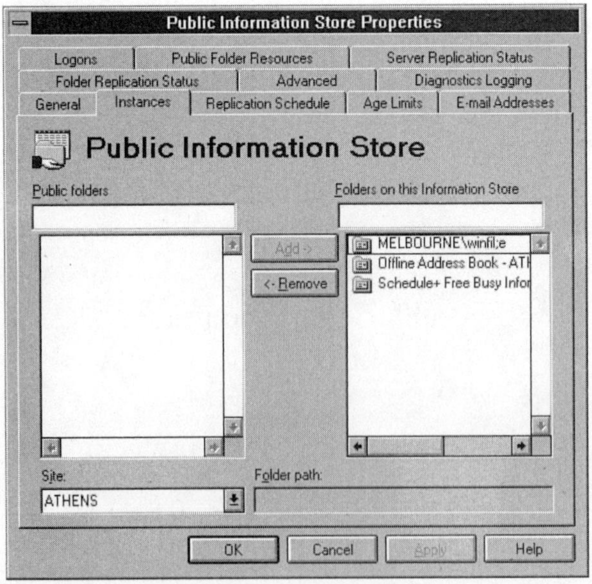

FIG. 14.14
Create public folder replicas on remote servers with this property page.

The left, Public folders display window lists all the folders in the currently selected site. The right, Folders on this Information Store displays the list of both public folders on this server and replicated to this server.

2. Use the Site pull-down menu to select a site in your organization. The public folders residing on that site are then listed in the left display window.
3. Select a public folder and click Add to mark that folder for replication to the local Exchange server.
4. To remove a public folder's instance from the local server, select it from the right display window, then click Remove.

NOTE You cannot remove a local public folder from the local Exchange server if it is the only copy of it in the local site. ■

5. Click Apply to set these properties and continue with other properties. If you are done with all settings, click OK to return to the administrator program.

The Replication Schedule Page

This property page allows you to set times when public folder replication messages are actually transferred. Take into consideration the potentially high volume of data that may need to be transferred from a large and heavily used public folder.

Setting the Replication Schedule:

1. Select the Replication Schedule tab of the Public Information Store Properties page. The dialog box in figure 14.15 appears.

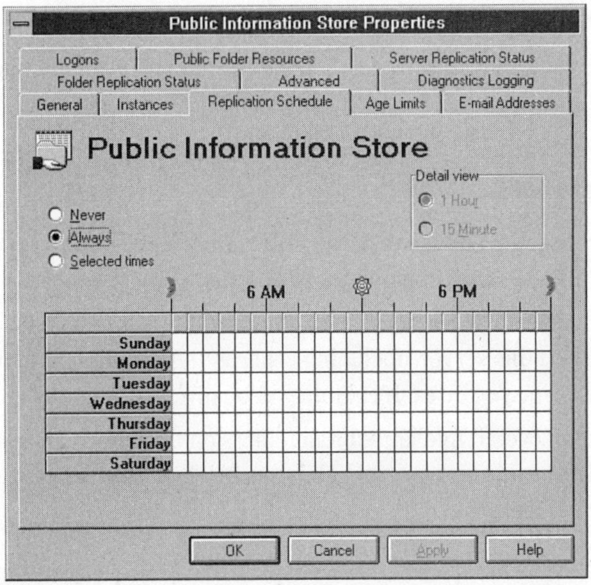

FIG. 14.15 Set public folder replication times for this server.

2. Select one of the three radio buttons that determine when this X.400 Connector connects.

   Never—This effectively disables public folder replication from this server.

   Always—Folder replication messages are sent every fifteen minutes. This time delay can be changed on this public information store's Advanced property page. By default, Always is selected.

   Selected times—Replication messages are transferred based upon the time grid on this property page.

3. If you choose Selected times, the Detail view radio buttons become available. Select either the 1 Hour or 15 Minute detail view and the time grid will change its scale accordingly.
4. If you choose Selected times, pick the time blocks for connection.
5. Click Apply to set these properties and continue with other properties. If you are done with all settings, click OK to return to the administrator program.

The Age Limits Page

The Age Limits property page allows you to define when information in a public folder should expire and be automatically deleted. This feature prevents public folders from becoming bogged down with megabytes upon megabytes of outdated, useless information.

Example

You set up a CLASSIFIEDS folder. You set the age limits for posting in the folder for seven days. Once a message has been sitting in a folder for a week, then it will expire and be automatically deleted by the information store.

Setting Age Limits:

1. Select the Age Limits tab of the Public Information Store Properties page. The property page in figure 14.16 appears.

   The main display window shows the columns of information about all the public folders on this server (including replicas). A description of the kind of information that is displayed by each column will be given later in this chapter.

2. To set an overall Age limit for all folders on this information store (days), select the checkbox and enter a number of days in which messages in all this server's public folders will expire.

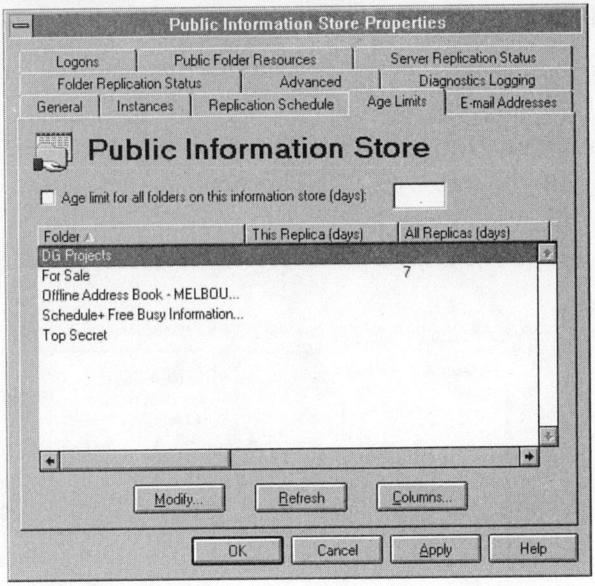

FIG. 14.16
Set the amount of time a message can exist in a public folder before it is deleted.

NOTE You can override this setting on an individual public folder on that folder's Advanced property page.

3. Select a public folder from the list and click Modify to set individual age limits for this folder. The dialog box in figure 14.17 appears.

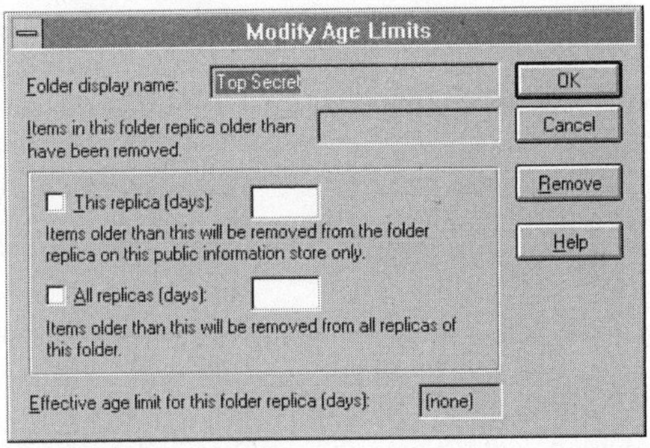

FIG. 14.17
Set age limits on an individual folder basis.

Click the This replica (days) checkbox to set an age limit or a public folder's instance on this server only. Click the All replicas (days) checkbox to set an age limit set for all instances of a public folder throughout your organization. Click the Remove button to delete the selected public folder instance from the information store. Click OK to set your choices (see fig. 14.18).

Part III
Ch 14

4. Click the Refresh button to update the display window with the latest information.
5. Click the Columns button to edit which columns are displayed and their width in pixels. More details on columns will follow.
6. Click Apply to set these properties and continue with other properties. If you are done with all settings, click OK to return to the administrator program.

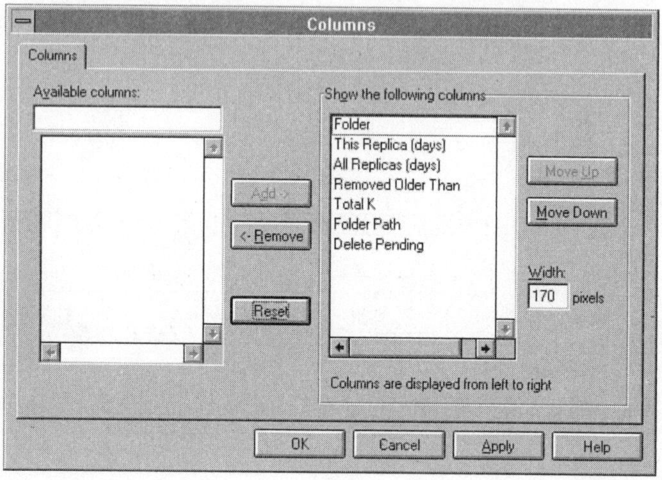

FIG. 14.18
Display columns available for the Age Limits property page.

Default Columns

By default, all available columns are displayed:

- Folder

  The Exchange administrator object display name for the folder.
- This Replica (days)

  Age limit set for a public folder's instance on this server only.
- All Replicas (days)

  Age limit set for all instances of a public folder throughout your organization.
- Removed Older Than

  Notifies that messages older than the number of days displayed have been deleted.
- Total K

  The sum of all messages in a public folder.
- Folder Path

  The location of the public folder (relative to this server or full X.400 address to another server).

- Delete Pending

  Normally "false," this column shows "true" when a folder or messages with that folder are scheduled to be deleted.

The E-Mail Addresses Page

E-mail addresses are used by the various Exchange gateways and connectors to identify specific directory objects to other messaging systems. There are three default addresses created each for MS Mail, SMTP, and X.400.

Setting public folder e-mail addresses:

1. Click the E-mail Addresses of the Public Information Store Properties page. The dialog box in figure 14.19 appears.

FIG. 14.19
Define e-mail addresses for this directory object.

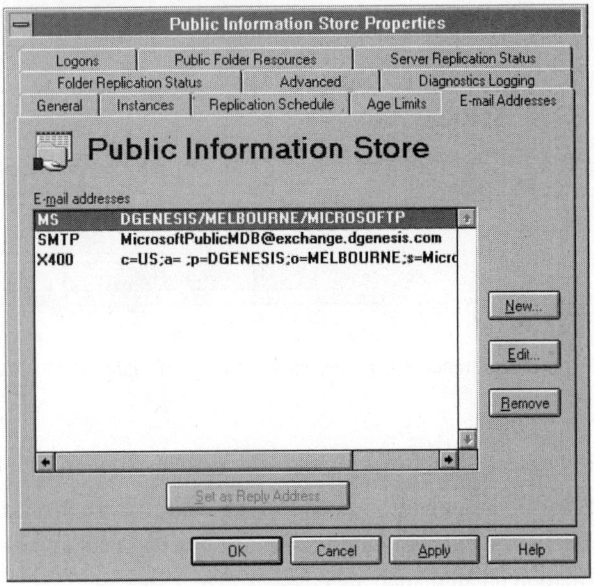

   The three default addresses (MS Mail, SMTP, and X.400) are displayed.

2. Click New to add a specific e-mail address for this information store. Select an existing address and click Edit to modify it, or click Remove to delete it.
3. Click Apply to set these properties and continue with other properties. If you are done with all settings, click OK to return to the administrator program.

The Logons Page

Use this property page to monitor which users are currently connected to a public folder.

1. Select the Logons tab of the Public Information Store Properties page. The property page in figure 14.20 appears.

FIG. 14.20
View users currently connected to public folders on this server. The main display window shows columns of information about connected users.

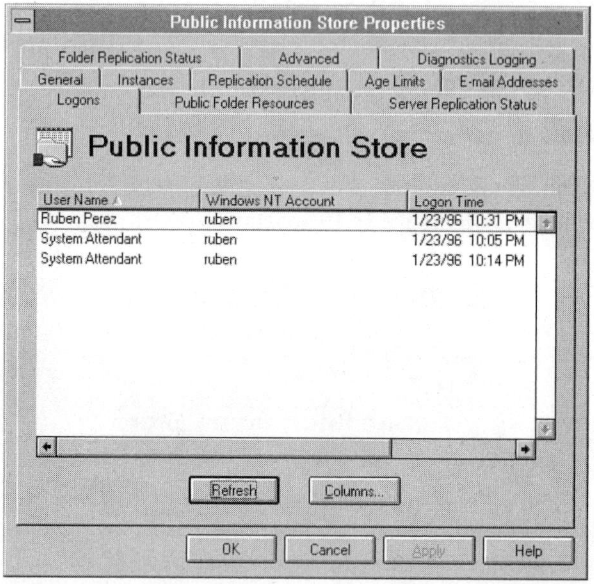

NOTE The System Attendant is always shown as a public information store logon.

2. Click the Refresh button to update the display window with the latest information.
3. Click the Columns button to edit which columns are displayed and their width in pixels. See the following for a description of each column heading and what type of information it can display (see fig. 14.21).
4. Click Apply to set these properties and continue with other properties. If you are done with all settings, click OK to return to the administrator program.

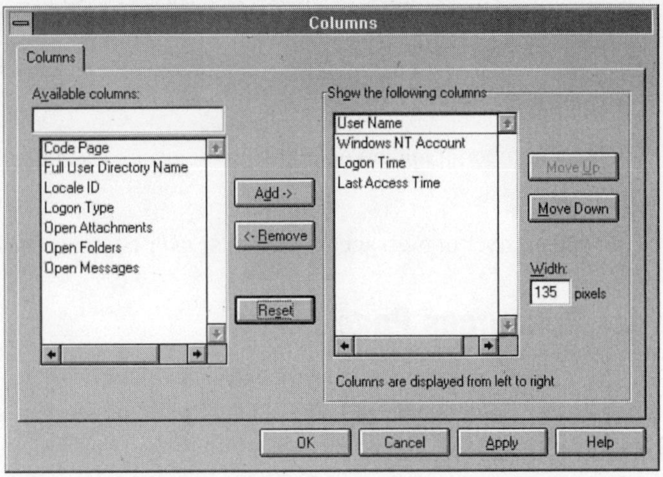

FIG. 14.21
Display Columns available for the Logons property page.

Default Columns

- User Name

  The name (display name) for the user logged on to this mailbox.
- Windows NT Account

  The Windows NT account of the user currently logged on to this mailbox.
- Logon Time

  The date and time the user logged on to Microsoft Exchange.
- Last Access Time

  [to be determined]

Optional Columns

These columns can be added if you want to view any of the following information.

- Code Page
- Full Mailbox Directory Name
- Locale ID
- Logon Type

- Open Attachments

  The total number of attachments a particular user currently has open.
- Open Folders

  The total number of folders open within the user's Exchange client for this user.
- Open Messages

  The total number of messages a particular user currently has open.

Public Folder Resources Page

This property page allows you to view the physical resources, e.g., hard disk storage space, used by the folders held on this public information store. It consists of one main display window that shows the public folders on the current server. The window is subdivided into various columns of information. The specific columns displayed are customizable both by information presented and width on the screen.

Note that the Schedule+ Free Busy Information and the Offline Address Book are in essence public folders as well and are listed on the Public Folder Resources property page.

Viewing Public Folder Resources information:

1. Select the Public Folder Resources tab of the Public Information Store Properties page. The property page in figure 14.22 appears.

   The display window shows all the public folders on this server.

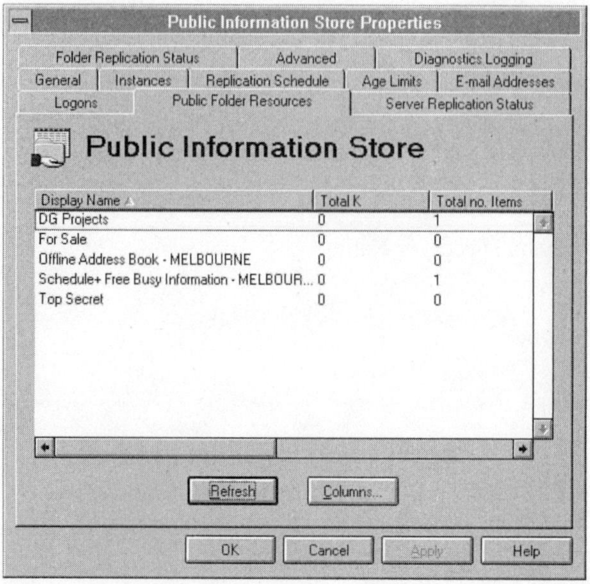

FIG. 14.22 View server resources used by each public folder on this server.

2. Click the Refresh button to update the display window with the latest information.
3. Click the Columns button to edit which columns are displayed and their width in pixels. See the following for a description of each column heading and what type of information it can display (see fig. 14.23).
4. Click Apply to set these properties and continue with other properties. If you are done with all settings, click OK to return to the administrator program.

Columns Using this option, you can select which columns are to be displayed and their width in pixels.

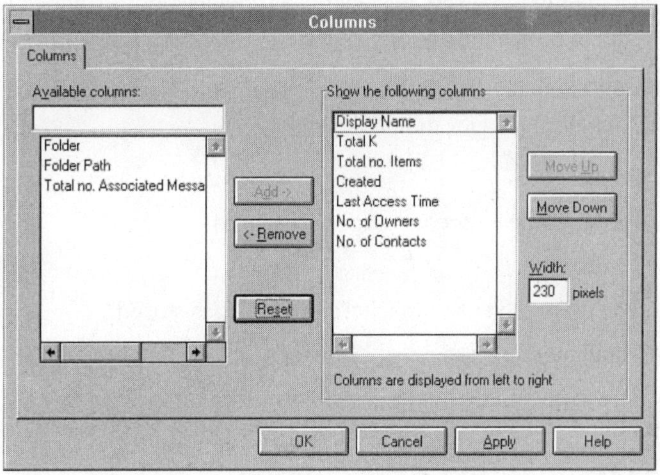

FIG. 14.23
Display columns available for the Public Folder Resources property page.

Default Columns Using this option, you can view/set the default columns of information that will be displayed for the public folder.

- Display Name

  The Exchange administrator program object display name for this public folder.

- Total K

  The total amount of disk storage space (in kilobytes) taken up by the contents of this public folder. This value includes any message attachments.

- Total number Items

  The sum of all messages and attachments stored in a mailbox.

- Created

  The date and time this folder was created.

- Last Access Time

  The last time a user logged on to this public folder.

- Number of Owners

  The number of users designated as Owners of this public folder. See section on defining roles for a public folder.

- Number of Contacts

  The number of users designated as contacts for this public folder. See section on defining roles for a public folder.

Optional Columns Using this option, you can select the optional columns of information that will be displayed for the public folder.

- Folder

  Folder name where messages are stored.

- Folder Path

  The system file path to where this folder is stored.

- Total number Associated Messages

  The sum of folder views and deferred action messages.

The Server Replication Status Page

This property page allows you to monitor the status of a public folders replication to the current public information store on the server level. Exchange servers are individually configured for transmitting updated public folder information to other replicas in remote sites. This property page is primarily a single-display window with various columns of information. The columns to be displayed are modified by none other than the Columns button. The information in this property page is used to not only verify that the selected remote public folders are indeed being replicated to this server, but to monitor details about message transmission time.

Viewing Server Replication Status:

1. Select the Server Replication Status tab of the Public Information Store property page. The property page in figure 14.24 appears.

FIG. 14.24
View the status of remote servers that replicate public folders to the local server.

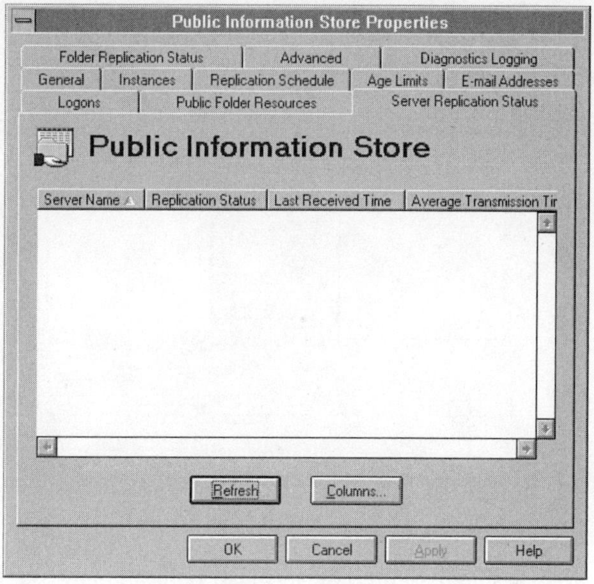

The display window shows all remote servers that replicate public folder data to this server.

2. Click the Refresh button to update the display window with the latest information.
3. Click the Columns button to edit which columns are displayed and their width in pixels. See the following for a description of each column heading and what type of information it can display (see fig. 14.25).
4. Click Apply to set these properties and continue with other properties. If you are done with all settings, click OK to return to the administrator program.

Default Columns

- Server Name

  Name of the Microsoft Exchange server replication public folder data to this server.
- Replication Status

  Notification of public folder replication status.
- Last Received Time

  The last date and time this information store received an update from the remote Exchange server.

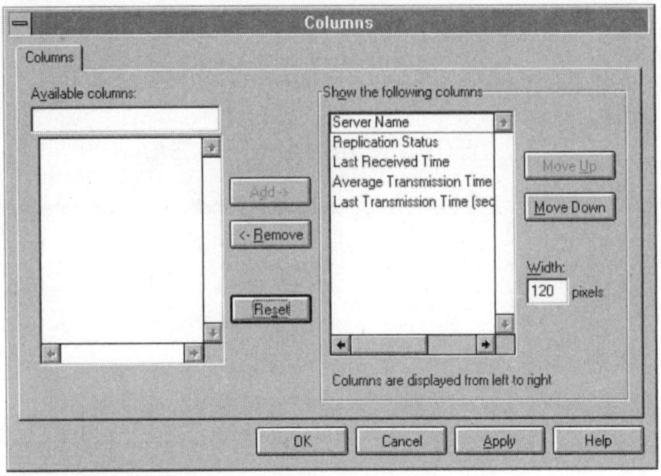

FIG. 14.25 Display columns available for the Server Replication Status property page.

- Average Transmission Time (sec)

  The average length of time (in seconds) replication messages have taken to transmit to this server.

- Last Transmission Time (sec)

  The length of time (in seconds) that the last replication message took to transmit to this server.

Optional Columns

There are no optional display columns on this property page. By default, all the columns that can be displayed are displayed.

The Folder Replication Status Page

This property page provides public information store monitoring capabilities on the individual folder level. This page is also one main display window whose information is displayed in columns.

Viewing Folder Replication Status:

1. Select the Folder Replication Status tab of the Public Information Store Properties page. The property page in figure 14.26 appears.

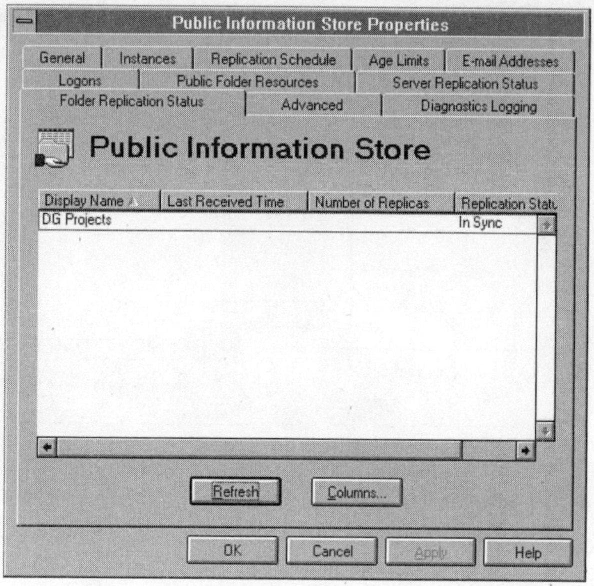

FIG. 14.26
View the status of individual folders replicated to the local server.

The display window shows all public folders replicated to this server's public information store.

2. Click the Refresh button to update the display window with the latest information.
3. Click the Columns button to edit which columns are displayed and their width in pixels. See the following for a description of each column heading and what type of information it can display (see fig. 14.27).
4. Click Apply to set these properties and continue with other properties. If you are done with all settings, click OK to return to the administrator program.

Default Columns

- Display Name

  The Exchange administrator display name for this directory object.

- Last Received Time

  The last date and time this public folder received an updated replication message.

- Number of Replicas

  The sum of all instances of this folder throughout the local site.

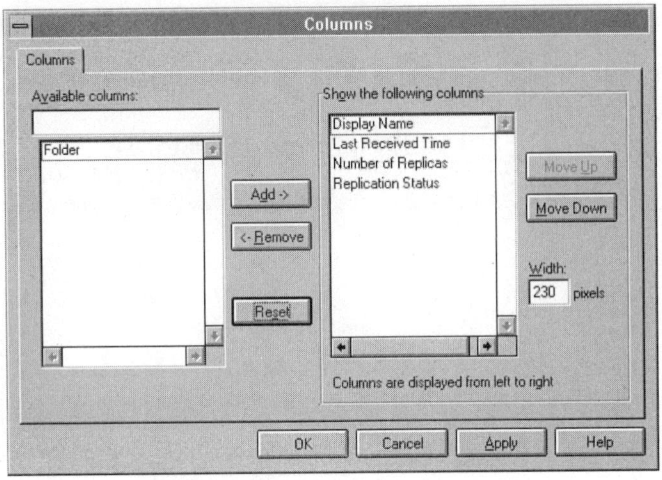

FIG. 14.27
Display columns available for the Folder Replication Status property page.

- Replication Status

  Notification of public folder replication status.

Optional Column

Folder—The public folder name

The Advanced Page

The Advanced property page allows you to make some specialized settings involving public folder replication. When a folder is replicated to a remote site, the actual replication data is a message addressed to the remote public information store. On this property page, you can set the upper limit for the size of the replication messages in order to better control messaging traffic.

1. Select the Advanced tab of the Public Information Store Properties page.
   The property page in figure 14.28 appears.
2. In the Replicate always interval (minutes) box, enter the interval (in minutes) between outgoing replication messages when the Always radio button is selected in the Replication Schedule dialog box. By default, this interval is 15 minutes.
3. In the Replicate message size limit (K) box, enter the maximum message size (in kilobytes) of an outgoing replication message. By default, this maximum is set at 100K. Messages are grouped up to or subdivided to fit that size.
4. To reset the values of the two boxes to their default settings, click the Default button.

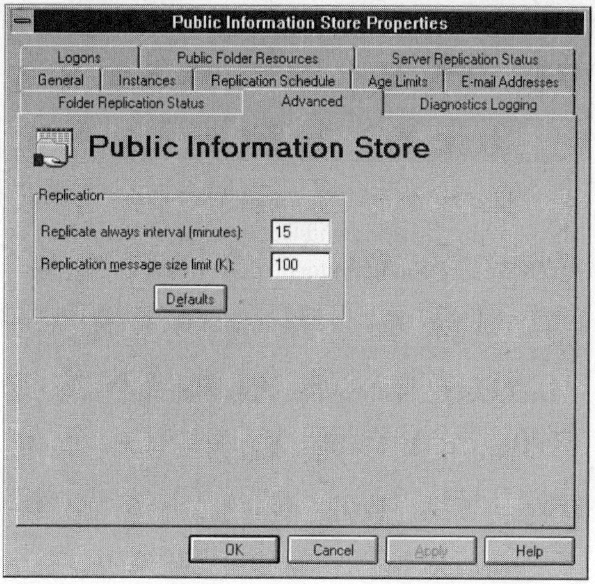

FIG. 14.28 The Public Information Store Advanced property page.

The Diagnostics Logging Page

This property page works in conjunction with the Windows NT Event Log to record various "events" that occur within the Information Store. This property page is identical to that one found on the Private Information Store Properties pages. Various levels of logging determine what constitutes an event and, therefore, what types of information are actually recorded. For troubleshooting purposes, you would want a very detailed record of occurrences within the Information Store, and hence set a high logging level. However, normally you would want to log only events that are critical, so set a lower logging level for everyday operation.

From Here...

The information stores are the Exchange databases that hold all the data in an Exchange organization. The private information store holds all the information in user mailboxes. The public information store holds public folders and also handles folder replication. Replication of public folders to other sites reduces network traffic between sites when a folder is used often. The information store configuration is handled through the following property pages:

1. Information Store Site configuration
2. Private Information Store
3. Public Information Store
    - Chapter 3, "Exchange's Integrated Server Components," provides a review of the information store and how it integrates into other Exchange components.
    - Chapter 15, "Creating and Configuring Recipients." Learn to set up the users' mailboxes held in the information store.
    - Chapter 26, "Diagnostic and Troubleshooting Tools," for troubleshooting information store errors.
    - Chapter 28, "Understanding User Interface Features," for creating public folders with the Exchange client software.

CHAPTER 15

Creating and Configuring Recipients

- How to create and configure a mailbox
- How to create and configure a custom recipient
- How to create and configure distribution lists
- How to create and configure a public folder

A recipient is any directory object designed to receive information. This chapter explains the administrative process of creating and modifying these objects. Several tools are provided with Microsoft Exchange to assist administrators in creating user mailboxes. The Microsoft Exchange Migration tool and the import command in the Administrator Program enable you to import directory lists in bulk from external systems, such as Novell NetWare or Lotus CC: Mail.

Recipients are managed from the Administrator Program. This Program displays recipient objects when the user clicks their container within the exchange hierarchy. Microsoft Exchange Server defines four types of recipients:

- Mailbox

  A mailbox is a receptacle for messaging data. Generally, there is one user per mailbox. However, more than one user can sometimes share a mailbox.

- Custom Recipient

  A custom recipient is outside the main Microsoft Exchange Server messaging site. This usually pertains to users on the Internet, or other foreign messaging system.

- Distribution List

  A distribution list is a group of many recipients. A message sent to a distribution list is forwarded to all its registered users.

- Public Folder

  A public folder is a receptacle for information shared among many users.

Each recipient has multiple property sheets that hold its settings. This section demonstrates how to create and configure each of the four recipient types that the Microsoft Exchange Server defines.

NOTE Whenever you create a new recipient of any sort, you must first select the recipient container in which you want to store this new object. If none is selected, you will be notified that Recipients cannot be created in the parent container.

Example:

Select New Mailbox from the Exchange Administrator file in the BOSTON site. You have not selected either the main Recipients container or any other custom container; therefore, the dialog box in figure 15.1 appears.

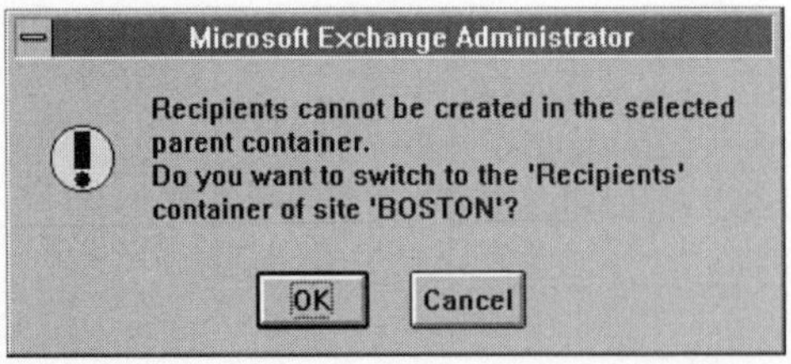

FIG. 15.1
This notice displays when the proper container for the object has not been selected.

Creating Mailboxes

The most common type of recipient is the mailbox. As mentioned previously, each mailbox generally has one user assigned to it. However, several users might share one mailbox. The term "mailbox" refers specifically to a Microsoft Exchange recipient on a Windows NT Server.

You can create a new mailbox using one of two methods:

1. Use the Windows NT User Manager to create an NT user account along with a mailbox.
2. Use the Microsoft Exchange Administrator program to create a mailbox for either a new or existing Windows NT account.

Creating a Mailbox with User Manager

Use the Windows NT User Manager to set up a new Windows NT account along with an Exchange mailbox. With the Microsoft Exchange Server installation you also get what is referred to as the Microsoft Exchange User Manager Extension (see fig. 15.2). This extension adds the menu *Exchange* to your Windows NT User Manager.

FIG. 15.2
The User Manager Extension lets you add and delete Exchange Mailboxes along with accounts in the Windows NT User Manager.

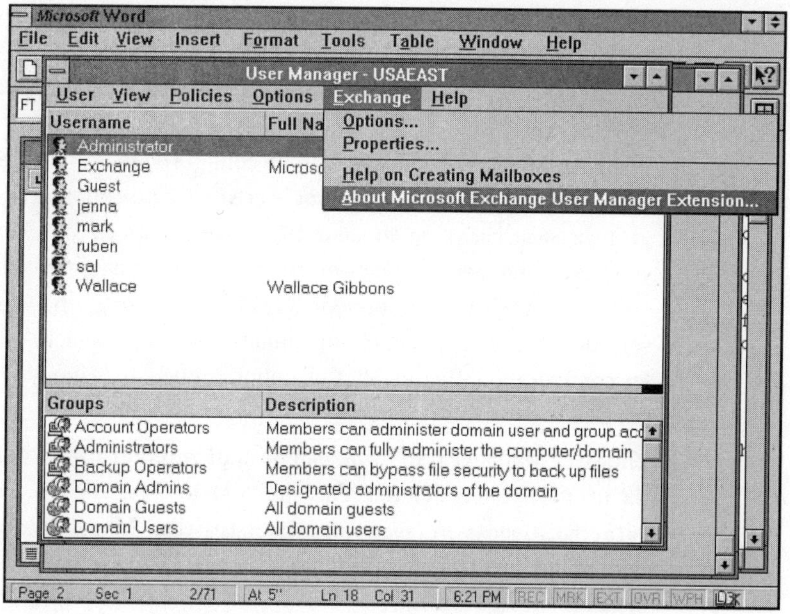

The *Exchange* menu enables you to view a user's mailbox properties without having to launch the Exchange Administration Program. More importantly, the *Exchange menu* integrates the creation of new Windows NT domain users with the creation of new Exchange mailboxes. You can use the following options to configure the Exchange User Manager Extension:

1. Select Options under the Exchange menu. The dialog box in figure 15.3 appears:

FIG. 15.3
You can select from the Options dialog box to configure the User Manager Extension.

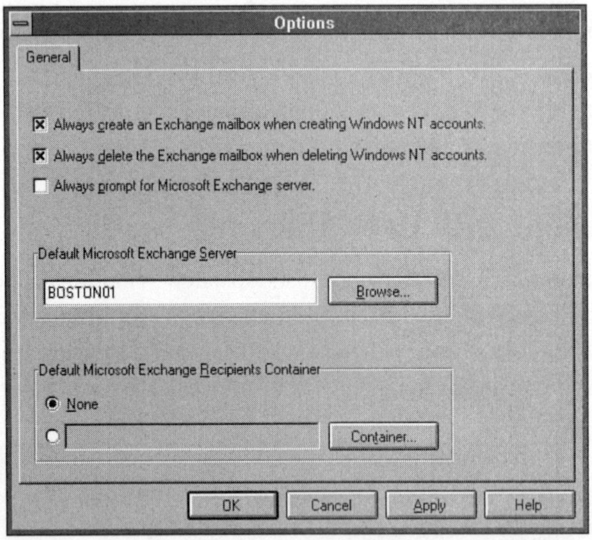

2. The User Manager Extension can be configured to always create an Exchange mailbox when a new user account is created. The option `Always create an Exchange mailbox when creating Windows NT accounts` sets up the User Manager to contact your Exchange Server. This selection also makes a user mailbox every time you create a new NT user. If immediately after you create a new user you check this selection, the standard Exchange mailbox property sheets will be presented to you for configuration. By default, this option is checked when you install Exchange Server.
3. The User Manager Extension can be configured to always delete the mailbox when the user account is deleted. The option `Always delete the Exchange mailbox when deleting Windows NT accounts` sets up the User Manager to contact your Exchange Server and delete a user's mailbox. By default, this option is checked when you install Exchange Server.

NOTE For the preceding option to function properly, you must be certain that the Microsoft Exchange Server is running properly.

4. Checking `Always prompt for microsoft Exchange server` brings up the Exchange select Server dialog box every time the User Manager attempts a connection to Exchange. This option is not checked by default.
5. The Default Microsoft Exchange Server box displays the Exchange Server in which the User Manager Extension creates new user boxes. You can type in a new name. Alternatively, you can click Browse to select a different Server.
6. Click Container to select a custom recipient container. By default, None is selected. This means that all new mailboxes become part of the general recipients container.
7. Click Apply to set these properties and continue with other properties. If you are done with all settings, click OK to return to the User Manager.

Creating Mailboxes in the Exchange Administrator

You will often want to create or administer several types of recipients. A more common way to do this would be to create a new user mailbox from within the Exchange Administrator program.

To create a new mailbox form within the Microsoft Exchange administrator, select the item **New Mailbox** from the administrator file menu. When the property pages for a new mailbox appear, you will be ready to proceed to the next step.

Configuring Mailbox Property Pages

No matter how the account is created, the property sheets associated with that mailbox are the same. The following is a list of property pages that we will cover in our discussion of mailboxes:

- General Information

  You use this to record basic mailbox information, such as name and location.
- Organizational Information

  For optional information about, for example, a company's organization. This might include a manager, or people who report to this mailbox owner.
- Phone/Notes

  You can use this to enter detailed telephone information and perhaps a long note about the user.
- Distribution Lists

  This category specifies the distribution lists to which this recipient belongs.

- E-Mail Addresses

  This page enables you to create, modify, and delete alternate addresses for this mailbox.
- Delivery Restrictions

  This defines from which addresses this mailbox will or will not accept messages.
- Delivery Options

  From here, you can give "send on behalf" permission and specify alternate recipients for messages sent to this mailbox.
- Custom Attributes

  This category enables you to add up to 10 administrator-defined fields used to keep additional information about the mailbox.

NOTE The field names are defined on the DS Site Configuration custom attributes page.

- Advanced

  This selection contains all settings relating to advanced administrator functions (trust levels, message sizes, storage sizes, text formatting, and hidden/not hidden status).

The General Page

You use the General Page to enter user data. The primary purpose of the General property page is to hold user information for a mailbox. In this place, you give the mailbox the name by which it will be known to all other users.

The key elements to a mailbox name are the Display Name and the Alias Name. Display Name is the name that appears in the Administrator window and in the Address Book. Alias Name is the string used to generate other addresses for this mailbox, such as Internet addresses.

For example, a suitable Microsoft Exchange Display Name could be Matthew Weed with the Alias Name MWEED. The Administrator Program and Address Book show the display name: Matthew Weed. The SMTP address for this account, however, is formulated as *aliasname@domain* or: MWEED@DGENESIS.COM.

NOTE A mailbox is often referred to by its user name, which is the same as its Display name.

The following explains how to set general properties for the mailbox:

1. Choose Recipients in the Exchange Server Administrator window. The list of mailboxes will appear on the right side of the window. Open the mailbox you want to configure.

NOTE If you have just created a new mailbox, you can omit the preceding step. The reason is that the property pages appear immediately after you create a new mailbox.

2. Select the General tab. The dialog box in figure 15.4 appears.

FIG. 15.4
This option lets you select the mailbox you want to configure.

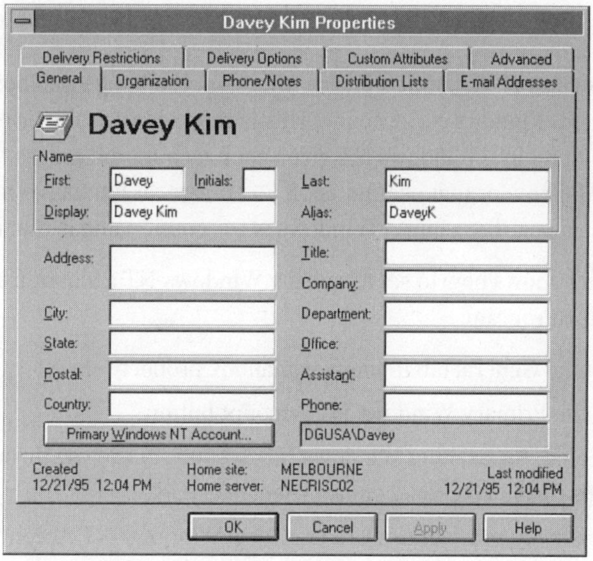

3. Enter the user's First name in the appropriate box.
4. Enter the user's middle initial in the Initials box.
5. Enter the user's Last name in the appropriate box.
6. Type an Alias that you will use to generate other e-mail addresses for this recipient.
7. Enter Postal information in the available Address boxes.
8. Enter appropriate Company and location (Department, Office) information for this user.
9. The Primary Windows NT Account sets the corresponding system account for this mailbox. The following section contains a more advanced description of this button.
10. Click Apply to set these properties and continue with other properties. If you are finished with all settings, click OK to return to the Administrator Program.

NOTE You can give a mailbox that is to be used by more than one person a generic name. A mailbox to be monitored by multiple people for purposes of technical support might be named Tech Support.

TIP Microsoft Exchange Server can automatically generate a Display Name and Alias Name when you type the user's first and last names.

NOTE Display and Alias are the only two required fields in the general property page.

Primary Windows NT Account Every Microsoft Exchange mailbox must have at least one associated Windows NT account. This is referred to as the primary Windows NT account. Logging into Windows NT gives your account full access to the Microsoft Exchange Mailbox for that user name. If you create an Exchange mailbox in the Windows NT User Manager, the primary Windows NT account name is that new account.

The following shows how to set a primary Windows NT account from the Exchange Administrator Program:

1. Select the General tab in the new mailbox property sheet.
2. Click the Primary Windows NT Account button.
3. Use Select An Existing Windows NT Account to browse through the Add Users and Groups dialog box. Select one. Then, click OK.

   Alternatively, you can use Create a New Windows NT Account to bring up the Create Windows NT account dialog box (see fig. 15.5).

FIG. 15.5
Create a Windows NT user account for an Exchange mailbox without using the User Manager.

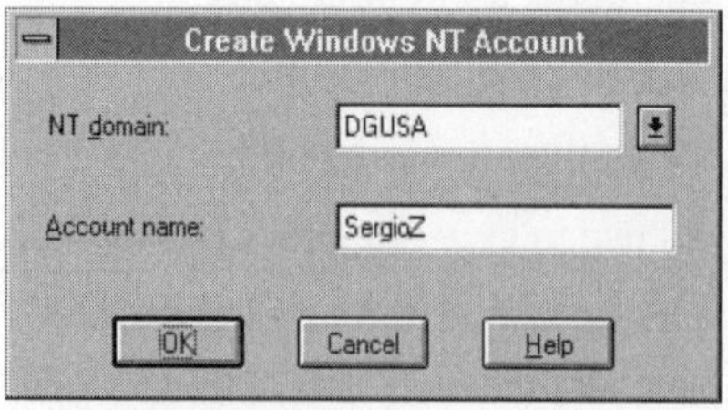

4. Pick the NT domain in which you want to create this account. Type a name in the Account Name box.
5. Click OK. The password for this newly created Windows NT account is the same as the mailbox's display name.

The Organization Page

This property page records data pertinent to how your company functions. The kind of information found in this place are names of individuals who report to this mailbox owner and the mailbox owner's manager. These individuals are all identified by their Exchange mailboxes. All this information is optional. The space is given to help you to be organized, however. It also provides for a specific definition of your organization with Exchange.

To set the Organization information, first specify the Manager of the mailbox owner:

1. Select the Organization tab. The dialog box in figure 15.6 appears:

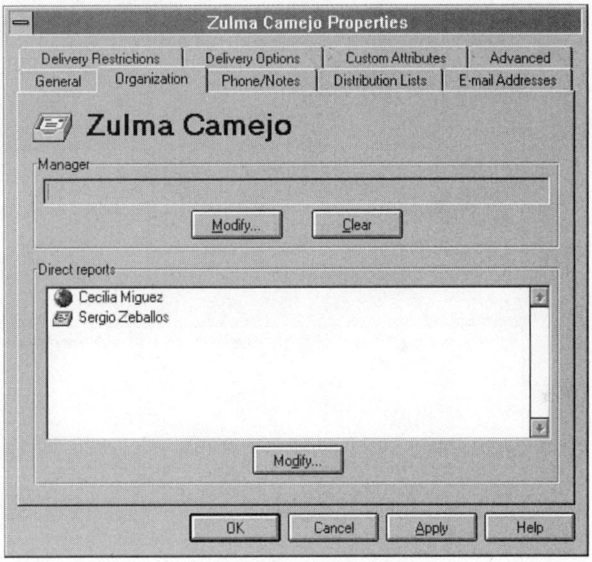

FIG. 15.6 The Organization properties let you define an executive hierarchy by Exchange mailboxes.

2. Click the Modify button under the Manager box. The address book displays. Select a recipient. Click OK. By default, the Manager space is blank.
3. To clear the Manager setting click the Clear button.

Next, specify a list of people who report to this mailbox owner:

1. Under the Direct reports box, click Modify.
2. On the left window select the appropriate mailboxes. Click Add to create a list on the right. Select and delete names manually in the right window to remove mailboxes from the list. Click OK to return to the Organization tab.
3. Click Apply to set these properties and continue with other properties. When you are finished with all settings, click OK to return to the Administrator Program.

The Phone/Notes Page

This property page gives you plenty of room to enter detailed telephone information concerning a mailbox user. There is also a large note space here to include any necessary comments. Once again, all these fields are optional.

The following explains how to configure the Phone/Notes property page:

1. Select the Phone/Notes tab of the Mailbox Property page. The dialog box in figure 15.7 appears.

FIG. 15.7 Include any relevant telephone data or notes.

2. Enter all relevant phone numbers in their appropriate boxes.
3. If you need an administrative note you can enter one in this place.
4. Click Apply to set these properties and continue with other properties. If you are finished with all settings, click OK to return to the Administrator Program.

The Distribution Lists Page

In this property page, you define this mailbox's membership to various distribution lists. Distribution lists are another type of recipient. The following discussion covers these lists in more detail.

You can add distribution list membership using the following steps:

1. Select the Distribution Lists tab in the user's mailbox. The dialog box in figure 15.8 appears.

FIG. 15.8
Define Distribution list membership for a mailbox.

The dialog box contains the distribution lists of which the user is a member. By default, a new mailbox is not a member of any of the lists.

2. Click Modify to change group membership. An address book window appears. Using this window you can add or delete your desired distribution lists. Click OK.

NOTE If no lists are available, and you want to create some new ones, see the instructions later in this chapter. These instructions explain how to define those recipients.

3. Click Apply to set these properties and continue with other ones. If you are finished with all settings, click OK to return to the Administrator Program.

The Delivery Restrictions Page

Delivery restrictions screen incoming mail. Using the settings in this property page, you can define specific senders from which this mailbox will reject mail. Alternatively, you can define a list of addresses from which this mailbox will only accept messages. The two options are mutually exclusive. However, Exchange enables you to select senders in both lists.

The following explains how to set these options:

1. Select the Delivery Restrictions tab. The dialog box in figure 15.9 appears.

   The left window lists only the senders that are permitted to send messages to this mailbox. Alternatively, the right window lists senders who will be rejected if they send messages to this mailbox. By default, they are both empty.

FIG. 15.9
The Organization properties enable you to define an executive hierarchy by Exchange mailboxes.

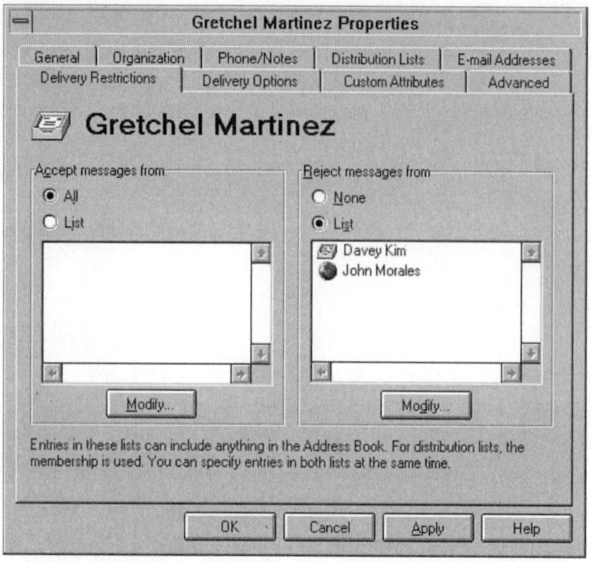

2. Click Modify under each window to add or delete senders. The address book dialog box will open. Type or select senders from the list. Alternatively, you can delete them in this window. Click OK when you are finished and want to return to the Delivery Restrictions property sheet.
3. Click Apply to set these properties and continue with others. When you are finished with all settings, click OK to return to the Administrator Program.

The Delivery Options Page

A Microsoft Exchange Mailbox can be configured with special options that provide some interesting functions. You can set two different delivery options on this property page:

- Alternate Recipient for a Mailbox

  Another recipient can be set up to receive mail intended for this mailbox.
- Send On Behalf Permissions

  Gives other users the right to send messages as if they originated from the primary user.

Alternate Recipient Occasionally, you will need to set alternate recipient for e-mail directed at a particular destination.

In our previous example, Sergio will be going on vacation for two weeks. Instead of bouncing the messages back with an auto reply, however, they can be redirected to an assistant's mailbox.

Use the following steps to set up alternate recipients:

1. Select the Delivery Options tab. The dialog box appears. The Alternate Recipient settings are in the lower left corner of the dialog box. By default, the None radio button is selected and there is no entry in the box below it.
2. Under Alternate Recipient click Modify. The address book dialog box appears. Select the recipient to which you want all messages from this mailbox redirected. Click Add. Click OK to confirm your selection and return to the Delivery Option property page.
3. Select the And Alternate Recipient check box to both redirect a message to the alternate recipient and deliver it to the principal mailbox. This essentially delivers two messages. By default, this box is not checked.

Send On Behalf This feature creates a situation in which one or many individuals are allowed to send mail "on behalf" of the primary mailbox. Authority is distributed across several users.

Example of using "send mail on behalf" feature:

Michael Navarro, a 3-D graphics technical director in Los Angeles, has a team of animators. Michael is currently the lead on a *special effects* project with a major studio. The animators are allowed to communicate electronically with the effects supervisor at the studio. Each animator has been given Send On Behalf privileges on the Michael Navarro mailbox. Animator Richard d'Andrea sends a message requesting information from the effects supervisor. The messages received by the effects supervisor are titled as sent by:

Richard D'Andrea on behalf of Michael Navarro

Use the following steps to set up Send On Behalf privileges:

1. Select the Delivery Options tab.

   The Send On Behalf settings are found in the top half of the property page. The "Give Send On Behalf Of Permission To" window displays all the users that have been granted this right.
2. Click Modify to edit the user list. The address book appears. In the left window, choose the user to which you want to grant this permission. Click Add to add users. Alternatively, you can delete the names from the user list on the right window to remove them. Click OK to confirm your selection and return to the Delivery Options property page.
3. Click Apply to set these properties and continue with other ones. When you are finished with all settings, click OK to return to the Administrator Program.

The Custom Attributes Page

This property page lets you define up to 10 extension fields for this mailbox.

Use the following steps to set up Custom Attributes:

1. Select the Custom Attributes tab. The dialog box in figure 15.10 appears:

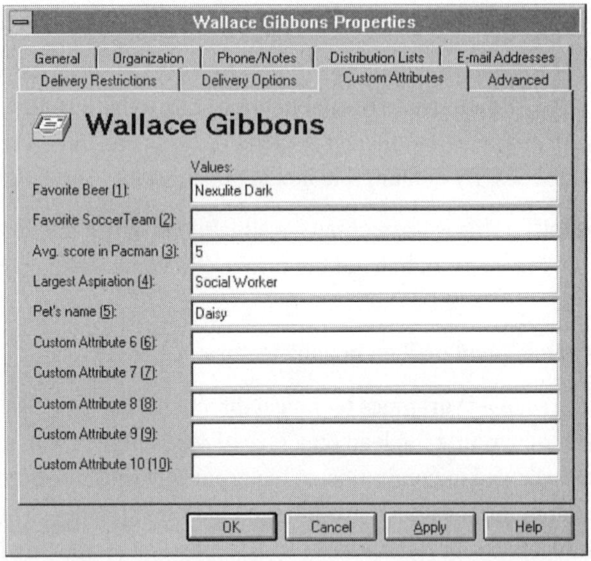

FIG. 15.10
Set values for the custom attributes designated for this site.

2. The dialog box lists all ten custom attributes on the left side of the box, and the user's values are entered on the right.
3. Type values for as many Custom Attributes as you want.
4. Click Apply to set these properties and continue with other properties. When you are finished with all settings, click OK to return to the Administrator Program.

The Advanced Page

Advanced properties are mainly concerned with the attribute information of a mailbox's system. The following are the advanced properties:

- Simple Display Name

  This name will be used by systems that cannot interpret all the characters in a normal display name, such as spaces.

- Directory Name

  Read only field. The name by which this object is known within its context in the directory. This name is presented for information purposes only and cannot be changed in this property sheet.

- Trust Level

  The directory replication trust level determines whether a recipient is replicated to another site. If the trust level assigned to the recipient exceeds the trust level set for the connector during Directory Synchronization setup, then the mailbox will not be replicated. Chapter 2, "Understanding Exchange's Organization and Sites," further discusses the application of trust levels.

- Message Sizes

  This property sets restrictions on maximum outgoing and incoming message sizes (in kilobytes) for this mailbox. Any message above the set limits in size are returned as nondeliverable.

- Home Server

  The Home Server is the Exchange Server on which this mailbox physically resides. The user must log on to the server listed to employ its client.

- Mailbox Options

  You can set the following two options:

  Allow Rich Text Format in outgoing messages.

  Hide the mailbox from display in address lists.

- Information Store Storage Limits

  You can set upper storage limits for this mailbox using this property. By default, a mailbox will use the values set on the Private Information Store property pages.

- Container Name

  This is the name of the recipients container in which this mailbox resides. This value is presented for information purposes only and cannot be changed in this property sheet.

- Administrative Note

  This note contains comments pertaining to settings on this page.

The following includes steps that help you to configure Advanced Properties:

1. Select the Advanced tab. The dialog box in figure 15.11 appears:
2. Enter a Simple Display name to be used by systems that cannot interpret all the characters in a normal display name.
3. Set the mailbox's Trust Level to the desired level.

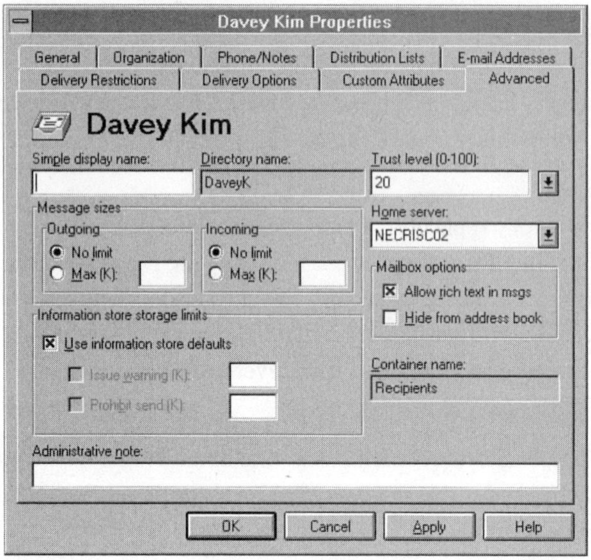

FIG. 15.11
The Advanced property page gives you control over several mailbox functions related to the system.

4. If you want to impose message transmission limits on this mailbox, click the appropriate Max (K) radio button. Enter the upper limit (in kilobytes) of message sizes you want to restrict.
5. If you want to change the serving on which the mailbox resides, select it from the Home Server pop-up menu. The entire contents of the mailboxes will be transferred to the new Server's information store.

NOTE This has the same function as selecting Move Mailbox from the Administrator Tools menu.

6. Select the mailbox options that you want: Check `Allow rich text in msgs` to provide for special message formatting options. This is the default setting. Check `Hide from address book` if you do not want this mailbox to appear in address listings.
7. Set mailbox specific `Information store storage limits` by clicking to remove the check in the Use information store defaults box. Type a storage size value (in kilobytes) in the Issue warning (K) at which users will be notified that their message storage is near capacity. Enter a value in the "Prohibit send (K)." When this maximum is reached, the user is blocked from sending mail from this mailbox. This will not, however, prohibit incoming mail. By default, these values are set in the Public Information Store properties for this Server. These values will affect this mailbox unless it is told otherwise.
8. Optional comments providing custom notes or instructions for a mailbox can be entered here (up to 1,024 characters). As an example, you can record the reasons for overriding information store defaults in this space.

9. Click Apply to set these properties and continue with other properties. When you are finished with all settings, click OK to return to the Administrator Program.

Creating Custom Recipients

Custom recipients are defined for sending messages to users outside the Microsoft Exchange organization global address list. Normally, these recipients are MS Mail users, SMTP users (Internet), foreign X.400 system users. You can also create custom recipients for any other third party connector or gateway. Once created, these recipients can be replicated across your organization as part of the global address list. They can receive messages from and send messages to a Microsoft Exchange Server. Custom recipient objects are identified by a globe icon in the Exchange Administrator program. Property pages for custom recipients are quite similar to those of standard Exchange mailboxes. The pages for custom recipients do not have as many advanced features as the latter.

The following steps help you to create a new custom recipient:

1. Select New Custom Recipient from the Administrator Program File menu. The New E-Mail Address dialog box in figure 15.12 appears:

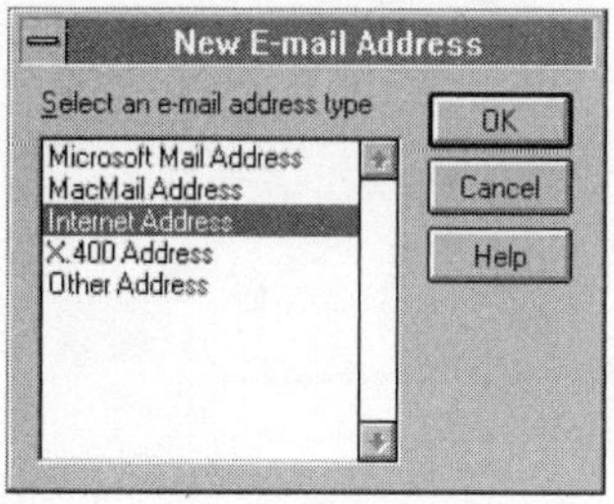

FIG. 15.12
Address types for all installed connections and gateways are displayed in this dialog box.

2. Select an e-mail address type for your new custom recipient. All installed connector types are listed. Click OK.
3. In the preceding dialog box, enter the appropriate delivery information for the selected address type.
4. Click OK to set address and proceed to the Exchange Custom Recipient Object property pages.

The following steps show you how to enter delivery addresses for specific custom recipients. Configuring an MS Mail custom recipient is discussed below:

1. Enter the correct name for this post office.
2. Enter the MS Mail Network name on which this user receives messages.

3. Enter the MS Mail Network name for the post office through which this user receives messages.
4. Enter the user's MS Mail Mailbox name on the preceding post office (see fig. 15.13).

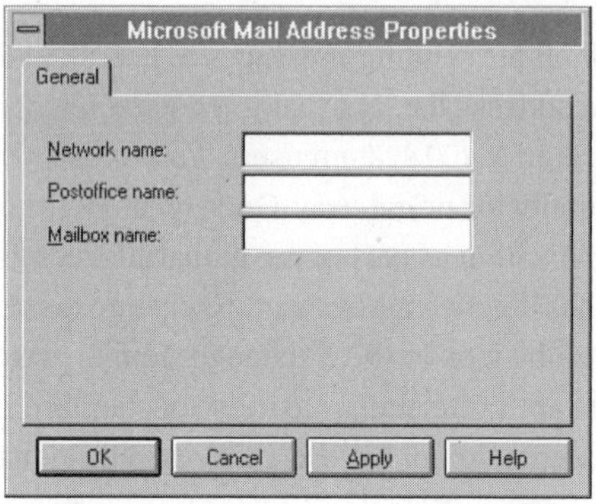

FIG. 15.13 You need to specify delivery information for an MS Mail (PC) post office recipient.

5. Click OK to proceed to the Exchange custom recipient property pages.

The following steps explain how to enter a custom MS Mail for an AppleTalk address.

1. Enter the user's Display Name (see fig. 15.14).

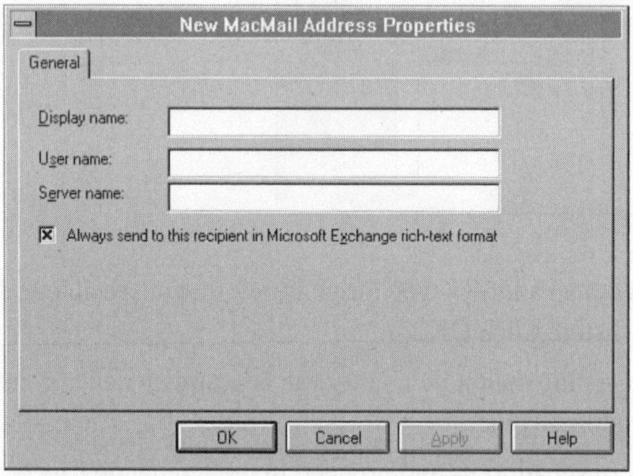

FIG. 15.14 You need to specify delivery information for an MS Mail (AppleTalk) Server recipient.

2. Enter the recipient's User Name as it appears on the Macintosh Server.
3. Enter the Macintosh Server name for this recipient.
4. Click Always Send to This Recipient in Microsoft Exchange Rich-Text Format to maintain special message formatting in messages transmitted to this recipient.
5. Click OK to proceed to the Exchange Custom Recipient property pages.

Follow these steps to enter a custom Internet or other SMTP address:

1. Enter an SMTP address in the single E-mail address box.
2. Click OK to proceed to the Exchange Custom Recipient property pages (see fig. 15.15).

FIG. 15.15
Entering a Custom X.400 recipient address.

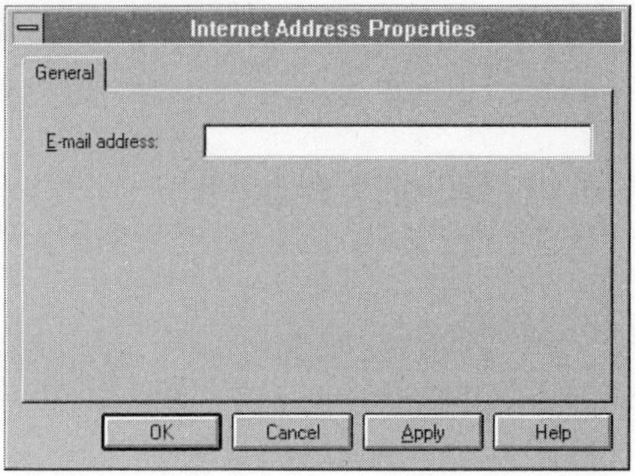

You must specify an Internet or other SMTP address in the window (must be in the user@domain format).

There are two property pages available to enter an X.400 address. The General page lets you define the specific address for a foreign X.400 recipient (see fig. 15.16). You can add more information for this recipient by using the Advanced page.

FIG. 15.16
This General property page defines a foreign X.400 recipient's delivery information.

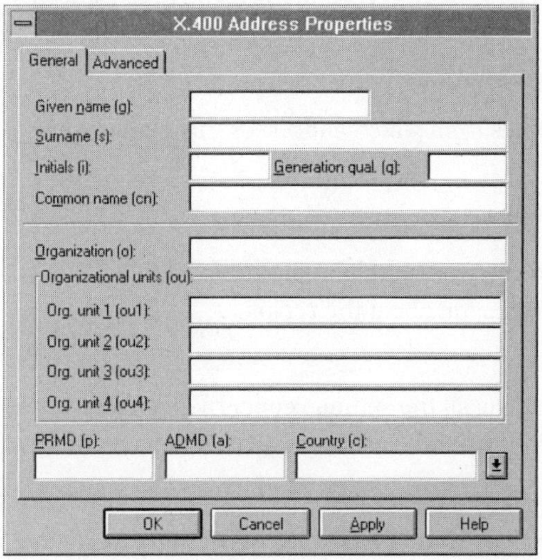

Configuring Properties for a Custom Recipient

After selecting the address type and entering delivery information for a custom recipient, you will be presented with the Exchange property pages for this recipient. You can also use this section as a reference for modifying custom recipient property pages after you have created the object.

The following explains how to complete the Exchange property pages for a recipient:

- General Information

  Records basic recipient information, such as name, location, title, and company. This section also enables you to change the e-mail address and its type for this custom recipient.

- Specifics About the Organization

  You can add optional information about your company's organization, such as a manager, and the people who report to this recipient.

- Phone Number and Notes

  In this place you can enter detailed telephone information and any additional notes about the user.

- Distribution Lists that Include the Recipient

  This page specifies the distribution lists to which this recipient belongs.

- E-mail Addresses

  This page enables you to create, modify, and delete alternate addresses for this recipient.

- Delivery Restrictions

  This page defines from which addresses this mailbox will or will not accept messages.

- Custom Attributes

  This page adds up to 10 administrator-defined fields that you can use to keep additional information about the recipient.

- Advanced Page

  This page contains all the settings concerned with advanced administrator functions, such as trust levels, message sizes, text formatting, and hidden/not hidden status.

The following sections explain the process of configuring custom recipient property pages. The specifics of each of the pages are discussed in depth.

The General Page

Select the General property page (see fig. 15.17).

This property page is almost identical to that of an Exchange mailbox. The main difference is the E-mail button in the bottom left corner of the window. When you click it, the dialog box in figure 15.18 appears:

FIG. 15.17
The General property page gives you control over several system-related mailbox functions.

FIG. 15.18
Choose to edit the current e-mail address, or create a new one.

NOTE Notice the globe icon denoting a custom recipient.

Select `Modify existing e-mail address` to edit the recipient address in the appropriate dialog box for the current address type.

Select `Create new e-mail address` to create an entirely new address using the same process described previously.

A box to the right of the E-mail address button shows the current address type and value of this custom recipient. Address types are abbreviated in the following way:

MS:	Microsoft Mail for PC networks
MSA:	Microsoft Mail for AppleTalk networks
SMTP:	Simple Mail Transfer Protocol addresses, for example, for the Internet
X.400:	Foreign X.400 addressees

The Organization Page

If this custom recipient has one or more managers, and certain individuals must report to them, enter these names in the spaces provided. This property page is functionally equivalent to a standard Mailbox's Organization property page.

The Phone Number and Notes Page

On this page you can enter detailed phone number information for this custom recipient. This property page is functionally equivalent to a standard Mailbox's Phone Number and Notes property page.

The Distribution Lists Page

You can add Custom Recipients to distribution lists as any other recipient. This property page is functionally equivalent to a standard Mailbox's Distribution Lists property page.

The E-Mail Addresses Page

This page holds a list of e-mail addresses automatically created for this directory object. You can alter the recipient's principal from this window, so that it is the same as the one on the General property page. These addresses will be used when routing messages from other connected mail systems, such as MS Mail. This property page is functionally equivalent to a standard Mailbox's E-mail Addresses property page.

The Delivery Restrictions Page

You can define other users within the Exchange organization that will not be able to send messages to this custom recipient by using the Delivery Restrictions page. The Accept Messages From and Reject Messages From windows are functionally equivalent to a standard Mailbox's Delivery Restrictions property page.

The Custom Attributes Page

Enter additional custom recipient data in the appropriate fields. This property page is functionally equivalent to a standard Mailbox's Custom Attributes property page.

The Advanced Page

Use this property page to create a simple display name for this recipient, if required. You also use this page to set a trust level as needed for either directory replication and synchronization, or both. Also, set an upper limit for the size of messages addressed to this recipient. Similar to a mailbox, you can select to allow rich text formatting for messages to this recipient, or choose to hide it from being displayed in the address book.

When you select the Advanced tab, the dialog box in figure 15.19 appears:

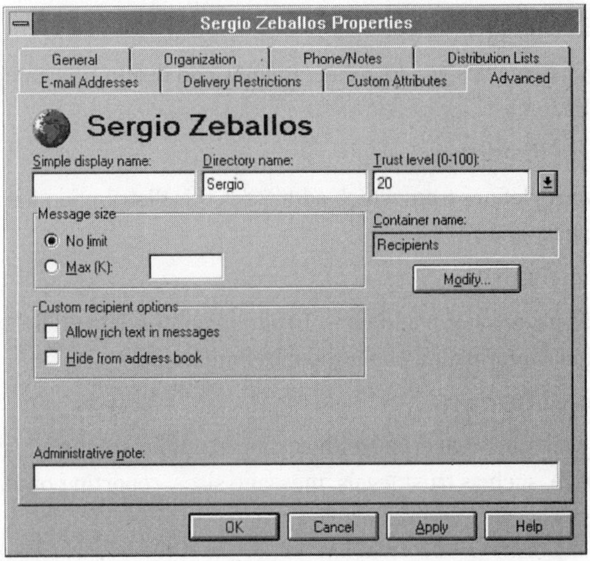

FIG. 15.19
You can set advanced properties for this recipient using the Advanced tab.

Because a custom recipient does not use storage space in a private information store, maximum storage options are removed from this page. Also, there is no option to change the home server for this recipient. The reason is that there are no messages being stored locally for this recipient.

NOTE Custom recipients do not have a Delivery Options property page. Therefore, you cannot specify alternate recipients. You also cannot give Send On Behalf privileges to that recipient.

Creating Distribution Lists

The following describes the function of the property pages for a Distribution List:

- General Information

  The General Information property page records basic recipient information, such as name, owner, and members. The General Information property page also allows you to select the expansion server for this list.

- Distribution Lists

  The Distribution Lists property page specifies the distribution lists to which this distribution list belongs. Lists can be nested within each other to develop a hierarchy for messages distribution.

- E-mail Addresses

  This page enables you to create, modify, and delete alternate addresses for this distribution list.

- Delivery Restrictions

  This page defines from which addresses this distribution list will or will not accept messages.

- Custom Attributes

  On this page you can add up to 10 administrator-defined fields that you use to keep additional information about the distribution list.

- Advanced Page

  All the settings concerned with advanced administrator functions are contained on this page, such as trust levels, message sizes, reporting options, and hidden/not hidden status.

The General Page

The following describes the function of the General Tab in the Distribution List property page:

1. Select the General tab in the Distribution List property page. The dialog box in figure 15.20 appears:

FIG. 15.20
The General property page gives you control over several system-related mailbox functions.

2. Enter a Display name for this distribution list as you want it to appear in the address book.
3. Enter an Alias name which will be used to generate other e-mail addresses for this distribution list.
4. The Owner box displays an Exchange user that has the right to modify a list's membership from within the Exchange client. Normally, only an administrator can modify a list's membership. Click Modify to open the address book. Select an owner from the list. Then, click OK. Use the Clear button to remove that user as the distribution list owner.
5. The Members box lists the current distribution list membership. Click Modify to bring up an address list. You can then click ADD to put new members on the list. Members can be mailboxes, custom recipients, or other distribution lists.
6. You can also select an Expansion Server for this list. By default, Any Server In Site is selected, and the distribution list will be expanded on the Server from which it was sent. Select a specific server from the menu and this distribution list will always be expanded there.
7. Enter any additional Notes in the box provided.
8. Click Apply to set these properties and continue with other ones. When you are finished with all settings, click OK to return to the Administrator Program.

The Distribution Lists Page

Lists can be nested by making them members of other lists. Click the Modify button to add or delete other distribution lists of which this list is a member.

The following illustrates how one list can be nested in another:

There are three new distribution lists in the DGENESIS organization. The first two lists are named DG ART DEPT and DG STORY DEPT. Each distribution list has a membership of about 25 to 30 other users, including mailboxes and custom recipients. The third address list created is named DG CREATIVE. This list only has five members. The members are the other distribution lists DG ART DEPT and DG STORY DEPT, along with three additional recipients meant to receive messages intended for these groups. Visually, the hierarchy resembles the one in figure 15.21.

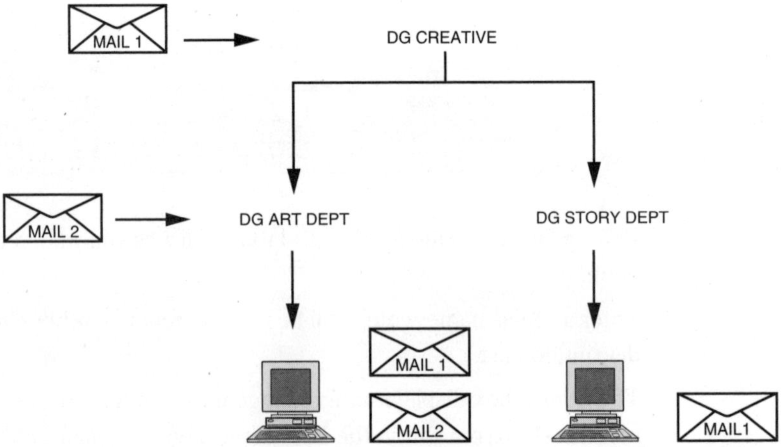

FIG. 15.21
Nested distribution lists can facilitate list management.

For comparison, examine the following three property sheets depicting this structure.

The DG ART DEPT and DG STORY DEPT Distribution Lists property sheets show the following membership information (see fig. 15.22):

The DG CREATIVE distribution list has both the DG ART DEPT and DG STORY DEPT and three additional recipients as its members. The property sheet for DG CREATIVE looks like figure 15.23.

Recipients within DG ART DEPT will now receive messages addressed to the DG CREATIVE list, as well. A similar result can be obtained by adding all the individual recipients to the DG CREATIVE distribution list. However, you would then have two lists in which to keep track of individual members. Nesting lists facilitates management by placing recipients into smaller logical subdivisions.

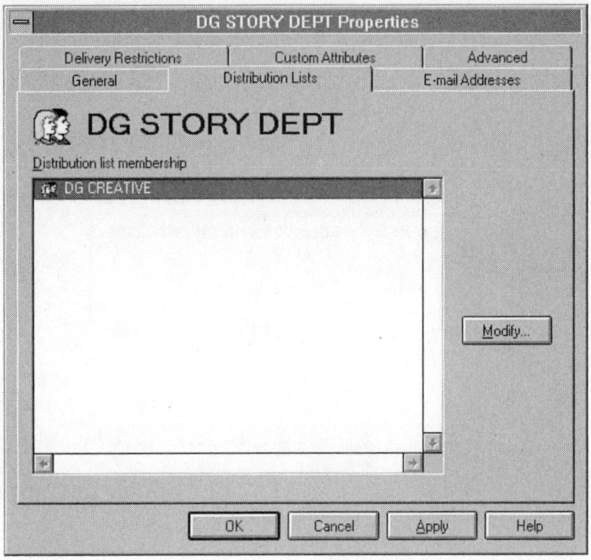

FIG. 15.22
A Distribution list can have distribution list membership, as well.

FIG. 15.23
Members of the top level distribution list hierarchy.

The E-Mail Addresses Page

Use this property page to establish alternate e-mail addresses for this distribution list. This property page is functionally equivalent to a standard Mailbox's E-mail Addresses property page (see fig. 15.24).

FIG. 15.24
The E-mail Addresses page displays alternate address data corresponding to all installed connectors and gateways.

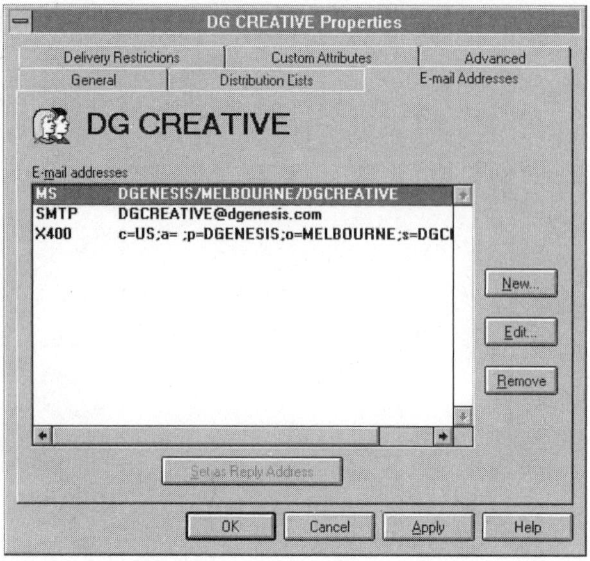

For Example, charlotte@ucla.edu, an Internet mail user, can address a message to DGCREATIVE@DGENESIS.COM. In effect, this user can send the message to over 50 members of this distribution list.

The Delivery Restrictions Page

You can define other users within the Exchange organization who will not be able to send messages to this distribution list. The Accept Messages From and Reject Messages From windows are functionally equivalent to a standard mailbox's or custom recipient's Delivery Restrictions property page.

The Custom Attributes Page

Using the Custom Attributes Page, you can enter additional custom recipient data in the appropriate fields. This property page is functionally equivalent to a standard mailbox's or custom recipient's Custom Attributes page.

The Advanced Page

The distribution list's Advanced property page (see fig. 15.25) is similar to Advanced property pages of other types of recipients. Simple display name, Directory name, Trust level, and Message size are the same settings found on the Advanced property pages of other types of recipients. The following are options specific to the Distribution List property page:

FIG. 15.25 The distribution list Advanced property page displays some settings that are similar to those of other property pages.

- **Report to distribution list owner**

  When checked, this option sends a message to the distribution list owner when a message that exceeds the specified size limit is sent to this list. By default, this is not checked.

- **Report to message originator**

  When checked, this option sends a message back to the message originator. By default, this option is checked.

- **Allow out of office messages to originator**

  When checked, this option responds with an Out of Office Message for any registered user who is a member of the distribution. By default, this option is not checked.

- **Hide distribution list from address book**

  As with other recipients, this prohibits the distribution list from appearing in the address book. Users will need to know the name of list to address it manually.

- **Hide membership from address book**

  When checked, the distribution list name itself is displayed in the address book. Users will be able, however, to view the individual members of the list.

Creating and Configuring Public Folders

Public Folders are created and designed from within the Microsoft Exchange client. Then, they are copied to a public information store. General configuration is handled through the Administrator Program. The following is an overview of the Public Folder property pages:

- General information on the folder

  This page gives the folder's name and display name, age limits, and specific client permissions.

- Replicas of the folder

  Add remove or copies of public folders on other severs within your organization.

- Folder replication status

  You can view and track the folder replication process for troubleshooting purposes using this page.

- Replication schedule

  This page helps you specify at which times information within public folders will replicate throughout your organization.

- Distribution lists

  A folder is a member of certain distribution lists. This page helps you specify to which lists it belongs. Any messages sent to the distribution list will also be stored in this public folder.

- E-mail Addresses

  This page enables you to create, modify, and delete alternate addresses for this public folder.

- Custom attributes

  This page lets you add up to 10 administrator-defined fields used to keep additional information about the mailbox.

- Advanced

  Contains all the settings concerned with advanced administrator functions, such as trust levels, message sizes, replication messages importance, storage limits, and hidden/not hidden status.

Configuring a Public Folder's Property Pages

Public folders are listed near the top of the Administrator's object hierarchy (see fig. 15.26). To view the public folder hierarchy in your organization, click the Public Folders object in the Administrator Program.

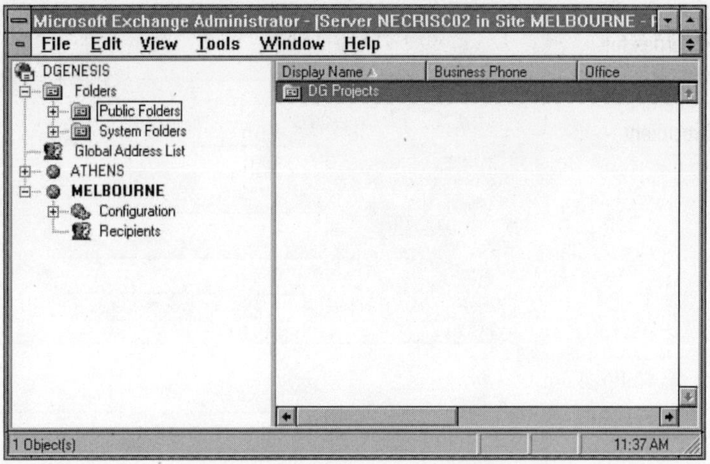

FIG. 15.26 View the public folders within your organization in the Administrator's hierarchy window.

To edit a specific folder within your site, open its property pages. You will be able to set all the options presented in the preceding list. To edit a public folder's contents, you must use the Microsoft Exchange client program and have appropriate client permissions. Another section later in the chapter discusses assigning client permissions. The next section covers the options available on the Public Folder property pages.

The General Page

The public folder is a unique recipient in that many different users can view and edit the information that it receives. As with other recipient types, the General property page enables you to set names for this object, as well as other general administrative notes. However, there are some very specific settings for this recipient type.

The following steps describe in detail how to set General properties for the public folders:

1. Select the General tab of the Public Folder property pages. The dialog box in figure 15.27 appears:
2. You can change the Folder Name in the appropriate box. This name is first assigned when the folder was created in the Microsoft Exchange Client program.
3. If you want to give the public folder a different display name for the address book, click the radio button marked Use This Name: under the heading of Address Book Display Name. By default, the Same As Folder Name button is selected.
4. You must enter a required Alias name used to generate additional e-mail addresses for this public folder.

FIG. 15.27
General properties for Public Folders are somewhat different from other recipient types.

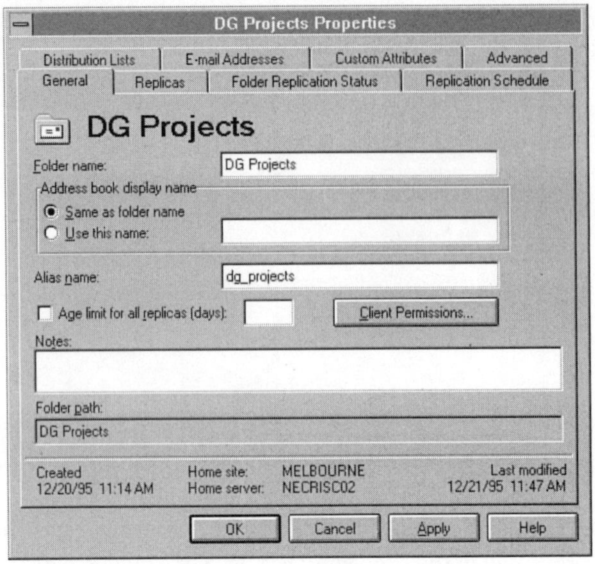

5. Click the `age limit for all replicas (days)` check box. On the right side of the check box enter the number of days in which a message will be automatically deleted. By default, there are no set age limits for a public folder, unless predetermined by public information store settings (see the scenario later in this section).
6. Enter any additional Notes in the space provided.
7. The Folder Path box displays the hierarchy of subfolders that leads to this public folder. If this is a main level folder, and not a subfolder, then only this folder's name is displayed.
8. Click Apply to set these properties and continue with other properties. When you are finished with all the settings, click OK to return to the Administrator Program.

Two important additional properties are specific to a public folder:

- Age limits
- Client permissions

Age limits determine the number of days that a message can remain in a public folder before it is deleted. This function helps to automatically purge the folder of outdated information. For example, if you set a folder age limit to one day, once that 24 hour period has expired, the message is deleted.

NOTE The Public Information Store has a similar age limit setting used for all the public folders it contains. The Public Information Store setting overrides any age limit set at the individual folder level.

Example:

The Public Information Store on Melbourne has an age limit setting of seven days on all its contents. DG Projects, a public folder held on the MELBOURNE Public Information Store, is set with an age limit of 10 days. The public information will override any individual settings. Any message in the DG Projects folder will be deleted after seven days.

Client Permissions

These are the available Roles:

- Owner

  This role marks the user as folder owner. This role also gives the user complete permission on this folder.

- Publishing Editor

  This editor is given all create, edit, and delete permissions on a folder. This role also gives permission to create subfolders. It does not, however, mark the user as the owner.

- Editor

  This role gives all create, edit, and delete permissions.

- Publishing Author

  Permission to create subfolders is given to the publishing author. Also, gives create, edit, and delete permission only to their items.

- Author

  This role gives permission to create, edit, and delete only their items.

- Reviewer

  Permission to read items is given to the reviewer.

- Contributor

  The contributor is given permission to create (though not to read) items.

- None

  No permissions are given on this folder. This role is often used as a default to limit access to a specific public folder.

The following steps help you to set up permissions:

1. Click the Client Permissions button on the Public Folder General property page. The dialog box in figure 15.28 appears:

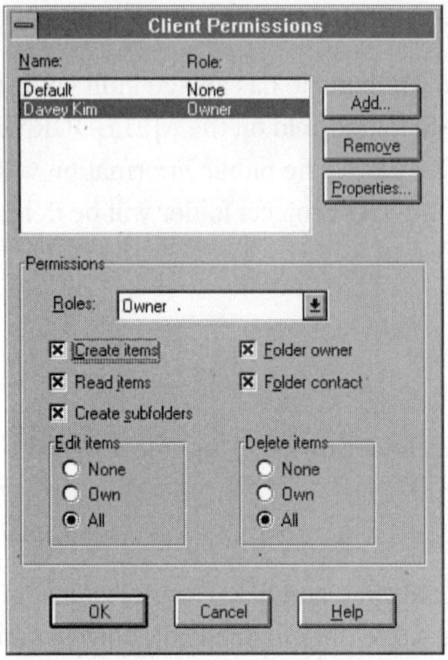

FIG. 15.28
Client Permissions determine what level of access a user has on a public folder.

The Name: and Role: columns display current users and their roles (see fig. 15.29). The Default role applies to any user not shown on this list.

2. Click Add to bring up the address list and add members to the Client Permissions list. Click a name. Then, click Remove to delete it from the list. Again, click a name. Then, click Properties to bring up that user's property pages.
3. The Roles pull-down menu displays preset roles for certain types of users. Clicking the menu pulls down the following list:

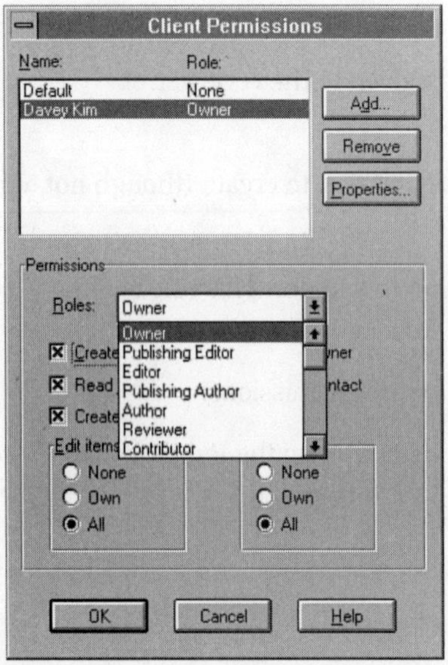

FIG. 15.29
You can use the Roles pull-down menu to give customized properties to a user.

Select a role from the menu. Note that the check boxes and radio buttons reflect the change in access rights for each role.

4. Alternatively, you can customize a role by clicking the available radio buttons and check boxes. If by clicking, you set a configuration that matches one of the predefined roles, that role will be displayed in the Roles pop-up menu heading. For example, you select the Author permission from the menu. The boxes and buttons display the permissions for the user role Author. When you click the Create Sub-Folders button, the name in the Roles menu changes to Publishing Author.
5. Click OK to set these permissions and continue editing other public folder properties.

The following list details the check box definitions:

- Create Items

  This check box gives permission to post items to the folder.
- Read Items

  When you check this box, you are given permission to open any item in a folder.
- Create Subfolders

  Check this box to give permission to make a subfolder of the main public folder.
- Folder Owner

  All permissions are given with respect to this folder.
- Folder Contact

  A user with Folder Contact status receives automatic error or conflict messages from the folder, such as replication errors, and oversize limit warnings. This user also receives users' requests for more access or other administrative tasks. Often, the owner and the contact are the same individual.

Radio buttons

The Radio button give users edit and delete permissions.

The following list outlines the scope of Edit permissions:

- None

  Users cannot make any modification to existing public folder items.

  Users cannot delete any folder items, even ones they have created themselves.
- Own

  The user can edit only items that they have created.

- All

  The user can edit any folder item, regardless of its creator.

The following list details the scope of Delete permissions:

- None

  Users cannot delete any folder item, even ones they have created themselves.
- Own

  Users can delete only items that they have created.
- All

  The user can delete any folder item, regardless of its creator.

The Replicas Page

This property page displays the destination servers to which a public folder will be replicated. You also can add or remove replicas throughout your organization using this window.

The following steps help you to configure replicas:

1. Select the Replicas tab from the public folder property sheets. The dialog box in figure 15.30 appears:

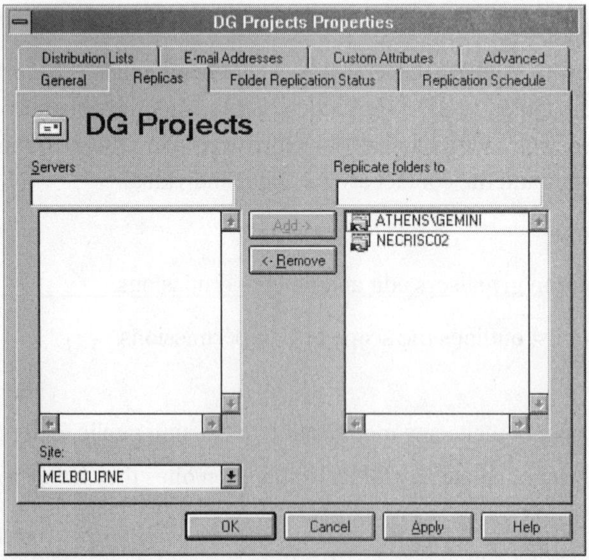

Fig. 15.30
View the public folders within your organization in the Administrator's hierarchy window.

The left side of the screen labeled Servers lists all the public folders. The right side of the screen labeled Replicate folders lists all the Servers to which this folder is replicated.

2. Using the Site pull-down menu at the bottom of the property page, select the site of the destination Server. Click and highlight the desired Server from the list of Exchange Servers on the left side of the window.
3. Click Add to include that Server in the replication list.
4. To remove a Server from the replication process, click its name on the right window. Then, click Remove.
5. Click Apply to set these properties and continue with other properties. When you are finished with all settings, click OK to return to the Administrator Program.

The Replicate Folders To box should now list every Server to which you want this particular public folder replicated. If not, repeat the preceding steps until all desired Exchange Servers are selected.

From Here...

This chapter showed you how to create and configure a mailbox, how to create and configure a custom recipient, and how to create and configure distribution lists.

For related information, read the following chapters:

- Chapter 18, "Setting Up Microsoft Mail for PC Networks"
- Chapter 19, "Setting Up Microsoft Mail for AppleTalk Networks"
- Chapter 20, "Configuring X.400 Connections"

CHAPTER 16

Site Connector and Dynamic RAS Connector

- How to install a site connector to link two Exchange sites over a high bandwidth connection.
- How to configure the Site Connector property pages.
- How to install a Dynamic RAS Connector and MTA transport stack.
- How to configure the Dynamic RAS Connector to transfer messages between sites.

This chapter is the first in this book that is dedicated to the specifics of linking two or more Microsoft Exchange sites. By now, you should have learned enough to be able to select the most appropriate connector between the Exchange servers in your organization. This chapter deals with the two connectors designed only to link Microsoft Exchange severs. Other connectors, such as X.400 or Internet Mail Connector, can be used both to link Exchange servers and to provide a gateway to foreign mail systems. The two connectors used only between Exchange servers are:

- Site Connector: full-time message link over high-bandwidth network links
- Dynamic RAS Connector: part-time scheduled message transfer over low-bandwidth lines

This chapter covers the basics of setting up a Site Connector and a Dynamic RAS Connector. Because a site can have any combination of connectors to a remote site, or even multiple connectors of a certain type, you will need to repeat the same steps outlined in this chapter each time you set up a new connector. ■

Understanding Site Connectors

The Microsoft Exchange Site Connector provides the most direct link between sites. Communication is handled through Remote Procedure Calls between servers in each site. Messages do not need to be converted to a different format (such as X.400) to be transmitted to a different site.

You should be familiar with the following concepts before you attempt to set up and configure a Microsoft Exchange site connector:

- *Target servers:* the list of Exchange servers in the remote site that will be involved in transferring messages to and from the local site.
- *Routing costs:* a number assigned to each connection on a relative scale from 1 to 100. Messages are first routed to connections that have the lowest cost; message transfer is distributed evenly across all connections that have the same assigned cost. You can set routing costs for a site as a whole as well as for individual Exchange servers.
- *Bridgehead server:* a specific Microsoft Exchange server in a site that is designated to establish communication with the remote site. Normally, the specific server that establishes this connection varies, depending on messaging traffic. Designating a bridgehead server is useful for controlling the message-transfer points between two sites.

Installing a New Site Connector

Installing a site connector to exchange messages between sites is a two-step process. First, you must set up a connector in the local site. The connector enables message traffic to the target site. Second, to receive messages from the remote site, you must install a corresponding site connector in the remote site. When you set up a new connection between sites, the Exchange Administrator program automatically prompts you to create the second site connector in the remote site. If you do not create a remote site (or cannot, due to access restriction in that site), you must coordinate your efforts with the remote site administrator to negotiate a successful connection between sites. The remote administrator must create a corresponding connector that links to your site.

Before you install a new site connector, make certain that the following conditions are met:

- The underlying network between two sites is properly configured and operational.
- All Microsoft Exchange services are running on both sites.

- You know the exact server at the remote site to which you want to connect.
- If you want to establish the corresponding site connector at the remote site, be sure that you have administrative access rights to the foreign Exchange server.

To create a new Site Connector, follow these steps:

1. Navigate through the Exchange administrator program's hierarchy, and click the Connections object (see fig. 16.1). The right display window shows all the connections currently running within this site.

FIG. 16.1
The Exchange Administrator program's display window shows all current site connections.

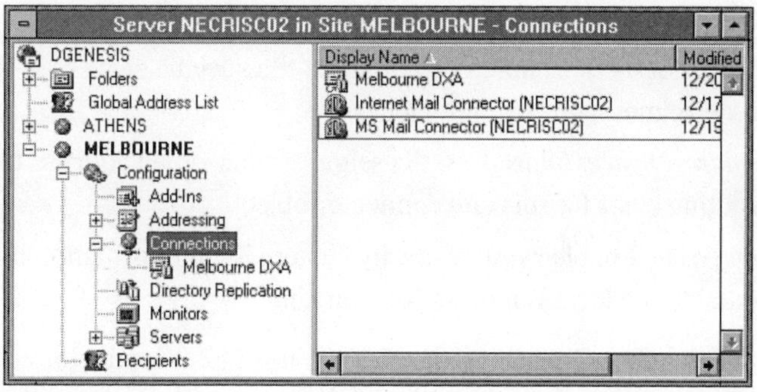

2. Pull down the File menu and choose New Other; then choose Site Connector from the New Other menu. The New Site Connector dialog box appears (see fig. 16.2).

FIG. 16.2
Enter the name of an Exchange server at the remote site.

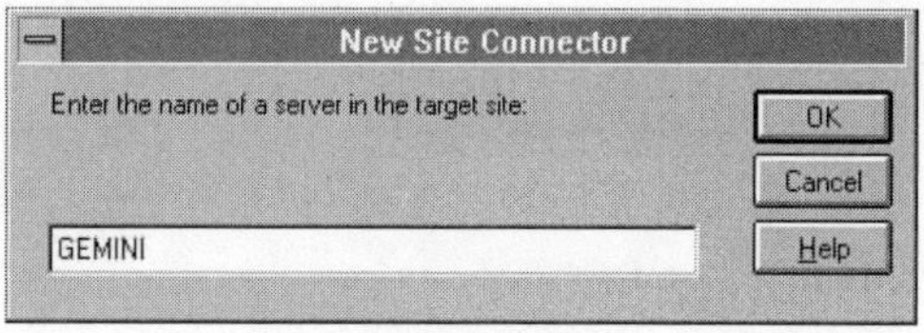

3. In the text box, type the name of a specific Microsoft Exchange server at the remote site.

NOTE The server name that you enter is used to identify the remote site and does not necessarily mean that this server is the machine that will handle message traffic between sites. Conceptually, a Site Connector resides at the site, not on any particular Exchange server.

4. Click OK. The Administrator program attempts to locate and access that server on the network.

If you attempt to create a site connector to a site where such a connector already exists, you will be notified of the situation and will not be allowed to create another connector.

Configuring Site Connector Properties

After creating a new Site Connector you will need to configure its properties.

The property pages for the Exchange Site Connector are as follows:

- *General.* Enables you to set an overall routing cost for this connector and designate a bridgehead server, if appropriate.
- *Target Servers.* Enables you to select the specific servers in the remote site that will receive messages from the local site.
- *Address Space.* Allows you to assign various e-mail address types and associated routing costs for this site connector object.
- *Override.* Enables you to specify custom login information if a target server is outside the local Windows NT domain.

General Tab The General tab is where you set Site Connector communication options. Primarily, you will define which site you are connecting to and which servers specifically will handle that connection. The following steps guide you through configuring the General Tab.

1. Click the General tab of the Site Connector property pages (see fig. 16.3).

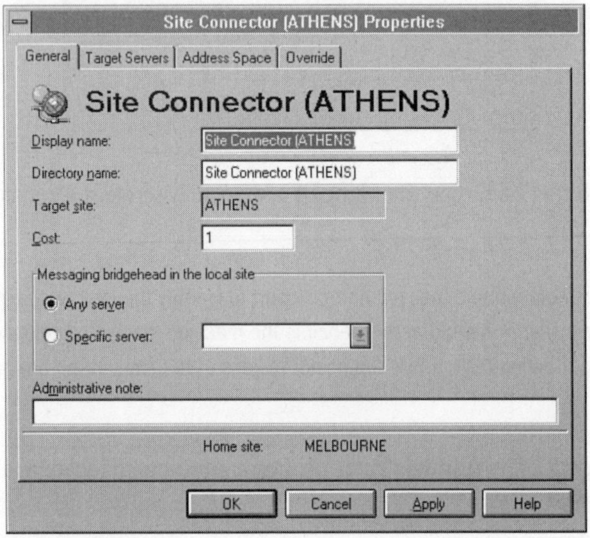

FIG. 16.3
Use the General Site Connector property page primarily to define the site to which you are linking.

2. If you want, type a new name for this site connector in the Display Name box. The default display name is in the format Site Connector (*site name*).
3. If you want, type a different directory name for this site connector in the Directory Name box. The default directory name is in the format Site Connector (*site name*).
4. The Target Site box shows the name of the remote site to which you are connecting. This data is provided for your information only. To change the target site at this point, you must click Cancel to exit the property pages and create a new site connector.
5. In the Cost box, enter a routing Cost for the site connector. An Exchange server uses this cost to determine whether to use this connection over other available connections. By default, a new site connector has a routing cost of 1.
6. If you want, specify a bridgehead server that will handle communication with the remote site. By default, the Any Server option is selected, and communication will be handled by the combination of target servers specified in the remote site's connector. If you select a specific server, that one machine will process all message transfer through the site connector.
7. If you want, make an entry in the Administrative Note box.
8. Click Apply to set these properties and continue setting other properties.
9. When you finish making settings, click OK to return to the Administrator program.

Target Servers Tab Use the Target Servers tab to set which remote Exchange servers will receive messages through this Site Connector. Servers that do not get listed are excluded from communication with the local site.

1. Click the Target Servers tab of the Site Connector property pages (see fig. 16.4).

   The Site Servers list on the left side of the dialog box shows all the available servers at the remote site. The Target Servers list on the right side of the dialog box shows the Exchange servers at the remote site which communicate to the local site through this site connector.
2. Select a server from the Site Servers list and then click Add to make it a target server for this site connector.

   To remove a server from the Target Servers list, select it and then click Remove.
3. The Target Server Cost section displays the routing costs for the selected target server. In the text box, type the desired routing cost for each server and then click Set Value to store that value.

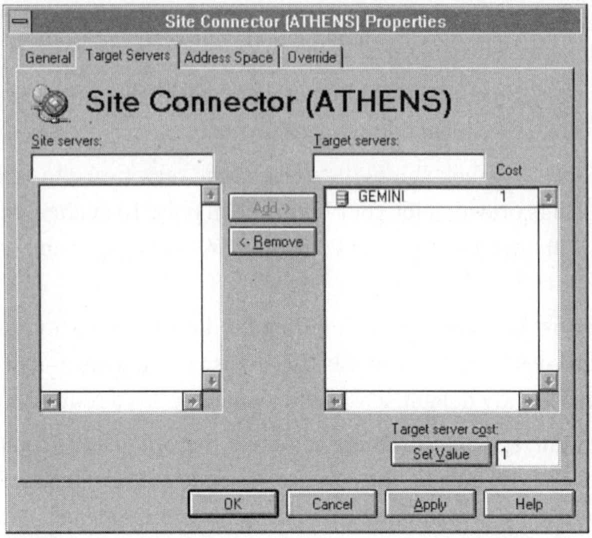

FIG. 16.4
Select the servers in the remote site to link through this Site Connector.

4. Click Apply to set these properties and continue setting other properties.
5. When you finish making settings, click OK to return to the Administrator program.

Address Space Tab The Address Space tab is where you tell Exchange which messages are routed through this Site Connector. Without an appropriate entry, messages will not find their way to the remote site.

1. Click the Address Space tab of the Site Connector property pages (see fig. 16.5).
2. Click one of the New address types (General, X.400, MS Mail, Internet) to add an address space entry for this connector. Select an existing address space entry and click Edit to modify it or click Remove to delete it.
3. Click Apply to set these properties and continue setting other properties.
4. When you finish making settings, click OK to return to the Administrator program.

Override Tab If the site to which you want to connect is not within the same Windows NT domain (or within a trusted domain), you must specify logon information for this site connector. This property page allows you to enter such data. Use the following steps:

1. Click the Override tab of the Site Connector property pages (see fig. 16.6).

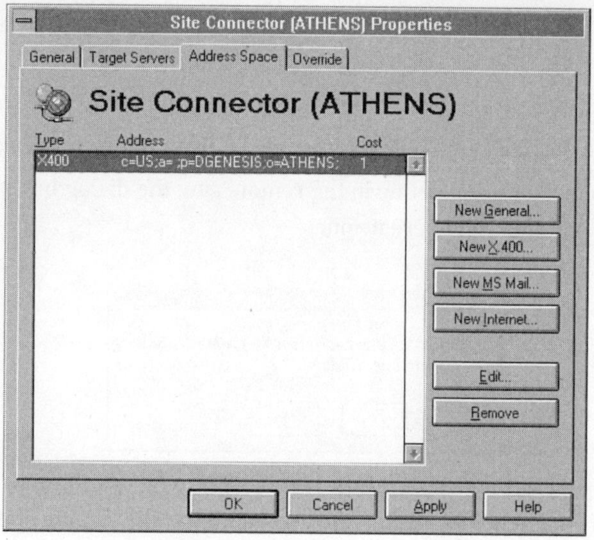

FIG. 16.5 Add or modify address-space entries to define message routing for this connector.

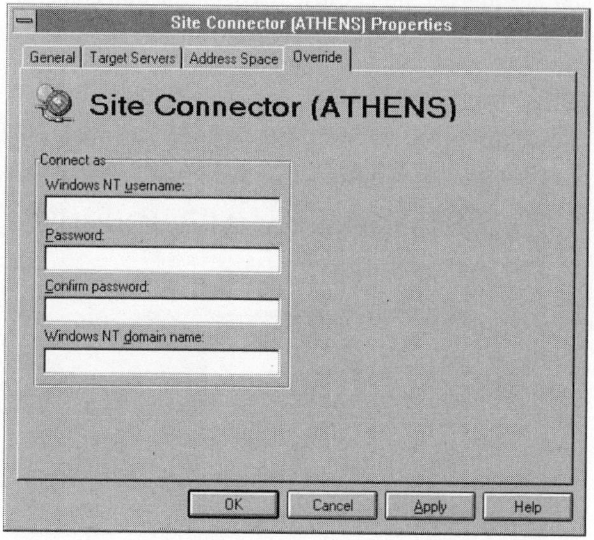

FIG. 16.6 Configure connector logon information to a remote Windows NT domain.

2. In the Windows NT Username box, type the name of the account that you want to use to log on.
3. In the Password box, type the password that is associated with that account.
4. In the Confirm Password box, type the password again.

5. In the Windows NT Domain Name box, type the domain in which the remote site resides.
6. Click Apply to set these properties and continue setting other properties.
7. When you finish making settings, click OK to return to the administrator program.

If a Site Connector is not set up in the remote site, the dialog box shown in figure 16.7 appears. It prompts you to create one.

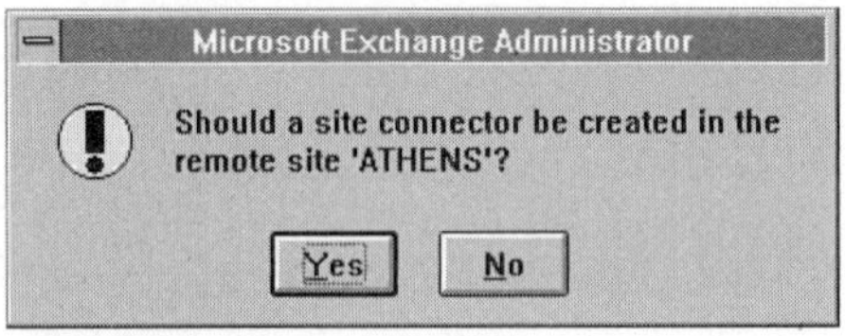

FIG. 16.7
Specify whether to create a corresponding site connector at the remote site.

Click No if you do not want to create and configure the remote site connector at this time. If you do click No, realize that message transfer will not occur until you set up that remote Site Connector at some late time. Click Yes to create and configure a site connector for the remote site at this time. The property page for the second site connector appears (see fig. 16.8).

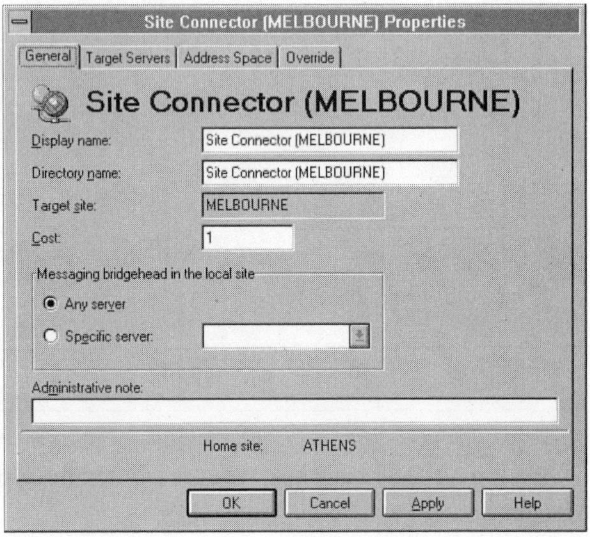

FIG. 16.8
General property page for the corresponding site connector at the remote site.

Configure this site connector following the procedure that you use to configure a local site connector. Keep in mind that the target servers now are Microsoft Exchange Servers that were the local servers in the previous connector configuration.

After you create and configure a site connector between two sites, the remote site appears in your Exchange Administrator program's hierarchy view. You can view all the Exchange objects at the remote site, but you cannot make any changes unless you log on directly to an Exchange server at that site. To share address lists with the connected site, for example, you must set up a directory replication connector to that site. See Chapter 17 for setting up directory replication between sites.

Deleting a Site Connector

If you want to remove a site connector that services message traffic between two sites, you first must determine what other services depend on the existence of that site connector. If other connections (such as a directory replication connector) rely on the site connector as the only link for message transport, you cannot delete that site connector; you first must delete any other dependent connections and then delete the site connector. If you do not want to delete the other connections, you must supply another link between sites that can service the other connections.

To delete a site connector, follow these steps:

1. Navigate through the Administrator Program's site display, and click the Connections object.
2. Select the Site Connector that you want to delete.
3. Pull down the Edit menu and choose Delete, or press the Delete key on the keyboard.

NOTE To disable all message transfers between sites, you must remove connectors from both the local and the remote sites. Log on to the remote Exchange server and then remove the site connectors, using the process described in this section. ■

Using the Dynamic Remote Access (RAS) Connector

The Microsoft Exchange Dynamic RAS Connector uses existing Windows NT Remote Access Services to facilitate temporary, low-bandwidth messaging links. The Dynamic RAS Connector establishes a temporary scheduled link to a remote Exchange site via a modem or any other RAS-compatible transport (e.g., ISDN or X.25), transfers messaging data, and then disconnects. This section covers installing and configuring the Dynamic RAS Connector to link your messaging sites.

Before installing a Dynamic RAS Connector, you must do the following things:

- Install the Windows NT Remote Access service on the Exchange server that will be establishing the connection.
- Enter a RAS phone-book entry for the remote Exchange server. Use your Windows NT documentation or on-line help to guide you through this process.
- Configure the hardware that is required for the remote access link (e.g., a modem or ISDN terminal adapter).
- Know the name of the remote server with which you want to establish the link.

Installing a Dynamic RAS Connector involves these steps:

- Install the RAS MTA transport stack. Because the MTA will use a transport that is not supported directly through Microsoft Exchange server, you must define an external (i.e., Windows NT Remote Access Service) transport stack to use in message transfer.
- Install and configure the Dynamic RAS Connector itself. Follow the steps in the following sections.

Installing the RAS MTA Transport Stack

You add the RAS MTA Transport Stack from within the Administrator program. Follow these steps:

1. From the Administrator program, select New Other from the File menu, then select MTA Transport Stack from the submenu. The New MTA Transport Stack dialog box appears (see fig. 16.9).

   The Type section of the dialog box lists the available MTA transport stacks on this Exchange server.

NOTE Only the RAS MTA Transport Stack is used for the Dynamic RAS Connector.

The Server section of the dialog box lists all the servers at the current site.

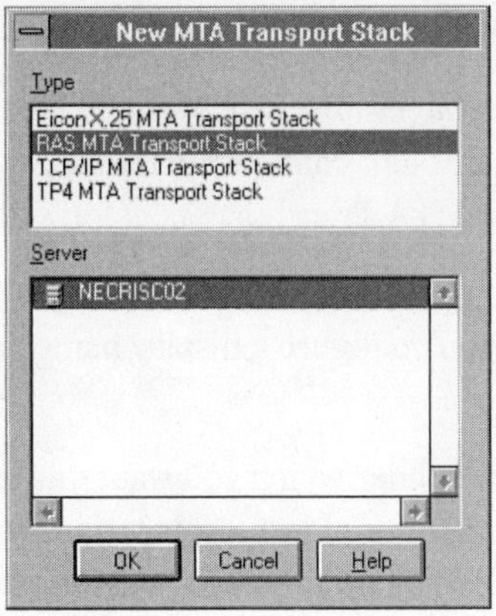

FIG. 16.9
The New MTA Transport Stack window is used by the Dynamic RAS Connector (and the X.400 connector) to select an underlying transport for message transfer.

2. Select RAS MTA Transport Stack from the list of available transports.
3. Select the server in your local site that will handle the remote-access connection. The transport stack will be installed on that server.
4. Click OK to accept the transport stack and Exchange server settings. The General tab of a new Dynamic RAS Connector appears (see fig. 16.10).

   The MTA Transport Stack has only two property pages to configure: General and Connectors. Configuration usually is a one-time process unless you change the local MTA callback number. Refer to the Connector property page to view the Dynamic RAS Connectors that use this MTA Transport Stack.

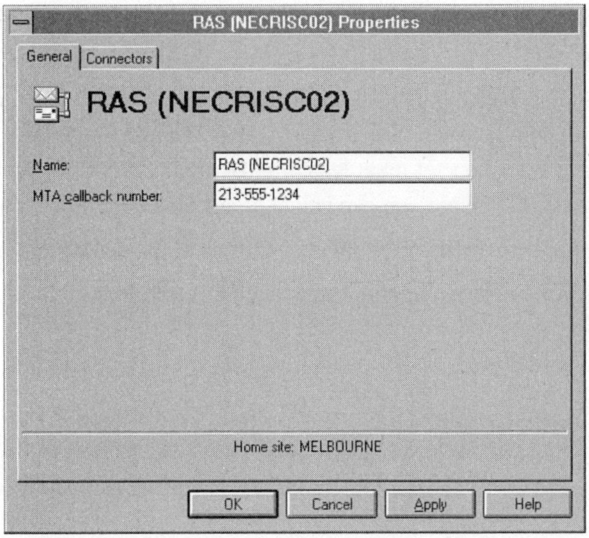

FIG. 16.10
The RAS MTA Transport Stack property pages.

Configuring MTA Transport Stack Property Pages

Settings in the MTA Transport Stack pages affect all Dynamic RAS Connectors that use it. The following section guides you through configuring the RAS Transport Stack. The process is similar to configuring MTA Transport Stack for X.25, TCP/IP, or TP4 connections as well.

General Tab The General tab lets you configure a display name and callback number for this RAS MTA Transport Stack.

1. In the Name box, type the name under which you want this transport stack to appear in the Exchange Administrator object display window. You cannot modify this name after you create it. By default, the stack is named in the format: RAS (*server name*).
2. In the MTA Callback Number box, enter the phone (or other device) number of the local Microsoft Exchange server.

NOTE The Windows NT Remote Access service uses a callback number as a means of authentication. The remote server receives a call, gets the callback number, hangs up, and dials the originator to establish a RAS link.

3. Click Apply to set these properties and continue setting other properties.
4. When you finish making settings, click OK to return to the Administrator program.

Connectors Tab

1. Click the Connectors tab of the RAS MTA Transport Stack dialog box (see fig. 16.11).

   The Connectors tab lists all the Dynamic RAS Connectors that use this transport stack. If you have set up the RAS MTA Transport Stack for the first time, the list is blank. After you set up at least one Dynamic RAS Connector, that connector is displayed in this tab; you can select it and then click Edit to modify its properties.
2. Click Apply to set these properties and continue setting other properties.
3. When you finish making settings, click OK to return to the Administrator program.

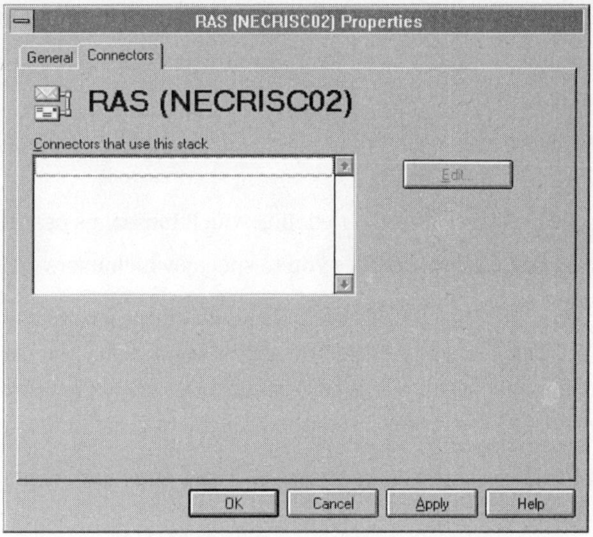

FIG. 16.11
The RAS MTA Transport Stack Connections tab lists all current Dynamic RAS Connectors.

Installing and Configuring a Dynamic RAS Connector

You create a new Dynamic RAS Connector from the Microsoft Exchange Administrator program. If you have not yet installed the RAS MTA Transport Stack, you must do so before proceeding with the following sections.

Installing a New Dynamic RAS Connector

Use the following step to install a new Dynamic RAS Connector.

Pull down the Exchange Administrator File menu and choose New Other; then choose Dynamic RAS Connector from the submenu. The tabs for the new connector appear.

Following are the tabs that you use to configure a Dynamic RAS Connector:

- *General.* Enables you to specify the name, remote server, MTA transport stack, maximum message size, and Windows NT RAS phone-book entry.
- *Schedule.* Enables you to set a connection schedule for this Dynamic RAS Connector.

- *RAS Override.* Enter alternative logon and RAS callback number infomation.
- *MTA Override.* Enables you to change the default MTA settings when you use this Dynamic RAS Connector.
- *Connected Sites.* Enables you to view, add, or modify addressing of the connected sites.
- *Address Space.* Enables you to define which messages pass through this connector.
- *Delivery Restrictions.* Enables you to specify which users can (and cannot) send messages to this Dynamic RAS Connector.

General Tab The General tab lets you set the communication methods for this Dynamic RAS Connector. Part of this configuration will be to enter the telephone number data for the remote site, so have that information available when configuring the following options.

1. Click the General tab of the Dynamic RAS Connector property pages (see fig. 16.12).

FIG. 16.12
Set general Dynamic RAS properties.

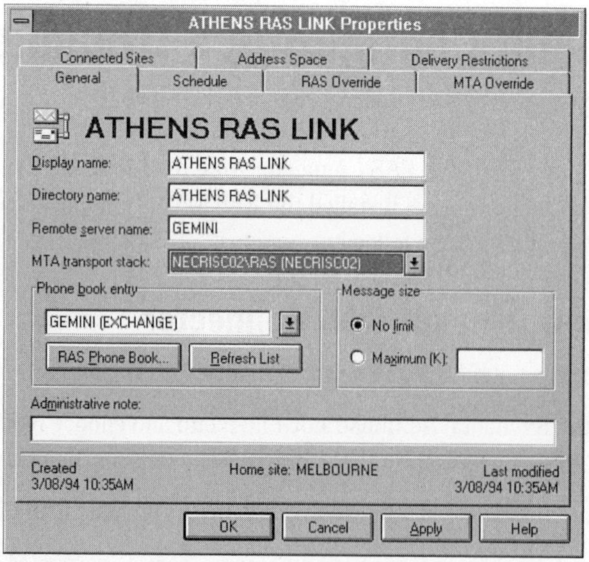

2. In the Display Name box, type the name that you want to appear in the Microsoft Exchange Administrator display window.
3. When you create a Dynamic RAS Connector, enter a name for it in the Directory Name box.

4. In the Remote Server Name box, type the name of the Microsoft Exchange server to which you are establishing a link.
5. From the MTA Transport Stack drop-down list, select the local Exchange server that will handle the remote access connection.
6. From the Phone Book Entry drop-down list, select the entry that dials into the remote server.

   If you have not yet created an appropriate entry, click RAS Phone Book to open the local Exchange server's phone book. In our example connector (see fig. 16.13), this brings up the Windows NT RAS phone book for NECRISC02.

FIG. 16.13
The Windows NT remote access service phone book shows an entry set to dial into a remote Exchange server.

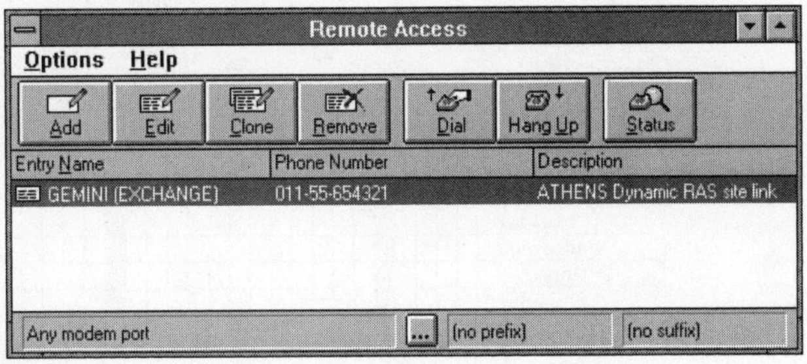

   If you have not yet done so, create a RAS phone-book entry, then close the RAS phone-book window. Click the Refresh List button to update the list with your new RAS phone-book entry.

TIP Setting an upper limit for message sizes often is a good idea. Particularly with a low-bandwidth link (e.g., a 28.8-Kbps modem), several large messages that have attachments could easily create a bottleneck through this connector.

7. If you want to set an upper limit for the size of messages that pass through this connector, click the Maximum (K) radio button, and in the text box, type the size limit (in kilobytes). A message that exceeds this maximum size will be returned as undeliverable. By default, the No Limit option is selected, and messages of any size can pass through the connector.
8. Make an entry in the Administrative Note box, if you want.
9. Click Apply to set these properties and continue setting with other properties.
10. When you finish making settings, click OK to return to the Administrator program.

Schedule Tab Use the Schedule tab to control how often the Dynamic RAS Connector becomes active and initiates a connection. Follow these steps:

1. Click the Schedule tab of the Dynamic RAS Connector property pages (see fig. 16.14).

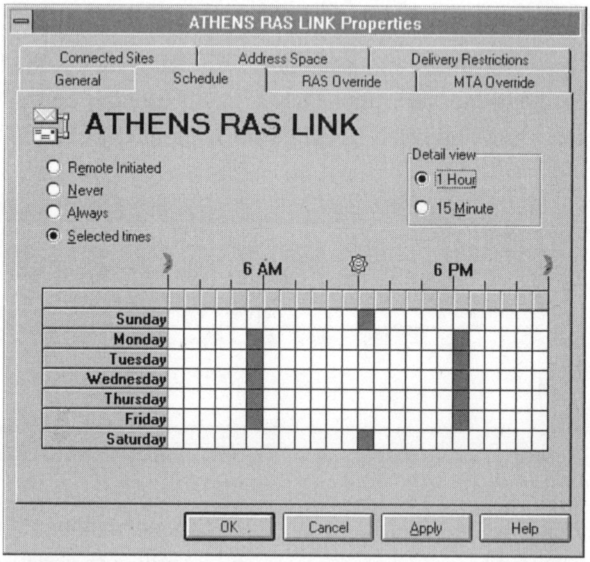

FIG. 16.14
Set connection times for this Dynamic RAS Connector.

2. Click one of the four options that determine when this Dynamic RAS Connector connects:

   - *Remote Initiated.* This option sends messages only when the remote MTA connects to this MTA. Both MTAs must have the two-way alternative option selected.

CAUTION

Only one MTA can be configured to be remote-initiated. Otherwise, if both MTAs are waiting for the other to initiate the connection, the messages will never be delivered.

   - *Never.* This option effectively disables this Dynamic RAS Connector.
   - *Always.* This option provides a remote access connection whenever messages need to be transferred. By default, this option is selected.
   - *Selected Times.* This option enables the Dynamic RAS Connector to initiate communication, based on the time grid.

3. If you chose Selected Times in step 2, the Detail View radio buttons become available. Choose either 1 Hour or 15 Minute; the time grid changes its scale accordingly.
4. If you chose Selected Times in step 2, choose the time blocks that you want to use for the connection. In figure 16.4, the Dynamic RAS Connector is set to initiate connections at 6 a.m. and 6 p.m. on weekdays, and at noon on weekends.
5. Click Apply to set these properties and continue setting other properties.
6. When you finish making settings, click OK to return to the Administrator program.

RAS Override Tab The RAS Override tab is designed to supersede RAS settings for both logon information and callback numbers. The following steps guide you through these settings.

1. Click the RAS Override tab of the Dynamic RAS Connector property pages (see fig. 16.15).

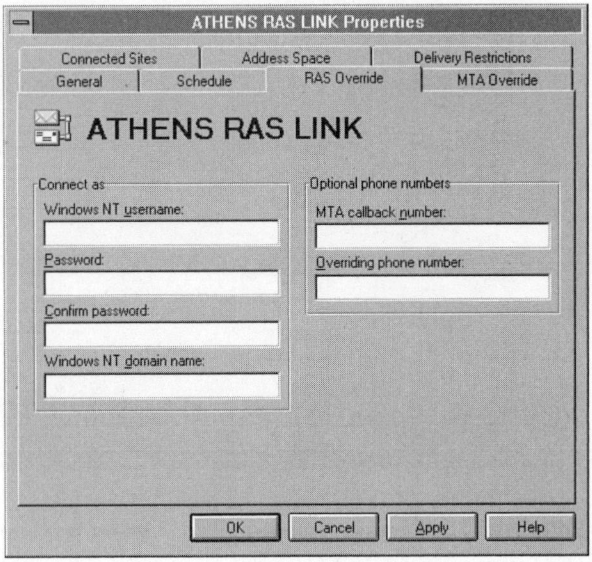

FIG. 16.15 RAS Override allows you to configure custom logon information from this tab.

2. In the Windows NT Username box, type the name that you want to use to authenticate this Dynamic RAS Connector.
3. In the Password box, type the password.
4. In the Confirm Password box, type the password again.
5. In the Windows NT Domain Name box, type the name of the domain in which the remote server resides.

6. In the Optional Phone Numbers section, type a phone number in the MTA Callback Number box.
7. Enter a different phone number in the Overriding Phone Number box.
8. Click Apply to set these properties and continue setting other properties.
9. When you finish making settings, click OK to return to the Administrator program.

MTA Override Tab Because of the typically low-bandwidth links associated with a remote access connection, it often is a good idea to set a different MTA configuration specifically for messages transmitted through this Dynamic RAS Connector. You set the MTA default configuration through the Site MTA property pages. Any setting in the MTA Override property page supersedes default MTA settings when the Dynamic RAS Connector negotiates a connection (see fig. 16.16).

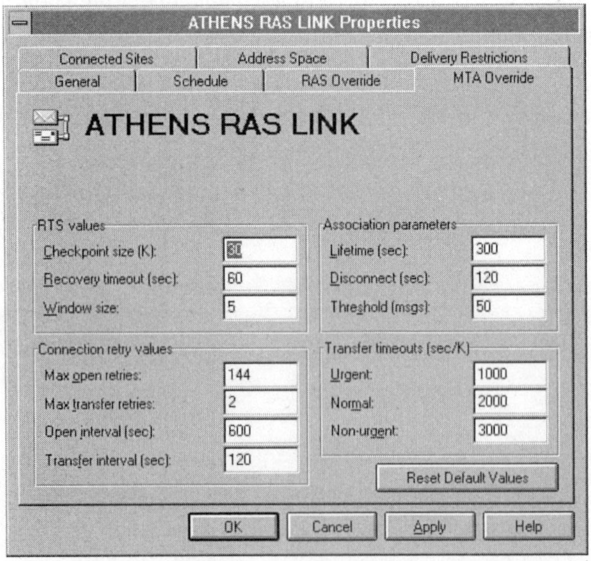

FIG. 16.16
Set specific override properties for the Message Transfer Agent.

Connected Sites Tab This property page lets you view which sites are linked via the current RAS Connector. Figure 16.17 shows a Connected Sites property page listing linked sites (blank if none).

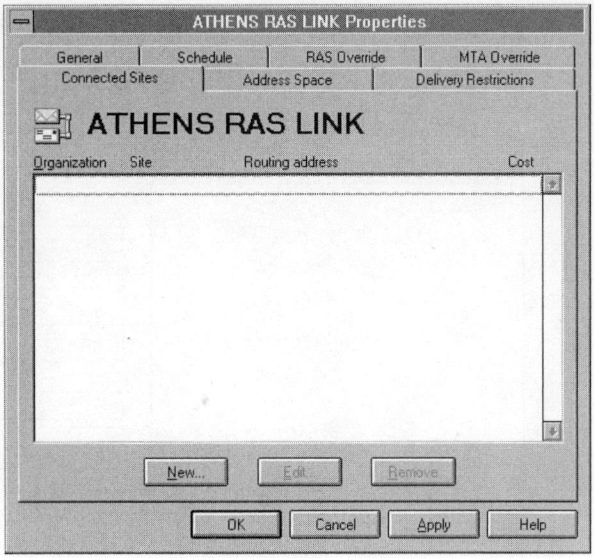

FIG. 16.17
View directly and indirectly connected Exchange sites.

Sites listed in the Connected Sites tab can receive messages from the local site via the current connector. If a site is not listed it may be available to view other links established via other connectors.

Address Space Tab The Address Space tab (see fig. 16.18) defines which recipients can be reached through this connector. Only enough addressing data is provided to distinguish messages that should be sent through this connector.

Routing costs are entered along with each Address Space entry.

Delivery Restrictions Tab The Delivery Restrictions tab specifies which users can and cannot send messages through this connector.

- *Accept Messages From.* Creates an exclusive list of recipients who have permission to send messages through this Dynamic RAS Connector.
- *Reject Messages From.* Lists specific recipients who are denied permission to send messages through this Dynamic RAS connector.

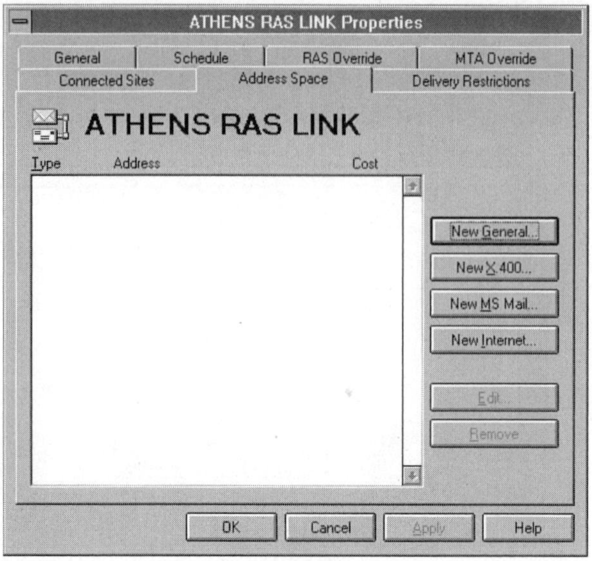

FIG. 16.18
Identify routes to this connector by using Address Space entries.

To set delivery restrictions, follow these steps:

1. Click the Delivery Restrictions tab of the Dynamic RAS Connector property pages (see fig. 16.19).

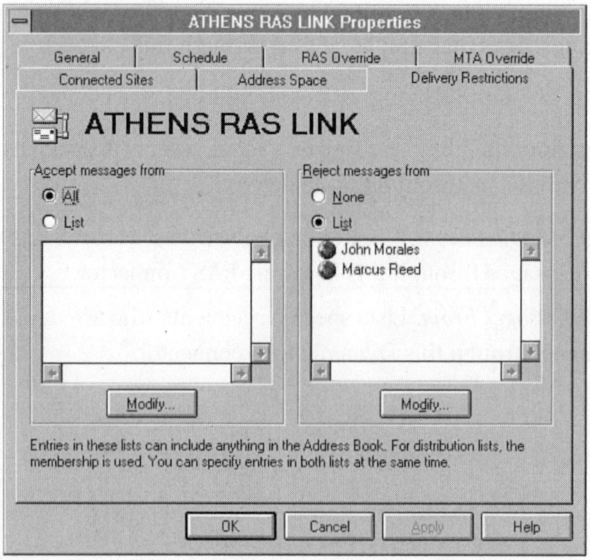

FIG. 16.19
Delivery restrictions allow you to specify who can access the Dynamic RAS Connector.

2. In the Accept Messages From or Reject Messages From section, click the List radio button.
3. Click the Modify button below each list to display the Microsoft Exchange address list.
4. Select the desired senders to include or exclude as per the above lists and then click OK.
5. Click Apply to set these properties and continue setting other properties.
6. When you finish making settings, click OK to return to the Administrator program.

From Here...

This chapter showed you how to link together two or more Microsoft Exchange sites. For related information, read the following chapters:

- Chapter 5, "Designing Exchange Topology," for broader consideration in planning your site and remote access connections.
- Chapter 13, "Message Transfer Configuration," for additional information on configuring MTA connection settings.

CHAPTER 17

Using Directory Replication and Synchronization

- **How to configure directory replication to share address lists within an Exchange site, between sites on the same network, and between sites on different networks.**
- **How to configure Exchange Directory Synchronization services including dirsync requestors, dirsync servers, and remote dirsync requestors.**
- **How to configure directory synchronization with Microsoft Mail for Appletalk networks.**
- **How to configure the Directory Exchange Agent (DXA) to handle directory synchronization on a server by server basis.**

In Chapter 2, "Understanding Exchange's Organization and Sites," you learned general concepts about how directory replication and synchronization work in an Exchange organization. This section teaches you how to set up and configure directory replication and synchronization in Microsoft Exchange Server. ■

This chapter assumes the following:

- That you have a basic understanding of Microsoft Exchange's directory architecture
- That Microsoft Exchange Server is installed and running on at least two sites
- That the external system is functional; you can send messages to it and receive messages from it

Understanding Exchange Replication

Just for a quick review, directory replication is the process by which Exchange Server shared updated user directory data. This process occurs between servers in an Exchange site as well as between servers in different sites throughout your organization. The following sections describe the steps you will use to set up replication between your Exchange servers.

Directory Replication Within a Site

Directory replication within a Microsoft Exchange Server site is automatic. The replication function is handled by the directory service and is always in operation while that service is running. This process requires no maintenance other than making certain that the servers in a site can exchange standard messaging information.

Mean time between replication requests is approximately five minutes, which means that a directory change effected on one server ripples through to each server in a site within five minutes. Network load and available bandwidth affect this process.

Following is an example of how a directory change propagates through an Exchange site:

- Administrator John creates a new mailbox recipient, Ginnie, on the server NEWYORK01.
- Upon creation, the new directory object is a legitimate candidate for directory replication.
- Within five minutes, user Eli on Microsoft Exchange Server BOSTON01 (a server at the same site as NEWYORK01) cannot only address Ginnie as a recipient, but can also see her name in the Global Address List.

NOTE Directory replication within a site is automatic. If you do not want a specific recipient to be copied during replication, you must make it hidden.

Replication Between Sites

The replication of directory information between two Microsoft Exchange sites is the second logical step in maintaining a cohesive directory structure within your organization. This section covers replication between the following:

- Exchange sites on the same network (LAN)
- Exchange sites on different networks

Directory Replication Connector

The principal tool used to set up directory replication is the directory replication connector. It handles the exchange of all directory information. As the administrator, you need only provide the site names and the names of the appropriate bridgehead servers to establish a replication connector.

Setting up replication between two Microsoft Exchange sites involves three steps:

1. Create a directory replication connector for both sites.
2. Identify the bridgehead server at each site that is responsible for transferring directory updates.
3. Establish a replication schedule to determine how often directory updates will traverse a site link.

The following sections provide details on configuration for specific situations. The general steps for setting up directory replication, however, are the same for all types of networks.

Directory Replication Between Sites on the Same Network

This section describes the procedure for using directory replication between two Exchange sites physically connected on the same local area network. Typically, this means high bandwith links between groups of servers in close geographical proximity. In the real world, this can be two distinct corporate divisions in the same building, for example. Whatever the case, your Exchange servers will be able to communicate with each other over your standard network connections and will not require the use of any additional transport mechanism.

The following is a list of requirements before setting up replication between sites on the same network:

- The messaging link between both servers is fully functional (sending and receiving messages). Usually, you use a site connector to establish such a link between sites on the same network.

- You have administrator permissions on each server with which you will be establishing a directory-replication relationship.

To set up directory replication between sites on the same network, follow these steps:

1. Open a New Directory Replication Connector from the Administrator program's File menu under New Other. The New Directory Replication Connector dialog box appears (see fig. 17.1).

FIG. 17.1
Use this dialog box to set New Directory Replication Connector options.

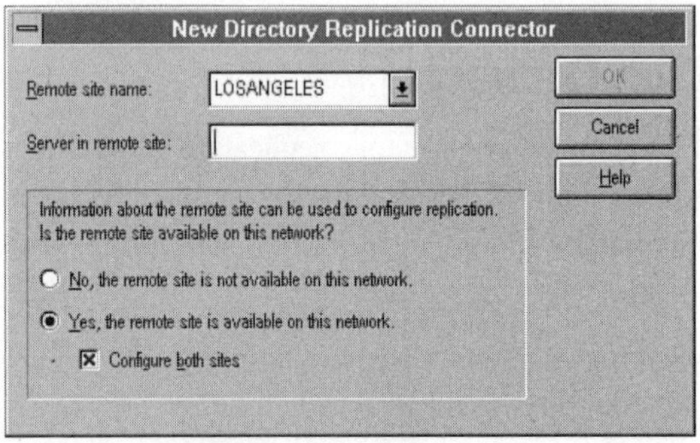

2. From the Remote Site Name drop-down list, select the site to which you want to connect.
3. In the Server in Remote Site box, type the name of the remote server.
4. Click the radio button labeled Yes, the Remote Site Is Available on This Network.

TIP You almost always choose this option when both sites are on the same LAN, because the option saves you time and reduces configuration errors. Only external situations, such as administrative security restriction within a company, might require separate configuration of such directory replication connectors. For example, an Admin on one site may not be given sufficient administrative privileges of the remote site to establish a connection alone.

5. Click the Configure Both Sites check box. This option automatically creates and configures a corresponding directory connector at the remote site.
6. Click OK to proceed to the Directory Replication Connector property pages.

NOTE Because both servers are on the same LAN, Exchange can locate the site and communicate with the remote server via remote procedure calls. You need to specify only the remote site's name in the New Site Connector dialog box.

To facilitate the interchange of directory data between sites, you must designate replication bridgehead servers. These servers process directory update requests from other bridgehead servers and also generate their own requests for updates. A one-to-one relationship must exist between bridgehead servers for sites that exchange directory information.

Following are a few example situations:

Example 1: You want to establish directory replication between the sites LOSANGELES and MELBOURNE. LA01 and MELBOURNE01 are the selected bridgehead servers. These servers will be the only replication point for Exchange directory information between the Los Angeles and Melbourne sites. You make no allowances for the use of multiple directory replication connectors to balance server load, link traffic, and so on.

In directory replication, you must designate a local bridgehead server and a remote bridgehead server when you set up a directory replication connector. *Local* and *remote* are relative terms. When you configure a directory replication connector between sites, the General tab of each connector shows different information for each end of the connection.

Example 2: You want to establish a directory replication relationship between the sites LOSANGELES and MELBOURNE.

The LOSANGELES Directory Replication Connector's General tab displays the following information:

Local bridgehead server	LA01
Remote bridgehead server	MELBOURNE01

The MELBOURNE Directory Replication Connector's General tab displays the following information:

Remote bridgehead server	MELBOURNE01
Local bridgehead server	LA01

You can create multiple directory replication links to one site if they originate from different sites. Directory information can pass between two sites at only one point, however.

Example 3: This example discusses the use of multiple directory replication connectors in a site. In this case, LOSANGELES is the site that has multiple connectors. MELBOURNE's bridgehead server (MELBOURNE01) replicates directory information with bridgehead server LA01 (see fig. 17.2).

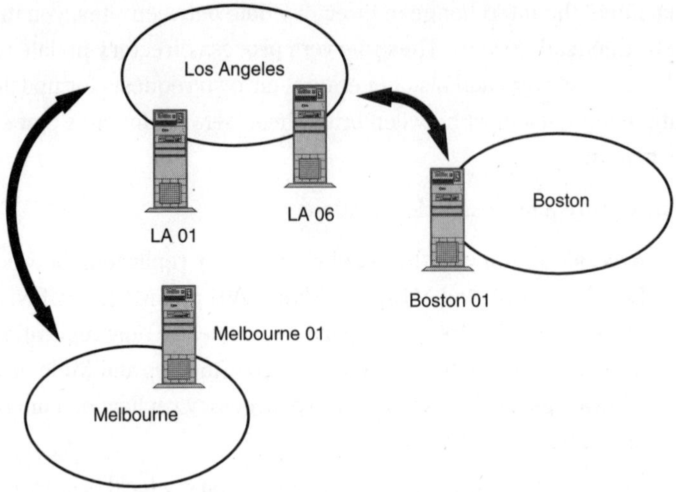

FIG. 17.2
Directory replication across multiple bridgehead servers.

Simultaneously, the BOSTON site replicates information to the LOSANGELES site. BOSTON01 is the bridgehead server for the BOSTON site. BOSTON01 links to a second bridgehead server at the LOSANGELES site: LA06.

A smaller organization could manage by setting up multiple directory replication connectors on one server. This procedure is not generally recommended but is an option for sites that have few users, infrequent directory updates, or a limited number of servers. In this case, both MELBOURNE01 and BOSTON01 can be bridgehead servers linked to LA01 (see fig. 17.3).

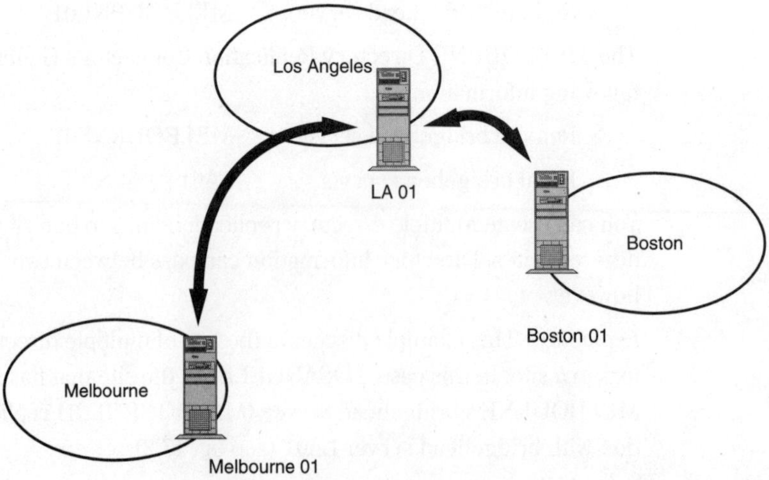

FIG. 17.3
Setting up multiple directory replication connectors.

In the preceding examples, directory information between the MELBOURNE and BOSTON sites is synchronized automatically by the sites' common link, LOSANGELES.

You set up bridgehead servers in the Exchange Administrator program. To designate bridgehead servers, follow these steps:

1. Click the General tab of the Directory Replication Connector Properties page (see fig. 17.4).

FIG. 17.4
General tab of the Directory Replication Connector Properties page.

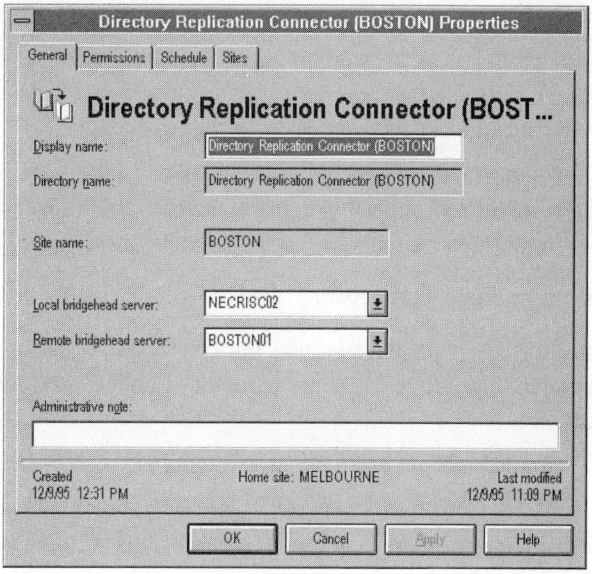

2. From the Local Bridgehead Server drop-down list, select the local server that will handle incoming and outgoing directory update requests. The default selection is the name of the Exchange server on which you are currently logged in.
3. From the Remote Bridgehead Server drop-down list, select the server at the remote site that will receive and request updated directory information.

After you establish a directory replication connector, you can change the local bridgehead server for that connector, but make sure that you update the remote connector to reflect the change. Usually it is best not to make such changes and to plan in advance for a situation that might require you to change this information. If you must change the local bridgehead server, this change will prompt Exchange to reinitiate the replication cycle.

Replicating Directory Information Between Sites on Different Networks

Sites located on different logical LANs can share directory information almost as easily as sites on the same LAN. Because you cannot use a site connector to link bridgehead servers, however, you must configure a custom connector to that site.

The following conditions must exist before you set up directory replication between sites on different LANs:

- The messaging link between both servers is fully functional (sending and receiving messages). This link can be set up with any available connector (Site, X.400, or Internet) that supports message transfer between sites.
- You know the e-mail address of the remote site bridgehead server's directory. The Exchange directory replication connector needs this address so that it knows where to direct replication messages. You must enter this information manually.

To set up directory replication between sites on different networks, follow these steps:

1. Open a New Directory Replication Connector from the Administrator program's File menu under New Other. The New Directory Replication Connector dialog box appears.
2. Click the radio button labeled No, the Remote Site Is Not Available on This Network. This will highlight the two input boxes below it.
3. In the Remote Site Name box, type the name of the remote site with which you are establishing replication.
4. In the Server in Remote Site, type the name of the remote bridgehead server.
5. Click OK to proceed to the Directory Replication Connector property pages.

Addressing Tab When you configure replication between two sites that are not on the same network, you must supply the e-mail address of the bridgehead's server directory. Follow these steps:

1. Click the Addressing tab of the Directory Replication Connector Properties page. The Addressing dialog box appears.
2. In a new connector, you see a blank address space for the remote bridgehead's server directory.

3. Click the Modify button. The New Entry dialog box appears.
4. Select the address type that you want to create. This type should be identical to the type of connector used to transmit normal messaging data between sites. LOSANGELES and MELBOURNE, for example, are linked via a private X.400 link, so the address selection in the New Entry box should be X.400.
5. The next dialog box will be different depending on what address type you selected in the preceding step.

Schedule Tab Directory updates transmitted between bridgehead servers are executed according to an administrator-defined schedule. You need to evaluate the following elements before you decide on an appropriate replication schedule:

- Expected replication traffic
- Network bandwidth between sites
- Server load on bridgehead servers
- Any scheduling constraints created by the type of messaging link

The first three items are related. If replication traffic is heavy between the two sites (if directory objects are frequently added, deleted, or modified, for example), this will affect available bandwidth. Sometimes, you have to have a frequent replication schedule to maintain an accurate global address list.

Scheduling constraints arise due to the type of site link used. This is especially the case when using part-time connections.

The site link between LOSANGELES and SANFRAN, for example, is established by a Dynamic RAS Connection. Three times a day, a modem connection to the SANFRAN site is established; the connection is maintained for 30 minutes and then closed. You must configure the directory replication connector to transmit data when the network connection is up; otherwise, the connector may attempt to transfer directory updates through a nonexistent link.

To configure the replication schedule, follow these steps:

1. Click the Schedule tab of the Directory Replication Connector Properties page (see fig. 17.5).

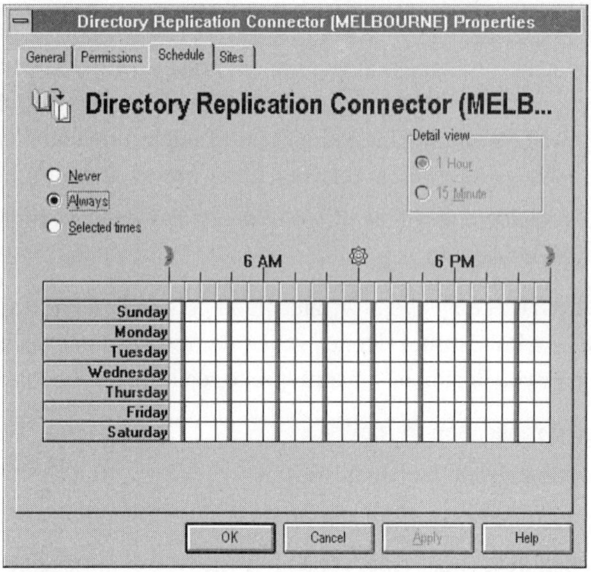

FIG. 17.5
Schedule tab of the Directory Replication Connector Properties page.

2. Click one of the three radio buttons in the top-left corner of the dialog box:
   - Never: disables directory replication
   - Always: updates the replication schedule every 15 minutes
   - Selected Times: allows you to specify the replication schedule manually
3. If you chose Selected Times in step 2, click one of the Detail View radio buttons (1 Hour or 15 Minute) to view the time grid in different increments.
4. Select the block(s) of time during which you want replication to occur by clicking the schedule grid.
5. If you are done configuring all other tabs for this connector, click OK. Otherwise, click another tab to continue making adjustments.

Following are two general recommendations on scheduling replication time:

- For international replication links, be sure to take into account the various time zones in which your site will operate. Off-peak hours for a server in London, for example, could fall in the middle of a high-message-volume time in New York.
- For sites that have a large number of frequent directory updates, you should opt for frequent replication, keeping in mind the fact that increased message traffic affects network performance.

Viewing a Site's Directory Data

After you configure both directory replication connectors and establish directory replication between two sites, you can view all sites with which you are exchanging directory data. This is the case because the local site receives directory updates from the immediately connected remote site, as well as from every other remote site with which that site is replicating data.

To view inbound and outbound sites, click the Sites tab of the Directory Replication Connector dialog box. Inbound sites are those from which the local site receives directory updates. Outbound sites are those to which directory updates are sent.

In an example earlier in this chapter, you created a directory replication connector to MELBOURNE to LOSANGELES. After the first successful replication request, you see the site names displayed in the Sites tab, as shown in figure 17.6.

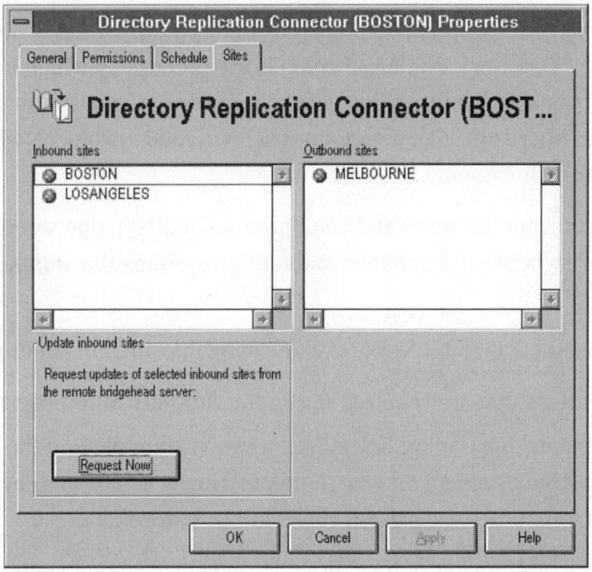

FIG. 17.6 The Directory Replication Connector Sites Properties page shows which sites are sharing directory information.

LOSANGELES is displayed in the Inbound Sites list; BOSTON also appears in the list because it is involved in the process as a whole. The Outbound Sites list displays only MELBOURNE because it is the one site that sends directory updates directly.

You also can use the Sites tab to request directory updates from selected inbound sites. You might need to request a directory update in the following situations:

- Your replication schedule is set to occur nightly, but you are aware that many changes were made at a specific site (perhaps a new Exchange server was created, with several new users), and you need to update the system immediately.
- A remote server was down during its scheduled replication time, and you need to force replication to maintain an accurate address list.

To request a directory update, follow these steps:

1. Click the Sites tab of the Directory Replication Connector dialog box.
2. Select the site from which you want to request directory updates. (You can select multiple sites by Shift+clicking them.)
3. Click Request Now.

Directory Synchronization

The third logical step to maintaining an up-to-date address list is directory synchronization (*dirsync*). Directory synchronization is the process by which a Microsoft Exchange server shares address information with other messaging systems. Dirsync in Exchange is based on the Microsoft Mail directory-synchronization protocol, which is widely supported by many messaging systems.

This section covers the setup and configuration of dirsync between Exchange and MS Mail, as well as between Exchange and foreign systems that support the MS Mail dirsync protocol.

Before you begin, you must verify the following information about your Exchange setup:

- All services that are required to run the Administrator program are up and running.
- A functional messaging link exists between your site and the systems with which you want to establish dirsync. A link is usually established by the MS Mail connector or by another specialized connector or gateway.

Following is a brief review of how directory synchronization works and of the tools that you use to set up dirsync in Microsoft Exchange.

The MS Mail dirsync protocol has two principal elements:

- *Directory Synchronization Requestor:* an agent that sends directory updates to, and receives updates from, a directory synchronization server
- *Directory Synchronization Server:* an agent that collects local address updates from requestors, compiles the updates into a master list, and sends the resulting modifications back to the requestors

Microsoft Exchange Server includes one principal component—the Directory Synchronization Agent (DXA)—that operates directory synchronization. The Exchange DXA can act as either a dirsync server or requestor. In standard MS Mail dirsync, the dirsync server maintains a server address list. Exchange uses the Global Address List to replace the server address list.

NOTE When Exchange receives external addresses that are imported during synchronization, the addresses are stored in the directory as custom recipients.

Directory Synchronization Requestor

A single Microsoft Exchange server can act as a requestor for multiple MS Mail dirsync servers. To avoid errors, make sure that you do not set up multiple dirsync requestors to connect to the same dirsync server.

CAUTION

Do not set up more than one dirsync requestor to the same dirsync server in your organization. Doing so can result in corruption of directory information, including duplicate entries when the two sites attempt to exchange updates.

Setting Up a Requestor in Microsoft Exchange

Follow these steps to create an Exchange requestor:

1. In the Administrator window, select a site in your organization.
2. Click the Connections icon. Your list of current connection objects appears.
3. Choose File, New Other, Directory Exchange Requestor. The New Requestor dialog box appears (see fig. 17.7).

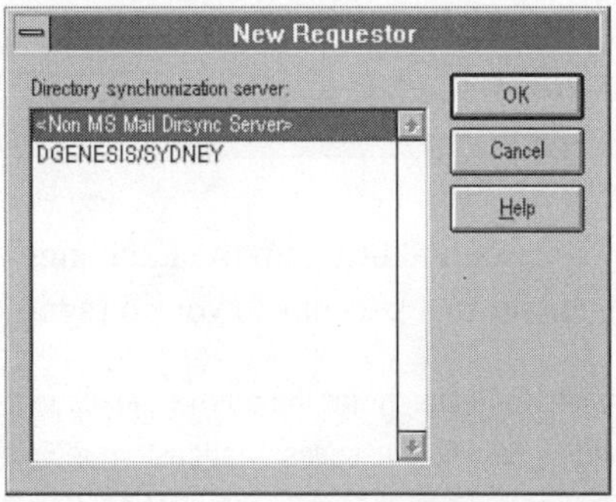

FIG. 17.7
This is the new Directory Exchange Requestor dialog box.

4. From the list of post offices defined in the MS Mail connector, choose the dirsync server that you will use. If you are setting up a requestor for a non-MS Mail system, select <Non MS Mail Dirsync Server> (this procedure will be detailed in the Requestor Configuration section).
5. Click OK. The Properties page for your new requestor appears.

Now you must set up properties in each of the available tabs, as described in the following sections.

General Tab The General tab allows you to name and configure the basic dirsync requestor properties. Follow these steps to configure from where to request directory updates and select the address types supported by this requestor.

1. Type the name of the requestor. You have 255 characters to give this requestor a name that should also identify the Exchange server site (see fig. 17.8). Check the Append to imported Users' Display Name box to add the requestor name to each custom recipient that is created in the DXA process.

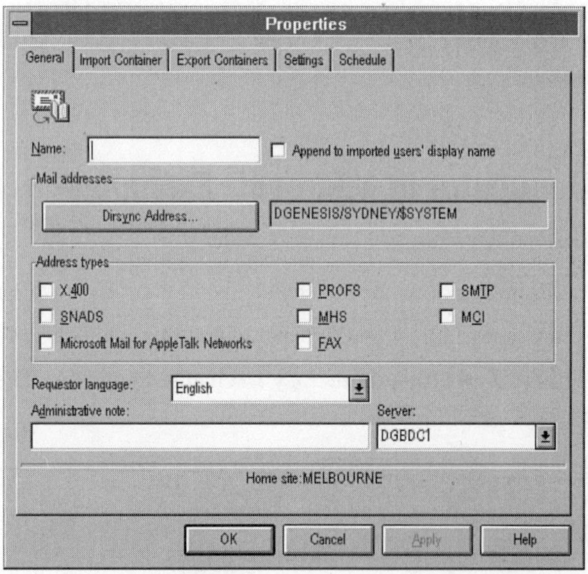

FIG. 17.8
The Dirsync Requestor General Properties page lets you set the nuts and bolts options for a dirsync requestor.

2. Click the Dirsync Address button to bring up the Exchange address list. From that list select the custom recipient that pertains to your dirsync server.

NOTE You must first create a Custom Recipient for the dirsync server with which this requestor will be exchanging dirsync messages. That custom recipient can be any MS Mail or compatible directory synchronization server in your organization. See Chapter 15 for information creating custom recipients.

3. In the Address Types section, check all the types that you want this requestor to obtain from the dirsync server. By default, MS Mail addresses are sent and received. If you choose an address type that the server cannot provide, the MS Mail default format (proxy) address is extracted instead.
4. The Requestor Language pull-down menu allows you to select the default address language template. Use the pull-down menu to choose a language template.
5. In the Administrative Note box, type any comments (up to 1,024 characters) that you feel are pertinent to this situation. The note is visible only in this tab.
6. The Server pull-down menu allows you to change the server at the local site that will handle this directory synchronization requestor. The default selection is the current server. Choose an Exchange server from the pull-down menu. A single Exchange server can be either a dirsync server or requestor, but not both. Also, only one requestor can be set up per Exchange server.
7. Click Apply to set these properties and continue setting other properties.
8. When you finish making settings, click OK to return to the Administrator program.

Import Container Tab An *Import Container* is the recipient container that receives imported information from a dirsync server. This tab allows you to assign trust levels to the imported directory objects.

Because trust levels are exclusive to Microsoft Exchange Server, any imported recipients will not have trust levels assigned. The import container setting gives that object a trust level that Exchange uses to determine replication security. As in any other case of trust-level use, only objects that have a trust level equal to or lower to the trust level of the next site are replicated.

See Chapter 12 for a discussion on how trust levels affect directory information sharing in an organization.

NOTE If you are using multiple requestors to multiple dirsync servers but do not want directory information to be shared between those dirsync servers, you must create a separate container for each group that is imported.

Suppose that you are using Exchange servers MELBOURNE07 and MELBOURNE08 as requestors to two Microsoft Mail network dirsync servers and that you do not want the MS Mail networks to share recipient information. You set each requestor to import to a diffferent recipient container in the MELBOURNE site, each with different trust levels. When synchronization occurs, each list of recipients is imported into its own container (with its own trust level). The information is not mixed and is not synchronized to the other MS Mail server because of the trust level settings.

The following steps describe how to configure the Import Container tab.

1. Click the Import Container tab of dirsync requestor property pages (see fig. 17.9).

FIG. 17.9
The Import Container tab.

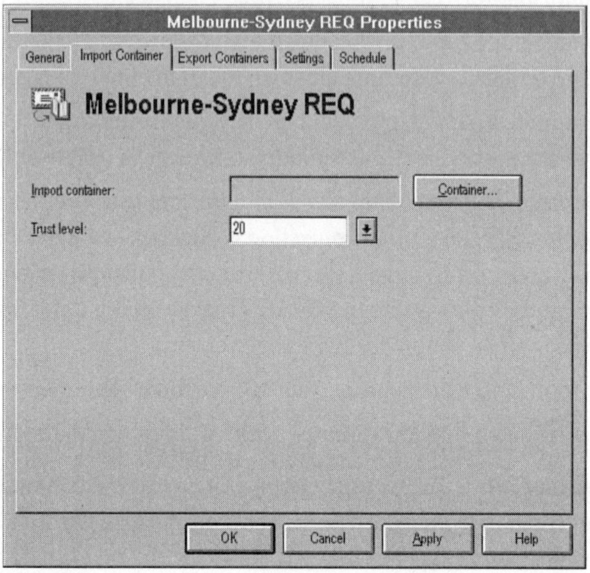

2. The Import Container page shows the current selected recipient. (The page is blank for a new setup.)
3. Click the Container button to display all container recipients. The Import Container Properties page appears (see fig. 17.10).
4. Select the recipient container in which you want all the custom recipients to be imported.
5. Click OK to return to the Import Container tab.
6. Enter a number in the Trust Level box. The default is 20.
7. Click Apply to set these properties and continue setting other properties.
8. When you finish making settings, click OK to return to the Administrator program.

CAUTION

After you choose a directory import container, you are stuck with it. The only way to alter where directory information is stored is to delete the requestor and set up a new one.

FIG. 17.10
Specify where you want incoming recipients to be stored.

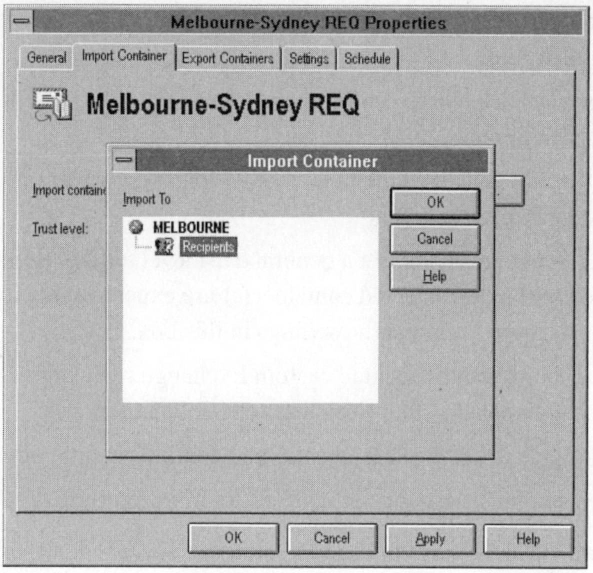

Export Containers Tab An *export container* holds the directory data that an Exchange requestor sends out during synchronization. By default, a requestor does not send out any containers. If you need to export directory information via a requestor, follow this procedure:

1. Click the Export Containers tab of the dirsync requestor's Properties page (see fig. 17.11).

FIG. 17.11
The Export Containers tab.

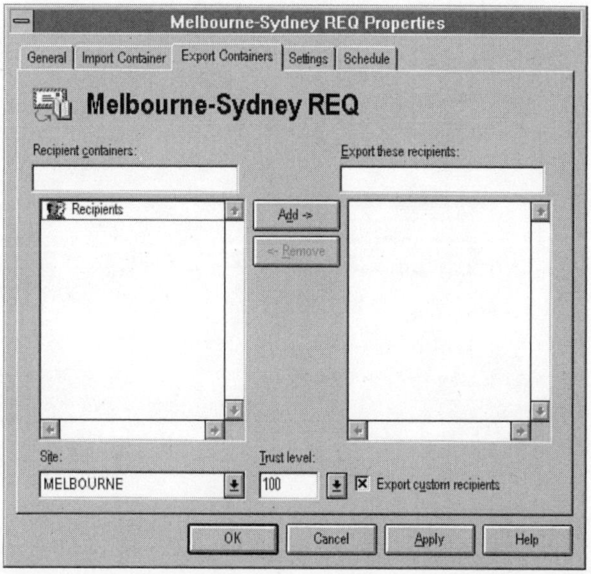

2. To start exporting from a container, select it in the Recipient Containers list and then click Add.

   To remove an exported container, select it in the Export These Recipients list and then click Remove.
3. Use the Site pull-down menu to view recipient containers from other sites and select those for export (optional).
4. In the Trust Level box, set a general trust level for this export function. Individual objects within the selected container(s) are exported only if their trust-level settings are equal to or less than the settings in this box.
5. If you do not want to include custom Exchange recipients in the export procedure, click the Export Custom Recipients check box to clear it.
6. Click Apply to set these properties and continue setting other properties.
7. When you finish making settings, click OK to return to the Administrator program.

Settings Tab The Settings tab allows you to set advanced properties for a directory synchronization connector.

To configure the Settings tab, follow these steps:

1. Click the Settings tab of the Directory Exchange Requestor Properties page (see fig. 17.12).

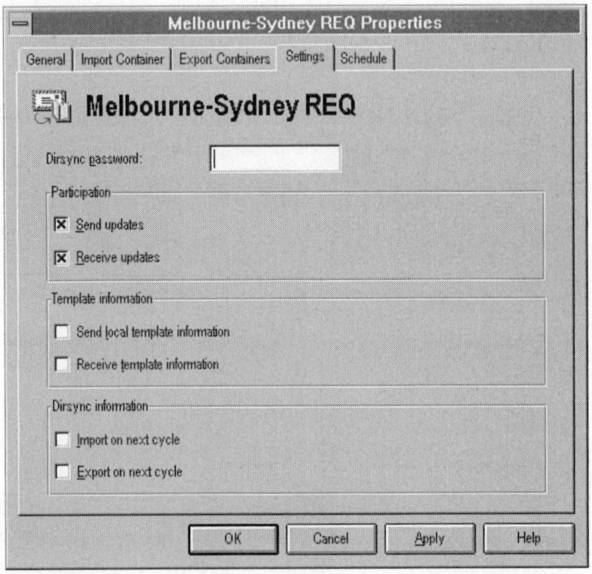

FIG. 17.12
The Settings tab.

2. The Dirsync Password box allows you to give this requestor a password to use when it sends directory updates to a dirsync server. Enter a password if one is needed to access the desired dirsync server. The password is selected when you set up the dirsync server on the remote system. If a password is not needed to access the dirsync server, then leave this space blank.
3. The Participation checkboxes let you define how this requestor is involved in synchronization. Click the appropriate checkbox for how you want this requestor to function:

   Send Updates—The requestor will export directory information to a dirsync server.

   Receive Updates—The requestor will import directory information from a dirsync server. By default both boxes are checked. If neither is checked, then the requestor will not operate.
4. (Optional) Choose one of the following Template Information options:
   - Send Local Template Information: exports address templates to the dirsync server
   - Receive Template Information: imports address templates from the dirsync server
5. Choose one of the following Dirsync Information options, which forces the connector to import or export (or both) all appropriate information to the dirsync sever:
   - Import on Next Cycle: requests every entry (of the selected address type) at the next dirsync sequence
   - Export on Next Cycle: sends addresses from the specified export containers to the dirsync server
6. Click Apply to set these properties and continue setting other properties.
7. When you finish making settings, click OK to return to the Administrator program.

Schedule Tab The Schedule tab allows you to set the time when update messages are transmitted to the directory synchronization sever.

NOTE The verification messages or updates from the dirsync server are handled automatically.

To set the requestor's schedule, follow these steps:

1. Click the Schedule tab of the dirsync requestor's Properties page (see fig. 17.13).

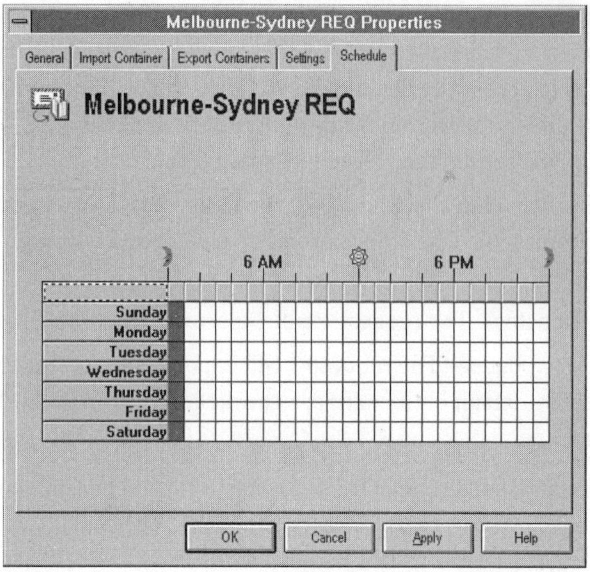

FIG. 17.13
The Schedule tab.

2. In the grid, click the boxes to select the time when you want directory update messages to be exchanges with the dirsync server. Update messages are sent at the beginning of the selected time. By default (if you don't select a specific time), dirsync messages are automatically scheduled for transmission at midnight.
3. Click Apply to set these properties and continue setting other properties.
4. When you finish making settings, click OK to return to the Administrator program.

This chapter has covered all the available options for configuring a Directory Exchange Requestor. You must now configure the MS Mail dirsync server to accept your new Exchange requestor. There are two primary settings to configure:

Password. You must configure the MS Mail Directory Exchange server to recognize your new Microsoft Exchange requestor. If you selected a password in the Settings tab, remember to include it in your configuration. Your MS Mail for PC documentation will guide you through this process.

E-mail address. When you configure your MS Mail dirsync server to recognize your new Exchange requestor, you need the MS Mail network and post office e-mail address of the local site. The local site's Site Addressing property pages contain this information.

Using Exchange as a Directory Synchronization Server

Another way to integrate Microsoft Exchange into directory synchronization with MS Mail-compatible networks is to set up a directory synchronization server (also called a dirsync server) on Exchange. Then you can use standard MS Mail requestors on remote machines to participate in directory synchronization.

Following are the general steps for setting up Exchange as a dirsync server:

- In the Administrator program, create a directory synchronization server for the local Microsoft Exchange server site. Configure its properties.

NOTE Although you can have multiple Exchange dirsync servers in your organization, you can have only one for each Microsoft Exchange site.

- In the directory, define a remote directory exchange requestor object that corresponds to each requestor that will link to this server.
- Configure each requestor on other systems that will use this server.

Creating and Configuring a Directory Exchange Server

When you create a new directory exchange server, it automatically gets an e-mail address based on the MS Mail address type for the local site. Because you can have only one directory exchange server per site, no addressing conflicts can exist.

To create a new directory exchange server in the Administrator program, choose File, New Other, Dirsync Server. If you have already set up another directory synchronization server in this site, the new Dirsync Server option is not available.

To configure an existing server from the Administrator program, follow these steps:

1. Click the Connections icon under the desired Exchange site.
2. From the list of connections icons, click the icon of your current dirsync server. By default, the name for this object is "DXA server."
3. Choose File, Properties to open the dirsync server property pages.

The following sections cover configuration of the dirsync server's property pages.

General Tab To set general Properties, follow this procedure:

1. Click the General tab of the dirsync server's Properties page (see fig. 17.14).

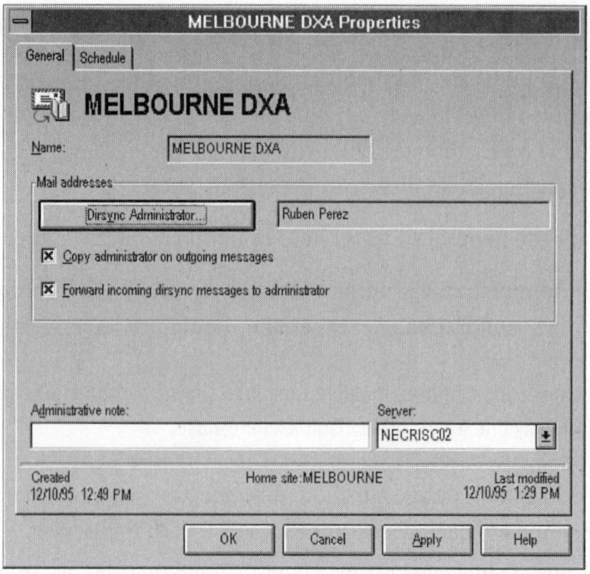

FIG. 17.14
The General tab of the DXA Properties page.

2. In the Name box, type a unique name for this dirsync server. (You are allowed to use 64 characters.)
3. (Optional) Select a dirsync administrator that will receive dirsync status and error messages and click the Dirsync Administrator button. The Exchange address List dialog box appears. Type or select a name (a user, public folder, or distribution list), and click OK. You return to the General tab.
4. To send a copy of each outgoing update to the administrator, click the Copy Administrator on Outgoing Messages check box.
5. To view each incoming update message from each requestor, click the Forward Incoming Dirsync Messages to Administrator check box.

NOTE By default, neither Copy Administrator on Outgoing Messages nor Forward Incoming Dirsync Messages to Administrator is selected. Typically, you would choose these options only for troubleshooting purposes.

6. If you want, enter comments (up to 1,024 characters) in the Administrative Note box. The comments will be visible only in this tab.
7. Use the Server pull-down menu to select the Microsoft Exchange server computer that will host the directory synchronization process. By default, the current Exchange server is selected.
8. Click Apply to set these properties and continue setting other properties.
9. When you finish making settings, click OK to return to the Administrator program.

Schedule Tab The Schedule tab defines when the directory synchronization server sends updates to its requestors. Server updates are independent of the schedule under which the requestors send their updates to the server. Directory updates are sent to requestors at the beginning of the scheduled hour.

To set the schedule, follow these steps:

1. Click the Schedule tab in the dirsync server property pages.
2. In the time grid, select the times when you want this dirsync server to send update messages to its requestors.
3. Click Apply to set these properties and continue setting other properties.
4. When you finish making settings, click OK to return to the Administrator program.

Defining Remote Directory Synchronization Requestors

Just as you do with a standard MS Mail directory synchronization server, you must identify and define each remote requestor that will be communicating updates to the local Exchange dirsync server. Setting up each remote requestor involves two steps:

- Define a remote dirsync requestor object in the Microsoft Exchange Server administrator program.
- Establish the permissions that these containers will use when importing and exporting addressing data.

These two steps make your Exchange directory synchronization server aware of its requestors. Review the following section to verify that a remote requestor is properly configured and able to communicate with the local Exchange dirsync server.

Creating and Configuring a Remote Directory Synchronization Requestor

To create a new remote dirsync requestor, follow these steps:

1. In the Administrator program, choose File, New Other, Remote Dirsync Requestor. The property pages for a new remote sirsync requestor appear.

NOTE The New Remote Dirsync Requestor command is unavailable until you set up a Microsoft Exchange directory synchronization server.

The following sections describe the tabs that you configure for a remote dirsync requestor.

General Tab To set general properties, follow these steps:

1. Click the General tab of the Remote Dirsync Requestor Properties page.
2. Type a display name (up to 255 characters) for this remote dirsync requestor. This name is displayed as the directory exchange server object name in the Administrator program.
3. Check the Append to Created Users' Display Name check box to add the name of this requestor to each recipient created when synchronizing addresses with this requestor. This is useful for keeping track of a recipient's origin.
4. Click the Dirsync Address button to bring up the Exchange address list. From that list select the custom recipient that pertains to the remote dirsync requestor.

NOTE You must first create a custom recipient for each remote dirsync requestor to provide address information about the requestor.

5. Enter a password in the password box if your Exchange dirsync server requests one during sychronization. By default, this box is blank. If you do use a password for security, remember to set the same password on the remote MS Mail requestor to avoid authentication errors.
6. The Request Address Type box specifies the format in which address updates are set. MS (the default) is used by MS Mail (PC) and other compatible directory exchange requestors. Select MSA if you are synchronizing directories with a Microsoft Mail for AppleTalk network.
7. The Requestor Language pull-down menu allows you to change the default language template.
8. Click the Export On Next Cycle check box to send all address information to the remote requestor during the next synchronization session. By default, this option is not selected. Keep in mind that all directory information is exported automatically when you first configure a remote requestor.
9. If you want, enter comments (up to 1,024 characters) in the Administrative Note box. These comments will be visible only in this tab.
10. Click Apply to set these properties and continue setting other properties.
11. When you finish making settings, click OK to return to the Administrator program.

Import Container Tab Much as you do in setting up directory exchange requestors, you use import containers to assign trust levels to objects that are being imported.

Because trust levels are exclusive to Microsoft Exchange Server, any imported recipients will not have trust levels assigned. The import container gives that object a trust level that you set in the Import Container tab. As in any other case of trust-level use, only objects that have a trust level equal to or lower than the next site's trust level are replicated. The following steps cover Import Container tab configuration.

1. Click the Import Container tab of the Remote Dirsync Requestor Properties page (see fig. 17.15).

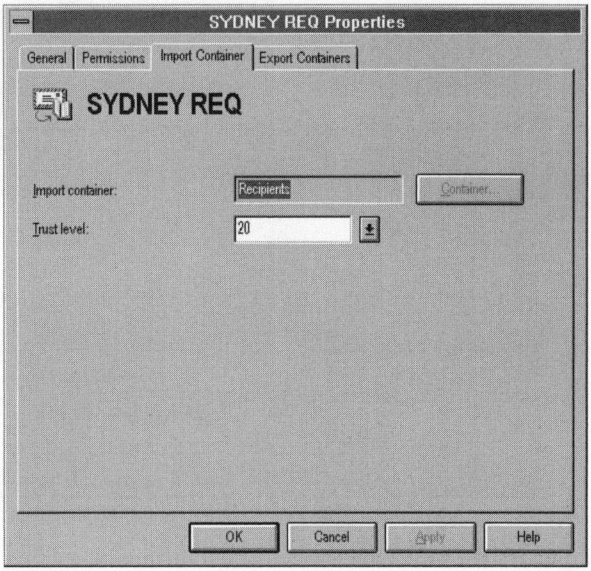

FIG. 17.15
Choose the container in which imported recipients will be stored.

Part III Ch 17

2. The Import Container box shows the name of the recipient container that stores the imported addresses. By default, this box is blank. Click the Container button to select a recipient container. All current recipient containers appear in a dialog box. Select one container to hold directory imports and click OK to return to the Import Container tab.
3. In the Trust Level box, assign a trust level to the import container. (The default setting is 20.) Remember that only objects that have a trust level equal to or lower than the setting in this box will be updated during synchronization.
4. Click Apply to set these properties and continue setting other properties.
5. When you finish making settings, click OK to return to the Administrator program.

NOTE You cannot modify import containers after you create them. If you must change where information is placed, you must delete the existing container and create a new one.

Export Containers Tab The Export Containers tab specifies what information is sent out to the remote requestor during directory synchronization. By default, no information from the local site is exported. To configure data export, follow these steps:

1. Click the Export Containers tab in the Remote Dirsync Requestor Properties page (see fig. 17.16).

FIG. 17.16
The Export Containers tab.

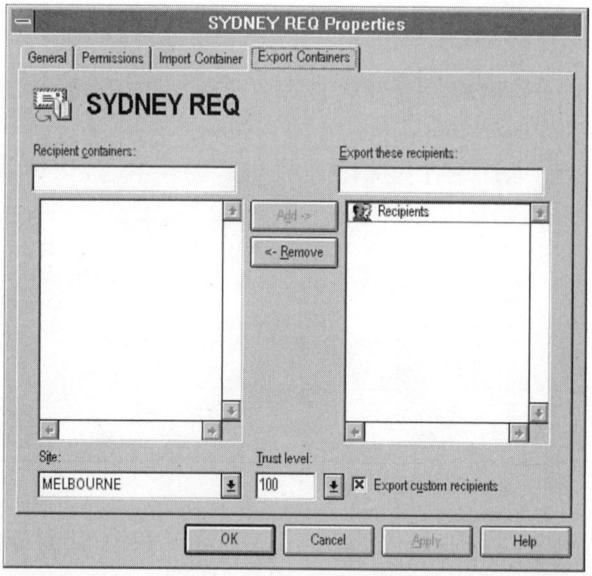

2. In the Export These Recipients list, select the container that you want to export, then click Add.

   To stop exporting a container, select it in the Export These Recipients list, then click Remove.
3. Use the Site pull-down menu to view other sites' containers, to which you can export recipients.
4. In the Trust Level box, set a trust level to limit replication of certain objects in the containers that you selected to export.
5. Click the Export Custom Recipients check box to include those recipients in synchronization. By default, this option is selected.
6. Click Apply to set these properties and continue setting other properties.
7. When you finish making settings, click OK to return to the Administrator program.

Configuring Remote Requestors

The final step in establishing directory synchronization between a Microsoft Exchange directory synchronization server and remote requestors is configuring the remote requestors on the MS Mail or compatible sytems.

The following sections provide general recommendations on configuring directory synchronization requestors on the following types of remote systems:

- Microsoft Mail for PC networks
- Microsoft Mail for AppleTalk networks
- Other foreign mail systems

Microsoft Mail for PC Networks 3.x Directory Synchronization Requestor

The requestor that you are most likely to set up is one for a MS Mail for PC network. Standard MS Mail requestor programs connect to Exchange directory synchronization servers through the MS Mail connector as though the requestor were of the standard MS Mail type. You need to configure the requestor from within your MS Mail administrator program. Consult your Microsoft documentation for the procedure.

Before you configure the requestor, make sure that you have met all of the following conditions:

> **TIP** You can test the operation of a MS Mail connection by entering the address of your recipient manually in the "to" line of the Exchange client.

- Exchange and the Microsoft Mail connector are properly configured and running.
- The Microsoft Exchange directory synchronization server is installed and running.
- MS Mail for PC Networks is set up and running correctly on its own.
- If your Exchange server and the MS Mail post office are not on the same logical network, the MS Mail external or multitasking MTA program must be set up and running correctly.

Directory Synchronization Between Exchange and Microsoft Mail for AppleTalk Networks

This section is dedicated to a discussion on address list sharing between Exchange and a Microsoft Mail for AppleTalk network. These solutions, though functional, are a poor substitute for the use of a Macintosh Exchange client directly. Primarily, these solutions will be used as a stop gap in preparation for an eventual complete migration to Exchange. Existing MS Mail AppleTalk servers can act as requestors to standard MS Mail (PC) dirsync servers. By pointing the Macintosh dirsync requestor to an Exchange dirsync server, your Mac servers can begin sharing address lists with your Exchange organization.

The first part of this section will cover the set up of a Directory Exchange Requestor in an MS Mail for AppleTalk network.

The directory synchronization requestor for MS Mail AppleTalk is installed with the Microsoft Exchange connection gateway.

Before you configure the MS Mail AppleTalk requestor, confirm the following situations:

- Exchange and the Microsoft Mail connector are properly configured and running.
- MSA (Microsoft Mail AppleTalk) is selected in the appropriate Exchange Remote Dirsync Requestor property pages. This setting is found under the General tab of this dirsync requestor.

CAUTION

If you do not set the requestor to receive messages in MSA format, duplicate entries are created in the MS Mail AppleTalk address list.

- The Microsoft Exchange Connection gateway software is properly configured and running on the MS Mail AppleTalk server.

If you have met all the preceding conditions, you are ready to continue setting up the directory synchronization requestor. If you have been looking at a Windows screen layout all day, the following steps could be a nice change of pace.

Requestor Configuration

When you set up directory synchronization, you need to configure three principal requestor options. You must log in as the network manager on your MS Mail AppleTalk server to make all configuration and administrative functions available. The next sections describe how to set the following:

- Install General Requestor Settings
- Identify the appropriate gateway
- Request the correct address types

General Requestor Settings

1. Open the Microsoft Exchange Connection folder on the Macintosh MS Mail server.
2. Click the Microsoft Exchange Connection Directory Exchange Requestor icon.
3. The first time you open a new requestor, a dialog box appears. Type your network manager password, and click OK.
4. The first time you set up a requestor a configure dialog box appears. Subsequently, you must select Application from the Configure menu.
5. The `Send Directory at` box allows you to enter the time when directory updates are sent to the Microsoft Exchange dirsync server. Use the 24 hour format hh:mm. By default this time is set to 4 a.m.
6. The `Receive Updates at` box allows you to enter the time when the requestor scans the Network Manager's inbox for directory updates.
7. In the Exchange Network box, enter the network name of the MS Mail connector.
8. In the `Exchange PO` box, enter the post office name of the MS Mail connector. This information is available on the Exchange MS Mail connector's Local Postoffice property page.
9. Use the `Exchange Password` box if you have also set a password in the corresponding Microsoft Exchange server remote dirsync requestor object. By default, this box is blank.
10. `DXA Mailbox` specifies the Exchange server mailbox to which the requestor will send update messages. By default this is `$SYSTEM`. Normally you do not want to change this setting.
11. The `Network Manager` box defines the MS Mail AppleTalk account to receive address list updates from the Exchange dirsync server. By default, this mailbox is Network Manager. The Password field is for the account specified in the Network Manager box.
12. `Requestor Name` refers to the corresponding remote directory exchange requestor as set in the Exchange server directory.

13. The `Fault Tolerance` check box enables tracking of address updates. Synchronization numbers are created and used to recover address when an error occurs. This will avoid having to do manual directory import and export. By default this is checked.
14. `Include Server In Friendly Name` sets all MS Mail AppleTalk addresses to display as *user@servername*. By default this is checked.
15. The `Export World List` check box when not checked will cease all updates being sent to the Exchange dirsync server. By default this is checked.
16. Click OK to save new settings and close the Configure dialog box. Click revert to keep previous settings.

If you are configuring this requestor for the first time, the Gateway dialog box appears.

NOTE If this not your first time configuring this requestor, then from the Configure menu choose Select Gateway.

In this dialog box, you must select a Gateway. This is the passage through which messaging data will reach the Exchange server. By default this is the connection gateway. Choose your preferred gateway and then click the Select button.

Address Filters Address filters allow you to specify the address types that you want to receive from the Exchange server.

To configure address filtering, follow these steps:

1. Open the Address filtering dialog box. If you just proceeded from gateway box, this is already open.
2. Check each address type you want to request from the Exchange dirsync server.
3. Click OK to save your settings and move on, or click Revert to return to the previous settings.

Starting the Requestor

1. Open the Microsoft Exchange Connection folder in Macintosh Finder.
2. Double-click the MS Mail Appletalk directory exchange requestor icon to start it. The requestor starts, and a status dialog box appears.

   The status display refreshes when the system receives directory update messages.

If the requestor is not given the network manager name and password, or if you are not currently logged in as a Network Manager, then the request will run as a foreground application, locking the desktop and preventing you from running other applications. However, if you have given the password, or are logged in as the Network Manager, then the application runs in the background.

To stop the requestor, choose File, Quit.

It is convenient to make the Macintosh dirsync requestor a startup item so you do not need to manually launch the application every time you restart the system. To make the requestor a startup item, follow these steps:

1. Make an alias of the directory exchange requestor. Do this by highlighting the requestor icon, then choose File, Make Alias.
2. Move the alias to the Startup Items folder inside the Macintosh System Folder.

Maintaining the MS Mail AppleTalk Requestor

As network manager, you may want to execute a few maintenance tasks as part of administrating Exchange directory synchronization from the MS Mail AppleTalk end. Those tasks are importing a complete list of addresses, exporting a complete local address list, and resynchronizing that information.

To import a complete list of known addresses, follow these steps:

1. Start the Exchange Connection Directory Exchange Requestor by double-clicking its icon in the Macintosh Finder.
2. Choose File, Import Directory. The Import Directory dialog box appears.
3. Choose Changes Since Last Update Only to immediately request the addresses that have changed since the last directory synchronization cycle.

   Alternatively, click the Complete Directory radio button and then click OK to import all available addresses of the selected type.
4. Click OK to finalize your settings.

NOTE To verify that imports have proceeded correctly, you need to start MS Mail AppleTalk manually and choose Mail, Gateway Recipient. A dialog box appears that lists the new recipients. All requested information should be available in this list after you receive an import confirmation message from the dirsync server.

Exporting Directory Information to Microsoft Exchange Server

The previous section described how to get MS Mail AppleTalk to receive addresses from Exchange. The following section describes how to update the Exchange address list with changes made on the MS Mail AppleTalk server. You will do this by telling the Exchange Connection software to export its contents to the Exchange dirsync server. The following steps describe the steps necessary to accomplish this:

1. Start the Exchange Connection Directory Exchange requestor by double-clicking its icon in the Macintosh Finder.
2. Choose File, Export Directory.
3. Choose Changes Since Last Update Only to immediately request the addresses that have changed since the last directory synchronization cycle.

   Alternatively, click the Complete Directory radio button to import all available addresses of the selected type.
4. Click OK to commence directory export.

After the Exchange server processes these update requests, it sends a confirmation message and a status report to the network manager's mailbox.

Another option is to export the local MS Mail AppleTalk addresses into a text-file format that the MS Mail (PC) import utility can read. Use this alternative when other methods are not operational.

To export the addresses (also called the word list) manually, follow these steps:

1. Start the Exchange Connection Directory Exchange Requestor by double-clicking its icon in the Macintosh Finder.
2. Choose Save to File from the File menu. A dialog box appears asking you for a location to save your exported information.
3. Select the folder in which you want to save your file.
4. In the Dump Work List Into box, type a file name. A unique identifiable name is recommended (perhaps including the date of the export for future reference).
5. Click OK to complete the export.

You can open the exported file with any text editor. All your addresses should be in that file, displayed in the following format:

A 30_character_alias MSMAIL:address

(MS Mail is the address type of this entry.)

Removing MS Mail AppleTalk or Exchange Server Addresses

Sometimes, you need to remove all MS Mail for AppleTalk recipients from the Exchange address list, and vice versa. This situation occurs when MS Mail AppleTalk users become full-fledged Microsoft Exchange clients.

To remove MS Mail AppleTalk recipients from the Exchange server address list, follow this procedure:

1. Start the Exchange Connection Directory Exchange Requestor by double-clicking its icon in the Macintosh Finder.
2. Choose Remove Mac Names from Exchange from the File menu. A confirmation dialog box appears to verify that you actually want to do this.
3. Click OK. Every MS Mail AppleTalk and gateway recipient is removed from the Exchange global address list.

NOTE If you suddenly realize that you really needed the addresses, you have to import them to restore the entries. Subsequent directory synchronization cycles do not replace deleted entries.

Removing Exchange Recipients from the MS Mail AppleTalk Local Address List

Follow this procedure to delete Exchange recipients from MS Mail AppleTalk:

1. Start the Exchange Connection Directory Exchange Requestor by double-clicking its icon in the Macintosh Finder.
2. Choose Remove Exchange Names from Mac from the File menu. A confirmation dialog box appears to verify that you actually want to do this.
3. Click OK. Every Microsoft Exchange recipient in the local directory is deleted from the MS Mail AppleTalk word list.

Resynchronizing Address Information

As directory synchronization occurs, updates are exchanged, and the network manager receives periodic messages confirming that the process is operational and that changes have been incorporated.

Sometimes, this process does not operate smoothly. In such cases, the requestor gives you the option of forcing resynchronization of the entire system manually.

If you believe that your system is out of sync, follow these steps:

1. Log on as network manager.
2. Start the Exchange connection directory exchange requestor by double-clicking its icon in the Macintosh Finder.
3. Choose Resync Cycle from the File menu. The Directory Exchange Requestor proceeds to restart its synchronization cycle.

The requestor receives the global address list from the Exchange server and resets the send/receive cycle.

If you get a message stating that the directory synchronization cycle is out of phase, you should initiate a complete directory refresh (import and export) between both systems. As described in the preceding sections, you should import the Exchange global address list and export the local address list to the Exchange dirsync server.

The MS Mail AppleTalk directory exchange requestor keeps a log of all its activities. This log is a text file stored inside the Preferences folder (in the System Folder). Any standard text editor displays this file.

NOTE This file logs all directory Exchange requestor activities, so the file could be very large if it is heavily used. Make sure that you delete or clear the file on a periodic basis. Confirming that synchronization is functional before you delete any log entries is a good idea.

Configuring Foreign Directory Exchange Requestors

Any foreign system that conforms with Microsoft Mail 3.x directory synchronization protocol can connect to an Exchange dirsync server. You probably need to consult your appropriate documentation for the process, but here are some general recommendations to follow before you configure synchronization with foreign systems:

- Make sure that all Exchange server operations are working correctly.
- Install and configure the correct gateway for Exchange communication with the foreign system.
- Properly configure the Exchange directory synchronization server and the appropriate remote requestor.

- Install whatever gateway the foreign mail system requires to communicate with Microsoft Exchange.
- Test to see whether standard messages can be transferred between systems. Because directories are not in sync, you have to enter the addresses manually.

Configuring Microsoft Directory Exchange Agent (DXA) Settings

The DXA is the Exchange component that actually runs the dirsync server and requestor. By default, the DXA is configured to allow both server and requestor processes to run. You can modify general settings for the DXA, as described in the following sections. The DXA is configured through an object named Directory Synchronization on each Exchange server in your site.

See Chapter 12 for more information on configuring all directory services on Exchange.

Configuring the Directory Synchronization General Tab

The Directory Synchronization General tab allows you to choose the server that carries out the DXA functions. Any server at the site is eligible, but always take into consideration other functions that a server is performing. To choose a server, follow these steps:

1. In the Administrator program, select a site in your organization.
2. Click the Servers icon to list the Exchange servers in this site.
3. Select the Microsoft Exchange server that you want to configure.
4. Select the Directory Synchronization object.
5. Click the General tab in the Microsoft Directory Synchronization object.
6. Use the Administrator Note box and type any additional comments you may want to add.
7. Click Apply to set these properties and continue setting other properties.
8. When you finish making settings, click OK to return to the Administrator program.

E-Mail Addresses Tab

The e-mail addresses are used to send and receive synchronization update messages. You will need the E-mail Addresses Properties page to create, modify, or delete these addresses. By default, Microsoft Exchange server automatically generates MS Mail (PC),

X.400, and SMTP addresses for each DXA. Several services, such as dirsync requestors and servers, use these addresses for communication with the DXA.

To create or modify Microsoft DXA addresses, follow this procedure:

1. Click the E-Mail Addresses tab.
2. To change an existing address, select it and then click Edit. The dialog box for its particular address type appears.
3. To create a new address for this DXA, click New. Select what type of e-mail address you want to add, then type in all necessary addressing information. Click OK to return to the E-Mail Addresses tab.
4. To delete an existing address, select it, click Remove, and click OK to confirm the deletion.
5. Click Apply to set these properties and continue setting other properties.
6. When you finish making settings, click OK to return to the Administrator program.

CAUTION

Many other Exchange services use these addresses. If you plan to change or delete them without appropriate consideration of such services, directory synchronization will fail.

Delivery Restrictions Tab

This tab is useful because it prevents messages that are unrelated to directory synchronization from being sent to the DXA. You also can set up delivery restrictions to allow messages to be sent only by specified senders. In the Delivery Restriction tab, you select specific addresses from which the DXA will reject or allow messages. By default, the DXA accepts messages from all senders. Such an open "door" could cause errors and delays in proper directory synchronization.

To set delivery restrictions, follow these steps:

1. Click the Delivery Restrictions tab of the Microsoft DXA.

   The left side of the tab lists the specific senders who have permission to send messages to the DXA. The right side lists senders who are not allowed to send messages to this DXA.

TIP Entering specific accepted senders is the most fault-tolerant approach to this setup. Be aware, however, that if you set up a new requestor without modifying the tab, all of that requestor's messages will be rejected.

2. To accept messages only from specific senders or to reject messages from specific senders (the settings are mutually exclusive), select List and click Modify. The Microsoft Exchange Address Book appears.
3. Select the specific container from which you want to view recipients in the Show Names From The: menu. The corresponding recipients are shown in the Type Name Or Select From List box.
4. Type **select** or a name from the list. If you can't see or remember the name you are looking for, you can use the Find button. The Properties button will display standard recipient properties for your selection.
5. Once you have selected a name or multiple names on the left, click Add.
6. Click OK to return to the Delivery Restrictions property page.
7. Click Apply to set these properties and continue setting other properties. If you are done with all settings, click OK to return to the administrator program.

Incoming Templates Tab

Incoming Templates are Address templates that take incoming address information and map it for specified Exchange server directory recipient attributes.

An address imported though synchronization with an MS Mail network, for example, could have the occupation and telephone attributes. For consistency, you would want to map the occupation tag to the Exchange Title attribute.

To map templates to Exchange server attributes, follow these steps:

1. Click the Incoming Templates tab of the Directory Synchronization Properties page (see fig. 17.17).
2. To modify an existing mapping, select it from the list and then click Edit. The Incoming Template Mapping dialog box appears.

   In the Map the String box, edit the template identifier string that MS Mail uses. In the To the Attribute box, edit the recipient attribute in which you want to store the incoming information. When you finish, click OK to return to the Incoming Templates tab.

NOTE All mapping strings must match the incoming strings.

3. To create a new mapping, click the New button. The Incoming Template Mapping dialog box appears. Type a string found in the incoming address information. Use the To The Attribute pull-down menu to select which Exchange attribute you want to associate with that string. Click OK to return to the Incoming Templates tab.

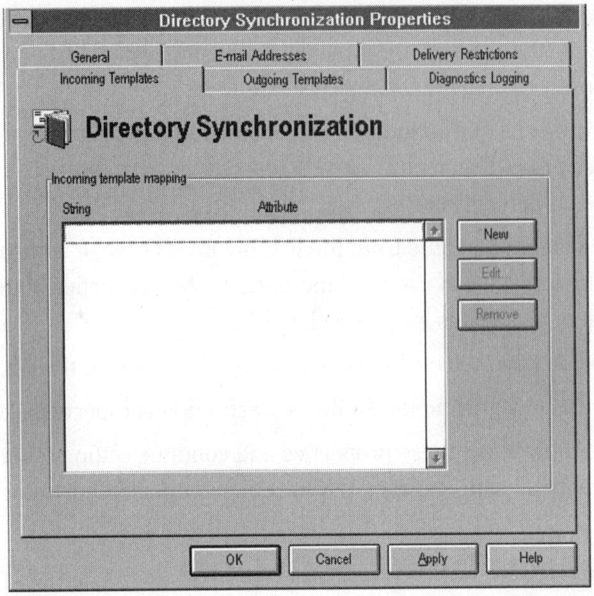

FIG. 17.17 Define Incoming Templates for synchronized addresses.

4. To delete an existing mapping, select it and then click Remove.
5. Click Apply to set these properties and continue setting other properties.
6. When you finish making settings, click OK to return to the Administrator program.

Outgoing Templates Tab

Outgoing template mappings are the inverse of the preceding function. You can map Microsoft Exchange server directory recipient attributes to outgoing MS Mail-compatible template information.

To map Exchange server attributes to an MS Mail template, follow these steps:

1. Click the Outgoing Templates tab of the Directory Synchronization Properties page (see fig. 17.18).
2. To modify an existing mapping, select it in the list and then click Edit. The Outgoing Template Mapping dialog box appears. In the Map the Attribute box, edit the recipient attribute that you want to map to the MS Mail template. In the To the String box, edit the MS Mail template identifier string in which you want to place outgoing-attribute information. When you finish, click OK to return to the Outgoing Templates tab.
3. To create a new mapping, click the New button. The Outgoing Template Mapping dialog box appears. Use the Map The Attribute pull-down menu to select which Exchange attribute you want to map to a string on the remote system. Type that string in the To The String box. Click OK to return to the Outgoing Templates tab.

FIG. 17.18
Outgoing Template Mappings translate Exchange attributes to a user-defined string.

4. To delete an existing mapping, select it and then click Remove.
5. Click Apply to set these properties and continue setting other properties.
6. When you finish making settings, click OK to return to the Administrator program.

As soon as you activate the directory exchange requestor for the first time, it exports a complete local address list to its Microsoft Exchange directory synchronization server. Also, the requestor sends out a request for entries in the Exchange address list. The Microsoft Exchange dirsync server returns a confirmation message, saying that it received the requestor's transmission; then that server sends all the data in the export container to the dirsync requestor.

Subsequent transmissions between dirsync requestor and server consist only of updates to the address lists. You can force the import or export of directory information manually, as well from the appropriate connector tabs.

Be aware that directory synchronization updates sent by the Exchange dirsync server are in the form of messages sent to the network manager's mailbox. From that mailbox, the messages are picked up by the Microsoft Exchange connection and synchronized into the local address list. These messages should not be modified or deleted; altering those messages interrupts the synchronization process and could produce data loss.

NOTE Large imports from the directory exchange server (several thousand entries) are known to take up to several hours. Be aware of such time requirements. Also be aware that during that time, no other messages will pass the Exchange connection gateway.

Starting Directory Synchronization

After you meet the preceding requirements, you can start the directory synchronization service. Follow these steps:

1. Open the Windows NT services control panel (see fig. 17.19) for the server on which you want to begin synchronization.

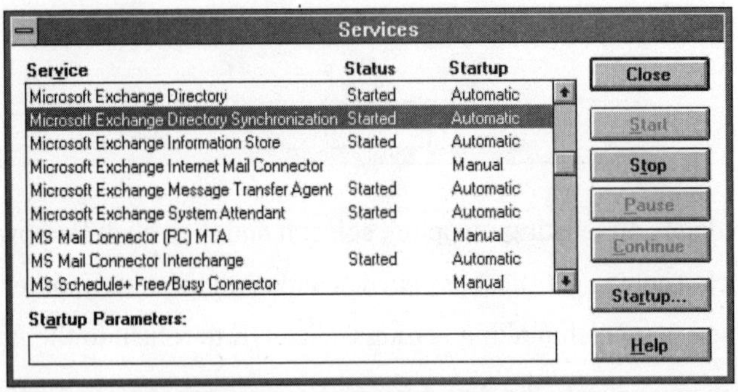

FIG. 17.19
Exchange services running under Windows NT.

2. Select the service name Microsoft Exchange Directory Synchronization.
3. Click Start. The service starts, and synchronization begins.
4. Close the services window.

NOTE If you set a specific time for directory synchronization that occurred while the service was stopped, a delay may occur until the first sync cycle actually begins. You can force immediate execution of a replication cycle in the property pages of the appropriate connector supporting synchronization.

Stopping Replication Services

Open the services control panel and click the Stop button to cease all replication procedures.

NOTE Notifying fellow administrators and users that synchronization will be shut down is a good idea.

From Here...

This chapter guided you through the process of establishing directory-sharing relationships between Exchange sites and between Exchange and other messaging systems. With this information, you can begin to structure your own directory-sharing architecture. Remember that the goal in directory replication and synchronization is to have the most complete and useful address lists possible without overloading server processing or network bandwidth in the process.

For more information, read the following chapters:

- Chapter 5, "Designing Exchange Topology," gives you a good understanding of the types of site connections that you need for efficient directory replication.
- Chapter 12, "Directory and System Attendant Configuration," guides you through configuring all settings pertinent to Exchange's directory system as a whole.
- Chapter 18, "Setting Up Microsoft Mail for PC Networks," shows you how to configure the MS Mail connector—an essential element of directory synchronization with Exchange.
- Chapter 19, "Setting Up Microsoft Mail for AppleTalk Networks," to learn about what is required to establish message traffic between Exchange and MS Mail (AppleTalk).

CHAPTER 18

Setting Up Microsoft Mail for PC Networks

- The MS Mail Connector Components
- Setting Up the MS Mail Connector
- Auditing the MS Mail Connector
- Directory Synchronization for MS Mail (PC)

As discussed earlier, MS Mail is a shared file system e-mail application. It relies on a series of flat configuration files to transfer data between the users on the post office. ■

Understanding the MS Mail Connector

The connection from Exchange to MS Mail requires several components. As discussed in Chapter 8, "Planning and Migrating to External Systems," Exchange can coexist or provide backbone support for MS Mail networks. The MS Mail connector is the message transfer component included in the Exchange server. It provides the MS Mail External and post office functionality to Exchange. External is a message transfer application, which runs in single threaded mode on DOS or as a multitasking application on OS/2. In the recent release of MS Mail v3.5, a set of Multitasking MTAs were ported to run on windows NT.

Figures 18.1 and 18.2 illustrate a visual comparison of the two message transfer agents.

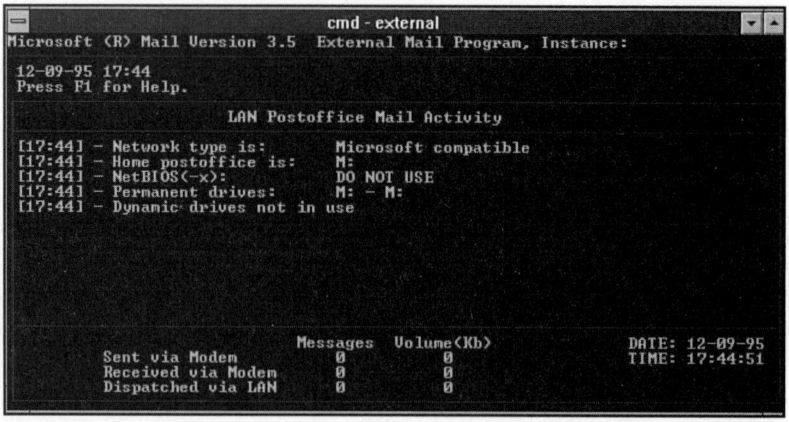

FIG. 18.1
The External application running on DOS.

NOTE The Exchange MS Mail Connector has a rich GUI interface that provides many new features.

In order to connect to an MS Mail post office on the same WAN/LAN, you must configure an MTA to do the following:

- Send and receive messages
- Convert the messages to the native format
- Deliver the messages to the destination post office and recipient

In Exchange, you configure the MS Mail Connector to receive messages from the Exchange MTA, convert the messages into the MS Mail format, and then deliver them to the target post office diagrammed in figure 18.3.

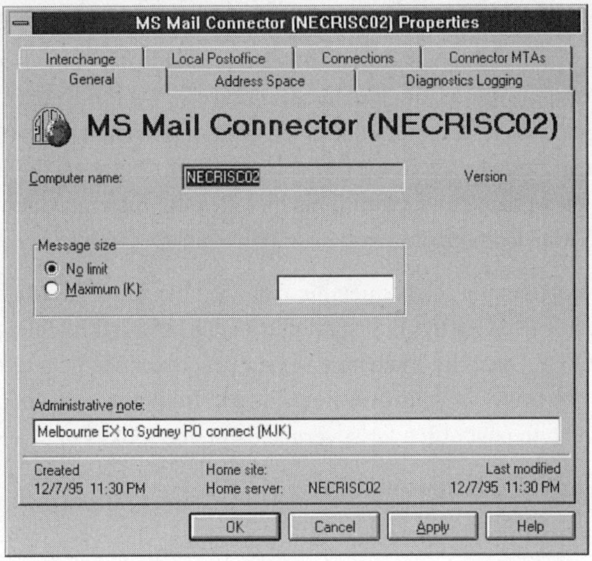

FIG. 18.2
The Exchange MS Mail Connector.

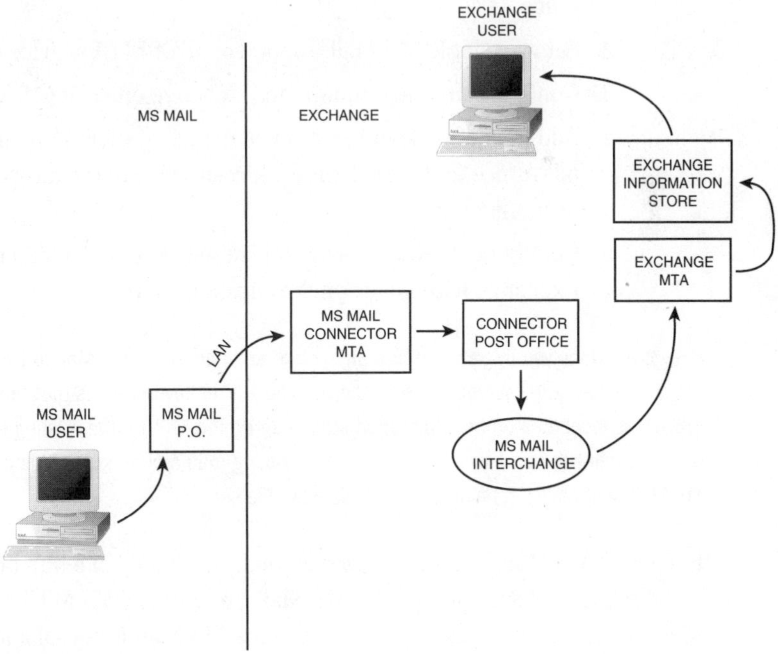

FIG. 18.3
The Exchange to MS Mail Architecture.

Exchange creates a local or "virtual" post office on the Exchange server. This post office models the MS Mail 3.x post office architecture. This post office becomes a shared file systems post office under the Exchange hierarchy. On the Exchange server, you have the information store, directory services, system attendant, and mail transfer agents. The Message Transfer Agent (MTA) communicates between the information stores and the different mail connectors. This includes the Internet Connector, the Connector, and the MS Mail Connector.

The core component of the connection from Exchange to MS Mail (PC) is the MS Mail Connector. It is used for the information transfer between Exchange and MS Mail sites and post offices. Once the Exchange server processes the data interchange, the MS Mail (PC) MTA can route the information to the MS Mail downstream post offices. Exchange serves as the hub post office for several clusters or spokes of MS Mail post offices.

Steps to connect Exchange to MS Mail:

- Configure the MS Mail Connector interchange.
  1. Define a connection to the directly connected downstream MS Mail post office.
  2. Set up a single MS Mail Connector (PC) MTA service for the network service.
  3. Configure message routing to Exchange on each MS Mail post office.
  4. Add the network and post office names of each of the downstream MS Mail post office to the Exchange address space of the direct connection MS Mail post office.
  5. Configure Directory Synchronization for the MS Mail post offices with the Exchange Directory Synchronization server.

NOTE Once you migrate the hub and spoke architecture of MS Mail to Exchange, the Exchange servers become the mail hubs. The key benefit is that the same server that processes local mail or the information store, can be the MTA for the existing MS Mail post offices. Exchange can easily incorporate into existing mail architectures. This includes existing MS Mail post offices running on Novell Netware file servers.

Exchange MS Mail Connector marries the functionality of a hub or gateway post office and the External application. The MS Mail Connector (PC) MTA component of the MS Mail Connector provides the functions of the MS Mail External and Multitasking MTA application. These include the following:

- Message delivery between MS Mail post offices and gateways
- Distribution of messages to recipients on MS Mail post offices on the same WAN/LAN

As you migrate from existing MS Mail shared file post offices, you may need to continue operating MS External and/or the Multitasking MTAs at the same time as the MS Mail Connector of Exchange. These older MTA applications do not provide the same rich feature set as the MS Mail Connector. The MS Mail Connector will allow you to integrate Exchange into any MS Mail environment using existing External or Multitasking MTA applications.

This example applies to all MTA connections including asynchronous modem connections and/or X.25 service.

NOTE With the Exchange server running on Windows NT, you can take advantage of the built in remote access services of the operating system. This way you can create a WAN environment without separate asynchronous connections. All the servers are networked together via a WAN/LAN. ■

The MS Mail Connector contains the following Exchange components:

- MS Mail Connector Interchange

  This is the Windows NT service which transfers and routes information between Exchange and the MS Mail Connector post office.

- MS Mail Connector Post Office

  The important thing to remember is that the MS Mail Connector post office resides on the Exchange server as a virtual post office to provide the translation between the native MS Mail message store and the native Exchange information store. This is a temporary information store for messages.

- MS Mail Connector (PC) Message Transfer Agent (MTA)

  This is a Windows NT service that connects the MS Mail Connector post office with one or more MS Mail post offices. This MTA also handles the mail transfer between post offices.

The message route from Exchange to MS Mail (PC) is as follows:

1. Exchange user creates a message addressed to an MS Mail (PC) recipient and submits it.
2. Exchange information store forwards message to Exchange MTA.
3. Exchange MS Mail interchange converts message to MS Mail format and drops the message into the Connector post office.
4. Attachments, OLE objects, and rich text formatting are saved and converted onto the Connector post office.
5. The Connector (PC) MTA delivers message to the destination MS Mail post office.

Setting Up the MS Mail Connector

As previously mentioned, the MS Mail Connector transfers information from Exchange and existing MS Mail (PC) post offices.

NOTE Each server in the organization can only run one instance of the MS Mail Connector. This instance can service more than one connection to MS Mail post offices and/or MS Mail gateways.

There are six key steps to setting up the MS Mail Connector:

1. Define the MS Mail Connector administrator mailbox.
2. Configure the general MS Mail Connector settings.
3. Connect to each MS Mail post office.
4. Configure the MS Mail Connector (PC) MTA for each post office communication. protocol: asynchronous, LAN, or X.25.
5. Launch the MS Mail Connector services.
6. Configure the directory services to include MS Mail post office recipients.

NOTE This chapter assumes that the connectivity exists between Exchange and the MS Mail post offices. If you need more information on connectivity between post offices, please see Chapter 9, "Installing Exchange Server."

There are two primary ways to connect to existing MS Mail post offices: LAN connectivity or remote connectivity, which includes asynchronous and X.25 connections shown in figures 18.4 and 18.5.

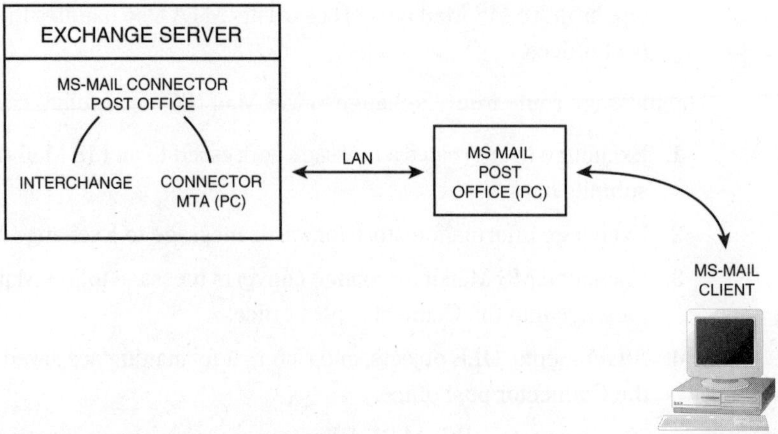

FIG. 18.4
Exchange to MS Mail post office via LAN.

FIG. 18.5
Exchange to MS Mail post office via asynchronous or X.25 connections.

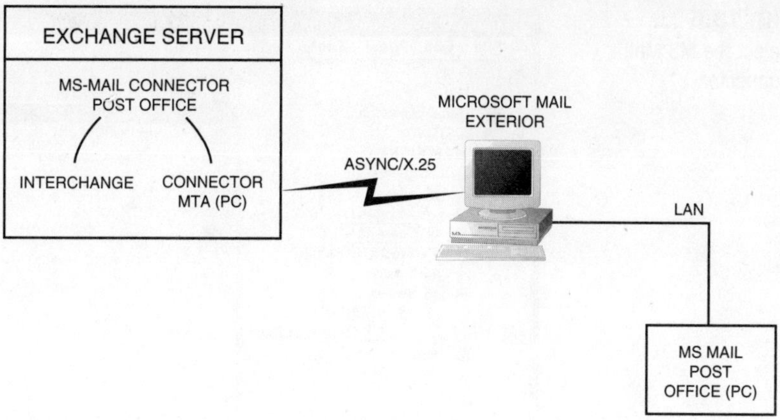

The main difference between connection methods is that with the remote connection, an additional instance of External must be running in order for the remote post office to transfer messages. This addition will require extra overhead for administration.

TIP If you have remote post offices with this configuration, you may want to either use NT Remote Access service to perform LAN based connections or migrate these post offices to Exchange ahead of other post offices.

Configuring the MS Mail Connector Interchange

The following are steps to configure the MS Mail Connector Interchange service:

1. Open the Exchange Administrator Application. This can be performed from the console on the Exchange server or from a workstation with connectivity to both the Exchange server and the MS Mail post office.
2. Choose the site from the organization list, the server name from the site, and the MS Mail Connector from the Connections list (see fig. 18.6).
3. Open the MS Mail Connector to configure the properties for the initial post office connection (see fig. 18.7).

   The Interchange tab allows you to select the "Administrator's Mailbox" which will receive system informational and alert messages from the Connector. These messages are typically due to nondelivery of mail (bounced mail) and failed messages.

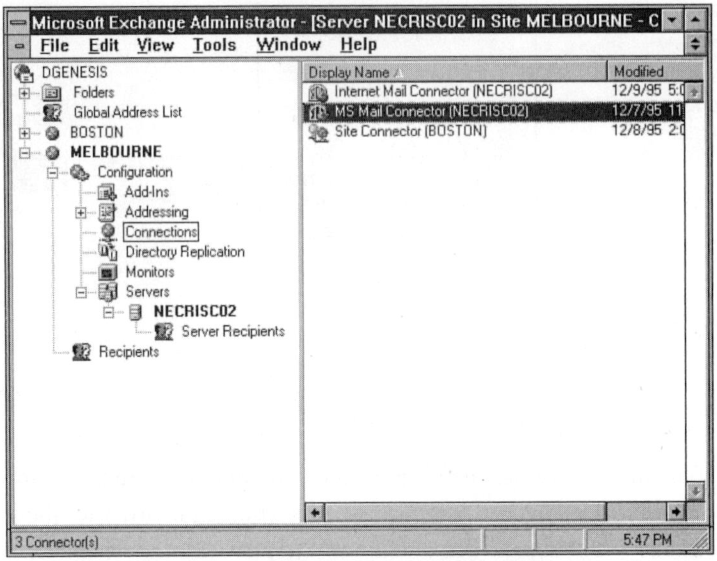

FIG. 18.6
Select the MS Mail Connector.

FIG. 18.7
The MS Mail Connector dialog box for (NECRISC02) with the Interchange tab selected.

4. Select the Administrator Account. This account can be a user, group, distribution list, or public folder (see fig. 18.8).

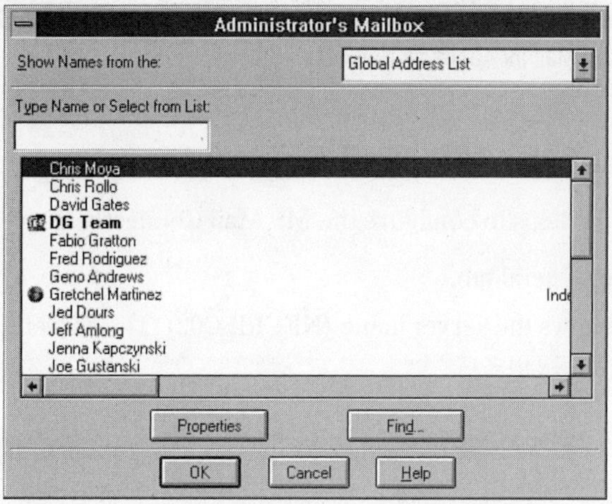

FIG. 18.8
Configuring the Administrator Account for the Connector.

5. Select OK to return to the Interchange tab.
6. From the Interchange tab, select the primary language for the recipients. The selected primary language is used for interoperability with MS Mail clients using an alternate language. This is useful for International users of Exchange. The default value is prompted from the Exchange server.
7. Select the "Maximize MS Mail 3.x Compatibility" check box. This option is used for OLE compatibility in messages transferred between the older version used in MS Mail clients and the new version of Exchange Clients.

   By selecting "Maximize MS Mail 3.x Compatibility," two versions of each OLE object are created. This option will increase or double the size of any OLE messages. If this option is not selected, MS Mail 3.x clients will not be able to view or save embedded objects originating from an Exchange client.

   If you want to enable "Message Tracking" for the MS Mail Connector, select "Enable Message Tracking." This option will record message information into the tracking logs. It can also debug problems when messages do not appear to be routing properly or it can be used to locate potential lost messages. The default for this option is "disabled." For more information on message tracking, see Chapter 25, "Monitoring Exchange Sites."
8. Click "Apply" to set these properties prior to defining the additional properties off the remaining tab menus.

NOTE The AppleTalk MTA Connector portion is discussed in Chapter 19, "Setting Up Microsoft Mail for Appletalk Networks."

General Setting of the MS Mail Connector

The following are steps to configure the MS Mail Connector Interchange service:

1. Select the General tab.

   This tab shows the server name (NECRISC02). The server name cannot be modified (see fig. 18.9).

FIG. 18.9
Use the General tab to set basic properties of the MS Mail Connector.

2. Define "Maximum Message Size."

   You can define an upper limit for messages transferred through the Connector or accept the default value of "No Limit." This option is useful if you want to restrict the size of the attachment transferred between systems. Attachments can easily reach megabytes of data in size.

   To limit the size, enter a maximum value between 0 and 9999999 kilobytes.

3. Type an administrative note or comment with respect to the MS Mail Connector. Include the initials of the technician working on the service. This comment can only be viewed from this Property page.

4. Click "Apply" to set the properties and configure the remaining Property pages.

NOTE You must first enter a value in the "Address Space" tab menu in order to define the MS Mail connection and close the connection property window.

Defining Post Office Connections

The following steps are used to set up the connections for MS Mail (PC) post offices over LAN, asynchronous, or X.25 connections. Each connection method will be described individually.

Creating a LAN Connection Use the Connections tab and Property page to create a LAN connection from Exchange to an MS Mail post office.

The following are steps to perform a LAN connection to an MS Mail post office:

1. Select the Connections tab.

NOTE You may want to clear the "Confirm Before Connection Changes Are Applied" check box, if you do not want to have additional confirmation messages displayed before changes are set.

This tab shows the organization and site name which is actively being configured (see fig. 18.10).

FIG. 18.10 Connections tab is used to define LAN connections.

2. Click the "Create" button to configure a new LAN connection post office (see fig. 18.11).

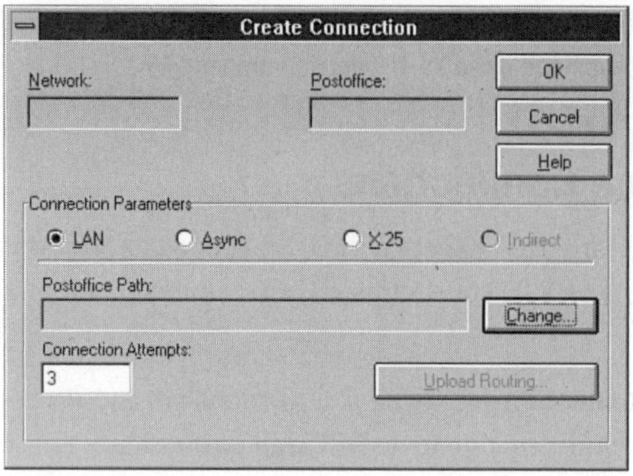

FIG. 18.11
Create connection to MS Mail post office.

3. Select "LAN" under the Connection Parameters window.
4. Click the "Change" button to specify the path to the LAN-based MS Mail post office.
5. In the Post Office Path dialog box, enter the complete path to the server, file share, and directory containing the MS Mail post office in the "Path" box.

   Use the following format:

   Microsoft Networking: \\server\share\path

   Novell Networking: \\server\volume\path
6. Specify a Network or Domain logon name and password in the "Connect As" and "Password" fields. You only need to complete these entries if any of the following are true:
   - The post office is on a server with share-level security; no domain security,
   - The post office is in an untrusted domain, outside the domain model for the Exchange rollout.
   - The Exchange service account is not a valid user on the target server.
7. Click "OK" to confirm entries. If the connection is valid, the network and post office names will be entered into the appropriate fields on the Create Connection dialog box.
8. Define the number of connection retries for messages being sent to this post office. If this value is exceeded, the message is returned to the sender with an undelivered notification. The default value is 3.

   An optional setting is to configure the routing information about the downstream post office from the one created. To import this information, follow these steps:
   - Click the "Upload Routing" button.

A "Downstream Post Offices Summary" dialog box appears with the routing information of any post office or gateway indirectly connected through this post office. If this post office is a "hub" for other post offices, this information should be uploaded. If the post office is a downstream post office, you may want to skip over these steps.

- Select any downstream post office you do not want to have uploaded. Choose the post office and click "Delete."
- Click "OK" to set the routing changes.

NOTE The information upload from this selection does not affect the configuration of the external options on the MS Mail post offices.

9. Click "OK" and return to the Connections Property page.
10. Click "Apply" to set the changes for the connection.

Creating an Asynchronous Connection Use the Connections tab and Property page to create an asynchronous connection from Exchange to an External MTA for an MS Mail post office (see fig. 18.12).

FIG. 18.12 Connections tab is used to define asynchronous connections.

Do the following to perform an asynchronous connection to a MS Mail post office:

1. Select the Connections tab.
2. Click the "Create" button to configure a new asynchronous connection (see fig. 18.13).

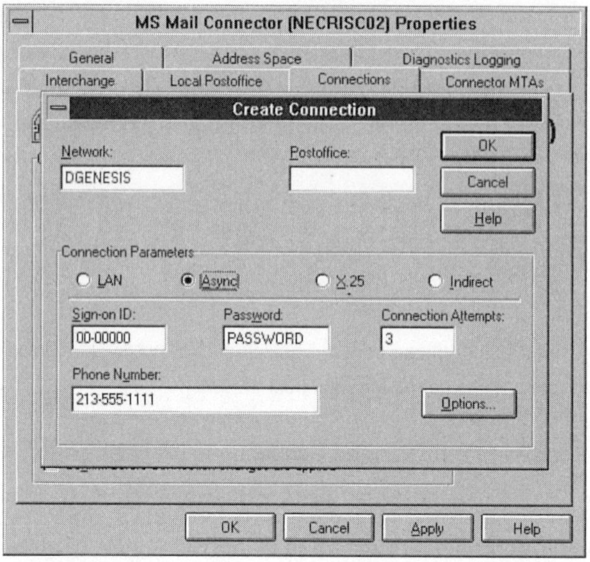

FIG. 18.13 New Connections dialog box with Asynchronous selected.

3. Select the "Asynchronous" radio button (see fig. 18.14)

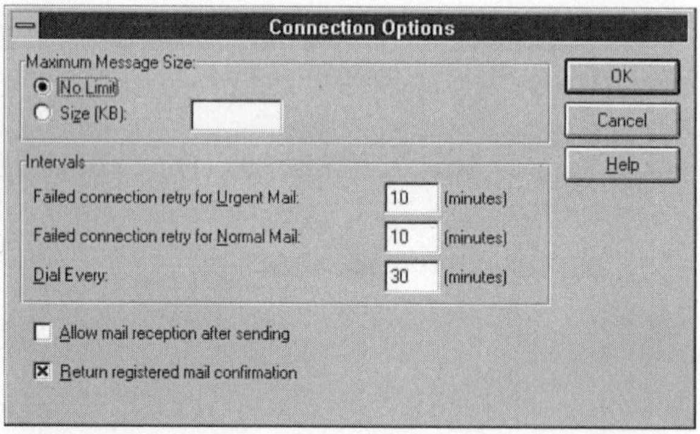

FIG. 18.14 Advanced options for the asynchronous connections.

4. Type in the Network name and post office in the respective field for the Asynchronous connection post office.

NOTE Unlike the LAN connection, you must enter the information for these values.

5. In the Sign on ID field, enter the serial number for the remote post office. The Sign on ID format is: ##-#####.
6. Enter the remote post office site password in the Password field.

7. Enter a value for the "Connections Attempts" box. The range is from 0 to 99. This value determines how many connection attempts Exchange will make to try to communicate with the remote post office, before returning the message to the original sender. The default value is 3.
8. Enter a phone number in the respective field. Make sure to add area code and any additional dialing prefixes. If you must dial a 9 to get an outside line, this must be included in the configuration. The phone number entered is the phone number for the remote post office MTA running the External application.

NOTE Make sure that the phone number you enter contains all prefixes. In addition, this number should direct Exchange to the remote MTA running the External application. ■

9. Click the "Options" button to enter additional configurations for asynchronous connections.
10. Enter a value for "Maximum Message Size." The default is set to "No limit" (see fig. 18.14). If you want to limit the message size to be transferred over an asynchronous connection, enter a value between 0 and 9999 kilobytes in the respective field. This limits the size of attachment data, without limiting routing data.
11. Enter a value for "Failed Connection Retry For Urgent Mail." The value ranges from 1 to 99 minutes between connection attempts for messages defined as urgent. The default value is 10 minutes.
12. Enter a value for "Failed Connection Retry for Normal Mail." This value ranges from 1 to 999 minutes between attempts to reconnect for messages defined as normal. The default is 10 minutes.
13. Enter a value for "Dial Every." This value ranges from 1 to 999 minutes between connections for regular calls.
14. Check the box in order to select "Allow Mail Reception after Sending." This allows messages to be transferred in a bidirectional single connection. This option offers faster and more efficient message delivery. If this selection is not made, connections are made on an individual basis for "Sending" and "Receiving" messages.
15. Check the box to select "Return Registered Mail Confirmation." This will allow message confirmations to be transferred over the connection and between mail systems.
16. Click "OK" to set changes.

Creating an X.25 Connection Use the Connections tab and Property page to create an X.25 connection from Exchange to an External MTA for an MS Mail post office. This connection is very similar to the Asynchronous connection. This section assumes that the X.25 protocol is already configured and running on this Windows NT server.

Do the following steps to perform an X.25 connection to an MS Mail post office:

1. Select the Connections tab (see fig. 18.15).
2. Click the "Create" button to configure a new X.25 connection (see fig. 18.16).

FIG. 18.15
Connections tab is used to define X.25 connections.

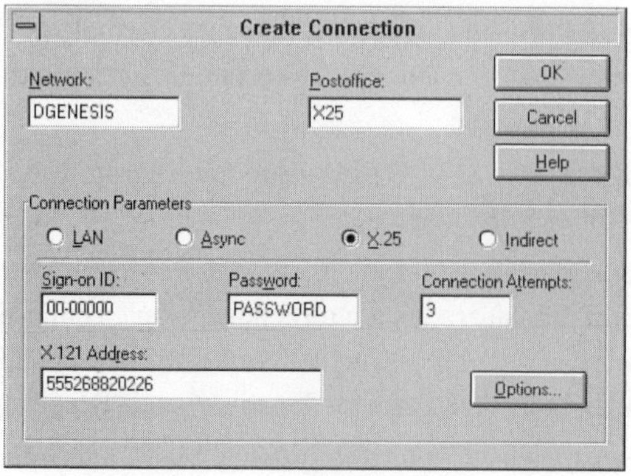

FIG. 18.16
New Connection dialog box with X.25 selected.

3. Select the "X.25" radio button. This brings up the additional configuration for the X.25 parameters.
4. Enter the Network and Post Office names in their respective fields.
5. Enter the sign on serial ID in the format ##-#####.
6. Enter the remote post office password.

7. Define the number of connection attempts. The default is 3.
8. Define the X.121 address. This value should include the entire X.121 address, consisting of up to 16 digits. The format should be as follows:

   [Area] [DNIC] [DTE Address] [sub-address]

   For more information on Exchange and X.25 support, refer to Chapter 20, "Configuring X.400 Connections."
9. Click "Apply" to set the specifications.

NOTE The "Options" dialog box for X.25 is identical to that for the Asynchronous connection.

Creating an Indirect Connection You can use the MS Mail Connector to act as a hub post office. The hub post office can be specified to feed various spokes, or indirect post offices.

Indirect connections are supported over the LAN or asynchronous or X.25 connections. They can be used to replace the External application running to service multiple downstream post offices.

Do the following steps to perform an indirect connection to an MS Mail post office:

1. Select the Connections tab.
2. Select the hub post office and then click Create to configure the indirect post office.
3. From the Connection Configuration dialog box, select the hub post office from the "Indirect Via" drop-down list (see fig. 18.17).

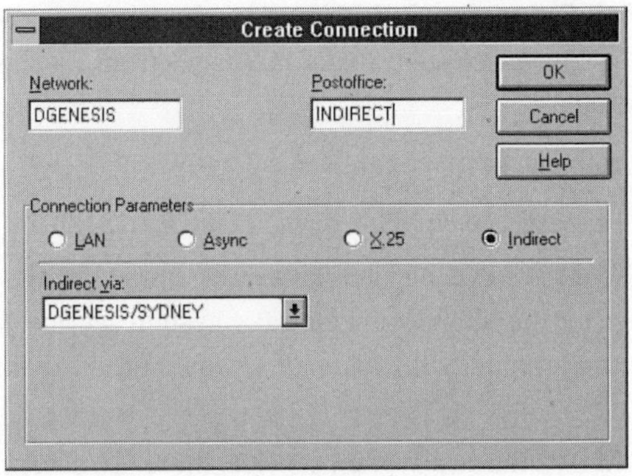

FIG. 18.17 Connection tab is used to define indirect connections.

4. Click "OK" to set the configuration.

These are the four options for MS Mail connections provided with Exchange.

The message queue is the final component of the Connections tab menu. The queue lists messages awaiting delivery by the MS Mail Connector. Figure 18.18 shows an empty queue after all pending messages were delevered. Normally, you would use the queue window to monitor the message load passing through your MS Mail Connector.

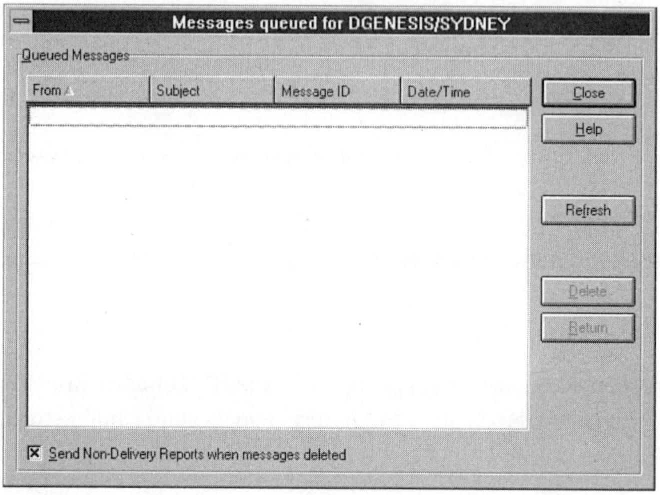

FIG. 18.18 MS Mail Connector message queue.

Configuring the Message Transfer Agent

The following steps are used to create the Message Transfer Agent services for connections over LAN, Asynchronous, or X.25. Each connection method will be described individually.

Creating an MS Mail Connector (PC) MTA Use the Connector MTA's tab and Property page to create the MTA services to transfer messages from Exchange to an MS Mail post office. Follow these steps:

1. Select the Connector MTA's tab (see fig. 18.19).
2. Click "New" to create a new MTA service (see fig. 18.20).
3. Enter a name for the MTA service. This name is used by the Windows NT operating system to register the MTA Connector as a system service. Once the service is defined, you cannot modify the name. You would have to remove the service and re-create it.

   Because the MTA runs as a system service, there are several character string limitations:

   - up to 30 characters, maximum
   - letters a–z in lowercase format

- letters A–Z in uppercase format
- numbers 0–9
- the <space bar>

If you use any other character string, the service will not be able to register with the operating system.

NOTE Naming the convention is important with services. If you preface the MTAs with "MS Mail Connector," they will interfere with the integrated Exchange Mail Windows NT services listed in the Control Panel–Services.

FIG. 18.19
MS Mail Connector MTA's tab menu.

FIG. 18.20
MS Mail Connector MTA's tab menu—New Service.

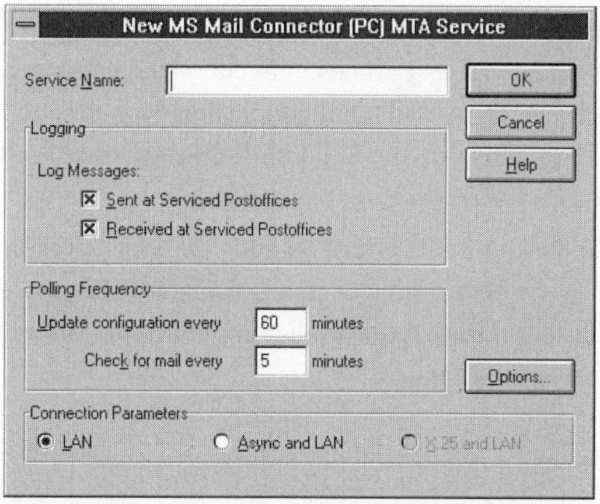

4. Select the “Log Messages Sent At Serviced Post Offices” check box. This option will set up logging in order to record each message transferred to the MS Mail post office environment.
5. Select the “Log Messages Received At Serviced Post Offices” check box. This option will set up logging in order to record each message transferred from the MS Mail post office environment.
6. Enter values for the “Update Configuration” field in minutes. This checks for updated information based on the interval minutes entered into this field. The default is 60 minutes.

NOTE If you enter a 0 in this field, you will stop the configuration from checking for messages.

7. Enter a value for the “Check for Mail Every” field. This field accepts values from 0 to 999 minutes. This is the polling interval for how long the MTA waits before rechecking for mail coming to the MS Mail Connector post office. The default value is 5 minutes.

   If you have multiple instances of the MTA service to service multiple MS Mail post offices and gateways, you may want to stagger this time interval so that each instance does not overlap. One service would check for mail every five minutes and the next service would check every six minutes.
8. Select the LAN option in the “Connection Parameters” section.
9. Define the MTA Connector options by clicking the “Options” button (see fig. 18.20).

   These options apply to both the LAN and the Asynchronous connection methods (see fig. 18.21). The first selection is for “Maximum LAN Message Size.” You can set an upper limit for the size of messages transferred through this MTA. The values range from 0 to 9999999 kilobytes and the default is “No Limit.”

   The next entry is used to define the “Close Post Office If” value. This value is used to close the destination post office connection when disk space utilization has reached whichever threshold point you designate from 0 to 999999999 kilobytes. Messages will queue up on the MTA until they are timed out or additional disk space is added on the destination post office.

   In addition to closing the connection, you can set a value for “Open Post Office If” disk space that has been added or made available. This value ranges from 0 to 999999999 kilobytes. Disk-space availability must rise above this value in order for message transfer to restart.

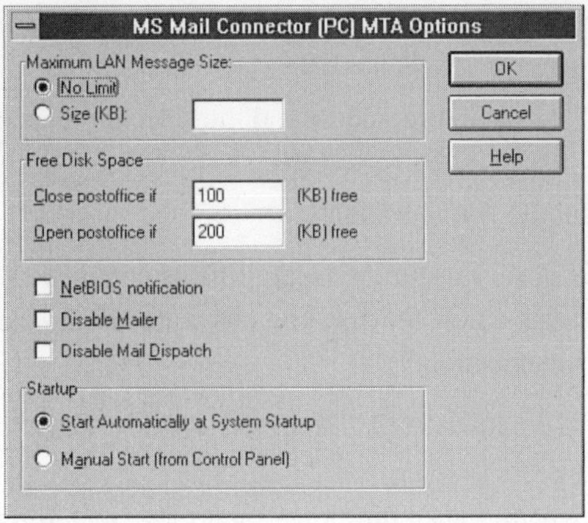

FIG. 18.21
MS Mail Connector MTA's tab menu—New Service, Options dialog box.

The next three check boxes are used for administrative notifications to the MS Mail LAN post office users. These have no impact for Exchange users. The first option is to check the "NetBIOS Notification" in order to have the MTA send a NetBIOS broadcast message.

The NetBIOS Broadcast will only work if the server and clients are running the NetBIOS protocol. In addition, you must start all the NT service MTAs prior to launching the External application on the destination post office for NetBIOS broadcasts to function properly. For more information, see the user manuals for the respective operating system to learn how to install NetBIOS.

Select "Disable Mailer" and "Disable Mail Dispatch" to stop mail notifications from being distributed via the External and Dispatch applications associated with the destination MS Mail post offices. These do not impact the Exchange users. For more information on the application, refer to your MS Mail Administrator Guide.

Select the "Startup" box to define the method that this NT MTA service will launch. The options are to have the MTA start automatically or manually.

Click "OK" to set these configurations.

10. Click "OK" followed by "Apply" to set all the configurations for this MTA service. If you modify these options for this service at a later point, you will need to stop and start the NT service in order to have the changes take effect.

To complete the MTA service, you need to define the post offices service by the MTA services.

1. From the MS Mail Connector property sheet, click the "List" button. The Serviced LAN Post Offices dialog box appears.

2. In the "Serviced LAN Post Offices" dialog box, select the post office to be serviced from the right panel of "Available LAN Post offices."
3. Click the "Add" button in the middle and the selection becomes a "Serviced LAN Post office."
4. Click "OK" to set the configurations.

If you need an additional service for an Asynchronous connection, you will need to modify an existing MTA or create a new service. The following are the configuration differences for the Asynchronous connection:

1. Click "Create" to create a new MTA service or click "Edit" to modify an existing MTA.
2. On the Property page, select the "Async and LAN" option (see fig. 18.22).

FIG. 18.22
MS Mail Connector MTA's tab menu—New Service via Asynchronous or X.25 connection.

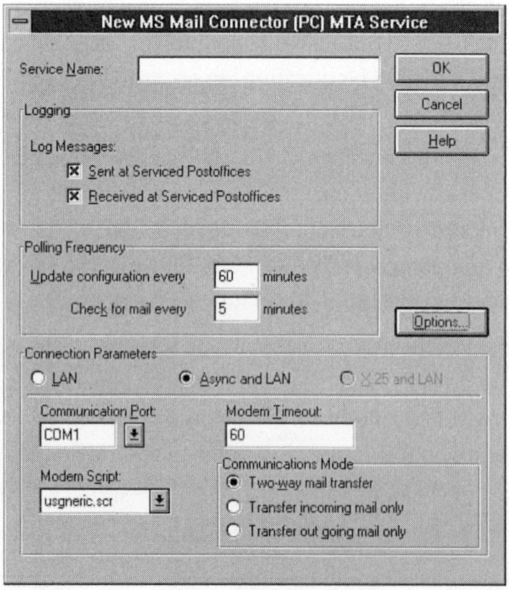

3. Enter the appropriate values for the following:

   Communication Port—This is the server communication port to be used for the MTA service. The default value is "COM1."

   Modem Script—This is used to define the initialization string for your particular modem.

NOTE If you have an existing modem that requires a customized script file, you can copy this script to the following path on the Exchange server:

%Exchangeroot%\connect\msmcom\maildata\glb

Modem Time-out—This is the value for the number of minutes the MTA will wait for a connection with the destination post office.

Communication Mode—This value defines whether the MTA will send and receive messages or only handle one-way message transfers.

4. Click "OK" to set the configuration settings.

   If this MTA has been modified, it will need to be stopped and restarted from the services control panel.

After you have configured all your MTA services and defined which post offices are serviced, you need to start the MTA NT services in order to begin message transfer. Do the following steps to start these services:

1. Open the control panel for the server services.
2. Locate the MTA service to be started, select the service, and click "Start." (See fig. 18.23.) The service will start and you can begin transferring messages between mail systems.

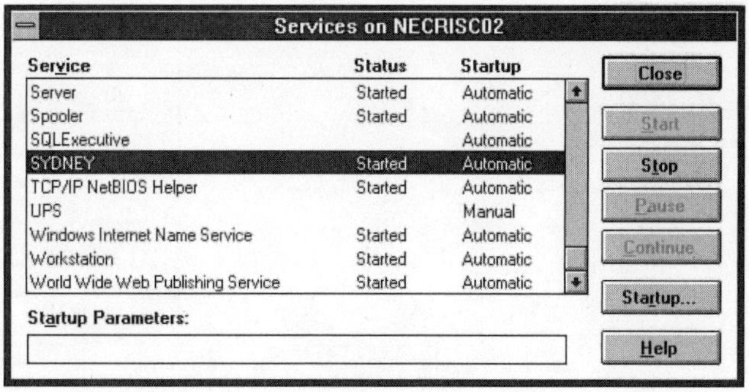

FIG. 18.23
MS Mail Connector MTA Windows NT service.

Defining the MS Mail Connector Address Space

The following steps are used to create the address space for the MS Mail post offices serviced by this MS Mail Connector.

Address space is used to properly route messages throughout the organization. If you have additional gateways installed, address space is important to ensure the proper message route.

1. Select the Address Space tab (see fig. 18.24).
2. Select the address space to be created. Your choice will depend on the type of gateway used to receive these message transfers. The address spaces are associated with a specific template for each connector. The template assists with entering the destination mail address. The options are:

New General—A blank template for creating a destination address when a template is not available. Typically each connector will provide an address template.

New Internet—A blank template to enter SMTP or Internet message routes.

New X.400—A blank template for creating an X.400 message route.

New MS Mail—A blank template to create an MS Mail message route. After the MS Mail Connector is configured to transfer messages through the associated MTA service, a message route is automatically generated in the MS Mail address space.

FIG. 18.24
MS Mail Address Space tab menu.

To create or edit the MS Mail address space, select the address space in the connection window.

In the Property page for the MS Mail address space, you must enter the network and post office of the destination MS Mail post office.

NOTE When you enter values for the address spaces, you can use wildcards. For example,

MS:DGENESIS\SYDNEY*

This address routes messages to all users on the destination post office.

All the address spaces will create a message route from this MS Mail Connector to the destination or foreign mail system. For more information on routing and addressing, see Chapter 23, "Exchange Maintenance."

Configuring the Local Exchange Post Office

When you use the MS Mail Connector for MS Mail (PC), Exchange must create a local or "virtual" MS Mail post office. This is known as the *local post office,* which was created automatically when you installed the MS Mail Connector. It was first configured when you set up the MS Mail post office interchange in the first part of this chapter.

The local post office is a working MS Mail post office. Exchange uses this post office to transfer messages to MS Mail post offices. The message first goes into the MTA and then gets transferred and converted into the local post office before being transferred out to the destination post office.

To configure the local post office, follow these steps:

1. Select the Local Postoffice tab (see fig. 18.25).

FIG. 18.25
MS Mail Connector local post office configuration.

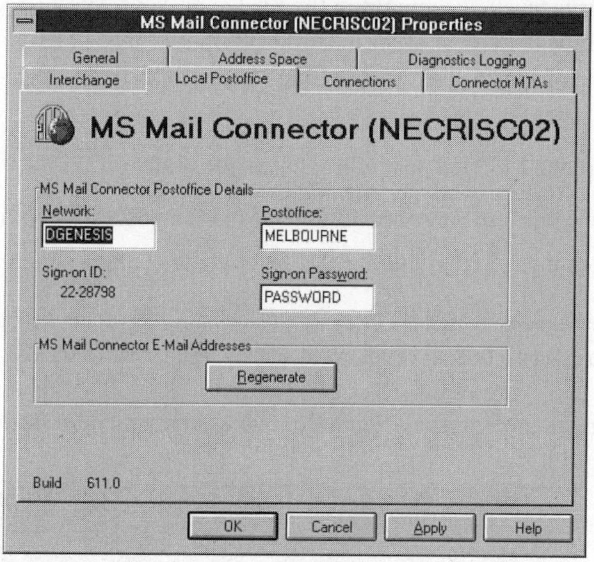

2. Enter the network and post office name for the local Exchange MS Mail post office interchange. These values can be changed. By default, Exchange enters the organization and site name into these fields.
3. Enter the password to be used by External MTA applications when you are connecting to and signing on to this local post office to transfer messages.

NOTE This is a good time to note the local post office Sign on Serial ID. You will need this information when you are configuring External to communicate with this local post office.

4. Click the "Regenerate" button under the MS Mail Connector Addresses heading. This selection will generate the proper addressing scheme to be used in routing messages through this local post office.

   If any changes are made to this local post office, you must execute the address regeneration. You will need to update the information on the remote External MTA, gateway, or post office as well. Additionally, if you change this information, you must stop and restart the NT MTA service and Connector interchange.

   A warning will appear to force you to confirm this action.

5. Click "OK" to accept configuration settings and apply them to the Connector.

Configuring the MS Mail Connector Post Offices and Gateways in PC Mail

Once you have finished configuring the Exchange MS Mail Connector, you must configure each MS Mail PC post office to work with the settings in Exchange. Refer to the MS Mail Connector's local post office settings to create an External post office site in MS Mail 3.x.

To configure the MS Mail post office, follow these steps:

1. Attach your Exchange server to the MS Mail post office with a network connection.
2. Launch the MS Mail Administration utility to configure the post office settings.

NOTE Once you have used the Exchange GUI interface, you will not want to have to go back to using the DOS character-based administration utility of MS Mail v3.x.

3. Toggle to the External-Admin Configuration menu item (see fig. 18.26).

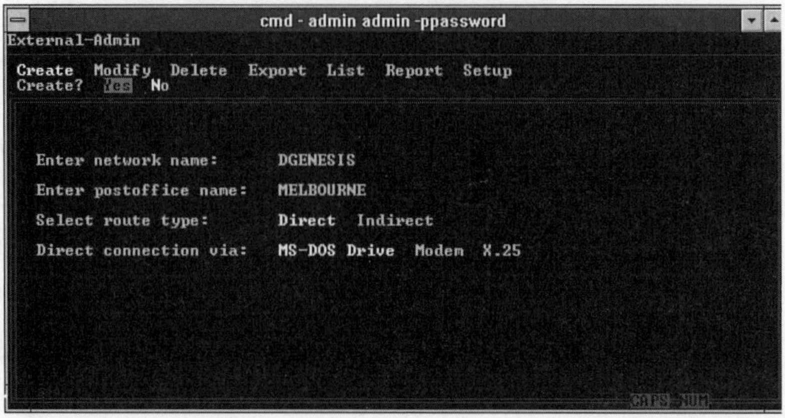

FIG. 18.26 Use the MS Mail Administration utility to configure the post office.

4. Select "Create" and define the network, post office, and route for the Exchange MS Mail Connector local post office.

   In this example, the MS Mail post office is called *Sydney* on the DGENESIS network. An External route has been added to the Exchange local post office called *MELBOURNE* on the same DGENESIS network. The connection type is direct. The only time you would use indirect is if you were routing MS Mail through another MS Mail hub post office prior to transferring the message to Exchange.

5. Select "Yes" to create the route and then exit the Administration application.

Once you have modified the settings for the post offices, if you have any MS Mail 3.x gateways, you will have to modify those as well. Because there are many different types of MS Mail gateways, you will be unable to describe the process for each one. The key components to modify are the network and post office names, sign on ID, and post office password. Refer to your user's manual for more information on configuring the gateway.

Managing the NT Service for the MS Mail Connector

Now that the MS Mail Connector is completely configured, you must start the connection service to begin transferring messages between Exchange and MS Mail.

To start the MS Mail connection services, follow these steps:

1. Open the Windows NT control panel or Windows NT Server Manager and select the "Services" option.
2. Select the MS Mail Connector Interchange service (see fig. 18.27).

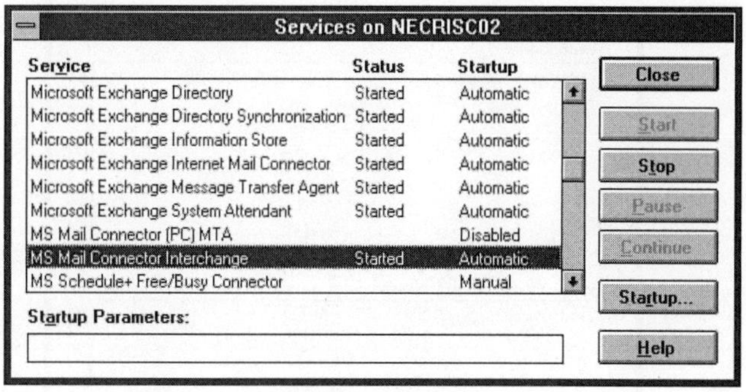

FIG. 18.27
Use the MS Mail Admininstration utility to configure the post office.

3. Click "Start" to launch the service.

NOTE The MS Mail Connector (PC) MTA is set to "disabled" because it is only used in the configuration of individual MS Mail MTA services. This service cannot be started.

4. Close the services window.

Testing the Connection Between Exchange and MS Mail

Now that all the services are running and messages are configured to route between Exchange and MS Mail, you should test the connection.

To test the message routing between Exchange and MS Mail, follow these steps:

1. Using the MS Exchange client software, create and send a message to a recipient with a destination on the MS Mail post office.
2. Verify in the MS Mail 3.x client software that the message has arrived.
3. Reverse this process to verify MS Mail to Exchange message routing.
4. If the messages do not arrive, the first place to begin diagnosis is in the Windows NT Server Event log for the Exchange server.

The MS Mail Connector interchange events is logged as "MSExchangeMSMI" for mail transfer between the Exchange information store and the MS Mail Connector local post office.

The MS Mail Connector (PC) MTA events are logged under the associated MS Mail MTA services names.

In this figure, you can see that the MTA has created a system message on the Exchange local post office with the respective name (see fig. 18.28).

FIG. 18.28
Windows NT event log for MS Mail Connector entries.

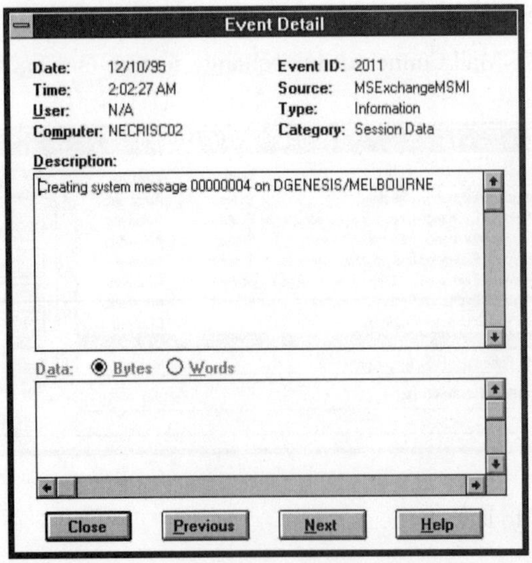

In this example, the MTA service is called "Sydney" and the event would be logged with this name (see fig. 18.29). As you can see, the MTA server, Sydney, has successfully started.

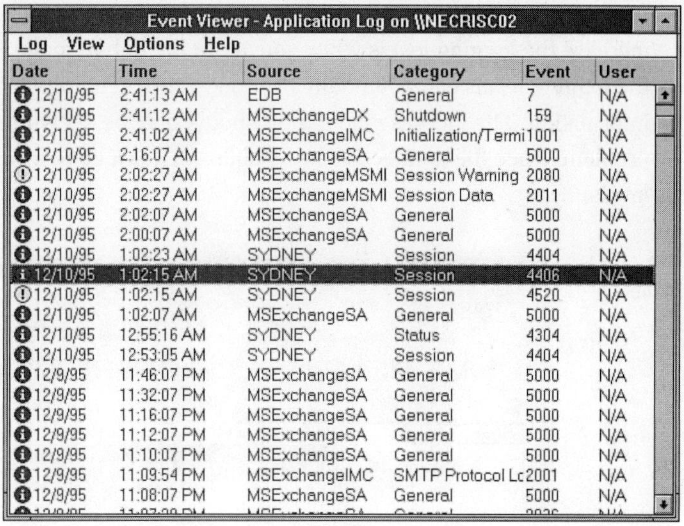

FIG. 18.29 The Windows NT event log will store a significant amount of events from the Exchange server. Each process has a unique service ID.

As you can see, Exchange provides numerous messages to the event log. If you have trouble with communication between Exchange and the MS Mail post office, you can adjust the sensitivity of the auditing levels.

Adjusting Audit Levels for the MS Mail Connector

To assist with debugging and routing problems between Exchange and MS Mail, you may want to increase the level of auditing for the MS Mail Connector.

To adjust audit levels, follow these steps:

1. Open the MS Mail Connector Property page and select the tab for "Diagnostics Logging." (See fig. 18.30.)
2. On the left panel are the services to be monitored and on the right are the category and logging levels. The service is the MS Mail Interchange Connector. The categories to adjust are MS Mail Interchange Connector, the MS Mail PC MTA, and the MS Mail AppleTalk MTA. (Note that the AppleTalk MTA will be discussed in the next chapter.)

   The levels indicate the level of granularity of information that you would like logged into the event viewer. The levels for the MS Mail Connector are None, Minimum, Medium, and Maximum. Typically you will have Minimum selected for the categories of the service that you are using. If you are not going to use the AppleTalk MTA, there is no need to turn logging on.

If problems do arise with the connections between Exchange and MS Mail, you can increase the logging levels while you are in the debug mode. Realize that increasing the logging levels can potentially overload your event logs with an abundance of information. The increase in logging should only be set while you are debugging a problem. Once the connection has stabilized, it is a good idea to reduce the logging levels.

FIG. 18.30 The MS Mail Connector tab menu for adjusting system auditing levels.

If you are still having problems with MS Mail message routing and the event logs are not providing the information necessary to solve the problem, try the following:

1. Delete and then re-add the MS Mail Connector, including all the MTA services.
2. See Chapter 26, "Diagnostic and Troubleshooting Tools."
3. Contact Microsoft Product Support Services.

Directory Synchronization

The final component to configure is the Directory Synchronization between the Exchange and MS Mail.

This section will assume that the Directory Synchronization server is already set up and running on Exchange. Each site can only run Directory Synchronization server. However, each server can support numerous directory requesters and remote directory requesters.

In addition, this section will assume that Exchange and the MS Mail post office can both send and receive messages via the Interchange Connector and the PC MTA. Directory Synchronization was explained in detail in Chapter 17, "Using Directory Replication and Synchronization."

Once the Directory Synchronization server is set up and configured on the Exchange server, there are a few steps needed to ensure the MS Mail post offices are included in the synchronization process.

1. Make sure that the Exchange Site Directory Synchronization service is installed and running (see fig. 18.31). Check your Windows NT system service list to confirm this.

FIG. 18.31
The Exchange Directory Synchronization server properties.

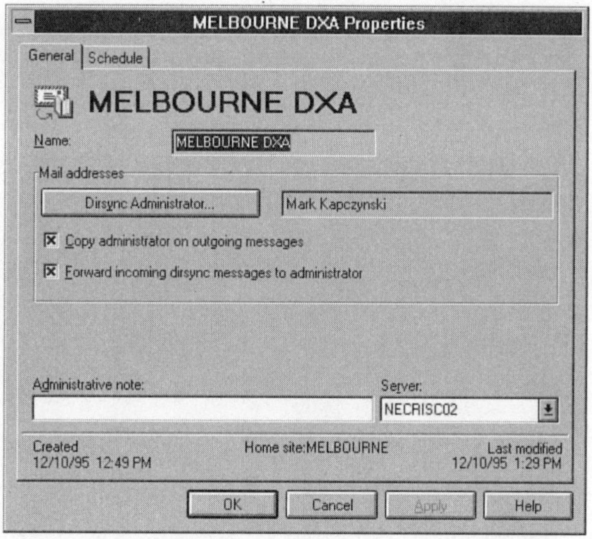

2. Install and configure a remote directory requester to synchronize the Exchange Global Address List (GAL) with the GAL on the MS Mail 3.x post office network (see fig. 18.32).

   The remote directory requester has all the information needed to communicate with the Exchange local post office prior to synchronizing with the connected MS Mail post office.

3. Open the MS Mail 3.x administration application and select the post office configuration options (see fig. 18.33).

   From this panel you can configure the directory synchronization options, as well as the use of the global address for the local post office.

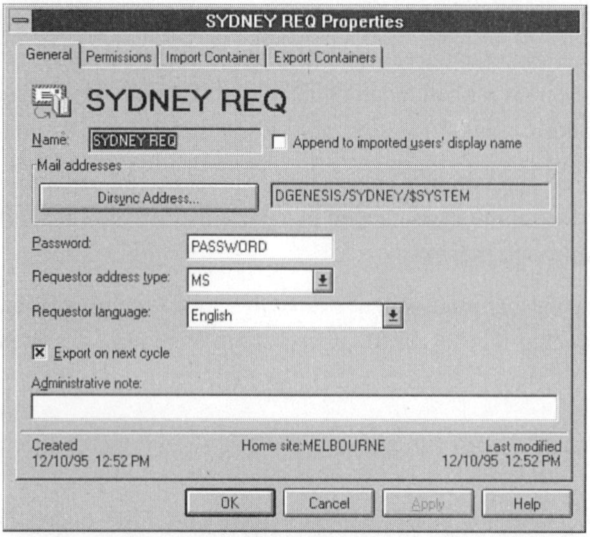

FIG. 18.32
The Exchange remote directory requester used to synchronize with foreign systems, including MS Mail 3.x.

FIG. 18.33
Configuration options in the MS Mail administration program.

4. From the "Dir-sync" menu, toggle to the "registration" menu to configure the Directory Synchronization server information.

   The information for the Directory Synchronization server will be the same as the Exchange MS Mail local post office. From this panel, enter the network, post office, and password for the server (see fig. 18.34).

5. From the "Global Address" menu in the post office configuration options, you will need to specify for the MS Mail 3.x post office to use the global address list.

Once the MS Mail administration is completed, you should stop and restart the Exchange Directory Synchronization Server service. As well, stop and restart the MS Mail Connector Interchange.

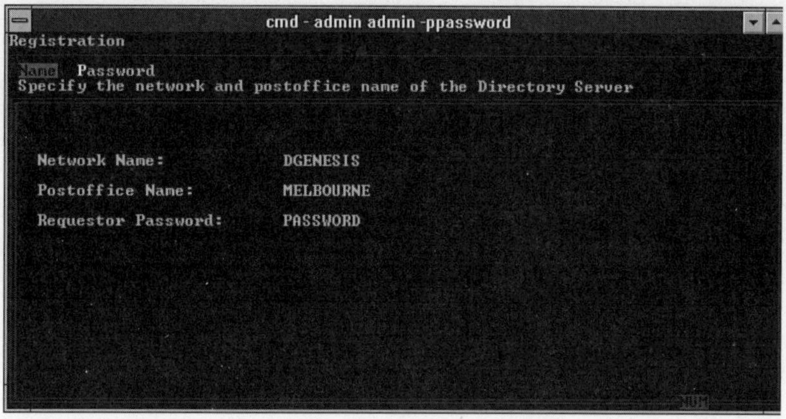

FIG. 18.34
Creating a Directory Synchronization requester in MS Mail.

As you can see, there are many components required to connect Exchange with MS Mail (PC) post offices. The message route includes the Exchange information store transferring messages to the Interchange Connector which converts the message to the local MS Mail post office, before the Exchange MTA transfers the message to the remote MS Mail Post office via a LAN connection or over an asynchronous or X.25 link.

From Here...

This chapter has explained the connection between Exchange and MS Mail (PC) post offices. For more information, see the following chapters:

- Chapter 6, "Planning Connections to Microsoft Mail Systems," will go into the steps associated with implementing the MS Mail Connector.
- Chapter 19, "Setting Up Microsoft Mail for AppleTalk Networks," will help you configure Exchange to work in an AppleTalk environment.
- Chapter 24, "Monitoring Your Organization," will cover foreign system connectivity beyond Exchange and MS Mail.

CHAPTER 19

Setting Up Microsoft Mail for AppleTalk Networks

- How to establish a network messaging link between your Windows NT and Macintosh server.
- How to configure the Exchange Microsoft Mail Connector to communicate with MS Mail (AppleTalk) servers.
- How to configure the Microsoft Exchange Connection on your MS Mail (AppleTalk) server.
- How to install and configure Connection Gateways on your MS Mail (AppleTalk) server.

In this chapter, you learn how to establish a messaging link between Microsoft Exchange and a Macintosh server running Microsoft Mail for AppleTalk networks. Unlike a MS Mail for PC network, MS Mail (AppleTalk) does not use the post office paradigm. Therefore, the process for connecting to an Exchange server is somewhat different. With respect to the Macintosh side, the Macintosh server believes it is communicating with a standard MS Mail (PC) postoffice. MS Mail for AppleTalk uses a special gateway component to communicate with the Exchange MS Mail Connector. With respect to the Exchange side, the Microsoft Mail Connector has specific configuration settings, and message queue for MS Mail (AppleTalk) connections. Any configuration specifically pertaining to Exchange communicating with MS Mail Post offices is not applicable. ■

Introduction to the Microsoft Mail Connector

In this section, you learn about the connectors used to establish a link between Exchange and Microsoft Mail (AppleTalk) servers.

The two core Exchange Microsoft Mail Connector components are the same:

- Microsoft Mail Connector Interchange: The Exchange service that routes messages between the Exchange server and the MS Mail connector post office.
- Microsoft Mail Connector post office: This component is an Exchange emulation of a true Microsoft Mail post office. It stores messages in transit to and from MS Mail (PC and AppleTalk).

Exchange also includes one additional component for communication with MS Mail (AppleTalk) servers:

- Microsoft Mail Connector (AppleTalk) message transfer agent: A Windows NT service that routes messages between the Microsoft Mail connector post office and the MS Mail (AppleTalk) server.

The following details the procedure for connecting Exchange to a Microsoft Mail for AppleTalk network:

1. Set up all necessary network connections between systems.
2. Install and set up the Exchange Microsoft Mail connector.
3. Place the Connector post office on a Macintosh accessible NTFS volume.
4. Configure the Exchange MS Mail connector to communicate with MS Mail (AppleTalk) servers. This includes starting the MS Mail (AppleTalk) MTA service.
5. Install and configure the Microsoft Exchange Connection software on the MS Mail (AppleTalk) gateway server.
6. Enter address space entries for the MS (AppleTalk) server. Test for correct message routing between systems.
7. If you want additional MS Mail (AppleTalk) servers to communicate indirectly with the Exchange server, install and configure the gateway access component on each Macintosh server.
8. Test transfer of messages to indirectly connected MS Mail (AppleTalk) servers if applicable.
9. Once messages are routed properly to all servers, proceed to set up directory synchronization to maintain up-to-date address lists among systems.

Installing Services for Macintosh

The following steps help you to configure your Exchange server to support Microsoft Mail for AppleTalk networks. Windows NT Services for Macintosh enable your server to communicate over Apple's native AppleTalk protocol. You must have an NTFS partitioned hard disk to support Services for Macintosh.

NOTE The following steps are quick guidelines to help you set up NT services for Macintosh. Consult your Windows NT Server documentation for more advanced configuration information.

1. Open the Network control panel on your Windows NT server. The Network Settings control panel appears (see fig. 19.1).

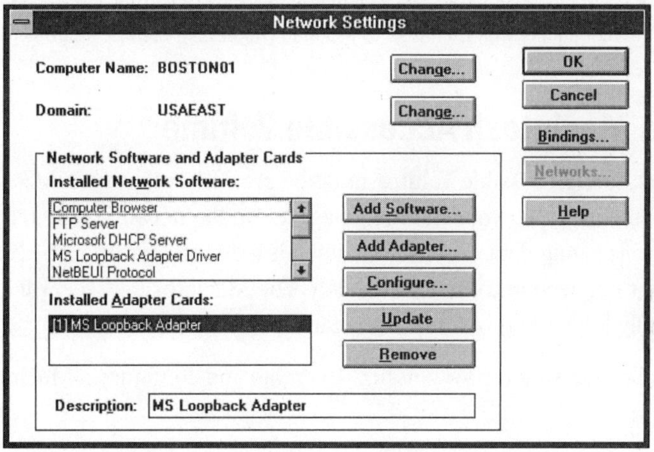

FIG. 19.1 The Windows NT Network Control Panel is part of your Windows NT server.

2. If Services for Macintosh is not listed in the Installed Network Software scroll box, it is not installed. Click Add Software. The Add Network Software dialog box appears (see fig. 19.2).

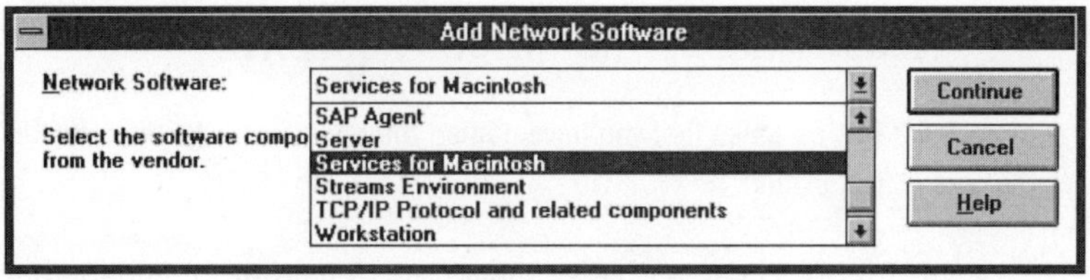

FIG. 19.2 Select Services for Macintosh among the list of available components.

Part III Ch 19

3. Select Services for Macintosh from the list of available network software. Click Continue.
4. Type the directory path to your Windows NT server software, for example, CD-ROM, floppy disk, or server volume. Click Continue.
5. After the services are loaded from disk and installed, you will return to the Network Settings control panel. Services for Macintosh should now be on the Installed Network Software list.
6. Click OK to complete service installation.
7. You will be prompted to restart your server to update the Network settings.

   Click Restart Now if this is appropriate. Alternatively, you can click Don't Restart Now to return to the Windows NT program manager.

NOTE If you choose not to restart immediately, remember that you will have to do so before continuing with Exchange to MS Mail (AppleTalk) configuration.

Creating a Macintosh Accessible Volume

A Macintosh Accessible Volume must be created so that your MS Mail AppleTalk server is capable of seeing your Exchange server on the network. Then, the two systems can trade messaging data. The volume itself is a directory within the NTFS structure configured for connection from a Macintosh. The Macintosh server will be configured to automatically log on to this volume on start-up.

The following steps show you how to create and configure a Macintosh Accessible Volume:

NOTE For more information on Macintosh Accessible Volumes, refer to your Windows NT Server documentation.

1. Open the Windows NT file manager.
2. From the file manager, you can find the following folder.

   :\EXCHSRVR\CONNECT\MSCON\MAILDATA

NOTE This assumes that you have named the main Exchange directory "EXCHSRVR" during installation.

3. From the MacFile menu, select Create Volume. The Create Macintosh-Accessible Volume dialog box appears (see fig. 19.3).

FIG. 19.3
You can create a New Macintosh-Accessible Volume from the MacFile menu.

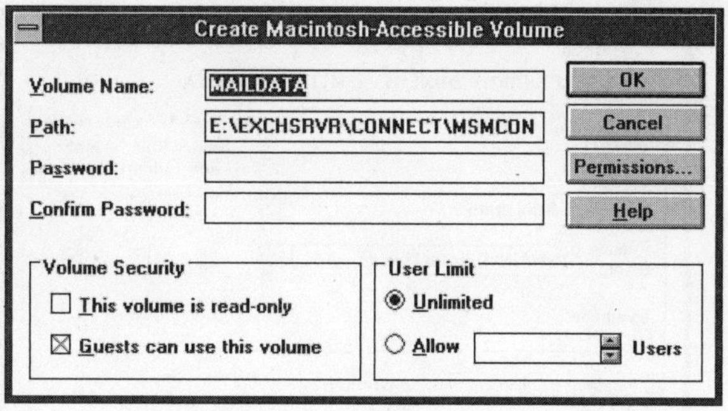

4. The Volume Name should be "MAILDATA."
5. You can enter a Password once. Then, you can enter it again in Confirm Password. The Macintosh server must use this information to connect to this volume. By default, no volume password is entered.
6. For enhanced security, clear the Guests Can Use This Volume checkbox.
7. Confirm that This volume is read-only remains unchecked.
8. Be sure that the Unlimited User Limit radio button is selected.
9. Click OK to create this volume and return to the file manager. Better yet, click the Permissions button to set access rights to this volume.

Configuring Macintosh-Accessible Volume Permissions

After creating a Macintosh-Accessible Volume you must define what users and groups have permission to access it. This is done in the Macintosh-Accessible Volume Permissions dialog box. This dialog box is almost identical to the Macintosh File Sharing dialog box. In this box, you select the Windows NT accounts that have access rights to this volume. The following steps will guide you in setting access rights to this volume:

1. There are two ways to open the permissions for a Macintosh-Accessible Volume. You can do this by clicking Permissions from the Create Macintosh-Accessible Volume dialog box. Alternatively, you can select the Volume from the file manager. Then, select Permissions from the MacFile menu. The Macintosh View of Directory Permissions dialog box appears (see fig. 19.4).
2. Use the... (ellipses) buttons to configure an Owner and Primary Group for this volume. These determine who is able to connect to this volume through the Macintosh Chooser.

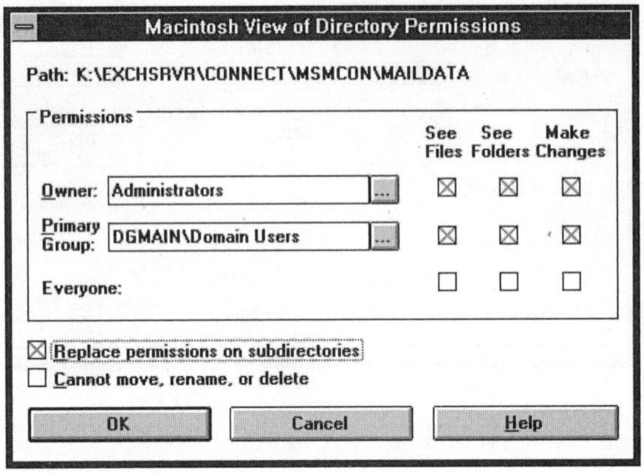

FIG. 19.4
You can set access permission for this volume.

3. Confirm that See Files, See Folders, and Make Changes permissions remain checked for the Owner and Primary Group.
4. Clear the check boxes pertaining to Everyone. This prevents anyone, except those users contained in Owner and Primary Group, from using this volume. By default, the Everyone permissions are checked.
5. Select the Replace permissions on subdirectories check box. This gives all directories within the current one permission settings identical to the ones on this page. By default, this box is not checked.
6. Click OK to set these permissions and return to the file manager.

Testing Connection to the Macintosh-Accessible Volume

You have completed the Macintosh-Accessible Volume configuration. This directory is now available for connection through the Macintosh Chooser. To confirm accessibility, you can test a manual connection, using the following steps:

1. Open the Chooser application from your Macintosh's Apple menu.
2. Click the AppleShare icon in the Chooser. Then, select the AppleTalk Zone, if applicable, in which your Exchange server is located.

   The Exchange server should now be listed in the Select a File Server display window.
3. Click the server's name. Then click OK.
4. On the connect dialog box, make sure the Registered User radio button is selected. Enter the user Name and Password for this server. Then, click OK.

5. After you are authenticated, a list of available Macintosh-Accessible Volumes displays in the Select the Items You Want to Use: window.

   Your newly created "MAILDATA" (or whatever customized name you chose) volume should appear on the list.

6. If your Volume is not visible, repeat the preceding steps for creating and configuring a Macintosh-Accessible Volume. Otherwise, proceed to the following section.

Configuring the Mail Connector for Use with MS Mail (AppleTalk)

Now that connectivity between Macintosh and Windows NT server has been established, the next step is to set up the Exchange MS Mail Connector to send and receive messages with the MS Mail (AppleTalk) server.

The following list details the property pages for the Exchange MS Mail connector. This list also discusses how they are configured to work with AppleTalk networks.

- *Interchange.* This page helps you set up the Microsoft Mail Connector (AppleTalk) MTA.
- *Local Post office.* Using this page, you set the local information that an MS Mail (AppleTalk) server uses to identify and connect to the MS Mail connector. Any standard MS Mail (PC) Post office uses this data to connect, as well.
- *Connections.* You can view the AppleTalk MTA's message queue using this page. All other options are reserved for MS Mail (PC) connections.
- *Connector MTAs.* This page is not used with respect to connecting to MS Mail for AppleTalk networks. Normally, this page defines which MS Mail (PC) Post offices are serviced by this Exchange server.
- *General.* You use this page for both PC and AppleTalk MS Mail connections to set an upper limit for message sizes.
- *Address Space.* On this page, you define which messages will be routed through this MS Mail connector to either type of MS Mail system.

- *Diagnostics Logging.* You define logging levels for the MS Mail (AppleTalk) MTA service on this page. You also configure logging for the Interchange activity and the MS Mail (PC) MTA on this page.

Configuring Exchange MS Mail Connector Properties

This section covers the installation of Microsoft Mail Connector properties primarily corresponding to communication with MS Mail (AppleTalk) servers. For a complete guide to the MS Mail connector, see Chapter 18.

The Interchange Page

The following steps guide you through the Interchange configuration:

1. Open the Microsoft Mail Connector property pages.
2. Select the Interchange tab. The MS Mail Connector (BOSTON01) Properties page appears (see fig. 19.5).

FIG. 19.5
You can designate mailboxes to be used by the MS Mail Connector Interchange property page.

3. You must set an administrator's mailbox if one has not already been defined. It will receive status notification from MS Mail Connector. If one is not defined, click Change. Then, select a mailbox from the address list.

TIP For a larger organization, it is a good idea to create a POSTMASTER account to receive the potentially large volume of status messages. This way, one administrator mailbox will not be burdened with an extra message load. Also, other administrators can view the delivery messages without logging on to a general administrator mailbox, or somebody else's personal mail.

4. Select the Primary Language for Clients from the pull-down menu.
5. Check the Maximize MS Mail 3.x Compatibility box to provide for OLE objects embedded in Exchange messages.
6. Unless you are currently using message tracking for troubleshooting purposes, make sure the Enable message tracking check box is cleared. For more information on message tracking for troubleshooting purposes, see Chapter 26, "Diagnostic and Troubleshooting Tools."
7. Configure the AppleTalk MTA settings. The following section discusses these settings.

Enabling the Microsoft Mail Connector AppleTalk MTA

You can open a messaging link between Exchange and MS Mail (AppleTalk). To do this, you enable the MS Mail Connector AppleTalk message transfer agent by following these steps:

1. Click the Configure button under the MS Mail Connector (AppleTalk) MTA. The MS Mail Connector (Apple Talk) MTA Options dialog box appears (see fig. 19.6).
2. Select the Enable MS Mail Connector AppleTalk MTA radio button under the Set Status window.

NOTE Enabling the AppleTalk MTA adds to the list of services in the Windows NT Services control panel.

3. Select the Start Automatically at System Startup radio button to configure this option. By default, this option is selected. Click OK to return to the Interchange property page.

FIG. 19.6
You can view and set MS Mail (AppleTalk) MTA service status.

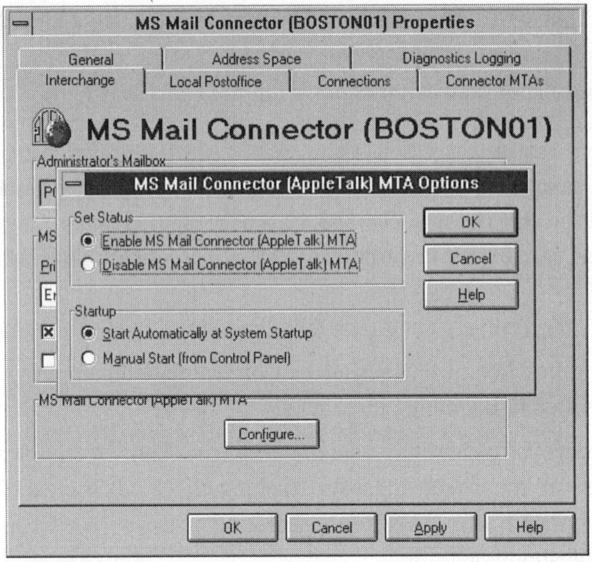

N O T E Normally, you will always set the AppleTalk MTA service for automatic startup. If, for example, you have a situation that requires some troubleshooting, and you want to have complete manual control over this service, select the Manual Start radio button.

4. Click Apply to set these properties and continue with other ones. When you are finished with all settings, click OK to set them and to return to the Administrator Program.

The Local Post office Page

The Local Post office information identifies the Microsoft Mail Connector Post office to the Macintosh MS Mail (AppleTalk) servers and any MS Mail Post offices on the network.

1. Select the Local Post office tab from the MS Mail connector property pages. The MS Mail Connector (BOSTON01) Properties page appears (see fig. 19.7).
2. Enter the MS Mail Network name for this post office. By default, this is the Microsoft Exchange organization name.
3. Enter a Post office used to identify this connector to other MS Mail servers. By default, this is the Exchange server's name.

FIG. 19.7
You can configure the local MS Mail Connector post office information.

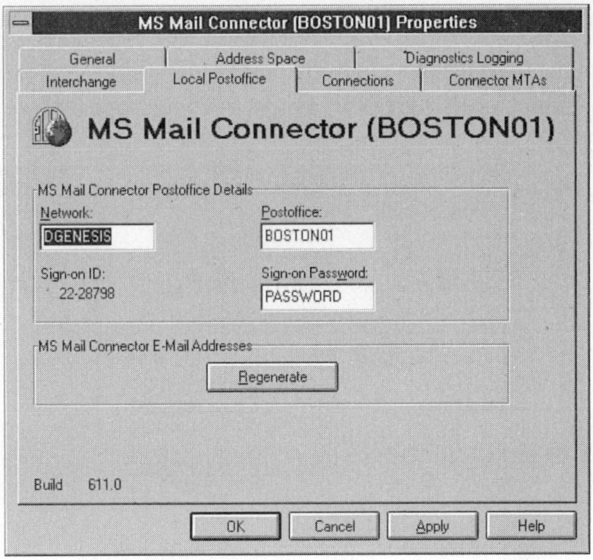

4. Enter a Sign-on Password used to authenticate other mail systems. By default, this is set to PASSWORD. You should change it for security reasons.
5. If you make any changes to post office settings, click Regenerate to rebuild addressing data.

NOTE For Local Post office information changes to take effect immediately, you must restart the Connector Interchange service as well as the MS Mail MTAs.

6. Click Apply to set these properties and continue with other ones. When you are finished with all settings, click OK to set them and return to the Administrator Program.

The Connections Page

The Connections property page only gives you the option of viewing the Microsoft Mail (AppleTalk) MTA message queue. The other options, such as Modify, Delete, and Create, are available only for Microsoft Mail (PC) connections. The MTA queue lists all outgoing messages awaiting transmission by the MS Mail AppleTalk message transfer agent.

To view the MS Mail (AppleTalk) MTA message queue, follow these steps:

1. Select the Connections tab from the MS Mail Connector Properties page. The MS Mail Connector (BOSTON01) Properties page appears (see fig. 19.8).

FIG. 19.8
You use this page to view the MS Mail connector AppleTalk message queue.

The Connections display window shows all current MS Mail connections.

2. Click the AppleTalk Mail entry in the window. The Modify and Delete buttons will dim.
3. Click the Queue button to bring up the Messages queued for AppleTalk Mail dialog box (see fig. 19.9).
4. The Queued Messages window shows the current messages awaiting delivery by this MTA.

From	The message sender
Subject	The information on the message's subject line
Message ID	The Exchange message identification code
Date/Time	The time the message entered the queue

5. Click Refresh to update the message list.

TIP The queued messages window is a listing of messages awaiting delivery at that moment. To get a more dynamic view of messages passing through the connector, you must repeatedly click the Refresh button. Clicking this button also gives you the latest updates.

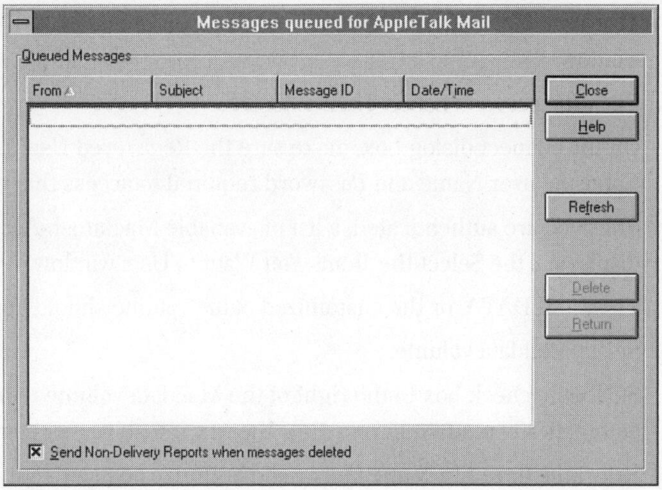

FIG. 19.9
The MS Mail (AppleTalk) message queue shows all the pertinent information on current messages.

6. Select a message. Then, click Delete to remove it from the queue. If Send Non-Delivery Reports when messages deleted is checked, the message sender will be notified of the deletion.
7. Select a message. Then, click Return to remove a message from the queue and return it to the sender.
8. Click Close to return to the Connections property page.

Macintosh MS Mail (AppleTalk) Configuration

This section describes the configuration required on the Macintosh side of the Exchange/ MS Mail (AppleTalk) connection.

The following are the Macintosh server configuration elements:

- Log in to the connector post office (Maildata volume).
- Log in to the Local MS Mail (AppleTalk) server as Network Manager.
- Install the Microsoft Exchange Connection Gateway.
- Configure the Gateway with the MS Mail client.
- Install the Macintosh Directory Exchange Requestor (DER). (optional)

Follow these steps to log in to the connector post office:

1. Open the Chooser application from your Macintosh's Apple menu.
2. Click the AppleShare icon in the chooser. Then, select the AppleTalk Zone, if applicable, in which your Exchange server is located.

The Exchange server should now be listed in the Select a File Server display window.

3. Click the server's name. Then click OK.
4. On the connect dialog box, make sure the Registered User radio button is selected. Enter the user Name and Password required to access this volume. Click OK.
5. After you are authenticated, a list of available Macintosh-Accessible Volumes displays in the Select the Items You Want to Use: window.

   The MAILDATA, or the customized name volume should appear on the list.
6. Select Maildata volume.
7. Select the check box to the right of the Maildata volume to have this volume automatically mounted every time the Macintosh server starts up.

   Select the Save My Name Only radio button to request your password when the volume attempts to mount at startup.

   Select Save My Name and Password to store your log-on data and then automatically authenticate your connection when the Macintosh starts up.
8. Click OK to mount the volume.

Installing the Microsoft Exchange Connection Gateway

The Exchange Connection Gateway is provided with your Microsoft Mail Connector software. Install it on your Macintosh MS Mail server to allow it to connect to the Exchange connector post office.

The following section assumes you have Microsoft Mail for AppleTalk Networks installed and properly running on your Macintosh server.

The following steps guide you through installing the Connection Gateway on your Macintosh server.

1. Log on to your MS Mail (AppleTalk) server as Network Manager.
2. Load the disk containing the Exchange Connection Installer. Open the installer application. The Connection Installer dialog box appears (see fig. 19.10).

   If no previous gateways have been installed, the Gateways Installed on This Server: window appears blank.
3. Select Install Gateway from the Gateway menu.
4. Select the GW icon from the dialog box. Then, click Install. The dialog box in figure 19.11 appears.

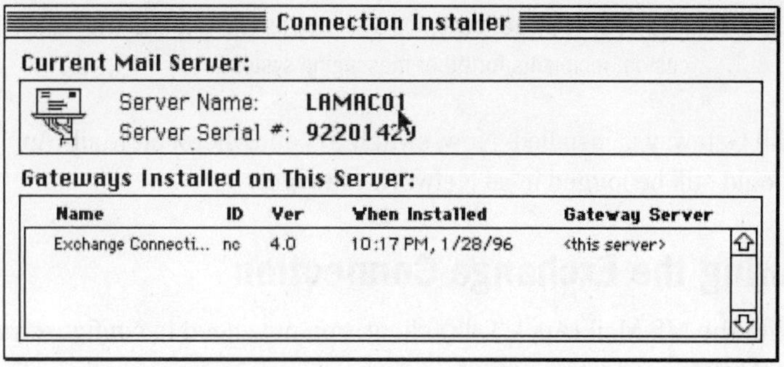

FIG. 19.10 View the installed gateways. This appears blank if there are none.

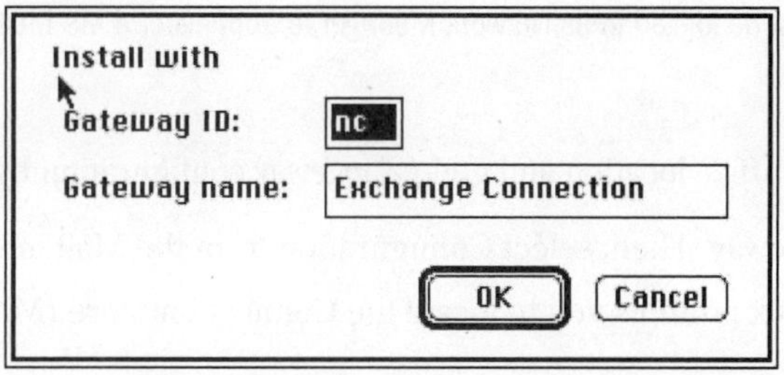

FIG. 19.11 You can enter Gateway Identification Information using this dialog box.

5. Enter a unique Gateway ID. This identifier is used by the MS Mail (AppleTalk) server to distinguish each gateway. By default, the ID for this gateway is NC.
6. Enter a Gateway name as it will be displayed in the gateway list. Click OK. The dialog box in figure 19.12 appears.

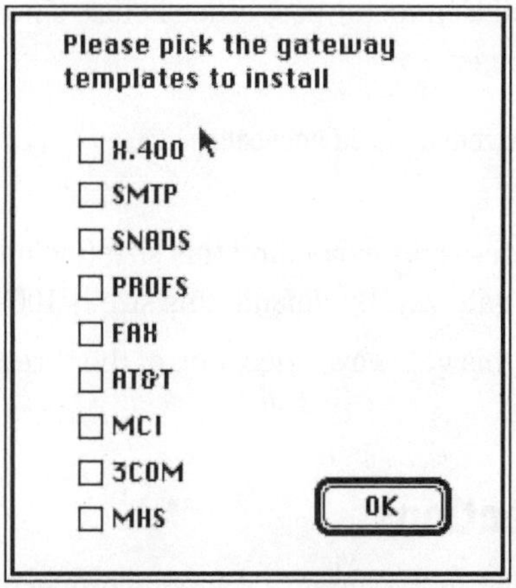

FIG. 19.12 You use this Gateway template to create external addresses.

7. Select which gateway templates to install for this gateway. Choose only those that you can access through this gateway, for example, those you use in your Exchange organization. Click OK.

NOTE A gateway template becomes available in your MS Mail (AppleTalk) client to create custom recipients for other messaging systems.

The Gateway is installed. Now, switch to your Microsoft Mail (AppleTalk) client which should still be logged in as Network Manager.

Configuring the Exchange Connection

With the MS Mail (AppleTalk) client, you now need to configure various gateway and post office connection options.

NOTE You must be logged in as Network Manager to administer a MS Mail (AppleTalk) server.

Specify the post office location and general gateway configuration by following these steps:

1. Select Gateway. Then, select Configuration from the Mail menu.

   A dialog box prompts you to locate the Connection Store (MacGate) directory. Click OK.
2. Scroll through the MAILDATA volume and locate the MACGATE folder. Click Open.
3. Enter a Blocking Factor value. This value limits the number of messages that can be transferred with each gateway cycle.
4. Enter an Aging Factor value. This is the amount of time, in minutes, that a message can remain in the MS Mail Connector post office before a notification message is sent to the Network Manager.

NOTE Setting the Aging Factor to zero turns off notification.

5. Set the Max Size value. Messages exceeding this size (including attachments) cannot pass through this gateway. By default, this size is 100 kilobytes.
6. Select a logging level for this gateway. Select one of the three radio buttons: Critical, Errors, or Details.

Scheduling Gateway Connections

This screen is functionally similar to Exchange's schedule property pages. Use this dialog box to configure at what times during the day this gateway connects to the MS Mail Connector post office. Your decision for the time of the day the gateway is to connect to the MS Mail Connector post office should be based on factors particular to your situation. For most, bandwidth, server loads, and connection costs (for example, over leased lines, or ISDN) are the limiting factors in this decision. If bandwidth or line costs are not an issue in your case, set the connection times as frequently as you want.

To set connection times, follow these steps:

1. Select Gateway. Then, select Connect Times from the Mail menu. A schedule grid appears for you to set connection times.
2. Select the radio button that determines how frequently you want this gateway to initiate connection.

   The Never button effectively deactivates the gateway.

   The Always button connects at the interval (in minutes) set at the bottom of this dialog box.

   At the Times Selected in the Chart Below defines connection times by those that are highlighted in the time grid.
3. Select the Connect Immediately When There Is Outgoing Mail check box to initiate a gateway connection as soon as a message is sent to the gateway.
4. If you chose the Selected Times option, use the time grid to mark the specific time you want the gateway to connect and transfer messages.

Installing an Access Gateway

After you have installed and configured the Connection Gateway, you can install additional access gateways on your MS Mail (AppleTalk) system. This enables other Macintosh MS Mail servers to communicate with Exchange and all its gateways and connectors.

You install an Access Connection Gateway by following these two steps:

- Extract the Access gateway from the Exchange Connection gateway.
- Install the Access gateway on another MS Mail (AppleTalk) server.

For step-by-step procedures for additional gateway installation, consult your gateway documentation.

From Here...

The information in this chapter bridged two distinct mail environments (Exchange and MS Mail for AppleTalk) with some external tools. However, most likely this will be just the first step in a full migration of Macintosh users onto Exchange. The upcoming release of a Macintosh Exchange client will provide for a better alternative for bringing Macintosh users onto an Exchange environment. As of this writing, the Macintosh client is in preliminary beta and will become a release product in the next two to three months.

For further related information, read the following chapters:

- Chapter 6, "Planning Connections to Microsoft Mail Systems," gives you a concept and planning guide with respect to how Exchange coexists with MS Mail environments.
- Chapter 17, "Using Directory Replication and Synchronization," discusses configuring directory synchronization between MS Mail (AppleTalk) and the Exchange server.
- Chapter 18, "Setting Up Microsoft Mail for PC Networks," gives you additional information on using the Microsoft Mail Connector.

CHAPTER 20

Configuring X.400 Connections

- How to install an MTA Transort Stack that corresponds to your current network environment
- How to Install a new X.400 Connector to establish messaging links between Exchange sites or between one Exchange site and a foreign X.400 system
- How to configure the various X.400 property pages for property operation
- How to test an X.400 Connector to verify proper message transmission

The Microsoft Exchange X.400 Connector is used to create a message route between two Exchange servers or between one Exchange server and another messaging system that complies with the X.400 standard. An X.400 connector is flexible due to its variety of available transport protocols. An Exchange site can utilize several X.400 connectors over various transport stacks, simultaneously providing multiple message routes as well as load balancing.

X.400 Supported Transport Protocols

The X.400 Connector can communicate over several network transport protocols. Out of the box, Exchange supports the use of the X.400 Connector with the following transport stacks:

- **TCP/IP.** Transmission Control Protocol/Internet Protocol. Uses the Windows NT TCP/IP services to establish communication over TCP/IP networks.
- **TP0/X.25 with the Eicon port adapter.** Transport Protocol 0/X.25. Both dial-up and direct connection over X.25 networks using the Eicon software and/or hardware solution. You may use multiple X.25 port adapters on each server, and each must have its own MTA Transport Stack (and appropriate hardware).
- **TP4/CLNP.** Transport Class 4/Connectionless Network Protocol. Exchange includes a setup driver that allows it to work with the TP4 interface on Windows NT.

Before you can install a new X.400 connection you must do the following:

- Make sure that the Exchange server has a necessary network transport protocol. For example, you must have the Windows NT TCP/IP protocols running and configured to successfully set up an X.400 connector with a TCP/IP Transport Stack.
- Configure and test all necessary networking hardware to confirm that a link exists. In the TCP/IP example, you can use the PING *IP ADDRESS* statement from the Windows NT command line to test this link.
- Know the exact X.400 address of the remote site or foreign system.

X.400 Connector Installation and Configuration

Whether installing an X.400 connection to another Microsoft Exchange server or foreign system, there are four primary steps to follow:

1. Install an appropriate MTA transport stack.
2. Install and configure a local X.400 connector.
3. Configure the X.400 connection on the remote Exchange site or foreign system.
4. Test the connection for message receipt and formatting consistency.

Installing an MTA Transport Stack

When you are certain that all applicable network software and hardware is installed on the Windows NT server that will be handling the connection, you are ready to proceed with installing an MTA Transport Stack. This section will first cover how to install the MTA Transport Stack and then how to configure the Property pages for each one.

The installation procedure is as follows:

1. From the Exchange administrator program File menu, select New Other, then select MTA Transport Stack. The New MTA Transport Stack dialog box appears (see fig. 20.1).

   The Type section of the dialog box lists the available MTA Transport Stacks on this Exchange server.

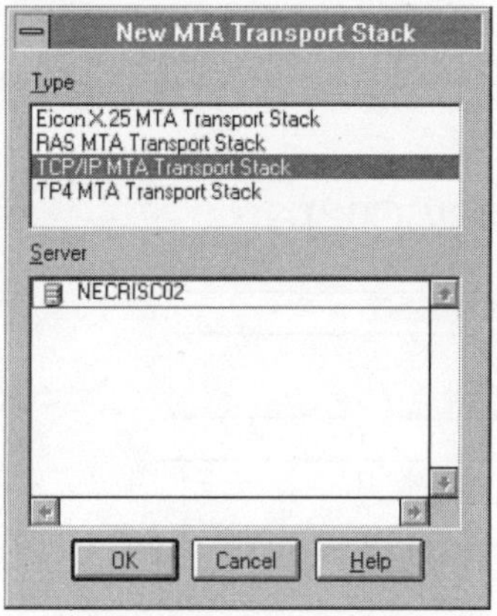

FIG. 20.1 The New MTA Transport Stack is used by the X.400 Connector (and also the Dynamic RAS Connector) to select an underlying transport for message transfer.

NOTE The RAS MTA Transport Stack is not used for X.400 connections.

   The Server section of the dialog box lists all the servers in the current site.

2. Click MTA Transport Stack. Select the server in your local site that will handle that type of connection. The transport stack will be installed on that server.
3. Click OK to accept the transport stack and Exchange server settings. The Properties page for the appropriate transport stack appear.

NOTE If all the necessary hardware/software for the network transport is not installed, you will get an error message stating that the required components are not ready. The MTA Transport Stack cannot be installed until these conditions are met.

Configuring MTA Transport Stack Property Pages

Each MTA Transport Stack has two corresponding Property pages: a General page that identifies specific local addressing data, and a Connections page that lists all the X.400 connectors using this transport stack for communication.

This section includes steps to set up a new TCP/IP transport stack. If you are not using TCP/IP as a network transport, then skip this section.

General Tab The General tab fulfills two functions for a new TCP/IP MTA Transport Stack. First, you can give it a name for display in the administrator program. Second, you can enter specific OSI address information if your network environment requires that you distinguish between applications that use the TCP/IP network transport.

1. Select the General tab in the TCP/IP MTA Transport Stack Properties page (see fig. 20.2).

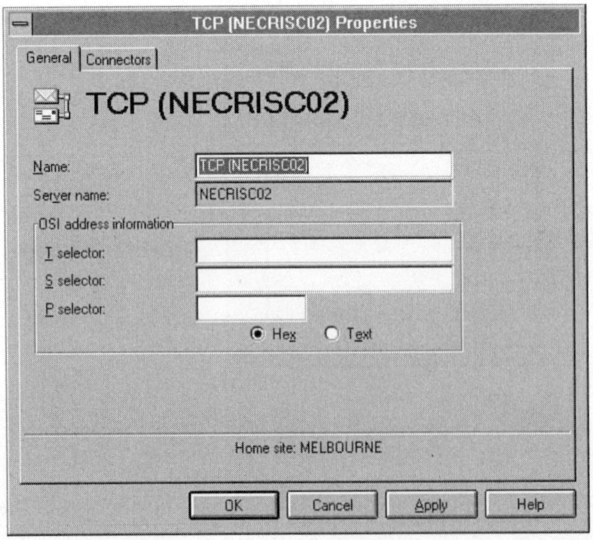

FIG. 20.2
Set the name and local transport information in this Property page.

2. Enter a Name for this MTA Transport Stack as you want it too appear in the administrator program's display window. By default, this transport is named as TCP (*server name*). You can only change it when you are creating a new transport stack.
3. The Server Name box displays the Exchange server on which this MTA Transport Stack is installed. The server cannot be changed at this point. To use a different server you must Cancel out of these Property pages and install a new MTA Transport Stack.

4. Under OSI Address Information, enter numbers required to distinguish Exchange from other services or applications using the TCP/IP Transport Stack. There is one box for each of the following three network layers:

   T selector: Transport Service Access Point (TSAP)
   S selector: Session Service Access Point (SSAP)
   P selector: Presentation Service Access Point (PSAP)

5. Select either the Hex or Text radio button, depending on the type of data you enter in the preceding boxes.
6. Click Apply to set these properties and continue with other properties. If you are done with all the settings, click OK to return to the administrator program.

Connectors Tab The Connectors Property page displays a list of every Microsoft Exchange X.400 connector that uses this TCP/IP MTA Transport Stack. You can open the Property pages for each listed X.400 connector from this page as well.

1. Select the Connectors tab on the TCP/IP MTA Transport's Properties page (see fig. 20.3). All X.400 connectors using this MTA Transport Stack are listed in the Connectors that use this stack window.

FIG. 20.3
A listing of X.400 connectors using this MTA Transport Stack (blank if no connectors are set up).

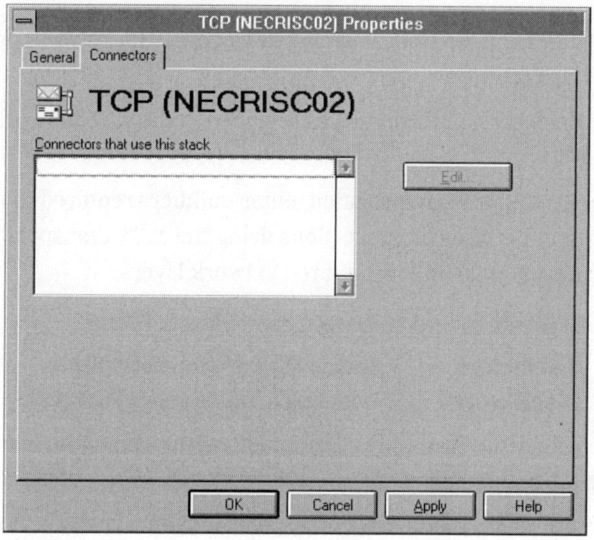

2. Select an X.400 connector name from the list (if any are available), then click Edit so that its Properties page appear.
3. Click Apply to set these properties and continue with other properties. If you are done with all the settings, click OK to return to the administrator program.

X.25 Transport Stack

This section includes steps to set up a new X.25 transport stack. If you are not using X.25 as a network transport, then skip this section.

General Tab The General tab fulfills two functions for a new X.25 MTA Transport Stack. First, you can give it a name for display in the administrator program. Second, you can enter specific OSI address information if your network environment requires that you distinguish between applications that use the X.25 network transport.

1. Select the General tab in the X.25 MTA Transport Stack Properties page.
2. Enter a Name for this MTA Transport Stack as you want it to appear in the administrator program's display window. By default, this transport stack is named as Eicon X.25 (*server name*). This name can only be changed when creating a new transport stack.
3. Enter the Call User Data as provided by your X.25 network provider. This can be up to 256 characters.
4. Enter the local X.121 Address as specified in the X.25 network set up under Windows NT.
5. Under OSI Address Information, enter numbers required to distinguish Exchange from other services or applications using the X.25 Transport Stack. There is one box for each of the following three network layers:

T selector:	Transport Service Access Point (TSAP)
S selector:	Session Service Access Point (SSAP)
P selector:	Presentation Service Access Point (PSAP)

6. Select either the Hex or Text radio button, depending on the type of data you enter in the preceding boxes.
7. Select the radio button that corresponds to your type of X.25 connection—Async Phone Line (Dial-up X.25) or Leased Line.

8. If you select Leased Line, enter the I/O port on which your Eicon adapter is installed.
9. Click Apply to set these properties and continue with other properties. If you are done with all the settings, click OK to return to the administrator program.

Connectors Tab The Connectors Property page displays a list of every Microsoft Exchange X.400 Connector that uses this X.25 MTA Transport Stack. You can open the Properties page for each listed X.400 connector from this page as well.

Use this Properties page to view which Microsoft Exchange X.400 connectors use this X.25 MTA Transport Stack. Follow these steps to view the list of connectors and open the Properties page for connectors on the list:

Using the Connectors Properties Page:

1. Select the Connectors tab on the X.25 MTA Transport's Properties page.

   All X.400 connectors using this MTA Transport Stack are listed in the Connectors That Use This Stack window.
2. Select an X.400 connector name from the list (if any are available), then click Edit so that its Properties page appear.
3. Click Apply to set these properties and continue with other properties. If you are done with all the settings, click OK to return to the administrator program.

TP4 Transport Stack

This section includes steps to set up a new TP4 transport stack. If you are not using TP4 as a network transport, then skip this section.

General Tab The General tab fulfills two functions for a new TP4 MTA Transport Stack. First, you can give it a name for display in the administrator program. Second, you can enter specific OSI address information if your network environment requires that you distinguish between applications that use the TP4 network transport.

1. Select the General tab in the TP4 MTA Transport Stack Properties page.
2. Enter a Name for this MTA Transport Stack as you want it to appear in the administrator program's display window. By default, this transport stack is named as TP4 (*server name*). You can only change this name when you are creating a new transport stack.

3. Under OSI Address Information, enter numbers required to distinguish Exchange from other services or applications using the TP4 Transport Stack. There is one box for each of the following three network layers:

   T selector: Transport Service Access Point (TSAP)
   S selector: Session Service Access Point (SSAP)
   P selector: Presentation Service Access Point (PSAP)

4. Select either the Hex or Text radio button, depending on the type of data you enter in the preceding boxes.
5. Click Apply to set these properties and continue with other properties. If you are done with all the settings, click OK to return to the administrator program.

Connectors Tab The Connectors Properties page displays a list of every Microsoft Exchange X.400 connector that uses this TP4 MTA Transport Stack. You can open the Properties page for each listed X.400 connector from this page as well.

1. Select the Connectors tab on the TP4 MTA Transport's Properties page.

   All X.400 connectors using this MTA Transport Stack are listed in the Connectors that use this stack window.
2. Select an X.400 connector name from the list (if any are available), then click Edit so that its Properties page appear.
3. Click Apply to set these properties and continue with other properties. If you are done with all the settings, click OK to return to the administrator program.

Installing and Configuring an X.400 Connector

When you have properly installed all the needed MTA Transport Stacks, you can create the actual X.400 connector that will transfer messages over that transport. You must have the following information in order to proceed in setting up a new X.400 connector:

- **A unique name for this connector**

  For identification in the Exchange administrator program.
- **Remote MTA name**

  String identifying the Message Transfer Agent on the remote Exchange site or foreign system.

- **Remote MTA password**

  String used to authenticate an X.400 messaging link (only needed if the remote MTA requires password authentication).
- **Stack address**

  The unique identifying address for the local X.400 connector.
- **Address space**

  Any address entry that will uniquely identify a message's route through this X.400 connector to a remote site or foreign system.

NOTE For an X.400 connection to be established, a connector must be set up on both sides of the link. For a Microsoft Exchange server, this means setting up a corresponding Exchange X.400 connector. For a foreign X.400 system, this involves using that system's administrative tools and entering appropriate addressing data for the Exchange server. (See guidelines near the end of this chapter).

Creating a New X.400 Connector

From the administrator program File menu, select New Other, then select X.400 Connector. The New X.400 Connector dialog box is displayed (see fig. 20.4).

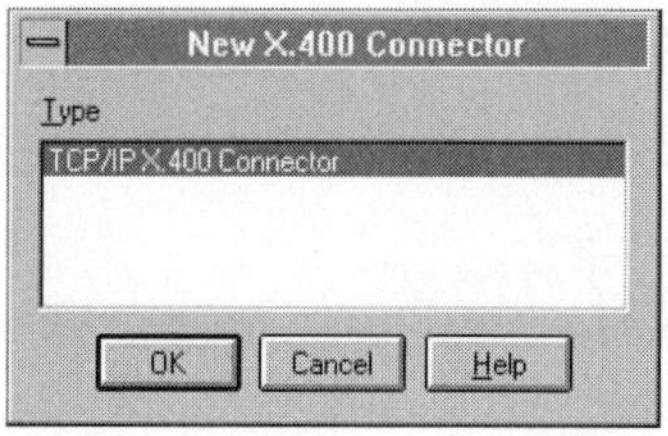

FIG. 20.4
Select an MTA Transport Stack for this X.400 connector.

The New X.400 Connector Type dialog box lists all the currently installed MTA Transport Stacks. Select one from the list and click OK. The X.400 property sheets open.

NOTE If you have not yet configured an MTA Transport Stack, you cannot continue from this point. Follow the instructions in the previous section to set up the underlying transport stack.

Configuring an X.400 Connector

The X.400 Connector property pages allow you to configure any X.400 connection, whether it be between two Exchange sites, or to a foreign X.400 system. The following is an overview of the X.400 property pages and the functions of each:

- **General**

  Set connector names, transport stack, and general X.400 message preferences.

- **Schedule**

  Set times when a local MTA will initiate communication with the remote site.

- **Stack**

  Set connection parameters for establishing a link to the remote Exchange server or foreign system. A different Stack page will be displayed, depending on which transport was selected for this X.400 connector.

- **Override**

  Change the default MTA attributes for messages routed through a specific X.400 connector.

- **Connected sites**

  Lists directly and indirectly connected to Exchange sites. Can also be used to set up indirect connection to sites.

- **Address space**

  Enter enough information to specify a message route through this connector.

- **Delivery restrictions**

  Define specific senders who will be allowed or denied permission to transmit messages through this connector.

- **Advanced**

  Set detailed X.400 communications specifications for this connector.

General Tab Use the X.400 General tab to set the principal communication options for a new connector. The following steps guide you through configuring the X.400 connector General tab.

1. Select the General tab of the X.400 Connector Properties page (see fig. 20.5).
2. Enter a Display Name for this connector as you want it to appear in the Exchange administrator display window.

FIG. 20.5
Select an MTA Transport Stack for this X.400 connector.

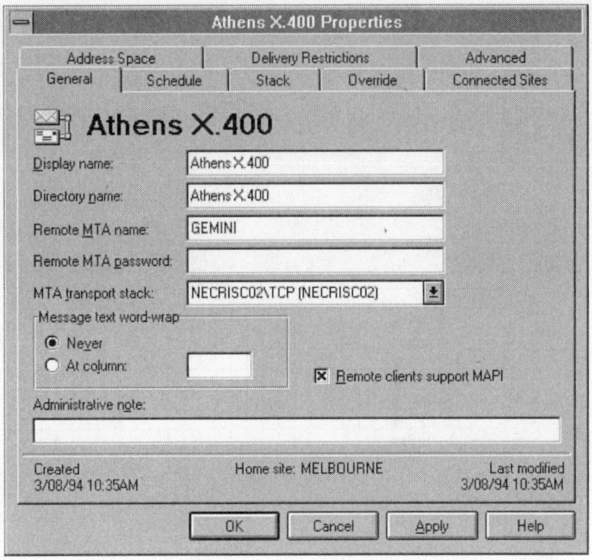

3. Enter a Directory Name used for addressing purposes.
4. Enter the Remote MTA Name in the box provided.
5. If required, enter a Remote MTA Password for the preceding remote MTA.
6. The MTA Transport Stack displays the currently selected transport for this X.400 connector. You can change the MTA Transport Stack with the pull-down menu.
7. Under Message Text Word-Wrap you can force a carriage return in all the outgoing messages by clicking the At Column button and entering the column number. By default, this is set to Never.
8. If your X.400 connection is to a foreign messaging system that does not support MAPI, clear the Remote Clients Support MAPI checkbox. All rich-text and other MAPI characteristics are removed from outgoing messages.
9. Enter any additional Administrative Note.

Schedule Tab Use the Schedule Properties page to control how often the X.400 Connector becomes active and initiates a connection.

1. Select the Schedule tab in the X.400 Connector Properties Page (see fig. 20.6).
2. Select one of the four radio buttons that determine when this X.400 Connector connects.

FIG. 20.6
Set connection times for this connector.

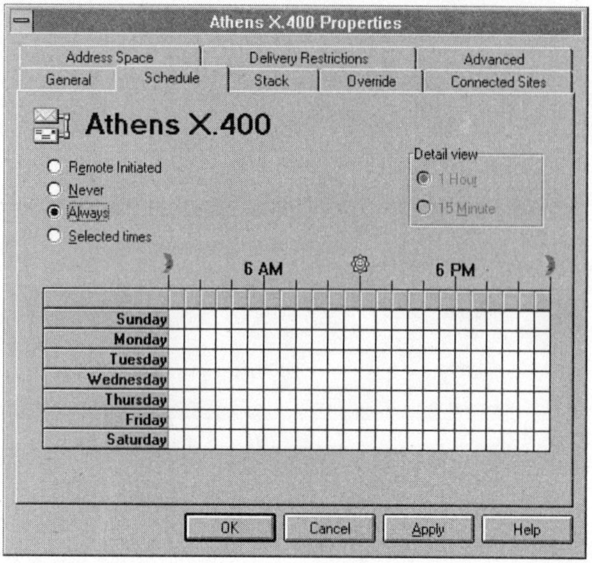

Remote Initiated—Send messages only when the remote MTA connects to this MTA. Both MTAs must have the two-way alternate option selected in the Advanced properties page.

CAUTION

Only one MTA can be configured to be remote-initiated. Otherwise, if both MTAs are waiting for the other to initiate the connection, the messages will never be delivered.

Never—A connection is never established. This option effectively disables this X.400 Connector.

Always—An MTA connection is established whenever messages need to be transferred. By default, this option is selected.

Selected Times—The X.400 Connector initiates communication based on the time grid on this Properties page.

3. If you choose Selected Times, the Detail View radio buttons become available. Select either the 1 hour or 15 Minute detail view and the time grid will change its scale accordingly.
4. If you choose Selected Times, pick the time blocks for connection.
5. Click Apply to set these properties and continue with other properties. If you are done with all the settings, click OK to return to the administrator program.

Stack Tab Each MTA Transport Stack has a different Stack page, primarily because each transport uses different addressing conventions. This section first covers the top section of the Stack Properties page which is unique to each transport. The second part of the page covers entering OSI information to identify a particular X.400 connector with the transport stack. The OSI information is common to all Stack properties pages and is covered only once following the address information section.

The X.400 Stack Properties Page

1. Select the Stack tab in the X.400 Connector Properties page (see fig. 20.7).

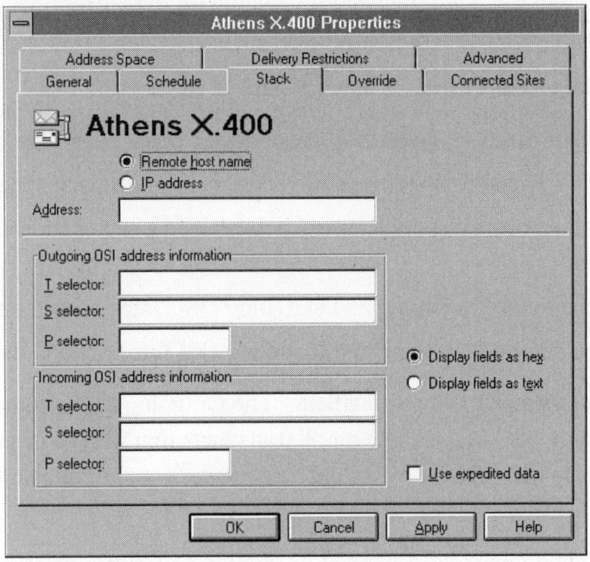

FIG. 20.7
Enter the TCP/IP addressing data for the remote MTA.

2. Select the appropriate radio button for the remote site's address. Use Remote Host Name if the remote server can be identified either through the Domain Name Service (DNS) or the Windows Internet Naming Service (WINS). Use IP Address if a host name is not available.

TIP Using an IP address will make for a slightly faster connection time to the remote system. However, using the IP address numbers may be too cryptic for administration purposes (that is, more difficult to remember and identify at first glance).

3. Enter the host name or IP address in the Address box.
4. Proceed to the "Outgoing and Incoming OSI Information" section later in this chapter.

X.25 Stack Properties Page

1. Select the Stack tab in the X.400 Connector Properties page. The X.25 Transport version of the Stack Properties page appears.
2. Enter your Call User Data as given by your X.25 provider.
3. Enter Facilities Data as specified by your X.25 provider. This contains a comma-delimited list of additional connection parameters.
4. Enter the X.121 Address of the remote server. This information can be obtained from the remote server's X.25 transport information.
5. Proceed to the "Outgoing and Incoming OSI Information" section later in the chapter.

TP4 Stack Properties Page

1. Select the Stack tab in the X.400 Connector Properties page.

   The TP4 Transport version of the Stack Properties page appears.
2. Enter the network service access point (NSAP) or the address of the remote X.40 system.
3. Proceed to the "Incoming and Outgoing OSI Data" section later in the chapter.
4. Proceed to the "Outgoing and Incoming OSI Information" section that follows.

Outgoing and Incoming OSI Information The Outgoing and Incoming OSI information, shown in figure 20.7, is the same for all transports that were previously covered. The following steps will cover how to configure the various outgoing and incoming information.

1. Under Outgoing OSI Address Information and Incoming OSI Address Information, enter numbers required to distinguish this X.400 connector from other services or applications using this transport stack. There is one box for each of the following three network layers:

T selector:	Transport Service Access Point (TSAP)
S selector:	Session Service Access Point (SSAP)
P selector:	Presentation Service Access Point (PSAP)

2. Select either the Display fields as hex or display fields as text radio button depending on the type of data you enter in the preceding boxes.
3. Select the Use expedited data checkbox if your network recognizes data packets identified for accelerated transfer. Some networks require the use of expedited data. Refer to your transport and network documentation for more information.

4. Click Apply to set these properties and continue with other properties. If you are done with all the settings, click OK to return to the administrator program.

Override Tab With the Override Properties page, shown in figure 20.8, you can set the connector-specific MTA. These settings only affect MTA links established through this X.400 connector.

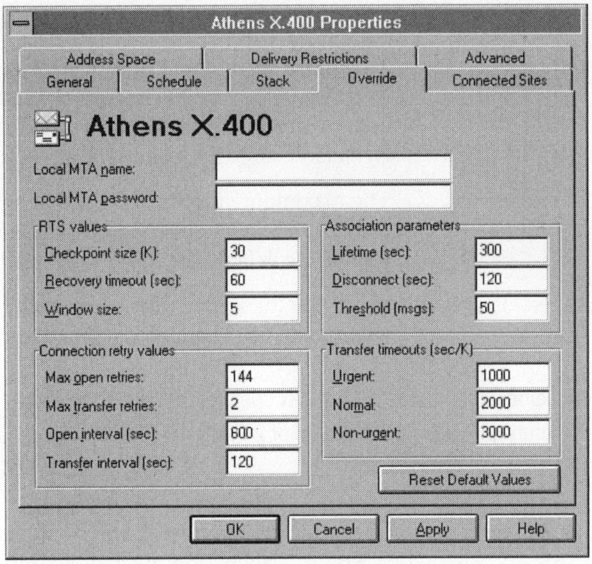

FIG. 20.8
Enter MTA override settings for this connector.

Enter a different Local MTA Name if the foreign X.400 system cannot accept the Microsoft Exchange server name. Sometimes the server name may be too long or contain characters (for example, spaces) that a foreign X.400 MTA cannot accept.

Enter Local MTA Password to require authentication when establishing communication from a remote system.

Enter specific MTA configuration variables. The following table lists each variable and its function within the MTA:

Part III Ch 20

Table 20.1 MTA Variables and Functions

Variable	Function
?RTS Values	
Checkpoint size (K):	The value used to verify packet transmission with returned checkpoints. By default, this is 30 kilobytes.
Recovery timeout (sec):	The time delay before retrying a broken transmission. By default, the delay is 60 seconds.

continues

Table 20.1 Continued

Variable	Function
?RTS Values	
Window size:	The maximum number of checkpoints that can be transmitted without acknowledgment. By default this value is 5 kilobytes.
Connection Retry Values	
Max open retries:	The maximum number of consecutive failed attempts before the MTA stops trying to open a communication channel with a remote MTA. By default, an MTA makes 144 attempts.
Max transfer retries:	The maximum number of consecutive failed attempts before the MTA stops trying to transfer a message packet. By default, the MTA makes two attempts.
Open interval (sec):	The delay (in seconds) between attempts to open a communication channel. By default, this delay is 600 seconds.

NOTE If you combine the default "144 Max open retries" with the default "600 second Open interval," it adds up to a total of 24 hours before a message is returned as undeliverable.

Variable	Function
Transfer interval (sec):	The delay (in seconds) between attempts to retransmit a failed message packet. By default, this delay is 120 seconds.
Association Parameters	
Lifetime (sec):	The maximum time that an idle connection between MTAs remains open. By default, an idle link is held open for 300 seconds after the last communication.
Disconnect (sec):	The maximum time allowed when establishing or terminating a connection before the session is ended independently. By default, this is 120 seconds.
Threshold (msgs):	The number of messages that must be queued at this MTA for it to initiate a link to a remote MTA. By default, 50 messages must be awaiting transmission.
Transfer Timeouts(sec/K)	
Urgent:	The delay (in seconds per kilobyte of total message size) between retries of urgent messages. By default, this delay is 1,000 seconds.
Normal:	The delay (in seconds per kilobyte of total message size) between retries of normal messages. By default, this delay is 2,000 seconds.

Variable	Function
?RTS Values	
Non-urgent:	The delay (in seconds per kilobyte of total message size) between retries of non-urgent messages. By default, this delay is 3,000 seconds.

Each item has a box to its right with a default numeric value. Replace any value with a number that will be used when establishing a connection through this X.400 connector. To return to the default Message Transfer Agent settings, click Reset Default Values.

Connected Sites Tab This Properties page lists other Microsoft Exchange sites that are available via this X.400 connector. This includes sites that are indirectly linked through this connector.

Here is an example of when to use this feature. Exchange site MELBOURNE is linked to site ATHENS via a public X.400 network. MELBOURNE, in turn, is linked to LOS ANGELES through a high bandwidth line using a site connector.

When data replication between sites occurs, information about indirectly connected sites appears in the Connected Sites window.

In this case, the indirectly connected sites are LOS ANGELES and BOSTON. A message sent from ATHENS to BOSTON is sent to the first site it is connected to and then forwarded to the next site, and so on, until BOSTON is reached.

Manually Modifying Indirectly Connected Sites

You may also manually insert an address entry for an indirectly connected site. This is done from the Connected Sites Properties page as well. This page may also be used to modify an existing route.

NOTE If you are using an X.400 connector to link to a foreign X.400 system, you can skip this section.

The following steps are used to add or modify connected site entries:

1. To create a new entry, click the New button on the connected sites Properties page. To change an existing entry, select it from the list and click Edit on the Connected Sites Properties page. The Properties page in figure 20.9 appears.

   The General page appears first.

2. Enter the Organization name in which the remote Exchange server exists. By default, your current organization is displayed.

3. Enter the name of the Microsoft Exchange Site in which the remote server exists. By default, this entry is left blank.

FIG. 20.9
Manually enter connected site information.

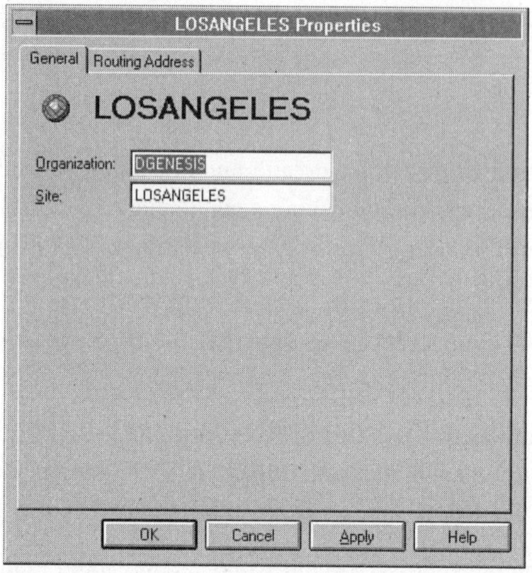

The following steps are to specify a routing address for an indirectly connected site.

1. Click the Routing Address tab (see fig. 20.10).

FIG. 20.10
Enter a routing address for the indirectly connected site.

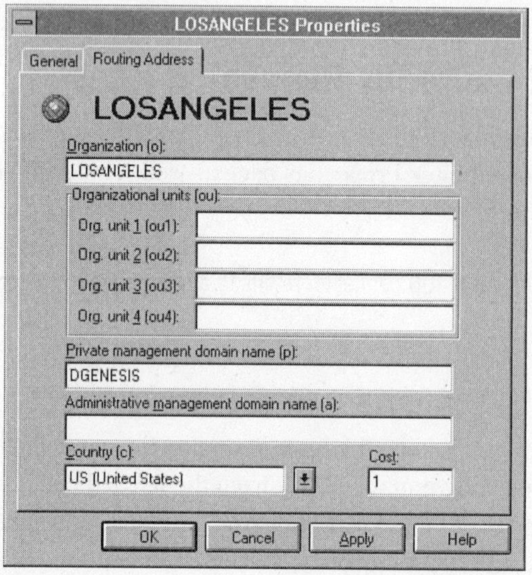

2. By default, the Organization name displayed is the site name you entered in the preceding General Properties page.

3. Enter X.400 routing information needed to connect to the remote server. The following is a list and description of the routing information required:

Organizational Units	Identify the Exchange servers via their valid X.400 names.
Private Management	Enter the PRMD of the remote Domain Name (PMDN) server.
Administrative Management Domain Name (ARMD)	Enter the PRMD of the remote server.
Country	An X.400 value that identifies the country of the server.
Cost	Standard Microsoft Exchange routing cost value. By default, this cost is 1.

To delete a connected site entry, select the site address entry from the connected sites Properties page. Click Remove. That remote site will no longer be available through this X.400 connector.

Address Space Tab This Properties page defines the messages that are routed through this connector. Only enough addressing data is provided to distinguish messages that should be sent through this connector.

Routing costs are also entered along with each address space entry.

Delivery Restrictions Tab This Properties page filters the individuals that can or cannot send messages through this connector. There are two easy-to-understand delivery options:

- **Accept Messages From:** Creates an exclusive list of recipients with permission to send messages through this X.400 connector.
- **Reject Messages From:** Lists specific recipients that are denied permission to send messages through this X.400 connector.

The following steps show how to set up the different delivery options:

1. Select the Delivery Restrictions tab in the X.400 connector Properties page (see fig. 20.11).
2. Click the List radio button under either Accept messages from or Reject messages from.
3. Click the Modify button underneath each list so that the Microsoft Exchange address list appears. Select the desired recipients to include or exclude from X.400 message transfer through this connector. Click OK.

FIG. 20.11
Delivery restrictions limit who can access this X.400 connector.

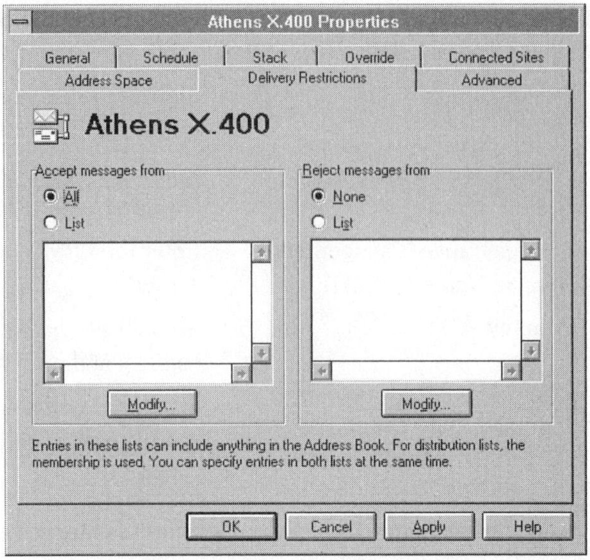

4. Click Apply to set these properties and continue with other properties. If you are done with all the settings, click OK to return to the administrator program.

Advanced Tab The Advanced tab is where you can control some of the finer points of X.400 connectivity with Exchange server. You will define which X.400 standard to utilize, and how various elements of the messages are transferred through the system.

1. Select the Advanced tab from the X.400 Properties page (see fig. 20.12).

FIG. 20.12
Set advanced communication and X.400 message properties.

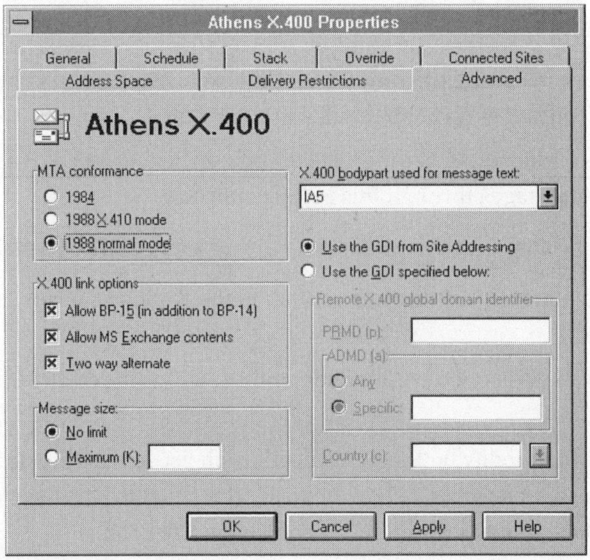

2. Under MTA Conformance, select the radio button pertaining to the correct X.400 standard you will be using. Exchange supports all the latest X.400 standards, but you must select the setting that conforms to what your provider uses. These are your three options:

   1984

   1988 X.410 mode

   1988 normal mode

CAUTION

To avoid message transmission errors, be sure to select the standard supported by your X.400 carrier and the remote X.400 system.

3. Under X.400 Link Options select all the checkboxes pertaining to features you want in this link.

   Allow BP-15 (in addition to BP-14)
   (only available if 1988 MTA conformance is selected)
   Use the BP-15 extension standard for message attachments.

   Allow MS Exchange Contents
   (use only when the remote system is a Microsoft Exchange server)
   Permits the transmission of MAPI message properties as an object of the X.400 message using the Message DataBase Encoding Format (MDBEF).
   Two-Way Alternate
   Permits both MTAs to take turns sending and receiving message data. Use when the remote MTA supports this functionality.

4. Under Message Size, click Maximum (K) and enter a value (in kilobytes) if you want to set a maximum for message transmission. By default, No Limit is selected and messages of any size can pass through this connector.
5. Under X.400 Bodypart Used for Message Text, use the pull-down menu to select the body part type used for the content of an outbound message. It must be supported by the foreign system. These settings do not affect inbound messages.
6. Select the Use the GDI from Site Addressing to use the Global Domain Identifier from the Site Addressing page to prevent message transfer loops.
7. Select Use the GDI Specified Below and enter the foreign systems GDI in the space provided. Obtain this information from the foreign system's configuration settings.

8. Click Apply to set these properties and continue with other properties. If you are done with all the settings, click OK to return to the administrator program.

Configuring a Foreign X.400 System

The specifics to configuring a foreign X.400 system vary from system to system. This section will provide you with general guidelines to follow when setting up a foreign X.400 system to communicate with a Microsoft Exchange server X.400 connector.

- Microsoft Exchange server supports a wide variety of X.400 content and body part types. It is a good idea to attempt to match X.400 capabilities exactly with a foreign system's settings whenever possible.
- If the local Microsoft Exchange X.400 connector is configured first, use the settings in the administrator program X.400 Properties page to retrieve settings for the foreign system.
- If the foreign system is configured first, obtain all the necessary settings for the local Exchange server.

Verifying Connections

When both ends of an X.400 link are configured, you must proceed to test the connection. Because X.400 performs message format conversions during transmission, you must not only make sure that a message is properly received, but that its contents are correctly formatted.

Messages sent to a remote Exchange site via an X.400 connector should be received in the exact same format as they were transmitted. This includes the transmission of all the attachments as well. All MAPI information should be preserved in the conversion and transmission process.

Here is a sequence you can use to test your X.400 link between sites:

1. Create and send a message to a remote site using the Exchange client. Include the following in the message:

   Rich text formatting (various colors, font sizes, and so on)
   An attached file (of any sort)
   An embedded OLE object (word processing document, spreadsheet, and so on)

2. Verify that the intended recipient receives the message in his or her inbox.
3. Check the message contents (including attachments and embedded objects) for data integrity.
4. Repeat the preceding steps by sending a message from the remote site to the local site.

When testing message transmissions to foreign X.400 systems, here are some important test steps to follow:

1. Create a message as previously described, with rich text formatting and attachments.
2. Verify that the message is delivered to the intended recipient.
3. Check that message for data integrity.

   A foreign system with a MAPI-based client should preserve all rich text formatting and attachments.

   A foreign system with a non-MAPI-based client should receive the message in plain text. Any attachments should be preserved and there should be an additional attachment that contains all the information this client cannot display.
4. Create and send a message from within the foreign system's X.400 client, addressed to a local Microsoft Exchange mailbox.
5. Verify that the local user receives all messaging data (including attachments).

From Here...

In this chapter you covered the following elements:

- Install and configure an X.400 MTA Transport Stack
- Install and configure an X.400 connector, using each type of MTA Transport Stack
- Guidelines for configuring a foreign X.400 system to communicate with an Microsoft Exchange server
- Test X.400 links between Exchange servers and between an Exchange server and a foreign X.400 system for message data integrity

The following chapters will provide more information on several of the items discussed in this chapter:

- Chapter 13, "Message Transfer Configuration," to learn about setting general Message Transfer Agent options that will affect message transmission over an X.400 Connector.
- Chapter 17, "Using Directory Replication and Synchronization," to learn about setting up directory replication between Exchange sites after they have a suitable messaging link system.

CHAPTER 21

Setting Up SMTP Connections

- Learning the Exchange Internet Mail Connector
- Setting up the Internet Mail Connector
- Auditing the Internet Mail Connector
- Configuring advanced options for the Internet Mail Connector

Today, the latest craze is the Internet. Exchange provides Internet electronic mail through the use of a robust Simple Mail Transfer Protocol (SMTP) connector service. The Internet Mail Connector service is used to allow Exchange clients to send and receive messages to and from people across the Internet. Clients do not need to be directly connected to the Internet to use this functionality.

This connector is one of the core components of the Exchange server; it integrates directly with the rest of the mail services. You can configure the connector as a stand-alone solution or use it as the backbone connectivity protocol. ■

Learning the Internet Mail Connector (IMC)

The Internet Mail Connector is a versatile connector that relies on industry standards to allow seamless integration with Exchange and existing SMTP mail systems. The connector provides message transferring with any other system that uses the SMTP protocol.

Internet Standards on the Internet Mail Connector

The Internet Mail Connector (IMC) is a Windows NT service that integrates into the Exchange architecture. Users from single or multiple Exchange or MS Mail 3.x sites can communicate with the Internet via the IMC.

NOTE Client workstations do not need to have an Internet connection to use the IMC Connector. ■

The functionality provided with the IMC Connector complies with Internet standards. The service relies on a set of standards that have been ratified over the past 30 years. These standards are a set of published documents known as *Requests for Comment* (RFCs). These are the guidebooks for developing applications to be used on the Internet. Following is a list of the key standards to which the Internet Mail connector adheres:

- *RFC 821.* This RFC is the Simple Mail Transfer Protocol (SMTP) standard. RFC 821 describes the message definitions for passing or transferring mail from one computer system to another.
- *RFC 822.* This RFC, which is the continuation of RFC 821, describes the message format and structure of the data in the message. The standard covers the header information (To, From, Subject, and message body data). This RFC deals with non-text attachments by decoding the data with uuencode and uudecode encoding. If you have an attachment, the IMC converts the attachment to text and populates the body of the message with the encoded data.
- *RFC 1521.* This RFC, which defines the standard for sending attachments over the SMTP protocol, is called Multipurpose Internet Mail Extensions (MIME). This RFC breaks down the components of a message and allows different portions to be sent in separate fields. With MIME, you can attach a variety of data types (such as Microsoft Word documents, video clips, and audio files) and transmit the data without conversion. This provides ease of use for sending data between sites.
- *RFC 1554.* This RFC defines the protocol used by the legacy Microsoft SMTP gateway for MS Mail 3.x. RFC 1554 defines the message format that is created when a message is transferred through the MS SMTP gateway. This RFC is similar to RFC 822, which provides for encoding attachments into the body of the message as text.

These RFCs allow for seamless integration with other SMTP mail systems across public and private Internet networks.

Internet Mail Connector Uses

Exchange supports a variety of connection methods, using IMC as the message connector.

The following are different ways to use IMC in a production environment:

- SMTP gateway to an MS Mail Network of post offices (see fig. 21.1)

FIG. 21.1
MS Mail users can leverage the gateway in Exchange to provide Internet connectivity.

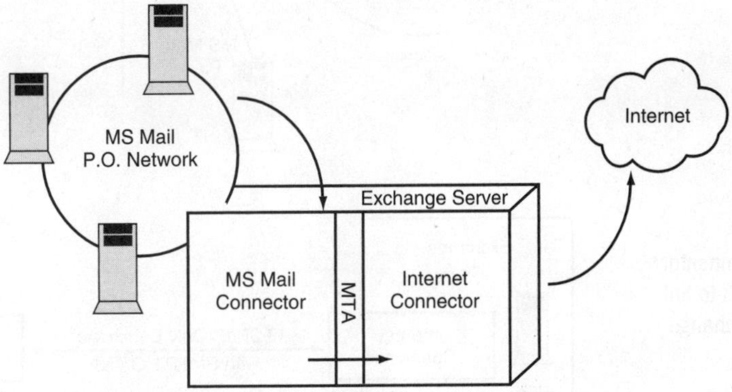

As described in Chapter 18, "Setting Up Microsoft Mail for PC Networks," MS Mail 3.x users can send and receive Internet messages through the MS Mail Connector on Exchange. In this example, Exchange acts as an Internet SMTP gateway. Exchange converts the messages to MS Mail 3.x format, using the MS Mail Connector interchange, and then transfers the messages to the MS Mail 3.x post offices with the MS Exchange MTA services.

- SMTP connector to an Exchange Network of post offices (see fig. 21.2)

  This example is similar to MS Mail 3.x use of the IMC Connector, providing SMTP connectivity from the native mail-system client to the remote SMTP mail-system recipient. This functionality is seamless to users. The advantage of having all Exchange clients using the connector is the fact that this architecture reduces the need for data-format conversions. At the same time that this connector services Exchange clients, it can service existing MS Mail clients. This example extends the preceding example by providing additional support for Exchange clients.

- Internet Mail Connector to link Exchange sites (backbone) (see fig. 21.3)

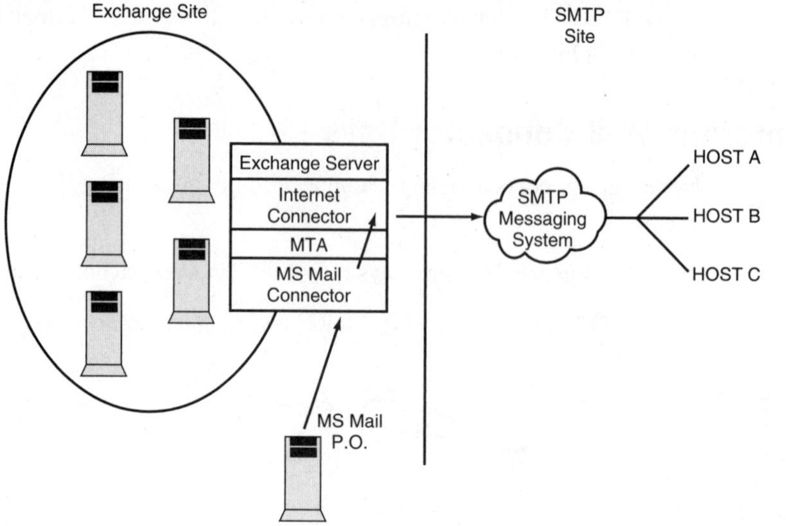

FIG. 21.2
The IMC integrates directly with the Exchange server.

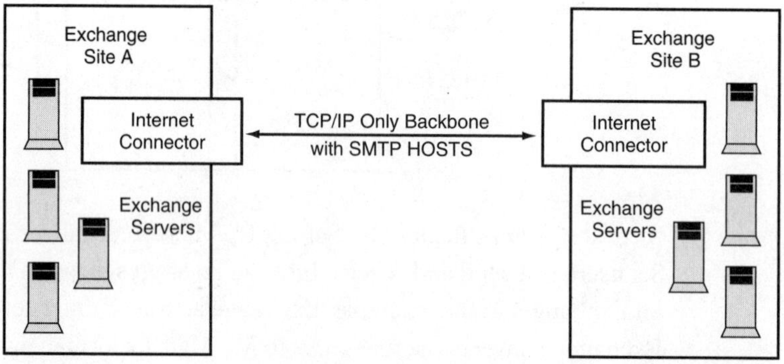

FIG. 21.3
The IMC Connector can be used to link multiple Exchange sites.

In this example, the IMC is used to link two Exchange sites. SMTP messaging is the backbone between the sites. Both Exchange sites need to be running the IMC locally. The IMC Connector then communicates with the destination IMC Connector. This is especially useful in organizations where MIS is geographically distributed. Each location can maintain its own Exchange messaging services and still provide connectivity with the other sites. Using the IMC to backbone sites puts additional overhead on the connector, which now is handling directory synchronization, folder replication, and message transfer through a single link.

Using the IMC Connector in this manner preserves the Exchange functionality of rich text-formatted messages, OLE objects, and public folder postings. This solution is a manageable solution for linking Exchange sites.

- Exchange server connecting to MS Mail 3.x with the IMC Connector (see fig. 21.4)

FIG. 21.4
The IMC Connector can be used to allow MS Mail 3.x to communicate with Exchange sites.

This example follows the backbone model. Instead of connecting with another Exchange site, however, the IMC Connector is used to create a backbone with an MS Mail site. The MS Mail site will be using the Microsoft SMTP gateway.

This solution permits immediate transmission of messages between Exchange and MS Mail sites. You do not have to configure the MS Mail Connector interchange, configure MTA services, or set up remote directory synchronization.

The MS Mail 3.x gateway product does not support many Exchange features, including OLE v2.0 objects, MIME attachments, directory synchronization through the MS Mail gateway, and multiple-host connections. The MS Mail gateway can communicate with only a single SMTP host, whereas the Exchange IMC Connector can have unlimited SMTP-host connections.

- Windows 95 client connecting to Exchange server over the Internet (see fig. 21.5)

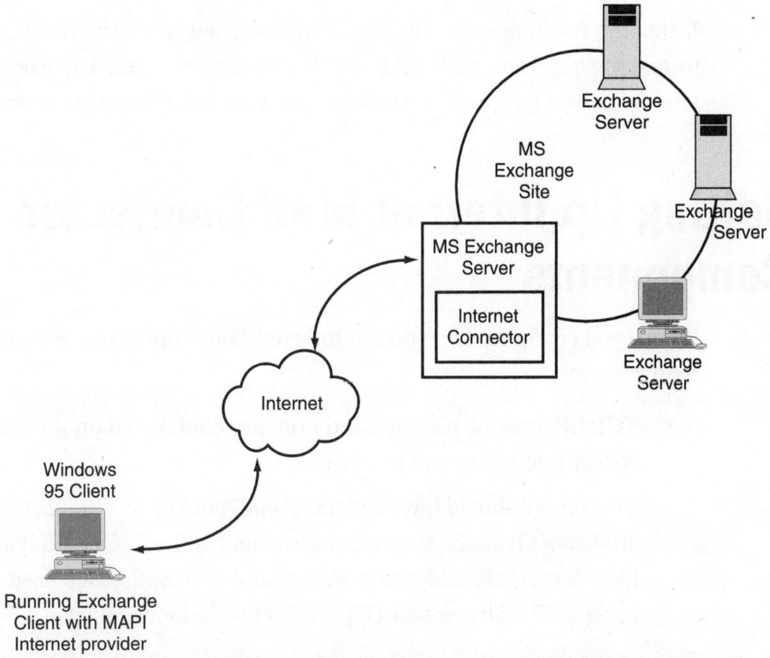

FIG. 21.5
The IMC Connector can send and receive message to Windows 95 client workstations.

This example focuses on the client connection with Exchange. A Windows 95 client with Exchange client software installed can access the Internet through a local service provider. After getting connected to the Internet, the client can transmit and receive messages through an Exchange Internet Mail Connector.

Setting Up the Internet Mail Connector Components

The Internet Mail Connector has many new features that are not available in the MS Mail 3.x SMTP gateway. These new features offer a balance of power and flexibility to route messages over SMTP networks. As described in the preceding section, you can use the IMC's rich feature set in many ways.

After it is configured, the IMC Connector transfers messages to remote SMTP mail systems by initiating a connection. When the connection is made, the messages are transferred across systems.

For incoming messages, the IMC Connector listens to a TCP/IP port for connection requests. In similar fashion, once the remote system establishes its connection with IMC, messages and data are transferred into Exchange.

Inside the Exchange site, the IMC Connector converts the message to an Exchange-format message and routes it to the Exchange recipient. The user will not notice any difference between an SMTP message and a normal Exchange message.

Setting Up Internet Mail Connector Components

Before you configure and run the Internet Mail Connector, you need to meet these requirements:

- TCP/IP must be installed and properly configured on the Exchange Windows NT server that is running the IMC .

  The server should have a static (nondynamic) Internet Protocol (IP) address. If you are using Dynamic Host Configuration Protocol (DHCP), you should exclude the IMC server's IP address from the pool of IP addresses used by DHCP. DHCP assigns IP addresses to TCP/IP clients automatically.

The reason for specifying a static IP address is that you are required to have a fully qualified Internet domain name. These values do not change dynamically with IP addresses; they are manually configured, and you would need to update them daily for the name to match the server's address.

- In the TCP/IP section of the NT server configuration, you need to enable Domain Name Server (DNS) lookups. The DNS matches common domain names (such as yourcompany.com) into a specific numeric IP address.

  You need to enter the host name and domain name of the IMC server (see fig. 21.6). In addition, you have to enter at least one value for the IP address of the DNS server. For more information on installing TCP/IP on an NT server, refer to your Windows NT user manual.

FIG. 21.6
These are the TCP/IP settings that enable DNS lookups on the Exchange server running the IMC Connector.

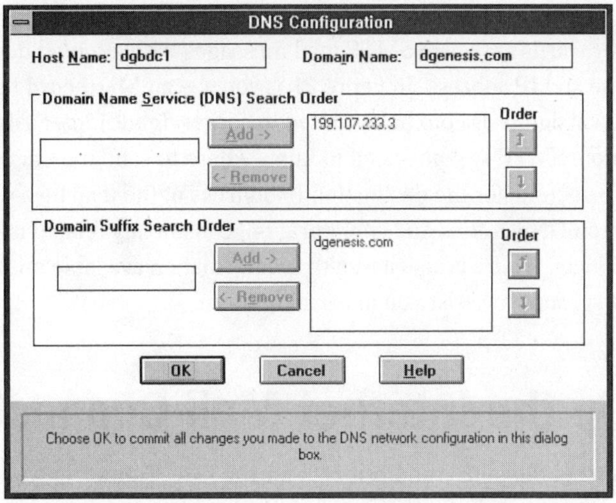

- Add the IP address, host, domain, and Mail Exchange (MX) entries in the DNS server.

  Use the IP address and the host and domain information from the Windows NT TCP/IP configuration to enter into the DNS. Adding these values to the DNS allows for name resolution. The DNS provides the function of mapping a "friendly" name to an IP address. This way, when a user enters a friendly name, such as dgbdc1.dgenesis.com, the DNS maps this name to its actual numeric IP address.

  Figure 21.7 shows an entry for a server name and then an associated IP address. In addition to the host name and IP address, add an address space entry in the IMC configuration for Internet bound Exchange messages to pass through this connector. This entry is called the Mail Exchange entry, or MX.

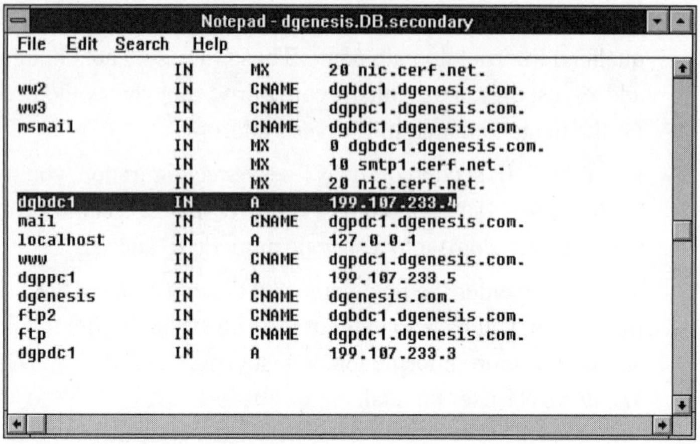

Notepad - dgenesis.DB.secondary

File Edit Search Help

```
                IN      MX      20 nic.cerf.net.
ww2             IN      CNAME   dgbdc1.dgenesis.com.
ww3             IN      CNAME   dgppc1.dgenesis.com.
msmail          IN      CNAME   dgbdc1.dgenesis.com.
                IN      MX      0 dgbdc1.dgenesis.com.
                IN      MX      10 smtp1.cerf.net.
                IN      MX      20 nic.cerf.net.
dgbdc1          IN      A       199.107.233.4
mail            IN      CNAME   dgpdc1.dgenesis.com.
localhost       IN      A       127.0.0.1
www             IN      CNAME   dgpdc1.dgenesis.com.
dgppc1          IN      A       199.107.233.5
dgenesis        IN      CNAME   dgenesis.com.
ftp2            IN      CNAME   dgbdc1.dgenesis.com.
ftp             IN      CNAME   dgpdc1.dgenesis.com.
dgpdc1          IN      A       199.107.233.3
```

FIG. 21.7
The DNS entries for server dgbdc1 in the domain dgenesis.com.

MX records associate SMTP mail messages with a routed destination host name and IP address. In figure 21.7, you see an MX record for mail destined for msmail.dgenesis.com to be routed to server dgbdc1.dgenesis.com. This way, when remote SMTP systems need to know where to send messages, they can look in the DNS records for the destination IP address of the mail messages. For more information on DNS entries and configuration, consult any related documentation for those products. There is also a wealth of information available on Internet web sites and newsgroups to assist you in learning more.

Setting Up the Internet Mail Connector

After you meet the initial requirements for the IMC Connector, you can begin to configure the connector. Following is a list of procedures to use as you configure the IMC Connector:

- Define an administrative message account
- Configure the address space serviced by the IMC Connector
- Specify the site address
- Configure connection options
- Define message-content options
- Set interoperability options
- Set specific IMC Connector message restrictions
- Management of SMTP messages

- Additional IMC Connectors
- Test the IMC Connector

You can configure all options from the Exchange Administrator program; select the Internet Mail Connector from the Connections section of the site hierarchy (see fig. 21.8).

FIG. 21.8
Selecting the Internet Mail Connector from the Exchange Administrator program.

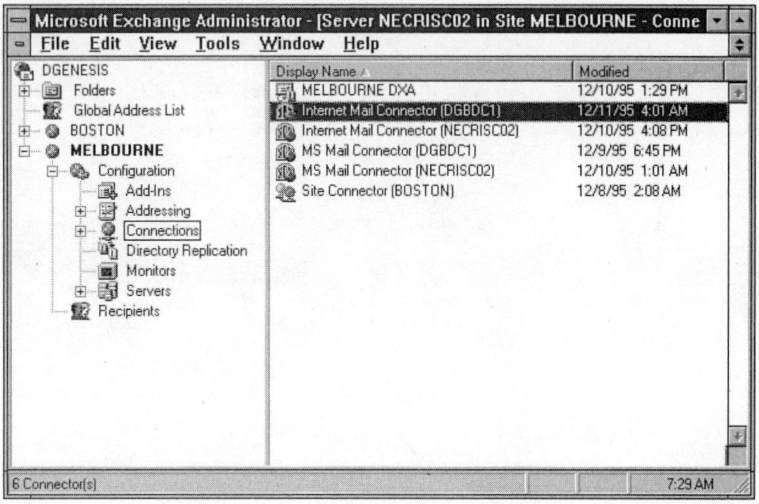

NOTE The IMC Connector is very complicated and has a multitude of options. Prepare yourself by setting aside a few solid hours to set up the IMC Connector.

Defining an Administrative Message Account

You must select an Exchange mailbox that will receive notification regarding the function of the Internet Mail Connector. This mailbox can be an administrators one or special account created for this purpose. Whichever option you choose, just make sure that the mailbox is checked periodically to catch important notfication messages sent by the connector.

1. Open the IMC Connector property pages (see fig. 21.9) for the server that you want to configure.
2. Click the Change button to the right of the Administrator's Mailbox box. The dialog box shown in figure 21.10 appears.

FIG. 21.9
A blank IMC Connector tab.

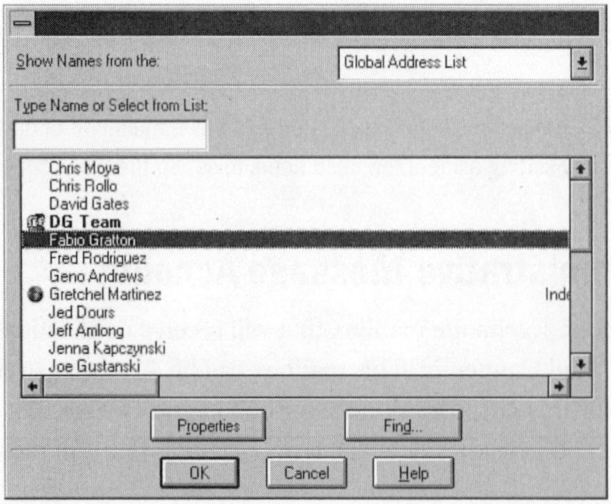

FIG. 21.10
Select the administrator message account.

The administrator message account is used to send notices of events associated with the IMC Connector and is similar to the postmaster account on the Sendmail system for UNIX. This account is the default account for message errors, bounced mail, problems with the connector, and other administrative notifications.

3. Define the notices to be sent to the administrator message account (see fig. 21.11).

From an administrative standpoint, selecting all the notifications is beneficial. If the volume of the notices is too excessive, change the administrator account to a public folder for the Exchange administrator group's use, or try to troubleshoot the cause for the notices before decreasing the notification settings.

FIG. 21.11
Define the notices to be sent to the administrator message account.

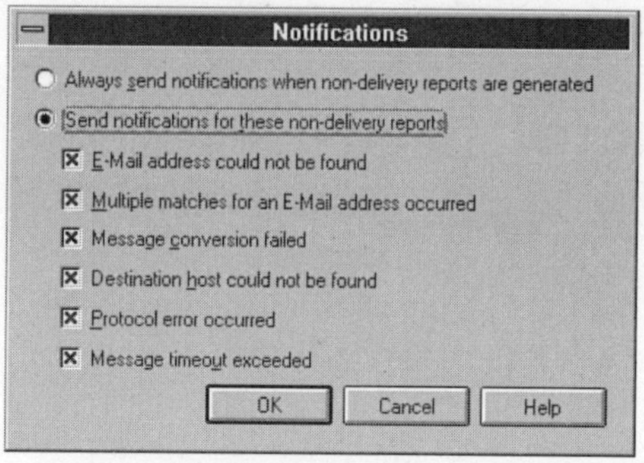

Configuring the Address Space Serviced by the IMC Connector

The address space entries for the Internet Mail Connector define which message are routed through it. You must make at least one entry in this page to activate message routing through the IMC. The following steps guide you through creating and editing address space entries.

1. From the IMC Connector property page, select the Address Space tab (see fig. 21.12).

FIG. 21.12
This property page displays Address Space entries for the IMC.

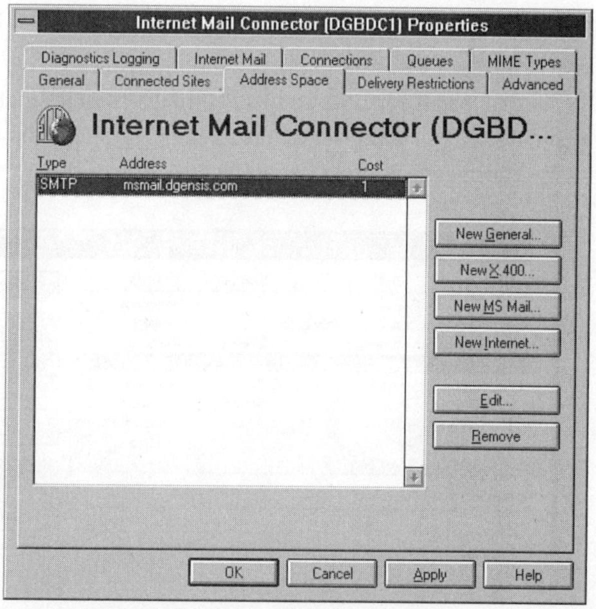

Part III
Ch 21

2. Click the New Internet address space button. The dialog box in figure 21.13 appears.

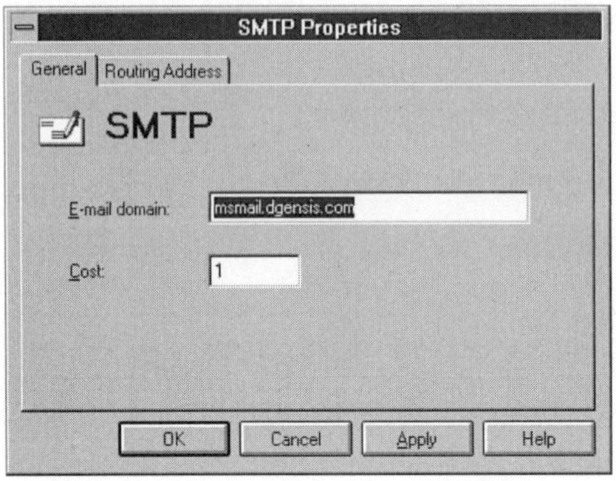

FIG. 21.13
Create a new Internet address space for the IMC Connector.

In the Address Space property page, you can enter multiple Internet domain names, MS Mail server names, X.400 names, or other connector names to route messages through this IMC.

3. Click OK to set the configuration.

Specifying the Site Address

1. From the IMC Connector property sheet, click Apply to set all the configuration settings. You see a reminder that you have to stop and restart the IMC Connector service.
2. Open the control panel services and locate the Exchange Internet Mail Connector service (see fig. 21.14). If the service is already running, stop the service, then restart it for your new setting to take effect.

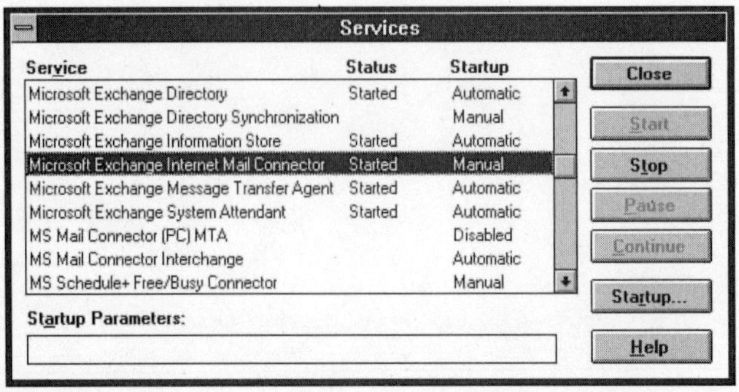

FIG. 21.14
NT service for the IMC Connector.

3. Select the "Site Addressing" icon in the Administrator program's display window and open its property pages.
4. Click the Site Addressing tab. The Services dialog box appears (see fig. 21.15).

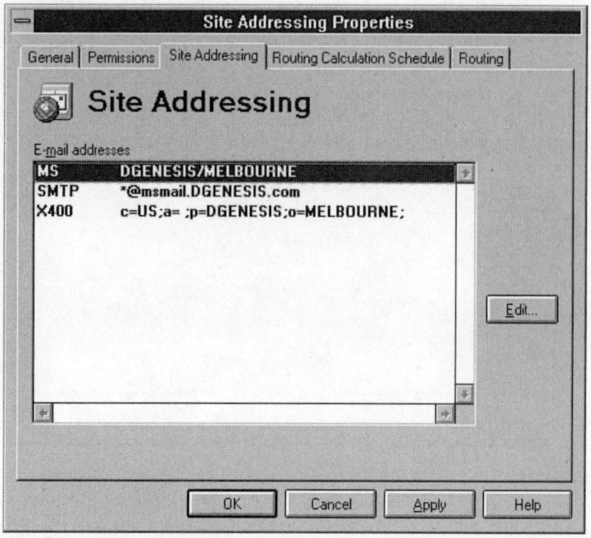

FIG. 21.15
Global site-addressing properties.

5. The addresses in the Services dialog box are the global settings for all recipients at this particular site. Make sure that the recipient address for the IMC Connector is the same as what is entered in the MX record of the DNS.

At this point, the IMC Connector should be up and running. The IMC Connector should be listening to port 25 of the TCP/IP protocol stack on the server—the port specified in RFC 821 for SMTP mail transferring. Now you can proceed to configure the additional options of the IMC Connector.

Configuring Connection Options

You can modify the settings for inbound and outbound transfer modes, connection limitations, delivery options, and message queues. Follow these steps:

1. From the IMC Connector property pages, select the Connections tab (see fig. 21.16).

FIG. 21.16
Configure the IMC Connector connections properties.

NOTE The None option is a great tool to use in debugging the IMC Connector. When this option is selected, you can keep the IMC Connector service running but restrict messages from being transferred from the site. Users will not notice any difference in their work, because messages will just queue up on the server until the transfer mode is reestablished.

2. In the Transfer Mode section, click a radio button to indicate whether messages will be incoming, outgoing, both, or neither.
3. Click the Advanced button to set the following options (see fig. 21.17):

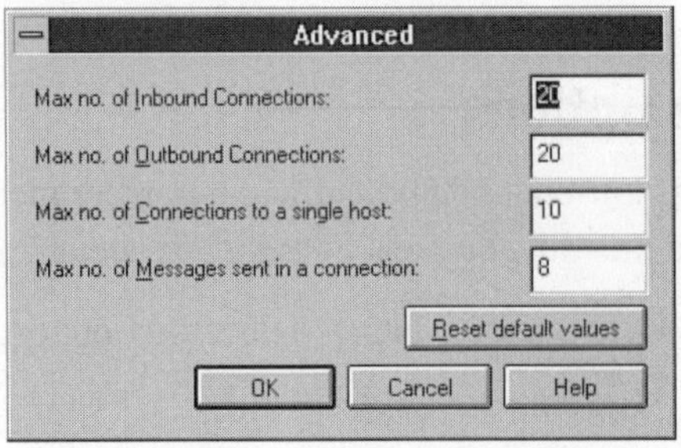

FIG. 21.17
Configure the advanced settings for the Transfer mode.

These options can be set based on the resources in your environment.

4. Configure the message delivery settings.

   The IMC Connector allows you to use the DNS to resolve SMTP Mail message routes or use a single SMTP relay host. If you choose the DNS option, the IMC attempts to connect with the various destination SMTP mail systems directly. If you do not want to have Exchange perform the actual message transfer to the remote hosts for performance or security reasons, you can specify an SMTP relay host. Exchange is not a relay host. A relay host has the capability to receive SMTP mail, look at the header destination information, and then perform the message transfer to the remote host. Typically, the smart host functionality is run on a UNIX server. The process is known as sendmail.

   The DNS option removes the need to have a UNIX server running sendmail just to relay messages to remote hosts.

   An additional option is to configure the message-delivery options based on domain. Message delivery can be based on Domain Name Service (DNS) lookup. The IMC Connector can perform a DNS request before forwarding messages to the appropriate destination. With the MS Mail 3.x SMTP gateway, you were forced to point the gateway to an existing SMTP relay host, which would actually deliver the mail to the final destination. The MS Mail 3.x SMTP gateway forced users to manage two servers to transfer Internet mail (see fig. 21.18).

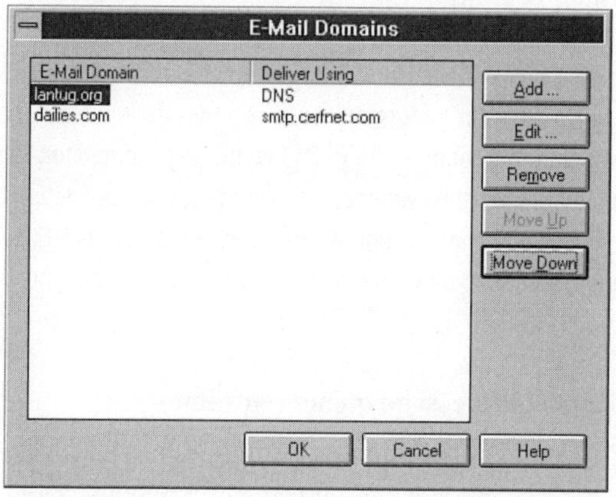

FIG. 21.18
Configure the advanced settings for the SMTP message delivery.

   This is useful if it appears the IMC is having a difficult time transferring messages to a particular remote host. You can configure an individual entry for that specific domain causing message transfer problems. Entries can be in the form of domain, sub-domains, and IP addresses. You can use wild cards as well.

5. Define inbound connections.

   You can configure the IMC to receive messages from all incoming hosts or reject remote hosts based on your input (see fig. 21.19).

FIG. 21.19
Configure the incoming connection to be accepted by the IMC Connector.

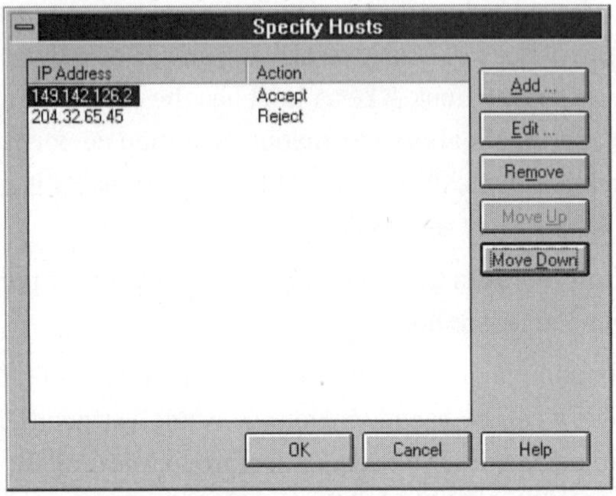

   You can specify entries only in the form of IP addresses and sub-net mask of the remote host to be rejected or accepted. This is useful when remote hosts are having a difficult time communicating with the IMC Connector or when a particular remote host has a history of transferring junk messages or corrupt data.

NOTE Typically, as your users subscribe to Internet listserv mailing groups, a wide variety of mail systems will attempt to communicate and transfer mail into the system. Some of these remote systems do not adhere to the RFCs like the IMC Connector. This can cause communication problems between the systems. Suppose that I speak English and am from the West Coast, and that my business partner speaks English and is from the East Coast. Both of us speak English, but we may not always be able to communicate if our accents affect our speaking abilities.

6. Define the Connector message queue retry intervals.

   This option is used to define the retry attempt interval for the IMC Connector, if it encounters a host to which it cannot transfer a mail message. The reason for the retry is that the remote host is too busy to process another communication request or is otherwise unavailable. The IMC Connector queues up the message and waits until the retry interval expires before trying to transfer the message to the remote host. The default setting retries the first time in 60 minutes; the subsequent retries are made at 150 percent of the set time interval.

If you use the default setting—the initial retry at 60 minutes—subsequent retries occur at 1 hour, 1.5 hours, 2.25 hours, 3.4 hours, 5 hours, 7.5 hours, and so on, for a total of 8 retries over 72 hours.

Select the message time-outs button to configure more specific retry intervals (see fig. 21.20).

FIG. 21.20
Configure the message time-out settings to drop remote connections from the IMC Connector.

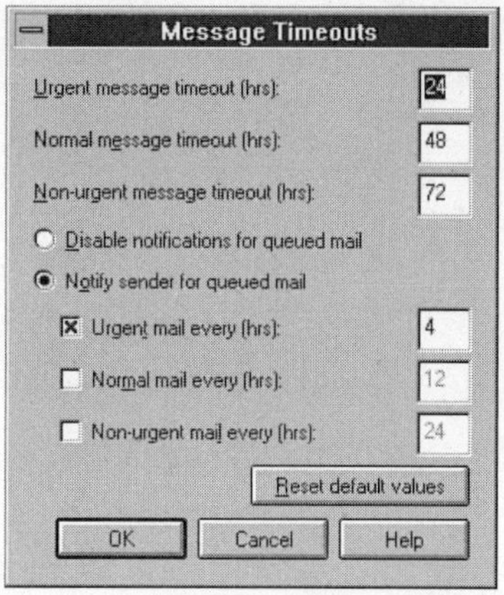

Notice the granularity of the message queue retries. You can configure a specific retry interval based on the priority level of the mail message.

Make sure to apply your configuration changes before you move to another configuration tab. Remember that you have to stop and restart the IMC Connector service after you complete your configurations.

Defining Message Content Options

This section explains how to configure the default message content format, Exchange rich text formatting options, and message formats for individual domains.

To configure the options for inbound and outbound messages, follow these steps:

1. From the IMC Connector property pages, select the Internet Mail tab.
2. The first option is to select the message content type for attachments. You have the option of configuring the IMC Connector to send and receive message via MIME or uuencode. MIME provides support for a variety of file formats, which do not get broken up or encoded into the mail message as in uuencode. MIME support separates the attachments from the text portion of the message, retaining the original format.

3. Choose the MIME character set translation standard (see fig. 21.21). The default option is to use the ISO 8859-1 standard for MIME outbound mail messages.

FIG. 21.21 Configure the MIME character set translation.

4. Use the pull-down menu to select the Non-MIME character set translation. The default option for uuencode messages is US ASCII for both inbound and outbound messages.

NOTE To send message content to the MS Mail 3.x SMTP gateway, make sure that you are using uuencode. The MS Mail 3.x SMTP gateway does not support MIME attachments. ■

5. Click the E-Mail Domain button. The E-Mail Domain dialog box appears (see fig. 21.22).

   This dialog box allows you to configure specific character sets, message content formats, and maximum message size for messages transferred through the IMC Connector.

6. Click Add to create additional e-mail domain entries, Edit to change an existing one, or Remove to delete one. When you are done with these settings, click OK to return to the Internet Mail Connector property pages. Figure 21.23 shows the Add E-Mail Domain dialog box after you click the Add button.

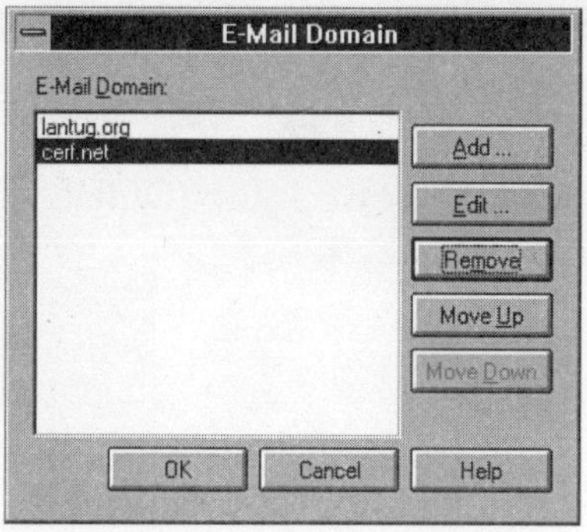

FIG. 21.22
Use this dialog box to specify message content by e-mail domain.

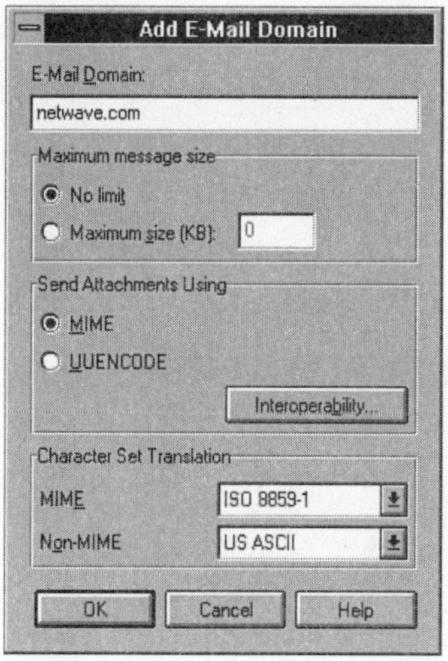

FIG. 21.23
Dialog box for creating a new e-mail domain configuration with message content options.

7. Click the MIME Types tab to define MIME attachment formats.

   From this property page, you can configure the MIME types (see fig. 21.24). MIME types include support for Microsoft Word documents, video files, audio files, HTML documents, binary executables, and other format types.

8. Click the New button to create an additional MIME type. The New MIME Type dialog box appears.

   In figure 21.25, for Microsoft Word, enter the MIME content type and the associated extension. The Microsoft Word MIME type is *application/msword* and the associated extension is *.doc*. When done, click OK to set the change and activate this new content type.

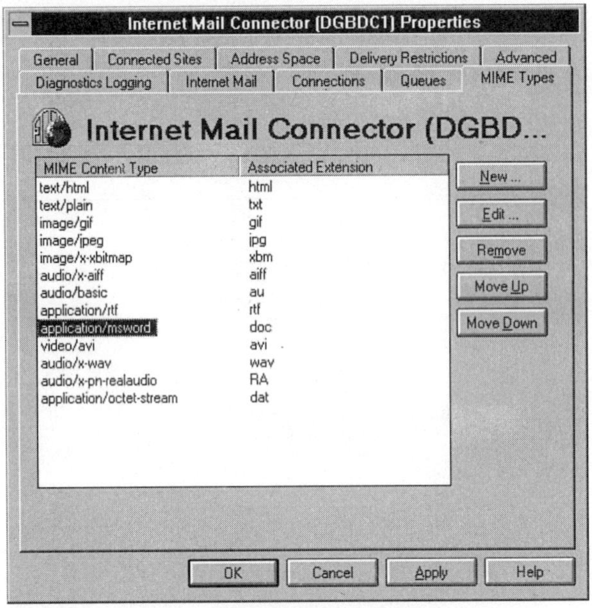

FIG. 21.24
Configure MIME attachment formats.

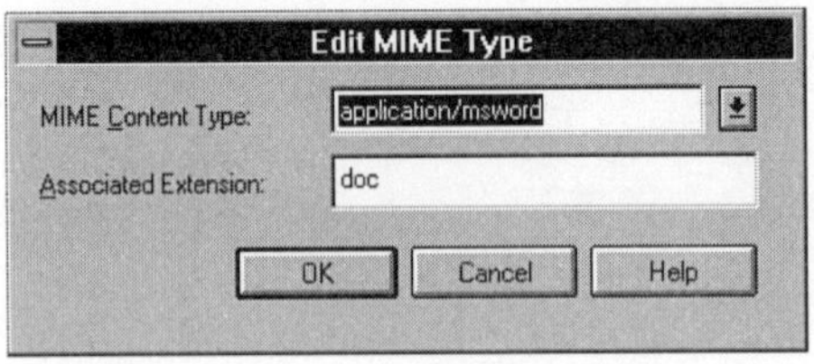

FIG. 21.25
Create a new MIME type or edit an existing type. You can configure for document formats, multimedia formats, or even application binary formats.

Setting Interoperability Options

Interoperability defines how display names are sent with outbound messages and how to set the maximum number of characters per line for outbound messages.

To set up the interoperability options for the IMC Connector, follow these steps:

1. From the IMC Connector property page, select the Internet Mail tab.
2. Click the Interoperability button in the message content section of the Internet Mail tab. The Interoperability dialog box appears (see fig. 21.26).

FIG. 21.26
Define the interoperability options for the IMC Connector.

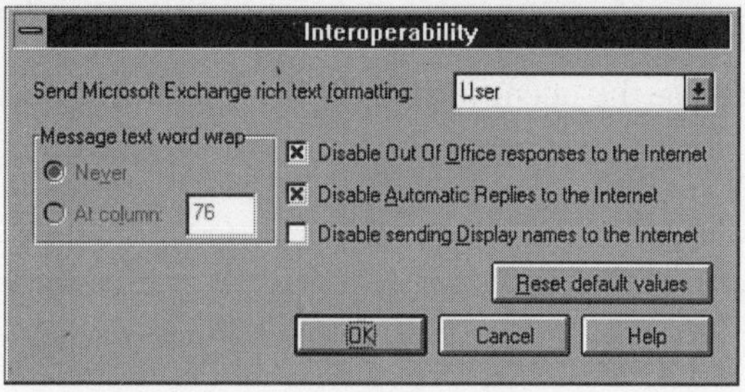

The IMC Connector sends outbound messages with the display name of the sender/creator and the sender's alias. The display name typically is the sender's full name, first and last. If you have a user named Fred Rodriguez, for example, his alias might be fredro and his display name, Fred Rodriguez. Use the interoperability settings to maintain uniformity.

You can set the following options to maintain interoperability: Message text word wrap, disable out of office response, disable automatic replies, and disable sending display names to the SMTP hosts.

In the example above, you should check the box to make sure to send the display names in the outbound messages.

In addition, you choose when to use MS Rich text formatting in messages (see fig. 21.27).

FIG. 21.27
Listed are the options of when to send RTF formatting in outbound messages.

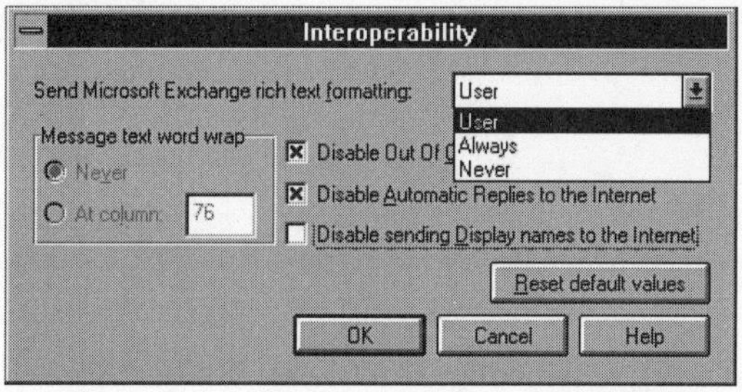

The three options allow the user to select when they wish to send RTF data, always send RTF data, or never send RTF data. If this IMC Connector only communicates with an MS Mail 3.x SMTP gateway, you should select the option to never send RTF data as the MS Mail SMTP gateway will not be able to understand this information.

3. Set the maximum number of characters per line.

   Also, if you choose the uuencode type in the Attachment section, the next window will give you the option to define the text word wrap. The default is set to 76 characters.

NOTE The MS Mail 3.x SMTP gateway expects to see 76 characters in incoming messages.

4. Define the Message size limit.
5. Open the General tab (see fig. 21.28).

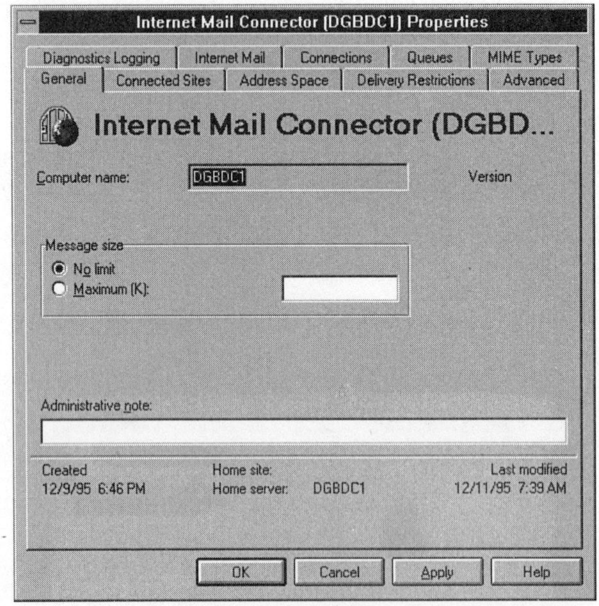

FIG. 21.28
The General tab allows you to set the maximum message size.

This option allows you to configure message limitations for the IMC Connector.

Defining IMC Connector Message Restrictions

These settings deal with the actual message settings for the IMC Connector.

1. From the IMC Connector property sheet, select the Advanced tab (see fig. 21.29). From this tab menu you can define the message parameters, maximum message transfer times, and the message transfer quotas.

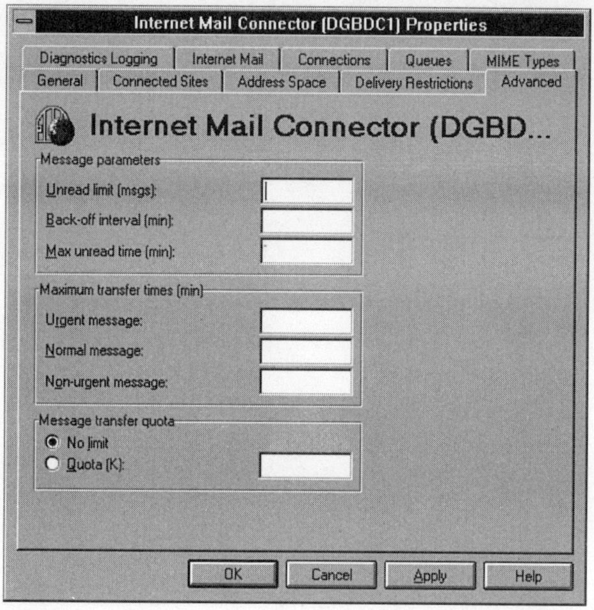

FIG. 21.29
The Advanced tab allows you to configure message transfer parameters.

Message parameters are used to limit the number of unread messages, to set the time to back off from message transfer, and to set a maximum unread message time. The values are set in the number of messages, and in the number of minutes.

The second portion of the Advanced tab menu defines the maximum transfer times broken down by urgent, normal, and non-urgent messages. These values are set in minutes. And can be used to close connections that would otherwise be held open for long periods of time. This quota helps to reduce the amount of traffic to single hosts.

The last set of values is used to set upper limits for the size of messages transferred from the IMC Connector to the remote hosts.

2. Click Apply when done modifying these entries to set your new values.
3. Next select the "Delivery Restrictions" tab menu (see fig. 21.30). Use this tab to restrict message delivery to certain users or to restrict those users from sending outbound SMTP mail through this IMC.

   You have the option to either grant users access to the ICM Connector or on the flip side, deny users access to the ICM Connector. On the left panel you can manage the usage by adding users who can connect. On the right panel, you choose who cannot connect. Figure 21.31 shows the two windows of the IMC's Delivery Restrictions property page.

FIG. 21.30
Users can be granted access rights to use the IMC Connector or restricted access to the IMC Connector.

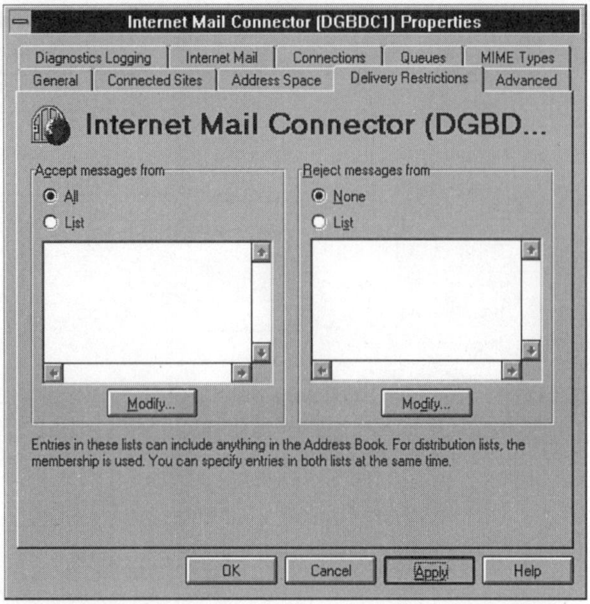

FIG. 21.31
You can manage access down to the user level.

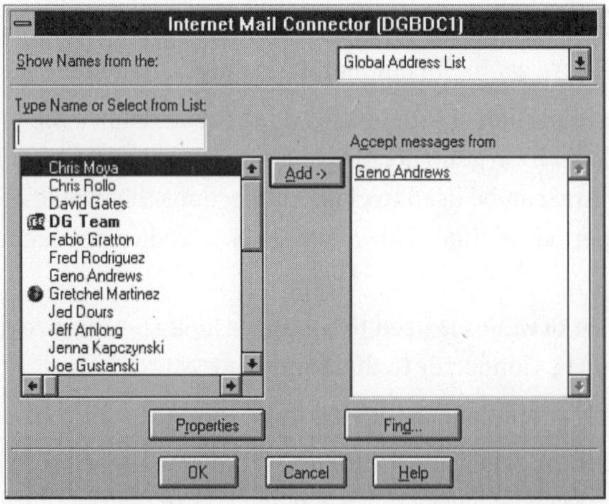

In addition to individual mailboxes, you can set delivery restrictions to distribution lists and custom recipients as well.

Managing SMTP Messages

After you configure the IMC Connector and have the NT service running, you can configure the following additional features to assist you in managing the connector.

1. From the IMC Connector property pages, select the "Internet Mail" tab.
2. Your first option is to check the "Enable message tracking" field. This will log information about the daily IMC transactions to a common log, that can be browsed to find transmission data on a particular message.
3. Your next option is on the Queues tab (see fig. 21.32). In this tab, you can get real-time statistics on the current processing of IMC Connector data.

FIG. 21.32
This tab provides real-time data about the status of messages in the ICM connector queue.

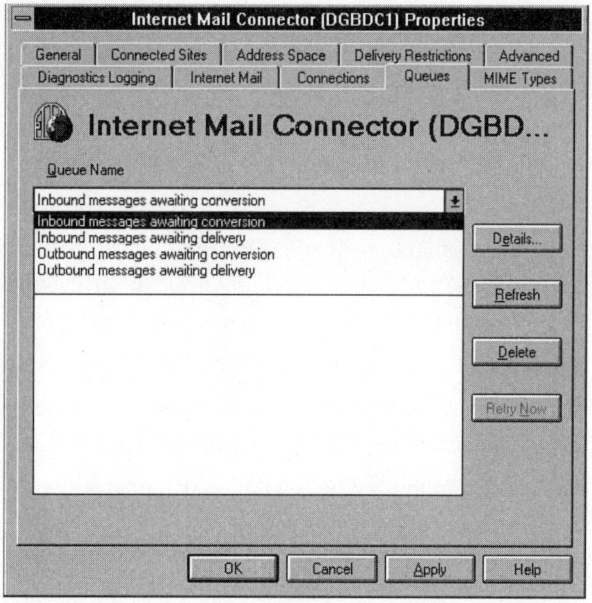

If you check the queue and see that several messages are waiting to be processed or transferred to another system, you can begin to diagnose where you may have a problem.

4. Select the Diagnostics Logging tab (see fig. 21.33).

FIG. 21.33
From this tab, you can specify what level of service logging you need for the IMC Connector.

Logged information gets written to the common NT event logs. On the left panel, the IMC service (known as MSExchangeIMC in the event log) is listed. The right panel lists the actual log category options. These include:

- Initialization/Termination monitors that the service starts and stops.
- Content conversion is the process of converting message data from native SMTP into Exchange native format and vice-versa.
- Addressing monitors the resolution of e-mail addresses with display names and foreign names.
- Message Transfer is the process that communicates with the remote hosts and transfers message from one system to the other.
- SMTP Interface event refers to the core application service operation.
- Internal processing is the service that routes the data inside of the IMC Connector.
- SMTP protocol log records all events having an impact from the protocol stack or network communication.
- Message Archival processes the IMC Connector temporary data while connections are being restored.

Typical configuration of auditing or logging is to keep each active process set to the minimum log level. In the event that the IMC Connector queue begins to back up, you may want to increase the logging level. Turning the logging on to maximum, will flood the event log with many additional messages for you to sort through. Once you have solved the problem, I would suggest returning your logging levels back to the minimum level.

5. Select the Connected Sites tab for the option to view the Exchage sites reached through this IMC. To configure routing to an additional site, click the New button at the bottom of the tab (see fig. 21.34).

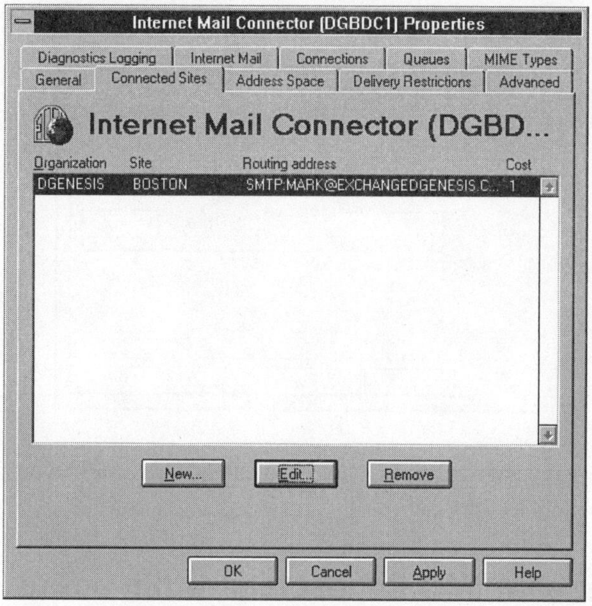

FIG. 21.34
This option shows the additional sites connected to the IMC Connector.

Adding a connected site creates additional routes for messages. Additional Exchange sites, as well as MS Mail 3.x post offices, can be routed to take advantage of the IMC Connector.

6. Enter the organization and site of the additional routed post offices when adding a connected site (see fig. 21.35).
7. After you enter the site name, click the "routing address" tab to complete the new message route. The Properties dialog box, shown in figure 21.36, appears.

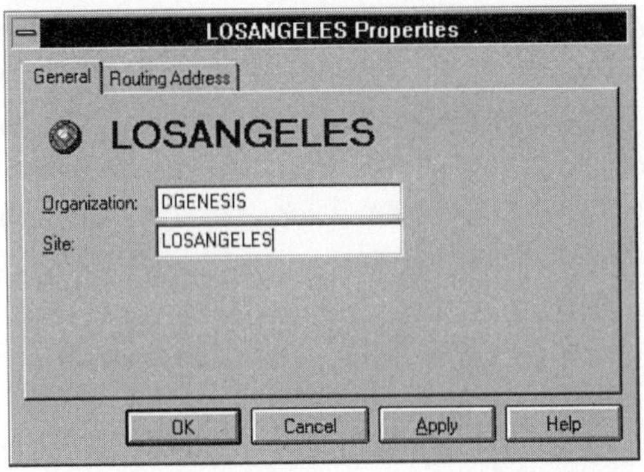

FIG. 21.35 Enter a value for the organization and the site.

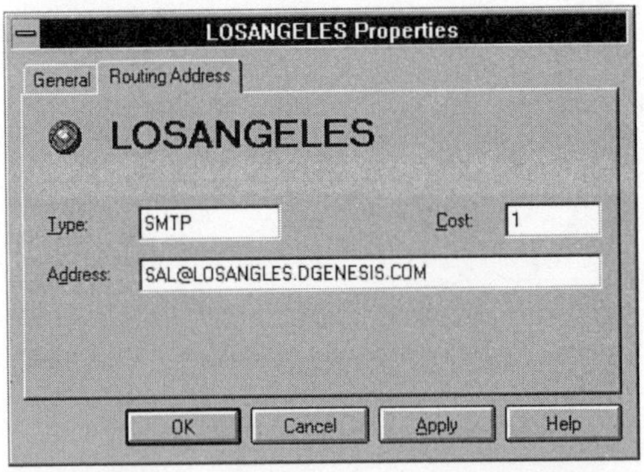

FIG. 21.36 Complete the message route with a message type and post office.

8. Enter a type of mail connection. You can add an SMTP type and include the destination mailbox address.

Defining Additional IMC Connectors within a Site

The IMC Connector runs as a single NT service per server. Typically, you have one connector per organization to service the public Internet connection. Additional connections may be needed if you are going to use an SMTP backbone to move messages throughout the organization. The IMC Connector is robust and can handle several thousand users. To balance the load, you can set up additional IMC Connectors to distribute the processing.

To allow coexistence between two or more IMCs you must perform the following adjustments:

1. In the Address Space tab, modify the entries for existing connectors to accommodate the address space of the new connector.

2. In the Connections tab, modify the maximum inbound and outbound sessions, along with what is specified in any new connectors.
3. Finally, for the new connector to resolve properly in the DNS, you must modify the DNS or host file to reflect a new connector's IP address.

Following are special routing suggestions for sites that have multiple IMCs:

- If your organization has multiple domains within the SMTP mail system, consider having each connector handle messages for one specific domain.
- If your site has relatively balanced incoming and outgoing SMTP messages, consider configuring one connector to receive SMTP mail and the other to send SMTP mail.

Testing the IMC Connector

When the configuration of the service connector is complete, the last thing to do (after you stop and restart the service) is test the connection. Use the following steps to test your Internet mail connection.

First, send a message from an Exchange client on your site to a remote SMTP server. Verify that the message was properly received.

Examine the body of the message to make sure that any attachments came through without a problem.

From the remote host, send a message back to the IMC Connector. Verify that the message was properly routed to the appropriate mailbox. If the message is delayed or does not reach the destination mailbox, you must track it down by using Exchange's troubleshooting tools. Refer to Chapter 24 for more information of such tools. A good place to start to verify the working state of the IMC Connector is first the IMC Queues tab and then the Windows NT Event Viewer for any alert messages.

From Here...

The IMC Connector is a full-featured SMTP Internet Mail Connector. The IMC Connector offers numerous configuration selections to give the administrator full control of the service. In addition to being a service, the IMC Connector architecture is scaleable to include MS Mail post offices, Exchange sites, and Internet access clients. The IMC Connector extends Exchange into the Internet.

This chapter explained the connection between Exchange and remote SMTP mail systems. For more information, see the following chapters:

- Chapter 8, "Planning and Migrating to External Systems," explains the steps associated with implementing the Internet Mail Connector.
- Chapter 24, "Monitoring Your Organization," helps you manage these server components.
- Chapter 26, "Diagnostic and Troubleshooting Tools," helps you to debug connectivity and message routing problems.

CHAPTER 22

Exchange Performance Tuning and Capacity Planning

- **Important performance optimizing concepts and definitions**
- **How to use the Windows NT Performance Monitor with Exchange**
- **Techniques to detect and remedy bottlenecks in hard disk usage, memory, and network usage**
- **How to use Loadsim to run performance tests on your Exchange servers**

At one time or another, everyone has experienced having to sit tight and wait—for example, at the doctor's office, or in traffic jams at rush hour. At such times, life seems to move too slowly. The same can happen with respect to computer operations that seem to take forever. In particular, this chapter discusses what situations can cause Exchange to operate sluggishly. Your time, and that of your users, is precious. The sections in this chapter give you tools to solve your problems. You also learn some answers to that simple question, "How many users can Exchange support?"

This chapter also touches on capacity planning so that your server and network can stay ahead of their workload. ■

NOTE The examples presented in this chapter might not completely match your environment. It is extremely important you recognize your environment's unique elements, and move with the most appropriate tuning strategy.

The "Art" of Performance Tuning

As you may have heard before, tuning is more of an art than a science. There are no mystic techniques that detect and tune all Exchange servers in all situations. A majority of the time, you'll find yourself learning how individual system components work together producing a result. Then, you must consider the trade-offs between the different results. For example, you may want to adjust your system components to provide more stability at the cost of slower performance.

Defining Users

Before you can answer the question, "How many users can an Exchange server support?" you need to understand the types of Exchange users in your organization.

Their usage patterns can range from reading and generating a few messages each week to hundreds every day. A small percentage of the user population, therefore, can be responsible for a majority of usage. It's a bit like driving in the left lane on the highway when you encounter some traffic. There's always one slowpoke who seems to cause the traffic to slow down.

Overall, you must understand the different types of users (light or heavy) within your organization, as well as their daily tasks.

Defining Servers

Obviously, each organization has purchased hardware specifically for its business needs. Consider a centralized company with one main location, and several warehouses and sales offices distributed throughout the country. The firm might house most of its computing power in corporate headquarters in the form of high-end servers. The company then places cheaper, low-end machines in the remote offices. The high-end servers meet the needs of power users in headquarters, while remote field personnel are satisfied with low-end machines to dial into and receive e-mail.

Another company might have several independent business units throughout the country. In this firm, middle-end servers are used to provide computing power as close to the customer as possible. Therefore, each business unit can provide the fastest service.

You need to understand your company's use of server resources, as well as distinguish between low- and high-end machines (CPU speed and RAM) as defined by your organization.

Defining Load

When monitoring a server, you will notice its workload rising as more users connect and begin to work on it. In addition, you might notice other remote servers connecting to the server (through Exchange's connectors), therefore generating even more load. However, the remote servers have users connecting and asking their local servers to perform remote tasks. These remote user requests are generating the load on your local server.

All server load, therefore, is ultimately generated by users' requests.

Direct versus Background Requests

When users ask the server to open an unread message, they cause the server to perform that task as a *direct* result of the users' request. As such, a server's workload rises in direct proportion to the number of users working directly with it. On an Exchange server that is only serving users, direct requests make up most of the load. Direct requests are also synchronous in nature. As illustrated in figure 22.1, all elements of the request initiate by user requests and are completed in the proper sequence.

FIG. 22.1
All elements of a Direct Request are completed in the order in which they are received.

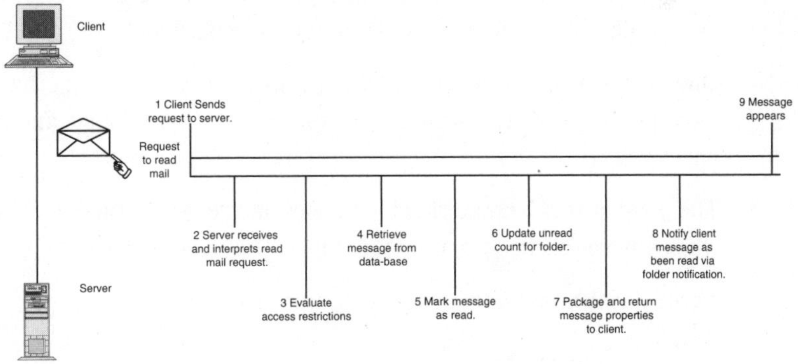

Background requests occur when a server is performing a task *related to* or *on behalf of* a user's request. Some examples of these tasks include replicating public folders and directory service information, expanding distribution lists, performing background maintenance, and transferring and delivering mail messages. Similar to direct requests, the load due to background requests is still proportional to the number of users directly connected. However, background requests occur asynchronously. Users, therefore, do not need to be directly connected to initiate this work.

In the context of background requests, delivering mail places most of the load on the server. The resources consumed for message delivery are directly proportional to the volume of mail generated by your users. Therefore, accurately determining what types of "users" are within your organization is key to tuning Exchange.

Remember, direct and background requests create different types of load on the server. You can measure this with the tools that this chapter describes.

How Many Users Can Exchange Support?

When a user initiates a request, the server uses one or more of its hardware resources to complete the task. Some examples of resources are the CPU, Memory, and the Network Card. Suppose a request requires one second of CPU time and two seconds of disk time—and that these cannot overlap. Assume also there is no other process that will interfere with this request's execution. The disk, therefore, is the "bottleneck" of the operation as it is the resource that expends the most time during a request's execution.

For example, two users issue the same request. Requests arrive at the server spaced three seconds apart. Each will be serviced and each user will not notice any unusual delays (other than the typical three-second response).

If the second request arrives one second earlier, however, a bottleneck momentarily forms as the server is placed under a slightly heavier load. Consequently, the second user notices a slightly longer (one second), delay in response time.

Once users begin to connect, and requests begin to queue up, the bottleneck becomes more pronounced. The server will experience a greater load, and there will be some unhappy users.

The point at which server load increases and response time becomes unacceptable is when you've reached the number of users Exchange, given the hardware, can support.

Three variables exist that will affect response time:

- User requests
- Number of users on one server
- Capacity of server hardware

As the number of user requests grows, so does response time. The same relationship is true for users per server. Hardware capacity has the opposite relationship: As it increases, so does its capability to handle more users and requests, therefore decreasing response time.

The next section shows you how to make your operation more efficient by tuning existing resources and planning for your users' demands.

Using Exchange's Performance Tuning Tools

Three tools exist that can help you tune your server, reduce response time, and make your operation more efficient.

- Performance Optimizer—this tool ships with Exchange and optimizes a server's configuration after asking a series of usage questions, for example, total number of users. This tool is the easiest to use and can be run immediately after Exchange's setup.
- Performance Monitor—this handy utility ships with Windows NT Server and provides several graphical views on Exchange and the way it utilizes hardware resources.
- Loadsim—this program ships with Exchange and generates the load of hundreds of virtual clients from one physical computer. You can configure the type of user, for example, light or casual. Loadsim determines the possible response time given your current hardware and software configuration.

NOTE For best results, use Loadsim after employing Performance Optimizer and Performance Monitor. ■

Using the Performance Optimizer

The Performance Optimizer automatically analyzes and optimizes key hardware for the best performance with Exchange.

The Optimizer first analyzes the server's logical drives. Then, it determines the most effective location for the MTA, information store, directory, and transaction log files. Specifically, the Optimizer locates the logical drive with the quickest sequential access time, and uses it for the transaction log files. The Optimizer then locates the logical drive with the fastest random access and uses it for the server's particular role. For example, a dedicated backbone server moving messages to other sites reserves its swiftest random access drive for MTA files. A public folder-only server will use its hard drive for the public information store files. Keep in mind that the Performance Optimizer can only examine a drive down to the logical, not the physical level. If you have divided your physical hard drive into sections or you have partitioned a RAID array into multiple logical drives, the Performance Optimizer cannot provide a drive configuration that will give you increased performance.

The Performance Optimizer also analyzes the total amount of physical RAM and determines the necessary amount of memory for the directory and information store.

Although you can run the Performance Optimizer immediately after setup, you should consider running it again after the following changes:

- Adding or removing a connector
- Changing a server's role within a site, for example, when a backbone server becomes a public folder server
- Changing or upgrading any major hardware component, such as RAM, CPU, hard drives, or network adapter

Using the Performance Monitor

An Exchange system should be structured so its resources are used efficiently and distributed fairly among the users. Performance Monitor (Perfmon) monitors specific system resources so you can meet your system structure goals.

Many times, you might be motivated to solve all problems the instant they appear. In fact, you might find your motivation dramatically increasing when users loudly display their unhappiness. To be prepared for such problems, you should first review Perfmon before moving too quickly in one direction. This can be accomplished by using the set of overview counters. Presented later in the chapter, these counters will keep you from plunging too quickly and deeply into a dilemma, only to discover that you've missed the problem. When your system is under a load you want to monitor, bring up all the overview counters in Perfmon. Then, you can determine which resource is being overworked.

Each section that follows has been listed in order of influence to Exchange's performance. Within each section, each counter is listed in the format *Object*: Counter. This will help you locate the particular counter within the Performance Monitor.

NOTE The "How to Detect "and "What to Do" sections presented a little later are by no means exhaustive. You might determine, for example, that you don't have enough RAM for Exchange, and that the suggestions listed in these sections do not adequately address the issue. You will want to investigate the issue further by referencing the Optimizing Windows NT volume included in the NT Resource Kit.

Using the Disk Subsystem

With most Exchange systems, the disk subsystem has the most influence on performance.

The primary consideration with the disk subsystem is not size but the ability to handle multiple random reads and writes quickly. For example, when Exchange users open their inboxes, the set of properties in the default folder view must be read for approximately the first 20 messages. If the property information is not in the cache, it must be read from the information store on disk. Likewise, a message transferred from one server to another must be written to disk before the receiving server acknowledges receipt of the message. This is a safety measure to prevent message loss during power outages. Now imagine the read and write activity of 300 heavy e-mail users on one server. Their combined requests would generate a multitude of random traffic on the disk subsystem.

CAUTION

Sometimes, you see extremely high %Disk Times and think that your subsystem is bottlenecked. However, you want to examine other overview counters before going in one direction. For example, when available memory drops to critical levels, NT will begin to page or write unused data or code to the hard drive to make room for more active programs. With extreme resource starvation, your disk subsystem can be reading and writing furiously and appear to be bottlenecked. Looking at other general disk counters in Perfmon will validate this illusion.

However, when you examine both memory and disk subsystem counters, you'll notice that during prolonged memory paging, disk activity increases.

The solution is to add more memory, not to increase your disk subsystem capacity.

The following sections will provide you with some information to help to detect hard disk bottlenecks and some tips on how to improve disk efficiency on your Exchange servers.

Physical Disk: % Disk Time

Disk Time is the percentage of elapsed time that the selected disk drive is busy servicing read or write requests. In other words, this counter provides an indication of how busy your disk subsystem is over the time period you're measuring in Perfmon. A consistent average over 95% indicates significant disk activity.

Physical Disk: Disk Queue Length

This counter measures the number of requests that are waiting to use disk subsystem. This counter should average less than 2% for good performance. Use the Disk Queue Length counter combined with the % Disk Time counter, to give you an exceptional overview of your disk subsystem's workload.

Both counters can monitor either your server's physically installed disk spindles or RAID bundles.

Inproving Disk Access Efficiency

Separate All Transaction Logs

The public and private information stores both utilize a transaction log that is written sequentially to disk. If possible, place the logs into separate physical spindles, preferably with the private store on the fastest drive.

Install Additional Hard Disks

You can separate Windows NT processes (paging file, event viewer log, Dr. Watson logs), and Exchange processes (message tracking logs, Microsoft Mail connection post office, directory database, Internet Mail connector logs) to enhance performance. You can also separate the public and private information stores transaction logs to separate disks or arrays for even more performance.

Overall, if you have a RAID subsystem, installing more drives yields faster throughput.

Install Faster Hard Disks and Drive Controllers

Choose a disk with a low seek time, which means the time required to move the disk drive's heads from one track of data to another. The ratio of time spent seeking as opposed to time spent transferring data is usually 10 to 1.

Determine whether the controller card does 8-bit, 16-bit, or 32-bit transfers. The more bits in the transfer operation, the faster the controller moves data.

Use RAID Disk Striping to Increase Performance

Use RAID 0 (disk striping) to increase overall capacity for random reads and writes. You will need at least two physical drives for RAID 0. Use RAID 5 (disk striping with parity) for slightly less performance, but more fault tolerance. You will need at least three physical drives for RAID 5.

If you implement RAID at the hardware level, choose a controller card with a large (4 megabytes) on-board cache.

Memory Considerations in Exchange

When Exchange runs, it only keeps portions of data needed, referred to as pages, in memory at any one time. When it needs a page of data that is not in RAM (page fault), NT will load that page into physical memory from a peripheral, which is usually the hard drive. The average instruction in memory executes in nanoseconds, which is one-billionth of a second, and hard drive seek and access times are in milliseconds. Therefore, NT must run 100,000 times slower than normal to retrieve a page from disk.

Keep in mind that Exchange needs a minimum of 32MB of RAM.

How to Detect Memory Bottlenecks

The following sections will assist you in detecting detrimental system performace caused by improper use of Random-Access Memory. Also, you will learn some techniques to better handle memory usage on your Exchange servers.

Overview counter—Memory: Pages/sec

Pages/sec reports the number of pages read or written to a disk to resolve page faults. You can turn this on when your system is under a typical load. If this counter averages above 5, a memory bottleneck is starting to form, and your disk subsystem is beginning to take a beating.

Add memory

You will want to add more memory until paging stops or occurs minimally. Afterwards, be sure to run Performance Optimizer to adjust Exchange's memory caches.

Use Multiple Paging Files

If your disk subsystem supports concurrent I/O requests, using multiple paging files usually improves system performance. Be sure to place the paging file on your fastest hard drive, and experiment with separating NT's paging file from Exchange's transaction log files.

Remove Unnecessary Services

Disable any unneeded services, protocols, and device drivers. Even idle components consume some memory and contribute to general system overhead.

The next section will discuss performance issues related to your network infrastructure.

Network Card Considerations with Exchange Server

A network by its heterogenous nature is full of potential performance bottlenecks. A company full of servers and clients talking in different protocols can often cause poor performance with Exchange. The following sections will help you to detect poor network performance with Exchange and help you improve it.

When a network bottleneck forms, one of the following three scenarios can result:

- Server Overload

  The server doesn't respond within a reasonable time to users' requests given its current capacity. Sometimes this is due to an overload of another resource, for example, the disk subsystem.

- Network Overload

  The network doesn't respond within a reasonable time. The reason is that the load of the users' requests has exceeded the capacity of the physical medium. In other words, the network has run out of Net Available Bandwidth (NAB).

  Although the counters presented in the following section will indicate that the network or a specific link is overloaded, you will want to use Microsoft's SMS product or a packet sniffer to be certain.

- Network Corruption

  The network is periodically transmitting corrupt data. In this case, the load is on both the server and the network due to the fact that each bad transmission requires a retransmission.

How to Detect Client Side Bottlenecks

The following counters are available to clients running NT:

NWLink: Bytes Total/sec (IPX/SPX)

Network Interface: Bytes Total/sec (TCP/IP)

NetBEUI: Bytes Total/sec

If you want to measure a client's workload, use the appropriate counter for your protocol. When your overview counters are generally idle, but your network counters are high, you can usually infer that your network has a bottleneck on the client end. This means that your client is doing most of its work gabbing with the network.

This counter also gives you an indication of how much load this client is placing on the network.

Redirector: Network Errors/sec

This counts serious network errors between the redirector and one or more servers. It applies to any protocol running on the client station, and shows if you have a network corruption problem. Each error is logged in detail in NT's Event Log.

This counter should normally be zero.

How to Detect—Server Side Bottlenecks

Server: Bytes Total/sec

This counter measures most of the meaningful server activity, and provides an insight into the server's load. It also provides an insight into how much load this server is contributing to the network's overall load.

Server: Sessions Errored Out

This counter measures the number of client sessions that are closed due to unexpected network errors. If this counter rises on one server, you might have a faulty network card. If the counter increases on several servers, check into the LAN infrastructure itself, such as routers, hubs, bridges, physical cabling, or connections, to determine whether you have a more serious network corruption issue.

This counter should normally be zero.

NOTE All of the following Exchange counters are available in Perfmon after you have installed Exchange.

MSExchangeMTA: Messages/sec

Messages/sec monitors the number of messages the MTA sends and receives every second. In other words, it measures the traffic generated by message flow. This is a quick way to focus on message traffic sent to other servers. For more specific information on message traffic, refer to the message tracking logs.

MSExchangeMTA: Messages Bytes/sec

Similar to the preceding counter, this counts the sums of the number of bytes in each message the MTA sends and receives each second. In other words, it reports the amount of message traffic measured in bytes.

MSExchangeISPublic: Rate of Open Message operations

This counter measures the rate at which messages are opened in the public folder. Overall, it measures public folder use. You can use this to determine whether public folder activity is balanced among servers.

MSExchangeDS: Reads/sec

This counter measures the amount of traffic generated by directory synchronizations.

NOTE You might be wondering what is a good figure for *Server*: Bytes Total/sec or for *MSExchangeMTA*: Messages/sec. The truth is that there is no simple answer. The reason is that your network has far too many variables.

Next, you might be wondering what are the maximum values. Again, there are no simple answers. For example, how could you find the maximum speed of your car? You can probably discover this by driving as fast as possible. But notice all the variables that will affect your maximum speed. Do you test drive the car up or down a hill, at sea level or at 10,000 feet? Whether you test drive on a cold or a hot day will affect the result. For example, cold air is denser and provides a performance boost, especially for turbo and supercharged engines.

The best approach is to drive your system through many conditions until you get a feel for its normal ranges or personality. To assist you in this process, you can use Loadsim which creates a synthetic load of hundreds of users on your system. While running your simulation, crank up Perfmon to monitor the load. ■

The following sections include suggestions that will improve network performance among your Exchange servers.

Apply Faster Hardware on Heavy Traffic Links

For the most leverage, you should apply hardware upgrades to machines generating the most traffic, as well as servers on the heaviest traffic links. This will provide a system-wide balance for your Exchange environment.

You can use a combination of the counters mentioned in the previous sections to determine which machine is generating traffic. A product such as Microsoft SMS can determine which network links experience the greatest load.

Segment your Network

If the *Server*: Bytes Total/sec or corresponding client counter begins to reach the maximum bandwidth of the network link to which your server is connected, you should consider segmenting your network. On an Ethernet segment, this value is approximately 1.2 megabits per second, once you include the overhead of the network.

Match the Network Card to the System Bus

If your client or server has a 32-bit bus, use a 32-bit adapter card. Overall, you should use the fastest network card and matching bus available.

Increase Your Bandwidth

If you determine your network is overloaded, increase its bandwidth by upgrading to faster network link technology; for example, Fast Ethernet, FDDI, or ATM.

Upgrade Your System Processor

Exchange is tightly integrated with NT. Therefore, it can take full advantage of a more advanced processor or multiple processors. You should eliminate all other bottlenecks before investigating the processor.

How to Detect Network Bottlenecks

Processor: % Processor Time or *System*: % Total Processor Time

Either one of these counters will determine whether your CPU is overloaded. These counters measure the total time your system is executing programs (non-idle threads). If either counter averages over 95%, your CPU is probably eperiencing a bottleneck. The System counter is useful for multiprocessor systems. The reason is that it averages the processor use for all installed processors.

When to Upgrade or Add Processors

You can upgrade to the fastest processor available. If this has been done, add additional processors if your hardware supports symmetrical multiprocessing. Keep in mind that NT Supports MIPS and Alpha, as well as Intel processors.

Overall, the addition of another CPU will typically give a better performance increase than upgrading to a faster single processor. The reason is that the multithreaded design of all Microsoft BackOffice products enables superior performance in a multiple processor environment.

Off-Peak Scheduling for the Processor

You might also consider scheduling processor intensive activities to off-peak hours.

Using Loadsim

Loadsim can help you measure the response time using an artificially generated server load. Loadsim can also measure "acceptability" by weighting certain actions that are perceived as more important by the user.

Calculating Acceptable Server Response Times

Loadsim measures two items with respect to an Exchange server: response time and "acceptability." To measure response time, Loadsim uses the 95th percentile. If the 95th percentile for a set of actions is one second, 95 percent of the response times are at or below one second. Only five percent (one in twenty) of the response times exceeded one second. To compare, the maximum response time is the 100th percentile. In other words, 100 percent of the response times are at or below the maximum.

To measure acceptability, Loadsim places a heavier weight on simulated actions that are perceived as more important to a real user. For example, most users expect quick responses when opening or deleting messages. They aren't, however, as affected by a small delay when sending mail. The actual actions and weights are categorized on the following table.

Table 22.1 Loadsim Can Give You Weight Values

Action	Weight
Read	10
Delete	2
Send	1
Reply	1
Reply All	1
Forward	1
Move	1

NOTE LsLog is a Loadsim tool that enables you to change the default percentile (95) and the weighted values for any action. For more information, refer to the Loadsim documentation and on-line help.

To arrive at the final number, Loadsim multiplies each percentile value by the corresponding weight. Then, Loadsim adds the results, and divides by the sum of all weights. This final number is referred to as the score, and represents the response time experienced by a simulated user.

The following list includes client requirements and recommendations that might make your Loadsim experience more productive:

- The test clients should have NT 3.51 or higher, a Pentium 60 MHz chip or faster, at least 32M of RAM, and a paging file of 100MB or more. If you want to simulate 200 or more users on one client, you'll need at least 64M of RAM.

- Avoid simulating more than 300 users per client. The DLLs responsible for client-to-server communication will fail to scale, and your test results will not be realistic. In other words, the response time for 500 simulated clients will not be accurate for 500 actual clients on separate machines.
- For best results, you should allow six hours per simulation to gather enough data for reliable, reproducible results. Only analyze the last four hours of the simulation. This enables the server to stabilize after all simulated users have logged on. Of course, you are free to develop your own standards. However, remember to allow enough testing time, especially when simulating fewer than 100 users.
- Run your initial tests on an isolated network which removes real-world traffic. Then, after gathering enough lab data, you might want to run some tests with a network load on the wire to determine whether your environment's network load will affect response time.
- Loadsim cannot perfectly simulate the network traffic of real users. Although 200 Loadsim users create 200 logical server connections, there is only one network card and physical wire. Therefore, simulated network overhead (as measured by Perfmon) will be lower compared to using separate client machines.
- Loadsim doesn't simulate all Exchange features, such as rules and PST-based users. Review the Loadsim documentation for a complete listing of simulated tasks.
- Loadsim isn't a perfect simulation of your environment. Its numbers are only good estimates. Despite this, you will still find Loadsim's data extremely useful.

Capacity Planning with Loadsim

It is possible to monitor Loadsim's actions with the Performance Monitor to determine which resource will be bottlenecked first as the number of users rises. This is especially useful for capacity planning.

You should also use Perfmon to separate client-side influences from the server side. Loadsim is executed from a client desktop. You should, therefore, use Perfmon before Loadsim to tune all major bottlenecks. Then, while Loadsim is running, use Perfmon to determine whether a client-side bottleneck is skewing your data.

Example of Using Loadsim

This test was run on a server with a Pentium 90 MHz CPU, 64M of RAM, a 32-bit network card with bus mastering, and a 32-bit controller card with 4M of on-board cache memory managing two 4.2 gig hard drives. This server was optimized by the Performance Optimizer and Performance Monitor before running the Loadsim test.

The following tables list the values for various Loadsim parameters. These values were used to configure Loadsim before executing the simulation.

Table 22.2 These Values Are for Various Loadsim Simulation Parameters

Initialize User Parameters	Value
Number of Non-Default Folders	40
Number of Messages per Folder	5
Number of Messages in the Inbox	4
Number of Messages in Deleted Items	1

Table 22.3 These Values Represent User Task Parameters

User Task Parameters	Value
Hours in Day	8
Originate New Mail (not Reply or Forward)	4x
Text only message	
1K text message	60
2K text message	16
4K text message	4
1K text message with attachment	
10K attachment	5
Excel attachment	4
Word attachment	2
Embedded bitmap	2
Embedded Excel Object	2
Recipients per New or Forward Message	3
Add Distribution List to Addressees	30%
Read New Mail	12x
Send Reply	7%
Send Reply All	5%
Send Forward	7%
Delete (move to Deleted Items Folder)	40%
Move Messages	20%
Load Attachments on Read Mail	25%
Maximum In box size in Messages	125
Other old mail processing	15x
Schedule + Changes	5x
Empty Delete Items Folder	1x
Messages sent per 8 hour day (computed average)	13.5
Messages received per 8 hour day (computed average)	68.8

NOTE Each simulated user executes one task at a time.

Each simulated user performs each task at randomly spaced intervals throughout each simulated day.

All tasks are completed within each simulated day. ■

Figure 22.2 illustrates Loadsim's results. The two important numbers are a response time of 1000 ms and 430 users per server. This is the crossover point at which response time becomes unacceptable.

Therefore, this server can support 430 users with a response time of one second or less occurring 95 percent of the time.

FIG. 22.2
This chart represents Loadsim's results.

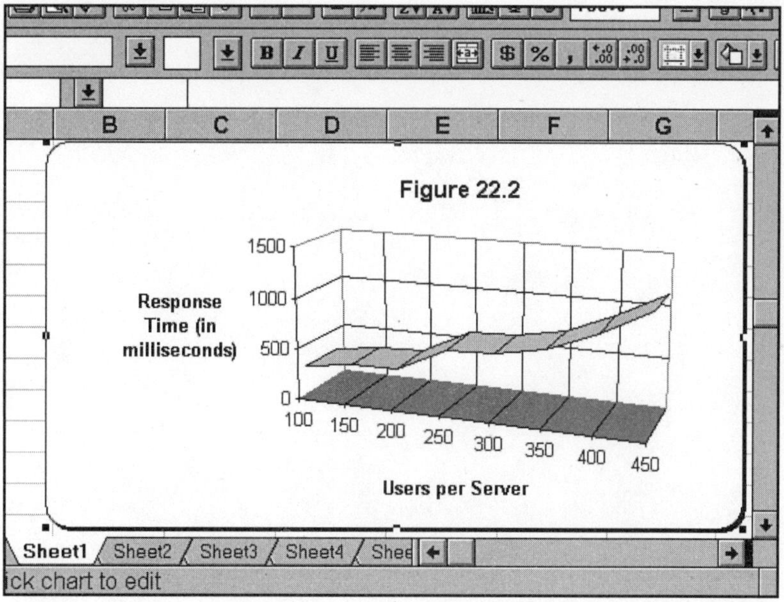

From Here...

You now know which components to measure, and how to use optimization tools. You also know the answer to the question, "How many users can Exchange support?"

This knowledge will enable you to solve the largest performance problems within your organization.

This chapter has addressed the topic of performance tuning and capacity planning. For more information, refer to the following chapters:

- Chapter 23, "Exchange Maintenance," for additional information about tools and techniques for optimizing your Exchange servers.
- Chapter 24, "Monitoring Your Organization," for information on additional utilities that assist you in watching over the servers and messaging links in your Exchange organization.
- Chapter 26, "Diagnostic and Troubleshooting Tools," which explains the tools and techniques you'll use when troubleshooting Exchange.

CHAPTER 23

Exchange Maintenance

- Adding, removing, and transferring users
- Creating templates to facilitate creating new mailboxes
- Monitoring mailbox and public folder usage
- Rebuilding routing tables
- Monitoring messaging your queues
- Maintaining replication and synchronization, and correcting inconsistencies
- Performing routine backups

After you plan and lay out your Exchange organization, the next step will be to establish the maintenance strategy for your organization. No matter how solid your design and implementation of the Exchange architecture, some tasks must be performed daily to maintain optimum performance and smooth operation.

This section will assist you in performing the routine tasks that will prevent messaging errors, help you fine-tune performance, and recover lost data when the worst happens. ■

Creating Different Server Recipients

During normal Exchange organization operation, there will be times when recipients created on one Exchange server need to be transferred to different machines.

Some common circumstances for relocating recipients are these:

- Internal reorganization: A user moves to a department in the company that is serviced by a different Exchange server.
- A server is down: A server must be taken offline for an extensive period of time.
- Optimum performance: After reviewing usage, you decide that for better performance, you need to switch a user's home server (or site).

Distribution lists and custom recipients are server-independent objects. They belong to a site as a whole, not to a specific Exchange server, and therefore, do not need to be transferred among servers in a site.

Moving Exchange Mailboxes

Mailboxes are the most common type of recipients. Moving a mailbox will also transfer its entire private information store contents (including attachments) to the destination server.

Because the Exchange information store uses intelligent storage for handling attachments addressed to multiple recipients on the same server, keep in mind that additional space is required to split these files. Consider the following example.

User A and User B on server BOSTON01 both receive a message with a 1 megabyte sound file attachment. The total storage space used on BOSTON01 to hold this sound is 1 megabyte. Both users are referencing the same instance of the file.

Suppose you transfer User A to server BOSTON05. The user's entire mailbox message contents and attachments are moved to BOSTON05's private information store. This means the 1 megabyte sound file now exists on both servers.

To move mailboxes to another server on the same site:

1. Use the Exchange administrator program and first select the site and then the server within that site where the mailboxes currently reside.
2. Select the mailboxes you wish to relocate. You can select a series of them by using Shift+click or a scattered assortment by using Ctrl+click.

3. When all desired mailboxes are highlighted, select Move mailbox from the administrator program's Tools menu. The following dialog box shown in figure 23.1 will appear.

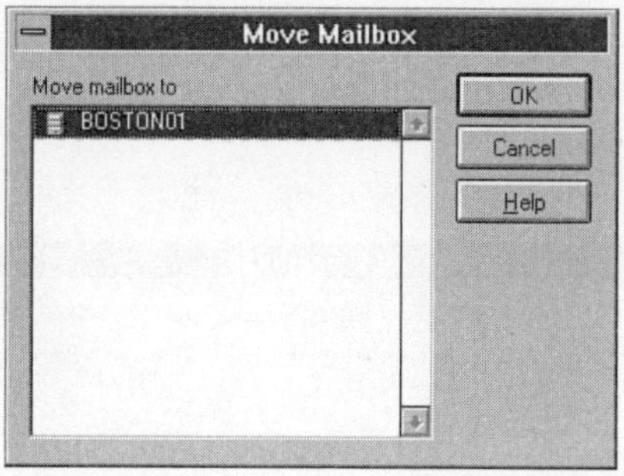

FIG. 23.1
Select the destination server in the Move Mailbox dialog box.

4. Select the destination server from the Move mailbox to server list. Click OK.
5. The mailboxes will be transferred immediately.
6. View the destination server's recipient container to confirm that the mailboxes now exist on the new server.

Messages in transit to a mailbox when it is moved to another server will be delayed until the appropriate routing information is properly updated.

To transfer a mailbox to a different site, you must use the Import/Export utility provided in the Exchange administrator program's Tools menu.

Moving Public Folders

Normally you will accommodate a wide number of public folder users by creating replicas of the folder across your organization. Then, according to the replication schedule, the folders will update each other with changes.

To create a public folder replica:

1. Using the Exchange administrator program, select the site where the public folders reside.
2. Select the Recipients container for that site.

NOTE Select Hidden Recipients from the View menu if your public folders are hidden in the administrator program display window.

3. Select the public folder you wish to replicate and open its property pages.

For more information, see Chapter 14, "Information Store Configuration."

Public Folder Replicas

Chapter 15, "Creating and Configuring Recipients," goes into more detail about configuring all aspects of the public folder recipient type. This section describes the Replicas property page for a public folder.

1. Select the Replicas tab of the public folder's property pages. The property page shown in figure 23.2 appears.

FIG. 23.2
Select the destination server for this public folder.

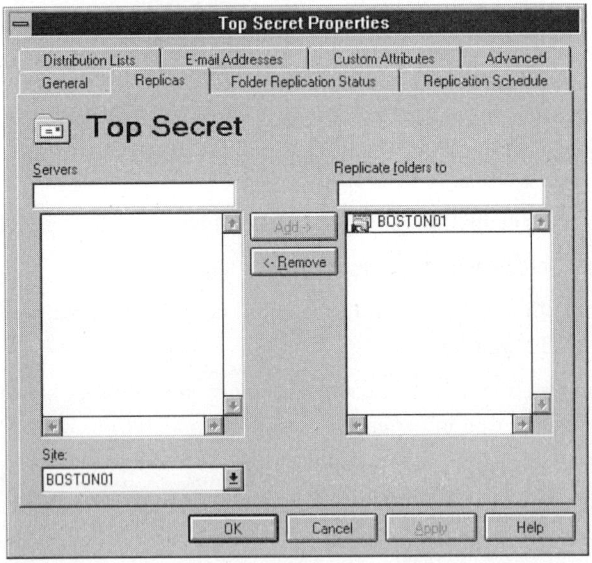

The Servers display window lists all Exchange servers in the site selected in the Site pull-down menu.

The Replicate folders to display window lists the Exchange servers currently selected as destinations for folder replicas.

2. Select a Site from your organization with the pull-down menu.
3. Select or type the name of the destination Exchange server within that site. Click Add.
4. To remove a destination server, select it from the right display window and click Remove.
5. Click Apply to set these properties and continue with other properties. If you are done with all settings, click OK to return to the administrator program.

CAUTION

Do not replicate the Offline address book public folder to any other server in your site. There must only be one instance of that folder in each site.

Moving a Public Folder with the Exchange Client Software

The Exchange Client (on Windows or Windows NT) can also be used to move public folders. You must have sufficient permissions on a specific folder in order to move it to a new location. Assuming you have the necessary permissions, to move a public folder with the Exchange Client software, do the following:

1. Expand the Public Folders object from the Exchange Client display window.
2. Locate the public folder you wish to move.
3. Click and drag it to its new location. You will see a progress box as the information store data is relocated.

Creating Mailbox Templates

A principal part of Exchange maintenance will be adding and deleting mailbox users. When adding a large group of recipients, you can avoid having to enter similar information (such as department or address) by using a mailbox template. You create a template mailbox by creating a dummy mailbox account (one not intended to receive messages) that will be copied when creating new users.

To create a mailbox template, do the following:

1. Using the Exchange administrator program, select a home site for this template mailbox in your organization.
2. Select New mailbox from the administrator program File menu, and the new mailbox property pages appear.
3. Give the new mailbox a Display name that will help you identify it as a template.
4. Enter all additional mailbox attributes that you want to include in the new group of mailboxes.

TIP Check the Hide From Address Book setting on the mailbox template's Advanced property page to prevent it from receiving mail. Then, temporarily make it visible when using it to import new users (unless you want all your newly created mailboxes to be hidden as well).

To use your template when creating a new user mailbox, follow this procedure:

1. Using the Exchange administrator program, select a home server for the new mailbox.
2. If the template mailbox is hidden, select Hidden Recipients from the administrator program View menu. Then select the Mailbox Template.
3. Select Duplicate from the Exchange administrator program File menu.
4. Enter the relevant user information for the new mailbox.

Performing Information Store Maintenance

The *information store* is the central storage facility for all Exchange messaging data. An information store can consume considerable disk space, depending on the size of your organization and the distribution of users per Exchange server.

The following property pages are important to maintaining the information stores:

- Private Information Store: Mailbox Resources: View Mailbox storage usage.
- Public Information Store: Public Folder Resources: View Public Folder storage usage.
- Exchange Server: Information Store Maintenance property page: Schedule hard drive optimizing for an Exchange server's information store.

Private Information Store Property Page

The Private Information Store property page allows you to view the physical resources used by each mailbox on a particular server. This property page lets you evaluate hard disk space usage and determine storage limits.

First, you must select the Private Information Store from a server within your site:

1. Navigate to your desired site with the Exchange administrator program.
2. Click the Configuration container of the selected site. All the site configuration objects appear in the administrator program's right window.

3. Open the Servers container. A list of Exchange servers in your site will be listed.
4. Click the server name on the Private Information Store you want to configure. The list of server objects is visible on the right display window of the Microsoft Exchange Administrator Program (see fig. 23.3).

FIG. 23.3 Select the Private Information Store object from among all the other server objects.

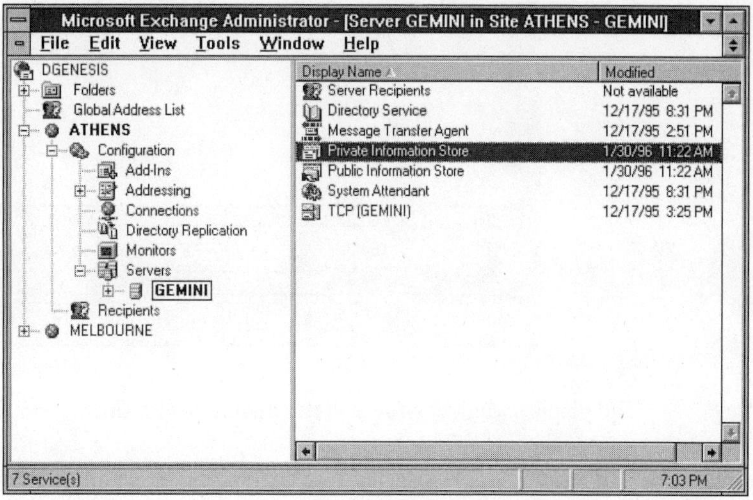

5. Click the Private Information Store object. Open its property pages.

Mailbox Resources Property Page The Mailbox Resources property page allows you to view the physical resources (e.g., hard disk storage space) used by the Exchange mailboxes on a server. It consists of one main display window that shows the mailboxes on the current server. The window is divided into columns of information. The specific columns displayed are customizable both by information presented and width on the screen.

NOTE A mailbox will only be displayed in this window after the first time a user logs on to it. If the mailbox has never been used, it will not appear on Mailbox Resources property page.

To view Mailbox Resources information, do the following:

1. Select the Mailbox Resources tab of the Private Information Store property pages. The following property page shown in figure 23.4 appears.

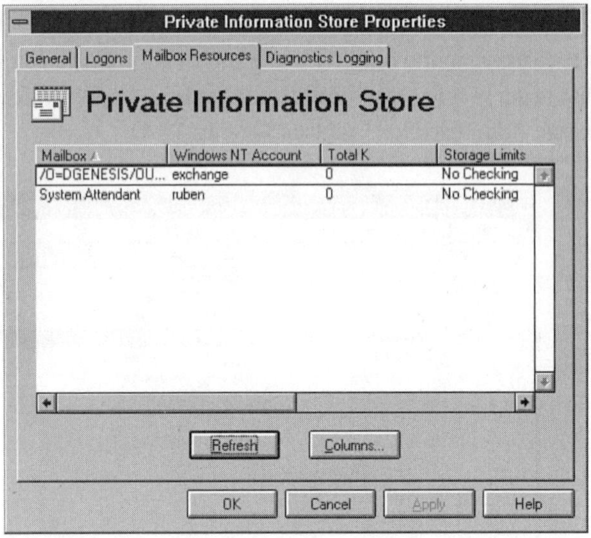

FIG. 23.4
Monitor mailbox storage requirements.

The display window shows all the mailboxes on this server that have been used at least once.

NOTE The Microsoft Exchange System Attendant and the Exchange account itself is always listed in this window as well.

2. Click the Refresh button to update the display window with the latest information.
3. Click the Columns button to edit which columns are displayed and their width in pixels. (See below for a description of each column heading and what type of information it can display.)
4. Click Apply to set these properties and continue with other properties. When you are done with all settings, click OK to return to the administrator program.

Default Columns Columns define what type of information is displayed in the standard dialog box. Default columns are preconfigured to display the most commonly needed information. Optional columns provide more detailed information that may be useful in troubleshooting errors. The following is a list of default columns:

- Mailbox: The Exchange administrator program object display name for this mailbox
- Windows NT Account: The Windows NT account of the user currently logged in to this mailbox
- Total K: The total amount of disk storage space (in kilobytes) taken up by the contents of this user's mailbox (this value includes any message attachments)

- Storage Limits: Any storage limits imposed on mailbox (e.g., Prohibit Send)
- Total number Items: The sum of all messages and attachments stored in a mailbox
- Last Logon Time: The last time a user logged in to this mailbox
- Last Logoff Time: The last time a user logged off from this mailbox

Optional Columns This following is a list of the optional columns to display in the dialog box.

- Full Mailbox Directory Name: The entire X.400 e-mail address for this mailbox
- Total number Associated Messages: The sum of stored views and deferred action messages (messages scheduled to be sent/processed at a later time) in this mailbox

Public Information Store Property Page

The Public Information Store property page allows you to view the physical resources (e.g., hard disk storage space) used by the folders held on an Exchange public information store. It consists of one main display window that shows the public folders on the current server. The window is subdivided into various columns of information. The specific columns displayed are customizable both by information presented and width on the screen.

The Schedule+ Free Busy Information and the Offline address book are in essence public folders as well and are listed in the public folder resources property page.

The Public Folder Resources Page The public folder resources page allows you to monitor what quantity of system resources is exhausted by the use of public folders on your system.

1. Select the Public Folder Resources tab of the Private Information Store property pages. The following property page shown in figure 23.5 appears.

   The display window shows all the public folders on this server, including those replicated from other servers.
2. Click the Refresh button to update the display window with the latest information.
3. Click the Columns button to edit which columns are displayed and their width in pixels. See the next page for a description of each column heading and what type of information it can display.
4. Click Apply to set these properties and continue with other properties. If you are done with all settings, click OK to return to the administrator program.

FIG. 23.5
View resources utilized by each public folder on this server.

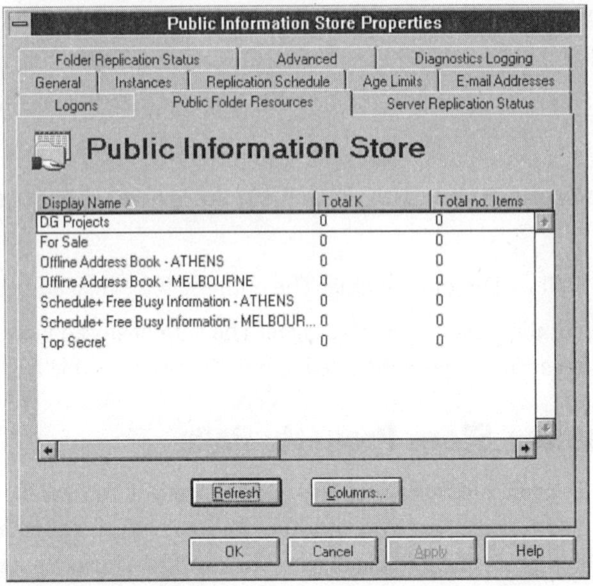

Default Columns Columns define what type of information is displayed in the standard dialog box. Default columns are preconfigured to display the most commonly needed information. Optional columns provide more detailed information that may be useful in troubleshooting errors. The folllowing is a list of default columns:

- Display Name: The Exchange administrator program object display name for this public folder
- Total K: The total amount of disk storage space (in kilobytes) taken up by the contents of this public folder (this value includes any message attachments)
- Total number Items: The sum of all messages and attachments stored in a mailbox
- Created: The date and time this folder was created
- Last Access Time: The last time a user logged in to this public folder
- Number of Owners: The number of users designated as Owners of this public folder (see section on defining roles for a public folder)
- Number of Contacts: The number of users designated as contacts for this public folder (see section on defining roles for a public folder)

Optional Columns The following is a list of optional columns that can be used to display additional information about server resources.

- Folder: Folder name where messages are stored
- Folder Path: The system file path to where this folder is stored
- Total number Associated Messages: The sum of folder views and deferred action messages

Compacting Information Stores Offline

Periodically you will want to perform a type of maintenance called *offline information store compacting*. This involves using the Windows NT *compact* command to optimize disk space allocation for an information store. It is important that you schedule this procedure at a time when message traffic is low or even nonexistent, because it involves stopping the information store service entirely.

The following command-line entry will compact the `expriv.eis` file (Exchange Private Information Store) and back up the original to a file named `expriv.bak`. The backup file is optional, but it is a good idea to create one every time you compact an information store for safety.

Here is an example command:

```
compact /s /b c:\exchsrvr\mdbdata\expriv.eis expriv.bak
```

where `EXPRIV.EIS` is the filename for the private information store and where `EXPUB.EIS` is the filename for the public information store.

The procedure for information store compacting is as follows:

1. Open the Windows NT services control panel and stop the Microsoft Exchange Information Store service (MSEXCHANGEIS).
2. Open a Windows NT command line window (or use the Run command from the Program Manager File menu).
3. Enter the compact command using the following syntax

   ```
   Compact [/s [/b] path\store [temporary_backup_file ]
   ```

   where `/s` specifies the file to compact

   where `/b` signals that a backup is to be made

4. Press Enter (or click OK if using the Run command from Program Manager) to start compacting.

NOTE Compacting a large information store could take a reasonable amount of time, so make sure to plan accordingly.

5. After the compacting process finishes, restart the information store service.
6. Test the information store for proper functioning by logging into it with an Exchange client and trying to view messages or connect to a public folder.
7. If the information store is functional, you may remove the backup (.bak) file.

NOTE While the information store service is stopped, all message transfer attempts to the store are refused. Also, server mailbox users will not be able to open the store through their client.

Maintaining Message Transfer Agents

The routing table is used by the Message Transfer Agent (MTA) to calculate delivery paths for each message. Whenever a change is made that affects routing (e.g., modifying address spaces for a connector), it will not take effect until the routing table has been rebuilt.

Normally, the routing table is rebuilt once per day. However you will be prompted to rebuild it whenever making a change that affects message routing.

You can also opt to rebuild the table manually, this way:

1. Select the General property page of the Message Transfer Agent property pages. The property page shown in figure 23.6 appears.
2. Click the Recalculate Routing button to begin rebuilding the routing table.
3. Click OK to return to the administrator program.

The MTA retrieves updated routing information from the routing table every 15 minutes. Therefore, it could take up to 15 minutes for routing updates to be utilized by the MTA.

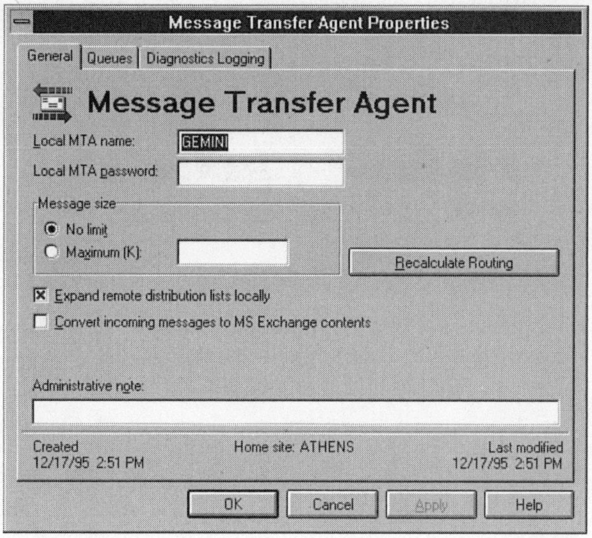

FIG. 23.6
Use the General Message Transfer Agent Properties page to recalculate MTA routing.

MTA Message Queues

The Queues property page lists messages awaiting delivery by the MTA. There are two primary windows in this property page. The Queue name window shows which queue you are currently viewing and the Message list box displays the messages in that queue. From this, you can view details about a specific message in the queue, change its priority for delivery, or delete it entirely.

Within the Message list window, there are three columns that contain information about a particular message:

- Originator: The original sender of the message
- Submit time: The time the message entered the queue
- Size: The size of the message in kilobytes

To configure the Queues property page, do this:

1. Select the Queues property page from the Message Transfer Agent property pages. The following Queues property page shown in figure 23.7 appears.
2. Use the Queue name pull-down menu to select which message queue to display. There are queues for the private and public information stores and any installed gateways.

FIG. 23.7
The message queue. It is blank because all pending messages have been delivered.

NOTE The Internet Mail connector and Microsoft Mail connector have separate queues that can also be accessed through their respective property pages.

3. Select a message and click Details to view additional information about it.

   The additional message information includes message originator, submit time, message size, and priority. This button is dimmed if no messages are in the queue. Other Message information includes the following:

   Next Retry Time: The next scheduled submission attempt

   Expiration: The time after which this MTA will no longer attempt to send this message and it will be returned as nondeliverable

4. Click the Refresh button to update the message list window with the latest list of messages in the MTA queue.

5. Click Priority to display the message's priority.

   Change the priority of a message if desired. It can be low, medium, or high. Messages are sent in order of this priority. A message's priority is set when a message is created.

6. Select a message and click Delete to remove a message from the MTA queue.

7. Click Apply to set these properties and continue with other properties. If you are done with all settings, click OK to return to the administrator program.

When dealing with MTA queue dialog boxes (or any other Exchange queue box), the messages you see on the list are a freeze frame of all queued messages at one point in time. To get a more dynamic view or to "catch" a message as it passes through the queue, you must continually press the Refresh button to get the latest updates.

MTA Diagnostic Logging

Logging falls mainly in the realm of troubleshooting and is discussed in chapter 26. MTA logs can be used for other purposes, such as billing and accounting for number of messages transferred.

Maintaining Microsoft Mail Connector

The Microsoft Mail Connector has its own temporary message store called MS Mail Connector post office. This gives the MS Mail Connector its own message queue property page on which to monitor message queue status.

To open the MS Mail Connector message queue window, do the following:

1. Open the MS Mail Connector property pages.
2. Select the Connections tab.
3. Select the MS Mail Connection to Monitor Message Traffic.
4. Click Queue. The MS Mail Connector message queue property page appears.
5. Select a sort order for the messages by clicking one of the categories on the top line of the Queued Messages window.

   Information displayed in the queue:

From	the original message sender
Subject	the data on the message's subject line
Message ID	the message identifier
Date/Time	the time when the messaged entered the queue

6. To remove a message, select it and then click Delete.

   If Send Non-Delivery Reports when messages deleted is checked, the original sender will be notified if his or her message was deleted from the queue. If it is clear, no notification will be sent when a message is deleted.
7. To return a message to its original sender, select it and then click Return.
8. Click Close to return to the MS Mail Connector Connections property page. Then, click OK to return to the administrator program.

NOTE As in the MTA queues property page, the view of queued messages is static. To update the display you must click the Refresh button.

Maintaining Directories

There are two components to each directory object saved in a server's information store: the object itself and a corresponding entry in the directory. Consistency adjustment corrects errors arising by mismatched directory information. This feature will either add or delete a directory entry to match the existence or absence of information store data.

The property page allows you to control at what point these inconsistencies are to be corrected. Figure 23.8 shows Advanced tab of the GEMINI Properties page where you configure directory inconsistency adjustment.

FIG. 23.8
This property page lets you adjust directory inconsistencies.

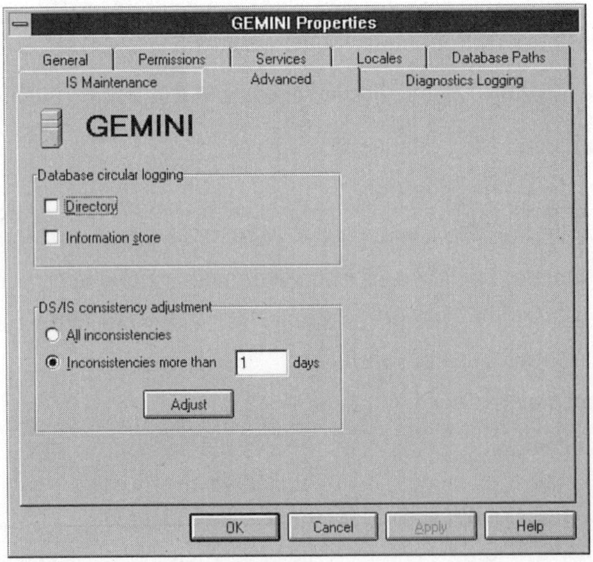

Select either All inconsistencies to correct them immediately or select Inconsistencies more than…days and enter the time an inconsistency can exist before it is automatically corrected.

Understanding Knowledge Consistency

Knowledge consistency for the local server is its awareness of other Exchange servers within a site and at other sites within your organization. The knowledge consistency operation is run automatically once daily, but if Exchange servers or sites were added and the local was not aware of those changes' servers (e.g., the local server was down during that time), then you may not want to wait for the automatic checking and do it manually.

Suppose Exchange server BOSTON01 is brought down for 2 hours for a memory upgrade. During the time of the upgrade, a new server, BOSTON08, is added to the site. When BOSTON01 is restored to proper functioning, it will not be aware of the existence of the new server until the knowledge consistency cycle is run at the end of the day. Knowing this, the administrator for BOSTON01 runs the knowledge consistency cycle manually from the Directory Service property pages to make BOSTON01 aware of the new server's existence.

Resynchronizing Replicated Directory Information

If a directory inconsistency is detected when checking manually, it is a good idea to manually execute all processes related to correcting inconsistencies. Use this sequence:

1. Check knowledge consistency from the directory service property pages and detect the error.
2. Manually update directory replication within the site by running Update Now also from the Directory Service property pages.
3. Open the Message Transfer Agent properties for this server and click Recalculate Routing from the General property page.

Although this sequence is optional and will be automatically executed within a 24-hour period, performing the tasks immediately will reduce the possibility of conflicts or errors.

Maintaining Directory Synchronization

When you have the Exchange MS Mail Connector configured as a Dir-Sync server, you must delete all the remote directory synchronization requestors that are part of the Dir-Sync server. More importantly, you must make sure that any Dir-Sync requestors on the remote MS Mail post offices are stopped or otherwise reconfigured to connect to a different Dir-Sync server.

CAUTION

Make sure to stop or redirect any MS Mail directory synchronization requestors relying on the local Exchange Dir-Sync server before you delete it. Otherwise, there will be messaging failures and possibly data loss resulting from the broken connectivity.

To delete an MS Mail connector Dir-Sync server, do the following:

1. Stop or redirect any MS Mail directory synchronization requestors that connect to the Exchange Dir-Sync server.
2. In the Exchange administrator program, select the site and the Directory Synchronization container that holds the Dir-Sync server.
3. Select each instance of a remote directory synchronization requestor and then select Delete from the Edit menu.
4. Select the Directory Synchronization container itself and then select Delete from the Edit menu.

Deleting Dir-Sync Requestor

In order to disengage Directory Synchronization between Exchange and a remote MS Mail Dir-Sync server, you must delete the Dir-Sync requestor on the Exchange server.

Follow this procedure:

1. In the Exchange administrator program, select the site and the Directory Synchronization container that holds the Directory Synchronization requestors.
2. Select the desired requestor to remove, then select Delete from the Edit menu.

Synchronizing MS Mail AppleTalk Directories

You can manually direct the Macintosh Dir-Sync requestor to request directory update and bypass its scheduled synchronization cycle:

1. On your MS Mail (AppleTalk) server, open the folder that contains the Microsoft Exchange Connection files.
2. Open the Exchange Connection DER file.
3. Select Import Directory from the Macintosh File menu. The dialog box shown in figure 23.9 appears.

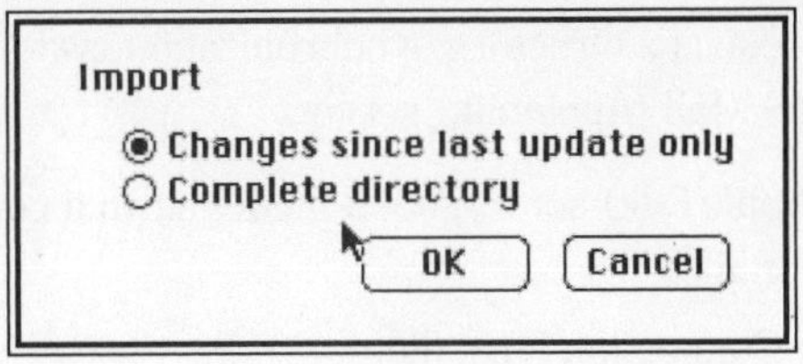

FIG. 23.9
Select how to request a directory update from the Dir-Sync server.

4. Select the Changes since last update only radio button to request only the addresses that have changed since the last synchronization cycle. Select the Complete directory radio button to request all directory information (more time-intensive) from the Exchange Dir-Sync server.
5. Click OK to execute the request.

Manually Exporting Directory Updates

You can direct your MS Mail (AppleTalk) server to send directory updates to an Exchange Dir-Sync server. Do this when you want to bypass the requestor export schedule:

1. On your MS Mail (AppleTalk) server, open the folder that contains the Microsoft Exchange Connection files.
2. Open the Exchange Connection DER file.
3. Select Export Directory from the Macintosh File menu.
4. Select the Changes since last update only radio button to export only the addresses that have changed since the last synchronization cycle. Select the Complete directory radio button to export all local directory information (more time-intensive) to the Exchange Dir-Sync server.
5. Click OK to execute the export command.

Resynchronizing Directory Information

If an error is detected in the Dir-Sync cycle, you can manually reset and execute a complete cycle. The MS Mail (AppleTalk) Network Manager receives confirmation messages on the Dir-Sync cycle. If notified that the server has not properly completed a cycle, you can manually force a synchronization adjustment with the Apple DER administrator program.

You can also check the Directory Exchange Requestor Log (in the Macintosh preferences folder) to verify that the synchronization process is functioning properly.

Do the following steps to restart a directory synchronization cycle between an Exchange server and a connected MS Mail (Appletalk) server.

1. On your MS Mail (AppleTalk) server, open the folder that contains the Microsoft Exchange Connection files.
2. Open the Exchange Connection DER file.
3. Select Resync Cycle from the Macintosh File menu.

Compacting Directory Information

Much like the information store, the Exchange directory can benefit greatly from offline compacting. The Microsoft Exchange directory service continually performs online compacting during its normal operation, but a dedicated, periodic, offline compacting will provide a more significant increase in performance. Not only will directory accessing speed improve after compacting, but hard disk space wasted through inefficient storage will be freed for use. Offline directory compacting requires stopping the Exchange Directory and Directory Synchronization services.

The following command-line entry will compact the `exdir.dsa` file (Exchange Directory service) and back up the original to a file named `exdirdsa.bak`. The backup file is optional, but it is a good idea to create one every time you compact an information store.

Here is an example command:

```
compact /s /b c:\exchsrvr\dsadata\exdir.dsa exdirdsa.bak
```

where EXDIR.DSA is the filename for replicated directory information and where EXDIR.DXA is the filename for synchronized directory information.

The procedure for compacting a directory is as follows:

1. Open the Windows NT services control panel and stop the Microsoft Exchange Directory service (MSEXCHANGEDSA) and the Directory Synchronization service (MSEXCHANGEDXA).
2. Open a Windows NT command line window (or use the Run command from the Program Manager File menu).
3. Enter the compact command using the following syntax:

   ```
   Compact [/s [/b] path\directory [temporary_backup_file ]
   ```

   where `/s` specifies the file to compact

   where `/b` signals that a backup is to be made

4. Press Enter (or click OK if using the Run command from the Program Manager) to start compacting.

NOTE Note: Compacting a large directory file could take a large amount of time, so make sure to plan accordingly. For a thousand users, for example, this process will take a couple of hours. ■

5. After the compacting process finishes, restart the Exchange Directory and Directory Synchronization services.
6. Test the directory for proper functioning by accessing into the local address list with an Exchange client.
7. If the directory is functional, you may proceed to remove the backup (.bak) files.

Working with Directory Event Logs

Part of maintaining a healthy Exchange Organization is working with the Windows NT Event Log. It is important to keep track of Event Log sizes (to set upper size limits and expiration dates for log entries) so as to not let the Event Log become too large. The two Directory Services to watch are these:

- MSExchangeDS: The directory service and directory replication process
- MSExchangeDX: Directory Synchronization

Logging levels for each service are set in the Diagnostic Logging property page. See Chapter 26, "Diagnostic and Troubleshooting Tools," for tips on using the Diagnostic Logging property pages for each service.

Backing Up Your Exchange Server

Probably the most important maintenance procedure for Microsoft Exchange organization is backup of information store and directory information. Few things on a user's computer are as important to him or her as his or her e-mail. Implementing a good backup strategy is well worth the effort. This section will provide a general conceptual guide to Exchange backup. For more detail in using the Exchange Backup utility, refer to your Microsoft Exchange server documentation.

Windows NT provides built-in tape backup and restore utilities that are supplemented by extensions installed with Exchange server. These utilities provide the basics for an adequate Exchange backup, but a full-featured backup software package would provide additional functionality and versatility. See Chapter 31, "Implementing Third-Party Integration Tools," on third-party integration for information about some forthcoming products that will facilitate backup beyond what comes with the basic Exchange and NT package.

This section describes backup and restore procedures directly relevant to maintaining Exchange information. For full NT server backups, refer to your Windows NT or third-party backup software documentation.

The version of Backup included with Microsoft Exchange is aware of the servers in your organization allowing you to do backups for a single server, server group, sites, or even an entire organization if necessary.

The main Exchange information you will want to back up is located in the following paths:

```
\EXCHSRVR\MDBDATA
```

and

```
\EXCHSRVR\DSADATA
```

Important Exchange files to be backed up are these:

- Information store databases: SYSTEM.EDB, PRIV.EDB, PUB.EDB
- Information store logs: EDB.LOG
- Directory database: SYSTEM.EBD (separate from the information store SYSTEM.EDB file), DIR.EDB
- Directory logs: EDB.LOG (separate from the information store EDB.LOG files)

When restoring lost data, the log files are played back to reconstitute the databases to the point of the last backup.

From Here...

This chapter showed you how to establish a maintenance strategy designed to ensure optimum performance and smooth operation. For related information, read the following chapters:

- Chapter 12, "Directory and System Attendant Configuration," provides more information on setting up and maintaining Exchange Directory services.
- Chapter 13, "Message Transfer Configuration," describes configuring messaging communication across your enterprise.
- Chapter 14, "Information Store Configuration," illuminates ways of working with both the private and public information store databases.

- Chapter 15, "Creating and Configuring Recipients," provides details about working with mailboxes and public folders.
- Chapter 24, "Monitoring Your Organization," to learn ways to monitor your systems and catch problems before they get out of hand.
- Chapter 26, "Diagnostic and Troubleshooting Tools," describes tracking down errors in an Exchange organization.

CHAPTER 24

Monitoring Your Organization

- Important terminology pertaining to monitoring your Exchange organization
- How to set up and configure link monitors to verify messaging connections
- How to set up and configure server monitors to verify proper operation of various system services
- How to use monitor status windows to read monitor data

Monitoring is the art of watching over your Exchange organization to identify and correct malfunctions before they become serious problems. An Exchange system consists fundamentally of Windows NT servers and links between them. Included with Microsoft Exchange server are two monitoring tools that service both components. They will be your eyes 24 hours a day to alert you when something goes wrong.

Exchange server includes two types of monitoring tools:

- Link monitor: Test messaging connections between Exchange servers in your organization.
- Server monitor: Test the status of Windows NT services on designated Exchange server.

Chapter 26, "Diagnostic and Troubleshooting Tools," will go into more detail on how to use the monitors to diagnose problems.

Understanding Exchange Monitoring Terms

The following terms are pertinent to using Exchange monitoring tools:

- Polling interval: the amount of time between system tests (time between ping messages sent or time between checking system service status)
- Warning state: a condition indicating that there potentially is a problem with a server or messaging link
- Alert state: a condition indicating that a serious problem exists within the server or messaging link
- Escalation path: the list of people, in order of notification priority, who receive alerts from a monitor
- Notification: the process of alerting a system administrator that a specific server or messaging link is functioning abnormally

Creating a Link Monitor

As an Exchange administrator, there are two fundamental ways that you may be notified of a downed messaging link:

- A user will try to send a message, it will come back undelivered, and you will receive an e-mail message from the user describing this fact.
- You can configure a link monitor to continuously watch that specific messaging connections are active and to detect unusual delays in message transmissions.

Link monitors watch for successful message connections between two points in an Exchange organization. They can also be configured to test connections to foreign messaging systems. Link monitors accomplish this by sending out a test message, called a *ping message*, and timing the round trip of that message.

A ping message sent by a link monitor is sent to test messaging connections. At the polling interval, a ping message is sent to every Exchange server and foreign system listed on the link monitor's servers property page.

To create a new link monitor, follow this procedure:

1. In the Exchange administrator program, select a site in your organization.
2. Open the Configuration container within the selected site.
3. Select the Monitors container; the right administrator program display window will show all the existing monitors (both link and server) in this site (see fig. 24.1).

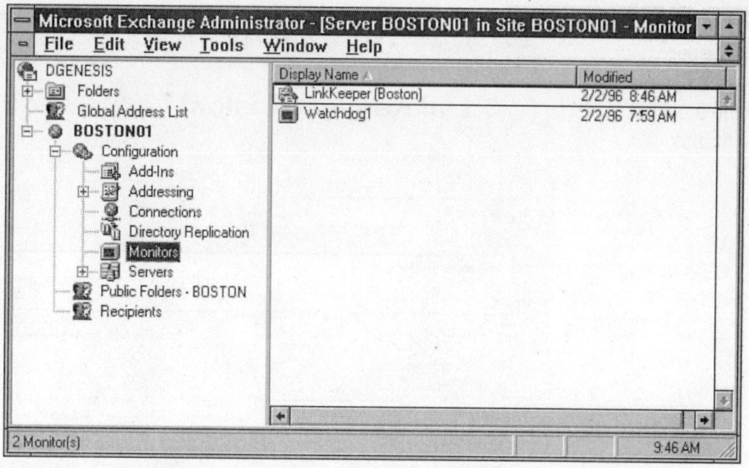

FIG. 24.1
The Monitor container shows all monitors in the selected site.

4. Select New Other, and then select Link monitor. The Link Monitor property pages appear.

Link Monitor Property Pages

The link monitor has several property pages:

- General: Name the monitor, set the polling interval, and optionally select a log file location.
- Notification: Specify how and to whom warning and alert messages are sent.
- Servers: Specify the local and remote Exchange servers and foreign messaging systems that will receive ping messages.
- Recipients: Configure ping messages to foreign messaging systems.
- Bounce: Enter time delay before a server enters a warning or alert state due to a non-returned ping message.

The General Property Page

1. Select the General tab of the LinkKeeper Properties page. The property page shown in figure 24.2 appears.
2. Enter a Directory name for this link monitor. (The directory name cannot be changed for a link monitor after it has been created.)
3. Enter a Display name as you want it to be shown in the administrator display window.

FIG. 24.2
The LinkKeeper Properties page lets you define a polling interval for this monitor.

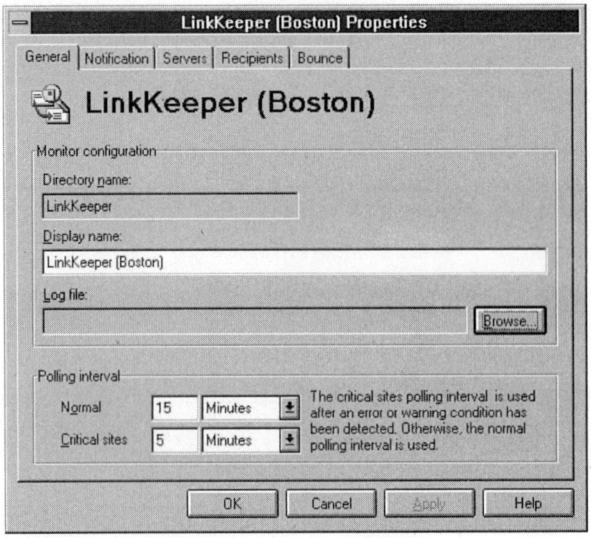

4. The Log File window shows the file name where monitor logs are being stored. Click Browse to select the file name and location.

NOTE Logging for link monitor activity is optional, so you need not specify a Log File location. ■

5. In the Polling Interval window, enter the units and time interval for Normal operation.
6. In the Polling Interval window, enter the units and time interval for Critical Sites.
7. Click Apply to set these properties and continue with other properties. If you are done with all settings, click OK to return to the administrator program.

The Notification Property Page

The Notification property page allows you to configure what happens when abnormal message link functioning is detected by a server monitor. There are three main types of notification:

- Launch a process: Load an external application. This option is often used in conjunction with paging software.
- Mail message: Automatically sends an e-mail message to a selected recipient describing the situation.
- Windows NT Alert: Use the Windows NT Messenger service to notify a certain user or group of users.

The Notification property page is primarily one main display window list where all notification objects are displayed (see fig. 24.3). By default, this window is blank, and no notification is specific.

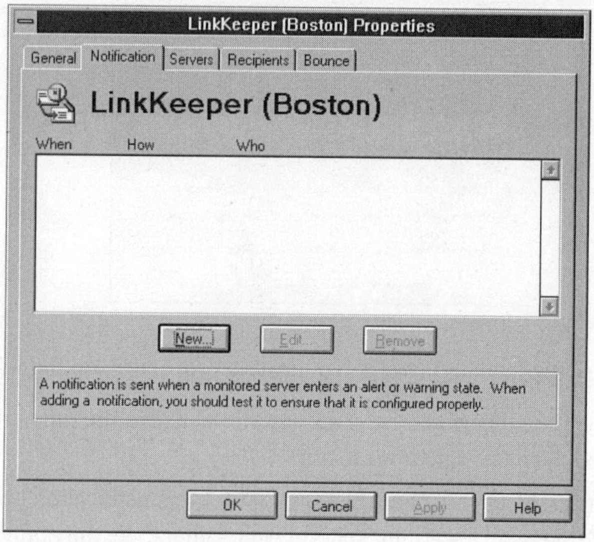

FIG. 24.3
The link monitor Notification property page shows who to contact in case of malfunctions.

Click New to define a new notification object. Select the type of notification (see fig. 24.4).

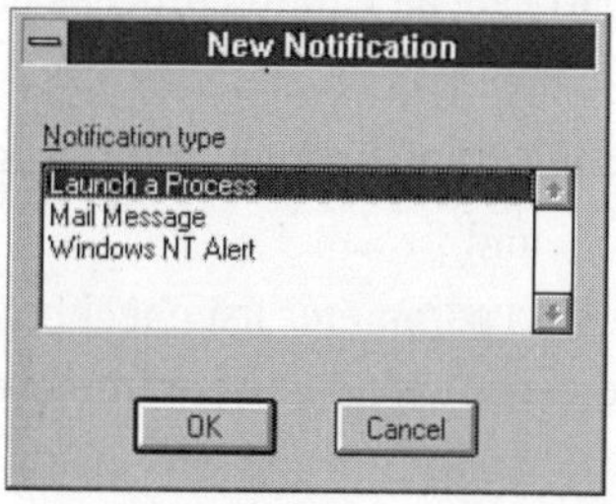

FIG. 24.4
Select a Notification type.

Launching a Notification Process Configuring an external notification application is as easy as choosing the application and setting the time delay for notification. You must configure that external process for the specific type of notification it provides (see fig. 24.5). All Exchange does is launch the process and pass along any additional required parameters.

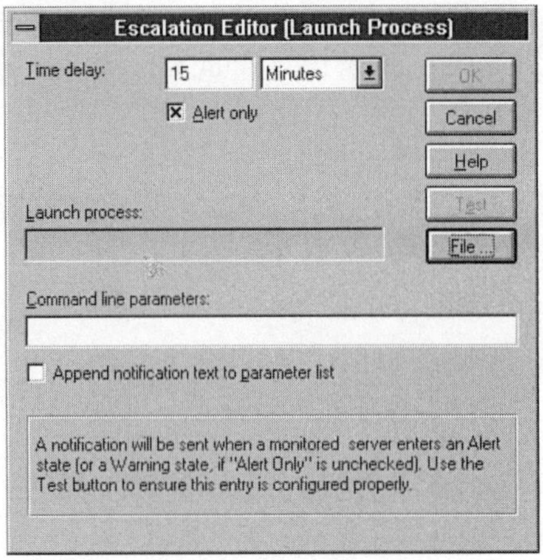

FIG. 24.5 Configure the parameters for the notification process.

To configure the Launch Process Notification properties, do the following:

1. In the Time delay box, enter a numeric value and the time units (seconds, minutes, hours) from the pull-down menu.
2. Clear the Alert only checkbox if you want this notification process to occur when the server is in a warning state as well. Otherwise, the notification process will only launch in an alert state after the time delay is exceeded.
3. Click the File button and navigate your directory hierarchy to locate the process you want to launch in this notification. The Launch process box will display this file once selected.
4. Enter any additional command-line parameters you want to pass to the notification process once it is launched.
5. Select the Append notification text to parameter list checkbox in order to attach the actual notification text to the above command-line parameters during the process launch.

NOTE If the external notification application is already configured, you may now use the Test button to verify property functioning.

6. Click OK to complete these settings and return to the Notification property page.

You can change a Notification by selecting it from the Notification list and clicking Edit. You can delete a notification by selecting it from the list and clicking Remove.

Using Mail Message Notification Mail notification will alert an administrator via e-mail that a server has entered an alert state (or warning state) due to excessive delays between message return.

To configure Mail Message Notification properties, follow this procedure (see fig. 24.6):

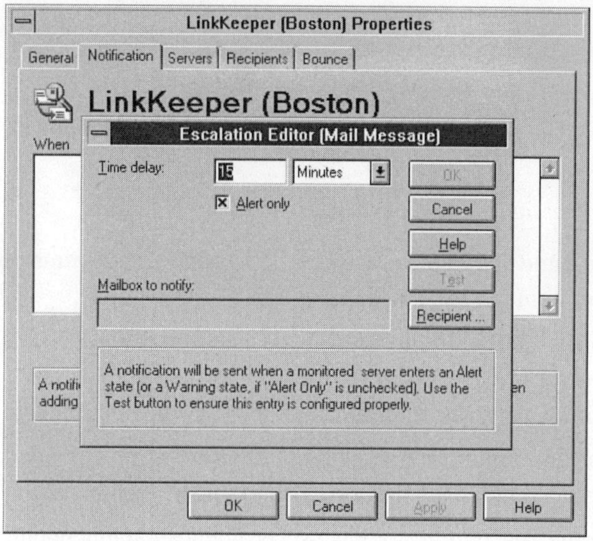

FIG. 24.6
Configure mail message Notification properties.

1. In the Time delay box, enter a numeric value and the time units (seconds, minutes, hours) from the pull-down menu.
2. Clear the Alert only checkbox if you want this notification process to occur when the server is in a warning state as well. Otherwise, the notification mail message will only be sent in an alert state after the time delay has exceeded.
3. Click the Recipient button and navigate the Exchange address lists to select a recipient for the mail notification.
4. Click the Test button to verify proper notification functioning. Check the destination address to verify message delivery.
5. Click OK to complete these settings and return to the Notification property page.

Using Windows NT Alerts Notification by Windows NT Alert (see fig. 24.7) is only useful if the recipient computer is turned on and a user is logged in to it. These alerts are transmitted via the Windows NT Message service and are displayed on-screen to a user.

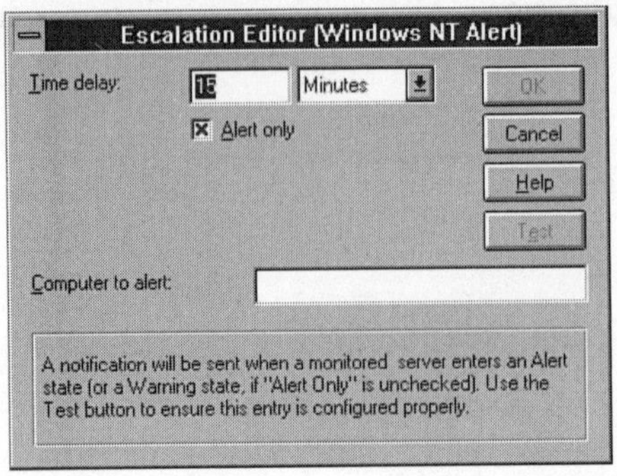

FIG. 24.7
Define Windows NT Alert parameters.

To configure notification properties for Windows NT Alert:

1. In the Time delay box, enter a numeric value and the time units (seconds, minutes, hours) from the pull-down menu.
2. Clear the Alert only checkbox if you want this notification process to occur when the server is in a warning state as well. Otherwise, the alert message will only be sent in an alert state after the time delay has been exceeded.
3. Enter the name of the Computer to alert in the box provided. Use the Windows NT server name (Exchange server name) for that computer.
4. Click the Test button to verify proper notification functioning. Check the destination computer to verify alert message delivery.
5. Click OK to complete these settings and return to the Notification property page.

The Servers Property Page

The Servers property page lets you determine which Exchange servers will be sent ping messages by the link monitor.

1. Select the Servers property page from the link monitor's property page.

   The property page shown in figure 24.8 appears.

   The left display window lists the Microsoft Exchange server in the site selected in the lower left pull-down menu.

   The right display window shows which servers will receive ping messages from this server.
2. Use the Site pull-down menu to select a site in your organization. The servers in that site will be listed in the left display window.

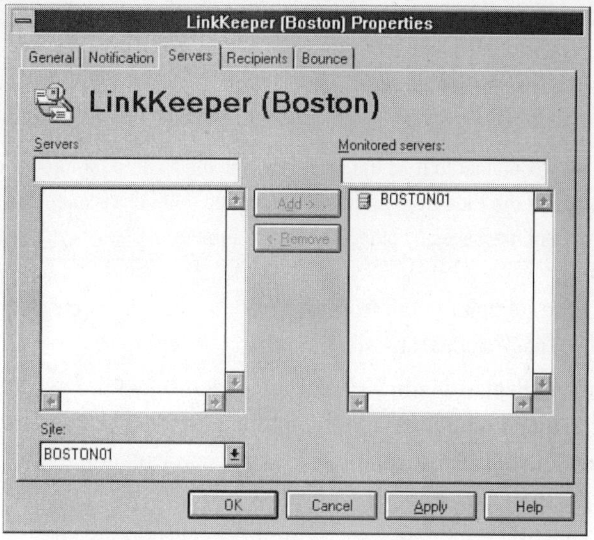

FIG. 24.8
Select which Exchange servers will receive ping messages.

3. Select an Exchange server from the Servers windows and click Add to enable monitoring for it.
4. To stop monitoring, click on a server from the right display window and click Remove.
5. Click Apply to set these properties and continue with other properties. If you are done with all settings, click OK to return to the administrator program.

The Recipients Property Page

The Recipients property page allows you to configure ping message recipients in foreign messaging systems. At each polling interval, selected foreign recipients will receive a ping message. You must configure each recipient as a custom recipient in the Exchange administrator program. The link monitor will look at the returned ping message subject line for confirmation of message integrity. Alternatively, you can have the link monitor look at the returned message's body.

For link monitoring, ping messages must be returned by a foreign system. You must write a script that will return the ping message. Another common solution is to send a message to a nonexistent address on that system; the system then returns the nondeliverable message to the link monitor.

NOTE Some systems do not automatically return messages sent to nonexistent addresses; they redirect them into a default mailbox. Make sure the foreign system is configured to bounce back messages sent to nonexistent addresses.

TIP Create a separate container to hold the custom recipients created for foreign system link monitoring. Also, set the Hide from address book option for each recipient, so they will not accidentally be sent messages by others in your organization.

1. Select the Recipients tab from the link monitor property pages. The Recipients property page appears.
2. In the left display window, click Modify and select the custom recipients you have created to get ping messages from this link monitor. The monitor will check the subject line of the returned message for confirmation of link status.
3. In the right display window, click Modify and select the custom recipients you have created to get ping messages from this link monitor. The monitor will check the body text of the returned message for confirmation of link status. Use this option usually when sending ping messages to a nonexistent address (when the subject line is not normally preserved).
4. Click Apply to set these properties and continue with other properties. If you are done with all settings, click OK to return to the administrator program.

The Bounce Property Page

The Bounce property page allows you the maximum allowable round-trips before a server enters a warning or alert state.

To define bounce times, follow this procedure:

1. Select the Bounce tab from the link monitor property pages. The property page shown in figure 24.9 appears.
2. Enter the number and select the time units (seconds, minutes, hours) to wait for a return message before entering a warning state. The default time is 30 minutes.
3. Enter the number and select the time units (seconds, minutes, hours) to wait for a return message before entering an alert state. The default time is 60 minutes.
4. Click Apply to set these properties and continue with other properties. If you are done with all settings, click OK to return to the administrator program.

After configuring all Link Monitor property pages, you must start the link monitor for it to carry out its functions. See "Starting and Using a Monitor" later in this chapter.

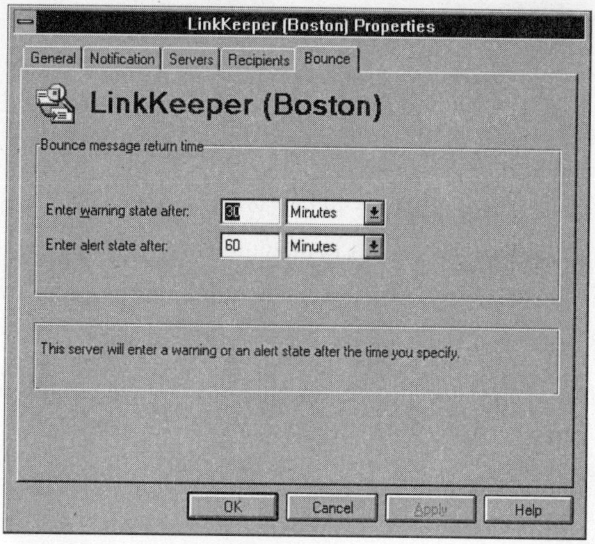

FIG. 24.9
Use this page to define threshold time before entering warning and alert states.

Creating a Server Monitor

A server monitor watches a selected list of Windows NT services for proper functioning. At each polling interval, the server monitor will check to see that the server is running by connecting to that server via a remote procedure call. The server's status is displayed in the server monitor's display window. You can also control (i.e., start, stop, pause) services via the server monitor display windows.

Additionally, these monitors can be used to monitor services that are not directly pertinent to Exchange if desired.

To create a new server monitor, follow this procedure:

1. In the Exchange administrator program, select a site in your organization.
2. Open the Configuration container within the selected site.
3. Select the Monitors container, the right administrator program display window will show all the existing monitors (both link and server) in this site.
4. Select New Other, then select Server Monitor. The Server Monitor property pages appear.

Server Monitor Property Pages

The server monitor has several property pages:

- General: Give the monitor a display name, set the polling interval, and select a log file location.
- Notification: Select alert type and delay times.
- Servers: Select which servers to monitor.
- Actions: Define procedure executed in case of malfunction.
- Clock: Set acceptable variations between system clocks.

If your organization includes different people who need to be notified of servers' malfunction, you must create separate server monitors. Also, if you want to set a different polling interval for a specific group of servers, you must create unique server monitors.

The General Page

The General property page allows you to name the server monitor and determine the polling interval and determine the location for a log file if one is desired.

To configure general settings for the server monitor, follow this procedure:

1. Select the General tab of the server monitor property pages. The property page shown in figure 24.10 appears.

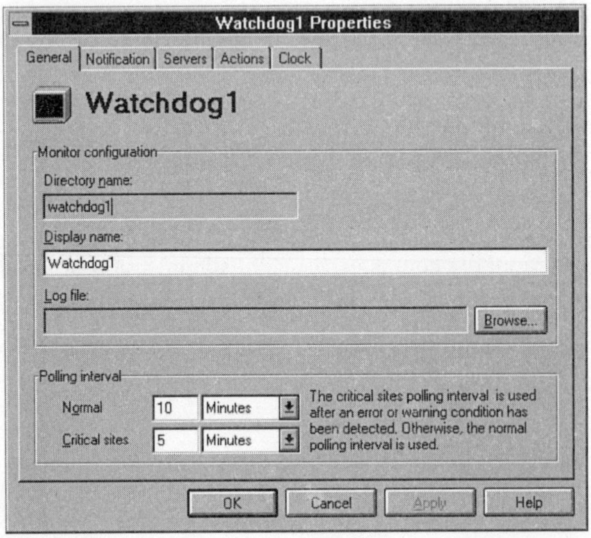

FIG. 24.10
Name this monitor and set its polling interval.

2. Enter a Directory name for this server monitor. (The directory name cannot be changed for a server monitor after it has been created.)
3. Enter a Display name as you want it to be shown in the administrator display window.
4. The Log File window shows the file name where monitor logs are being stored. Click Browse to select the file name and location.
5. In the Polling Interval window, enter the units and time interval for Normal operation.
6. In the Polling Interval window, enter the units and time interval for Critical Sites.
7. Click Apply to set these properties and continue with other properties. If you are done with all settings, click OK to return to the administrator program.

The Notification Property Page

The Notification property page allows you to configure what happens when abnormal functioning is detected by a server monitor. There are three main types of notification:

- Launch a process: Load an external application. (This option is often used in conjunction with paging software.)
- Mail message: Automatically send an e-mail message to a selected recipient describing the situation.
- Windows NT Alert: Use the Windows NT Messenger service to notify a certain user or group of users.

The Notification property page is primarily one main display window where all notification objects are displayed. By default, this property page is blank.

Click New to define a new notification object. Select the type of notification.

Launching a Notification Process Configuring an external notification application is as easy as choosing the application and setting the time delay for notification. You must configure that external process for the specific type of notification it provides. All Exchange does is launch the process and pass along any additional required parameters.

To configure Launch Process Notification properties, follow this procedure:

1. In the Time delay box, enter a numeric value and the time units (seconds, minutes, hours) from the pull-down menu.

2. Clear the Alert only checkbox if you want this notification process to occur when the server is in a warning state. Otherwise, the notification process will only launch in an alert state after the time delay is exceeded.
3. Click the File button and navigate your directory hierarchy to locate the process you want to launch in this notification. The Launch process box will display this file once selected.
4. Enter any additional command-line parameters you want to pass along to the notification process once it is launched.
5. Select the Append notification text to parameter list checkbox in order to attach the actual notification text to the above command-line parameters during the process launch.

NOTE If the external notification application is already configured, you may now use the Test button to verify property functioning.

6. Click OK to complete these settings and return to the Notification property page.

You can change a Notification by selecting it from the Notification list and clicking Edit. You can delete a notification by selecting it from the list and clicking Remove.

Using Mail Message Notification Mail message notification will alert an administrator via e-mail that a server has entered an Alert state (or Warning state as well, if desired).

To configure Mail Notification properties, follow this procedure:

1. In the Time delay box, enter a numeric value and the time units (seconds, minutes, hours) from the pull-down menu.
2. Clear the Alert only checkbox if you want this notification process to occur when the server is in a warning state. Otherwise, the notification mail message will only be sent in an alert state after the time delay has been exceeded.
3. Click the Recipient button and navigate the Exchange address lists to select a recipient for the mail notification.
4. Click the Test button to verify proper notification functioning. Check the destination address to verify message delivery.
5. Click OK to complete these settings and return to the Notification property page.

Using Windows NT Alerts Notification by Windows NT Alert is only useful if the recipient computer is turned on and a user is logged in to it. These alerts are transmitted via the Windows NT Message service and are displayed on-screen to the specific user.

To configure notification properties for Windows NT Alert:

1. In the Time delay box, enter a numeric value and the time units (seconds, minutes, hours) from the pull-down menu.
2. Clear the Alert only checkbox if you want this notification process to occur when the server is in a warning state. Otherwise, the alert message will only be sent in an alert state after the time delay has been exceeded.
3. Enter the name of the Computer to alert in the box provided. Use the Windows NT server name (Exchange server name) for that computer.
4. Click the Test button to verify proper notification functioning. Check the destination computer to verify alert message delivery.
5. Click OK to complete these settings and return to the Notification property page.

The Servers Property Page

The Servers property page lets you determine what servers are being monitored by the server monitor.

1. Select the Servers property page from the server monitor's property page.
   The property page shown in figure 24.11 appears.

   The left display window lists the Microsoft Exchange server in the site selected in the lower left pull-down menu.

   The right display window shows which servers are being monitored.
2. Use the Site pull-down menu to select a site in your organization. The servers in that site will be listed in the left display window.
3. Select an Exchange server from the Servers windows, and click Add to enable monitoring for it.
4. To stop monitoring, click on a server from the right display window and click Remove.
5. To define specifically which services are monitored on each server, use the Services button. (See the procedure in the next section.)

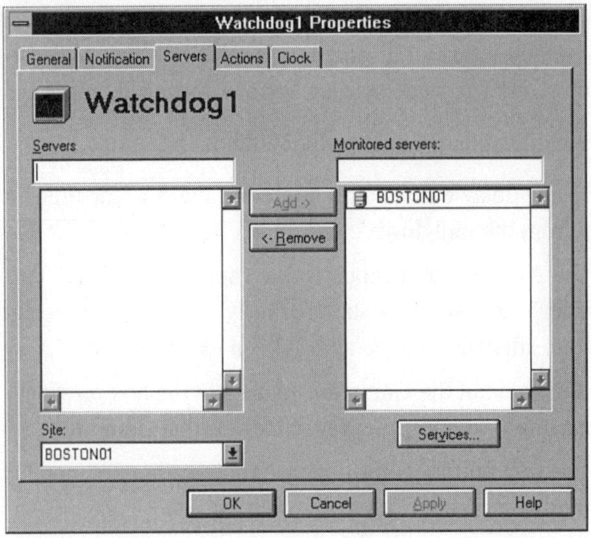

FIG. 24.11
Select which servers this monitor will watch.

Configuring Monitored Services You can determine specific services to be monitored for each selected Exchange server. By default, only the core Microsoft Exchange services (Directory, Information Store, and MTA) are configured for monitoring. Monitored services can also be configured on the property pages for each individual Exchange server.

To configure monitored services with the server monitor, follow this procedure:

1. On the Servers tab of the Server monitor property pages, select a server to configure.

   Click the Services button. The dialog box shown in figure 24.12 appears.

   The Installed services window shows all the system services running on this Windows NT server.

   The Monitored services window shows the system services currently being watched.

NOTE This dialog box is identical to the Services tab in an individual server's property pages.

2. Scroll through the list of installed Windows NT services and select which to monitor. Click Add.

FIG. 24.12
Add or remove services to be monitored.

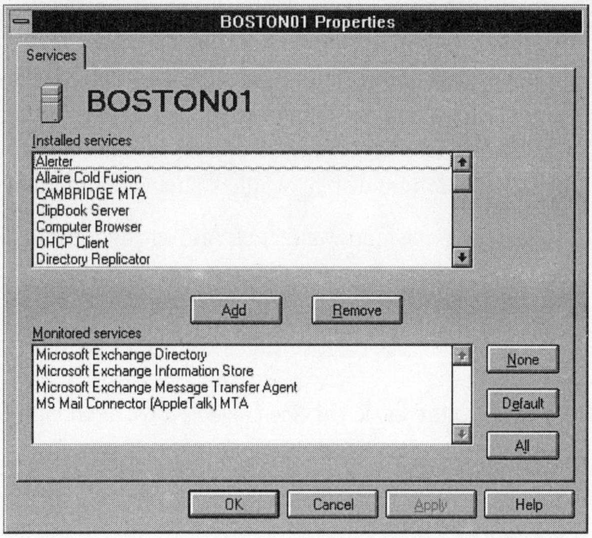

3. To remove a service from the Monitored services list, select it and click Remove.
4. Click None to remove all services from the monitored services list.
5. Click Default to keep only the Microsoft Exchange Directory, Information Store, and Message Transfer Agent services on the monitored list.
6. Click All to include every Windows NT service in the Monitored services window (this is usually not a good idea, except under very special circumstances).
7. Click Apply to set these properties and continue with other properties. If you are done with all settings, click OK to return to the Server Monitor's Servers property page.

Configuring Monitored Services from Exchange Server Property Pages To open Server property pages, follow this procedure:

1. Navigate to your desired site with the Exchange administrator program.
2. Click on the Configuration container of the selected site. All the site configuration objects appear in the administrator program's right window.
3. Open the Servers container. A list of Exchange servers in your site will be listed.
4. Click the server name on which the Private Information Store you want to configure is located. The list of server objects is visible on the right display window of the Microsoft Exchange administrator program.
5. Open its property pages by selecting Properties from the administrator program file menu or by pressing Alt+Enter.
6. Select the Services tab.

The Services Property Page

The Services property page allows you to define what services will be checked by a Microsoft Exchange server monitor. It is identical to the page found on the server monitor Servers page. The top display window shows all services currently installed on this Windows NT server; the bottom display window shows the monitored services.

Select a service from the top window and click Add to add it to the list of Monitored Services.

Select a service from the bottom window and click Remove to take it off the list of Monitored Services.

Click Default to return to the basic services selected by Exchange Server.

Click None to remove all services from the monitored lists.

The Actions Property Page

Use the Actions property page to define what steps are to be taken when a monitored service ceases to function. By default, no action is taken when a service goes down (except notification). Settings on this dialog box apply to all Exchange servers selected on the Servers property page. If you want to define different actions for different servers, you must create additional server monitors. There are three action choices to configure:

- Take no action: Literally, to do nothing in response to a stopped service. (Normal notification functions will still occur.)
- Restart the service: Initiate a service restart command.
- Restart the computer: Initiate a server restart command.

First attempt actions are executed the first time a service is polled and found to be in a warning or alert state. Second attempt is after the second, and Subsequent attempts are any time after the first two.

To configure Actions, follow this procedure:

1. Select the Actions tab from the Server monitor property pages. The property page shown in figure 24.13 will appear.

NOTE Actions defined in this property page are performed in addition to any notification action.

2. Next to First attempt use the pull-down menu to select an appropriate action. By default, Take no action is chosen.

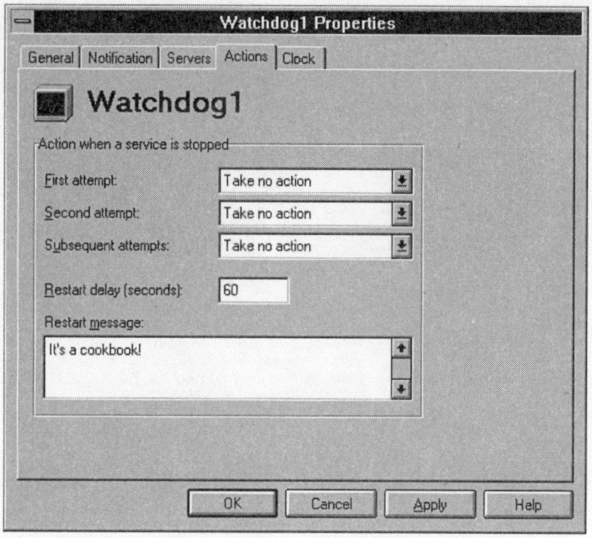

FIG. 24.13
Define what actions the server monitor should take upon detecting a service malfunction.

3. Next to Second attempt use the pull-down menu to select an appropriate action. By default, Take no action is chosen.
4. Next to Subsequent attempts use the pull-down menu to select an appropriate action. By default, Take no action is chosen.
5. Enter a Restart delay (in seconds) that the server will wait before initiating a restart command. By default, this value is 60 seconds.
6. Type Restart message that will be displayed by the server when a restart server action is initiated.
7. Click Apply to set these properties and continue with other properties. If you are done with all settings, click OK to return to the administrator program.

The Clock Property Page

The Clock property page configures system clock monitoring. Proper system clock synchronization is essential to running an efficient Exchange organization. So many connectors, gateways, and general maintenance processes depend on system-clock-based schedules that incorrect time setting could create many problems. The monitoring computer will generate an alert if both computers' system clocks are off by the predetermined number of seconds.

To set clock monitoring, follow this procedure:

1. Select the Clock tab of the Server Monitor property pages. The dialog box shown in figure 24.14 appears.

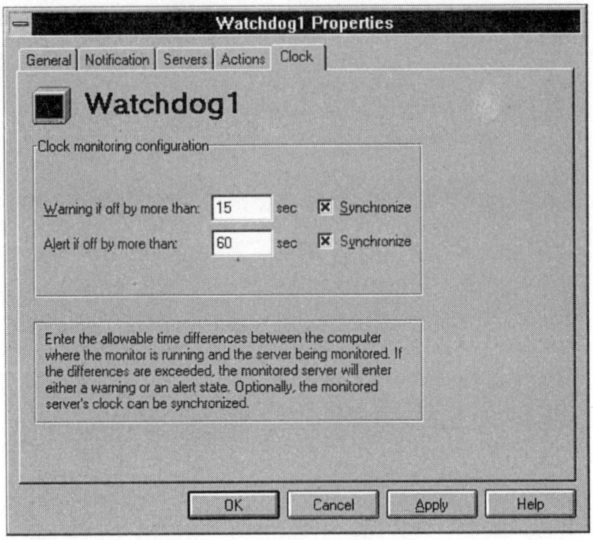

FIG. 24.14
Make sure clocks in your organization are properly synchronized.

2. In Warning if off by more than, type the maximum amount of time (in seconds) that the two clocks can differ before entering a warning state.
3. In Alert if off by more than, type the maximum amount of time (in seconds) that the two clocks can differ before entering an alert state.
4. Clear the Synchronize checkboxes to prevent the clock from adjusting to the monitoring computer's clock. By default, this option is selected.
5. Click Apply to set these properties and continue with other properties. If you are done with all settings, click OK to return to the administrator program.

Starting and Using a Monitor

After creating a monitor, you must start it in order for it to perform its functions. You can start a monitor manually from the administrator program or automatically from the command line. The monitor's window must be open at all times when running (minimized is OK).

Automatically Starting a Server Monitor

You can configure a server monitor for automatic startup by creating a program item for it in the Program Manager Startup group. The following sequence automatically starts the administrator program and designated monitors when logging in to Windows NT.

1. In the Windows NT Program Manager, open the Startup program group.
2. Select New from the Program Manager File menu.
3. Select Program Item from the New Program Object dialog box. Click OK.
4. Enter a Description for this startup item.
5. Enter a command line following this format: **path\admin.exe / m[sitename]\monitorname\server**

   Example command-line entry:

   ```
   E:\exchange\bin\admin.exe /mMELBOURNE\watchdog1\NECRISC01
   ```

   Optionally, multiple monitors can be started with this command-line entry by adding an extra `/m` and identifying the monitor.

   Example:

   ```
   E:\exchange\bin\admin.exe /mBOSTON\watchdog1\BOSTON01 /
   mBOSTON\linkkeeper\BOSTON01
   ```


Manually Starting a Server Monitor

To start a monitor manually from the administrator program, follow this procedure:

1. Using the Exchange administrator program, select the site in which the desired server monitor resides.
2. Open the Configuration container for the selected site.
3. Click on the Monitors container for this site. The right administrator display window will show all the monitors you have created in your site (whether started or not).
4. Select the server monitor of your choice. From the administrator program Tools menu, select Start Monitor (see fig. 24.15).
5. In the Connect to server dialog box, select which server to connect to as a home server. Click OK to start the monitor. The server monitor's display window appears.

NOTE You must connect to a specific server in order to execute server-based operations (e.g., sending mail).

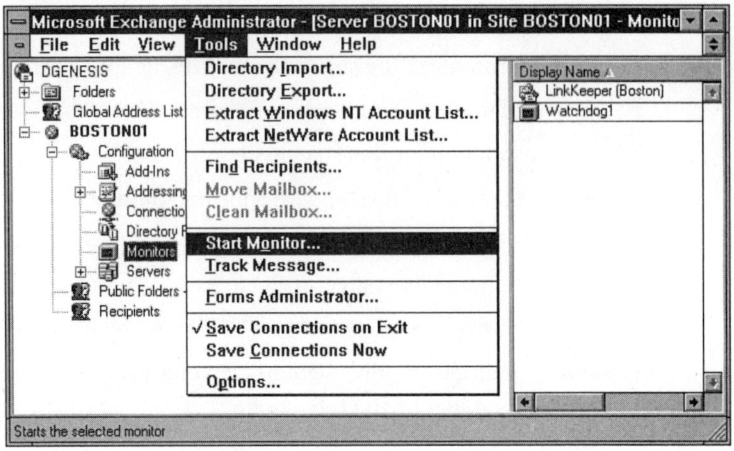

FIG. 24.15 The administrator program's Start Monitor command.

Using Monitor Status Windows

Monitor status windows are your portal through which you view the current condition of monitored links and servers. The status windows periodically update and display data on their operation. With enough strategically placed monitors, you can get an overall feel of your organization's messaging conditions from a single machine in your enterprise.

Reading the Link Monitor Window

The Link Monitor window displays the condition of monitored links. Each line in the display represents one link. You can sort the display using the Column heading buttons. You can also change the width of the columns to make the display easier to read (see fig. 24.16).

FIG. 24.16 A functioning Link Monitor window.

The Columns indicate the following things:

- Icon: Visually represents the link status

Up	Link is operational
Down	Link is not operational
Exclamation point	Warning state
Question mark	Link not yet monitored

- Server: The Server that sent the ping message and to which it is expected to return
- Last Measurement: The time the last ping message was sent
- Last Change: Time that the status of the link changed
- Last Time: The round-trip time of the last ping message sent from the sending server
- Comment: A description of the monitored link condition

Reading the Server Monitor Window

The Server Monitor window displays one line for each server being monitored. The status of the server, as represented by the icon, reflects the status of all server components. If any component is down, the server is considered to be down (see fig. 24.17).

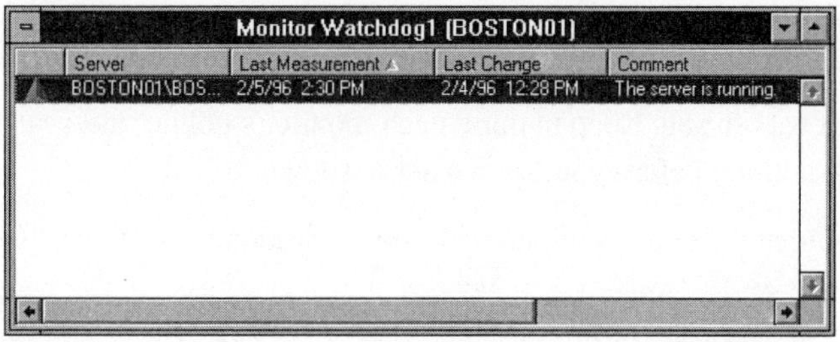

FIG. 24.17
A functioning Server Monitor window.

The Columns indicate the following things:

- Icon: Visually represents a server's status

Up	Server is operational
Down	Server is not operational
Exclamation point (!)	Warning state
Question mark (?)	Server not yet monitored

- Server: The name of the server being monitored
- Last measure: Time the last Remote Procedure Call was sent to test the status of Windows NT services
- Last change: Time the condition of service on a server changed

Double-clicking on a status message in either a link or server monitor will bring up property pages with status information. See Chapter 26, "Diagnostic and Troubleshooting Tools," for an explanation of these property pages.

Stopping a Monitor for Maintenance

When bringing an Exchange server down for maintenance, consider the effects on monitors watching the server. Any server monitors will notice the halted services, initiate notifications, and enter an alert state. Any link monitors watching messaging connection through this server will enter alert mode and send out applicable notifications as well.

To prevent these problems, you can put a server into maintenance mode. When a monitor polls a server in this mode, it knows not to go through the normal alerts and warnings routine.

The command to specify a maintenance mode for a server is as follows:

```
ADMIN /t
```

After this command is executed, each monitor learns of the server's maintenance status at the next server poll. Keep in mind each monitor's polling interval to be sure that all monitors are notified before you bring a server down.

The command can be modified with these additional switches:

`-n`	halts notification processes on a monitor, but keeps monitor initiated repairs
`-r`	keeps monitor initiated notifications, but halts repair processes on a monitor
`-nr`	halts both notification and repair processes
`-t`	resets the monitor to normal mode

To confirm that a monitor has received a maintenance notification, open a link or a server entry in the monitor and select its Maintenance property page. The checkboxes will give you this information.

From Here . . .

In this chapter, we have covered the two types of Exchange monitors. You will use these tools as your virtual eyes and ears watching over your Exchange servers and messaging links. Various notification options can be configured to alert you in the event a malfunction or aberration in standard perfomance occurs. However, these monitors are just additional tools at your disposal, not substitutes for good site and link planning and implementation.

- Chapter 12, "Directory and System Attendant Configuration," describes in detail ways of using the Server property pages to configure monitored services.
- Chapter 26, "Diagnostic and Troubleshooting Tools," provides more information using monitors to diagnose problems.

CHAPTER 25

Monitoring Exchange Sites

- Understanding elements of NT's security
- Understanding elements of Exchange's security
- Installing and managing the Key Management Server

Exchange relies on the C2-level security included within Windows NT for a portion of its structure. C2-level security is a U.S. Department of Defense rating defined. It provides for discretionary access control (users, groups, etc.), object reuse protection (protecting deleted data), mandatory logon, and auditing of security related events. Windows NT can provide user authentication, resource access, and auditing. Each of these areas is described in this chapter. Exchange increases security with digital signatures and message encryption. ■

Understanding NT Authentication

Every user, process, and service is required to enter a unique login name and password to gain access to the system. The operating system's interactive two-step security process of checking the login name with the password is known as *authentication.*

Microsoft Exchange Server enables the operating system to ascertain the identity and handle the validation of users and processes. The identity is the username and the validation is the user password. The operating system then will establish the security context, which explains and controls what kind of access will be granted to the user or process.

When a user or process logs in to the Windows NT server, there is no need for any other usernames or passwords to achieve access to Microsoft Exchange Server. This feature is unlike other types of message-system security features.

For example, a LAN Administrator on a Novell Netware 3.1x located on Server1 and the Microsoft Mail 3.x post offices and utilities are located on Server2. The administrator is required to enter a username and password for initial access to Server1. An additional username and password is needed for access to the directory structure on Server2. Moreover, a third username and password is needed to finally access the Admin program. Other message systems, such as Lotus cc:Mail, have similar security policies.

Defining NT's Domain Architecture

Each user or resource within a single location, such as the Microsoft Exchange Server, is a member of a particular *domain*. A domain is either a single Microsoft Windows NT server or multiple Windows NT servers that use the same security scheme and user-account database. Only one username and password is required to recognize, authenticate, and establish a connection to all the Windows NT servers and their resources in the domain.

Multiple domains or separate domain remote sites can connect by way of a trust relationship. This connection between the domains allows users on one domain the capability to access resources within the other domain. When the domains are in a trusted relationship, one domain (*trusting domain*) trusts the other (*trusted domain*). Any user located in the trusted domain can gain access to objects within the other domain.

For example, a user at Digital Genesis located in Los Angeles who logs on to Domain A wants access to a resource on Domain B. Because Domain B located in Boston has a trusted relationship with Domain A, the Domain B resources are available to this user. This situation is known as *passthrough authentication*, which allows having only one user account on one domain and the capability to access resources on the other.

The Types of NT Accounts

Window NT accounts are the principal structure upon which authentication is based. Accounts consist of the two main elements: the user ID and the associated password. These two fundamental bits of information provide the key to access various services. There are two main types of Windows NT accounts:

- User Accounts
- Service Accounts

User Accounts

Single and multiple user accounts can be associated with a Microsoft Exchange Server mailbox. The user attempting to establish a connection with a Microsoft Exchange Server must be located within the same domain as the Microsoft Exchange Server to which the user is trying to connect. If the user and the Microsoft Exchange Server are located on different domains, the domains must be in a trusted relationship.

As another example, a user on Domain A at Digital Genesis in Los Angeles wants to acquire access to a Microsoft Exchange Server located on Domain B in Boston, but in this case, Domain A and Domain B do not have a trusted relationship. The user on Domain A cannot establish a connection with the Microsoft Exchange Server located on Domain B.

Service Accounts

On the Microsoft Windows NT server, an assortment of services is initiated when the system goes through its startup process. The Microsoft Exchange Server information store service and MTA established connections are good examples of services that run on a Microsoft Windows NT Server. These services, through a user account known as a service account, log on to the system and start up automatically.

The service account is an important feature to the Microsoft Exchange Server. Create this account before beginning the installation of Microsoft Exchange Server. This account affects the installation of—and communication establishment between other—Microsoft Exchange Servers. When you install and join a new Microsoft Exchange Server to a site with an existing Microsoft Exchange Server, the service account is requested to complete the installation. The service account must be the same on all servers within a site. Without this account, Microsoft Exchange Servers in the same site will not be able to communicate with each other. If a site extends over multiple domains, only one service account is needed, provided that a trust relationship exists between domains.

Introduction to NT's Access Control

When a user logs on to a Microsoft Windows NT Server, the security features of the operating system look to the security context (covered previously in this chapter) for information determining the permissions to access specific network resources. A *permission* controls access to individual objects located in the system that use specific authorization information. Each object is different and, subsequently, has different levels of permissions.

The following list shows the variety of permissions to control access that Microsoft Exchange Server offers:

- Mailbox
- Public Folder
- Directory
- Group

Each of the permissions is discussed in detail in following sections of this chapter.

Mailbox Permissions

The Administrator program is the application used to grant permissions to log on and gain access to a Microsoft Exchange Server mailbox. One mailbox can have either one or multiple user accounts with the user permission set for it.

Microsoft Exchange Server reviews all user accounts for the user permission when a log-on is attempted. After the review completes, it verifies whether or not the user attempting to log on has this permission.

Public Folder Permissions

Using the Microsoft Exchange Client, the owner of a public folder can grant permission to the following areas to access it:

- Mailboxes
- Distribution lists
- Public folders

As stated above previously, different objects have different levels of permissions. The owner of a public folder can grant others the following permissions:

- Create items
- Read items

- Edit items
- Delete items

The public folder, similar to other Windows NT resources, reviews the user accounts for permissions for this resource. Then, the folder verifies that the object trying to access it has the appropriate permissions.

As an example, Digital Genesis has created two differing distribution lists within a Financial public folder on the Microsoft Exchange Server—Accounting and Accounting Managers. The permissions can be modified on the Financial public folder so that members of the Accounting group have Read Access, and the Accounting Managers may have Read and Write permissions.

Directory Permissions

Applying permissions to directories is different than applying permissions to public folders. With directories, the permissions are granted directly to the user's account database. Within the administrator application, although all users can see the directory listed, unless the users have the correct permissions, they cannot view the data inside the directory. A good example of a directory permission is *Add Child*. With this permission on the Recipient Container, a user can create mailboxes.

Roles are another way of making administrative tasks easier. Roles consist of built-in groups of certain kinds of similar permissions. For example, the following list shows the built-in permissions for the Admin role:

- Add Child
- Modify user attributes
- Delete
- Logon

Organizing NT Groups and Permissions

Sets of user accounts with similar network resource needs can be placed into a *group*. This action simplifies the administrative task of adding permissions to individual users. If a group named MIS is created, all members of this group automatically have the permissions that are granted to the group, and these permissions are applied to the individual user. Any users accounts that are created after the group was created, or existing users who become additional members of this group, will have the same group permissions applied. Likewise, if the permissions of the group are modified, all members of the group will have their permissions changed. Microsoft Windows NT Server offers built-in *local* and *global groups* with the capability to also create local and global groups. When possible, a good recommendation is to use groups. Using groups diminishes the amount of time spent dealing with administrative tasks.

Local Groups

Only the domain where the *local group* exists will contain the definition of resource permissions for this group. Additionally, no matter which domain the local group is located in, permissions can be granted only to that particular domain's resources. Local groups may contain the following:

- Other users
- Global groups from the same domain
- Users from trusted domains
- Global groups from trusted domains

NOTE Local groups cannot contain other local groups from the same domain.

Global Groups

Groups that can use resources within other domains are known as *global groups*. Global groups consist of a group of user accounts that was given access to permissions and rights for the following:

- The global group's own domain
- Servers and clients of the domain
- Any trusting domains

Global groups also can be members of local domain groups.

In essence, the creation of global groups allows sets of users from within a particular domain and the available use of network resources, from both inside and outside the domain.

Using NT's Auditing Capabilities

Microsoft Windows NT has built-in auditing capabilities that allow the operating system to track events that occur within the system to detect security breaches. This tracking is an advantage for the Microsoft Exchange Server system. As discussed previously, the operating system handles the identity and validation of users for Microsoft Exchange Server. Moreover, the Microsoft Windows NT Server operating system can be modified to audit the Microsoft Exchange Server event services and directory objects. These events show up in the *Windows NT event log.*

NOTE Microsoft Exchange Server Administrators do not require permissions to administer to the Microsoft Windows NT Server. ■

Using Exchange's Advanced Security

As mentioned previously, Exchange uses several of NT's built-in C2-level security features. To augment this security, Exchange adds digital signatures and message encryption. To enable these advanced security features, you must designate one server within your organization that manages a special security database. This server is known as the Key Management (KM) Server. Before discussing how the KM Server works with digital signatures and message encryption, make sure that you understand keys, tokens, certificates, and Exchange's revocation list.

Keys

Each mailbox created within Microsoft Exchange Server is given two pairs of electronic keys. One key pair, used for signing and verifying actions, is created by the Microsoft Exchange Client. The other pair, used for encrypting and decrypting operations, is generated by the KM Server. The *private key* is known only by the user, and a *public key* is known by the public (it can be accessed by other mail users). This key-type of security features is known as *public/private key technology*, a data-encryption industry standard.

The Microsoft Exchange Client, located on the user's local hard disk, stores the private keys in an encrypted security file (with the extension, .EPF), within the client's local directory structure. The private encryption key is used for decrypting messages destined for the user's mailbox. The private signing key is used for signing messages when they are sent.

For every message recipient, each of their public encryption keys is used when the original message composer sends an encrypted message. The multiple public encryption keys are used to complete the encryption process. When each recipient receives the encrypted message, his or her public signing key is used to verify the identity of the message sender or composer.

Another key used by the Microsoft Exchange Server is the *bulk encryption key*. This key is used in conjunction with both the public and private encryption keys. The bulk encryption key is used to encrypt the original message. The key then is placed into a *lockbox*, where it is kept to protect the key during transit. If the message has multiple recipients, a lockbox is attached to the message for each of the recipients. When the message is received at the recipient's location, the bulk encryption key is extracted from the lockbox and used to decrypt the original message.

Certificates

The Certificate Authority (CA) is the Key Management Server component that generates signing and encrypting certificates. Certificates bind the user's public key to the user's mailbox. The CA certifies the genuineness of those public keys created for users. Users have two kinds of certificates—an encryption certificate and a signing certificate. The *encryption certificate* is an attribute of the mailbox and contains the user's public encryption key. The signing certificate is contained in the user's security file on the local hard disk drive. It holds the user's public signing key.

The certificate also contains the following information:

- A unique serial number, generated by the CA for each certificate
- The CA's directory name (DN)
- The user's directory name (DN)
- The expiration date of the user's public key

Exchange also supports the revocation of security certificates. This action permanently deactivates the security certificate for a mailbox. This should be done only when you are absolutely sure that you do not need to recover the security keys in the future. When the security certificate is revoked for a mailbox, anyone attempting to open an encrypted message previously sent from this mailbox is prompted with a warning, informing him or her that the message was secured with a revoked security certificate.

The revocation list contains the serial number and expiration date of all revoked certificates. This makes sure that the revoked user's mail account cannot be used by unauthorized personnel. The user then can be reconfigured for advanced security and another certificate issued. Reconfiguration will issue another token, and also another certificate serial number and expiration date.

You may want to consider revoking advanced security when the following situations exist:

- Users feel their security was compromised because it appears that someone is signing messages on their behalf or because someone has gained access to their security files and passwords.

  For example, a Digital Genesis salesperson's laptop was stolen in the field. You should revoke this salesperson's certificate to ensure that that person's security certificates are in the relocation list. Then you should reconfigure the user for Exchange's advanced security, generating a new security certificate for the user.
- An employee leaves your organization, and you want to ensure that the digital signatures and encrypted messages from this user are identified as invalid.

All revoked certificates originate in the KM Server database and are distributed to all the clients. Each client caches the original list and receives a daily update from the KM Server. For performance reasons, revoke users judiciously. When a message reaches its recipient and the signature is verified, it must be checked against the list before the message can be decrypted. The more certificates that are contained in the list, the more advanced security and performance of the client will degrade.

Tokens

When a mail administrator activates advanced security for a user, a temporary security *token* is generated. This random eight-digit code not only enables digital signing and data encryption, but also can be recovered if lost.The token should be loaded on the local workstation. Tokens are used only once, to secure a connection with the KM server and complete the advanced security setup for Microsoft Exchange Server advanced security users.

Key Management Server

One Microsoft Exchange Server integrated component is the Key Management Server, which is the central point for advanced security within the system. The Key Management Server provides the following services:

- Certifies public signing and encryption keys
- Creates public and private encryption keys

- Maintains backups of private encryption keys and public signing keys
- Generates tokens
- Maintains the original copy of the revocation list

All private encryption keys, public signing keys, and the revocation list are stored in the key management database. For additional security, the KM Server database itself is encrypted.

Each user that you want to use advanced security must be configured after the KM Server is configured. The users are given a temporary token to allow access to the KM Server so that the advanced security features setup can be completed.

When the Key Management Server is properly set up and advanced security is activated, users can take advantage of Exchange's digital signatures and message encryption.

Digital Signatures

Microsoft Exchange Server provides *End-to-End Authentication* and *Data Integrity* through the use of Digital Signatures, which are based on a user's signing keys. Two processes, signing and verifying, are involved.

When a message is to be sent, the sender selects Digitally Sign Message. It then will have a "signature" placed on it. The signature, or signing key, claims that the message was derived from the indicated source. The name on the header is matched with the sender's name. This matching prevents forgeries. Before the recipient can receive the message, the destination verifies the signature on the message.

After the message is signed, it is transformed to *message hashes*, which are a unique representation of a message. Moreover, the hashes are then encrypted. The original message and the encrypted hash message are then sent with the signing certificate to the destination. The signing certificate contains the sender's signing key.

When the message reaches its recipient, the message is verified when user chooses Read Digital Signature from the toolbar. First, the sender's certificate is checked against the revocation list. If it is on the list, the recipient is notified that this user was revoked from the system. Next, the original message is hashed as the encrypted hash message is decrypted. These two messages, both in hashed states, now can be compared to each other. If the hashes don't match, the message has been modified in transit and the user is notified. This feature allows for built-in data integrity verification. See figure 25.1 for an illustration of how messages are sent and received by using digital signatures.

FIG. 25.1
Sending and receiving a message with a digital signature.

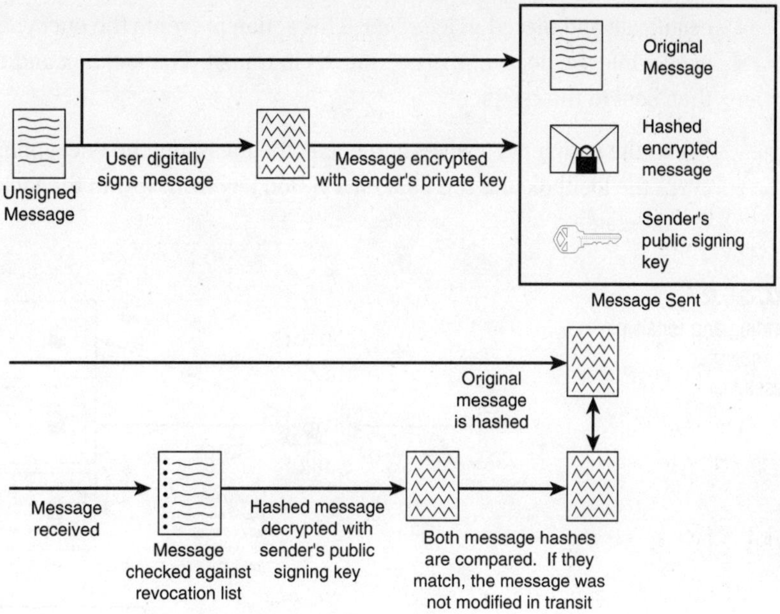

Introduction to Data Encryption

Microsoft Exchange Server provides confidentiality by encrypting the destined message. When the message is sent, the data-encryption security feature scrambles the message. If you viewed the message in this scrambled state, it would resemble a bunch of random alphanumeric characters. When the message is received at its destination, it is decrypted and put back together in the original format.

Microsoft Exchange Server supports the following two standards to complete this security task:

- CAST encryption algorithms
- Data Encryption Standard (DES)

NOTE The Data Encryption Standard (DES) is available with Microsoft Windows NT Server software in Canada and the United States.

When a user chooses Secure Message with Encryption from the toolbar, all of the recipients' certificates are retrieved from the directory. Next, a bulk encryption key is created to encrypt the message. Finally, the user's public encryption key is extracted from the certificate and placed in a *lockbox*. This action prevents the encryption key from being used while the decrypt the message is in transit. The lockbox and the encryption key are then sent to the recipient.

When the recipient receives and opens the message, the encryption key is used to decrypt the lockbox and the bulk encryption key from within the lockbox is used to decrypt the message.

FIG. 25.2
Sending and receiving an encrypted message.

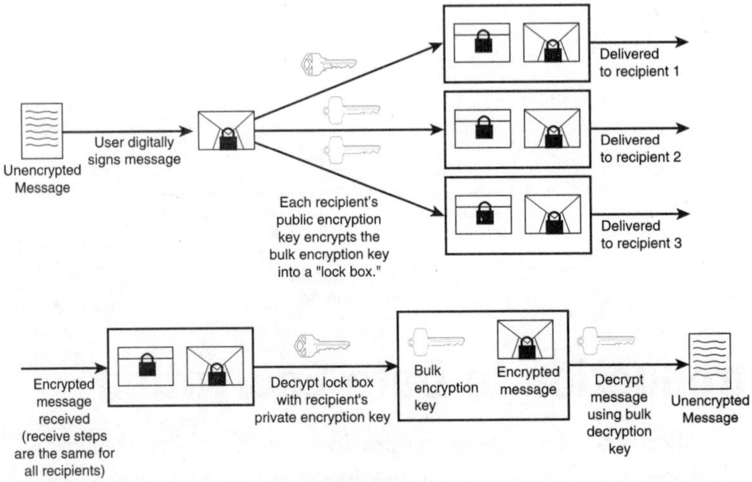

Using Key Management Server

The Key Management Server, which is a component of Microsoft Exchange Server, is the central point for advanced security. The following steps show what is involved to set up and maintain Microsoft Exchange Server advanced security:

- Selecting the server to manage the key management database
- Installing the Key Management component software and enabling individual users to take advantage of advanced security features
- Configuring remote sites to use advanced security
- Verifying that the Key Management component is functioning correctly
- Viewing security logs for errors or attempted breaches, and periodically clearing the logs of unneeded information
- Backing up and maintaining the key management database

Selecting the Server to Manage the Key Management Database

Only one Microsoft Windows NT Server in the organization that is running Microsoft Exchange Server can become the Key Management Server (KM Server) and manage the Key Management advanced security database. Having multiple KM Servers can cause authentication and encryption errors. When deciding which Microsoft Exchange Server to use as the KM Server, keep the following important points in mind:

- Advanced security administration can be done only from within the site where the KM Server is located.
- The server should be physically secure, such as placed in a locked room or area with restricted access.
- The Key Management database should be backed up regularly.
- The server must be using the NTFS file system for maximum security.

Installing the Key Management Component Software

In order to install the Key Management component software, the setup process asks for two passwords. One password is copied to a floppy disk. This option can be deselected on the property page during the beginning of the setup. If the copy is deselected, the setup process displays the password on-screen. It's recommended to write down this password.

Do the following steps to install your Key Management component software:

1. Launch SETUP.EXE from the Microsoft Exchange Server CD-ROM for your appropriate CPU (\SETUP\i386\EXCHKM for Intel processors).
2. Choose Continue to bypass the Welcome screen.
3. Enter Full Name and Organization information, and then choose OK to continue.
4. Confirm Full Name and Organization information.
5. Choose OK to bypass the Product ID information.
6. Setup shows a screen with the default directory (`C:\SECURITY`). If the default directory is OK, press continue and skip to step 10.
7. Click the *change folder* icon to change the directory to which setup will install the files.
8. Select the directory in which install needs to install the files.
9. If directory doesn't exist, choose OK to confirm its creation.

10. Choose OK to continue.
11. Click the Typical button to execute the install. KM Server then installs with all options.
12. The next screen asks about the Country Code selection and the creation of *KM Server Startup floppy disk.* Accept defaults, choose OK, and skip to step 15.
13. If you need to change the country code, select the correct country code.
14. If the decision is made to go with a diskless setup, deselect (clear the check box) the box beside the option. Choose OK to continue.

NOTE If there is not a KM Server Startup floppy disk created, the password for the Key Management Server Service is displayed on the screen.

Important: Please write this password down somewhere. This password cannot be changed with reinstalling the component. This password is needed by the KM Server Service to start up. This is the password that would otherwise be placed on the floppy disk.

15. If defaults were accepted from step 12, a request to insert a blank floppy disk in drive A appears. Insert the blank floppy disk and choose OK.
16. To complete a successful setup, click OK.

Starting the Key Management Server Service

The Key Management Server Service must be started to enable and configure advanced security for individual users.

NOTE If a KM Server Startup Floppy Disk wasn't created, the password that was displayed on-screen during the setup process must be input within the startup parameters for the KM Server service.

1. Log on to Microsoft Windows NT Server as Administrator.
2. Select the Main program group, then Control Panel, and finally Services.
3. Locate the Key Management Server service entry, highlight it, and click the Start button. Refer to the preceding Note regarding diskless KM Server setups.
4. After displaying a message about starting the services, the Key Management Service status changes to Started.
5. Close the Services applet and exit Control Panel.

Changing Your Advanced Security Administrative Password

The Key Management Server requires an Advanced Security Administrator's password to modify any security-related items. This password is separate from any other passwords, which were explained in previous chapters. This password is specific for security-related administrative tasks.

If this is a new install or if the advanced security password has never been changed, take the following steps:

1. Launch Microsoft Exchange Server Administrator program.
2. Connect to a Microsoft Exchange Server.
3. Click on the Configuration container.
4. Choose the Encryption object and open its property pages.
5. Click the Security tab.
6. Choose Key Management Administrators.
7. Enter the Advanced Security Administrator password.

NOTE If the password has never been changed for any reason, the default password is PASSWORD.

8. Click Change Password, type the old password into the Old Password box, and then type your new password in the New Password box. You then are asked to verify the new password.
9. Choose OK to save the changes.

Enabling Advanced Security Features for Individual Users

To allow users to digitally sign and encrypt messages, advanced security must be enabled for each recipient. With the KM Server in production, after the advanced security setup process for a user is initiated, an RPC call is made to the KM Server, which generates and returns a token.

Configuring Remote Sites to Use Advanced Security

Users located in remote sites cannot be directly set up for advanced security because the KM Server uses RPC calls, but the users still can be set up for advanced security in an indirect manner. The Key Management Administrator can input the names of the users located at remote sites from a site that contains the KM Server. The tokens are generated for the individual users in the same manner that users located in the local site are generated. Then, the tokens must be securely transferred to the individual users for final setup of the client. Such transfers of token information are done "out of band" by a phone call, fax, or alternative means of comunication.

Verifying That the Key Management Component Is Functioning Correctly

The Microsoft Windows NT Server logs information about the Key Management Server in the applications Event Viewer, which includes information regarding the KM Server functions and duties. If the option is used when launching the KM Server (this is done in Control Panels, Services icon, within the startup parameters option), the events also will be shown in the KM Server command box.

1. Open the Administrative Tools program group from the Windows NT Server Program Manager.
2. Launch the Event Viewer.
3. From the Log menu, select Applications.

All log information regarding the Key Management Server that is being recorded in the Event Viewer is identified by an MSexchangeKM entry in the source column.

Viewing Security Logs for Errors or Attempted Breaches

Events that are generated by the Key Management Server are related to granting and revoking of permissions, security violations, and the internal operation of the KM Server. All events logged can be viewed in the Event Viewer.

Backing Up and Maintaining the Key Management Database

All advanced security data is stored in the SECURITY\MGRENT folder. This directory structure should be backed up on a regular basis. Any Microsoft Windows NT-compatible backup application can be used to archive the advanced security directory structure.

The two services that must be running at the start time of the backup are the Information Store service and Directory service.

From Here...

This chapter described the rich security features available within NT and Exchange. With the proper use, you can guarantee your users a robust messaging system while maintaining message integrity and system security.

For related information, see the following chapters:

- Chapter 22, "Exchange Performance Tuning and Capacity Planning," describes how to tune Exchange after applying security.
- Chapter 23, "Exchange Maintenance," provides the information you need to maintain your Exchange installation.
- Chapter 24, "Monitoring Your Organization," provides the tools to monitor all changes to your Exchange system before and after applying security.
- Chapter 26, "Diagnostic and Troubleshooting Tools," details several problem situations and their solutions.

CHAPTER 26

Diagnostic and Troubleshooting Tools

Message Tracking

A powerful way to find link malfunctions.

MTACHECK

A method to scan the database for damaged objects, remove them, and rebuild the queue.

ISINTEG

A utility that performs diagnostics and repair functions on the IS databases.

Diagnostic Logging/ Windows NT Event Viewer

Microsoft Exchange Server is an intricate product that consists of many components, so it is important in any pilot or installation that you set aside enough time for planning and installation. Many tools exist that can help you plan and analyze a Microsoft Exchange Server installation. This chapter familiarizes you with some of the tools Microsoft Exchange provides for diagnosing and troubleshooting various components of Microsoft Exchange within your organization. ■

Tracking Exchange Messages

Tracking a message through a Microsoft Exchange system can be a powerful way of finding link malfunctions. Message tracking can assist support professionals in pinpointing the exact servers or links at fault. It can also be used to determine the quality of service of the Microsoft Exchange system in areas such as performance, round trips between two servers, alternate route setup, and usage and reliability issues such as lost mail. Exchange provides tools to follow a message through its journey to verify transmissions at certain points of your organization. Here are some common uses for Exchange message tracking:

- Analyzing a message's path through the system to test for proper routing
- Determine the time delay for messages to pass through each connector in their path
- Finding mail that was not appropriately delivered (also called "lost" mail)

All message tracking information is stored by the system attendant on each server when tracking is enabled. The Exchange Server component that actually writes the entries to the log file is the System Attendant.

The location of this log is

driveletter:\EXCHSRVR\TRACKING.LOG

Tracking logs are kept for an entire day and a new log is created the next day. Tracking must be enabled on each component through which the message flows occur.

For example, to track a message to a remote site connected via the Internet, you would need to enable MTA tracking on both Exchange sites and the Internet mail connector used at each site.

As explained earlier, Message tracking is a powerful tool to debug any problems with the Exchange System. Following is a discussion of how to enable Message Tracking on various Exchange Components:

- *Message Transfer Agent.* To enable tracking for every MTA in a site, select the Enable Message Tracking check box on the MTA Site Configuration General property page.
- *Information Store.* To enable tracking for every information store in a site, click the Enable Message Tracking check box on the Information Store Site Configuration General property page.
- *Microsoft Mail Connector.* To enable tracking for an MS Mail connector, click the Enable Message Tracking check box on the MS Mail Connector Interchange property page. You must enable tracking individually for each MS Mail connector in each site.

- *Internet Mail Connector.* To enable tracking for an Internet Mail Connector, click the Enable Message Tracking check box on the Internet Mail Connector Internet Mail property page. You must enable tracking individually for each Internet Mail Connector in each site.

Message tracking allows support professionals to view, sort, and filter the information collected by each individual server or the messages sent, received, and delivered by the server. Here is how you would use the Message tracking tools from the Exchange administrator program (see fig. 26.1).

FIG. 26.1
Open the tracking tools from the Exchange Administrator program.

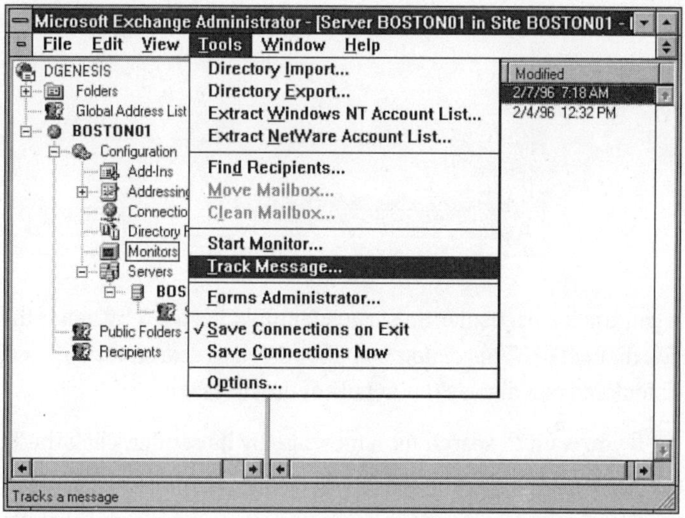

1. Choose Tools, Track Message from the administrator program menu. The Connect to Server dialog box appears.
2. Choose a server in your site to connect to. Preferably, connect to a server with either the sender or recipient of the message you want to track in its address list. The Select Message to Track dialog box appears.
3. In the Select Message to Track dialog box, find the message you want to track. You are given the option to search for messages either by sender or recipients. (In this search tool, the sender or recipients must be listed in the address lists available to this Exchange server.)

   If the recipients you need are not listed in the address book, or if you already have a Message ID to use for tracking, click cancel on this page and proceed to the advanced search page (see fig. 26.2).

FIG. 26.2
Search for message either via sender or recipients (must be visible in the address book).

You can track a particular message identified in step 3 by using the Select Message to Track dialog box. This dialog box allows you to search for a message by either sender or recipient and can display the details of the message:

1. If you want to search for a message by its sender, click the From button and select a sender from the address book.

   If you want to search for a message by its recipients, click the Sent To button and select a recipient (or group of recipients) from the address book.
2. In the Look Back box, enter the number of previous days you want to search for messages. Keep in mind that message tracking must have been enabled on those days for a log to have been created.
3. To connect to a different Exchange server use the Browse button.
4. When all of your parameters are set, click the Find Now button. All tracking logs for the number of days selected will be searched sequentially. The results are displayed in the bottom window (see fig. 26.3).
5. Select a found message from the list and click Properties to view further property details about it (see fig. 26.4). Click Close when you are done viewing the message's details to return to the Select Message to Track dialog box.

FIG. 26.3
A successful search displays the message matching your criteria in the bottom display window.

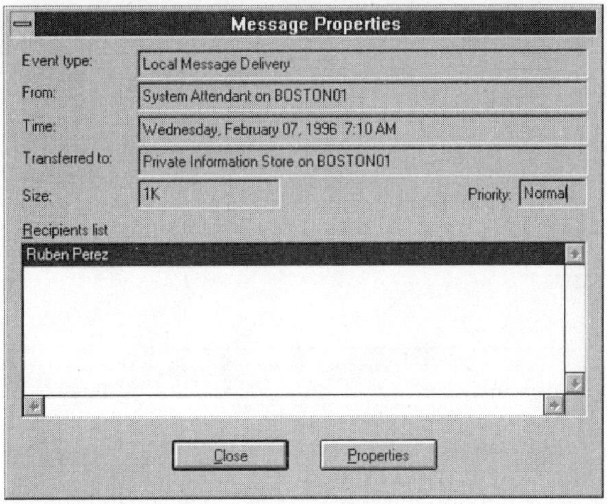

FIG. 26.4
The Message Properties dialog box shows you unique information about the messages your search found.

6. Click OK to return to the Message Tracking Center dialog box.

   In the Message Tracking Center dialog box, the Message ID field is now filled in with the appropriate information from the selected message and the Track button is now available.

Using the Message Tracking Center

The Message Tracking Center windows can trace a message (that is found in the search windows from the previous steps) through its path. It executes searches on all the message logs of the Exchange servers that handled it. This includes from the point it originated on an Exchange server (or entered the network through a connector or gateway) to the point it was delivered (or left the network).

Clicking the Track button in the Message Center dialog box (see fig. 26.5) performs the actual track on the message and fills in the information in the Tracking History box. The Tracking History box displays the steps taken in the process of delivering the message, including the action performed and the Exchange Server involved. A message's Tracking History is the sequence of steps taken to reach a destination.

FIG. 26.5
The Message Tracking Center lets you search for a message in various ways, then trace its route once it is found.

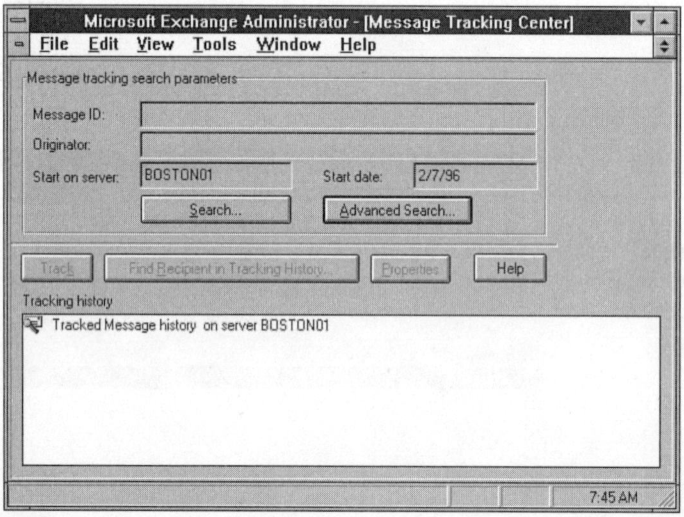

There are two parts to the Message Tracking Center: the message search utilities that also display message details, and the Tracking tools for those messages.

Once a message has been tracked, two additional buttons become available in the Message Tracking Center dialog. What follows is a discussion of the first button—this button can search for messages and display message details:

1. The Message Tracking Search Parameters window displays the current message resulting from the search (blank if none). Click Search to bring up the Select a Message to Track dialog box (see previous page).
2. Click Advanced Search to find a message based on different parameters. The dialog box in figure 26.6 appears.

FIG. 26.6
Search for a message using more advanced parameters.

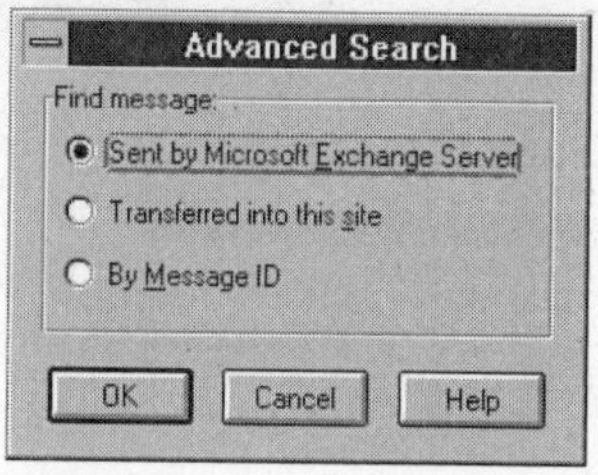

Sent by Microsoft Exchange Server

Selecting Sent by Microsoft Exchange Server from the Advanced Search dialog box brings up the Select System Message to Track dialog box (see fig. 26.7), which helps you find messages originating from core Microsoft Exchange components. Typically, these are warning and status messages from the Exchange server to an administrator.

FIG. 26.7
Search for a message by using more advanced parameters.

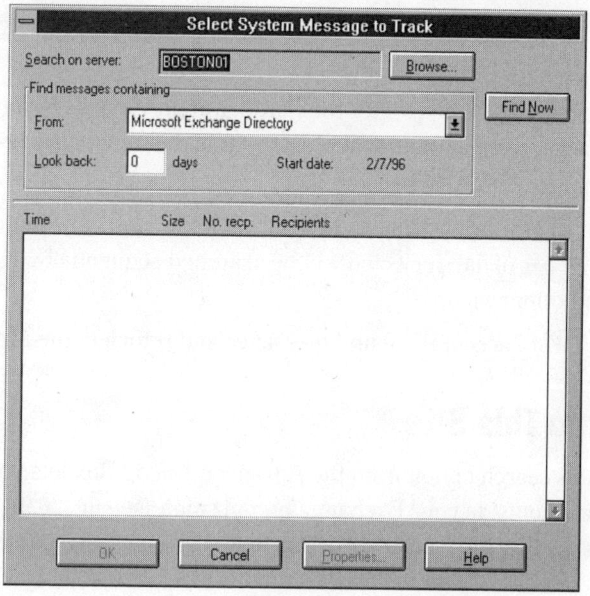

1. To search on a different Exchange server, use the Browse button (see fig. 26.8).
2. Use the From pull-down menu to choose which Exchange component (Directory, Information Store, System Attendant, Directory Synchronization Agent) to scan for as the message originator.

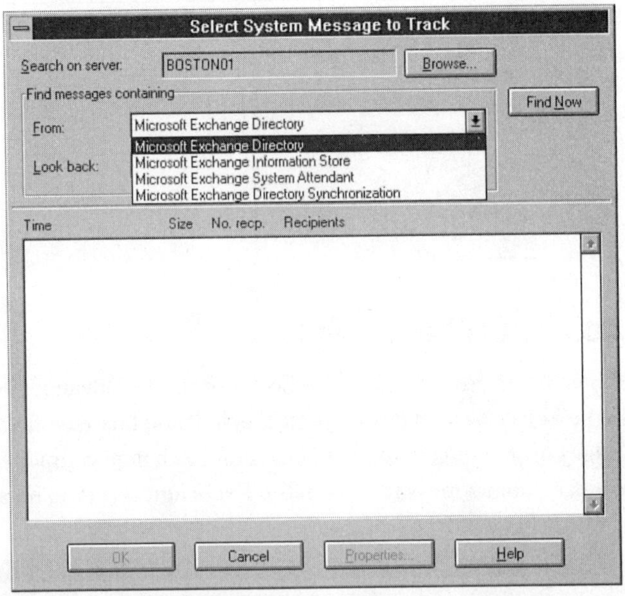

FIG. 26.8
Select an Exchange component that could have originated the message.

3. In the Look Back box, enter the number of previous days you want to search for messages. Keep in mind that message tracking must have been enabled on those days for a log to have been created.
4. When all of your parameters are set, click the Find Now button. All tracking logs for the number of days selected will be searched sequentially. The results are displayed in the bottom window.
5. Click OK to accept the found messages and return to the Message Tracking Center.

Transferred into This Site

Choosing this search option from the Advanced Dialog Box lets you search for a message that originated outside your Exchange organization (see fig. 26.9). You can filter this search by selecting the connector or gateway that a message passed through to enter the system.

FIG. 26.9
Find a message originating outside the organization.

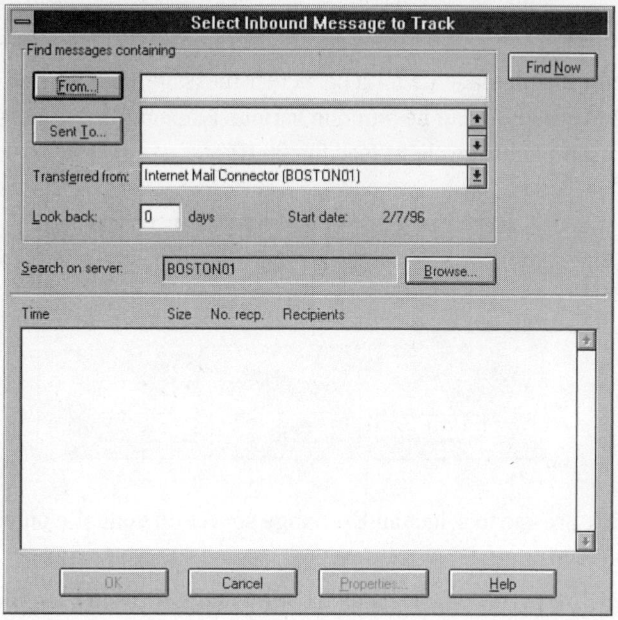

1. If you want to search for a message by its sender, click the From button and select a sender from the address book. Normally, you will not use this option if the sender is not a custom recipient in the address list.

   If you want to search for a message by its recipients, click the Sent To button and select a recipient (or group of recipients) from the address book.
2. Use the Transferred From pull-down menu to select a connector in your site as the inbound gateway for the message you are searching for.
3. In the Look Back box, enter the number of previous days you want to search for messages. Keep in mind that message tracking must have been enabled on those days for a log to have been created.
4. To connect to a different Exchange server use the Browse button.
5. When all of your parameters are set, click the Find Now button. All tracking logs for the number of days selected will be searched sequentially. The results are displayed in the bottom window.
6. Click OK to accept the found messages and return to the Message Tracking Center.

By Message ID

If you know the message ID for a particular message, you can find it by selecting this option. A message ID can be found in various Exchange logs, message queues, and also in the Microsoft Exchange client (see fig. 26.10).

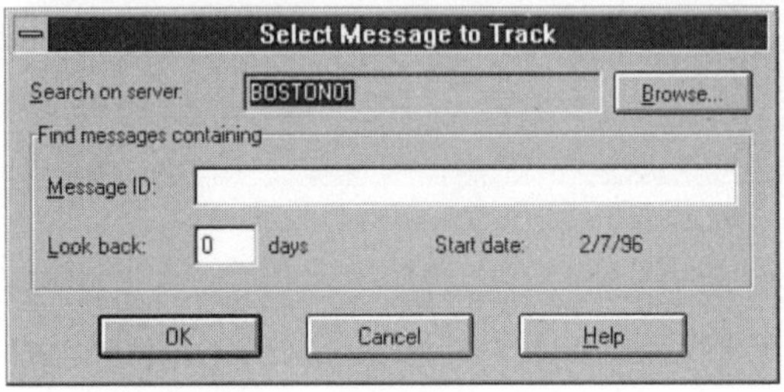

FIG. 26.10
Search for a message by its Exchange Message ID.

1. Click Browse to select an Exchange server on your site on which to search for the message.
2. Type (or paste if you've copied the message ID from a log file) the message ID into the Message ID text box.
3. Enter a number of days to Look Back into a log file. Start Date will display the first day to start looking for a message.
4. Click OK to search for the selected message and return to the Message Tracking Center.

Tracking a Message

After finding the message that meets your criteria, click Track from the Message Tracking Center dialog box. Assuming all the necessary tracking check boxes were activated, the display window will show you the path of the selected message from the first instant it entered the Exchange organization, to when it was delivered (or left the organization through a connector or gateway).

You can view details about the message route by clicking and expanding the message view in the display window.

Additional Exchange Core Component Troubleshooting Tools

Following is a discussion of some of the Core Troubleshooting Tools to diagnose problems with MS Exchange. These are: MTACHECK and ISInteg.

MTACheck is a support tool that assists the administrators in diagnosing the MTA queues. *ISInteg* is a support tool run on an offline information store that checks the consistency of the information store.

If the MTA queues become corrupt or unable to process a message, it is possible for the MTA to be unable to start. In these situations, a utility called MTACHECK.EXE which can be found in the \exchsrvr\bin directory can be used to repair the problem.

MTACHECK.EXE will check the consistency of the MTA queues, check the integrity of all objects, and if necessary, delete corrupt objects. Under most circumstances, the MTACHECK.EXE program will resolve any issues with a problematic MTA.

MTACHECK

A message transfer agent uses message queues to store messages. The queues are in essence databases that store messages awaiting delivery to their intended destinations. Occasionally, parts of these databases can become corrupt and cause message transfer errors. MTACHECK scans the queue database for damaged objects, removes them from the queue, then rebuilds the message queue for correct operation.

MTACHECK can be used primarily in two types of situations:

- Routine tests of MTA queue databases for message integrity.
- Troubleshooting an MTA that has spontaneously stopped and will not properly restart. Running MTACHECK may clear the problem and enable the MTA to restart.

MTACHECK places removed data in a directory called MTACHECK.OUT.
The MTACHECK.OUT directory is created in the path:

\EXCHSRVR\MTADATA\MTACHECK.OUT

The data files are created in that directory and given the name: DB*.DAT

MTACHECK creates one file for each damaged piece of data removed.

CAUTION

When removing damaged message files from the queue, MTACHECK may remove messages that cannot be recovered.

MTACHECK is run from the Windows NT command line of the Exchange server you want to scan. The executable is located in the directory:

driveletter:\EXCHSRVR\BIN\MTACHECK.EXE

First, you must manually stop the Message Transfer Agent Service before running this utility (MTACHECK will remind you if you forget). Then, delete the current contents of the MTACHECK.OUT directory. If it is the first time MTACHECK is run, the MTACHECK.OUT is not yet in existence.

NOTE The MTACHECK.OUT directory is automatically created when MTACHECK.EXE is run.

Use the following procedure to run MTACHECK on an Exchange server:

1. Stop the Message Transfer Agent service.
2. Remove or delete the contents of the MTACHECK.OUT directory.
3. Run MTACHECK.EXE from the Windows NT command line.
4. Analyze the results and restart the MTA service when appropriate.

Optional switches

Use these switches to modify the MTACHECK execution.

/v	Start verbose display. Displays progress messages more frequently and in more detail.
/f *filename*	Saves progress messages to the specified filename.

`MTACHECK /v /f MTACHECK.LOG` is an example of a command that uses both of these switches. It enables the verbose status display, and it stores that display in a file called MTACHECK.LOG.

ISINTEG

The ISINTEG utility performs diagnostic and repair functions on the Exchange Information Store databases. This is a function similar to that performed by the MTACHECK utility.

Situations that would warrant use of this utility are

- The Information Store service will not start properly.
- After recovering an information store database with software other than the built-in Windows NT backup utility

There are three main modes of operation for the ISINTEG:

- *Test Mode.* Runs diagnostic scan of the Information Store databases to detect errors.
- *Test Mode and Fix.* Runs the same diagnostics as normal, but proceeds to fix whatever it can in the process.
- *Patch Mode.* Used when recovering an information store database with a software other than the built-in Windows NT backup utility.

ISINSTEG is run from the Windows NT command line of the Exchange server you want to scan. The executable is located in the directory:

driveletter:\EXCHSRVR\BIN\ISINTEG.EXE

Optional Switches

Use these switches to modify the ISINTEG execution.

Switch	Description
-?	Displays this options list
-pri	Runs diagnostics on the private information store; by default, this is the test that will run
-pub	Runs diagnostics on the public information store
-fix	Runs diagnostics and corrects any errors that it can (also called Check & Correct)
-verbose	Displays more detailed diagnostic information
-l (*filename*)	Stores log information under a different file name; by default, INISTEG.PRI and INISTEG.PUB are the log files
-test *testname*,...	Runs a specific ISINTEG test; all available tests can be viewed with the -? switch

Using Diagnostic Logging

Diagnostic logging is a tool that lets you zero in on messaging problems that plague your system. These logging settings are set in the Diagnostic Logging property page for each component. Diagnostics are logged into the Windows NT event logs, which can then be viewed with the NT Event Viewer.

The following Exchange components have a diagnostic logging property page for their pertinent system services:

Directory Service

Directory Synchronization

Internet Mail Connector

Information store (both public and private)

Microsoft Mail Connector

Message Transfer Agent

TIP The Diagnostic Logging property page for each Exchange server shows a unified list of that server's logging settings.

Subcomponents and Categories

Categories are the various functions of each Exchange service. You specify various levels of logging on a per-category basis. Different categories within a service (or subcomponent of that service) can be logged separately to track a problem to a specific function.

Some services (for example the Information store) also have subcomponents. Subcomponents are logging subdivisions beneath each Exchange service. Each Subcomponent also has a set of categories that can be logged individually.

For example, the Information Store service (MSExchangeIS) has three subcomponents. Each subcomponent (System, Public, and Private) pertains to roles of that service. Each subcomponent also has a set of categories pertaining to its specific functioning. The three categories of the Public subcomponent are

Replication Status Updates

Incoming Messages

Outgoing Messages

You would set a logging level for each category depending on the type of problem you are encountering.

Logging Levels

Each Exchange component enables you to set various levels of logging. These levels determine what type and how critical an event must be before it is recorded. Every logging level includes events from the level above it. The following are the logging levels available for all Exchange components:

None (level 0)	Log only critical events or error events. By default, this is set for every Exchange component
Minimum (level 1)	Log only very-high-level events.
Medium (level 2)	Log important sequences of events.
Maximum (level 5)	Log everything. This will log the complete operation of the service and even include certain lines of code from a service. Use only when you have narrowed the problem down to a couple of categories.

The level numbers pertain to what Windows NT defines the event to be.

Your decision to change logging levels should be based on tracking down a problem to a particular service and category. If you have a suspicion that a certain component is the culprit for a certain error, then start increasing logging levels gradually for a fewer number of categories.

For example, say that you are not properly receiving Internet mail anymore, yet all other types of messaging data are delivered without any problems. This would naturally suggest that you should increase the logging levels on all the categories of the Internet Mail Connector and not initially on the MTA or Information store. Then you proceed to narrow down the list of categories and increase the logging levels as you get closer to the source of the problem.

NOTE Use the high logging levels (maximum and medium) sparingly and only when you have narrowed down the problem to a few categories. These settings generate a large amount of events and tend to fill logging space quickly.

Using Windows NT Event Viewer

Anyone familiar with Windows NT administration will attest to the helpfulness of the Event Viewer. Whenever there is a problem on a server, this is always a good first way to look for it. This tool is invaluable for churning through the various Events generated by Microsoft Exchange's system services.

For review, an *event* is any notable incident within the Windows NT operating environment. Critical events will trigger an immediate on-screen notification to the administrator. However, the more run-of-the-mill events are only logged. These need not necessarily be errors, just occurrences worth recording. Windows NT logs three main types of events:

- *System events*—Status of system services and other system operations
- *Security events*—logons and permission auditing
- *Application events*—operational errors

Which events are actually logged is determined by the logging levels set for each Exchange component.

Please refer to your Windows NT documentation for an in-depth explanation of the Event View. Also, it will teach you the best way to use that tool to interpret the Events generated by Exchange's and other programs' services

From Here...

This chapter familiarizes you with some of the tools Microsoft Exchange provides for diagnosing and troubleshooting various components of Microsoft Exchange in your organization.

For more information, read the following chapters:

- Chapter 24, "Monitoring Your Organization," tells you how to implement a monitoring scheme to help you detect common errors before they become serious problems.
- Chapter 26, "Diagnostic and Troubleshooting Tools," gives you specific troubleshooting scenarios that may pertain to your situation. Also, further information on diagnostic logging.

PART IV

Exchange Client Software and Scheduling

CHAPTER 27

Installing and Configuring Exchange Clients

- Before Installing the Exchange Client
- Installing the Microsoft Exchange Client
- Configuring the Exchange Client

With the overwhelming amount of information being sent and received by the computer user today, an easy-to-use and easy-to-install messaging interface has become essential. The Exchange Client has met this criterion very nicely. With its ease of installation and configuration, the Exchange Client can be used as a single source for many, if not all, of your messaging and group-wide applications.

The Exchange Client is a flexible interface to not only Exchange, but your other mail systems as well. With the correct configuration, your client can become a powerful universal messaging tool. This chapter will cover how to get the Exchange client up and running under various configuration options.

Preparing to Install Your Exchange Client

Before running the setup program there are a few questions to consider that will affect your client installation strategy. Do you want your installation to be server based, or do you want all the executables to reside on the client? Do you want to install from CD or over the network? One last question for an administrator: Would you like to preconfigure client options or have the users choose their own settings?

The answers to these questions will determine your approach to setting up the Exchange Client software.

Each of these areas will be covered in detail to make the answers to these questions a little clearer.

Installing Using an Installation Share

An installation share allows you to run the setup files directly off a hard drive without necessitating the use of CD or floppy disk. An installation point to run setup can be located on a server or on the local machine. After loading all of the files, you then, in the case of a file server, share the directory with an appropriate title.

You first need to copy the Microsoft Exchange Client software from whatever source (CD-ROM or floppy) onto your hard drive.

If you are installing from a CD-ROM, copy the contents of the appropriate client directories from the Exchange Client's CD. For example, to load the Windows 95 client onto an installation share, you would copy the entire contents of the WIN95 subdirectory to the hard drive.

If you are installing from a floppy disk, start by creating a new directory on the destination hard drive to hold the install files.

Second, copy the contents of each Exchange Client installation floppy into an appropriately named new subdirectory; for example, DISK1, DISK2, etc.

To run an installation from the server, find the SETUP.EXE file and execute it. The setup application will run as normal from that point on.

Weighing Server-Based Installation Advantages and Disadvantages

With a server-based installation all users use a server-based copy of the Exchange Client. There are advantages and disadvantages to this scenario:

- Why—Less configuration on the clients. All settings can be maintained on the server. More change control over the installations.
- Why Not—More LAN traffic; each time a user loads the Exchange Client, it must run across the network. Users may see a dramatic decrease in performance. Client cannot function while server or network is down. Does not take advantage of Client server model efficiently.

Creating the Network Share

On server, create a directory for each client. For example, create a share called DOSCLNT for all DOS clients to be run off a server. You will need to do the same for Windows 3.x, Windows 95, and Windows NT.

CAUTION

The share points you are currently using as operating system network shares will not be available for users. You will need to create new ones.

It is a good idea, if you have the drive space, to create duplicate shares for these clients during install. You can then have existing users mount one and have migrating users mount the new share.

NOTE Each operating system version must have its own separate shared install on the server.

For Windows 3.x or Windows 95 machines that are currently running from a server-based install, the computer setting up the Exchange Client share must be running the same shared copy of Windows. All Exchange Client files must be placed in the Windows SYSTEM folder on the client's home server or the setup will fail.

After the client installation directories are created you can load the appropriate files. This is done by running an administrative setup (setup /a).

1. Connect to the Client installation share.
2. Change to the appropriate client for your operating system.
3. In a Program Manager shell choose File, Run. Or, in the new Windows 95 shell choose Start, Run.
4. In the Run dialog box, type **setup /a**.

Usage: setup [/A] [/G filename [/Q[0|1|T]] [/R] [/U[A]] [/Y]

Translation:

/A = Administrator mode.

/G filename = Generate a logfile of this installation and write to this file.

/Q0 = Quiet installation show exit.

/Q1 = Quiet installation hide exit.

/QT = Quiet installation hide all display.

/R = Reinstall the application.

/U = Uninstall application but leave shared components.

/UA = Uninstall all components of application.

/Y = Run install without copying files.

Preconfiguring the Client for an Over-the-Network Install

The Microsoft Exchange Setup Editor (see fig. 27.1) allows you to preset options that will be used during a server of local-based share client setup. This utility allows you to predefine most of the default options during the setup process. The following screens and text will guide you through this procedure.

FIG. 27.1
The Microsoft Exchange Setup Editor.

Start the process by choosing the Select Client Installation button (see fig. 27.2), or select the text from the File pull-down in the Microsoft Exchange Setup Editor.

NOTE This step selects the location of the *EXCHANGE.STF* file that will be modified by the Setup Editor.

Enter or find the path that contains the client setup files. You may enter the path manually by typing in the directory where your server-based client setup files are located, or you can search for an installation point by double-clicking the directories highlighted in the box.

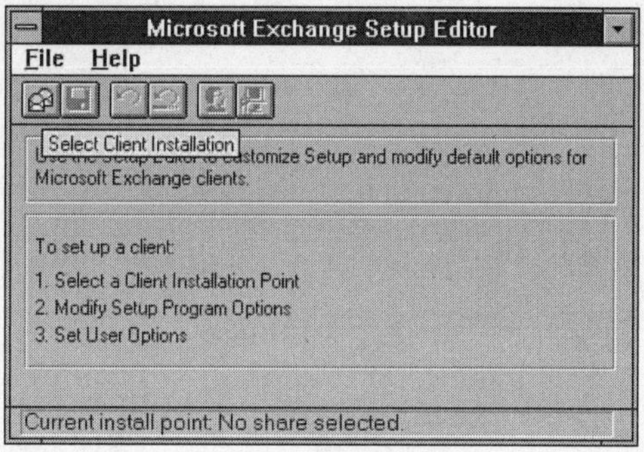

FIG. 27.2 Select Client Installation Button.

NOTE You may also search for a directory where the setup files are located by using the Network button. Then specify a network server on which the files reside.

After you have selected the client installation directory, you are able to modify the default settings of the desired setup share. This step is initiated by either selecting the Modify Setup Program button or selecting the Modify Setup Program text from the File pull-down menu.

The General Page

Under the General tab (see fig. 27.3) you can specify whether you want the person installing the Client, from this share, to be able to choose additional modes of installation besides Typical:

- Custom—Enables the person installing the Client to add and remove components from the Client. This option is recommended for experienced users only because essential portions of Exchange can also be deleted from the Client setup.
- Laptop—Loads a minimal amount of files. This option should be checked if you have users with smaller hard drives or portable computers.

In the Miscellaneous section of this tab you can specify in which Program Manager Group the Exchange icons will be installed. This section enables you to customize the name of both the group or *.grp name and the title of the group itself. You can also specify a directory other than default. This might be useful if you have multiple clients, as in the case of a multi-boot machine; for example, Windows 95 and Windows NT.

FIG. 27.3
The General tab of the Setup Program Options dialog box.

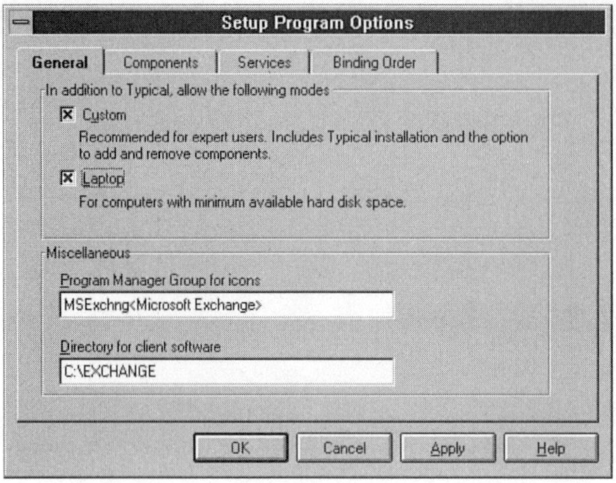

The Components Page

Under the Components tab, you have the ability to change which components of Exchange and Schedule+ will be installed on the client machine during setup. This is done by checking or unchecking the box to the left of the component you wish to change. You can do this by double-clicking the square or clicking the Select/Clear Component button at the bottom of the dialog box (see fig. 27.4).

FIG. 27.4
The Components tab of the Setup Program Options dialog box.

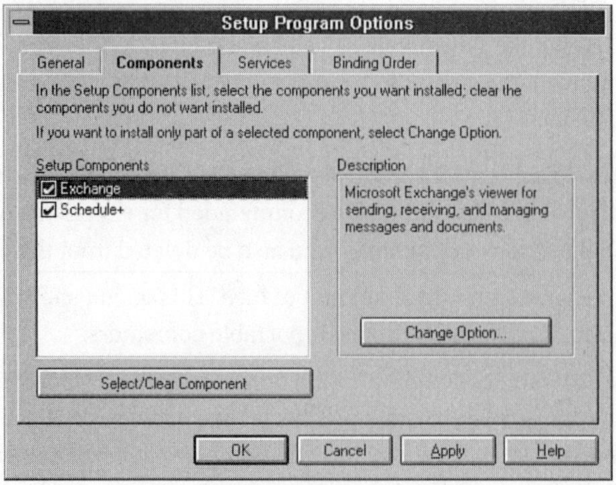

NOTE There are multiple layers of components when the Change Option button is available (not grayed out). The specific selections available under Select Components are discussed in detail later in this chapter under the Installing the Exchange Client section.

The Services Page

Under the Services tab (see fig. 27.5) you may add and remove information services to be installed on the client, allowing the client to have only the services that exist in your environment. For example, if there is to be an Exchange Server only and no Microsoft Mail Post Office, you can specify this here. This specification takes out any guesswork on the part of the person configuring the client on the desktop, who may not know what information services are available.

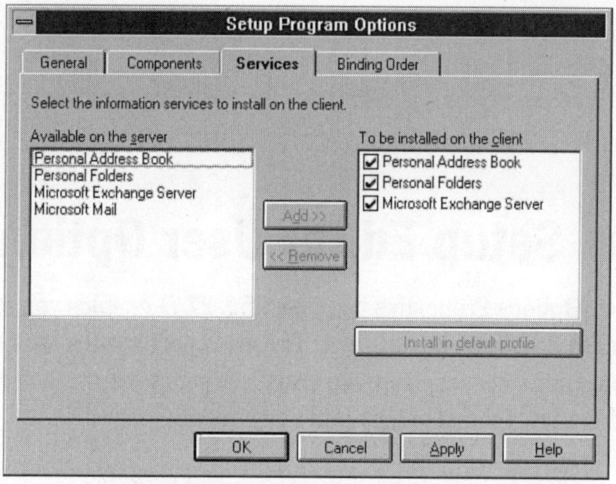

FIG. 27.5
The Services tab of the Setup Program Options dialog box.

The Binding Order Page

From the Binding Order property page (see fig. 27.6) you have the flexibility of promoting, demoting, adding, or deleting protocols. The Remote Procedure Call (RPC) protocols are used to communicate with the Exchange Server over the network.

Move Up—Promotes the selected protocol in the binding order.

Move Down—Demotes the selected protocol in the binding order.

Remove—Deletes the selected protocol from the bindings list.

Add—Allows you to specify additional RPC protocols in the protocol stack from a specified computer on the network.

NOTE It is important to specify only the protocols used in your networked environment. If the binding order has unused protocols (especially if they are high in the order), the Client will attempt to communicate with the server until it times out, then try the next protocol in the stack. This process causes slow response times in the Client server communications.

Part IV Ch 27

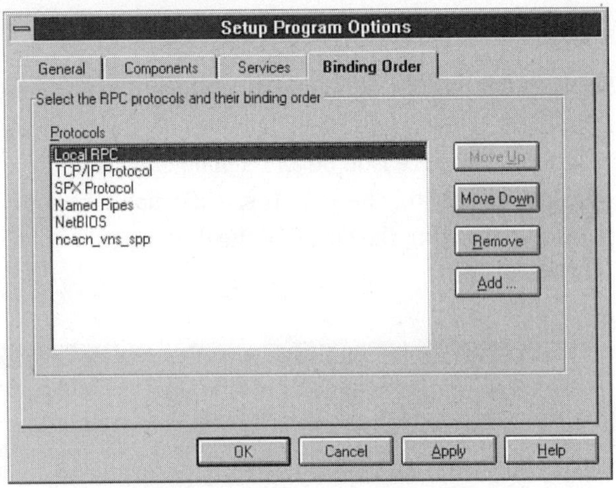

FIG. 27.6
The Binding Order tab of the Setup Program Options dialog box.

Setting the Setup Editor User Options

The Set User Options Properties page (see fig. 27.7) enables you to specify a few of the initial settings of the Exchange Client. These property pages are General, Read, Send, Spelling, and Home Server. They are initial settings because they are user-definable on the Client from the Tools, Options pull-down menu.

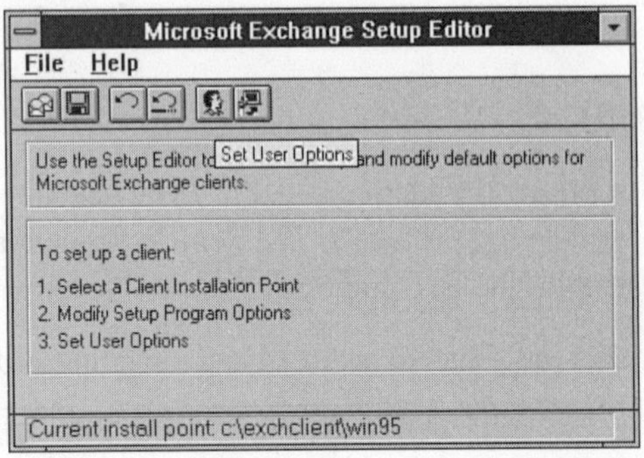

FIG. 27.7
Set User Options button on the Microsoft Exchange Setup Editor Properties page.

The General Page

The General tab enables you to modify the look and feel of the Exchange Client interface:

When a new item arrives

- Play a sound—This is a user definable sound file.
- Briefly change the pointer—Changes the pointer into a flying envelope when new mail arrives.

- Display a notification message—Displays a text dialog box and has a button which enables you to read the message now.

Deleting items

- Warn before permanently deleting items—Displays the Are you sure dialog box before permanently deleting the item(s).
- Empty the `Deleted Items` folder upon exiting—Permanently discards all contents of the Deleted Items folder when exiting mail. This is a good idea if you have limited space on your hard drive.

Show ToolTips on toolbars enables you to turn off ToolTips by default.

NOTE ToolTips are the text captions that appear when you leave your pointer above a button on the toolbar.

`When selecting, Automatically select entire word` (see fig. 27.8) enables you to turn off this option. This feature selects the entire word when part of the word is highlighted during editing.

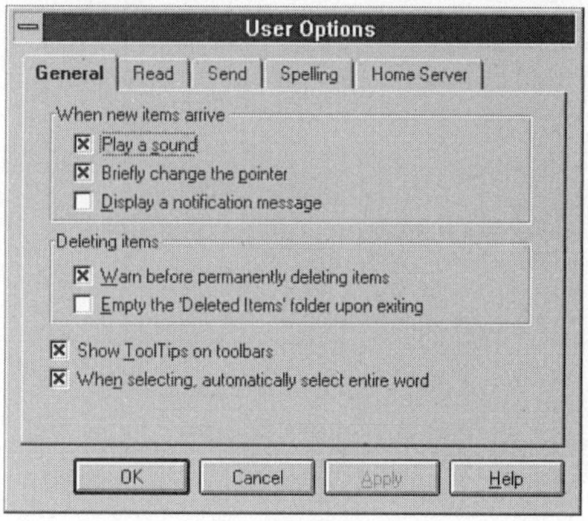

FIG. 27.8 The General tab of the User Options dialog box.

The Read Page

This screen (see fig. 27.9) enables you to modify what will happen to the message after you have read its contents. This property page contains both radio buttons and check boxes. Radio buttons (the round buttons) allow you to choose only one of the options, whereas check boxes (the square boxes) allow you to select any, all, or none of the items listed.

After moving or deleting an open item

- Open the item above it—Opens the object immediately above the item you are viewing in the folder contents list.
- Open the next item below it—Opens the object immediately above the item you are viewing in the folder contents list.
- Return to Microsoft Exchange—Takes you back to the Exchange Client folder in which you were working.

When replying to or forwarding an item

- Include the original text—Keeps all of the original text and places it, by default, at the bottom of the message.
- Indent the original text—Places a space in front of the original text to differentiate it from the reply or forwarding text.
- Close the original item—Closes the original text when the user chooses reply or forward.

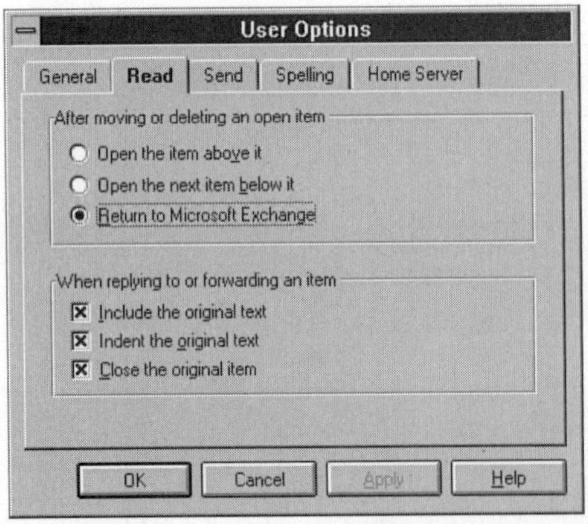

FIG. 27.9
The Read tab of the User Options dialog box.

The Send Page

The Send property page (see fig. 27.10) enables you to set the default actions regarding sent messages. These actions include receipt, sensitivity, importance, and disposal of the message after it is read.

Request that a receipt be sent when:

- The item has been read—Returns a receipt after the recipient has opened your message for reading.
- The item has been delivered—Returns a receipt after the message has been delivered to the intended recipient.

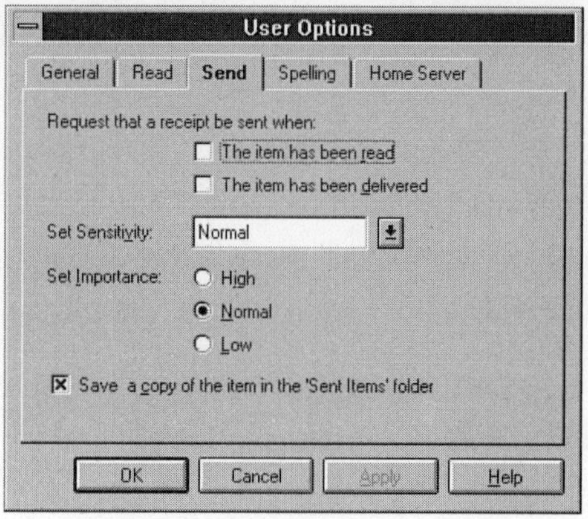

FIG. 27.10
The Send tab of the User Options dialog box.

Set Sensitivity:

NOTE Sensitivity refers to the optional column that can be added to the folder list view in the Exchange Client. The message sensitivity is set to one of the following choices:

- Normal—Nothing is displayed in the sensitivity column. Any recipient can modify the original text when replying or forwarding.
- Personal—Personal is displayed in the sensitivity column. Any recipient can modify the original text when replying or forwarding.
- Private—Private is displayed in the sensitivity column. Recipients are not allowed to modify original text.
- Confidential—Confidential is displayed in the sensitivity column. This sensitivity level should be used in accordance with your company's guidelines.

The Spelling Page

The Spelling property page (see fig. 27.11) enables you to set default options regarding spell-checking. The spelling options are applied to the text of messages that are being sent, replied to, and forwarded to. The following are brief explanations of the available options:

General options

- Always suggest replacements for misspelled words—If the word is not found by the spell-checker, a list is displayed to choose a replacement or allow you to add the word to your personal dictionary.

- Always check spelling before sending—Runs spell-checker automatically when you choose send.

When checking, always ignore

- Words in UPPERCASE—Does not spell-check words in all uppercase letters.
- Words with numbers—Does not spell-check words containing numbers.
- The original text in a reply or forward—Spell-checks only new text added in a reply or forward. This saves a lot of time when replying to large messages.

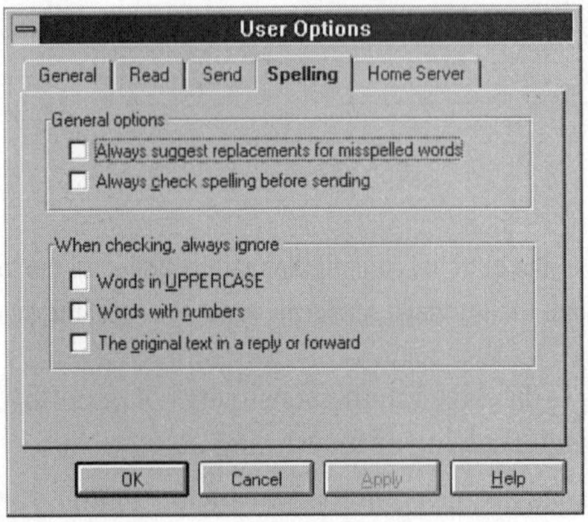

FIG. 27.11
The Spelling tab of the User Options dialog box.

The Home Server Page

The Home Server property page (see fig. 27.12) enables you to enter the default Exchange Server to which this client will connect.

NOTE This server name does not have to be entered with the normal Universal Naming Convention (UNC) backslashes (\\).

The Use network security to log on to Microsoft Exchange box enables you to choose whether or not to use Windows NT account security to access Exchange accounts on the server.

Select OK to exit out of User Options.

When you are satisfied with all of the settings in the Setup Editor, you need to save the changes to disk by selecting either the Save button or choosing Save from the File pull-down menu.

FIG. 27.12
The Home Server tab of the User Options dialog box.

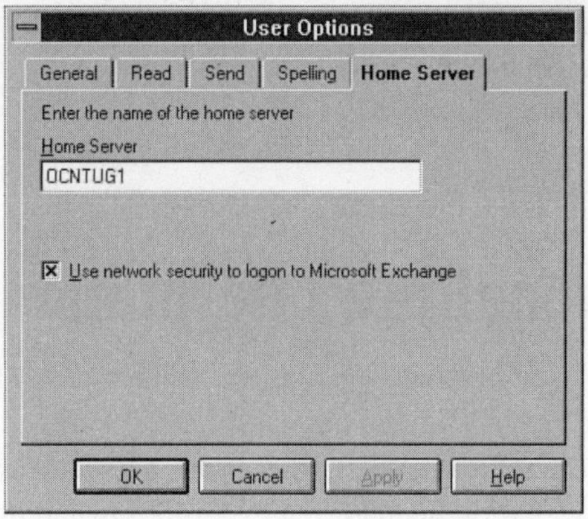

Exchange Client System Requirements

The following are not minimum, but suggested, requirements. The Exchange Client will probably run on a lesser machine. You might not be pleased with the performance if you load it on lower hardware.

Hardware:

- 486 or Higher Processor
- 16M of RAM
- 12M to 22M of available Hard Drive

Software:

- DOS 3.1 or later
- Windows 3.1
- Windows for Workgroups 3.11
- Windows 95
- Windows NT 3.51

Exchange Client Inbox Backward Compatibility

The Exchange INBOX that comes bundled with Windows 95 must be upgraded to the Exchange Client version supplied in the release version of the product. Due to the massive improvements to the inner workings and the user interface, all client software must be upgraded. This also includes upgrading Schedule+ to the current version designed to work with Exchange Server. More on Schedule+ is discussed in Chapters 29 and 30.

Saving Your Personalized Information

On the bright side, all of your personalized files you had under the Exchange Client in Windows 95 can be used again. With the new client, just specify where these files are located. If upgrading to the same directory where your personal files are makes you nervous, you can move the files with the following extensions to another directory:

- .PST—The file where all of your personal folders and messages are stored.
- .PAB—The file where all of your Personal Address Book entries are stored.
- .SCD—The file where all of your Schedule+ information is stored.

NOTE If you are upgrading your client from Microsoft Mail 3.x, you will need to save your *.MMF and *.SCH files. These are your mail folders, messages, and Schedule+ information. These files will be used to migrate all of your information into your new Exchange Client.

Installing the Microsoft Exchange Client

The entire install or setup process is very easy. All you have to do is follow the dialog boxes' instructions. Ample help and various tips are available as you follow the setup screens.

NOTE The Windows 95 setup screen is depicted in the figures. There are some differences between the older Program Manager style interface and the new shell found on Windows 95. Any differences will be addressed in the appropriate steps in this chapter.

The first step in the Microsoft Exchange Setup procedure is to select the directory or folder you want the client to be installed into (see fig. 27.13). You can either go with the default, which is C:\EXCHANGE, or you may change that by selecting Change Folder.

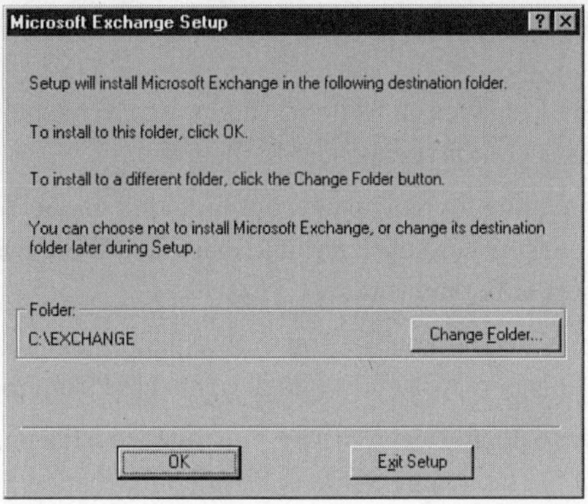

FIG. 27.13
Select the Destination Folder in which to store your messages.

Choosing an Installation Type

At the next screen you are presented with three choices.

1. *Typical* takes the most commonly used settings and installs them.
2. *Custom* gives you the opportunity to pick and choose the components you require.
3. *Laptop* installs the options that are most commonly used by mobile computing users.

Choose the installation method that fits your needs. If you are the adventurous sort and want to see all of the options available, go down the custom path. This option enables you to pick only the options that fit your requirements. If you don't know if an option is what you need, check help or follow the guides that are displayed in the box on the right.

At this point you have two options:

1. Change Option (see fig. 27.14) allows you to go deeper into the highlighted choice (if suboptions are available).
2. Select All does just what it says; it picks all of the options available. Selecting Change Options will reveal what choices are available to you behind the Exchange line.

At this screen you can specify what components of the Exchange Client you wish to load (see fig. 27.15):

- Microsoft Exchange—The Client software.
- Information Services—Messaging options (Change Option available).

- Spelling—Helper application that can automatically check your spelling before you send an item.
- Help—Extensive help files on all items within the Exchange Client; recommended, especially if this is your first exposure to the Client.
- Shiva—This is a utility for dial-up networking found on the Windows and Windows for Workgroups Clients. It enables you to dial into a Windows NT Remote Access Server to connect to the network.
- Personal Address Book—Enables you to save names and addresses in a file for easier access. This is very useful while disconnected from the network.
- Personal Folders—Enables you to save messages to a file on a specified local hard drive instead of the Exchange Server's Private Information Store. This is also very useful when not connected to the network.
- Microsoft Exchange Server—This option tells setup that you will be entering an Exchange Server later on during the install.
- Microsoft Mail—This option enables you to use your new Exchange Client with a Microsoft Mail 3.x server.

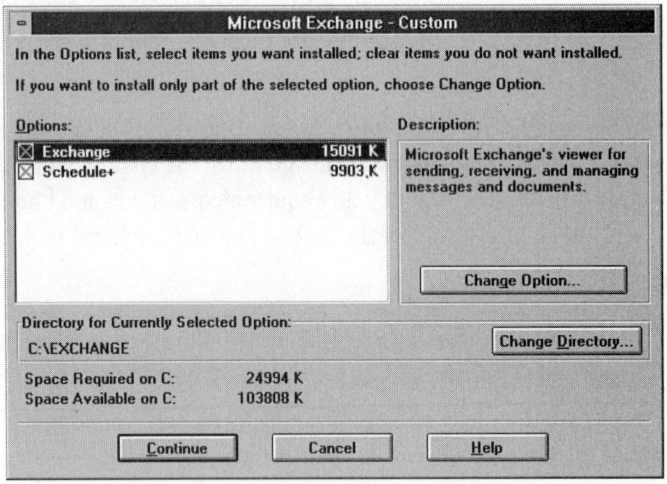

FIG. 27.14
The Custom options screen allows you to change Exchange and Schedule+ settings.

FIG. 27.15
Exchange Information Services available during setup.

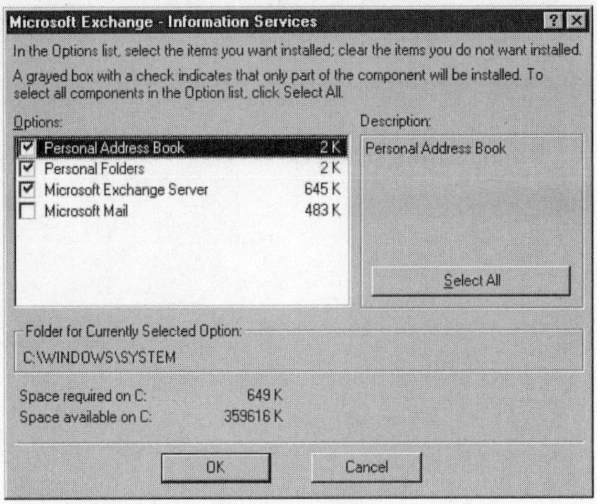

After selecting OK at the Information Services screen, the Schedule+ Options list appears. This list offers some very nice features that the developers have added to make life easier (see fig. 27.16):

- Microsoft Schedule+ Program Files—required executables and libraries.
- Print Layouts and Paper Formats—This option loads a variety of different formats for printing your schedule and contact list for popular styles of personal organizers.
- Help—This is always a good thing to load with a new program.
- Additional Importers and Exporters—You can select this one if you are using a Personal Data Assistant (PDA) and want to merge information to or from Schedule+.
- Seven Habits Tools—This is a personal productivity utility designed to help you organize and focus your time. The Seven Habits Tools are located under the Tools Menu and include a Mission Tab, Roles Tab, Goals Tab, and Wisdom Tab.

NOTE If you have any questions about any of these features please refer to Chapter 30, "Using Advanced Schedule+ Components."

After you have made all of the selections you want to use during setup, you can choose OK at each of the screens and continue with the install. At this point you see the setup progress bar and the various screens introducing the latest features. When you see the Completed Successfully screen, hit OK and you return to your desktop display.

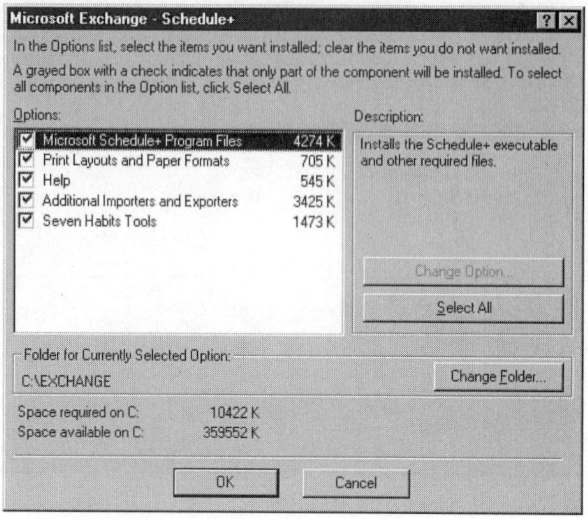

FIG. 27.16
Options available for Schedule+ during setup.

Configuring the Exchange Client

Now that you have installed the Client, you need to configure it to work with your messaging environment. Start by installing some of the most common services to see how this is done. If you have any other Messaging Application Programming Interface (MAPI) compliant messaging service, the configuration will be essentially the same.

Knowing Your Messaging Services

Before you start configuring your Exchange Client, take a few minutes to inventory what messaging services you will want to access. Due to the Exchange Client's many capabilities, you can receive messages from many sources besides the Exchange Server. One can also choose:

- Internet Mail (POP3 Server)
- Microsoft Fax
- Netscape Internet Transport
- Lotus Notes Mail
- Microsoft Network Online Service
- CompuServe Online Service
- Other MAPI-Compliant Mail Packages

Creating Your Client Profile

Your profile tells Exchange what services you are going to be using as well as where your personal files are located.

The first time you start up the Exchange Client after a fresh install, you will see a blank profile dialog box. You need to click Add to start including options to your personal profile (see fig. 27.17).

FIG. 27.17
The point where you add your information into your profile.

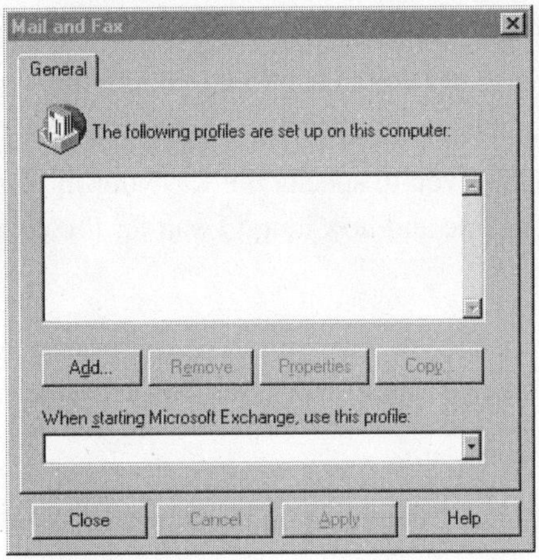

The next screen you see is the Inbox Setup Wizard dialog box. From here you can place check marks next to the information services you wish to use. You also have the choice of manually configuring the information services (see fig. 27.18). This option enables you to answer questions in a non-wizard style manner. The preferred method is to check the boxes and press the Next button.

FIG. 27.18
Information services available to add to your profile.

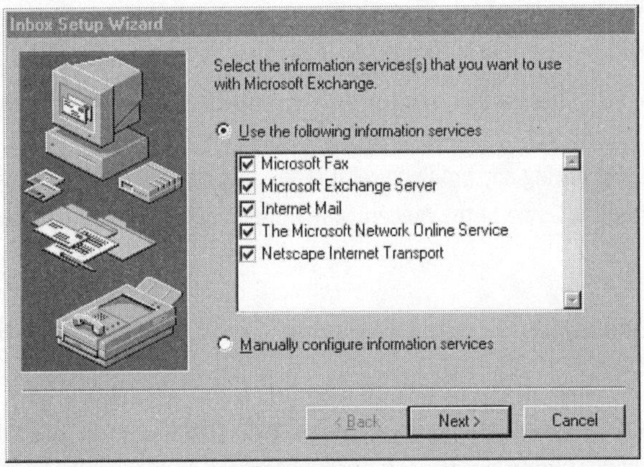

Following the Inbox Setup Wizard to the next screen, you see the first selection in the list of Information Services. The Microsoft Fax setup screen enables you to choose a fax modem to utilize for the faxing service. If you have already installed a modem on your computer, the Setup Wizard will fill in your default modem for you. From this point you are able to look at the properties of your fax modem; or if one is not yet installed, you can do so by selecting Add.

When you select properties for your fax modem you have the ability to change your

- Answer mode—Answer after <number> of rings.
- Speaker volume—This allows you to set the speaker volume on your fax modem. It also gives you the option of turning off the speaker after the connection is made.
- Call preferences—Enables you to specify the way your modem will handle the connection to the phone line and how long to wait for the fax machine on the other end.

NOTE If you have an answering machine or similar service, remember to make the answer after <number> less than the number of rings you have for that service to pick up or you won't receive many faxes. ■

In the advanced modem settings dialog box you have even more options:

- Disable high speed transmission—You could use this if attempts to send at a higher speed fail due to a poor connection or other line problems.
- Disable error correction mode—If error correction is causing problems with sending or receiving faxes.
- Enable MR compression—If your fax-modem supports hardware data compression, you can enable this option.
- Use Class 2 if available—Check to see if your fax-modem supports Class 2. If it does, this would be the place to enable it during faxing.
- Tolerance—This can be set to high, medium, low, or very low.

NOTE If you are having any problems with faxing, please check the owner's manual of your fax modem. Some of the preceding features may not be compatible with all fax modems. ■

If you select Add at the Microsoft Fax setup screen, you are given the following two choices:

1. Fax Modem—A physical device attached either to your machine or shared through the network. Using a network-shared fax modem usually requires a software package that resides on both the client and the server.

2. Network Fax Server—A special fax software component used mostly in large companies to accommodate large amounts of faxing data. This software resides on a network server and is used to route or distribute faxes to individuals or nodes (see fig. 27.19).

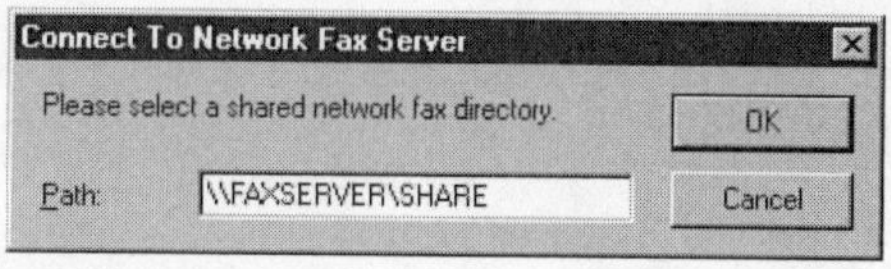

FIG. 27.19 Where you enter a path to the fax server's share.

At this dialog box, enter the path to the Fax Server's share directory. This is usually dependent on the software preferences.

The next screen enables you to choose whether you want the fax modem to pick up every incoming call. Remember, if you choose to have the fax modem answer, set the number of rings to a reasonable amount to allow you or your answering machine to pick up if necessary (see fig. 27.20).

NOTE Communications-sharing devices are available to alleviate the problem of having a dedicated fax modem. The communications-sharing device recognizes incoming fax calls and routes them to your fax modem for pickup.

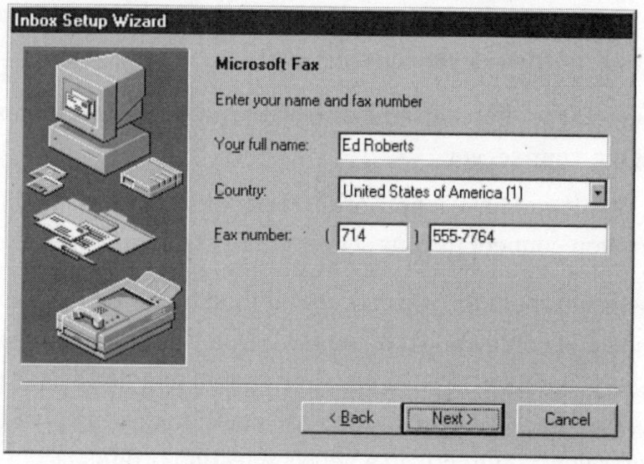

FIG. 27.20 Microsoft Fax–Personal Information.

At the next screen enter your name and fax number. When you are done, continue to the next screen by pressing Next.

1. Enter the name of your Exchange Server (see fig. 27.21). You do not have to enter the normal backslashes.
2. Enter the Mailbox Name. This is set up on the Exchange Server and is usually either a common name or a company standard name.

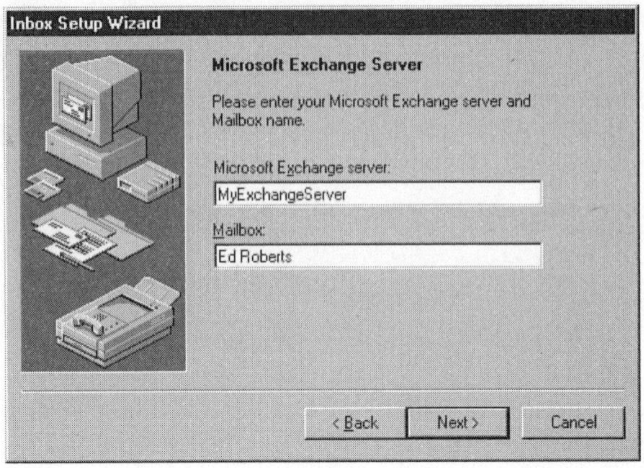

FIG. 27.21
Where you enter your Exchange server and your mailbox name.

You are now asked if you will be traveling with this client. This is a good question. How should you answer?

- Yes—You will not be hassled about being offline when you are not connected to the network.
- No—If you are using a computer that will normally be connected to a network. This will bypass some of the offline, mail-related issues.

If at the last screen you chose yes, you will travel with this computer, you are then asked how you will connect to the Internet Mail server. The best way to answer this question is to consider your normal mode of usage.

- Modem—If you dial in from home or are on the road a lot and use your modem to connect to your server.
- Network—If you have a network interface card in your mobile computer and this is the way you connect to your server while in the office.

When you select modem for your access method to the Internet mail server, you will be given the choice of connections. If you have Dial Up Connections already defined, the Wizard will let you choose from a pull-down list. If you don't have predefined Dial Up Connections (see fig. 27.22), or want to use another existing Dial Up Connection, choose New. This will allow you to create a new connection profile.

The next screen asks you to enter the name or IP address of your Internet Mail server. This is the server on which you have an Internet or SMTP style mail account.

The server from which you would like to receive your Internet mail needs to support POP3 mail. This is a standard that allows other servers to interface and receive mail as a proxy service.

FIG. 27.22
Are you going to be using Dial Up Networking?

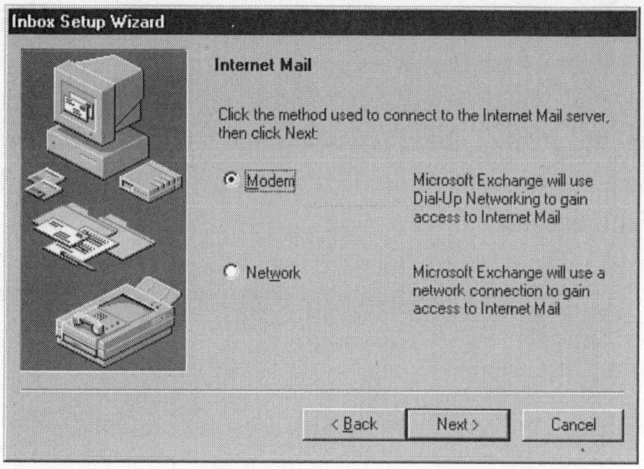

The next screen gives us the option of either choosing Off-line or Automatic.

- Off-line—Will use the Remote Mail feature of the Exchange Client. This feature enables you to view the headers and sizes of messages before downloading them.

NOTE This option is especially nice when on the road with a slow modem and someone tries to send you a 10MB PowerPoint presentation.

- Automatic—Downloads all incoming messages (regardless of size) and sends all outgoing mail. This method is fine if you have a fast modem and adequate space.

The next screen asks you to enter your account and name (see fig. 27.23). Your e-mail address is either the account or alias defined on the POP3 server. This will be in the normal Internet mail format of username@domain. Your name may already be entered from a previous setup or you may enter it now.

FIG. 27.23
This screen holds your Internet mail account information.

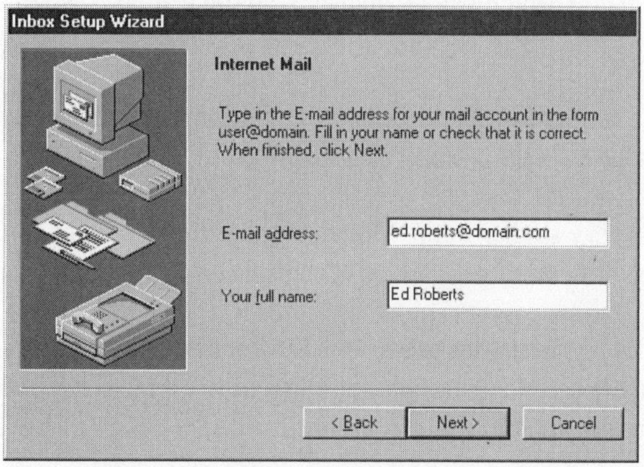

NOTE The name you enter will be displayed as the sender on all of your Internet mail, so put in a nickname if that is what you prefer.

Now you are at the point of entering your actual Internet mail account information. The Mailbox name is the account on the POP3 server (see fig. 27.24). The Password is the password for this account.

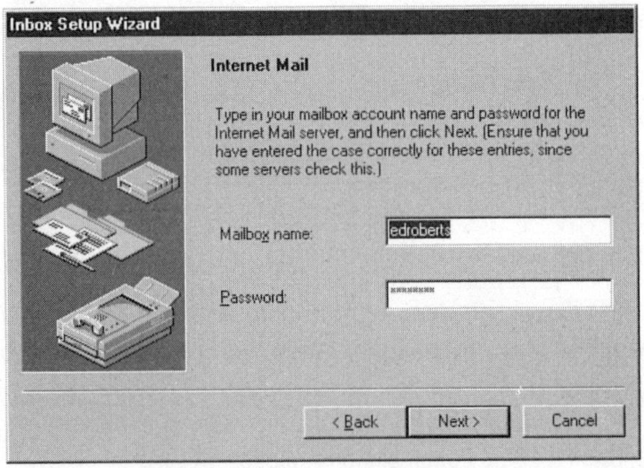

FIG. 27.24 Enter your Internet mail (POP) account information.

NOTE Ensure that you enter the account name and password correctly (including case-sensitivity) due to most POP3 servers being located on UNIX servers. The UNIX operating system is case-sensitive in all fields.

The next screen is a desirable option because Netscape is such a popular tool right now, and it also supports Internet mail. The Inbox Setup Wizard enables you to configure the Mail and News portions of Netscape in the next couple of screens. This screen asks you to enter your name, which will be displayed in the from box when sending mail through Netscape.

NOTE There are no setup options during this Wizard for Microsoft Internet Explorer because it uses the Exchange Client for all messaging services to the Internet.

This screen is very similar to the Internet mail setup screen encountered earlier. In this case you must either enter the name of the server or the IP address (see fig. 27.25).

NOTE Netscape differentiates between the SMTP and POP3 servers for sending or receiving mail (see fig. 27.26). Be aware that just because a server has SMTP installed does not mean that it also has POP3.

FIG. 27.25
Enter the name of the SMTP server used for outgoing Internet mail.

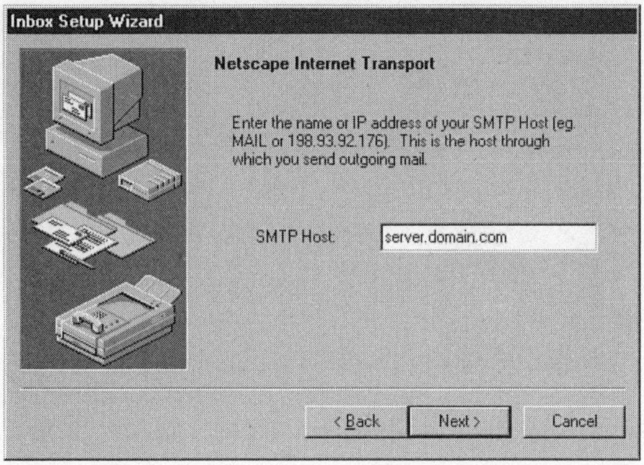

FIG. 27.26
This screen asks for your POP3 mail server. Like the previous screen, this may either be the name of the server or IP address.

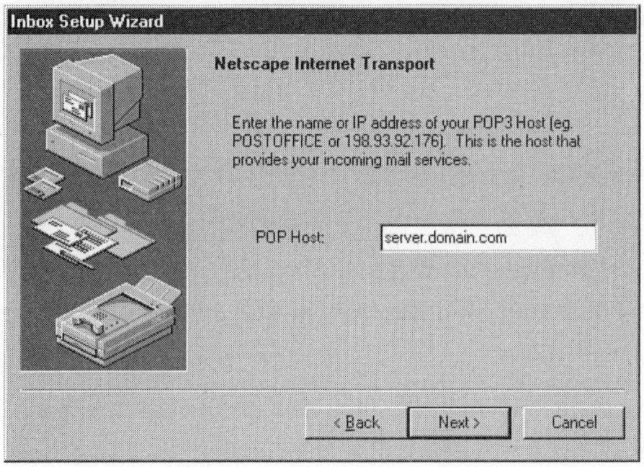

On this screen enter your account and password. Remember that case-sensitivity still applies due to the server.

This screen allows you to enter the address for an Internet newsgroup server (see fig. 27.27). If your organization maintains a news server, then use that address. Otherwise you will need to use your Internet access provider's news server. Again this can either be a domain name or IP address.

Now you are given the chance of either using a preexisting Personal Address Book or creating a new one. You can either enter the path to your old Personal Address Book if you have one, or Browse for it. If you do not have a Personal Address Book, as is the case of a new install, you can choose Next and one will be created for you in the default location.

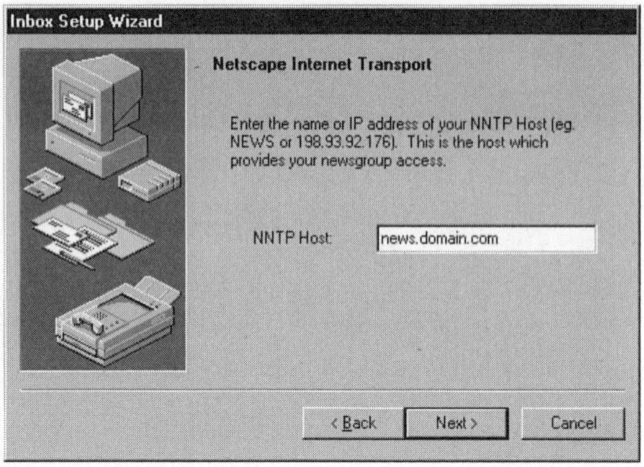

FIG. 27.27
Enter the Internet address of your provider's newsgroup server.

NOTE If you want to keep your Personal Address Book in another directory, you may enter it here. This is a good idea if you store all data files in a certain place for backup or security reasons.

The next-to-the-last screen enables you to specify whether you want the Exchange Client to start up when you first log on to your computer.

Congratulations! You have made it to the wrap-up screen. All you have to do now is select Finish to start using your Exchange Client with all of the services you selected and configured.

By configuring your Exchange Client, a new profile has now been created. In figure 27.28 you see the profile that was created in this chapter.

FIG. 27.28
This screen lists all your Mail and Fax profiles.

If you are not connected to the network, you may receive the option to Work Offline. If you will be connecting to the network, choose Connect; otherwise, choose Work Offline and use Remote Mail to send and receive your messages with your Exchange Server (see fig. 27.29).

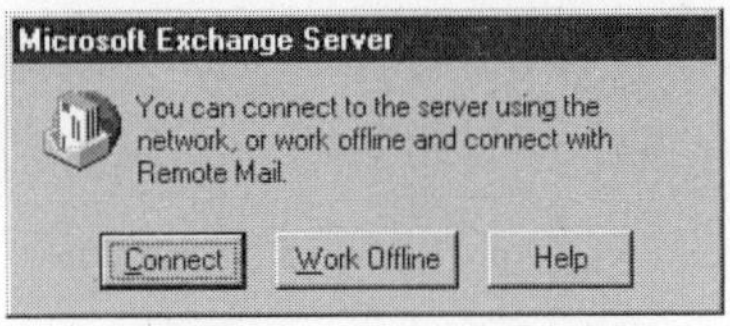

FIG. 27.29
Use this dialog box to select working offline.

NOTE You can access the Exchange Client Profiles by clicking the right (or alternate) mouse button on your Inbox icon, then selecting properties.

You are now ready to run your Exchange Client. All you have to do is double-click your Microsoft Exchange icon, and you are on your way to utilizing the full power of this versatile tool.

From Here...

This chapter has covered the installation and configuration options of the Exchange Client. The steps included in this chapter were:

- Planning the Exchange Client rollout to meet your organizational needs.
- Installing the Microsoft Exchange Client on your platform.
- Configuring the Exchange Client to work in your messaging environment.

Installing and configuring the Exchange Client takes planning and some knowledge of your messaging environment. You will find a wealth of information in other related chapters in this book.

- Chapter 28, "Understanding User Interface Features," continues explaining the use and options of the Client.
- Chapter 30, "Using Advanced Schedule+ Components," covers all of the features of Schedule+ and its interaction with the Exchange Client.

CHAPTER 28

Understanding User Interface Features

- Key User Interface Features
- Special Client Features
- Customizing the Exchange
- Client functionality in other Exchange compliant applications

This chapter will cover the many features of the Exchange Client. With all of the messaging systems and groupware services on the market today, the easier to use the interface, the less confusing the environment has to be. With the addition of task automation, this user interface is one of the most powerful and easiest to use. ■

Key Features of the Exchange Client

The Exchange Client has many easy-to-use features. This chapter discusses the features in detail, giving suggestions and instructions on their usage. The key features to be covered are:

- Single Location for Information
- Easy-to-Use Interface
- Creating Custom Views
- Integration with your Desktop Applications

Single Location for Information

With the Exchange Client's flexibility in the ability to access a variety of information systems, the Client can be your one-stop shop for all of your information. You can receive not only e-mail but various forms of data, voice, pager, images, and workflow applications.

The Client Viewer: An Easy-to-Use Interface

On the user's desktop, easier is better. When you start your Exchange Client (see fig. 28.1) you see icons and folders that seem familiar. That is because they are the same icons you see in your other Microsoft applications. This makes everyday tasks much less burdensome.

FIG. 28.1
The Exchange Client main view.

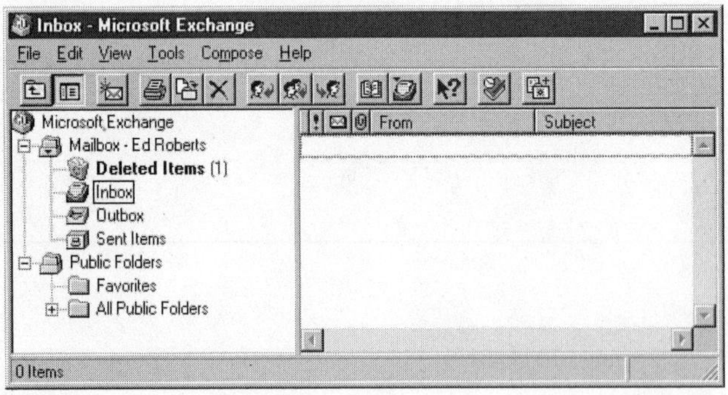

This section will cover what you see in the default Client setup and what features are available. First look at the folder list located on the left:

NOTE If you do not see the folder list, choose the View menu, then select Folders.

- Top Level—This icon will be the mail system you chose in your profile. There are several, including Microsoft Exchange, Microsoft Mail 3.x, and Lotus Notes.
- Mailbox—Your mailbox name, with a plus sign to the left and a down arrow on the icon. This signifies there are sub-folders. By clicking the down arrow or plus sign the sub-folders will be shown.
- Deleted Items—This is the recycle bin of the Exchange Client.

NOTE If there is a number beside any of the sub-folders, this is an indication that there are objects stored inside.

- Inbox—This is where all messages, faxes, voice mail, etc., are received and kept until either moved or deleted.
- Outbox—Used as a spooling folder when online. When offline, it is used to store your messages until you reconnect to the network.

NOTE When there is mail spooling or being stored in the Outbox, it will turn red.

- Sent Items—If you choose to save sent items, this is where they are stored. If you choose not to save sent items, this folder is emptied when you log out of the Client.
- Personal Folders—Are owned by the user of this profile. The owner can create, move, and delete them at will.
- Public Folders—Are stored on the Exchange Server as a repository for all Exchange users to store messages of interest to multiple parties. The public folders can be restricted to certain groups or users. This will be covered later in this chapter.
- Folder Contents List—Located on the right of the screen, this area contains information about the object stored in the highlighted folder.

NOTE The Folder Contents List may be set to full screen within the Exchange Client. This is done by choosing the View menu and clicking Folders.

Creating Custom Views

Now that you have seen how the Exchange Client looks with the default settings, you can start to customize the interface to meet your personal tastes.

Customizing Folders If you do not see Personal Folders, follow the steps below. If Personal Folders is present, skip to Adding a Folder or Sub-Folder.

1. From the Tools menu in the Client, choose Services and then choose Add.

2. In the Available Information Services box, select Personal Folders, and then choose OK.
3. In the File Name box, type the name of a personal folder file with a .PST extension, select the location of the folder you would like to place the file in in the Look In box, then choose Open.
4. In the Create Microsoft Personal Folders dialog box, enter the name you want to appear as the title of the new folder, decide whether you want encryption, and set the password to this folder.

NOTE If you do not want a password, leave the boxes blank.

5. Choose OK until you are back to the Exchange Client.

Adding a Folder or Sub-Folder You can add folders and sub-folders to help sort and store your messages. Use the following steps to add folders.

1. In the folder list, select the location (your mailbox or a folder) for the new folder, and then choose New Folder from the File menu.
2. Type the new folder name, and then choose OK.

NOTE To create a Public Folder, you must have Create Sub-Folder permissions for the folder one level up.

Deleting a Folder or Sub-Folder Select the folder you want to delete, and then choose Delete from the File menu, or click the Delete button. You can also drag the folder to the Deleted Items folder.

NOTE When you delete a folder, all sub-folders and items in the folder are moved to the Deleted Items folder, unless you are deleting a public folder.

Adding Files to a Folder You can also store files in your folders. All you have to do is drag a file from either File Manager or Explorer onto the folder where you want to place the object.

NOTE The folder will turn dark when you are directly over it with your cursor.

Customizing the Folder Contents List

The Folder Contents List shows details about the object contained in the highlighted folder in the folders list. By default, this list shows the following columns:

- Level of importance—This column shows whether the object's header reflects a high, medium, or low priority.
- Item Type—This icon represents the type of object stored in the folder.
- Attachment—When there is an attachment to an object, a paper clip icon will be present in this column.
- From—This is the originator of the object.
- Subject—The name of the message or object.
- Received—This is the date/time stamp of the message or object.
- Size—The number of bytes contained in the message or object.

Adding, Deleting, or Moving Columns

To make the Folder Contents List more to your liking you can add, delete, or move columns (see fig. 28.2). You can also resize the column to make it fit your display.

FIG. 28.2
The Columns dialog box lets you add, remove, or resize the columns in the client view window.

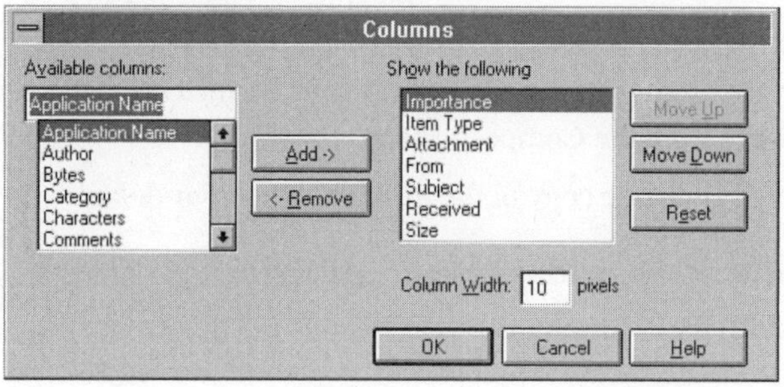

To Add a Column:

1. From the View menu, choose Columns and then select the column you want to add from the Available Columns box.
2. Choose Add and then OK.

To Remove a Column:

1. From the View menu, choose Columns and then select the column you want to remove from the Show The Following box.
2. Choose Remove and then OK.

To Resize a Column:

Place the cursor over the side of the column heading you want to change and drag the split bar by holding down your left mouse button. When the line is where you want it, let go of the button.

To Change the Order of the Columns:

1. From the View menu, choose Columns and then select the column you want to move from the Show The Following box.
2. To move the column to the left or right in the Folder Contents List, choose the Move Up or Move Down button and then choose OK.

NOTE The Move Up button moves columns to the left, while the Move Down button moves them to the right.

Customizing the Toolbar

The toolbar allows access to commands without having to find them by selecting the pull-down menus. The menu bar in the Exchange Client by default has the following buttons on the toolbar:

- Up One Level—Opens the folder directly above the folder you are in, if one exists.
- Show/Hide Folder List—This is the same as selecting Folder from the View menu.
- New Message—Opens a New Message Form. This is the same as selecting New Message from the Compose Menu.
- Print—Prints one copy of the active item to your default printer.

NOTE You must have an active printer to use this option.

- Move Item—Moves the active item, either a folder or an object, to a specified location. This is the same as selecting Move from the File menu.
- Delete—Deletes the active folder or item, the same as File, Delete.

NOTE You can also delete an object by dragging it onto the Deleted Folder.

- Reply to Sender—Opens a copy of the active message that is preaddressed to the sender, the same as selecting Reply to Sender from the Compose menu.
- Reply to All—Opens a copy of the active message preaddressed to the sender and all recipients, the same as Reply to All from the Compose menu.

NOTE When you use Reply to Sender or Reply to All, any attachments are replaced by markers stating the name and type of attachment.

- Forward—Opens a copy of the active message that you can then address and send to other users, the same as Forward from the Compose menu.

NOTE When you use Forward, all attachments are included in the message being sent. You can forward multiple messages by selecting them in the Folder Contents List. Each message will be sent as an attachment in a new message.

- Address Book—Opens the Address Book, where you can view information about users, distribution lists, and public folders, the same as Address Book from the Tools menu.
- Inbox—Displays the contents of your Inbox in the Folder Contents List. This is especially helpful if you have a large number of folders and you have to scroll to find the Inbox.
- Help—Changes the mouse pointer to a Help pointer. To use the Help pointer, click the button, then place the pointer over a command or other screen element to display the corresponding Help topic.

NOTE The Help button remains selected and the Help pointer remains active until you click something, or press ESC.

- Add to Favorites—Adds the selected Public Folder to your Favorites Folder. This provides an easy way to view and access public folders that you use frequently.

NOTE Unlike a normal Public Folder, when a Favorites Folder contains information it will turn to bold text.

- Show Schedule+ —This toolbar button opens your Schedule+ application. This is a very easy way to toggle back and forth between your schedule and your mail.

Adding or Removing a Toolbar Button

By adding or removing buttons on the toolbar you can tailor this feature to fit your work habits.

Adding a button:

1. Either double-click the desired toolbar background or select Customize Toolbar from the Tools menu (see fig. 28.3). The following dialog box appears.
2. Select the button that you want to add from the Available Buttons box, then drag it to the Toolbar Buttons box, or choose Add.

Deleting a Button:

1. Either double-click the desired toolbar background or select Customize Toolbar from the Tools menu.
2. Select the button that you want to remove from the Toolbar Buttons box, then drag it to the Available Buttons box, or choose Remove.

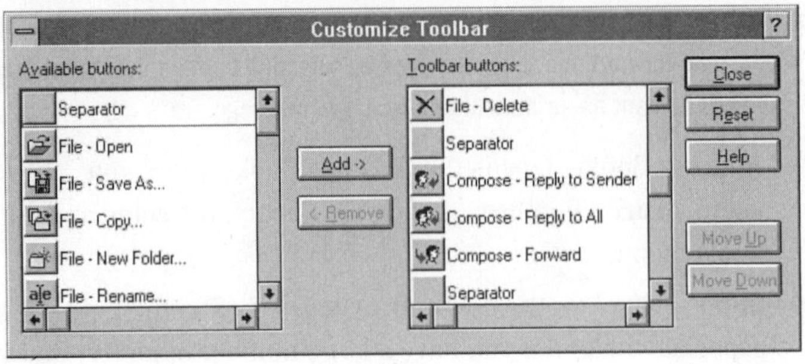

FIG. 28.3 Customize the Toolbar to have your most frequently used options just one click away.

Resetting Buttons to Default Settings:

1. Either double-click the desired toolbar background or select Customize Toolbar from the Tools menu.
2. Select the Reset button from the Customize Toolbar dialog box.

Integration with Your Desktop Applications

The Exchange Client is very much a part of your working environment. As such, it should blend in seamlessly with your other desktop applications. Microsoft has done an excellent job of integrating its products with Exchange Server. In this section we will cover some of the highlights of the Client's integration.

- Sending a Document from within an Application
- Routing a Document
- Posting Documents to a Public Folder
- Attaching Documents from within an Application
- Adding Exchange Options to the Microsoft Office Toolbar

Sending a Document from Within an Application

To send a document as an attachment with your Exchange Client follow these steps:

1. Choose Send from the File menu.
2. The document is placed as an attachment in a new message dialog box.
3. You can now enter the recipients in the To box and add any comments to the message.
4. Click the Flying Envelope and it will be placed in the Outbox for spooling to the network.

Routing a Document

To route a document to any number of recipients, follow the instructions below:

1. Choose Edit Routing Slip from the File menu. The Routing Slip dialog box appears.

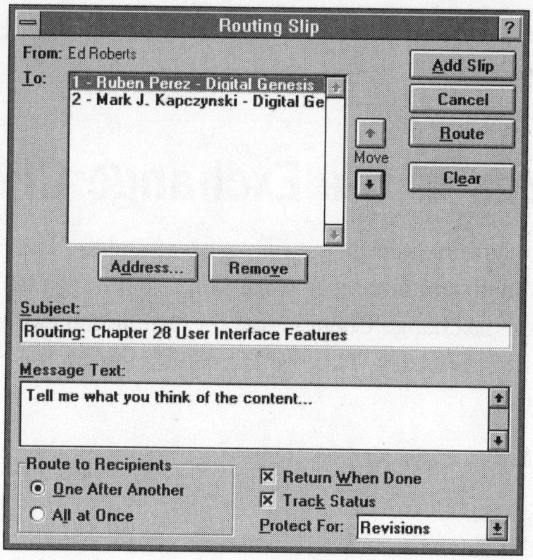

FIG. 28.4 The Routing Slip dialog box.

2. Click the Address button. This brings up the Address Book dialog box. Choose the people you want to send this document to or enter a new person by clicking the New button.
3. The Subject field is filled in from the property sheet of the document you are sending. This field is editable.
4. The Message Text field is what will appear in the body of the message that is routed.
5. Route to Recipients can be toggled to either One After Another or All at Once.
6. You can check either Return When Done or Track Status.
7. To protect the document for changes, select one of the options in the pull-down.
8. At this point you can do one of four actions:
   - Add Slip—This saves the changes and allows you to route them at a later time by selecting Send from the File menu.
   - Cancel out of the form without making changes.
   - Route the document. This will insert the document in a New Message form. It can then be sent to the named recipients.
   - Clear all fields to start a new route slip.

Posting Documents to a Public Folder

Your document can be placed in a Public Folder on the Exchange Server for viewing. Here's how:

1. Select Post to Exchange Folder from the File Menu.
2. This places the document in the Public Shortcuts Folder under Public Folders on your Exchange Server.

Special Features of the Exchange Client

The Exchange Client now includes some very powerful tools. The utilities that have been popular in the UNIX mail community for some time are now available in Exchange. The major advantage in the Exchange Client is that they are much easier to use. There is no script editing, just fill in the boxes. This section takes a look at the advanced features of the Exchange Client.

- Auto Assistants
- Using Filters
- Remote Functionality
- Profiles and Information Services

Utilizing Auto Assistants

Auto Assistants help you manage your incoming mail, handling messages as they arrive in your Inbox. These actions include responding to, filing, and routing items. The Auto Assistant checks to see if the message meets specific conditions. The two Auto Assistants are the following:

- Inbox Assistant—Manages the mail coming into your Inbox on a daily basis
- Out of Office Assistant—Manages your mail when you are out of the office

Both Assistants use the same basic principles. Both are configured to accomplish tasks by using rules.

Each rule is applied to incoming mail and consists of two parts:

1. Conditions—The characteristics of the message or form
    - Who the message is from
    - Who it is being sent to

- Words in the subject box
- Words in the body of the message

2. Actions—What happens when the rule's conditions are met
    - Moving items to a particular folder
    - Copying items to a particular folder
    - Forwarding items to another person
    - Deleting items

All rules are processed on the Microsoft Exchange Server. This allows the Auto Assistant to continue running even if you have not started your Exchange Client. If the rule's actions can be performed without user intervention, the rule is completed entirely in the Microsoft Exchange mailbox. Examples of this are receiving alerts or moving a message into a set of personal folders. Remember, the personal folders reside on your client.

NOTE If you set up more than one rule, they are performed in the order listed.

Adding a Rule to the Inbox Assistant

To show how easy it is to use the graphical interface of the Inbox Assistant, here is a step-by-step example.

NOTE You need to be connected to your Exchange Server before you can add or edit an Auto Assistant.

1. Start or open your Exchange Client.
2. Select the Inbox Assistant from the Tools menu (see fig. 28.5). The following dialog box appears.

FIG. 28.5
The Inbox Assistant dialog box showing currently defined rules (blank by default).

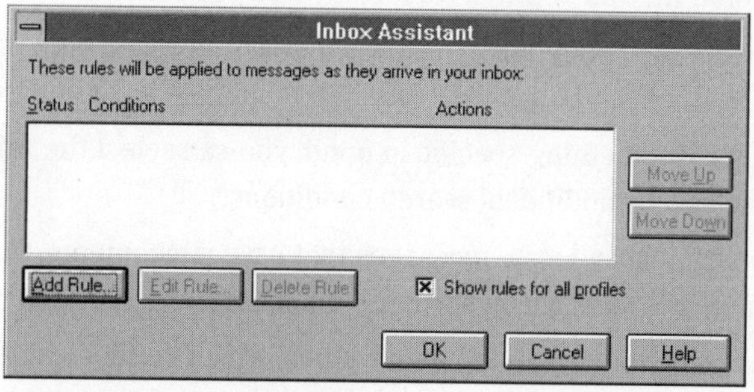

3. Click the Add Rule button. The Edit Rule dialog box appears.

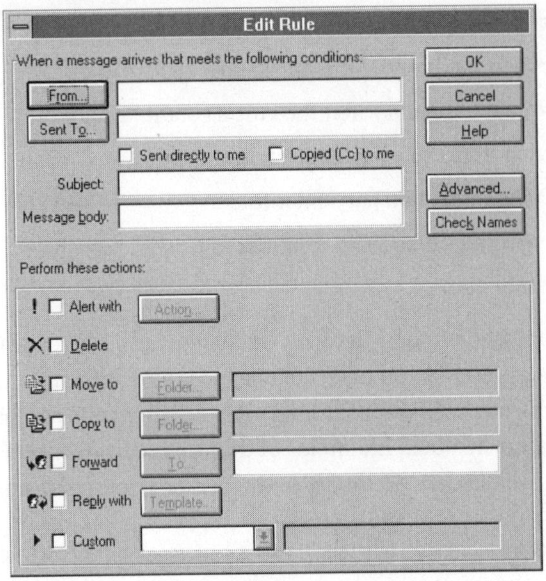

FIG. 28.6
Define rules to affect the messages in your Inbox.

4. In the From box enter the name, or alias, of the person who will be sending the item.
5. In the Sent to box enter either your name or an account owned by you such as Sales, Tech.Support, or Admin.
6. If you would like to be notified if the message is either sent to you directly or copied (CC) to you, check the appropriate box.

NOTE You can check both boxes. The Assistant will also check for your name in distribution lists.

7. In the Subject box type a word or words, with multiple strings separated by a semicolon (;), that you wish to include as a condition.
8. In the Message body box type a word or words, again with multiple strings separated by a semicolon (;), that you wish to include as a condition.
9. If you have something specific in mind, you can select the Advanced button, where you can specify additional search conditions.

   Example: You can locate messages that have attachments, that are a particular size, or that do not meet the conditions you specify.
10. At this point you can also Check Names, which verifies names in the From and Sent To boxes by checking them against the address lists in your Address Book.

NOTE If a matching name is not found, or if there are multiple matches for the same name, the Check Names dialog box is displayed, where you can select the correct name or create a new one.

11. You are now at the Perform these actions: box. Place a check in the Alert with box, which activates the Action button.
12. By clicking the Action button you are sent to the Alert actions dialog box. In this box you can specify the text contained in the alert message and specify which sound will be played when the conditions are met.
13. Next on the list of actions is Delete.

NOTE This item is mutually exclusive. You cannot choose this item if you have chosen Alert, Copy, or Move.

14. If you have not chosen to delete the item, you can now Move the item to one of your Personal Folders or to a Public Folder for which you have permission.
15. You may now Copy the item(s) to a folder.

    Example: You move the message to a Personal Folder and want to copy it to the bulletin board in a Public Folder.
16. Once you are done handling the item, you can choose to Forward it to one or many recipients.
17. If you are setting up an auto reply service, you can choose the Reply with button and specify a Template.

NOTE The Template can have additional recipients and attachments.

18. The final option in the Edit Rule dialog box is Custom.

NOTE Custom actions are add-ons that are not provided by the Microsoft Exchange Client.

19. Then select OK until you are back to the Exchange Client.
20. The Inbox Auto Assistant is now ready to handle any messages meeting the criteria you specified.

Adding a Rule to the Out of Office Assistant

When the need arises, say a vacation or holiday, you can set up your Exchange Inbox to answer your mail with a friendly reminder you are out. The following example configures the Out of Office Assistant to answer any messages while you are away.

1. Start or open your Exchange Inbox.
2. Select the Out of Office Assistant from the Tools menu. The Out of Office Assistant dialog box appears.

FIG. 28.7
The out of office assistant minds your mailbox automatically while you are away, or do not want to be disturbed.

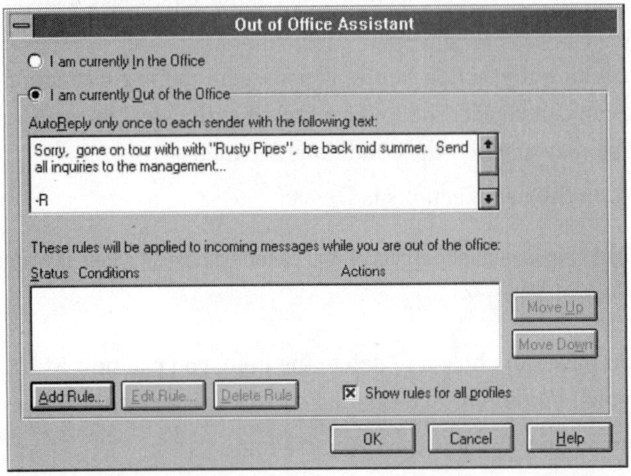

3. In the Out of Office Assistant dialog box click the button that says you will be Out of the Office.

NOTE Clicking I am currently In the Office will disable the Auto Assistant from replying to your messages.

4. You may now type a message in the AutoReply box. This will send a reply only once to each sender.

NOTE This may be enough if you want a quick reminder. If you would like to handle the message in any other way, please continue.

5. When you select Add Rule, you are presented with the same options that you are given during the Inbox Assistant.
6. In this case, select any messages Sent directly to you, or copied to you.
7. You can now Move or Copy the message into a predefined folder or leave it in your Inbox.
8. You can also Forward the messages to someone reading your mail while you are out.
9. Another option is to Forward the message to an address you can read while you are away—unless you are on vacation and don't want to think about work.

10. Probably the best feature for your needs, in this case, would be Reply with. You can send a message stating when you will be back and whether or not anyone will be replying to messages.
11. Click OK until you are back at the Exchange Client.

NOTE If there are any options that require more explanation, please refer to the steps in Adding a Rule to the Inbox Assistant.

Using Filters in Your Exchange Viewer

Filters can be very useful if you have many items in your Exchange Client. If you are looking for items sent by a certain individual, on a certain subject or date, you can use a filter.

To filter messages, forms, and files in a folder:

1. Choose Filter from the View menu.
2. Fill in and check all that apply to your search.

NOTE If you enter more than one condition, the filter shows only the items that meet all conditions.

Example: Typing John Smith in the From box and Sales Report in the Subject box will filter all items except those that are from John Smith and have Sales Report as part of the subject.

3. Choose Advanced to set a filter for items based on other conditions, such as size or date. You may also set a filter for items that do not meet specific filter conditions.
4. Choose OK.

To remove a filter:

1. Choose Filter from the View menu.
2. In the Filter dialog box choose the Clear All button.
3. Then press OK.

Remote Functionality

The most efficient way to work when you are not connected to a local area network is to dial in. When you work away from the office, at home or on the road, you can do most of your work offline. When you need to send and receive mail, or to update information in your offline folders, you can use a single command to connect to your server and perform the actions you want. You then disconnect and continue working offline.

Working with Offline Folders

The recommended way to work offline is to use offline folders. An offline folder is a snapshot of a server folder that you work with offline. You add, delete, and modify the contents of an offline folder exactly as you do with the server folder.

To Make a Folder Available Offline, take the following steps:

1. In the folder list, select the mailbox folder or Favorites Folder for which you want to create an offline folder.
2. From the File menu, choose Properties, and then select the Synchronization tab (see fig. 28.8).

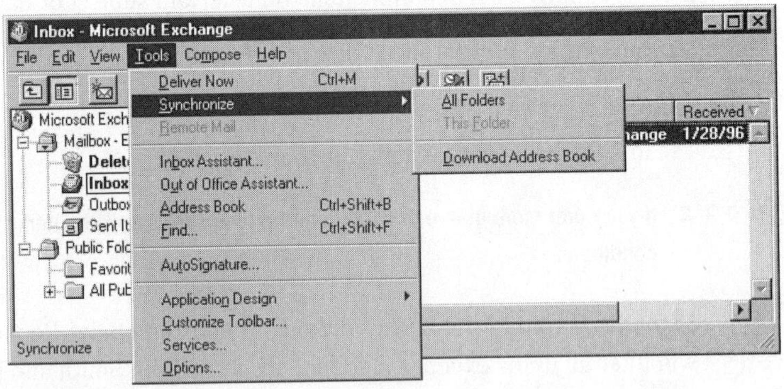

FIG. 28.8 Choosing the Synchronize menu option.

3. Under This Folder Is Available, select When Offline Or Online.

NOTE If you do not have an offline folder file, you are prompted to create one. Choose Yes and follow the instructions on your screen. For additional information, click the Help button.

4. Choose OK.

To Update Offline Folders:

1. Select Synchronize from the Tools menu.
2. Choose either All Folders or This Folder.
3. Exchange will synchronize the folder you chose or all offline folders.

NOTE Offline folders are available only if you use Microsoft Exchange Server. If you do not use Microsoft Exchange Server, you can work offline using Remote Mail.

Using Remote Mail

You can use Remote Mail to view the headers of new items in your server Inbox. You then select specific items to transfer to your offline Inbox. Because you download only the items you specify, this method can be faster than synchronizing your offline Inbox, which downloads all new items. You can also use Remote Mail to send mail you compose while offline.

NOTE When you start your computer offline, you must attempt to log on to Microsoft Windows or Windows NT (the connection will time out). If you don't do this, you will not be authenticated by your domain controller, and you won't be able to connect to your mail server.

Using offline folders or Remote Mail is the most efficient way to work with Microsoft Exchange away from the office. Because you work offline and connect to your server only as needed, long-distance telephone charges are minimized and demands on your server are reduced. However, to work with Public Folders for which you do not have offline folders or to use Schedule+, you must use a continuous dial-up connection. For information, see the topic "Working with a Continuous Dial-Up Connection."

Profiles and Information Services

The Exchange Client is very flexible. It can be used by more than one person or possess multiple configurations per user. This is accomplished with Profiles. The Client can also be used to access multiple sources of information. This option is configured through a feature called Information Services.

Introduction to Profiles

A Profile contains information services that control the way the Client works. When you install the Microsoft Exchange Client, you are prompted to create a messaging Profile. A Profile Wizard helps you set up your Profile. This is covered in Chapter 27, "Installing and Configuring Exchange Clients."

Generally, the Profile that you create during installation is the only Profile you will need, unless:

- More than one person uses the same computer; each person should have a Profile to keep mail private and secure.
- You need to work with a different set of services; you can create an additional Profile with those custom services.

NOTE You can start the Client with the default Profile you have specified. You can also be prompted to select a Profile each time you start the client.

TIP Being prompted to select a Profile is a good idea when you use multiple Profiles, or when there are multiple users per computer.

Understanding Information Services

Information services provide great flexibility in the Exchange Client; they

- Control how your messaging applications address and route your mail.
- Enable you to modify where your mail and folders are stored.
- Specify the location for incoming mail, your Personal Address Book, and any sets of personal folders that you have created.
- Enable you to send faxes or connect to other mail systems such as Exchange, Microsoft Mail, the Internet, or a variety of MAPI-enabled mail systems.

NOTE Before you can use an information service, you must add it to your active Profile.

From Here...

The Exchange Client has many valuable features. With the few items covered in this chapter, it is already apparent how powerful a tool it can be. There are many other ways the User Interface can be used to enhance your working environment. By following the online help and the Microsoft documentation, you can do virtually any form of information sharing.

These features reveal how the Exchange Client integrates tightly into your information-sharing environment. Try some of the sample applications that come with the Exchange Server to see the true Client/Server integration of this application.

- See Chapter 15, "Creating and Configuring Recipients," to set up accounts to be used with Auto Assistants.
- See Chapter 27, "Installing and Configuring Exchange Clients," for explanations on how to configure other Exchange Client components.
- See Chapter 29, "Integrating Schedule+ with Exchange Server," to see what issues you will face when performing the task of rolling out Schedule+ to your enterprise.

- See Chapter 30, "Using Advanced Schedule+ Components," to see how the Exchange Client interacts with Schedule+.
- See Chapter 31, "Implementing Third-Party Integration Tools," to see how other applications can be used to enhance your environment.
- See Chapter 33, "Introduction to Exchange Forms Development," to learn more about the integration of forms in Exchange.

CHAPTER 29

Integrating Schedule+ with Exchange Server

- Getting everyone on board
- Compatibility issues
- Permissions issues and privacy

Before you roll out Microsoft Schedule+ as part of your migration to Exchange, you need to take a few things into account. This chapter covers those issues in depth, provides some examples of real-world situations, and recommends some solutions to tough problems that you are certain to face.

Schedule+ Compatibility

Schedule+ Version 7.0 ships with the Exchange CD-ROM as well as with Microsoft Office for Windows 95. This version is incompatible with the versions that shipped with Windows NT Server, NT Workstation, and all versions of Microsoft Office before the Windows 95 version.

The product was completely revamped, its interface was changed, and more than 100 changes were made to enhance functionality and ease of use. Backward-compatibility issues arise with every software product, however, and Schedule+ is no exception. You must make sure that everyone in your organization is using the most current version.

If you used Schedule+ before Exchange, you can easily export your data to the new version so that you won't lose any data. The tool that you use is Microsoft Schedule+ Interchange, which is explained in Chapter 30.

Another issue to deal with is the Macintosh. In some organizations, "religious wars" are waged over which platform is better for the end users as a desktop operating system. Most IS organizations agree that homogeneity would be a nice thing, but it rarely happens. Usually, only the largest organizations are able to justify standardization, because the support costs are so high. Small and medium-size organizations tend to allow a mix of PCs and Macintoshes because they want the employees to be comfortable with their computing environments.

A Macintosh Exchange Client software version ships 90 days after the public release of Exchange. To play it safe, wait for the client to come out and test it thoroughly before implementing Schedule+ in a heterogeneous Mac and PC environment. Make sure that both products have the same features and that the menus and buttons are the same. Documentation and training are somewhat more difficult to develop, in addition to educating the IS staff to support both platforms. You don't want to roll out software that people won't be able to use effectively.

Getting Everyone on Board

Getting the entire organization to accept electronic scheduling can be a daunting task for any IS group. This section covers some points that you should be aware of before you try to sell the organization on using Exchange and Schedule+ for electronic scheduling.

People resist change. In most cases, getting people to switch to a computer-based solution for scheduling is difficult, because scheduling is very personal to most people. Scheduling is something that people do every day; when they make appointments, they look at their day planners and find an appropriate time to schedule the engagements. People are used to the way in which they already work, so getting them to switch takes good salesmanship, a direct order, or a mixture of both methods. Rollout or implementation approaches are covered in more detail later in this chapter.

Getting your users to understand the benefits for both themselves and the organization is your goal. Getting everyone on board is important, because the success and effectiveness of the rollout depend on user participation and enthusiasm. For the introduction of any software to be successful, proper hardware, software, and training resources are required.

Training is the key element in this equation, because in the case of Schedule+, no additional hardware is required. You just need to purchase licenses for each copy of Schedule+ that you are going to run on the client. If the workstations in your organization already have licenses for Microsoft Office, the users are already licensed to run Schedule+.

You want to make certain that you give your users the correct amount and quality of training on this product. If your company makes a large investment in administrator and user training for Exchange, you want to make sure that you can leverage or take advantage of all that training by having people use all of the software features, such as scheduling, to their fullest potential. This achieves maximum return on the investment that your organization has made in Exchange technologies.

Rolling out Schedule+ only to have people not use it—or, worse, having only some people use it—is your worst nightmare, because Schedule+ is so integrated into Exchange. When User A schedules a meeting, for example, he sends an e-mail message about the meeting to User B. If User B accepts the invitation but then never launches Schedule+ to check his schedule, business suffers and productivity slips.

Conversely, if you get everyone using the product, you have a robust environment, in which productivity and effectiveness rise. Meetings become much easier to schedule, and tasks get accomplished on time.

You want to relate the concept or idea of a computer working environment to your users when you train them. The Exchange Client and Schedule+, combined with Microsoft Office, provide a tightly integrated environment in which users can remain all day. When the phone rings, Schedule+ is right there on users' desktops, enabling users to get contact management information, appointment times, and add tasks to their lists of things to do.

Suppose that Tom calls Jane, asking her who the East Coast sales representative is and what his fax number is. Jane, who is using Windows 95, selects Schedule+ from her taskbar, because it was already open. She pulls up "Find" from the "Edit" menu, clicks the "Contact List" radio button, and types in **east coast** and clicks "Start Search." Within seconds, the name and phone number pop up and Tom is on his way. From within Schedule+, Jane clicks the Exchange icon which brings up the client. From there, she e-mails Tom the information just to be sure. While in the client, she notices there is a new scheduling-related message in her box because of the special icon in front of the entry. Upon reading the message, she accepts an invitation for a meeting, and it is automatically scheduled for her. In the meantime, Jane's secretary has booked two appointments for her.

Scenarios such as the preceding example make the case for companywide use of Schedule+ as a desktop environment. The capability of Schedule+ to assign permissions to other users, as well as its breadth of scope, give users what they need to be productive. High levels of participation make scenarios like this commonplace within an organization. The technology needs to weave itself into the corporate culture.

Widespread acceptance of Schedule+ is the key to the success of the application implementation for several reasons. These reasons vary in importance from organization to organization, depending on the flexibility and knowledge of users, size or number of users, platform, and many other factors. After you read some of the examples in the following sections, you will get a better idea how to approach a Schedule+ rollout as part of the Exchange rollout.

Shared Schedules

You can give other users permission to view various aspects of your schedule. You may want to allow your secretary to make appointments for you, for example, but not to access your to-do list. The permissions system of Schedule+ is very flexible. You have complete control over the accessibility of a users schedule to a target set of users.

Group Meetings

Schedule+ makes scheduling group meetings very easy. Integration with the Exchange client enables you to generate e-mail to all the participants, both attendees required and optional, that when the message is read and accepted, automatically schedules the meeting on the participant's schedule. The system knows when people are busy and suggests an appropriate time when everyone can attend. This feature takes the guesswork and hassle out of planning meetings.

Microsoft provides the Meeting Wizard to help you plan your group meetings, schedule resources, and pick the right times. This walks a user through the key elements when scheduling a meeting; this includes attendees, resources like conference rooms and audio/visual equipment, and meeting agendas.

Contact Management

Have you ever written a letter and wished that you could paste the addressee into the letter from a database without a great deal of work? Schedule+ provides this function through its Contact List. You can enter information on all your personal contacts here in the Contact List and paste it directly into Microsoft Word, or other windows based application.

In addition, the Schedule+ Interchange allows you to import database information from any database that supports ASCII text files. This is the Contact List repository. By using the Text Import Wizard, you can easily step through the process to migrate all data from a Microsoft Access database, for example, and use all the contact information in Schedule+ and Word documents.

Another useful feature enables you to publish enterprisewide phone-book lists of contact information for the company or organization. You can post this ASCII text file in a public folder and load the contact list information into Schedule+, providing immediate access to the addresses and phone numbers of everyone in the company. It saves data-entry time and assuredly saves paper in the process. You can write scripts to automate the entire process so that updates can occur without inconvenience to the user.

To-Do Lists

Some people like to use sticky notes or post-it notes, to-do pads, or handheld Personal Directory Assistants (PDA), but having an integrated list of tasks right in your working environment makes things much easier. Schedule+ enables you to configure advance warning times or reminders and organize your tasks under or by project headings to give you an organized to-do system.

The task manager in Schedule+ provides a way to track the percentage complete, as well as any contact information related to a certain project. When the task manager is tied into the permissions features of Schedule+, you can have the following scenario.

Joe has his to-do list organized under several project headings. He becomes ill. Because Joe gave Tom rights to see his to-do list, Tom is able to pick up where the project left off, because the name of the contacts involved, as well as the status of all the pieces of the project, were entered into Schedule+..

This scenario is a very realistic scenario if Schedule+ is widely adopted in your company and becomes part of the way that people work every day.

Extensive Printing Capabilities

Schedule+ provides many ways or pre-defined reports to print scheduling and contact information, ranging from printing the Contact List to printing daily, weekly, and monthly views of your schedule.

Enterprise Event Scheduling

Because Schedule+ is tightly integrated into Exchange, an entire year's worth of holidays and events for an organization can be entered one time, by one person, and distributed throughout the enterprise through the use of public folders. An example of this would be a business enterprise pay schedule and company vacation days on an annual basis. This way you can provide valuable information about companywide dates or events without having to publish paper calendars. This method of distribution is also more dynamic and can change as needed.

Scheduling of Resources

In many organizations, many resources need to be reserved, including conference rooms, audio/visual equipment, chairs, and tables. Schedule+ gives you the opportunity to create a schedule for these resources, allowing people to see when the resources are free, and make the reservations themselves. By using the permissions options of Schedule+, you can create a secure, tamperproof way to free time for the people who normally would reserve those resources for you. This eliminates the need in a company to have a person manually scheduling these types of resources.

In addition, the Meeting Wizard included with Schedule+ can automatically select a time when the resource is free if the resource is a "required" attendee. The wizard searches the Schedule+ system to find the next availability for the resource. The wizard will then make a recommendation of a meeting time when the resource can be used.

Now think about what happens if people don't use the program, or if some people use it and others don't. Meetings will be harder to schedule, because everyone involved can't rely on the participants to read the e-mail messages generated by Schedule+. Also, the Meeting Wizard might select a time when someone can't attend a meeting, because that person didn't enter his or her appointments into the system.

These issues are at the heart of the success or failure of Schedule+ implementation. It is imperative that everyone be committed to using the system every day; if they do not, it will make things harder, not easier. There are a couple of traditional approaches taken when deciding under what conditions to introduce new software. They are discussed in the next section of this chapter.

The "No Other Way" Strategy In this strategy, a group of users—usually, the people who head departments or divisions—decides to introduce a new software package. This group structures communications in such a way that people must use the package to receive important information.

An example of this is the original introduction of e-mail into departments. The heads of the department decided that e-mail was the way to go, and provided the tools and training needed to make the transition. To garner support for the idea, they stopped sending paper memos regarding the times of meetings, and the status of projects. The people who weren't reading their e-mail were reprimanded for not showing up or being unprepared. This forced the late-comers to start reading e-mail. There was really no other way.

The use of Schedule+ can be effective regardless of the size of the organization because it forces compliance indirectly. Most people will be turned off if you just order them to do something. If you give the people who support the technology the freedom to use that technology en masse, the latecomers will see the light or the benefits of the technology. These new users will be ostracized from the group and ultimately will fall behind the technology. In addition, some late adopters of the technology wind up being the biggest supporters of technology developments; they just need to see all the benefits the software brings with it.

In some ways, this strategy may seem to be a bit forceful, but it allows users to decide for themselves to some degree. The key is getting support for the product with the user community in the preinstallation or planning phase of the Schedule+ rollout. A successful implementation requires involvement, not only from the IS department, but from the user community to drive the details of how the product will be used on a day to day basis.

The "We're Doing It This Way" Strategy In some organizations, and especially in large organizations, information-technology policy is set from the top down. A huge capital outlay must take place when a technological direction is decided upon, so there is no room for IS or end user non-compliance with the corporate technology policy. Therefore, a great deal of research is done in these organizations to make sure that the company is moving in the right direction and that any changes that are made will result in productivity increases, cost reductions, and worker satisfaction. Beta tests are orchestrated, surveys are done, and some minor training is conducted by the team of peers from IS and the end user community charged with deploying this technology.

When a decision is made from IS, the upper management of a business unit, or another managerial body, users have no choice about whether to comply with the policy, which becomes "the way things are done." This type of policy makes training very effective, because everyone will be using the same product, usually on the same platform.

An example in which this strategy is apparent is in the choice of word processors and spreadsheets. Most large organizations pick one product for several reasons and make it the standard; everyone just goes along. Another example is when companies have standard forms for expenses and office supplies. Those forms are the way that the company does business, and employees have to use them. The incentive is, "If you want your money back, you must fill out this expense report." This managerial approach is not the friendliest one, but it tends to achieve the desired result if the proper training mechanisms are there to empower the user.

The "Sales" Strategy Some organizations attempt to sell users on a concept, figuring that if the users feel that they are part of the decision-making process, the implementation will be more accepted, and, therefore more successful. In addition, the common thinking is that if users embrace the concept of a proposed change, the implementation will go much more smoothly than if the change was forced down users' throats.

The only problem with this approach is that if users don't particularly like the proposed solution for the wrong reasons—such as resistance to change in general, intimidation due to the scope of the software, or software complexity—you are getting slanted feedback. Be careful to pay attention to the tone of the comments that you are getting. As you talk with your users, keep in mind that your perspective as an information-technology professional is much different from theirs. Although you may see cost savings, increased productivity, and cutting-edge technology, they may see your proposed change as a completely new way of working that is counterproductive.

You can find examples of this in the implementation of carpool, telecommuting, and recycling programs in organizations. The organizers of those programs often ask for input from employees before they establish the programs. As it relates to information systems, this approach is often taken in the design of front ends or user interfaces for database applications, Web pages, and help-desk systems.

These approaches should help you decide exactly how you want to implement the installation if you indeed decide to use Schedule+. Remember that you don't have to install and use Schedule+ to use Exchange. Perhaps a phased approach is right for your situation. Some users get information overload, and putting them through too much training in too short a time can result in burnout. In addition, extra time is available to the IS staff for supporting these users when you use a phased approach of implementation. You get to find out what the frequently asked questions (FAQs) are and can post those questions in a Exchange public folder when you implement Schedule+.

Although the topic of group scheduling discussed previously pertain to the Exchange features of Schedule+, this product is still powerful for individual scheduling. If motivated users want to use Schedule+ to keep track of their days, contacts, and tasks, they can do that. Just make sure that those users do not use the functions that interact with other users, because the other users might not be using the program.

Given the fact that a local copy of their schedule exists, the user has the ability to use Schedule+ without employing the resources of the Exchange at all. If you want to use the Exchange server, however, Schedule+ keeps both the local and the server copies of your schedule in synchronization and is completely configurable. You can have Schedule+ resynchronize every so many minutes or upon exiting the application or system. You also have the option of initiating synchronization manually.

Viewing Other Users' Schedule+ Schedules

Schedule+ allows you to view other users' schedules, contacts, tasks, and events. This ability to view other schedules is a concern for the information-policy-making body of your organization, because certain privacy issues go along with permissions. Some of these issues are discussed in the following sections.

Read Permission Issues

When you assign read permissions to users, they cannot only see that something is on your calendar, but also see all the information related to that entry. You have to keep these read permissions in mind when you configure permissions, because sensitive information can be compromised if the Private check box in the read permissions configuration section is not used. You can easily forget to check that box and even more easily forget that other users may have read access to your schedule.

A worker might give his boss read access to his schedule, for example, so that the boss will know the status of projects and when the subordinate is busy. The worker might just put "Interview with Company B" in his schedule, and that can lead to major trouble. This example shows that the information available to be seen by other users can comprise personal information.

Modify Permission Issues

Giving a user modify permission means that he or she can move appointments around without your knowledge or approval. This set of permissions can open the door to finger-pointing when meetings are missed and deadlines aren't met.

You must structure your information policy in such a way that users cannot modify a schedule without verbal approval. This security model gives the system a deterrent that will make people think twice before making unapproved changes. Users will be forced to confirm changes made to their personal schedule by other users in this example.

Create Permission Issues

Giving a user create permission enables him or her to make appointments and enter information into your schedule. In most cases, this set of permissions is great for executives who have secretaries, or if two people share a schedule, or if you are scheduling a resource such as a conference room or an overhead projector.

You must understand the difference between create and modify permissions. Suppose that you want to set up Schedule+ so that people can schedule their own reservations. You assign create rights to the global group of users called Everyone so they can make reservations freely. This group simplifies wide scale distribution of permissions.

That part is simple. The hard part is making sure that no one has permission to modify someone else's reservation. The permissions in schedule+ get so granular, down to the object level. You have to keep close track or unwanted reservations or appointments might start moving around without your control or approval.

The preceding example isn't meant to deter you from deploying the product; it is meant to point out the difference between create and modify permissions and to stress the need to keep a close eye on permissions.

When they are planned and used effectively, the security permissions features of Schedule+ can be a real boon to productivity. These features allow people to delegate tasks to others and stay focused on what they need to do. They also facilitate a basic reservation system for conference rooms and equipment, eliminating the need for manual scheduling.

From Here...

We've tried to point out some potential points of concern when deciding whether or not to deploy Schedule+ across the enterprise along with Exchange. These include:

- User participation and acceptance
- Training
- Information Policy
- Schedule+ as a working environment

By getting together with your users and information policy-making bodies you can come to an informed decision about what do and when. We discussed the three different approaches to instigating change when it comes to software. These consist of:

- The We're Doing it this Way Approach
- The No Other Way Approach
- The Sales Approach

In addition, some issues about permissions and privacy were discussed. These issues are at the forefront of a lot of discussion regarding groupware technologies like scheduling. You want to have the greatest number of features that can make information accessible to more people to make them more productive. After reading this chapter, you will have a lot more to bring to the table for discussion about how you might proceed.

The following chapters provide more information related to Schedule+:

- Chapter 9, "Installing Exchange Server," covers some issues that you should consider before installing Exchange.
- Chapter 28, "Understanding User Interface Features," provides in-depth view of the key features and functions of the Exchange Client.
- Chapter 30, "Using Advanced Schedule+ Components," provides detailed descriptions of all the key features of Schedule+.

CHAPTER 30

Using Advanced Schedule+ Components

- Schedule+ key features
- Schedule+ integration with Exchange
- Schedule+ flexibility

While most of the chapters so far have focused on back-end administration of Exchange, this is a good chapter for end users. If you are an administrator, you may want to point out this chapter to your users for reference and to your training staff to aid in the preparation of training materials, because it offers step-by-step guides through many of Schedule+'s features. The figures in this chapter help you become familiar with the layout of Schedule+, its expansive features, and ease of use.

As a client component of Exchange, Schedule+ offers individual and group scheduling, contact management, and day planning across the enterprise. On the back end, it takes advantage of all the features of Microsoft Exchange Server, such as directory synchronization, global address books, e-mail, and fault tolerance.

The power of Schedule+ is in its ability to provide access to information for anyone who needs it, while still maintaining privacy and security. By replicating the local copy of your schedule with the Exchange server's copy, Schedule+ allows you to share information even when you are not in the office. Schedule+ is not just an application; it is a working environment. ■

Using Key Features

Schedule+ offers many features to the user for organizing information. We will be discussing the key features of Schedule+ in great detail, giving step-by-step instructions on their use. The features covered will include:

- Scheduling and planning appointments
- The meeting wizard
- Scheduling recurring appointments
- Events
- Scheduling tasks
- Scheduling recurring tasks
- Events
- Views
- Tab gallery
- Contact management
- Finding information
- Schedule+ Interchange
- Access permissions
- Printing
- *The Seven Habits of Highly Effective People*
- Configurability

Scheduling and Planning Appointments

The main job of Schedule+ is to keep track of your day. The main screen shows your calendar for the day when you load the program. From this screen, you can begin to schedule appointments, move to other days, show different views, and so on. Figure 30.1 shows this layout.

In addition to the basic characteristics of a meeting—like start time, end time, description, and location—Schedule+ provides some additional parameters that prove useful when scheduling appointments. These include, but are not limited to, the following:

- Whether the appointment is an all-day affair
- Whether to sound a reminder chime and when
- Whether an appointment is tentative
- Whether the engagement is private or not
- Whether to make an appointment recurring

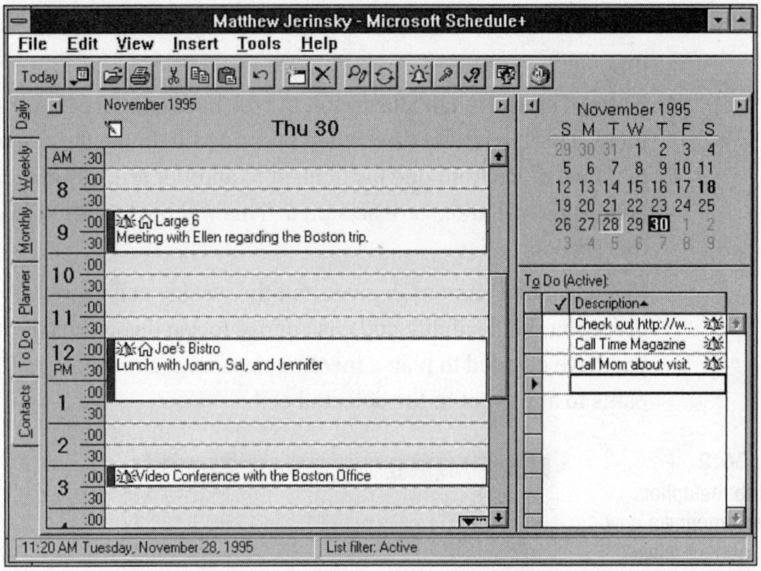

FIG. 30.1
The Schedule+ main screen lays out your day in a notebook-style format.

From the main screen, shown in figure 30.1, there are several ways to make an appointment. You can either double-click in a certain half-hour time interval, or you can hold down your left mouse button and drag the pointer to cover the entire time period of the engagement. Once highlighted, clicking the right mouse button brings down a menu from which you select New Appointment. The Insert menu at the top of the screen also provides a way to enter a new appointment. After either of these steps has been taken, you are presented with the screen shown in figure 30.2.

This screen contains all the information for the appointment. If you used the first method, double-clicking an interval, you can set the start and end time on this screen. If you chose the latter method, the correct starting and ending times will already be correct.

There are three or four tabs associated with a particular appointment:

- General: The General tab is the default tab that is selected whenever a new appointment is created. It shows the essential items such as meeting time, duration, location, and description, with all the options discussed above. This is the only tab that requires input. Other tabs are optional.

- Attendees: The Attendees tab gives you the ability to invite other people to the meeting (see fig. 30.3). By using the Invite Others button you can ask other people to join you for a meeting. Just highlight their names and click the Required or Optional buttons, depending on whether the person must be at the engagement or his or her attendance is optional. This feature can be used to keep people informed that there's a meeting happening without requiring their attendance. If you invited your boss as an optional attendee, he or she would stay abreast of what was happening in your department, even without really having the time to attend every meeting.
- Notes: The Notes tab allows you to type in comments about the particular appointment. This tab is also used when pressing the Invite Others button on the Attendees tab. Invitations from one participant to another are automatically pasted into this area when invitations are accepted. This will be discussed in greater detail later in this section.
- Planner: The Planner tab gives you the weekly cell view of your entire calendar. This gives you the flexibility and ease of use to see if you are free at a certain time, once you have decided to plan a meeting, or accept an invitation. It shows all the participants to any event in the selected cell.

FIG. 30.2
The tab metaphor makes entering a new appointment quick and simple.

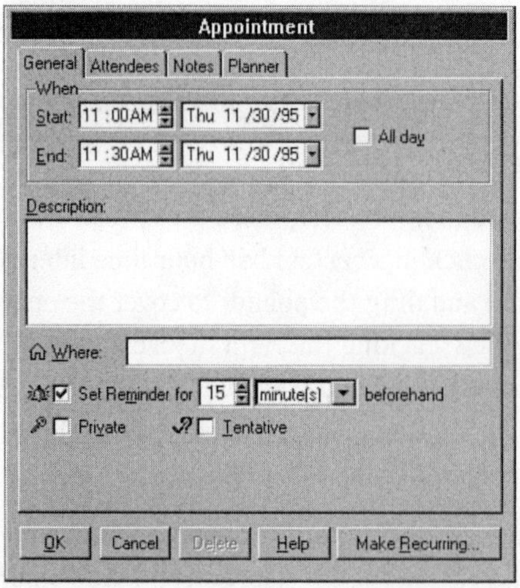

You can invite other people on the network to participate in a particular event. When you click the Invite Others button, Schedule+ presents the list of users in the global address book; however, you can drop-down the list box to use your personal address books instead, just as you can in the Exchange Client.

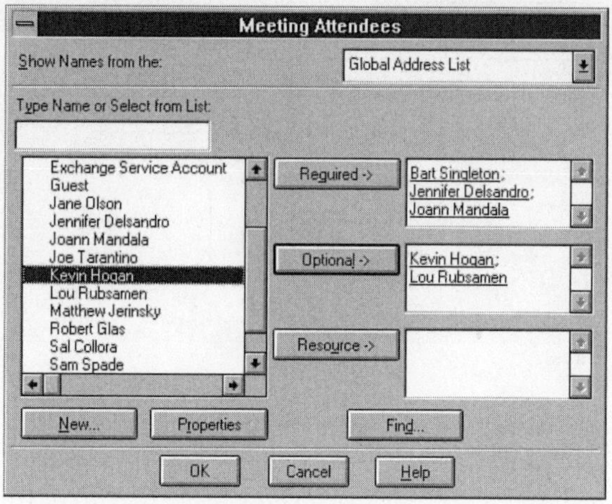

FIG. 30.3
Use the Attendees tab to invite people to a meeting.

TIP You can use both global and personal address books when inviting people to meetings by using the drop-down box in the upper right corner of the window.

After you choose the invitees, an e-mail message window is displayed, allowing you to explain what the meeting is about or to give any additional information. The participants, be they optional or required, are automatically entered into the To: field. Also, you can see that the optional participant, Bart in this case, has been filled into the cc: field. This shows the integration of Schedule+ into Exchange. At the top of the screen, you can see that the time and date have been filled in automatically and that the e-mail message form automatically popped up.

After the invitation message has been sent, it shows up in the recipients' inboxes just like any other message, except it has a special icon to indicate that it is a Schedule+ request.

When the invitation message is opened, Schedule+ is launched and shows the e-mail message that was sent, along with a request to accept, decline, or make a tentative agreement to attend the meeting. Schedule+ checks your schedule to see if you are free and lets you know whether something is already in that time slot, making it an easy choice. You can also view your schedule from here. This is useful if, for instance, you needed time to prepare for a subsequent appointment and the requested meeting would cut into that preparation time. Figure 30.4 gives an example of the choices available to you at this point.

After Joe accepts the invitation, the appointment gets pasted into his schedule automatically (see fig. 30.5). This is one of the most powerful features of Schedule+. In the process of accepting, Joe fired off an e-mail message to Kevin saying that he could make it. This allows Kevin to count on Joe's attendance.

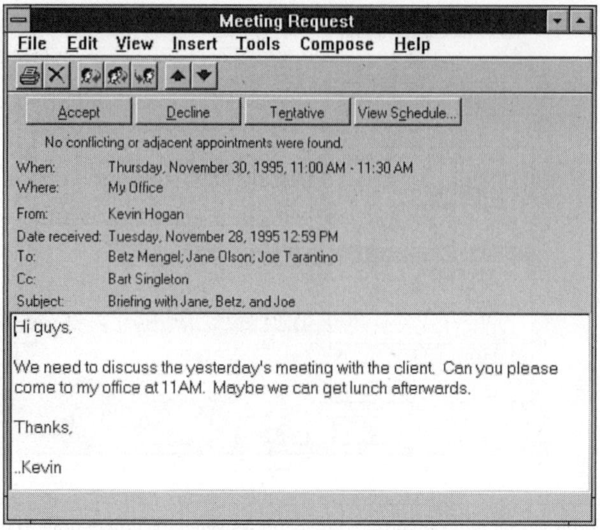

FIG. 30.4
You can either accept or decline an invitation by just clicking the appropriate button.

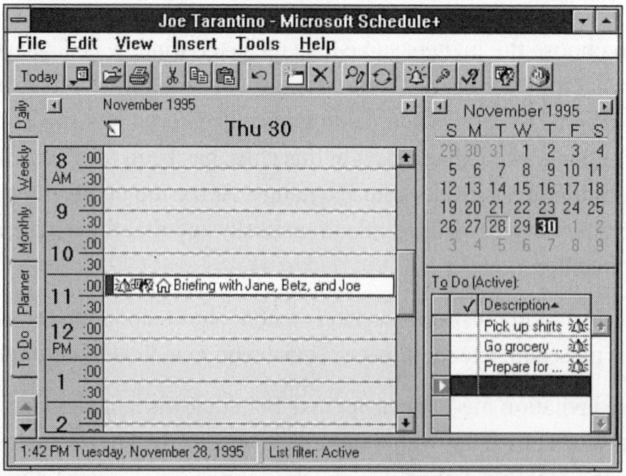

FIG. 30.5
Schedule+ automatically places the meeting in your calendar when you accept an invitation.

Schedule+ automatically enters accepted appointments into your schedule and sets the Notes tab to include the e-mail message that was tacked onto the invitation. This is useful because sometimes it is easy to forget why a meeting was called, and the invitation message often contains that information.

The Meeting Wizard

The meeting wizard is a utility that makes it very easy to schedule a meeting between several people across the network. The previous section was doing it the hard way—if you can believe that! The meeting wizard can be accessed by choosing Make Meeting, either from the Tools menu or from a selected time period on the calendar.

You can select location, resources, required, and optional attendees. Clicking Next brings you to a screen where the attendees are selected. They can be keyed manually into the window and then checked using the Check Names button, or, more easily, they can be picked from either the global address list, or your personal address list by clicking the Pick Attendees button. This brings you to the selection window as shown in figure 30.6.

FIG. 30.6
You can select the attendees from the global address list.

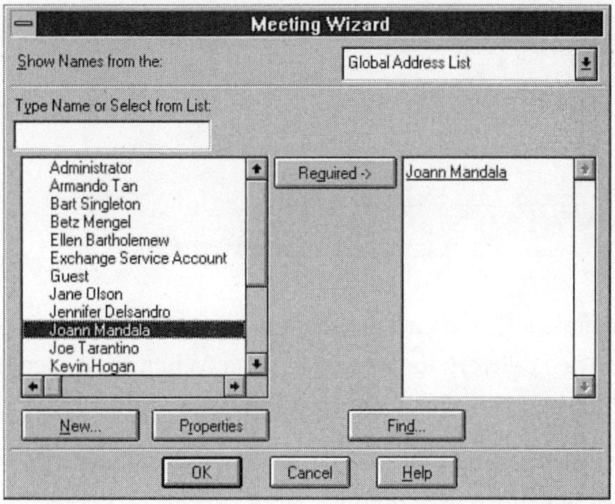

This screen should be very familiar to you by now. It is used whenever recipients need to be selected. The next thing you need to do is fill in any optional attendees, the same way you select required attendees: just pick them from the list.

The next page the wizard brings up has travel time and appointment duration information on it. The wizard asks what times and days are acceptable. With this information, the wizard goes to the Exchange server and checks whether people are free at the requested times.

If you have optional attendees, the wizard will ask if you want to get Free/Busy information for them. This is really situation-specific. For example, if you would like to have the remote possibility that your boss will make an appearance at a meeting, but he or she isn't required to attend, you would want to schedule the meeting at a time when he or she is free. If he or she isn't free, there is no possibility of even poking his or her head in at the meeting. If you choose not to check other people's schedules, the optional attendees will still be invited. After you've made your selection, the wizard will show you a planning grid.

The grid shown in figure 30.7 indicates the times that others are busy or free. The wizard suggests a time that is conducive to not only your own schedule but also the schedules of all the required participants (and optional participants if you instructed it to do so). If you aren't comfortable with this time for some reason—maybe it is too early—you can click the Pick Next Time button, which will bring up the next available time.

FIG. 30.7
The wizard suggests a time for the meeting.

After you click Finish, the wizard presents a screen where you type an e-mail message that the wizard then delivers to the participants. When they accept, an entry will automatically be added to their schedules and you will get a reply.

The meeting wizard makes it a real snap to schedule a meeting among many people. The key to making this feature of Schedule+ work is that the people you want to invite to meetings regularly have to keep the electronic schedules up to date. The Exchange server will take care of the rest. It keeps track of all the Free/Busy time information by always keeping the server copy of the user's schedule in synchronization with the user's local copy. If every individual's schedule is up to date, effectively scheduling meetings using the wizard is really simple.

Our example did not include scheduling equipment or locations. If you want to use those features, your Exchange administrator needs to create Exchange accounts for the rooms and pieces of equipment that are going to be reserved. If those resources are kept in the global address book, they can be scheduled across the enterprise by all users with the permission to do so. When using these features, the wizard adds a page or two asking you the device or resource for which you wish to make a reservation.

Scheduling Recurring Appointments

Schedule+ makes it simple to fill recurring tasks and appointments into your schedule. This is particularly useful for scheduling status meetings. Think about the contrast with a paper appointment book. On paper, you must write in each iteration of the same meeting on the same day each week. Sure, you could just assume that you'll have the meeting and not write it down, but does everyone in the office know that? What happens if it slips your mind and you make another appointment in its time slot?

Schedule+ offers two ways to schedule a recurring appointment such as a status or staff meeting. One way is to select Recurring Appointment under the Insert menu. Another way is to click the Make Recurring button when scheduling a regular appointment. Either method produces an appointment dialog box that contains four tabs. The four tabs for a recurring meeting are a bit different than those for a regular meeting: here there is no Planner tab, and there is a When tab. The When tab, shown in figure 30.8, is the key to recurring events.

FIG. 30.8
Setting times and dates for recurring events.

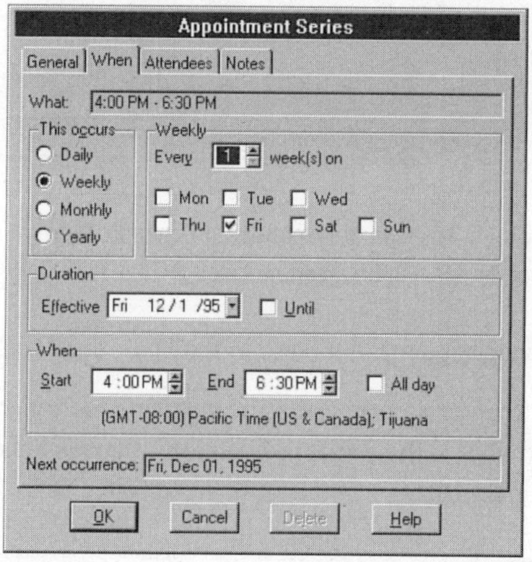

The result, the completed schedule, is shown in figure 30.9. Take a look at the figure. You can see in the monthly calendar on the upper right that all the Fridays are shaded, indicating something is scheduled then. In addition, looking at the daily appointment, you will notice the circular arrows that indicate a recurring appointment.

TIP You can make changes to recurring appointments by using the Edit Recurring selection under the Edit menu.

Entering Schedule+ Events

Events are engagements that have no specific time of day attached to them. For example, if a seminar will occur on a certain day, or a certain movie is being released, and you want to be reminded of them, they wouldn't be classified as appointments or tasks, but would be considered events.

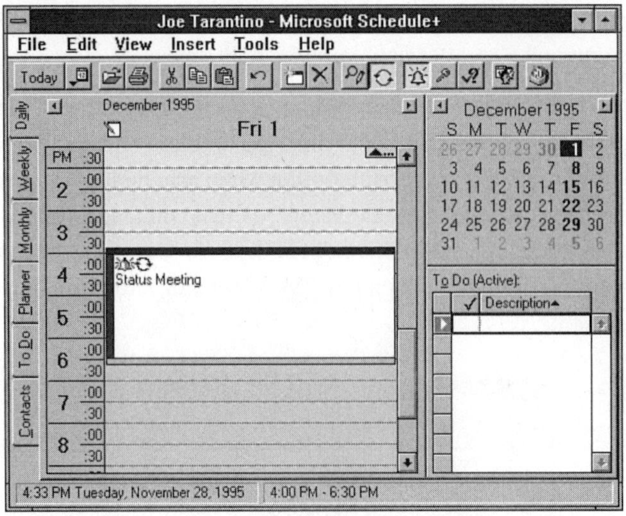

FIG. 30.9
Recurring appointment scheduled for the month.

NOTE Events do not show up in any kind of Free/Busy information. They are simply reminders of things that may be happening on a certain day.

Events show up above your appointment book in the Daily and Weekly views.

There are several ways to enter an event into the system. One easy way is to single-click the pen-and-paper icon that is to the left of the date; this causes Schedule+ to display a drop-down menu (see fig. 30.10).

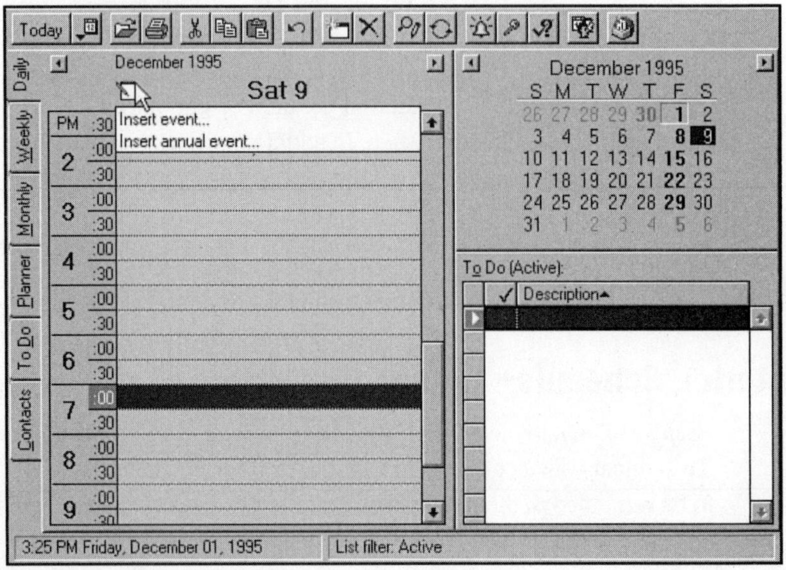

FIG. 30.10
Clicking the event icon drops down a menu.

From the drop-down menu, select Insert Event. This will bring up the main event editing window. It is here you set all the properties of an event (see fig. 30.11).

FIG. 30.11
The main event window is where you will enter your event times and descriptions.

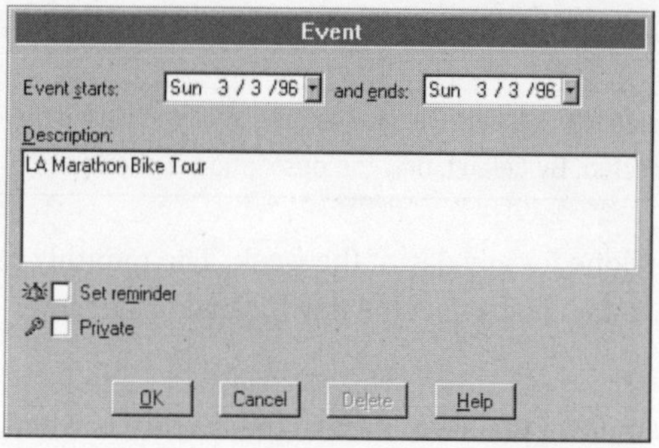

The Set reminder and Private checkboxes carry their usual standard meanings. The figure shows that no reminder is necessary, but you can set the reminder for minutes, hours, days, weeks, or months ahead of time.

There is a special kind of event called an Annual Event. You can use this feature to easily schedule occasions like birthdays and anniversaries. There are three ways to insert an annual event into your schedule. You can click or right-click the event icon under the month, you can use the Insert menu, or, if you already have events entered for a certain day, you can click that event to get a drop-down menu. Type in the description, pick the date, choose your reminder settings, and click OK. Your annual event then appears at the top of the day for which it is scheduled.

NOTE There are several ways of executing the functions of Schedule+. Use the method that seems most comfortable to you. There is no single, right way, as all methods lead to the same windows.

Scheduling Tasks

Schedule+ provides a flexible To Do List system. It is an organized, entry-based system that helps you keep track of things you have to do during the day or series of days, just like all those sticky notes surrounding your computer monitor and inside your wallet. You can do things like set priorities, set the number of days a task should last, note when the task should be completed, and fill in the percentage of completion of a chore. The To Do List provides a more complete view of the information than what appears when the Daily tab is selected on your calendar. The Daily tab only shows the description field.

When you use Schedule+ on a regular basis, viewing the To Do List on the Daily tab is of great assistance because you have a constant reminder right on the screen that you have to get certain tasks completed that day. Adding a task is very simple from the Daily tab: select one of the rows with the left mouse button and type in a description.

TIP Under the View menu, selecting Columns will give you the ability to view more To Do List fields while the Daily tab is selected. By default, only the description is shown.

Adding a task can be done for any day of the week. The monthly calendar is right above the To Do List for that day. Just select the day the task is due, and complete the same procedure.

A good, practical example of the usefulness of this feature is when you first get into the office in the morning. Fire up Schedule+, and when you are looking over your schedule for that day, you can start entering the things you have to get done, right on the same screen. You'll find that always having the reminder in front of you throughout the day will really help, especially if you have the habit of leaving Schedule+ open all day as previously discussed. When you work in a hectic environment, the morning is usually the calm before the storm, when all your thoughts are in order. As the day goes on, things can get lost in the shuffle, but Schedule+ will keep you right on track.

TIP You can use your right mouse button to pull a menu to access more complex task properties. Select New Task.

In addition to using the simple entry method, putting a task on your To Do List using the To Do tab is also very easy. Simply click the To Do tab. It displays the screen in figure 30.13. From there, position the pointer somewhere in the main window, and click your right mouse button. From here, you have a few options. You can organize your To Do List into Projects or you can just list Tasks quickly. Projects are headings that categorize your tasks. For example, if there are certain activities that you perform every day, such as checking voice mail, e-mail, and writing reports, these tasks can be placed under a project title called Daily Activities. In addition, you can have a project called Home that lists all the chores you need to complete for home, like grocery shopping and going to the dry cleaner.

You can forego using project titles altogether and just list the things you need to get done under the project title of None (the default). You will see later how that method is quicker if you enter your tasks on the Daily tab of your calendar.

Using Project Titles We will now enter a new task into the schedule with a project title, step-by-step. First, let's use the To Do tab on the calendar to enter tasks, so select that tab. Then, position the pointer anywhere on the grid and click the right mouse button.

This will drop down a menu. Remember that you can also use the Insert menu at the top of the screen to enter new projects and tasks. Now follow this process:

1. Select New Project.
2. Enter a name for the project (in this case, Home).
3. Set a priority (determine whether the project is private), and click OK. The priority should be 1–9, A–Z, and privacy hides the information from other people on the network. If you give your secretary or associate permission to view your schedule, any item marked as private will not be displayed.
4. Select the newly created Home project row, and click the right mouse button.
5. Select New Task to bring up the screen shown in figure 30.12. The items on the screen are very straightforward.

TIP The right mouse button is context-sensitive and will provide a customized menu, based on where the pointer is located.

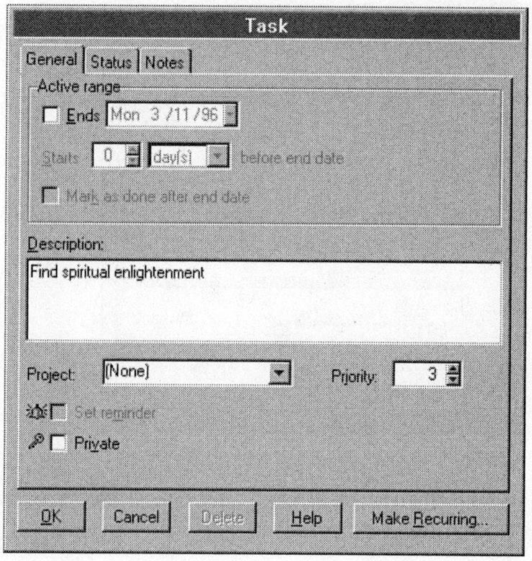

FIG. 30.12
The General tab contains overview information about a new or existing task.

6. Fill in the desired values.
7. Move to the Status tab and fill in values for the percentage complete, days of effort, contact information, billing information, mileage, and your role in the task.
8. Press the OK button to enter the task under the current project.

You can add additional tasks and projects using the procedures just described. Schedule+ has an ingenious way of completing tasks as well as entering them. When a certain task has been completed, clicking in the checkmark field crosses the item off your To Do list. The entry is not removed, but it is crossed out. This is useful for those times when you can't remember whether you paid your bills or not, or when you paid them.

The status items provide the timely information you need when you are working on many different projects. Sometimes you will not enter the status information, but it is nice to know it is there and that Schedule+ can serve as a way to keep track of your tasks when there are several of them at once. It is also handy when you are given the permission to view someone else's To Do List. For example, one person takes minutes during a meeting and records the progress of all the action items; that person can enter the information into other people's To Do Lists (see fig. 30.13). The information can prove very useful and productive in a collaborative environment. This is really the power of Exchange: it links people to each other in every way.

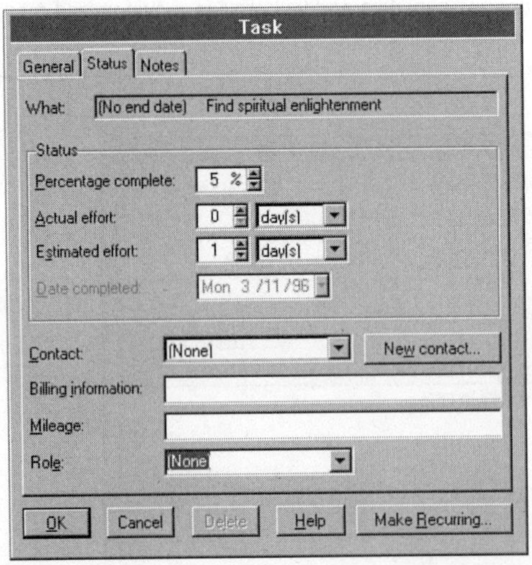

FIG. 30.13
The Status tab gives detailed information about the progress of a task.

The Notes tab provides a way for you to enter additional descriptive information, or any ancillary information related to the task. This tab is provided throughout Schedule+ and Exchange for free-form text entry to complement the database-style field entries.

Turning a Task into an Appointment A key feature you can use when putting tasks on your To Do List is to turn the task into an appointment. This is useful for when you know you have a job that needs to be done and you know what that job entails, but you don't have any time-specific information. You can place the item on your To Do List, make notes, give a description, but leave off the time information. Later, when you get the details, you can put the item onto your appointment calendar. To access this feature, you select the task you want to convert into an appointment, click your right mouse button, and choose Appt. From Task from the menu. This will bring up the standard appointment schedule window.

By using the To Do list to its potential, you can have this kind of handy information at all times. For maximum benefit, it is important to have policies in place so that people throughout your organization are required to use the system.

▶ **See** the section titled, "Getting Everyone on Board," in Chapter 29, "Integrating Schedule+ with Exchange Server," for more information about setting company policies, **p. 706**

Scheduling Recurring Tasks

Filling in recurring tasks is almost the same as entering appointments, except that tasks are related to the To Do List rather than the appointment calendar. Choose the To Do tab on the left side of the calendar window, position the pointer in the main window, and click the right mouse button, and choose Recurring Task.

TIP You can use the menus for this function by selecting Recurring Task from the Insert menu.

A dialog box pops up with four tabs. The names of these tabs should be familiar to you, but because this is a recurring task, the entries on the General and When tabs are a bit different, to reflect the time intervals at which these tasks must be accomplished.

The General tab has an entry at the top of the window that explains when the tasks occur. Other than that, the General tab is the same as the nonrecurring General tab. The When tab gives you the opportunity to enter the times when the task will occur. You can choose daily, weekly, monthly, or yearly and control things like when the recurring task will start and when it will end. This screen also tells you when the next occurrence is taking place. The complete screen is shown in figure 30.14.

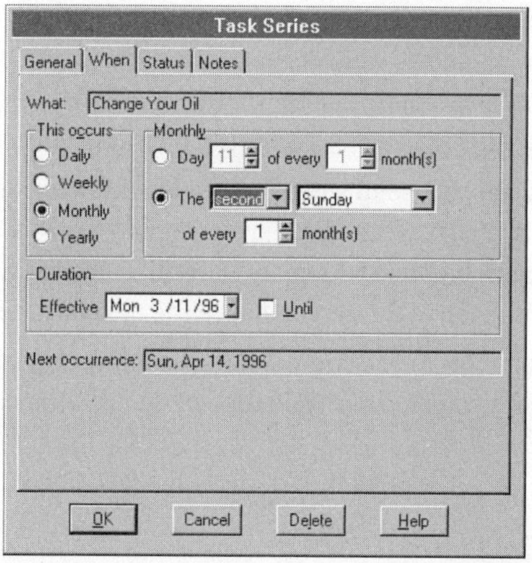

FIG. 30.14 Using the When tab, you can set the times when tasks occur.

The Status and Notes tabs are the same for recurring tasks as regular tasks. Refer to the previous section for descriptions of these tabs.

Schedule+ provides a robust To Do List system that enables you to remind yourself of tasks that need to be accomplished on a particular day. The system is easy to use, is as straightforward as using sticky notes around your monitor, and provides much more power.

Using Views

The Schedule+ window is divided into several views. View is just another way of describing all the different tabs on your screen. For example, selecting the Daily tab is the same thing as the Daily view.

The Schedule+ window comes configured with six default views: the Daily, Weekly, Monthly, Planner, To Do, and Contacts views. In the next section, you will see all the different views that are available in addition to the default views.

- The Daily View: You have already seen plenty of examples of the Daily tab. It is shown in many of the figures in this chapter and is the default view. In the Daily view, your day is on the left side of the screen, with the right part of the screen divided vertically between a monthly calendar used for navigation on the top and the To Do List shown in the lower portion of the screen. You use the arrows located at the top of view above the date to move from day to day.

  This view is where most of your activity will probably take place. It consolidates a lot of disparate information. You are kept abreast of your events, appointments, and things to do all from this one screen. In addition, the monthly calendar gives you the long-term picture, shows which days you are free, and allows quick navigation. To move from month to month, use the arrows above the calendar.

- The Weekly View: This view gives you the picture of how the week is shaping up (see fig. 30.15). It is most useful when previewing the week ahead. For example, if you know you have a busy week ahead, you can make sure to enjoy the upcoming weekend a little more because you know you will be having a busy week. You can use the arrows at the top of the screen to see the next or previous weeks.

  Another good use of the Weekly view is for scheduling appointments when people say they would like to meet at a certain time period. If someone wants to have a breakfast meeting, you can check the Weekly view to see what particular morning you are free. This view makes it very simple.

- The Monthly View: The Monthly View gives you the appointments and events scheduled for an entire month (see fig. 30.16). It looks much like the old paper calendars where you would keep track of birthdays and anniversaries.

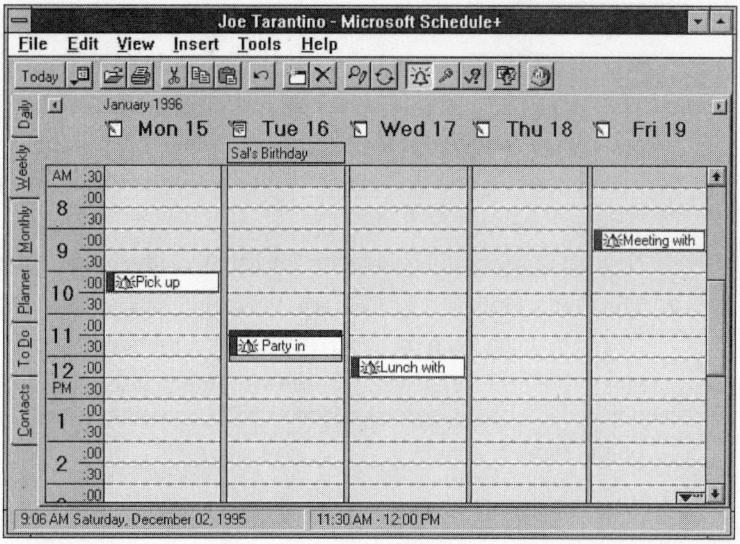

FIG. 30.15
The Weekly view gives you the week at a glance.

FIG. 30.16
The Monthly view gives you the long-term picture.

Events show up with an asterisk in front of them, and appointments show up with the time in front of them.

- The Planner View: The Planner is really useful for project management. You can see the upcoming period of time and schedule meetings. It shows you which meetings require your attendance, which are optional, and whether resources are reserved for the particular meeting.
- The To Do View: This view gives you an extended look at the tasks you need to accomplish. It gives much more information than the Daily view.

  The additional attributes shown are priority, the ending date, the duration, the percentage complete, and the project to which the task belongs.

  ▶ **See** the "Scheduling Tasks" section to get a complete description of how to use the To Do View, **p. 727**

  New categories can be added to the list by double-clicking one of the column titles.
- The Contacts View: The Contacts View functions as your address book (see fig. 30.17). You can keep track of names, phone numbers, and addresses for both home and business. In addition, important dates and notes can be entered. You see detailed information about all your contacts on one screen using the series of tabs on the right.

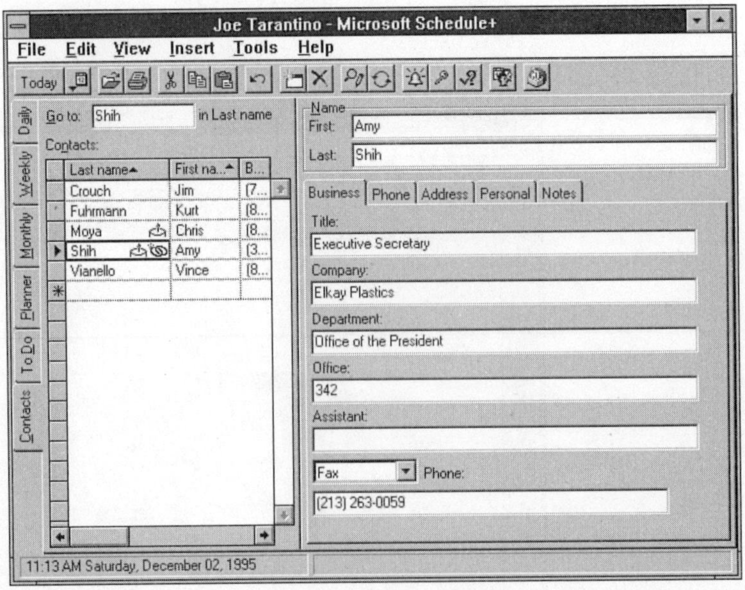

FIG. 30.17
The layout of the Contacts View enables you to enter and find information quickly.

See the "Using Contact Management" section for step-by-step instructions on how to use the Contacts View, **p. 739**

You can find information by quickly navigating through the list of contacts on the left, or by entering the last name directly into the window at the top of the screen. Just entering the first few letters brings you directly to the right place.

Using the Tab Gallery

The Tab Gallery gives you the ability to customize your main Schedule+ window. You can customize what tabs are available, to be more in tune to the way you work. For example, if you really like to work with a Weekly View, but you also want to see your To Do List information, you can replace the default Weekly Appointments tab with the Weekly Schedule tab. If you have a separate contact management system already in place, you can choose to delete the Contact tab from your main screen and replace it with something else.

To use the Tab Gallery, select it from the View menu at the top of the screen or right-click any one of the tabs along the left side of the notebook (see fig. 30.18).

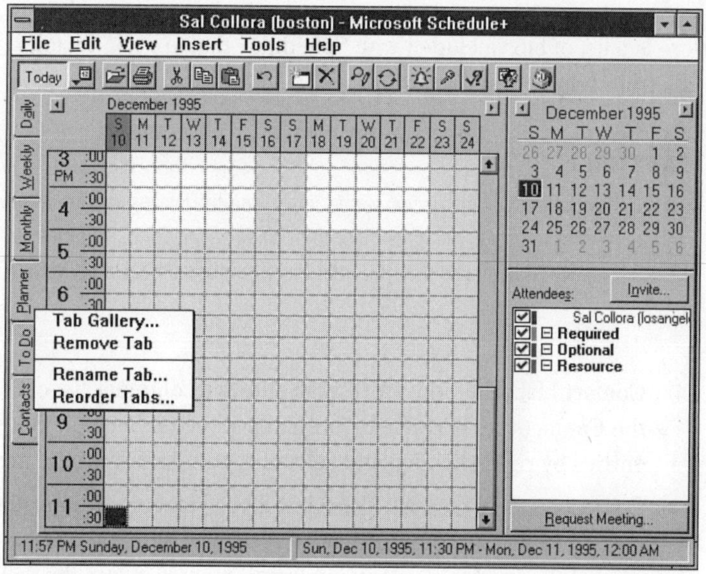

FIG. 30.18
Getting into the Tab Gallery is simple. Just right-click any tab.

The Tab Gallery presents a list of available tabs, showing a thumbnail view of each and a textual description. Use the Add and Remove buttons to move tabs from one window to the other, and use the Move Up and Move Down buttons to establish the order in which you want the tabs to appear on the screen (see fig. 30.19).

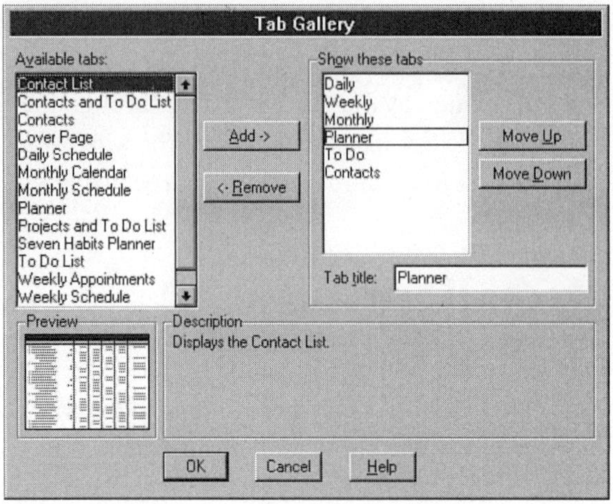

FIG. 30.19
Use the Tab Gallery window to add and remove views from Schedule+.

NOTE Each tab has a screen name that may be different from the name listed in Available Tags box. You may notice that when you add a tab, a duplicate entry will exist. Just remove the duplicate. You can also change the screen name to something you are more comfortable with if you wish. ■

Here is a list of tabs included with Schedule+ that are not defaults (you must use the Tab Gallery to select these views):

CAUTION

You can have as many tabs as you want, but be careful. Having too many views will make Schedule+ more confusing to use. If you have more than six or seven views, you must scroll through your tabs on the main screen. This makes things a little more cumbersome. Unfortunately, Schedule+ does not layer the tabs.

- Contact List: The Contact List tab shows a columnar list of contacts. It differs from the Contacts tab because it doesn't have the tabbed edit fields. You can edit the entries by right-clicking, and selecting Edit Item from the menu.
- Contacts and To Do List: This view gives you contact information and the related tasks (see fig. 30.20). Schedule+ will display all related tasks for a specified contact entry. It looks at the contact information entered into the task if it exists. There is an entry for All that will display all tasks.

NOTE When presented with columns that appear with buttons at the column heading, right-clicking will bring up a menu allowing you to sort, group, and arrange your fields. This applies in every context. ■

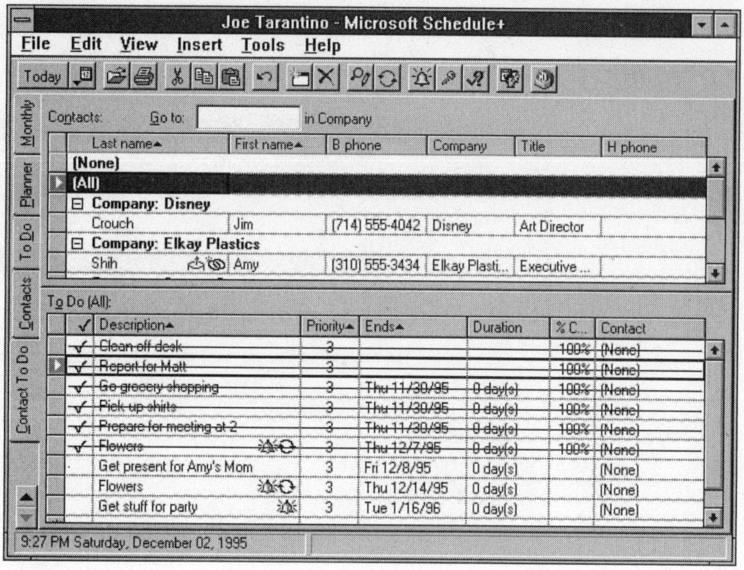

FIG. 30.20
The Contacts and To Do List view joins the information based on contact information stored in the task entry.

- Monthly Schedule: This view combines the Monthly and To Do List views (see fig. 30.21).

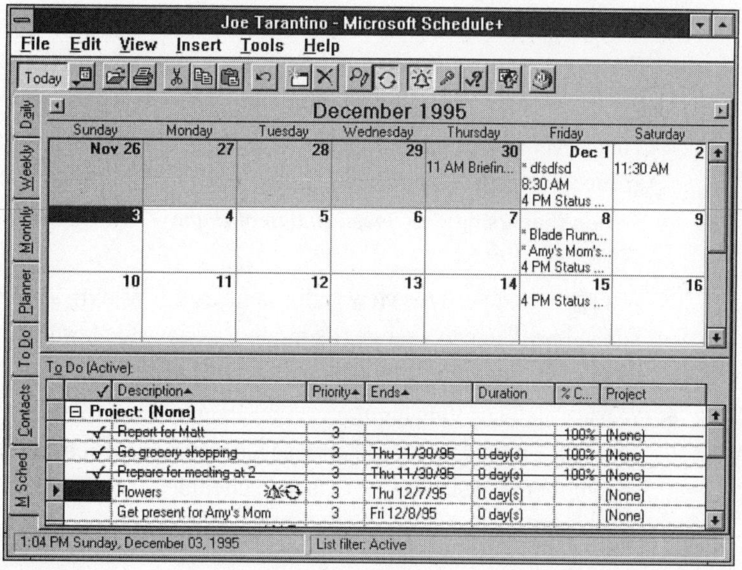

FIG. 30.21
You can move the horizontal line in the middle of the screen to resize each part of the window.

- Projects and To Do List: Rather than display tasks hierarchically like the To Do View, the Projects and To Do List View lays out each of your projects in a separate window. Selecting a particular project brings up all the related tasks in the bottom window.

This is particularly useful when using Schedule+ for small project management purposes. See figure 30.22.

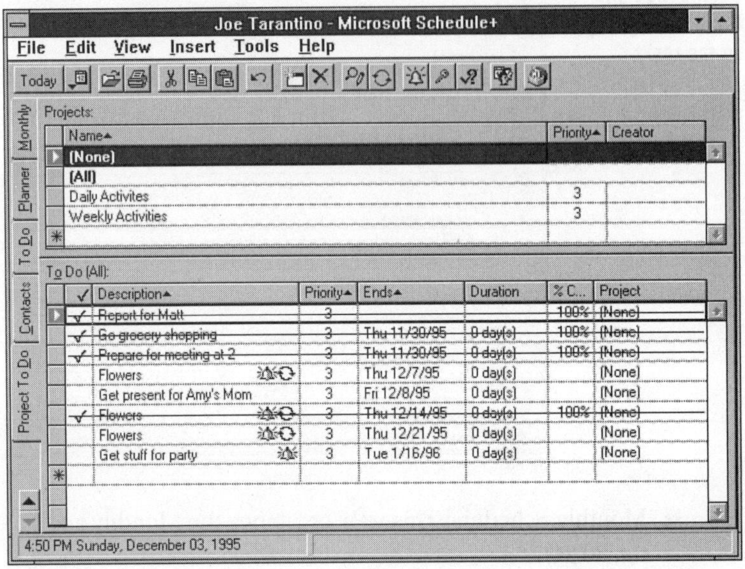

FIG. 30.22
You have easy access to all your projects and their related tasks using the Projects and To Do List View.

- Seven Habits Planner: The tab is based on the book *The Seven Habits of Highly Effective People* by Stephen R. Covey. By going through the series of wizards under the Tools menu, you'll get a better idea of how to prioritize your life and your day.

  This view displays appointments for up to seven days as well as the To Do List grouped by your Seven Habits Roles.

  ▶ **See** the "Using *The Seven Habits of Highly Effective People*" section later in this chapter, **p. 748**

- Weekly Schedule: This view is the same as the Weekly View, except that it adds the To Do List. You can change the number of days to view by using the Number of Days selection under the View menu. See figure 30.23.

- Yearly Calendar: Viewing the yearly calendar gives the longest-term picture that Schedule+ provides. It can serve as a navigation device, and it shows the days that appointments, tasks, and events are scheduled.

NOTE The right mouse button loses some functionality here. In order to add a new appointment, event, or task on the selected day, you must use the Insert menu.

The Tab Gallery provides many different ways of viewing information. Schedule+ was made to be very flexible in this manner. It is meant to be a daily environment where the user feels comfortable, and the utility of each view varies with the user.

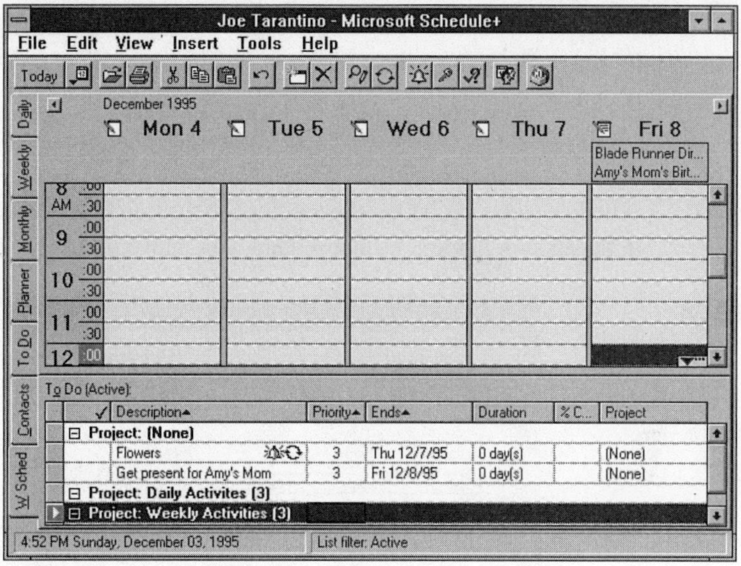

FIG. 30.23
You can use this view to enter new appointments as well as projects and tasks.

Using Contact Management

Schedule+ provides a full-featured contact management system. It functions just like the cardfile on your desk except that it provides many more fields of information and is completely searchable.

▶ **See** the next section for more information on searching, **p. 741**

Selecting the Contacts View on the notebook will bring you into the contact management screen (see fig. 30.24). It is separated into four distinct parts:

- The Go to field in the upper left part gives you the ability to find an item quickly.
- The Contacts listing under the Go to field on the left is a list of all your contact names.
- The upper right part shows the full name of the selected contact.
- The lower right part contains all the tabs where you enter information.

Five separate tabs in the Contacts view categorize all the fields Schedule+ offers:

- Business: The Business tab contains all the information regarding a person's company. Just start typing into the fields.
- Phone: The Phone tab provides a way to enter all the relevant phone numbers on one screen. You can enter business, fax, assistant, home, cellular, and pager numbers.

- Address: You enter both business and home addresses in these fields. There is multi-line support for the address to accommodate floor numbers and department names.
- Personal: You enter birthdays and anniversaries at the Personal tab (see fig. 30.25). These are automatically placed into your schedule as events. You can use any of the schedule views to change the notification time on those events. (Since the default notification is 15 minutes beforehand, you may want to change it.)

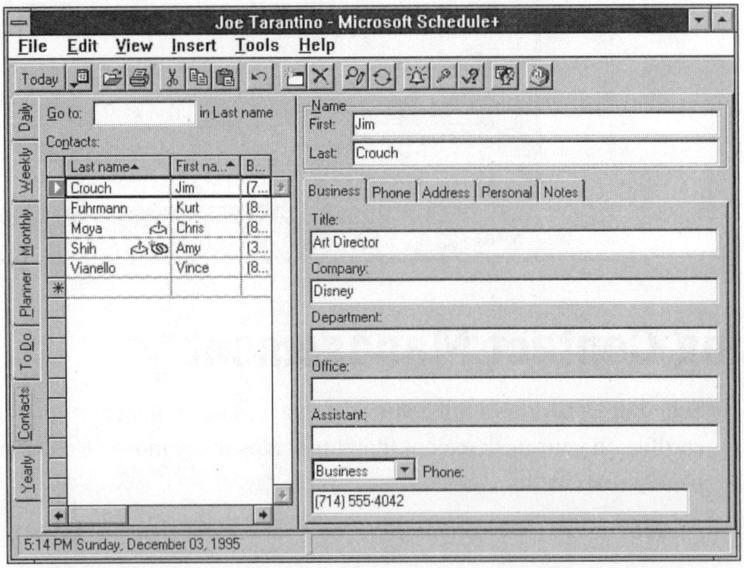

FIG. 30.24 Schedule+ provides robust contact management through the Contacts View.

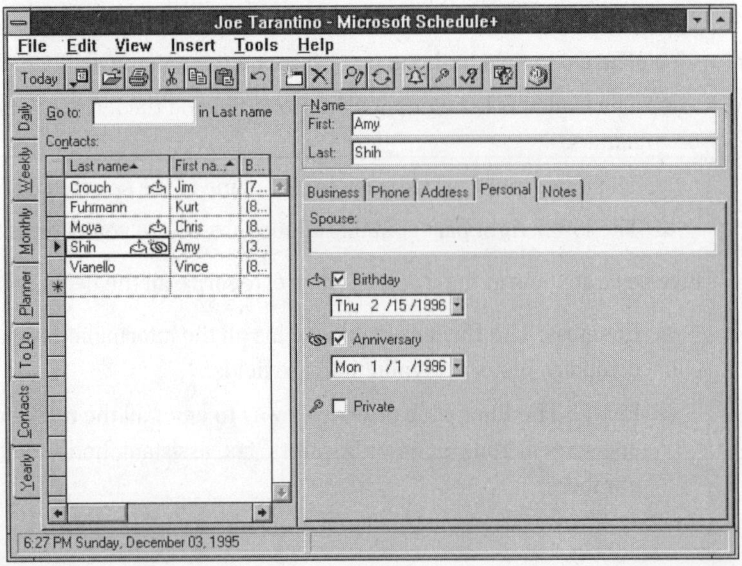

FIG. 30.25 With the Personal tab you can enter anniversaries and birthdays, and have them integrated into your schedule as events.

This screen also contains a field for the name of the contact's spouse.

▶ **See** the section entitled "Entering Schedule+ Events" earlier in this chapter for more details, **p. 725**

- Notes: The Notes tab is used for typing any notes about the contact. In addition, there are four user-defined fields that let you keep track of things that might be important to you.

TIP The four user-defined fields available for each contact can be used to tag each contact with different criteria which can then be used to group and sort the contacts into categories. For example, users can separate their "business" contacts from their "personal" contacts by entering these keywords in the User 1 field and then grouping the contacts by this field. Other uses include being able to identify those contacts which require a specific action item such as a follow-up letter or phone call.

Schedule+ offers basic contact management functionality that is integrated into Schedule+, Exchange, and other OLE applications.

Finding Information

Schedule+ offers different ways to locate information after it has been entered into the system. Because there are so many views in Schedule+, the searching facilities are very powerful, fast, and flexible. If you select Find from the Edit menu, the window shown in figure 30.26 appears.

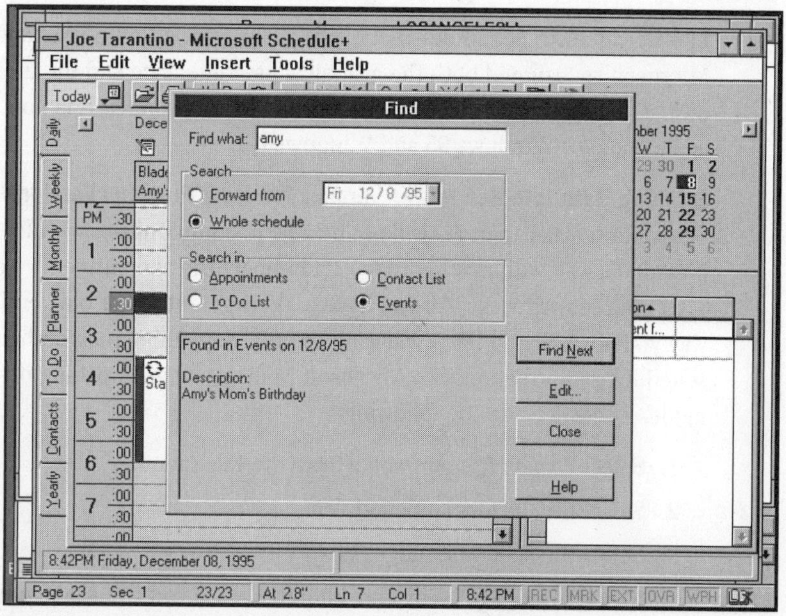

FIG. 30.26
You can enter a search string and find information from many sources.

You can control three properties of any search:

- What to search for
- Scope of the search
- What kind of information you want to find

These are entered and selected in the top three sections of the window shown in figure 30.26. The fourth section shows the results of the search.

You use the Find Next button to cycle through all the matches to your query. At any time, you can click the Edit button to change the properties of the item showing in the window. When you edit an item, it appears in its native edit window, as shown in figure 30.27.

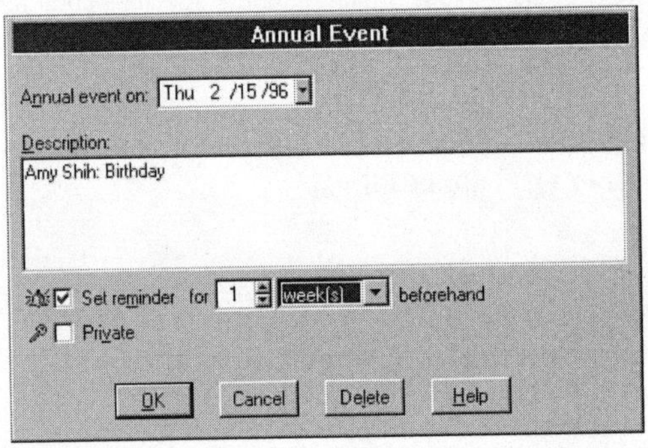

FIG. 30.27 When you edit an annual event, it pops up in the Annual Event edit window.

Schedule+ Interchange

In order to make Schedule+ more robust and tie it into the Exchange architecture, Microsoft redesigned both the graphical user interface and the file structure of Schedule+. The outcome was 100 enhancements to the product. It is now available as a 32-bit application for Windows 95 and Windows NT.

Bringing Data into Schedule+ Version 7.0 from Previous Versions Any version of Schedule+ earlier than 7.0 will not be able to communicate with Exchange. Microsoft has provided a way within Schedule+ 7.0 to import the appointments from previous versions. This is an easy process. All you have to do is get into your old version of Schedule+ the way you normally do. This will vary slightly, depending on whether you link your scheduling information with Microsoft Mail or you are working off-line in stand-alone mode. Either way, do the following:

1. Select Export Appointments from the File menu.
2. Select the file format Schedule+.
3. Select the schedule range All.
4. Include Daily Notes by checking the box if you want to export that information.

Figure 30.28 shows an example of what this screen will look like. It is a very simple process to save all your appointments into a file so Schedule+ 7.0 can import your data.

FIG. 30.28
Exporting data from previous versions of Schedule+ is quick and easy.

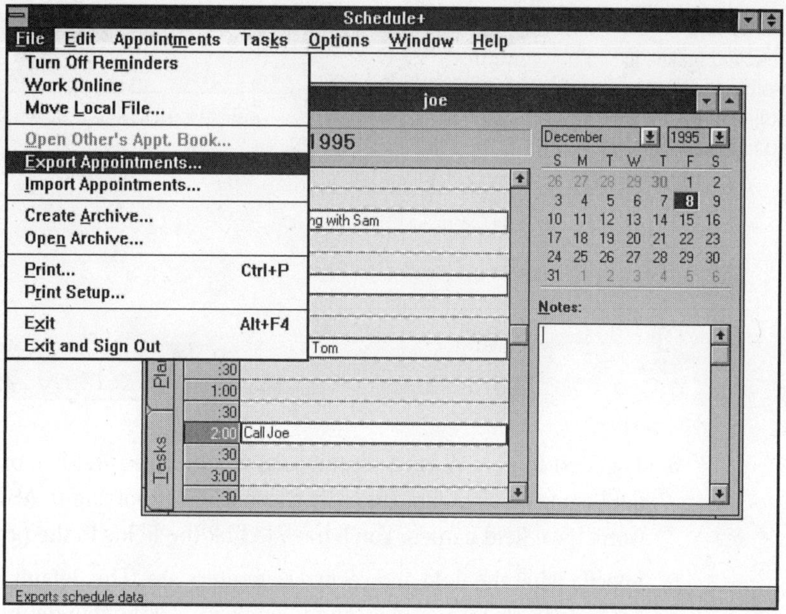

Duplicate appointments are put next to appointments that are already scheduled.

Another use of Schedule+ Interchange is the distribution of company holidays, days off, birthdays, and events. You can also distribute a company phone list this way. The file can then be e-mailed or posted in a public folder.

Importing Files to Schedule+ from Databases In addition to importing files from older versions of Schedule+, the Interchange feature can be used to import database files into any one of the containers in Schedule+: the Appointment Book, the To Do List, the Event List, or the Contact List. If you already have an Access database, for example, that contains all your contact information, you can export the file to an ASCII delimited text file and import it directly into Schedule+. Here's the process.

1. Begin by writing down the name and order of the fields in your Access table. This will be useful later.
2. Export the data from Access as an ASCII text file. (Refer to the Access on-line help for instructions on how to do this.)
3. Schedule+ provides a wizard to help you import text data. From the File menu, select Import and scroll to Text, which makes the wizard pop up.

4. Input the name of the ASCII text file containing the information you want to import, and click Next to bring up the screen shown in figure 30.29.

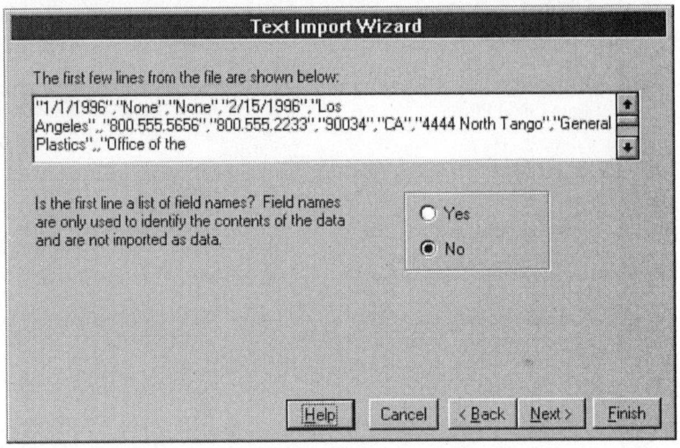

FIG. 30.29
The wizard makes it possible to use the first line of the file as field names.

5. The Text Import Wizard screen asks whether the first line of the file contains the field names. Select No. (In most cases when exporting to ASCII from Access you won't have field names. You'll have to link the fields to the proper data later.)
6. Specify what the field and record delimiters are. The default in most cases is to separate fields by commas, and to enclose each field in double quotation marks. Keep these defaults, and click Next.
7. At the screen shown in figure 30.30, you must select where you want the information to be placed. In this case, select Contact List because we are assuming that the Access database was a list of names and phone numbers.

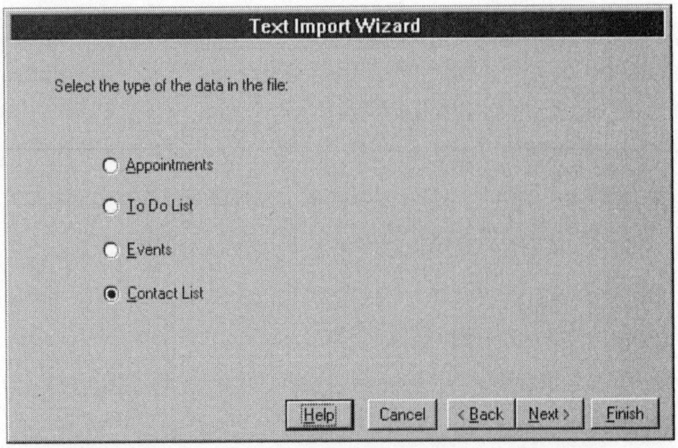

FIG. 30.30
You must select what kind of information is being imported.

8. Link the data with the field names in the Contact List. This will be very easy because you've written down the order of your fields in the Access file. Just go through each one as shown in figure 30.31 and select the proper field.

FIG. 30.31
Associate data values with field names.

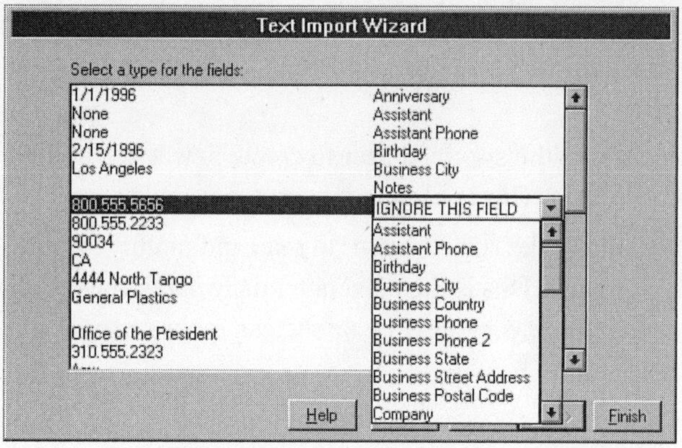

9. Click Finish, and the items will appear in your Contact List. It is as simple as that.

You can also use Schedule+ to export data using a similar wizard.

Access Permissions

Access permissions are configurable for every object in the Exchange environment, and Schedule+ is no exception. You can assign rights to other users to view various parts of your schedule with varying authority. For example, you can give your boss read access to all the appointments in your calendar while keeping your contacts, tasks, and events private. You can hide things from even your boss by marking them as Private in the properties window for the item.

Assigning permissions to users is straightforward; however, knowing what each of the permissions give access to is very important, so as not to compromise your privacy.

Setting permissions is done through the Tools menu. When you select Set Access Permissions, the window shown in figure 30.32 appears.

What follows is a description of each kind of permission. With the exception of Custom, selecting an option in the User Role box will gray out all the fields below it. For example, if you select Read, it will enable read access for Appointments, Contacts, Events, and Tasks. Custom lets you set each one individually. Also, Delegate and Delegate Owner permissions enable the checkbox labeled User meeting requests sent to me.

- None: Gives no access to the specified user. If this user tries to access your schedule, he or she will get an Access Denied message.
- Read: Gives the specified user read-only access to any item not marked Private in the item description. This is good for when you want your fellow employees to know what you're doing, while you retain the ability to hide the text of any particular

description as needed. If you mark an item Private, another user looking at your schedule will know you have something scheduled, but he or she won't know what it is.

- Create: Allows the specified user to create new items and read existing ones not marked Private. This is useful for secretarial applications.
- Modify: Allows the selected user to read and modify existing items, except for items marked Private. This is the most potentially dangerous of all permissions because if you give it to someone else, he or she can make changes to your schedule without you knowing.
- Delegate: Allows the selected user to send and receive messages on your behalf. A delegate cannot read an item marked Private. This is another potentially dangerous attribute. Use only if you completely trust the person. It can lead to problems. It is useful for planning meetings when you are without a computer: you can call your delegate and have him or her send out a message for you.
- Owner: Allows the selected user to modify all of your schedule.

NOTE This permission enables the user to view your private data, and assign permissions.

- Delegate Owner: This is the same as owner, except the user can send meeting messages on your behalf.
- Custom: Allows you to define the level of permission for each of the scheduling categories. This is a very powerful feature because it enables you to give certain privileges to certain users.
- User receives meeting requests sent to me: Gets selected whenever you use any of the delegate permissions, because for all intents and purposes you may as well be that user, so why not receive his or her meeting requests. You can accept or decline as that user.

Depending on the permissions assigned to you, you can open other users' schedules. To do this, select Open and Other's Appointment Book from the File menu. You can also just press Ctrl+O, select the user from the list, and click OK. You now can perform operations on that user's schedule. If you have Delegate or Delegate Owner permission, you can send out messages on behalf of that user.

In addition to these user permissions, there are three Global Permissions you can set, just by clicking the Global tab:

- Disallow Overlapping Appointments: Prevents you from scheduling two things on the same date at the same time. This is useful for maintaining the integrity of your schedule and avoiding conflicting appointments.

- Disallow Recurring Appointments: Removes the ability to schedule a recurring appointment.
- Show *n* Months Worth of My Free/Busy Information: Enter a value depending on how far ahead you would like others to be able to see your schedule. This option is useful in those situations where you would really like to keep your schedule open just in case something comes up. By keeping this number small, you only share a limited amount of information about when you will be free.

As you can see, the permissions capabilities of Schedule+ are extensive and robust and tie heavily into the Exchange server.

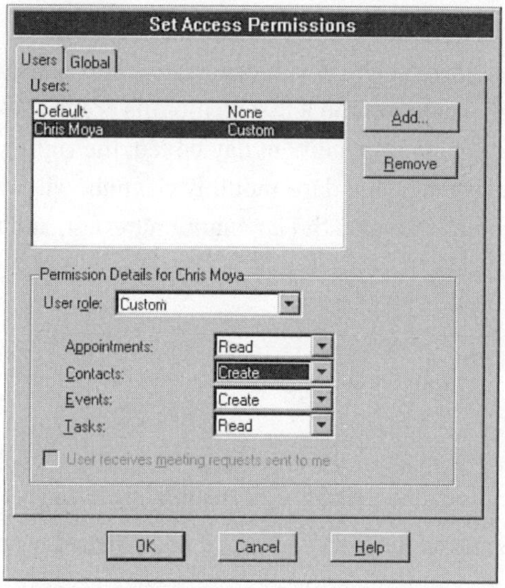

FIG. 30.32
Permissions are a powerful tool that lets others view certain aspects of your calendar.

Printing Your Schedule+ Information

There are times that you are going to be without computing resources. Whether you are at home, on the road, in a meeting, or your computer is busy recalculating a massive spreadsheet, there will come a time when you need to have your schedule on paper. Schedule+ gives you the ability to print out a wide variety of scheduling information in a variety of different formats:

- All Text: Prints all data pertaining to that day.
- Contact List: Prints a report of all contacts, sorted by Company. Any entries that do not have a company field value are listed first and sorted by Last Name.

- Daily Dynamic: Presents the time of day on the left with all relevant information provided in each time period. What makes this report dynamic is that the time periods will be adjusted so that all time periods that have appointments and events are shown. The To Do List appears on the right side.
- Daily Fixed: Differs from the Dynamic in that the times on the left do not shift. Instead, a separate section is added on the upper right labeled Other Appointments.
- Monthly: Prints the standard monthly calendar with the previous and next months on the banner of the page. Any appointments, events, or tasks are put into each cell of the calendar.
- Monthly—small header: Same as Monthly, except the previous and next months are not printed.
- Monthly on Tri-fold graphical: Very informative report consists of two pages. Page one contains a daily layout on the left. The months are in the middle, with the current month shaded and the current day boxed; the right side shows the To Do List. Page two consists of a standard monthly calendar without the previous and next months. Each cell contains the appointment, event, and task information for that day.
- To Do List—mini.
- To Do List—normal.
- To Do List—text.
- Weekly—5 day: Lays out the 5 days of the week as columns, with the time of day running down the side, and provides all relevant information for each day and time.
- Weekly—7 day: Same as the 5 day, except it adds Saturday and Sunday.
- Weekly—7 day with calendar: Adds a banner with a monthly calendar to the standard Weekly—7 day report.

Using *The Seven Habits of Highly Effective People*

Microsoft Schedule+ includes a series of wizards to help you organize your life as well as your day. In his book *The Seven Habits of Highly Effective People,* Stephen R. Covey outlines a philosophy that helps people organize and prioritize the various aspects of their lives. Schedule+ can be used with Covey's principles in mind. On the Tools menu, two options relate to Covey's principles. If you choose Seven Habits Quick Start, the Seven Habits Wizard (see fig. 30.33) will ask you a series of questions and provide feedback based on your answers that will allow you to organize your time effectively.

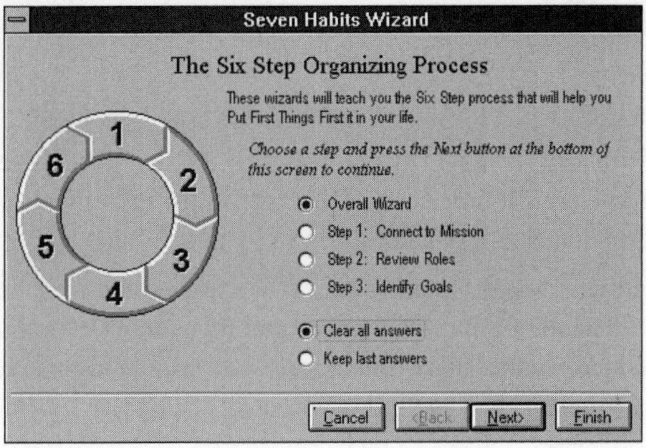

FIG. 30.33
The Seven Habits Wizard will lead you to other wizards that will help you do some self-evaluation.

The point of the exercises is self-reflection to get you to improve your quality of life, maximize your effectiveness, and learn a little something about yourself. The screens presented by the wizard lead you to self-understanding that will embody itself in the way you work every day. Completing all the wizards takes some time. You can always select Save Your Answers on the opening wizard and go back to answering later, but it is better to complete the reflection in one session.

When you have completed all the wizards, you'll have the tools to prioritize the things that are really important to you, and it will show in your attitude. You'll wind up with a personal mission statement, roles you will play, goals you'll strive to achieve, as well as bits of wisdom from historical figures. You'll come away from the experience with a different perspective.

Configuring Schedule+

Schedule+ provides a high degree of customizability. This is accomplished through the Options window. To get into the window, select Options from the Tools menu. This will bring up the screen shown in figure 30.34.

The General Tab

The General tab is shown in 30.34. Its options consist of the following:

- Calendar Name: This is the name that appears on the bar on the top of the screen. It can be set to anything you want. It defaults to your name in the Global Address List.
- Week starts on: The day you select will appear first in the navigation screens, as well as the weekly and monthly tabs. The default is Sunday.

- Day starts at: The time you set here will sit atop your schedule in the daily and weekly views. The default is 8:00 AM.
- Day ends at: The time chosen here will cause any time after it to appear shaded in your views.
- Appointment book time scale: This controls the increments of time you see in your view. The default is a half hour.
- Appointment drag-drop time scale: When you extend a meeting by dragging the border to another time, you'll notice that the amount of granularity you get is 15-minute increments. This is the default drag-drop time scale value; you can change this value to suit your needs if you wish.
- Prompt to archive data over *n* months old: The system will prompt you every *n* months to move your old data off your active schedule to a local or network disk for recordkeeping purposes. Having Schedule+ prompt will keep your data current and remove any outdated appointments. You can always load the data from the disk if you need it later for reporting purposes.
- This account is for a resource: You can create accounts for resources like overhead projectors and conference rooms. If the Schedule+ is being used for that purpose, check the box.
- Set Daily Reminder: Selecting this checkbox will provide a pop-up window at the beginning of every day telling you what tasks you have scheduled for that day. The default is checked.
- Enable Reminders: If this box isn't checked, Schedule+ will not sound or display an alarm. The default is checked.
- Sound Audible Alarm: Select this checkbox to have a sound accompany the alarm pop-up windows. The default is checked.
- Automatically accept meeting requests: This is not checked by default. It is probably wise to keep it that way, so that you have full control over which appointments you attend and which ones you don't.
- Automatically remove canceled meetings: This is unchecked by default. You might want to check this box if you work in Schedule+ throughout the day. It will free time in your schedule and avoid waste of time used in planning for a canceled meeting.
- Send meeting requests only to my delegate: This feature is used in conjunction with the Delegate Access Permission if you don't want to receive meeting requests but want them to go to your delegate.

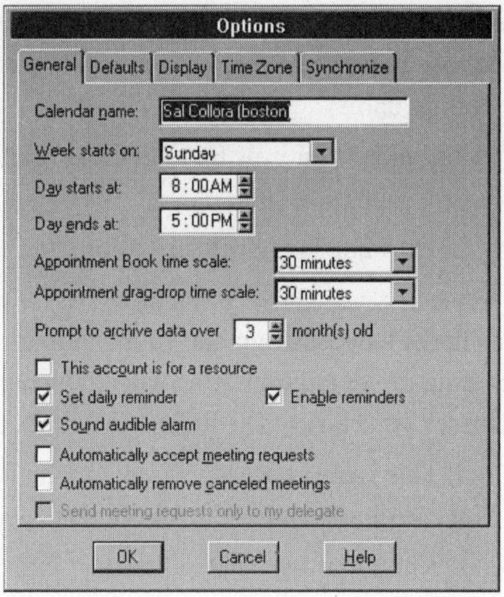

FIG. 30.34
The Options window allows you to configure Schedule+.

The Defaults Tab

The Defaults tab controls default behaviors for commonly used elements used in the General tabs of appointments, events, tasks, and contacts. Its options consist of the following (see fig. 30.35):

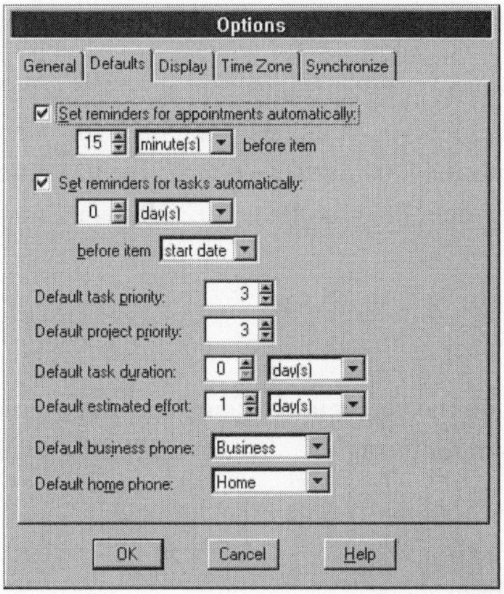

FIG. 30.35
The Defaults tab gives you control over the default values of commonly used parameters.

- Set reminders for appointments automatically: This determines whether Schedule+ sets a reminder for each appointment by default and the time period before the appointment when the user is reminded. The default value is 15 minutes.

- Set reminders for tasks automatically: This parameter is identical to the above, except that you can choose to be reminded before the start date or the ending date (because tasks have ending dates).
- Default task priority: This value is entirely up to you. You can select 1–9 or A–Z. The default value is 3.
- Default project priority: This value is entirely up to you. You can select 1–9 or A–Z. The default value is 3.
- Default task duration: Tasks have starting dates and ending dates; therefore, they also have duration. Setting the default duration will enable you to automatically set a reasonable ending date for your tasks. The default is 0 days.
- Default estimated effort: This value represents how much effort will go into a task. The default is 1 day. You can change it to suit your needs.
- Default business phone: When you are entering contact information, there exists a field for Business Phone. In today's society, people tend to have many different phone numbers. If you tend to communicate with people by fax, you might want to make Fax their default business number. The default value is Business.
- Default home phone: Just as in business, sometimes you communicate with people more on their cellular phones when you make personal calls. You can make Mobile or Pager the default home phone number. The default is Home.

The Display Tab

The Display tab lets you control the way things appear on the screen. From font size to the colors of objects, this tab lets you configure Schedule+ the way you want to see it. When you combine this with the flexible views offered by Schedule+, you have a lot of control over the way things look. Refer to figure 30.36 for what's available on the Display tab.

The Time Zone Tab

The Time Zone tab gives you the ability to configure a primary time zone and a secondary time zone, as well as account for daylight savings time (see fig. 30.37).

The ability to have a secondary time zone is great for people who travel all the time. By choosing Second Time Zone from the View menu, you can configure Schedule+ to display your appointments in two time zones.

This tab also shows the current time in your primary time zone.

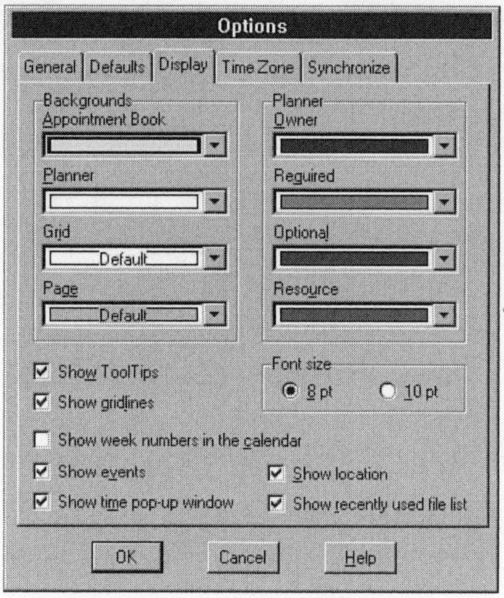

FIG. 30.36
The Display tab lets you see Schedule+ the way you want it.

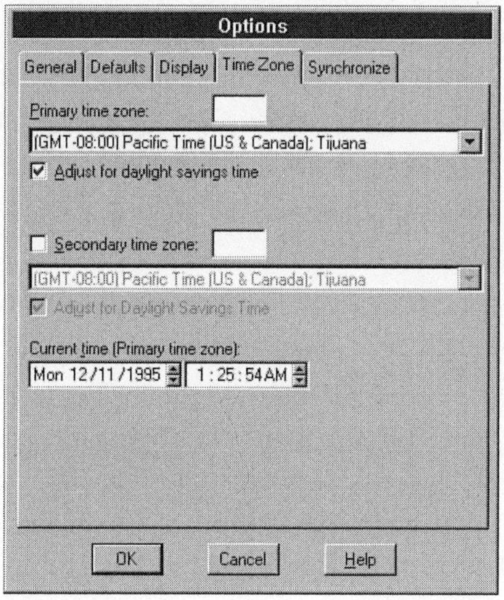

FIG. 30.37
The Time Zone tab lets you configure Schedule+ to let you schedule appointments for a second time zone if you need to travel often.

The Synchronize Tab

In order to provide its group scheduling capability, Schedule+ needs to synchronize the Exchange server copy of your schedule file with the one on your hard disk. This is configured in the Synchronization tab (see fig. 30.38). It offers the following options:

FIG. 30.38
Configuring the synchronization of both copies of your schedule file is made simple by this tab.

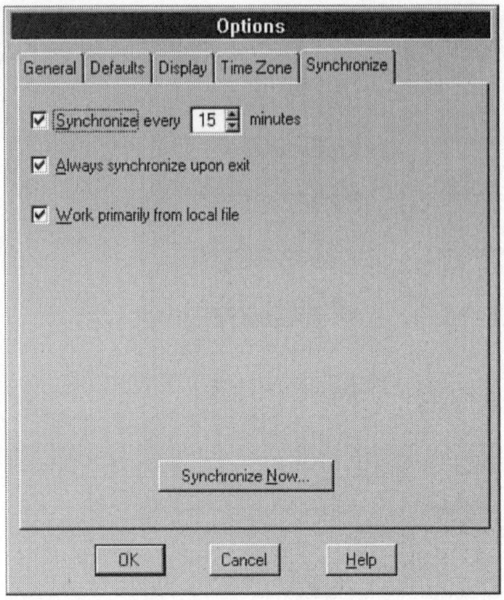

- Synchronize every *n* minutes: This option can be set for any amount of time you wish. However, there are a few things to keep in mind. Setting it too low will create network traffic and ultimately serve to annoy and disrupt you. Setting it too high may make it difficult to keep your two files in close enough sync at any given point in time. The default is 15 minutes, and that should be sufficient in most cases.
- Always synchronize upon exit: This is a good feature and should be left at its default value of checked.
- Work primarily from local file: Checking this box writes all data to your local file first, allowing you to synchronize the server file according to the schedule. This is the default mode of operation and should be left alone.
- The Synchronize Now button: You can use this button to manually initiate the synchronization of the two versions of your schedule file. You may want to do this after a lot of activity so the rest of the network users will know not to try to invite you to meetings at those times.

From Here...

Network scheduling can be a very valuable tool in your organization. Although an entire book can be devoted to the topic of Schedule+, we've described the basic features of Schedule+ to give you a head start on understanding what a powerful environment Exchange and Schedule+ provide.

We've explained how Schedule+ integrates into the Exchange client and server architecture. In addition, these features show how flexible this piece of software is. You can do a lot with Schedule+, as long as you use your imagination to come up with novel uses of the technology, like global phone books and enterprise-wide event scheduling with Exchange public folders. Follow those ideas to squeeze more mileage out of the Schedule+ features.

- See Chapter 28, "Understanding User Interface Features," for an explanation of how to use this other Exchange client component.
- See Chapter 29, "Integrating Schedule+ with Exchange Server," to see what issues you will face with the task of rolling out Schedule+ to your enterprise.

PART V

Third-Party Integration and Application Development

CHAPTER 31

Implementing Third-Party Integration Tools

- Workflow technologies
- Document imaging strategies
- Information sharing resources
- Information providers
- Communications and gateways to extend Exchange

By now, we have discussed all the core functions of Exchange provided in the shipped version. Although Microsoft has an extensive array of features built into the application, it cannot deliver all the features that end users need in their environment.

Third-party developers are essential resources in the deployment of Exchange in your environment. You saw that Exchange is more than just a messaging system. Exchange is an application framework. Third-party developers can extend the framework to provide a wide array of solutions on top of your core Exchange architecture.

Using Workflow Technologies to Extend Exchange

Workflow was discussed briefly in Chapter 1, "Overview of Microsoft Exchange" as it pertains to the Exchange universal inbox paradigm. Workflow sometimes is confused with electronic forms and forms routing. *Workflow* consists of a strict set of rules to a process. It extends the function of group collaboration.

Workflow is composed of several other key technologies: e-mail, imaging, document management, and databases. The end result is that it should streamline business processes and reduce system costs by using workflow servers to perform tasks based on the business model (see fig. 31.1). These applications will be integrated with the Exchange client and will provide an agent running on the Exchange Server to process and manage the workflow.

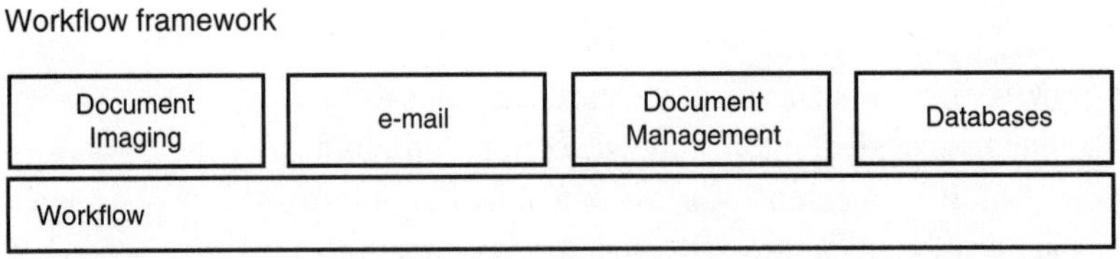

FIG. 31.1
Workflow framework and technologies.

The following is a list of workflow technology solutions. Each product mentioned has a description of the components, as well as integration with Exchange. The products include Exchange client software integration and data routing to external database sources (see fig. 31.2).

- *Action Technology*—Action promotes its ActionWorkflow System. Together with Microsoft, it is working on the workflow API (WAPI). Action has numerous partners to include Watermark Imaging, Saros, PC Docs, and FileNet. Action is a leader of the Workflow Coalition. This organization is promoting a common framework for workflow-enabled application. Action takes full advantage of Exchange's Groupware and Universal to provide an interface to the workflow of the business.

  Action uses the Exchange inbox to start workflows and then receive status reports via e-mail. The Action Workflow Manager Server triggers the appropriate business rules with respect to the business model. The Workflow Manager can populate a database with the information or route a request by way of e-mail to a subsequent recipient. This takes advantage of the existing network.

  For more information:

  http://www.actiontech.com

- *FileNet*—FileNet also has a high-end workflow solution named Workflo. FileNet and Action both work together and are competitors. FileNet, however, positioned itself as the complete workflow solution. As mentioned previously, workflow includes e-mail, images, documents, and databases. FileNet has solutions to address all the components. The other components are discussed in following sections of this chapter.

  Both Action and FileNet are leaders in the Windows-based workflow market.

  For more information:

  http://www.filenet.com

- *Axonet Information Center*—Axonet has a product named MegaFlow. This product is a simpler workflow manager. It doesn't have built-in support for the various workflow data types. However, it is extensible by way of OLE, and it supports RTF from the client side.

  For more information:

  http://www.tiac.net/users/axonet/

FIG. 31.2
Workflow business process.

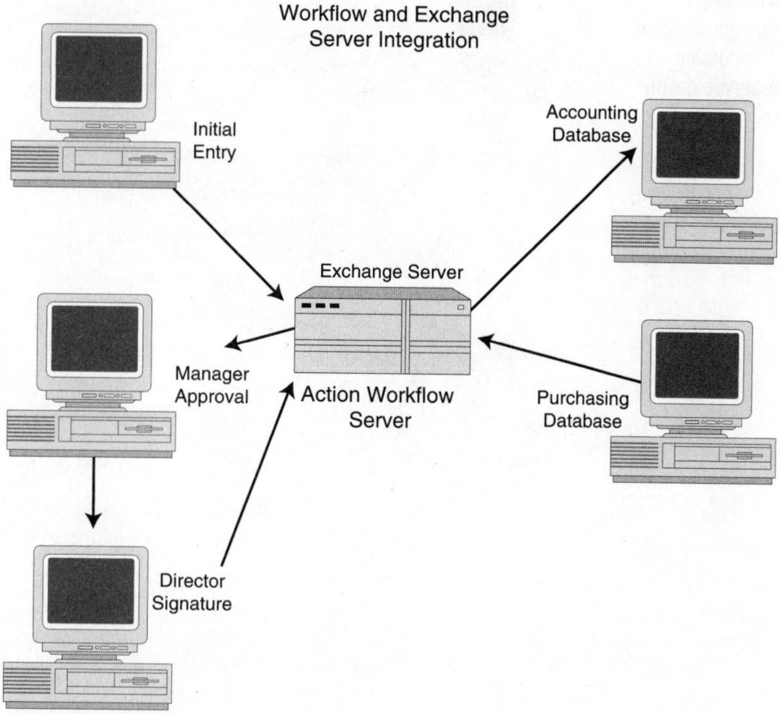

Document Imaging and Management with Exchange

Document imaging is the capability to take an object, scan it, and store the image for later use on the computer system.

Document management is the capability to take existing data in a variety of formats—including scanned images, audio and video files, word processing documents, and more. After the system has stored the object, the object is cataloged and managed for later use. This includes user-defined fields, object-file type conversions, object indexing, and security permissions.

Both of these technologies are complementary and separate. Document imaging involves capturing the object from an external source: paper, fax, and so on. The image must be processed and stored. You then would store the image into a document management system, which will contain more than just this one kind of data object (see fig. 31.3).

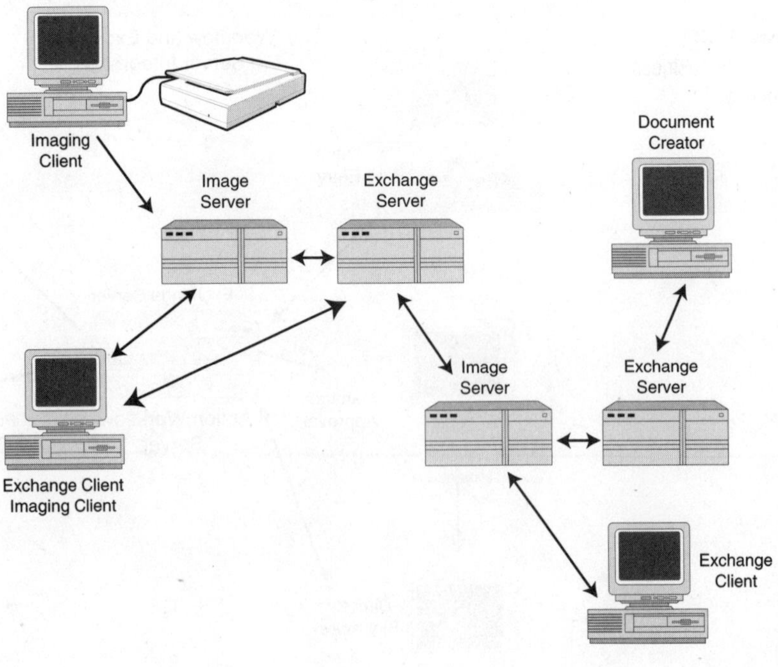

FIG. 31.3 Document imaging and document management with Exchange.

The following is a list of document imaging and document management technology solutions. Each product mentioned has a description of the components as well as integration with Exchange. The products include Exchange client software integration and server connections to external image repositories.

- *Watermark Imaging*—They are the primary NT-based, Exchange Server-enhanced, document-imaging solution. Watermark recently was acquired by FileNet to provide the complete workflow solution, as described in the previous section.

  Watermark can distribute scanned papers or faxes throughout the organization. This capability leverages the Exchange e-mail topology. Watermark provides the capability to e-mail a pointer into the storage system, to limit the amount of data transferred across the network, and to avoid duplicate copies.

  For more information:

  Phone: (617) 229-2600

- *Unisys*—Unisys recently has announced a solution integrated with Exchange's groupware function. The product is Unisys InfoImage Folder. The name indicates its positioning in the Exchange Universal inbox. InfoImage Folder will compete with the Watermark imaging system.

  For more information:

  http://www.unisys.com or **http://www.microsoft.com/exchange/**

There are several document management solutions, which are described in the following list:

- *Saros*—Saros, recently acquired by FileNet, provides a document management solution, Saros Mezzanine. This product has a library metaphor for storing documents and data objects. The data objects are checked in and out. Mezzanine manages this procedure. Saros integrates with Exchange—a user can e-mail a document or object into the Saros library without having the client software installed on the PC. Users also can e-mail pointers to files inside of Saros without having to check out a document and e-mail the entire file to the recipients. This setup eliminates multiple copies of files. Saros has both the client e-mail integration and an NT server product as the library.

  For more information:

  http://www.saros.com

- *FileNet*—In addition to leveraging the acquisition of Saros, FileNet has acquired Greenbar Software to provide a Computer Output to Laser Disk (COLD) solution. FileNet will use this application as a tool for distributing printed reports. The reports will originate from their Workflo System, which provides FileNet two document management solutions, one for documents and one for system reporting.

  For more information:

  http://www.filenet.com

- *PC Docs*—PC Docs provides a set of electronic tools for publishing documents and accessing the information through the Exchange inbox. From within Docs Open, you can publish a document to a public folder and then allow users to interact and discuss the document. Docs Interchange for Exchange consists of two agents, distribution and mail. The distribution agent will replicate by using the Exchange replication technology. It also allows for seamless integration between the Docs Open library and Exchange. Documents can easily be replicated into the Exchange folders. The mail agent allows Exchange client users to e-mail a query to the Docs Open library and access the Docs Open database. This doesn't require a user to have the Docs Open client on his or her workstation, just Exchange. Users can request documents be e-mailed back to them from the Docs Open library by way of the Docs Exchange Interchange.

  Watermark imaging is an imaging partner with PC Docs. From Watermark, you can send the scanned images into Docs Open.

  For more information:

  http://www.pcdocs.com

- *Common Ground*—Common Ground recently was acquired by Hummingbird Communications. Common Ground for Exchange provides a publishing and document management solution. Users can share access to documents by way of the Exchange network. Users can access the Common Ground Digital Papers directly from their Exchange client.

  For more information:

  http://www.commonground.com

Information Sharing

Information sharing is the capability to have group discussion forums with threaded conversations about a document, topic, or project. This capability is similar to an Internet News Group. This technology is the basis for groupware. Groupware provides a central repository for threaded conversation. The paradigm is activity that is classified as *one-to-many*. In this way, a user can write to one place, and then many people can access and comment on the information. Groupware is a base feature of Exchange. However, in this first release of exchange, there is little support for threaded conversation (see fig. 31.4).

FIG. 31.4
Groupware: one-to-many conversations.

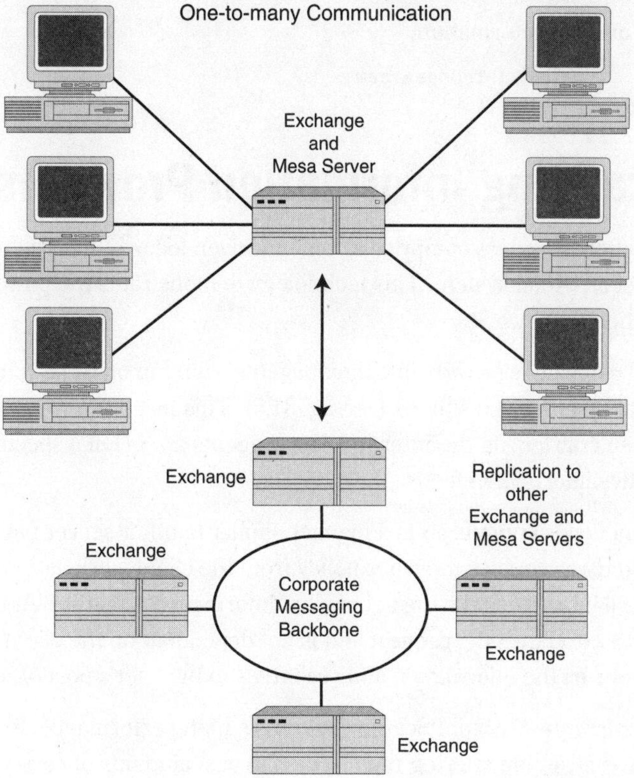

- *Mesa*—Mesa has a product named Conference Plus. This application is an add-in to the Exchange client. Another folder appears in the Universal inbox, representing Mesa. After you click to open this folder, you can access the information with the threaded conversations.

  Mesa writes its information to the MAPI v1.0 Exchange data structure. Mesa was one of the first third-party developers that worked on Exchange solutions by using MAPI. Its MAPI Message store runs as another Exchange service, taking full advantage of the rich administration and replication tools.

  From the client, Mesa allows direct access to Conference Plus folders by way of the Exchange inbox as a root-level folder. Mesa then provides an Exchange Interchange that provides two-way replication between Conference Plus folders and Exchange

Mesa message stores to address existing users of Mesa. Finally, a migration utility is included to assist with converting folders from Conference Plus to the Exchange MAPI message store architecture.

Mesa is currently working on an Exchange Interchange for Internet News Groups, Lotus Notes, and other interchanges as needed in the marketplace.

For more information:

e-mail: **`info@mesa.com`**

Understanding Information Providers

Information providers comprise a content-driven focus of Exchange. Exchange is more than just an e-mail system. This technology demonstrates the power of this client-server application framework.

Several companies provide intelligent agents, running on the Exchange Server to retrieve information of a given subject (see fig. 31.5). This technology can parallel what is known as a "web crawler" on the Internet. These agents are given a specific topic and poll their respective information feeds.

This function is configured in a manner similar to other server-based rules on Exchange. The end user accesses the rules policy from the client workstation with the Exchange Universal inbox and tells the agent what information to gather. At this point, the agent on the server executes the request and is not dependent on the client to be connected. The agent returns the information and resources to the user's post office information store.

- *Fulcrum*—Fulcrum Search Server is a high-performance, text-indexing and retrieval engine offering rapid access to vast amounts of corporate information stored in documents or databases. It supports ODBC connections to data sources. Users in a workgroup-computing environment have flexible access to large amounts of data.

  "Fulcrum Find" provides content-based indexing and retrieval of information in public folders, attachments, or e-form data. The server-based component is an Intuitive Searching engine, which is used to return specific subjects of content to the user. The search can be performed across multiple servers or on the desktop. The result set is a hierarchical list with the most number of hits at the top of the list. The user then can select the information source and read the content. Additionally, Fulcrum Find supports SQL statement calls to optimize the performance of a search query.

  For more information:

  `http://www.fulcrum.com`

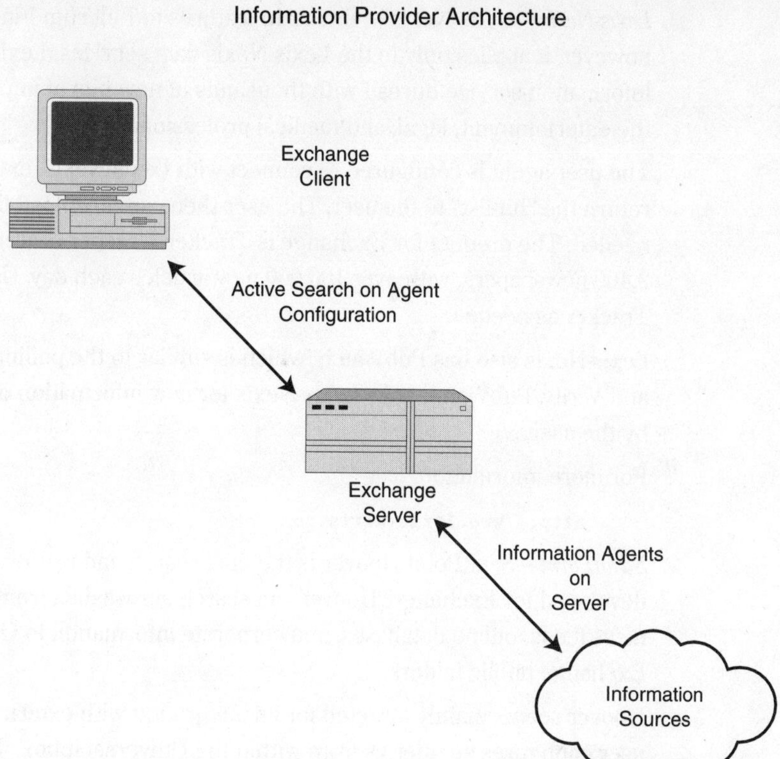

FIG. 31.5
Information providers for Exchange Server.

- *Verity*—Verity Topic agents compete with Fulcrum. Verity goes beyond the corporation to provide a rich, integrated search and retrieval engine that can be directed to external data sources such as Reuters and the public Internet. Similar to Fulcrum, Verity has a server process that runs on the Exchange Server, which gets configured from the client PC running Exchange. The server automatically notifies the user when the information needed is located. The agents also can poll specific data sources and, when new information is found, automatically retrieve this data for the user.

  The user can configure the agents remotely from the client or e-mail an agent or a query to be processed. The user can configure several agents to execute from the desktop or the server with the flexibility of the output format and location. Verity also can transmit the output of a query via fax, pager, e-mail, or public folder. Verity Topic can access data sources that include Exchange folders, attachments, ODBC data sources, Lotus Notes, and Acrobat Catalogs.

  For more information:

  `http://www.verity.com`

- *Lexis-Nexis*—Lexis-Nexis is similar in features to Fulcrum Find and Verity Topic; however, it applies only to the Lexis-Nexis data services. Lexis-Nexis is an information-service bureau with thousands of new bits of information daily for the entertainment, legal, and medical professions.

  The user agent is configured to connect with Lexis-Nexis, execute the query, and return the "hit-list" to the user. The user then can download the information that is needed. The product for Exchange is Tracker. Tracker searches across an index of 2,400 newspapers, with over 100,000 new articles each day. Users can customize Tracker as needed.

  Lexis-Nexis also has PubWatch, which is similar to the polling feature of Fulcrum and Verity. PubWatch polls Lexis-Nexis for new information on the subject entered by the user.

  For more information:

  `http://www.lexis-nexis.com`

- *SandPoint*—SandPoint Hoover is the final search and retrieval engine currently developed for Exchange. Hoover can search across data from multiple media, live news feeds, online databases, and corporate information in ODBC data sources or Exchange public folders.

  Hoover seems mainly targeted for its integration with external data sources. The user configures all queries from within the Universal inbox. The agent can search across over 5,200 data sources, including *The Wall Street Journal, Forbes, Dow Jones, Business Week*, and more.

  For more information:

  Phone: (800) 775-4442

Communications and Gateways for Exchange

Communications and gateways provide ways to extend Exchange in legacy systems or to provide new functionality from the inbox. These technologies include wireless access to Exchange mail servers, X.25 support for international message transfer, and public and private network and systems. For Gateways, several third-party developers will extend Exchange with paging servers, fax servers, voice message servers, and connections into legacy mail systems, including Profs and All-in-One.

Communication Support for Exchange

Communications gateways and service providers for Exchange provide the backbone for accessing the Exchange message stores by way of wireless networking protocols (see fig. 31.6) from a client PC or the technology to allow standards-based transmission of Exchange messages over X.400 and X.500.

FIG. 31.6
Wireless Networking Services for Exchange Server.

Wireless Access to Exchange

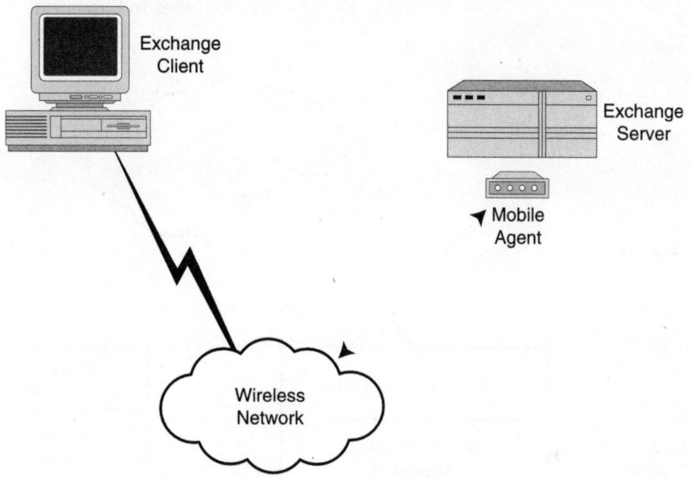

The process follows this scenario: a request is made from the mobile user on its PC with the Exchange inbox. The request is encapsulated in a message and transferred by way of the wireless network to a server-based agent. The agent then de-encapsulates the messages and performs the action dictated in the message. At this point, it communicates with the Exchange Server to send or retrieve mail, change a server-based rule, or perform another Exchange task.

The key standards for wireless technology are ARDIS, CDPD, GSM and Inmarsat. The following list breaks down the technologies and service providers for wireless communication.

- *Inmarsat*—This is a standard satellite network provider with worldwide capability. Inmarsat is perhaps the largest provider worldwide, serving 50,000 users on land, on sea, and in the air. It provides both narrow-band and ISDN connections. It has worked closely with other wireless providers—AT&T, Vodafone, and Ardis—to create a set of standards for wireless networking. The goal was to split client and server functions from the network-layer transports.

Inmarsat (see fig. 31.7) developed a solution to give the user a common interface to messaging—Exchange client viewer. It extends the MAPI interface with a wireless interface to provide ease of future development efforts over wireless networking. The technology is known as Inmarsat Wireless Messaging. The technology is composed of enhancements to the client, a middle-layer agent, and a server component. The technology interpolates with other wireless networking standards—ARDIS, CDPD, and GSM.

FIG. 31.7
Wireless networking technology by Inmarsat.

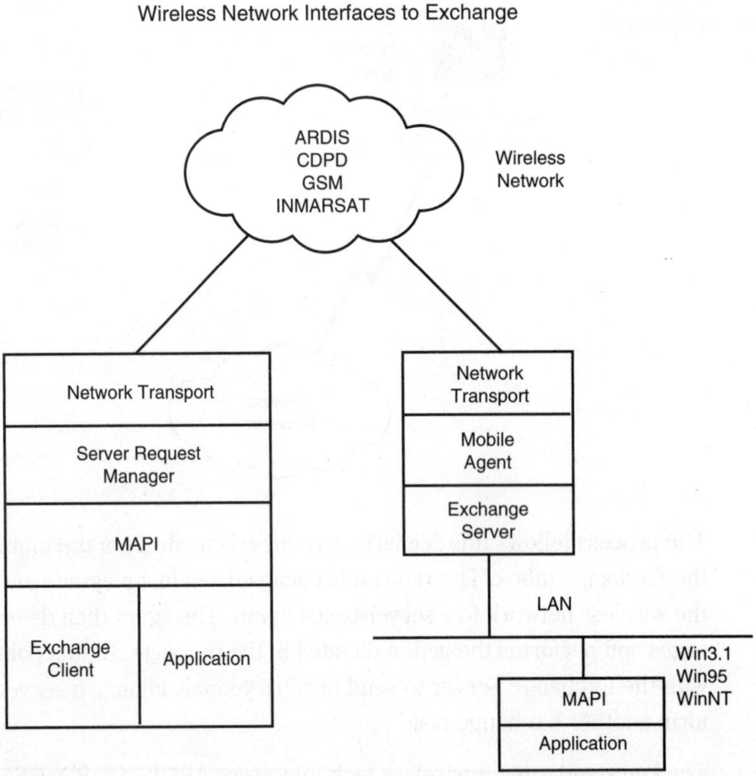

The key elements to user interface are remote copy of message headers, remote copy of messages, remote deletion of messages, remote forwarding of messages, and remote configuration of user rules and filters. The server request manager interfaces with the Exchange Server. The purpose is to process client-side requests from the mobile agent. It performs this process by using standard MAPI transport providers.

The mobile agent interfaces with the client and the server request manager. The mobile agent is responsible for interacting with Exchange on behalf of the mobile user. The agent handles authentication, server-based rules and filters, logging NT server events, and providing NT performance counters.

For more information:

http://www.worldserver.pipex.com

- *Vodafone Group*—Vodafone and Paragon Software have an Exchange Middleware messaging solution for wireless networking. Vodafone follows Inmarsat's wireless messaging technology to provide users with wireless access to Exchange around the world. Vodafone has 40 GSM roaming agreements to provide worldwide coverage. GSM is an organization that provides a standard for wireless communication, which is growing at the rate of 10,000 new customers each day. Based on the number of GSM agreements, Vodafone is a leader in wireless communication.

  Paragon provides Precis Link, which is a MAPI-based remote access standard for Exchange. Precis Link provides similar functionality to Inmarsat, with offline message processing, to include rules, filters, forwarding, and deleting.

  Vodafone Networking uses advanced mobile communications of Short Message Server (SMS) and high-speed circuit switched data by way of its digital cellular networks. Precis link leverages these communication methods to allow users to access Exchange servers over satellite, digital cellular, and mobile-radio systems. Precis provides an easy interface for developers to leverage wireless networking, without needing full knowledge of the transport.

  For more information:

  http://www.vodafone.co.uk

- *AT&T*—AT&T wireless services provides wireless access for users into Exchange servers. AT&T relies on the communication standard, CDPD, or Cellular Digital Packet Data. Currently, CDPD is deployed only in the United States. CDPD makes wireless data communication ready for end users. It's based on the TPC/IP protocol. This offers easy integration with existing infrastructures. CDPD offers transfer rates of up to 19.2 kbps, enhanced security, and the capability to support voice and data. Forty-seven of the top fifty cities in the U.S. already have CDPD service available. AT&T's service hopes to provide a cost-effective solution for the workgroup model by allowing filed sales and support personnel to easily connect to resources.

Similar to Inmarsat and Vodafone, AT&T allows users to download headers before retrieving messages, remote administering rules and filters, and configure support for attachments. It provides server-based agents to perform tasks for the client.

The rough cost of the AT&T service depends on data transferred per month. A sample rate is 500kb per month for $50. Please contact AT&T for current pricing information.

For more information:

```
http://www.airdata.com
```

- *Eicon*—Eicon provides WAN services for the NT operating system. This is useful for the X.25 transport protocol support necessary for some X.400 and X.500 connections to value-added networking providers.

  EiconCard for NT extends the TCP/IP stack included with NT over X.25, frame relay, and PPP and ISDN connections. It offers a high-capacity, robust implementation of X.25 for Exchange servers. As illustrated in figure 31.8, NT now can be extended as a WAN IP router. EiconCard can take full advantage of the Microsoft back office remote access support.

FIG. 31.8
WAN service for NT by Eicon.

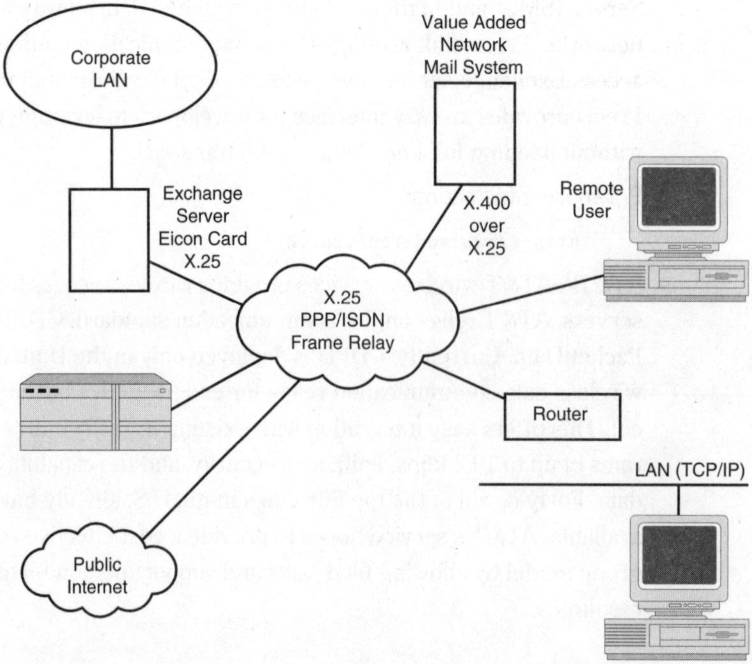

For more information:

`http://www.eicon.com`

- *Sprint*—Sprint provides Sprint Message Xchange service for Microsoft Exchange. SMX currently is used to link together various mail systems over Sprint's private network services. SMX now links Exchange LAN sites with other MS Mail, Lotus, and Exchange LAN sites. This method is effective to link LANs by outsourcing some of the messaging backbone to Sprint.

  Sprint's network extends to 140 countries, which is a tremendous benefit if a company has both U.S. and European offices and wants to link together its Exchange LANs. Sprint acts as the Middleware network to support the connection, which is a huge cost savings to the companies because they can connect to Sprint in native Exchange formats without maintaining extra X.400 gateways. Sprint provides addressing templates for recipients on X.400, the Internet, fax, and telex.

  For more information:

  `http://www.sprint.com`

Besides Sprint, several other value-added networking providers are working on supporting Exchange backbones. Services in the works will provide companies with links from Exchange into legacy systems, Profs, All-in-One, and Officevision; into other LAN mail systems such as Lotus and Cc:mail; and into other forms of messaging—EDI, fax, telex, CompuServe, X.400, and the Internet. A good way to think about these public and private networks is as a way to out-source gateways and address/message conversion processes. By supporting native Exchange formats, the providers can allow easy integration from the corporate LANs into trading and business partners.

Gateway Support for Exchange

Gateways and connectors (see fig. 31.9) are used to extend Exchange into existing LAN-based mail systems or legacy host systems. They also can provide new types of functionality to enhance messaging within the organization. Besides new Exchange gateways, the existing MS Mail gateway is accessed from Exchange. You can access these through the MS Mail PC connector.

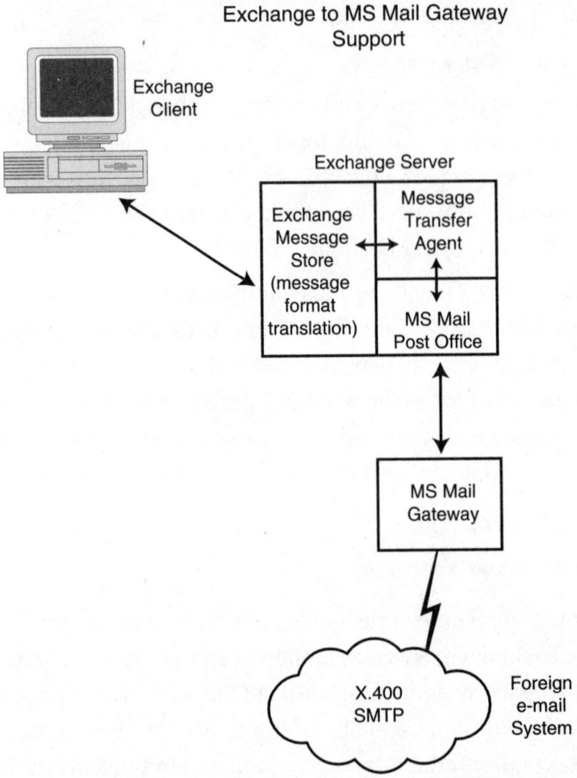

FIG. 31.9
The MS Mail gateways for Exchange Server.

- *Attachmate*—Attachmate is providing Profs and SNADS gateways for Exchange. These tools are used to extend Exchange into legacy SNA environments to link users with Profs and OfficeVision mail systems or use the SNA transport to communicate with other servers.

  The gateways are known as Zip! Office gateways for Exchange. These gateways allow users on VM/CMS host systems to share messages with Exchange clients (see fig. 31.10). The gateway routes messages and status reports between Exchange and the host systems. Host users can use Profs, CMS Notes, or CMS Reader to read and create messages. This gateway also is used for processing SENDFILE or PUCH requests from VM to the LAN.

  Exchange manages the in- and out-bound messages for the Zip gateway. Exchange stores the out-bound messages in its MTS Out folder. The Zip gateway polls this folder and, when it finds a message, processes the message. After the gateway has the message, it translates the message and attachment to be forwarded to the host system.

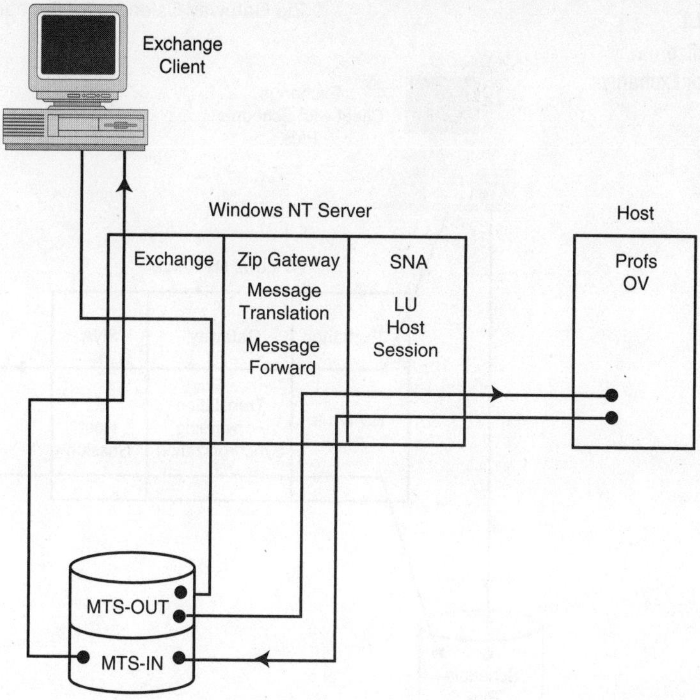

FIG. 31.10
ZIP! Office gateways for Exchange Server.

NOTE Due to message formats on the host systems, only one attachment can be sent in the body of a message. If multiple attachments must be sent to a host recipient, multiple messages must be used.

The Exchange Server with the Zip gateway running also must be able to connect to the host through an SNA gateway or be channel-attached to the host with SNA Server installed locally.

Besides the messaging gateway, Zip supports scheduling across systems (see fig. 31.11). Schedule Plus and Profs Calendar Users can be part of the same calendar network. The gateway routes calendar requests between the two systems, including scheduling meetings between platforms, viewing free/busy times, and logging appointment data in each system's calendar.

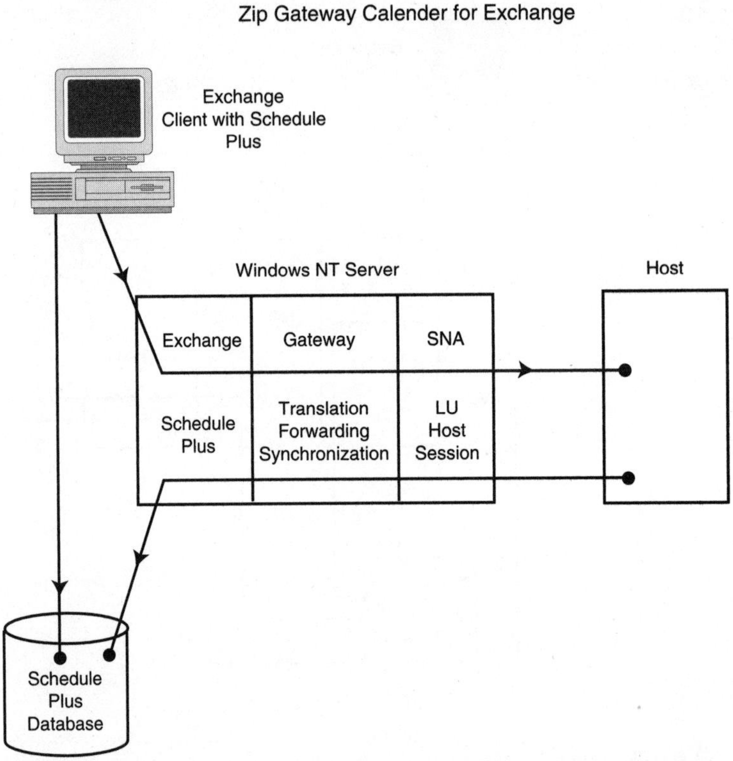

FIG. 31.11
The Zip! Office Calendar for Exchange Server.

The calendar look-ups happen in real time. A request is made from the Schedule plus client and is communicated to Exchange. After the request is in Exchange, the Zip gateway translates the request into a native host format and forwards the schedule request to the host system.

The Zip gateway is an NT service and is integrated with the Event Log, Performance Counters, and Process Viewer. Multiple gateways can be installed on the same server hardware. This is similar to the MS Mail PC MTAs, which can run multiple instances of the MTA on a single NT server. The gateway also comes with its own configuration utility, to set the configuration information for delivery, message translation, nodes, address space, and queue status.

For more information:

`http://www.attachmate.com`

- *Alisa*—Alisa Systems supports Digital's All-in-One and Vmsmail mail systems. The Alisa Gateway is an NT service, running on the Exchange Server. The gateway supports messaging with attachments of documents and binary files. The DEC and Exchange directories will be synchronized and usernames are mapped into the native format for the system. The gateway can be managed by using native Exchange and NT administration tools.

  For more information:

  `http://www.alisa.com`

- *RightFax*—RghtFax has a fax gateway solution for Exchange. This gateway runs as an NT service for integration with the NT directory services and Exchange. The fax gateway consists of a client and server set of components.

  From the client, a user can create an e-mail message. When defining the recipients, the user can specify users to receive the same mail message by way of fax. The mail message doesn't need to be configured in any different manner. When the message is received by the Exchange Server and the recipient list is parsed, the server recognizes the fax recipient and routes the message through the fax gateway.

  On incoming faxes, RightFax supports DID lines for individual caller fax identifiers, which requires additional hardware to support phone-line trucks or direct connections to the phone systems coming in via T1 connections. One fax server can service over 700 DID lines. For a large organization, this capability allows every individual to have a direct fax line. When the fax server actually receives the incoming fax, it resolves the destination user recipient on the Exchange mail system by the DID identifier. The user receives faxes just as he or she does an e-mail message or other inbox application.

  The RightFax client becomes integrated with the Exchange inbox on the desktop. This client has numerous advanced features, including support for DTMF, OCR, Imaging letterhead, signatures, voice prompting, group send options, delayed transmissions, and support for complex graphics. Additionally, you can send document attachments by way of fax without doing the conversion on the client PC. The conversion is handled by the server gateway.

  For more information:

  `e-mail: dts@rightfax.xom`

- *Integra*—Integra recently purchased WinBeep Software. WinBeep provides an NT server-based pager gateway for Exchange. Similar to the fax gateway, from the Exchange client a user can send a message with a destination recipient through e-mail, fax, or pager by using the WinBeep Exchange pager gateway.

  The pager gateway is being developed by WinBeep at Integra technologies. The pager gateway will plug into Exchange just like any other gateway or connector. It will be administered from the Exchange administration utility.

  The pager gateway also can be used in conjunction with server-based rules. One example is if you use an alphanumeric pager, you can set up your e-mail to be forwarded to your pager when you are out of the office.

  Because the paging gateway is a rich, tightly integrated NT service, you can configure the SQL server to send reports and alerts by way of MAPI to the pager gateway to notify an administrator or manager of a situation.

  The Integra pager gateway works with several paging service providers: Ameritech, Comtech, MobileComm, PageMart, PageNet, Skytel, Southwestern Bell, Message Center, and USA Mobile. Additionally, it supports wireless communication through several protocols: ARDIS, DTMF, IXO, and TDP.

  For more information:

  Phone: (800) 905-5062

- *Octel*—Octel developed a framework for voice messaging on top of the Exchange platform. The Unified Messaging Strategy consists of using the e-mail backbone for Exchange to connect to PBX phone switches and route voice mail directly to the desktop in the Exchange client inbox (see fig. 31.12).

  Octel positions the phone systems as an extension to the messaging architecture of an organization. From within the inbox you may receive e-mail, faxes, documents, and now voice mail. Voice mail also can be accessed 24 hours a day by touch-tone phone. Voice mail has many of the same communication properties that e-mail uses. Voice-mail messages are stored and forwarded between users as needed. The messages also are routed by content or request.

  Octel provides a client component to integrate with the inbox so that the voice-mail messages appear as e-mail messages. The users simply open the message to play the voice mail. The user also can reply to the original message or create a new voice message from the same interface. Exchange then handles the routing via mail or via the phone switches. The client also includes telephone dial-in support. The user dials into the Octel system to retrieve message information. The message information includes voice, fax, and e-mail messages. Voice messages can be easily played back over the telephone. Fax messages can be routed to an alternate fax number or forwarded to another user. E-mail messages can be read back to the user over the telephone via the text-to-speech hardware on the system.

FIG. 31.12
Octel Voice-Mail gateway for Exchange Server.

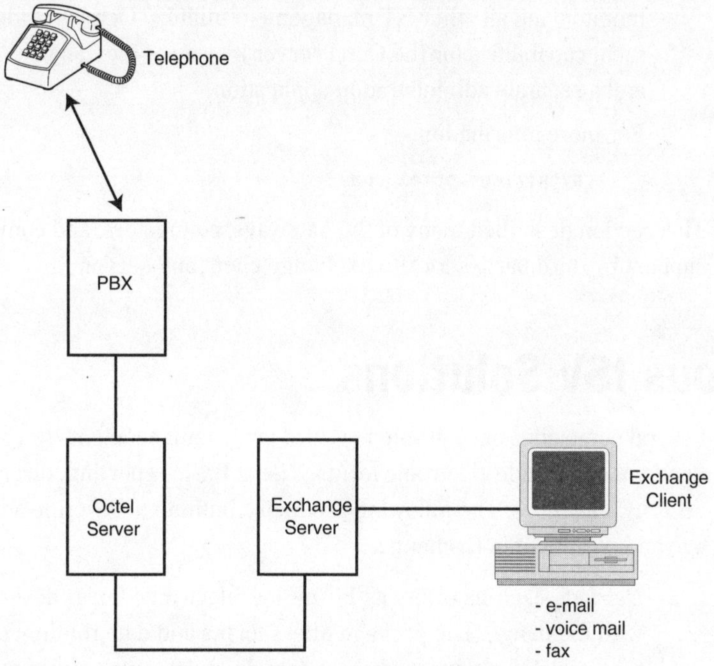

The Octel Server provides in- and out-bound voice functionality. It acts as a voice-mail gateway to external systems. The user can create a voice-mail message from the desktop and have Octel route the message to the destination to be played back for the user. This Octel system can take advantage of multimedia PCs but doesn't require them. If a user has sound capabilities on the PC, the voice-mail message can be played back from the PC. If the user doesn't have sound capabilities, when he or she opens the e-mail note that contains the Octel message, Octel dials the user's phone number from the PBX and plays the message back over the phone.

The key to this strategy is that Exchange and NT will handle all the directory services for the enterprise. The Exchange account that originates from the NT Domain account also will be used for the voice mail system. A component of the user account includes the voice-mail system information. However, all the voice-mail data is stored inside the Exchange message, in a compressed format. Octel also plans to include faxing as a functionality of this Unified Messaging Strategy.

The Octel server supports voice, fax, text-to-speech, and voice recognition. This includes support for DTMF, DID lines, PBX connectivity, and open computer-industry standards for customization. The server is based on Windows NT and takes full advantage of the user accounts, NT registry, Event Log, performance monitor, and all other NT management utilities. Octel provides additional management capabilities for the Octel server by way of Exchange's Administration utility and a separate administration application.

For more information:

http://www.octel.com

This section described many of the gateways, connectors, and communication protocols support by third parties for the Exchange client and server.

Various ISV Solutions

Several companies have developed third-party enhancements to Exchange. These enhancements include electronic forms, Visual Basic reporting, directory service providers, security, and more. The following products continue to describe additional ways to leverage an investment in Exchange.

- *Delrina*—Delrina offers its FormFlow electronic forms designer package for use with Exchange. The package offers forms and data routing, using the Exchange topology. This forms package offers database connectivity, multi-platform support, printing, and scalable architecture.

  For more information:

  http://www.delrina.com

- *Crystal Reports*—Crystal reports announced a reporting tool for use with Exchange that allows easy integration and access to the Exchange MAPI information store. Crystal Reports provides access to Exchange reporting mechanisms and data exporting from the information store. This added capability allows the user to query, print, and modify data from the desktop. The amount of data within the information store is unlimited; it can be e-mail messages, e-forms data, system information, documents, voice mail, and more. Crystal Reports enables you to build interfaces to this information by using Exchange and Visual Basic. The information will be useful to both end users and system administrators.

  For more information:

  Phone: (800) 663-1244

- *Nortel Entrust*—Northern Telecom's Entrust security technology provides the software-based encryption and digital signatures services. Security is important because it provides a wrapper around confidential or sensitive data. The content of the message is guaranteed by a digital signature. The digital signature ensures the identity of the sender.

  With Entrust's security in Exchange, Exchange can be used for electronic commerce, electronic transfer of funds, or database transactions. Nortel provides a solution for large-scale management of cryptographic keys. The automated key management is invisible to the end user, yet provides privacy into a distributed computing environment.

  Entrust provides support for RSA, DSA, DES, and CAST security algorithms.

  For more information:

  `http://www.entrust.com`

- *Hitachi*—Hitachi has announced a directory synchronization system, Syncware, for Exchange. Syncware synchronizes Exchange with all other e-mail systems in the environment. Syncware is the server component that will provide the directory services function. Additionally, there is Agent@Exchange, which is the directory services agent that runs on Exchange to export the directory information to Syncware.

  Some features of Syncware include a streamlined user interface, enhanced rule mapping to convert names, and network monitoring and testing tools. A messaging administrator can tell at a glance the status of the synchronization throughout the enterprise. It integrates with cc:Mail, MS Mail, QuickMail, Lotus Notes, Groupwise, Beyond Mail, Davinci, Officevision, and SMTP mail.

  The key benefit to this is the complex address translation that Hitachi has simplified for managing several directories. The conversion rules are built into the system, but can be modified for special use. The product consists of a server and agent model that is mail-enabled. Syncware agents are installed on each mail system, and the server is installed on a UNIX workstation. Each agent monitors which addresses get changed on the system. When a change occurs, it is forwarded via e-mail to the server. After the server is done processing the directory updates, it propagates the changes to the other mail systems. With this solution, Exchange can plan an active role in a mixed-mail enterprise environment.

  For more information:

  `http://www.hitachi.com`

NOTE Electronic data interchange is discussed in Chapter 32, "Using Electronic Data Interchange."

Exchange provides the MAPI v1.0 API to use for application enhancements or custom solutions for Exchange. Beyond MAPI, Exchange SDKs (software development kits) are available for developing custom applications, external gateways, or integrated applications.

We mentioned several third-party solutions for Exchange. This list is by no means complete. Please contact Microsoft for continued updates to the list of ISV's developing third-party application for Exchange at the following Web page:

`http://www.microsoft.com/exchange`

Exchange provides a robust messaging and groupware framework. Third-party developers are working to extend the framework with workflow, document imaging, document management, information sharing, information agents, communications connectors, gateways to external systems, and more. Microsoft provides the MAPI 1.0 application programming interface to allow additional developers to leverage the Exchange framework as needed.

From Here...

This chapter explained how Exchange can be extended by using third-party applications. For more information, see the following chapters:

- Chapter 1, "Overview of Microsoft Exchange," describes the Universal inbox paradigm.
- Chapter 32, "Using Electronic Data Interchange," explains how to use the Exchange Server for Electronic Data Interchange transactions.

CHAPTER 32

Using Electronic Data Interchange

- What is EDI?
- Defining Exchange's role in EDI
- Third-party EDI development

Exchange is a powerful electronic mail messaging platform. As you have seen, many Independent Software Vendors (ISV) are developing third-party solutions to extend and enhance Exchange's core technology. A new area where Exchange has been gaining momentum is in Electronic Data Interchange (EDI). Exchange enables Microsoft to enter this high-end commerce transaction system running most corporations around the world.

EDI is a strategic direction for Microsoft. EDI over Exchange complements Microsoft's Internet commerce strategy to provide a completely integrated solution. ■

What Is EDI?

EDI is an architecture for providing electronic commerce between trading partners. Trading partners are business organizations that wish to share commerce data via electronic means. One example is that a grocery store chain and a food manufacturer could be trading partners. Using EDI, when the store needs to order more food for the shelves, the products and amounts can be shipped directly to the manufacturer for order processing and shipment. In figure 32.1, an example of an EDI data flow is displayed.

FIG. 32.1
This figure shows an EDI dataflow diagram.

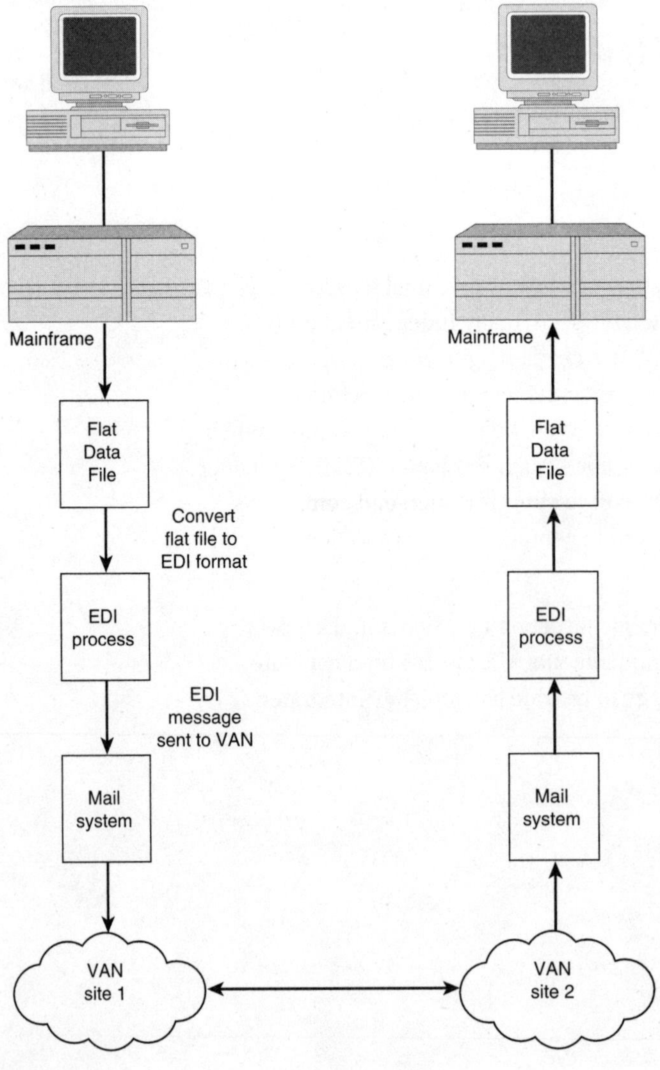

EDI is a complement to electronic mail as it promotes a paperless system. EDI applications today are complex, proprietary, archaic, and customized for specific systems and industries. Several standards have been drafted to define EDI in the marketplace. X.435 was specified in 1990. The X.435 standard is an extension to X.400 incorporating electronic commerce requirements. The original specification was to be used with X.400 P2 protocols which were standardized in 1984. X.435 today supports X.400 P22 protocols dated 1988.

NOTE Microsoft Exchange Server Message Transfer Agents (MTAs) are certified to this X.400 P22 protocol standard. This will ensure interoperability for customers. Only digital messaging MTAs have received this certification.

Using EDI requires an application environment. A typical EDI architecture will have an e-mail client communicating with the mail server (see fig. 32.2)—in this case, an Exchange server. The mail server must support X.400 or SMTP addressing and connections. This is handled through the use of a gateway product running on the mail system. Exchange offers X.400 and SMTP connectors built into the server software package.

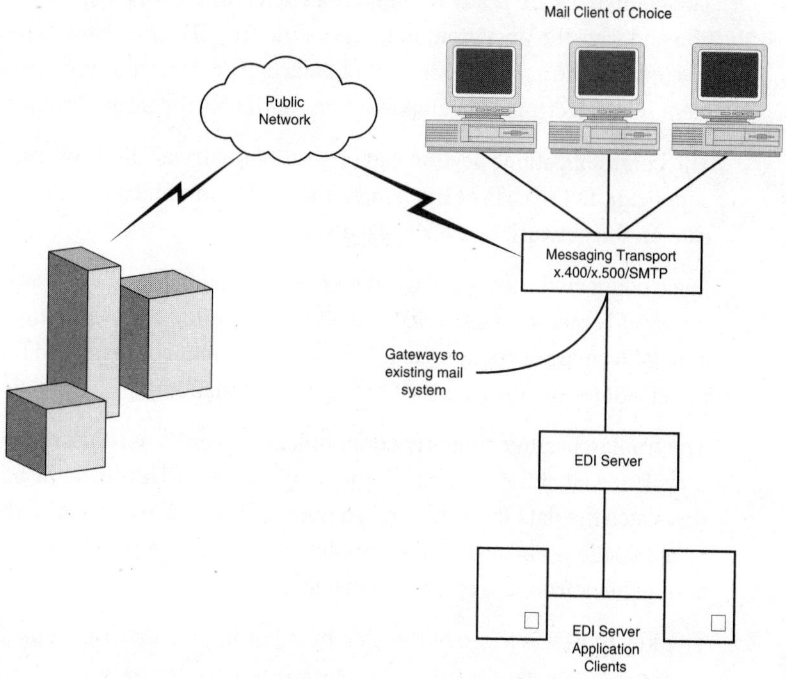

FIG. 32.2
This an example of an EDI architecture.

At the same time that mail is able to travel over X.400, EDI-enabled applications must generate EDI data files or preformatted EDI data packages. These packages are then sent over the same exact X.400 or SMTP connections. Depending on the final destination of the message, it may pass through an additional gateway to reach an existing mail system or traverse a Value added Network (VAN) to reach a trading partner. Between the EDI application and the X.400 connector is an EDI server. Third-party solutions are being developed to leverage Windows NT and Exchange to perform the function of EDI server. This EDI server is used to translate flat data files into EDI packages to be forwarded to the mail connectors. These products will be discussed later in this chapter.

The EDI Process

EDI starts with a trading partner agreement between you and your trading partner. This is an agreement between companies as to the computer systems and technology to be used for the EDI dataflow. They must make a combined decision about the EDI standard to be used for the transactions, the information to be exchanged, the VAN, and scheduling of the information exchange.

The companies are ready to then create a document of an invoice in the business application and save the document in the system. The EDI translator automatically reformats the invoice into the agreed-upon EDI standard. The translator creates and wraps the document in an electronic envelope that has an ID for the target trading partner.

The communications portion can be part of the translation software or a separate gateway connector. In the case of Exchange, the EDI communication gateway begins to communicate on the network or over a dial-up line.

Once connected with the VAN, the envelope containing the document is then transmitted to the VAN messaging service. Several VANs today are beginning to support native Exchange formats to reduce the need for data format conversion. The VAN reads the ID on the envelope and distributes it to the correct mailbox.

The trading partner similarly communicates over its network or over a dial-up line and downloads all of the contents of the mailbox. The EDI translator opens the envelope and translates the data from the agreed upon EDI standard format to the format to be read by its application. The process is complete when the company's accounting department creates a check from the electronic invoice.

The key to EDI is to reuse the data by inputting the data only one time. The EDI and messaging systems handle the rest of the work. Data moves without intervention from the business application to the trading partner's application.

EDI Application and Translation

As you can see, EDI is a simple, yet extremely complex system. EDI translation software must integrate with EDI application software. It is important to rely upon industry standards to maintain this type of EDI relationship.

After defining the document in the business application, you use an EDI mapper to create a map or relationship of the business document. With the mapper, you describe or associate the relationship between the datafields in your business application and the selected EDI standards. The mapper or association manager is an integral part of the complete EDI solution.

If both the EDI translator and business application are on the same type of computer, the data will move faster and more easily from one process to another.

EDI General Components

In an EDI deployment, several key elements are needed. The following list is an introduction into the key technology used in EDI:

- EDI translation management software manages the method in which data is communicated throughout the EDI dataflow.
- Mappers or association management implementations or integration vary significantly from one translator to another translator. These mappers handle data mapping between fields in an EDI dataflow.
- Communications software is modular to the translator. Exchange and MAPI provide a programming tool that enables you to develop custom applications and make system calls to the communication protocols.
- Modem connectivity with a high baud rate provides more data throughput.
- VAN networking with Exchange partners provides the easy integration for EDI with a variety of worldwide trading partners.
- WAN networking is the notion of extending an existing WAN to link into trading partners' LANs.

EDI Glossary

The following is a list of the various terms used in the world of EDI. This list is an introduction to the basics of EDI. If you are considering using EDI to resolve business data management between you and a trading partner, please see **http://www.microsoft.com/exchange** for more information or contact your local Microsoft Consulting Services office to discuss your implementation in detail.

Common EDI terms:

ANSI. American National Standards Institute. A private, nonprofit membership organization that coordinates the development and approval of voluntary consensus standards in the United States.

ANSI ASC X.12. ANSI Accredited Standards Committee X.12. The committee was chartered by ANSI in 1979 to develop uniform standards for the electronic interchange of business documents.

DEX/UCS. Direct Exchange UCS.

DISA. Data Interchange Standards Association Secretariat for ANSI ASC X12.

DSD. Direct Store Delivery.

ECR. Efficient Consumer Response. Utilized in the Grocery Industry to determine consumer response to products, marketing, and promotions.

EDI. Electronic Data Interchange. A generic term for computer-to-computer transmission.

EDIA. Electronic Data Interchange Association. This group wrote the original UCS and WINS standards; they currently act as Secretariat for the Ocean, Rail, Motor, and Air EDI standards. They also host the annual Pan American EDI conference—one of the world's largest.

EDICA. Electronic Data Interchange Council of Australia. The Australian EDI administrative organization.

EDICC. Electronic Data Interchange Council of Canada. The Canadian EDI administrative organization.

EDIFACT. EDI for Administration, Commerce, and Trade. This is the International EDI Standard set by the U.N. and administered in the U.S. by DISA.

EFT. Electronic Funds Transfer. The electronic transfer of funds from payer to payee through the banking system.

Hub. Also known as sponsors, hubs are large companies, active in EDI, that strongly encourage their paper-based business partners to begin using EDI.

ISO. International Standards Organization.

JIT. Just-In-Time Manufacturing.

NEX/UCS. Network Exchange UCS.

NRF. National Retail Federation.

POS. Point-Of-Sale.

Proprietary Standards. Industry-specific or company-specific data formats that do not comply with ASC X.12 standards.

Trading Partner. Vendor or other party with whom business is conducted.

Transaction Set. A complete business document, for example, an invoice, a purchase order, or a remittance advice.

VAN. Value added network.

The EDI Process

The EDI process is a very complex and integrated system to architect, configure, deploy, and coordinate. Because of the proprietary computer systems, the integration with a value added network provider (VAN), and the coordination of standards with the trading partners, the process can be detailed.

The process can be broken down into two components: the sending system and the receiving system.

The Sending system follows the data flow shown in figure 32.3

The following is a step-by-step breakdown of an EDI dataflow. You will see the main steps in an actual dataflow. This is a technical overview of these steps. These steps can be applied to any set of EDI trading partners.

1. Data is extracted from the corporate application in its native format. As the data is extracted, it is ordered into the message format. This file is saved on a record-based, user-constructed file. This file is called an Interface file.
2. The translation software processes parse through a table based on the message structure and Interface files specific for the EDI engagement. Translation software is the software that formats data into the specified EDI format. It is also used to extract data out of an EDI format. During the parsing process, data validation checks are made, codes are converted, partner profiles determined, and then the data is formatted based on the EDIFACT syntax specification.
3. This file, the Interchange file, containing the formatted data is ready to be transmitted via the messaging transport via X.400 into the VAN.
4. Before sending the Interchange file, the data file is encapsulated with an envelope, defining the communication protocol and destination. The file is then transmitted. This process is called the Communications interface.

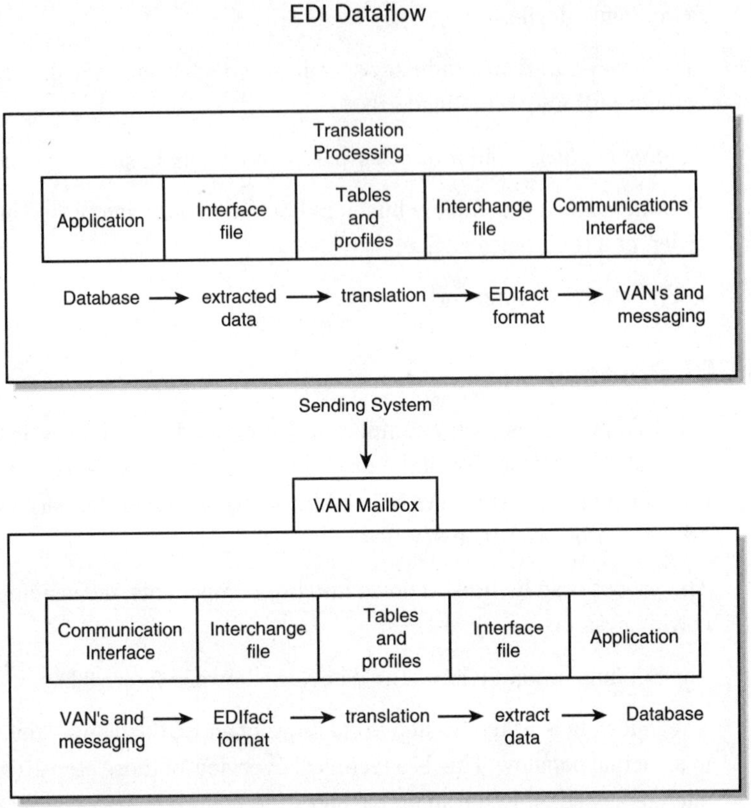

FIG. 32.3
This is a complete EDI data flow diagram.

The Sending system adheres to the following data flow:

1. The Interchange file can be received directly or via the VAN. From the VAN, the trading partner will connect to the VAN and retrieve the data from a predefined mailbox. This requires special software to enable the trading partner to access a VAN mailbox. This is also handled in the communication interface.
2. The Interchange file is downloaded and the data is extracted according to the message specification. Data validation is managed according to the known properties of the message. These are mandatory, conditional, range, and radix. The codes are then translated into a format used by this trading partner in-house.
3. The data sets are placed in an interchange file for use in the in-house system. Additional data validation may be required in order to ensure data integrity.
4. The final step is to upload the data into the in-house system.

Exchange Integration with EDI

EDI typically relies on X.400 as the network transport and addressing scheme for conducting transactions. Exchange has X.400 built right into Exchange platform.

For X.400 support, Exchange can use X.25 protocols, or run over TCP/IP or connect with TP4. One example would be to use X.400 addressing and connectivity over an IP-based network. In this case, Exchange server could communicate with X.400 over the public Internet. The X.400 support is bundled into Exchange server (see fig. 32.4). This does not require a third-party gateway.

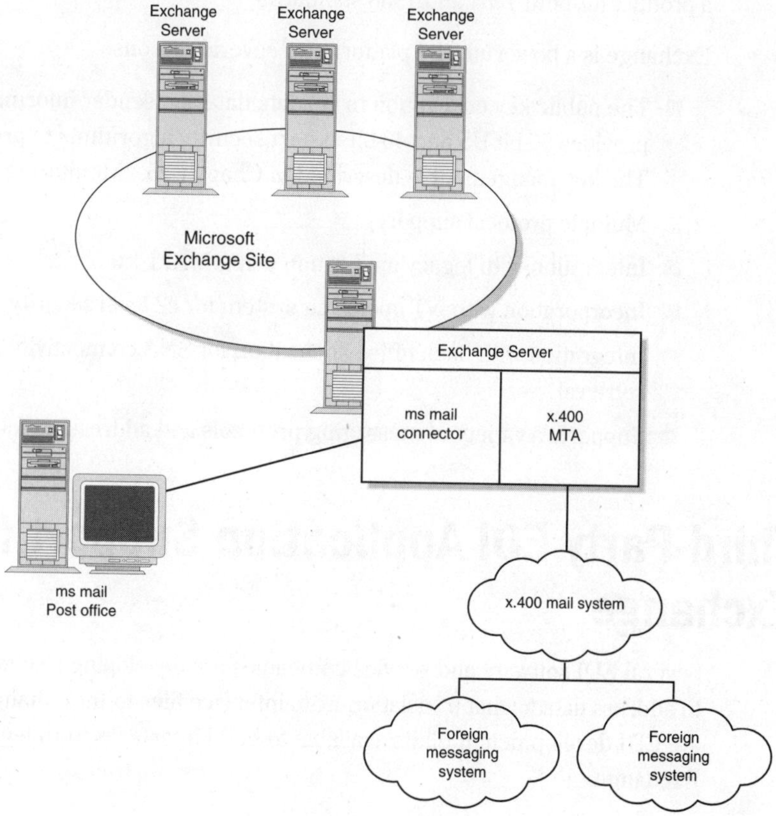

FIG. 32.4 X.400 support in Exchange is built into the core product.

Microsoft Exchange's role is to provide a secure messaging transport over X.400 for delivering EDI documents. On the client side, several third-party developers have EDI-enabled applications to work with MAPI and the Exchange client.

NOTE Currently, X.500 standards exist; however, most organizations have not deployed X.500-based global directory services. X.500 is an elaborate directory standard. Most vendors have their own X.500 interpretation; this includes Exchange, Digital's Mail Bus, Novell's NDS, and more. The interface that these X.500 vendors provide is via X.400. To clarify, you would use X.400 to communicate with a proprietary X.500 directory. X.500 standards are the core logic for today's business enterprise messaging systems.

The Exchange Message Transfer Agent is completely standards-based. It is certified for 1984 and 1988 X.400 standards. This will maintain interoperability for customers, VANs, and trading partners. With this level of certification, Microsoft is the first vendor to certify a product for both 1984 and 1988 standards.

Exchange is a powerful EDI platform for several reasons:

- The public key encryption to validate data and sender information. Exchange provides 56-bit US and 40-bit export security algorithms to provide data encryption. The key mangement is described in Chapter 25, "Monitoring Exchange Sites."
- Multiple protocol support
- Integration with legacy application using MAPI 1.0
- Incorporation with NT operating system for c2 level security
- Integration with back office application for SNA connectivity and for SQL data retrieval
- Supports a variety of messaging protocols and addressing formats

Third-Party EDI Application Support for Exchange

Several EDI software and service companies are developing Exchange EDI software tools to address data format translation from interface files to Interchange files. As well, there are EDI development toolkits available to build interfaces from legacy systems into Exchange.

The following is a list of independent software vendors (ISV) with EDI solutions for Exchange. The companies provide X.400 messaging services as well as EDI application development tools.

- Mpact Immedia

  Mpact has been a leader in electronic commerce software. It will offer transaction-based network services based on the Exchange server product. Mpact will leverage the power of Exchange in addition to the native X.400 communication support. The product will be Interconnexions. This will integrate Mpact's EDI system software with its VAN service to the Exchange messaging backbone.

  Mpact also provides EDIkit. EDIkit enables developers to integrate EDI into a business application. EDIkit provides interface support for MAPI, which can be linked to any application using "C" runtime environment to make EDI CMC calls in the application. The ease-of-use once integrated for the end-user is to have a print option. When the print option is selected, the data is extracted and translated into EDI and passed on to the messaging system.

  JetForm Corporation, a company developing an electronic forms solution for Exchange, will integrate as well with EDIkit. The JetForm user interface will feed data into the business application. From there, the data is EDI accessible. Mpact will provide an appellation development workbench with a set of APIs to use in application development.

  For more information about any of these technologies, you can contact Mpact Immedia at **http://www.mpact.ca**.

- EDISYS

  EDISYS is the creator of VediX, Visual EDI for Microsoft exchange Server. Vedix allows for flexibility in application development to be able to EDI-enable a business application. This product uses Exchange to provide a robust and easy interface, multi-platform support, and multi-applicaiton integration. It is a state-of-the-art EDI translator that reads the interface file and performs the table and profile look-up to translate the file for a native data format into the EDIFACT standard data format. In addition, it provides easy setup and maintenance of trading partner profiles and translation maps for use in data mapping.

  For more information, you can contact EDISYS at +44-0-1296-330011.

- ISOCOR

  Isocor provides the Isocor Messaging for NT Product line. The suite of applications is used for developing messaging servers, client tools for Microsoft MAPI on Windows 95, directory synchronization with Lotus and CC:Mail, and directory administration tools for X.500-based directories. It serves as a high-speed backbone for EDI on top of Exchange.

- ISOTRADE is the product specifically for EDI-based applications including TSI and Sterling. MAPIWARE are service modules for MAPI on Windows 95 used to extend MAPI for use with X.400, X.500, EDI, and several security modules used with ISOTRADE.

  ISOTRADE supports the global EDI standard X.435 messaging RFC. It installs directly onto the Exchange server running Windows NT. It will convert EDI transactions from X.12 and EDIFACT data formats to X.435 for electronic mail distribution using Exchange. The X.435 standard is encapsulated into the X.400 standard messages. Several VANs have already committed to supporting Exchange and EDI solutions. These are AT&T, GE, and SITA. This system can also route the EDI messaging over an X.400 connecting with TCP/IP. Many translation and business application developers support ISOCOR. These include American Business Computer, EDI/Able, EDS, Sterling, TSI, and others. From within one of these EDI applications, it can communicate with the ISOTRADE module running on the server.

  ISOTRADE is a good model for how Microsoft Exchange is non-proprietary. It supports all of the EDI applications just listed. The leverage that it has is that, relying on Exchange, it can pass EDI messages over X.25, TP4, or TCP/IP using X.435.

  For more information, you can contact Isocor at **http://www.isocor.com**.

Exchange provides a robust messaging framework to build interfaces for EDI applications. As you have seen, several companies are providing EDI application software, as well. VANs will provide native Exchange connectivity. EDI is a powerful way to extend and leverage the role of Exchange in the enterprise.

NOTE EDI is a very difficult subject to cover in just one chapter. If you are interested in learning more about EDI, you might like to read some EDI text books, as well as research how EDI can be interfaced with your legacy business application. EDI solutions are very expensive and require special attention from application development to implementation. Make sure you discuss any EDI solution with the application development specialists from your department.

From Here...

This chapter has explained how Exchange can be used for EDI applications. The next chapter concludes this book on Exchange, by providing some insight to the future of the product. For more information on extending Exchange services, see the following chapters:

- Chapter 1, "Overview of Microsoft Exchange," describes the Universal Inbox paradigm.
- Chapter 31, "Implementing Third-Party Integration Tools," presents several third-party products to provide additional leverage for Exchange in your business enterprise.

CHAPTER 33

Introduction to Exchange Forms Development

- How to install the forms designer software.
- An overview of the forms environment.
- How to plan and design forms for use in your organization.
- How to use the Forms Designer to build and customize forms.

This chapter introduces you to the world of making custom Exchange applications without prior programming experience. However, if you're already familiar with Windows and Visual Basic, you'll have a very easy time using the Forms Designer interface.

The Exchange Forms Designer lets you lay out all the different fields on your form, link them to Exchange objects, and designate actions on events. Without any previous programming experience, you can create applications that will make your organization more productive. Many example applications are provided on the Exchange CD-ROM. You can use these predesigned forms, and modify them for your use. They are located in the \EXCHANGE\FORMS directory of whatever drive you have installed the client applications.

See the section "Installing the Forms Designer" for more information on installation.

The Forms Designer enables the creation of two types of forms:

- Stand-alone forms

  These forms are not associated with any particular folder. They facilitate the input of information with the intent to send it to an individual or group of users. These applications include message-taking, office supply requisitions, and vacation requests.

- Folder forms

  These forms facilitate the input of information into a public folder where permitted users can view the information in an organized way. These applications include group discussions, bulletin boards, and enterprise-wide groupware databases. Filters can be applied to move data into sub-folders, and views can be applied to group or soft information.

Among the potential custom applications you can create are *electronic forms*. For example, in many organizations there are standard forms that are routed to specific individuals. Using the Forms Designer, you can create a travel-request form, time-off request form, or office-supply requisition. These applications take the work out of making simple requests. In addition, with the integration of *public folders*, the forms are easy to distribute throughout the organization. You no longer have to make sure that everyone has the most up-to-date form, and that they have enough copies. Distributing the forms electronically makes it easier for the user, and easier for the recipient who receives all the forms. He or she can easily organize and process all the requests in the universal inbox.

Another strong suit of the Forms Designer is to maximize the effectiveness of public folders. By designing an application, you can make it really easy to enter data into a public area. A great example of this use is for those organizations that post a lot of memos. Instead of printing out the memos and distributing them through the mailroom or by e-mail into everyone's inbox, you can just create a public folder called "Company Memos" and then write an application that lets the user enter the memo into some structured fields. Once the user executes the form, the memo is posted to an appropriate sub-folder under the main "Company Memos" folder. The sub-folder could be based on a field on your form that had a drop-down list of company departments. Using this system, everybody wins. The mailroom folks have less junk mail to route, the people in the copy room have less to copy (which saves toner), and most importantly, paper is saved, which is good for the environment as well as the bottom line. ■

Installation of the Forms Designer

As mentioned throughout this book, the Forms Designer is a *client application*. It is installed with Schedule+ and the Exchange Client. However, you may not have installed it when you installed the other components. What follows is an installation procedure:

1. Run the Exchange Setup Program.
2. Choose Complete/Custom from the menu provided.
3. From the Complete/Custom window, choose Change Options.
4. In the Options box, select Forms Designer and Sample Applications, and choose OK.
5. Choose Continue.
6. Choose Continue.

If you had any previous version of the Forms Designer on your drive, Setup will detect and overwrite it with the new version. Any forms you create will not be overwritten by any new versions you may install.

Along with the application, all the different sources of help are installed. There are three different sources of help when you are designing applications: Cue Cards, On-line Help, and On-line Documentation.

These various sources of on-line help are a great supplement to this chapter. You will get the context-sensitive help you need, and at the same time you'll get more step-by-step tutorials to walk you through all the functions. The on-line manuals give you access at your fingertips. Most of the time, someone else has the manual when you need it.

Using Forms in Your Organization

Exchange's structure provides for many different uses of the containers in the hierarchy. You can design applications that leverage this flexibility. Two possible ways of using the Exchange framework are for discussion and reference purposes.

Discussion Applications

In many organizations, several different teams are working on different projects. As they get ideas, they usually send out an e-mail to all the people involved. As the weeks go by, everyone winds up with many e-mail and voice-mail messages that have no structure. Many are simply carbon copies, forwarded messages, or replies. It usually means going back and sifting through all the messages looking for information.

Some groups use a *bulletin board* or *internal newsgroup* to help centralize all the data. The only problem with this solution is that most e-mail packages that provide bulletin board capability have poor security. You can't control who can post, read, or modify. When using Usenet-style newsgroups, you can't control who can read and post very easily. You would have either have to set up passwords, or host entries for each machine to read or post. It isn't very easy or robust.

Using a custom Exchange application for discussion, you gain all the access control that is inherent in Exchange and NT Server. You can allow only members of the proper teams to access their information. In some cases, you would want to allow read-only access to people in other groups to promote team cooperation. Exchange's public folder structure is flexible enough to allow this.

Not only that, using a custom application can structure the data. The forms you create can contain certain fields, and also contain information about threads. The ability to structure information in different views gives the user the ability to chose a report sorted by date, author, or subject. You can also use structure subjects if you want to keep discussions along a certain topic.

Some of the most common uses of discussion applications are customer-support databases, brainstorming applications where team members can input ideas as they come to them, frequently asked questions lists, and meeting-summarization applications.

Reference Repositories

Exchange serves as a great repository of documents and objects as well as e-mail. You can easily write applications that provide easy access to all your standard documents throughout the enterprise. Many organizations have several standard documents such as policies and procedures manuals, style guides, and computer-usage guidelines. In addition, many organizations have standard Word document templates that they use. These objects can be placed in an Exchange public folder and made available right on the user's desktop.

Explaining the Forms Environment

A few pieces of the Forms environment need to be explained in the scope of the large Exchange picture. These components consist of

- Forms Libraries
- Views
- Rules

- Permissions
- Items

Forms Libraries

When you create a form, you save and install it into a folder forms Library. The properties of the forms saved into a particular folder are dependent on the properties of the folder. This includes access permissions. When the user chooses New Form on the Tools menu in the Exchange Client, he or she is presented with a list of forms available in the folder.

The Global Forms Library The Global Forms Library houses all the forms that you want to make available to everyone in the enterprise. These forms could include vacation-request forms, corporate memos, or telephone message forms.

The Folder Library Every folder, either public or private, has a forms library associated with it. You can save forms into one of your private folders, but they will only be shared with anyone to whom you have given access to your folders.

By putting forms into a public folder, you allow robust sharing based on the permissions of the folder, which are generally easy to change if the need arises. When new users are added to the Exchange system, their group memberships can determine which public folders they have access to.

For example, say you had a group called Directors that contained people at or above the level of director in your organization. You could create a folder that contained a form they could fill out that would make it easy to enter product data sheets, and store them in a public folder so that all people at that level or above could view and modify them. The folder you set up has the permission properties set to only allow members of the NT group Directors to view and modify.

The Personal Forms Library This library is not shared with any other user. It contains the forms the person uses most often. If you have functions that you perform every day, and create a form to automate those tasks, you would place the form in your personal library. In addition, you can use these forms when working off-line as long as your default information store resides on your local disk.

Views

Since forms reside in folders, it is pertinent to discuss folder views. Global views apply across all forms and folders, and folder views apply only to the selected form containing the view.

Think of views as the different reports generated off of a database. In the old days, you had to write different report specifications to get the data you wanted presented in the order you wanted.

Views allow you to order information and present it to the user the way he or she would like to see it. When you establish a form, you create structured fields within it that lend themselves very nicely to the four kinds of views:

- Filtering

  Using filtering gives you the ability to only view information that meets certain criteria. Let's go back to our Directors example. If you want, you can set a filter to only display product descriptions of a certain product line, rather than the whole line.

- Sorting

  This view allows you to sort on any field. In our example, you can easily sort by part number or department number if you like. Even better, you can sort by director name, which lets you easily see which director was responsible for which products.

- Grouping

  Grouping lets you use a hierarchical model like the Windows Explorer in Windows 95, or the File Manager in Windows NT. You can click a certain title or expand or collapse the information. You can group the items by product line, and then filter down to more specific product information for each product in that particular line.

- Columns

  You can format the data in your folder like a spreadsheet. This makes it very easy to read, and very familiar to a majority of users. You can place all your fields in any order you wish across the screen.

Views are created outside the form, in the Exchange Client. Once you install a form into a folder form library, all its fields are published to the library, allowing you to easily set up views later on in the Client.

Rules

Just as views are folder properties that apply to form, so too are rules. Rules are a powerful feature in Exchange that allow you to control what happens to an item once it is submitted to a folder.

Many e-mail packages have this functionality in some form. However, in most cases, you must be logged into your mail application for the rules to take effect. Also, most e-mail packages lack the ability to do this with bulletin board-type functionality.

With Exchange, an example of applying rules to a form entry would be that any item meeting certain criteria can be moved to a sub-folder, or e-mailed to someone else as a carbon copy, or even deleted if you so wish.

This functionality gives you much more control over the organization of your data, and even helps reduce redundant entries. It cuts down on administration because everything is automatic once the rules are established. For more information on rules see the section entitled "Setting Folder Rules," later in this chapter.

Permissions

By establishing folder permissions, you control who has access to any of the forms contained in that folder's Library. You also control what the user can do in the folder. You can set options to allow read, write, and edit access. In addition, you can select pre-defined roles that allow the administrator to quickly establish a set of permissions for the user.

You can also delegate any user as an owner of a certain folder. This enables that user to give other users access permissions. This is analogous to Windows NT Server permissions that allow multiple users to be administrators for a certain domain. Giving someone else ownership permissions allows for multiple administrators and the delegation of responsibilities.

Items

An easy way to think of items is to think of database tables. In a database, tables consist of records, which consist of fields, which have values. Exchange forms work the same way. Folders contain items, that contain fields, that have values. It's very straightforward. An item is like a record in a database.

Explaining the Form's Components

If you are familiar with Visual Basic at all, this section will make a lot of sense and be refresher material. If you've never used Visual Basic, this section will provide very important information that will aid you in understanding the form design process.

The reason we mentioned Visual Basic is that Exchange forms are Visual Basic Version 4 executable programs. They do not need to be run independently of Exchange, as the Exchange Client takes care of this process. Using forms is completely transparent to the user.

The Forms Designer serves as a front end to Visual Basic, so non-programmers can create robust applications using a simple tool without the advanced knowledge needed to use Visual Basic.

Using Visual Basic comes with some consequences. One thing is that non-Windows clients will not be able to use Exchange forms because there is machine-executed code involved, and non-Windows platforms cannot run this code.

On the flip side, however, companies that have in-house Visual Basic expertise can build robust, enterprise-caliber applications that take full advantage of object linking and embedding, as well as SQL Server access. For example, you could have an Exchange application that relies on the Global Address Book for addressing information, but at the same time writes fields to a SQL Server database somewhere on the network.

An Exchange form is made up of the following components:

- The Form Itself

  The form's appearance and behavior are set through its properties that will be discussed in the next section. You can use a form within a folder, as a part of another application, or as a stand-alone application.

  The form itself acts as a shell that encases its components. It is at the top level of the hierarchical structure of the form. Forms contain windows, that contain fields.

- The Form Windows

  Forms can contain multiple windows that are used for different functions. One window might contain addressing information, while another might be an output window. Windows allow you to keep the screen neat and logically organized by function. Keep this in mind as you design your forms.

  By using multiple windows in the same form, as opposed to multiple forms, you keep greater control. It is easier to pass information between windows than between forms.

- The Window Fields

  Each window presents information as fields. You determine which fields will appear in which windows. You can either create new fields in each window, or carry over field values from other windows in the same form.

  Fields are not limited to input and output. They can be menus and toolbars. They can initiate actions by having events assigned to them. The field's actions are governed by its properties.

Setting Properties of Form Components

Setting a form's properties is the most daunting task facing the form designer. It is through these properties that the application takes the desired effect. Properties sheets are the means by which the Forms Designer accomplishes its magic, without the need for writing code. Depending on the properties of each object, certain actions will bring about certain results.

As indicated by the title of the section, setting up the properties of each component is made easier because the properties are organized by Form, Window, and Field. The properties you can set for an item will vary with the item.

Form Properties

The general properties of forms consist of the display name, the icon the user will see, the version of the form, the item type associated with the form, and a brief description.

In addition to the general properties, the event properties control what happens when a user takes a certain action on the form. For example, if the user clicks a "Submit" button, you could have the form display a confirmation window showing the value of all the current fields.

Window Properties

The general properties of a window are the name, tab order of the fields in the window, caption, and the WinHelp filename.

You can also control resizing options, borders, and colors of the window with the format properties.

Field Properties

In addition to the standard general properties like field name, caption, and location, fields allow you to set initialization values. This allows you to set default values to all the fields in your window. If you have a radio button in your window, for example, you can set whether it is selected by default or not.

All of these properties will be discussed in greater detail when we actually go through the design of a real form. Each property will be explained in detail. What is important at this stage is that you get the feel for what needs to be done when designing a form.

Installing Forms

Upon the creation of a form, a form project file with an .EFP extension is created. It is very similar to a Visual Basic project file.

When you choose the Install command from the Forms Designer, several things happen that are transparent to you. The form files are taken by the installation routine and Visual Basic project files are created. This enables you to use these .MAK files and use them within Visual Basic 4 to extend your applications at a later time.

Once that happens, the form is compiled into a .EXE file, just like when you use the "Make .EXE" command from the File menu in Visual Basic. In addition, a configuration file with a .CFG extension is created. This is used by the forms library for installation.

After that step is completed, the form gets installed into the forms library of your choice. You will now be able to access your form from the folder you chose.

Planning Your Exchange Form

You now have all the information you'll need to create an application. The information in this section will give you a general overview of the steps you will follow to create an application from beginning to end.

When designing a form, you should follow these simple steps:

- Define the purpose of the application

  This sounds very obvious, but this simple step will help you stay focused. By determining what the form will do, you'll give yourself information that will aid in the design. For example, if the application is a simple message-taking application that will be available to everyone in the organization, you may want to keep the design very simple, and you will know that the form will most likely wind up in the global forms library, so you might want to contact the administrator of the system to get permission to post it there.

- Define the fields

  Defining the purpose of your form will give you a good basis for what fields you should include on the form. To continue the example from above, you might want to include the time the person called, their name, company, the message, and whether to call them back or not.

  It is a good idea to come up with a logical structure of the field, which will help you lay them out on the screen and decide whether you need more than one window.

- Creating a folder for your application
- Create the form

  Using the Forms Designer, create the actual screen that will contain the fields. Drag and drop the objects onto the window on the form. This part of the Forms Designer feels very much like a drawing program. Make sure the form has a logical flow to it, and that all fields are appropriately marked.

- Set the properties of all objects

  Once you create the form, you need to go back and set the properties of all the objects on your form, including the form itself. Although some people like to set the properties of each object when it is created, doing it in two steps allows people to collaborate on the layout and confirm all the field choices and names before moving forward.

- Install the form

  Once you set properties on the objects on your form, you need to install it in order to test functionality of the application. If the application spans multiple forms, be sure that all the forms are installed in the folder. It's a good idea to keep the application in a personal folder so no one else can access it while it is being debugged and tested.

- Test the form

  In order to make sure your form performs all the functions you intended, in the way you intended, you need to test the form extensively. Things to look for are whether the screen layout is correct, required fields are in fact required, and that button groups work properly.

- Design the views

  As explained before, views let you order the data for your users. Once the form is installed, you need to establish the views that will better facilitate the purpose of the form. You can sort, group, filter, and make columns. Once you register your forms with the folder, users can access the views from the Exchange Client.

- Move or copy the form

  Once the views are designed, and further testing is performed, you can move or copy the form into its final destination folder. In your first step, if you remember, you knew who would be using the form, so you contacted the administrator to get permission to post the form into the proper public folder. You will now use that permission, and post the form. Planning ahead will save you a lot of time.

- Set folder properties

  Now that the form is in a public place, you can set the properties that will do such things as define a default view and whether or not the form is accessible. This is a good feature if you have not completely finished the testing process.

- Set permissions

  As stated throughout this chapter, you can set the permissions of the public folder that houses your forms. If you only want certain users to access your applications, or want the form to be read-only for certain people, you can set the permissions to reflect your wishes.

- Set folder rules

  You can set rules to specify actions for incoming data based on conditions. You could use this feature to eliminate duplicate data, generate carbon copies to certain recipients automatically, or move data to sub-folders.

You are now ready to create applications using the Microsoft Exchange Forms Designer. The next section will go into detail with a step-by-step tutorial. A sample form will be created from scratch, showing you how the outline above will help you design custom applications.

Creating the "Web Site Button" Form

You are now ready to design a form from scratch. We're going to try to follow the outline for designing forms described above as closely as possible.

- Defining the purpose

  Many organizations that have World Wide Web sites on the Internet choose to advertise their sites on other servers. These companies must come up with forms that enable the technical staff to communicate effectively and quickly with the media department that purchases the space on others' Web sites.

  The form we're going to design facilitates that need. It makes it very easy to let the technical staff know exactly what's needed by the company housing the hypertext links.

- Defining fields

  We've already stated the purpose of the form rather clearly, so we'll move on to defining the fields we'll use on the form.

TIP It is a good idea to collaborate with all the departments involved with the fields on the form at design time. They can provide a lot of key insights that will make the form much more useful to all the parties involved. For this form, the media, creative, and account departments need to be involved in the form-layout process.

The fields are shown in the following table:

Table 33.1 Web Site Button Form Field Names and Descriptions

Name of Field	Purpose
To	Addressee on the technical staff
Date	Date the note was sent
Subject	User definable subject field
Company	Company from whom you leased space
URL	Web site URL the button will reside on
OurURL	URL the button will point to
Size	Pixel size required by the company
StartDateEffective	Button start date
EndDateEffective	Button end date
Transport	Type of media required, if any
Address	E-mail address of company
Contact	Name of contact person
ContactPhone	Phone number of contact

This table is exactly what you should draw out before ever loading the Forms Designer. The field names will be used later in the field properties definitions. The purposes of each field will also help you and your colleagues better design the form and add fields later.

- Deciding where the form will reside

  You now have to determine where your form will reside. For this application, you will just store the form in a folder forms library. This is because there's a person in the media department who coordinates all the Web site space lease agreements, and starts the routing of the form. He or she will use this form from a private folder. When troubleshooting the form, it is much safer to keep the form in a private folder until it is ready.

  You don't need to do anything special to use your Folder Forms Library. The form-installation procedure will do this for you. If you were using a public folder, you would have to obtain permission from the Exchange administrator to create the public folder and write items into it.

- Creating the form

You are now ready to launch the Forms Designer and start drawing out your form. We will go through step by step. Figures will be used to walk you through each step. Each figure will be the result of the step before it. For example, step one will yield the figure immediately following it.

1. Double-click the Forms Designer icon. The Microsoft Exchange Forms Designer dialog box appears (see fig. 33.1).

TIP You can use any of the sample forms provided to familiarize yourself with the different kinds of forms.

2. Choose the Form Template Wizard (see fig. 33.2) and click Next.
3. Select To Another User (send) and click Next.
4. Select To Send information and click Next (see fig. 33.3).
5. Choose One Window and click Next (see fig. 33.4).
6. Type **Website Button Form** in the Name field (see fig. 33.5), and **This form is used to send detailed information to the technical staff to expedite Web site media buys** in the Description field .
7. Click Finish (see fig. 33.6).

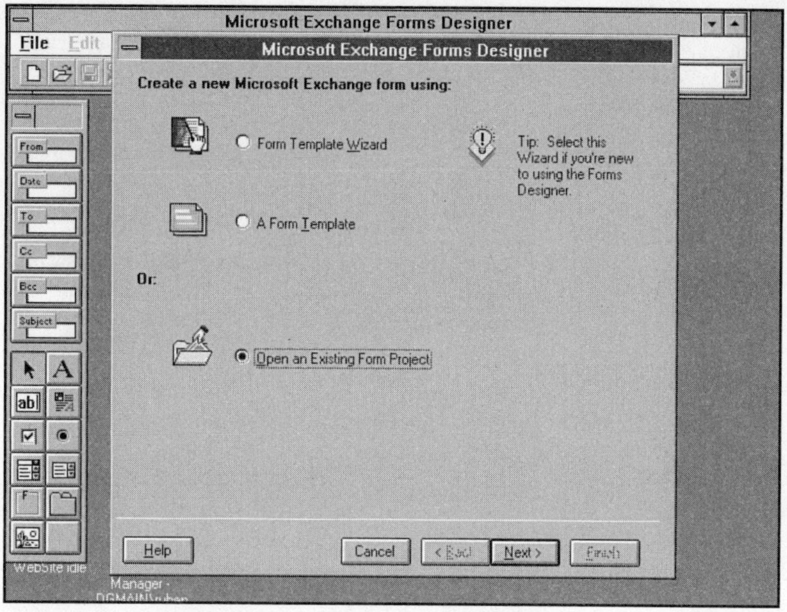

FIG. 33.1
You can use the Wizard, open a template, or use an existing application.

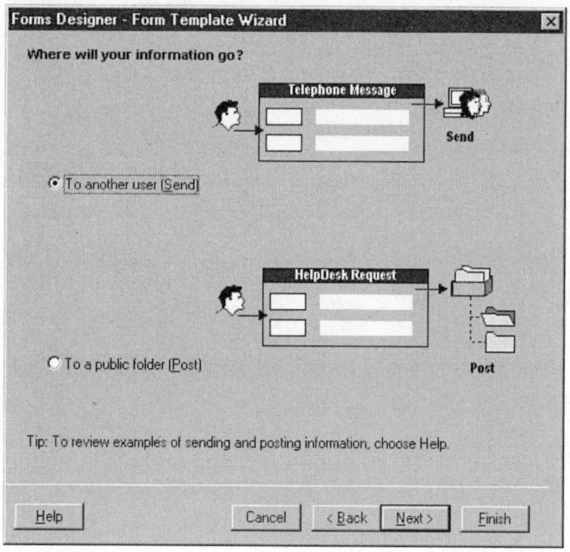

FIG. 33.2
The Wizard gives you the choice of using the form to send to another user, or to post to a public folder.

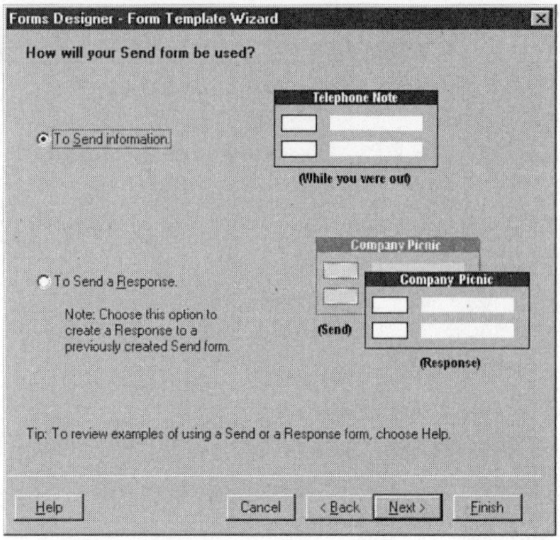

FIG. 33.3
You can either use the form to send information, or let the user enter a response to an existing item.

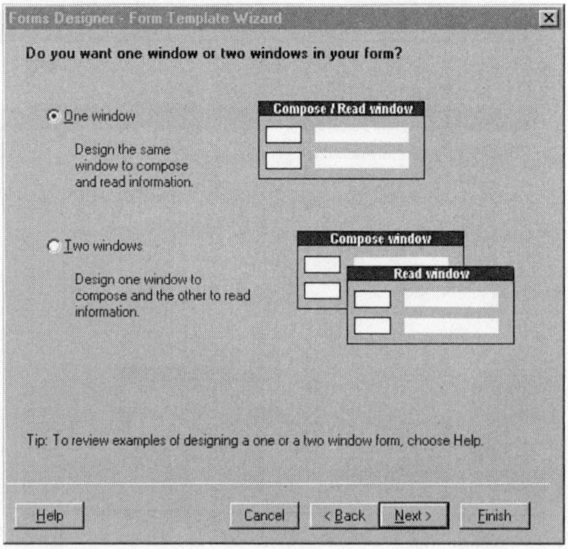

FIG. 33.4
The name and description given to the form will determine how the user sees it in the Viewer.

FIG. 33.5
The Finish screen of the Wizard shows you the next steps you'll need to take when designing your form.

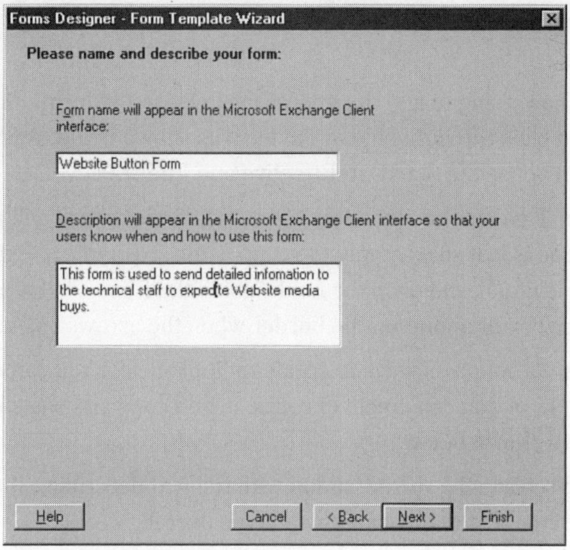

FIG. 33.6
Clicking Finish will lay out the default fields onto the form and bring up the screen where you can add fields to it.

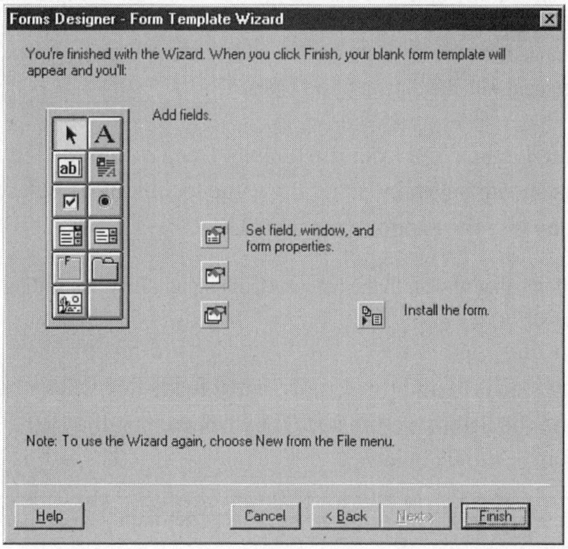

8. Our form does not require a "cc" field. Click in the middle of the field, and hit the DEL key.
9. We are now going to add the necessary fields to the form. First, select the Frame tool, and click the right side of the form as shown below. A frame will be created. This will house the StartDateEffective and EndEffectiveDate fields.
10. Now you'll create the text entry boxes for the fields that will go inside the frame. The frame is just an easy way to group fields. To create a text entry field, click the Entry Field tool, and drop the fields inside the frame. Then resize the fields as necessary by dragging on the border when the arrows appear.

    There are a couple of ways to create multiple fields. You can either create each one separately, or you can create one, size it, and copy and paste it. The final product will be what's shown below.

    You can replace the word Caption with the text describing the field. Just click in the box with the text of the caption and type over it.
11. We will now create a Listbox containing the name of the companies we usually deal with when we buy space. You can always add new companies easily.

NOTE You could use an Entry Field for this field, but for this example, it is good to try to experiment with the different field types.

Select the Listbox tool from the toolbar. Drop it onto the left side of the form, and size it as shown below by using the same technique as before. In addition, type **Company** into the caption (see fig. 33.7).

NOTE The items that appear in the listbox will be input later when setting properties for each field.

12. The next step is to add three more entry fields that will sit between the frame on the right, and the listbox on the left. They will contain the URL, OurURL, and Size fields. The result is shown below.

TIP It is a good idea to save your form at this point. Select Save from the File menu, give your form the name WEBFORM, and click OK.

13. Let's now create the frame for the Transport field. This will consist of creating a frame with three radio buttons. The frame caption should read "Transport" and the three radio buttons should have the captions "America Online," "Compuserve," and "Internet," respectively.

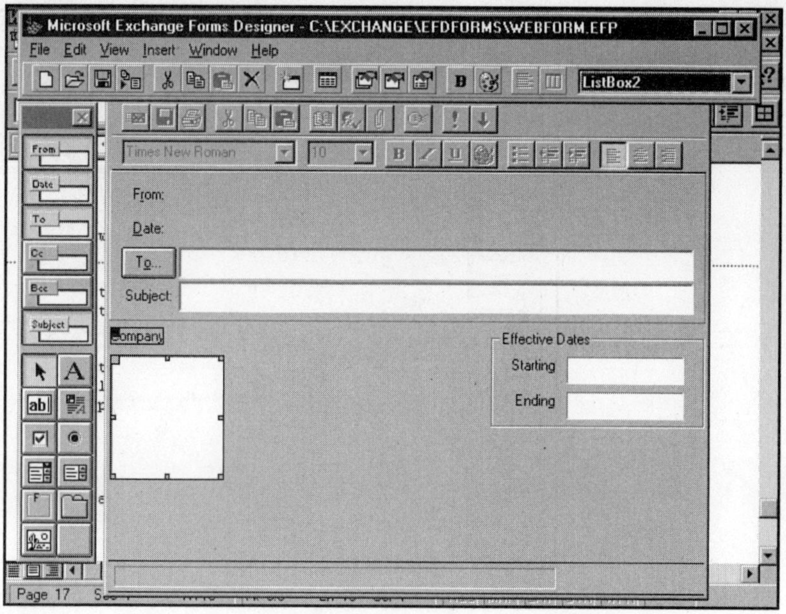

FIG. 33.7
You now have four elements on your form: a frame, two entry fields, and a listbox.

NOTE You'll notice that the listbox containing the company field has been extended. It is very easy to control the length of the box by just dragging on the border.

As a reminder, click within a caption to change the text, and drag the edges of the box to resize. To move boxes around, click somewhere inside the box when the cursor is an arrow and drag the item around the form. If you are familiar with Windows applications, this should be familiar to you.

14. You only need to create three more fields: entry fields that will hold the Address, Contact, and ContactPhone fields. They are shown in the figure 33.8.

Setting the properties of all objects on the form

Now that the form has all the objects laid out on the screen, the next step is to make them actually perform functions. You do this through the use of properties. The various objects on the form, including the form itself, the windows, and the fields all have properties that define their use.

We'll first set the properties for all the fields on the form. The reason the fields come first is that each field is given a name in the properties field that will make it easier to reference when setting Window properties.

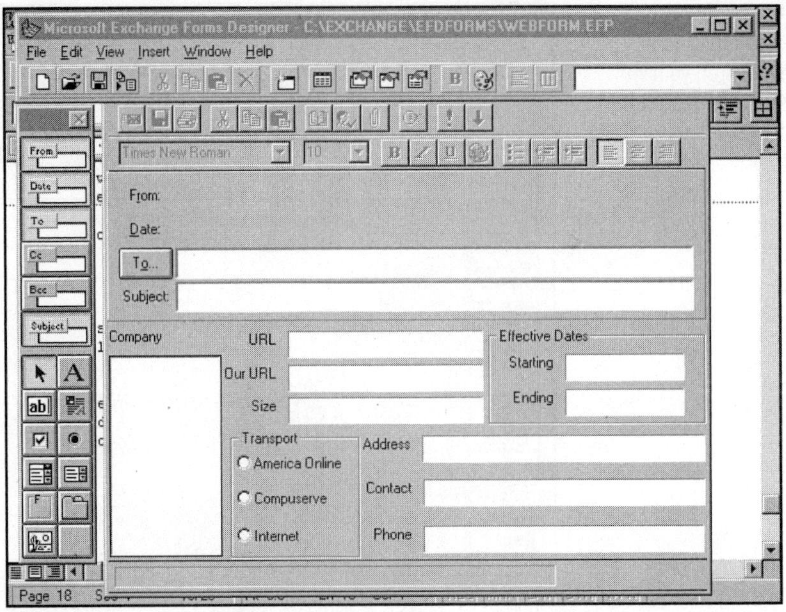

FIG. 33.8
The form is now completed.

1. Double-click in the Company field; the properties screen will appear as shown below. There are tabs of information: General, Format, and Initial Value.

TIP You can select the field and press F4 instead of double-clicking the object. For fields in tight areas of the screen, this is the preferred method, because double-clicking in these areas sometimes yields strange results such as the selection of text.

2. On the General tab, enter **Company** into the Reference Name field. The reference name is simply the variable name assigned to the field. You will use this when determining things like tab order.
3. Check the Required checkbox (see fig. 33.9). This field is required because without a company name, the rest of the fields cannot be complete. The purpose you established earlier will aid you in determining whether a field is required or not.
4. Click the Format tab. This tab controls the font, alignment, appearance, and style of the field value and the caption. The formatting defaults are correct for our purposes for this application.
5. Click the Initial Value tab (see fig. 33.10). This tab differs for each kind of field. Since we are using a listbox in this case, this tab gives you the opportunity to fill in the values in the list and select a default. Fill in the values according the figure shown below. These are the names of some popular Web sites that sell advertising space.

FIG. 33.9
The General Properties are complete for the Company field.

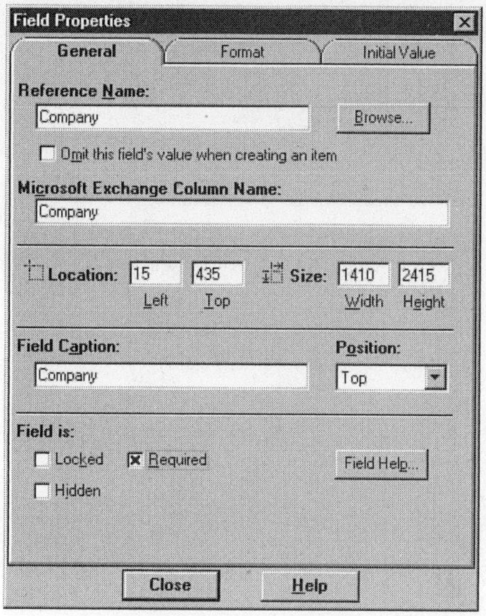

FIG. 33.10
Highlight any entry and click the Set selection to initial value button to make it the default.

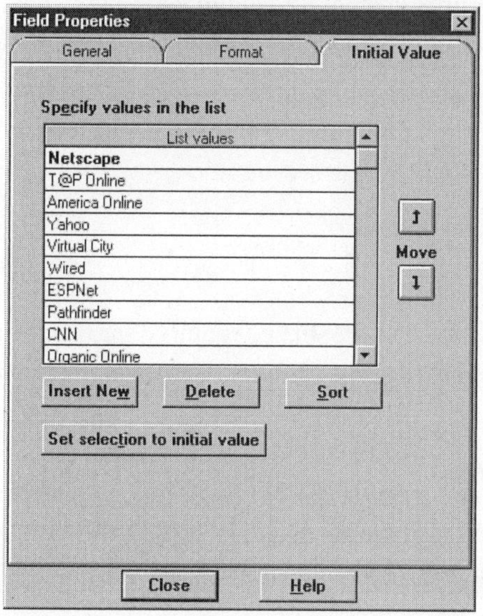

6. Push the Close button.
7. Move the pointer over the URL field and double-click.
8. On the General tab (see fig. 33.11), type **URL** as the Reference Name.
9. Check the Required checkbox.

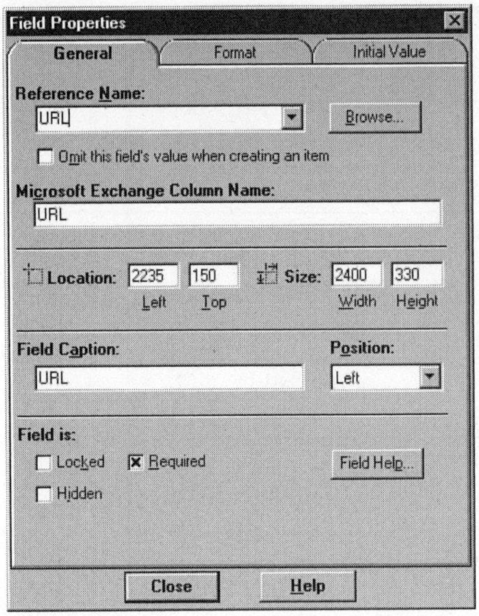

FIG. 33.11
The General tab contains the same information regardless of field type.

10. Complete the procedures in steps 7 through 9 for all the fields remaining on the form. The Reference Name will match the Caption in the General tab of all the fields (excluding spaces).
11. Double-click the Internet radio button in the Transport frame.
12. Click the Initial Value tab.
13. Click the selected radio button.
14. Select close.

You've now completed all the form properties required for this form. For other forms, you'll probably need to set other properties, and this example provides you with a good starting point.

Setting Window Properties

Forms contain fields and windows. Just as fields have properties, so do windows.

1. Select Window Properties from the View menu.
2. Type **WebButton** into the Window Name field (see fig. 33.12).
3. Type **Web Button Form** into the Window Caption field.
4. Establish the tab order by selecting fields and clicking the button marked >>. Follow the figure below for an example of the field order.

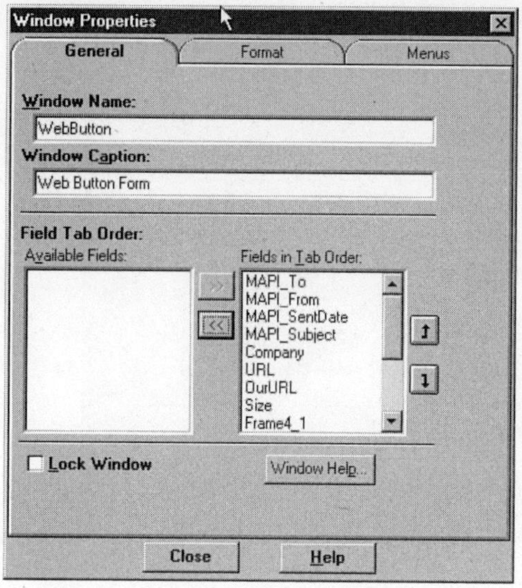

FIG. 33.12
The layout of the window is determined by its properties.

5. Click the Format tab (see fig. 33.13). This tab contains properties for window behavior. Things like background color, window icon, and title-bar icons are set using this tab.
6. Click the Formatting toolbar checkbox in the Window Options section. Since all the necessary fonts are configured for each field, you don't need the Formatting toolbar for this specific application. It has been removed to show you the variations you can make to a form. (You can leave it if you wish.)
7. Change the Window Sizing Options dropdown box to Resizeable. Your properties sheet should be identical to the one below.
8. Click the Menus tab (see fig. 33.14). You can add and modify menu items here. For our form, we will not need to modify this at all. Refer to the on-line help and Microsoft documentation for more information on modifying menus.
9. Click the close button.

The Window Properties have now been set. This is the second tier of properties you need to set for your form. We will now move on to the third and final set of properties that will control how the form itself interacts with the user.

Setting form properties

We'll now set the form properties. We'll again follow the step-by-step model, using various figures to keep you on track.

1. Select Form Properties from the View menu.

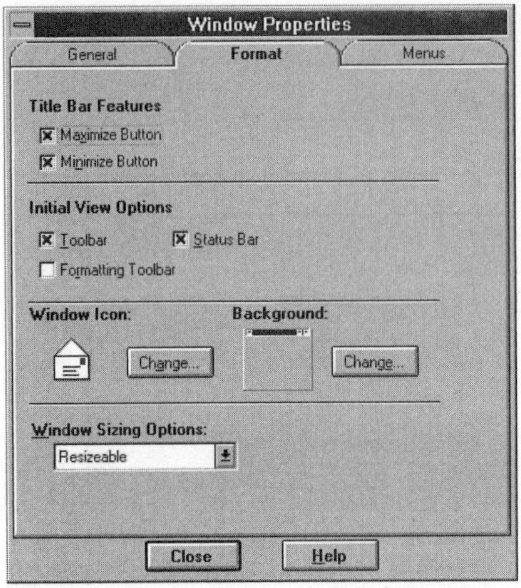

FIG. 33.13 Your Format properties are now complete.

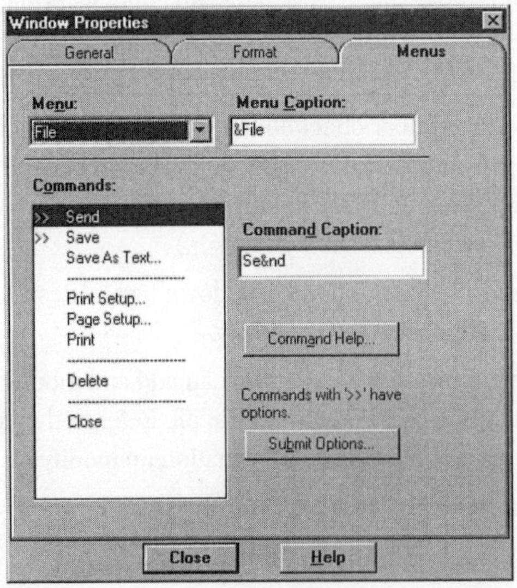

FIG. 33.14 The Menus tab gives you the opportunity to change the menus at the top of the screen.

TIP You can also press Ctrl-F to get to the Form Properties.

This will bring up the properties that define your form. As you can see, the General tab (see fig. 33.15) contains the Form Display Name and Description you entered in the wizard. There are no other mandatory properties you need to set for this application.

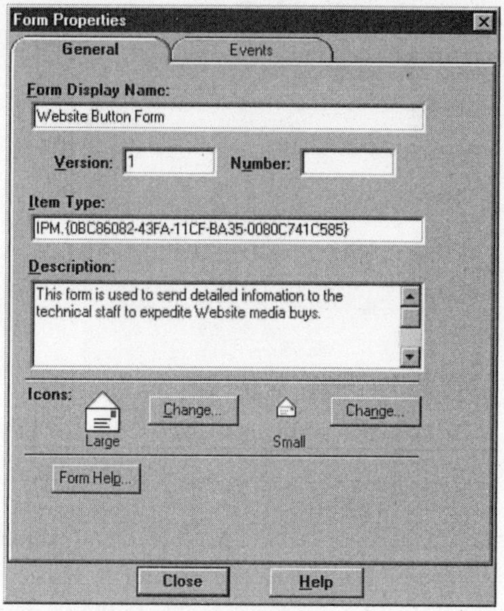

FIG. 33.15
You use the General tab to control how the user sees your form.

NOTE Although the icon and help settings are set here, they are not modified for this application. Please refer to the Microsoft documentation and on-line help for more information on setting up help for your applications.

2. Click the Events tab (see fig. 33.16). You use this tab to define how the form will react to different events the user generates. This particular form requires no modification of these properties. See the Microsoft documentation and the on-line help for a full description of these fields.
3. Click the close button to return to the main editing window.

All of the needed properties are now complete for this form. From here, we'll continue on our list of steps that need to be followed when creating custom forms with Exchange.

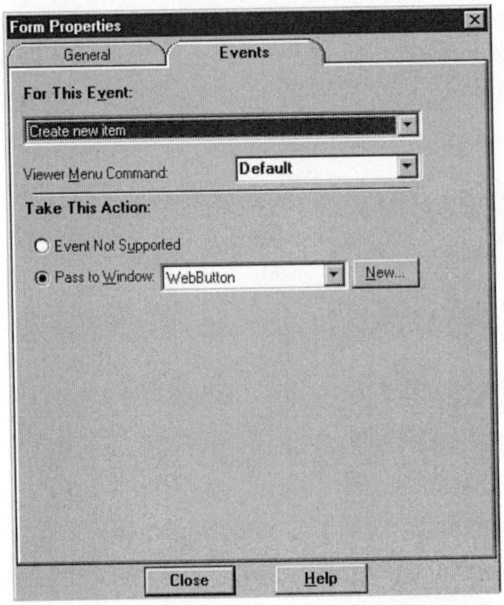

FIG. 33.16
The Events tab is used to control how the form will react when different events are triggered.

Installing the form

When you install a form, Visual Basic code is generated and an executable file is generated that Exchange will run when someone calls the form. This code can be called up within Visual Basic later on to add more functionality to the form or application.

1. In the Viewer, create a new private folder called **Web site Buttons** (see fig. 33.17) in your Mailbox container.
2. Choose Install from the File menu. This will initiate the process of calling Visual Basic and compiling the form. After the computer finishes all those steps, a prompt will come up asking you where to install the form.
3. Click the Folder Forms Library radio button, and select Web site Buttons from the list of folders. If the list doesn't appear, click the plus symbol to expand the tree of folders.
4. Click OK.

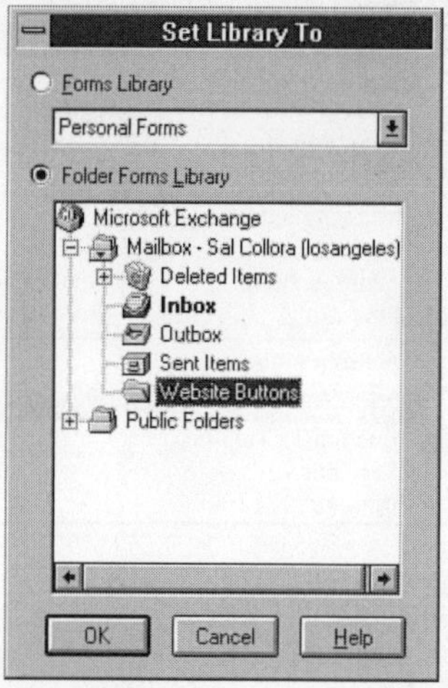

FIG. 33.17
The installation procedure does all the work for you. All you have to do is select where you want to reside.

Testing the Form

You now need to run through the form to make sure everything works properly. This is really not a step-by-step process. Look for the following items:

- Required in the Field Properties are actually required to submit the form.
- Button groups only let you select one button.
- Form layout is correct.
- Fonts look appropriate at all resolutions.

To use the form, select New Web site Button Form from the Compose menu in the Viewer.

Designing the Form Views

The Column Name property of each field becomes very important when designing views. You can group, sort, and display information by any one of the column names you defined in the design phase.

Our Web site Button form (see fig. 33.18) is used to send structured data to another user. We've created a folder for the form, and will now design a view. When the user receives a Button Form in his or her inbox, dragging into this folder will make the item conform to the default view.

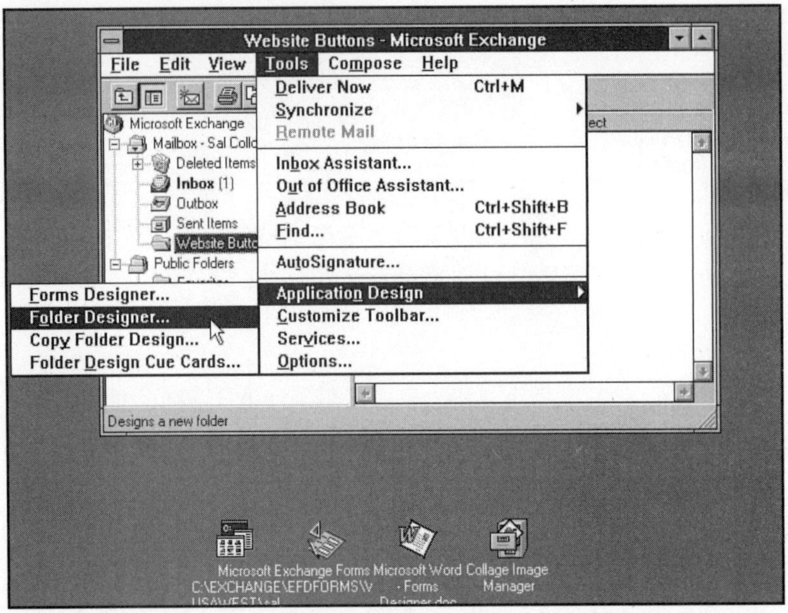

FIG. 33.18
Designing views is made easy by the Folder Designer.

1. From the Tools menu, choose Application Design, then Folder Designer.
2. Click the Views tab (see fig. 33.19).

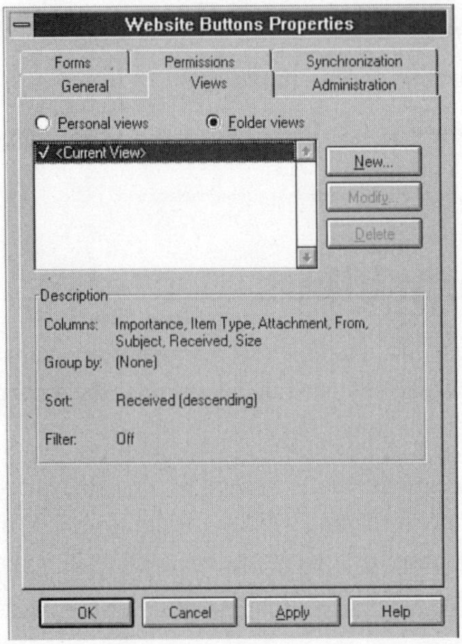

FIG. 33.19
The Views tab displays the views available, and provides a textual description of each.

3. Click the New button.
4. Type **by Company** in the View name box.
5. Click the Columns button.
6. Highlight each of the entries in the Show the Following list and click the Remove button so the list is empty.
7. Click Company in the Available Columns list, and click the Add button.
8. Click Transport in the Available Columns list, and click the Add button.
9. Highlight Transport in the Show the Following list, and click the Move Down button.
10. Click Address in the Available Columns list, and click the Add button.
11. Highlight Address in the Show the Following list, and click the Move Down button.
12. Click Sent in the Available Columns list (see fig. 33.20), and click the Add button.
13. Highlight Sent in the Show the Following list, and click the Move Down button.
14. Click OK.

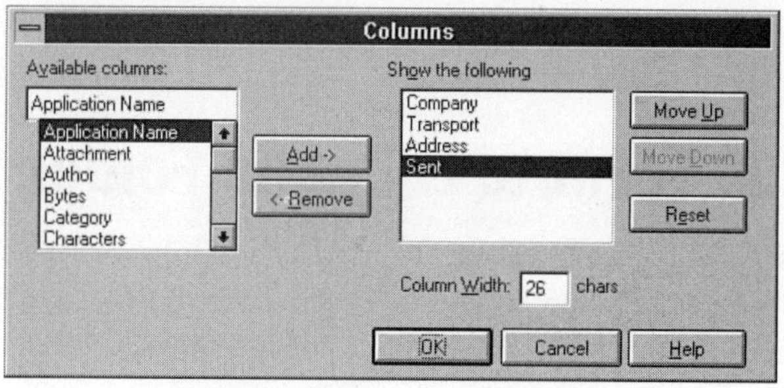

FIG. 33.20
The layout of the columns included in the view should look like this after steps 5-12 are completed.

15. Click Sort.
16. Drop down the list, and select Sent.
17. Click the Descending radio button.
18. Click OK.
19. Click OK.
20. Double-click the by Company entry in the list to place the checkmark next to it. It is now the default view.
21. Click OK.

All the entries in this folder will now be displayed according to the view you created (see fig. 33.21).

FIG. 33.21
Views determine how the items appear in the folder.

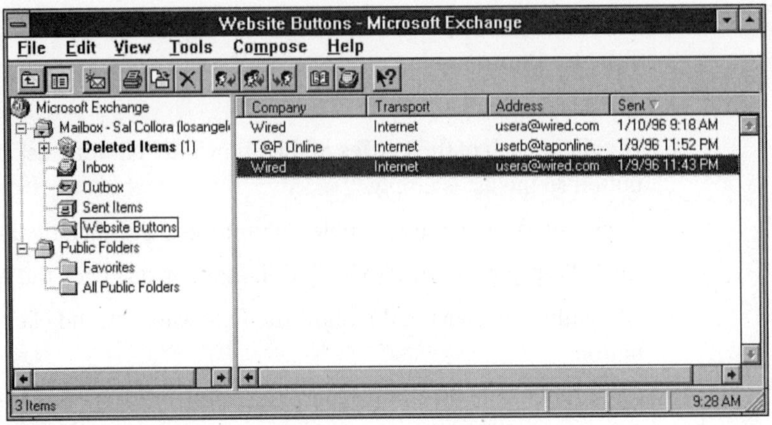

You have now completed all the necessary steps for the Web site button form. The next steps are provided for demonstration only, since this form is a send form, which is intended to simplify sending structured information to a particular user.

You can, however, make the public folder the recipient of the message. This would enable a centralized repository of all the Web site Button buys.

Copying the Form to a Public Folder

Our Web site Button Form will only be used by a couple of people, so putting it into a public folder isn't really appropriate; however, for the purposes of illustration, we will go through the steps of copying a form into a public folder.

In some organizations, administration of these folders is centralized and information policy prevents the administrator from giving users permission to manipulate public folders. The user must pass the folder on to the administrator, and have the administrator perform the following steps.

In some cases, however, a new public folder will be created, and permission will be granted to the user to manipulate the folder and its forms library. The tutorial below assumes you have all the proper permissions.

1. Select the Web site Button Form folder.
2. Choose Copy from the File menu.
3. In the Copy box, select the public folder you would like to copy the Web site Buttons form into. In this case, it's the All Public Folders folder. Yours may vary.
4. Click OK.

Setting the Folder Properties

Now that the form has been moved to a public folder, you must now set the properties for that folder.

1. Right-click the Web site Button folder and select Properties.
2. Select the Administration tab (see fig. 33.22).
3. Select by Company as the Initial view on folder. This will ensure that all items in that folder conform to the view we defined earlier.
4. Select Move/Copy in the Drag/Drop listbox.
5. Select the All users with permission radio button in the This folder is available to box.

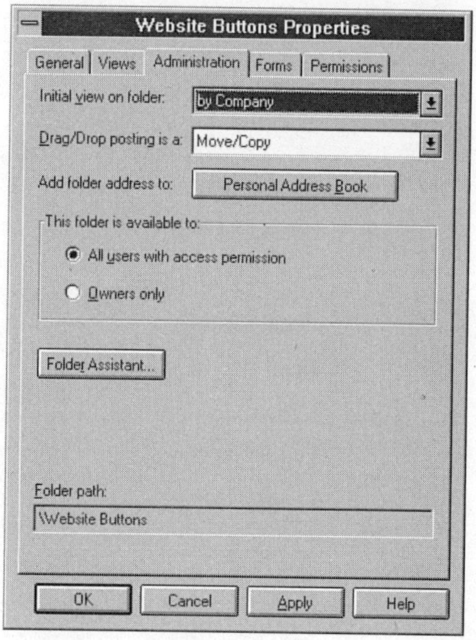

FIG. 33.22 The Administration tab should now be completed as shown above.

6. Select the Forms tab.
7. Click the Only forms listed above radio button. This ensures that only the Web site button form will be allowed in this folder. This protects against someone putting in some other kind of form, like a Vacation/Absence form in the Web site Button folder.

Setting Folder Permissions

1. Click the Permissions tab (see fig. 33.23).
2. Click the Default user and change the Role to None. These are the properties for all users. Changing the Role to None means that users have no privileges in the folder.

   The following table lists all the Roles and their associated permissions.

Table 33.2 Roles and Permissions

Role	Permission
Owner	All
Editor	Create Items
	Read Items
	Edit All Items
	Delete All Items
Author	Create Items
	Read Items
	Edit Own Items
	Delete Own Items
Publishing Editor	Create Items
	Read Items
	Edit All Items
	Delete All items
	Create Subfolders
Publishing Author	Create Items
	Read Items
	Edit Own Items
	Delete Own Items
	Create Subfolders
Reviewer	Create Items
	Read Items
Contributor	Create Items
None	No Permissions granted
Custom	Enables you to set permissions that do not match a predefined role

3. Click the Add button.
4. Select the users you want to have access to your folder and click the Add button.
5. Change the Role of each user you've added to Author. This allows them to Create and Read items in the folder. As you can see, each user can only edit and delete their own items.

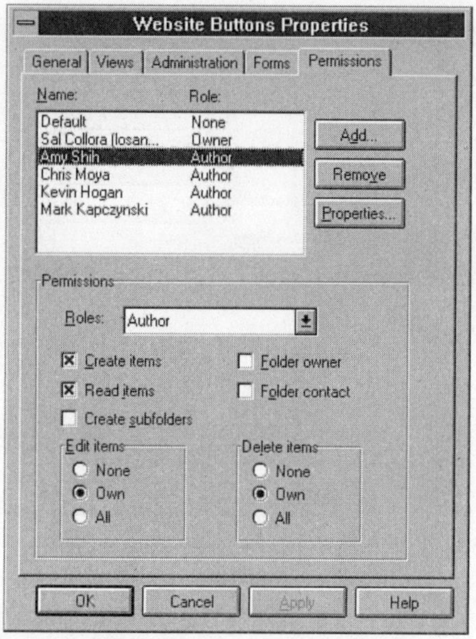

FIG. 33.23
The Permissions tab enables you to control who has access to your form, and what operations each user can perform within the folder.

Setting Folder Rules

You can use rules for any folder, including the inbox. Rules process incoming items by running them through a series of criteria. The rule itself is the action to take upon the meeting of those specified criteria.

Some organizations have people with certain contacts or specialties. You can set up rules to copy messages to certain users with those specialties.

We're going to set a rule that will forward all Web site Button requests for ESPNet to Ruben Perez because he processes all the ESPNet dealings. The user you choose will obviously depend on your own site.

1. Right click the Web site Button folder and select Properties.
2. Select the Administration tab.
3. Push the Folder Assistant button.

4. Click Add Rule.
5. Click the Advanced button.
6. Click the Folder: Web site Buttons radio button in the Show properties of group.
7. Select the Company Checkbox.
8. Select ESPNet the listbox (see fig. 33.24).

FIG. 33.24
The Advanced properties you select fields on the form as search criteria.

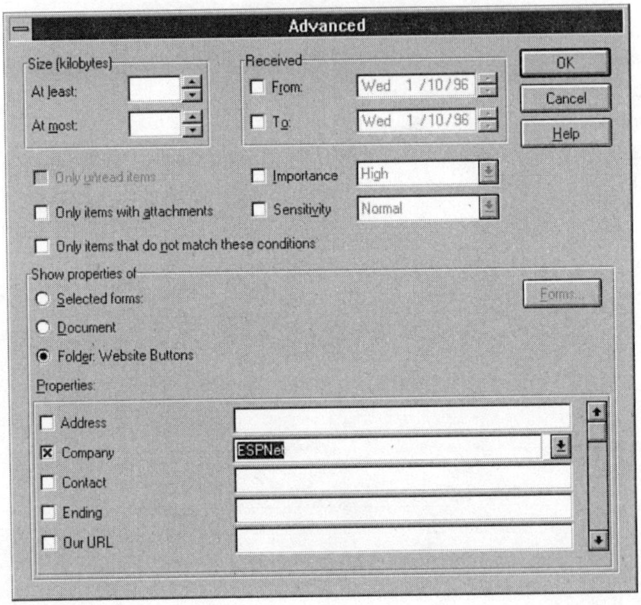

9. Click OK.
10. Click the Forward checkbox (see fig. 33.25).
11. Click the To button.
12. Select the proper user from the list and click the To button.
13. Click OK.
14. Click OK (see fig. 33.26).
15. Click OK.

We've now completed all of the steps in the folder design process. Your form will now make it a lot easier to expedite Web site Button requests. The purpose of using this kind of application was to show you how you automate any kind of process.

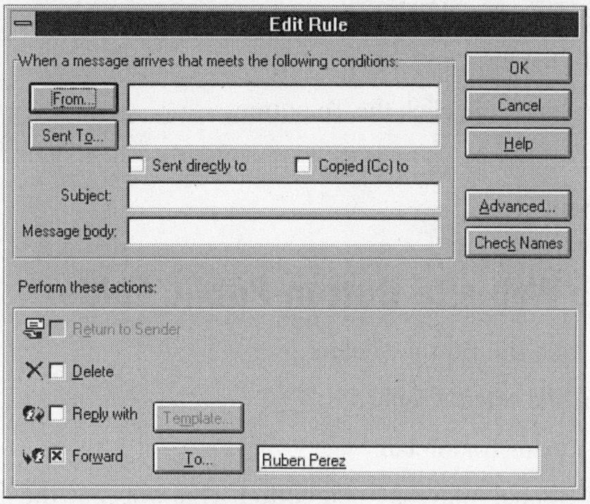

FIG. 33.25
You've now set up a complete rule. All ESPNet requests will be forwarded to the user you chose.

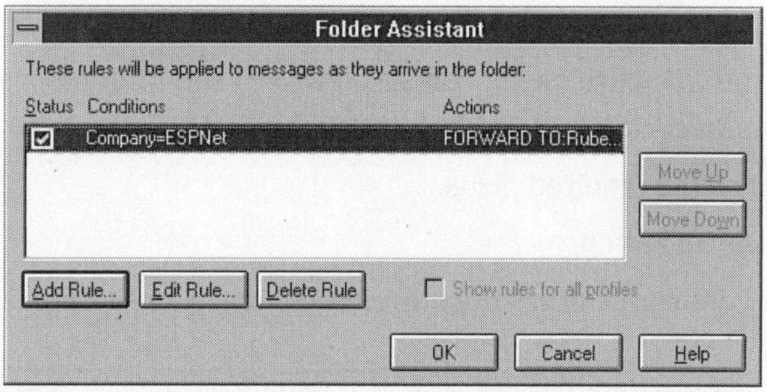

FIG. 33.26
The newly created rule is now added to the rule list in the Folder Assistant.

The Exchange CD ships with many examples of common office forms. Using what you have learned here, you can go about modifying those for your own purposes.

Using Your Form

Now that you've created a new form and placed it in a public folder, accessing it and using it are a snap.

Addressing to a Person

1. Select the Web site Buttons Folder.
2. From the Compose menu, choose New Web site Button Form. The form will pop up on your screen.

3. Fill out all the required fields.
4. Click the To button.
5. Select a recipient and click the To button.
6. Click OK.
7. Click the Send icon.

Addressing to the Web site Button Public Folder

1. Select the Web site Buttons Folder.
2. Right-click, and select Properties.
3. Click the Administration tab.
4. Click the Personal Address Book button. This will copy the name of the folder to your Personal Address Book so you can send an item to the folder.
5. Click OK.
6. From the Compose menu, choose New Web site Button Form. The form will pop up on your screen.
7. Fill out all the required fields.
8. Click the To button.
9. Select Personal Address Book from the Show Names from listbox (see fig. 33.27).

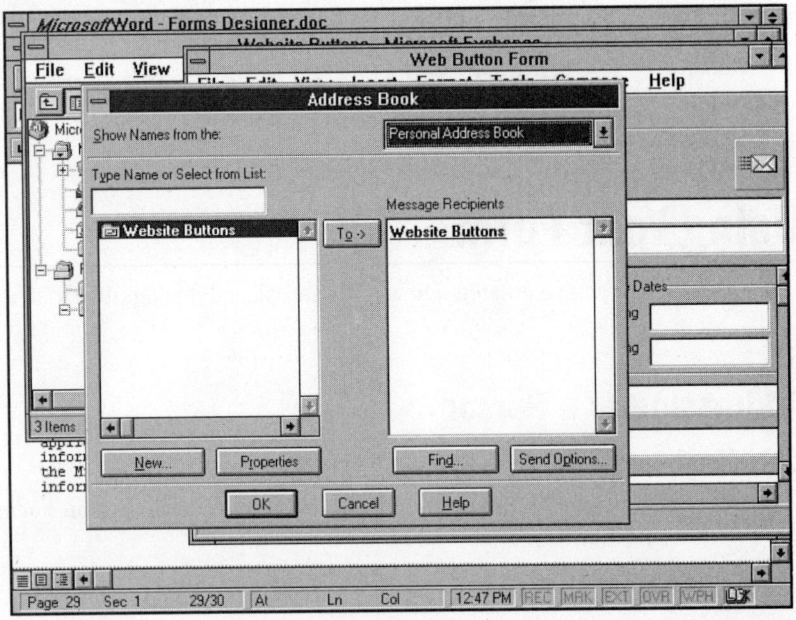

FIG. 33.27
The Web site Buttons folder is now in your Personal Address Book.

10. Select the Web site Buttons entry.
11. Click the To button.
12. Click OK.
13. Click the Send icon.

Extending Forms with Visual Basic

Since forms are Visual Basic applications, you can actually use Visual Basic to extend the functionality of forms beyond what the Forms Designer offers. The Forms Designer simply gives you a "No Programming" environment where you design very powerful applications without typing one line of code.

We will only be covering a brief overview of what you need, what goes into using Visual Basic to modify applications, and why you would want to. You can refer to the Microsoft documentation and Visual Basic documentation for specifics on using Visual Basic for MAPI and OLE applications.

Anyone who wants to use VB to extend an application created with the Forms Designer should be very experienced with Visual Basic, as well as MAPI and OLE. Forms are 16-bit applications, therefore, you can only use the Visual Basic for Exchange that gets installed when installing the Exchange Client and Forms Designer or 16-Bit Visual Basic 4.0.

Potential Uses of Visual Basic with Exchange Forms

You might be asking yourself, why would I want to use VB to extend forms? Here are just a couple of examples of how VB can improve your forms.

- You can use a form to enter data into external databases. For example, if you have a form for ordering office supplies, you can extend the form so that once the purchasing supervisor reviews the requisition and approves it, the data gets entered into a Microsoft SQL Server database automatically and the purchase order generated with the daily run.

  By using public folders, you can distribute the application throughout the Exchange network without actually copying the .EXE file on all the servers in your network for all your users to access. In addition, when the form gets modified, all the users on the network will get the most up-to-date version of the form automatically without the need to redistribute. All of that is controlled by the synchronization within Exchange.

- You can include OLE controls in a form that can take data from OLE-compliant applications such as Excel. For example, if you want your form to grab the latest data from a spreadsheet and paste it into the form, you can write code that reads the contents of the OLE control into a file, and then reads the file into the form using OLE Messaging functions.

  You can use this function to send hourly time sheets to a user in native Excel format. The form can contain a blank Excel worksheet that has the header cells filled in with the days of the month, and you just fill data right into the worksheet. The recipient can then either cut, copy, and paste the data, or save it directly as an Excel file.

Modifying Applications

When you install a form using the Forms Designer, several files get created in a directory called <FORMNAME>.VB. These files are those used when extending forms with Visual Basic (see fig. 33.28).

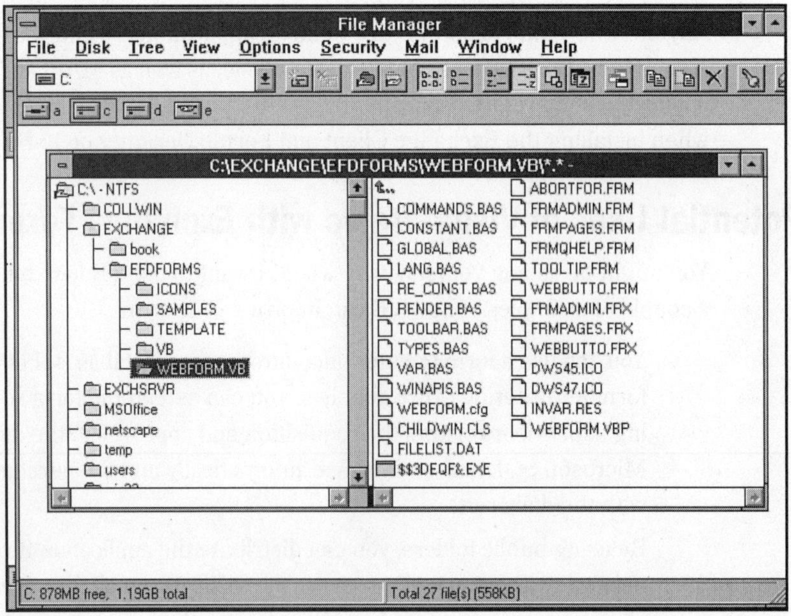

FIG. 33.28
The WEBFORM.VB directory contains all the files used by Visual Basic.

When using VB, only the <WINDOW NAME>.FRM files and the <FORM FILE>.CFG files are modified. Once you finish using Visual Basic to modify your form, you need to register all the new fields and properties in your form with Exchange. You will need to modify the .CFG file directly in Notepad or Wordpad to add all the objects and properties so they are recognized by Exchange.

From Here...

As stated earlier, we could devote an entire book to forms and application design under Exchange. We've tried to provide the information you need get your feet wet. You can always refer to the Microsoft documentation and the on-line Help for more information.

Having read this chapter, you should now understand the following:

- Forms are ways of posting data to a folder or sending structured information to a user or users.
- Forms are Visual Basic executable files.
- The Forms Designer provides a non-programming interface for creating forms.
- Forms are stored in libraries.
- Forms are composed of windows and fields.
- Forms, windows, and fields all have properties that control their behavior.
- Placing forms in public folders gives users across the enterprise access to the forms and the data contained within them.
- Forms can be extended with Visual Basic.

Index

Symbols

A

E

F

G

J-L

M

N

O

Q-R

S

T

U

Complete and Return this Card for a *FREE* Computer Book Catalog

Thank you for purchasing this book! You have purchased a superior computer book written expressly for your needs. To continue to provide the kind of up-to-date, pertinent coverage you've come to expect from us, we need to hear from you. Please take a minute to complete and return this self-addressed, postage-paid form. In return, we'll send you a free catalog of all our computer books on topics ranging from word processing to programming and the internet.

ɪr. ☐ Mrs. ☐ Ms. ☐ Dr. ☐

ɪame (first) ______ (M.I.) ___ (last) ______

ɪddress ______

______

ɪity ______ State ___ Zip ______ ______

ɪhone ___ ___ ____ Fax ___ ___ ____

ɪompany Name ______

ɪ-mail address ______

. Please check at least (3) influencing factors for purchasing this book.

- ɪront or back cover information on book ☐
- ɪpecial approach to the content ☐
- ɪompleteness of content ☐
- ɪuthor's reputation ☐
- ɪublisher's reputation ☐
- ɪook cover design or layout ☐
- ɪndex or table of contents of book ☐
- ɪrice of book ☐
- ɪpecial effects, graphics, illustrations ☐
- ɪther (Please specify): ______ ☐

. How did you first learn about this book?

- ɪaw in Macmillan Computer Publishing catalog ☐
- ɪecommended by store personnel ☐
- ɪaw the book on bookshelf at store ☐
- ɪecommended by a friend ☐
- ɪeceived advertisement in the mail ☐
- ɪaw an advertisement in: ______ ☐
- ɪead book review in: ______ ☐
- ɪther (Please specify): ______ ☐

. How many computer books have you purchased in the last six months?

- ɪhis book only ☐
- books ☐
- 3 to 5 books ☐
- More than 5 ☐

4. Where did you purchase this book?

- Bookstore ☐
- Computer Store ☐
- Consumer Electronics Store ☐
- Department Store ☐
- Office Club ☐
- Warehouse Club ☐
- Mail Order ☐
- Direct from Publisher ☐
- Internet site ☐
- Other (Please specify): ______ ☐

5. How long have you been using a computer?

- ☐ Less than 6 months
- ☐ 6 months to a year
- ☐ 1 to 3 years
- ☐ More than 3 years

6. What is your level of experience with personal computers and with the subject of this book?

	With PCs	With subject of book
New	☐	☐
Casual	☐	☐
Accomplished	☐	☐
Expert	☐	☐

Source Code ISBN: 0-7897-0687-3

7. Which of the following best describes your job title?

Administrative Assistant .... ☐
Coordinator .... ☐
Manager/Supervisor .... ☐
Director .... ☐
Vice President .... ☐
President/CEO/COO .... ☐
Lawyer/Doctor/Medical Professional .... ☐
Teacher/Educator/Trainer .... ☐
Engineer/Technician .... ☐
Consultant .... ☐
Not employed/Student/Retired .... ☐
Other (Please specify): ____________ ☐

8. Which of the following best describes the area of the company your job title falls under?

Accounting .... ☐
Engineering .... ☐
Manufacturing .... ☐
Operations .... ☐
Marketing .... ☐
Sales .... ☐
Other (Please specify): ____________ ☐

9. What is your age?

Under 20 .... ☐
21-29 .... ☐
30-39 .... ☐
40-49 .... ☐
50-59 .... ☐
60-over .... ☐

10. Are you:

Male .... ☐
Female .... ☐

11. Which computer publications do you read regularly? (Please list)

____

Comments: ____________

Fold here and scotch-tape to mail.

NO POSTAGE NECESSARY IF MAILED IN THE UNITED STATES

BUSINESS REPLY MAIL
FIRST-CLASS MAIL PERMIT NO. 9918 INDIANAPOLIS IN

POSTAGE WILL BE PAID BY THE ADDRESSEE

ATTN MARKETING
MACMILLAN COMPUTER PUBLISHING
MACMILLAN PUBLISHING USA
201 W 103RD ST
INDIANAPOLIS IN 46290-9042